SOURCES IN THE HISTORY OF THE
Modern Middle East

SOURCES IN THE HISTORY OF THE
Modern Middle East

Akram Fouad Khater

North Carolina State University

HOUGHTON MIFFLIN COMPANY   Boston   New York

Vice President and Publisher: Charles Hartford
Editor-in-Chief: Jean Woy
Senior Associate Editor: Fran Gay
Associate Project Editor: Lindsay Frost
Editorial Assistant: Teresa Huang
Production/Design Assistant: Bethany Schlegel
Manufacturing Manager: Florence Cadran
Senior Marketing Manager: Sandra McGuire

Printed in the U.S.A.

Library of Congress Catalog Card Number: 2001131516

ISBN: 0-395-98067-4

56789-QF-09 08 07 06 05

CONTENTS

PART III
The Rise of Postindependence States, 1950–2000

247

PART IV
The Middle East Today

315

PREFACE

Students of Middle Eastern and North African history have been more separated from their subject matter than is the case with the study of American or European history because of unfamiliarity with the languages, customs, and culture of this part of the world. Consequently, they have had to struggle to glimpse and hear the voices of real human beings within the stories they read about this area. Without access to relatively unfiltered voices, most students have been hard-pressed to understand and explain the behavior and actions of individuals and groups. In other words, they have mostly been learning only a part of the history of the Middle East and North Africa. This text is meant to overcome that hurdle.

The idea behind the book emerged out of my own experiences as a professor of Middle Eastern history. Early on in my teaching career I relied mainly on secondary sources to teach. My goal, as is the goal of most who teach this subject, was to help students understand the way the modern Middle East—as a set of political, social, economic, and cultural spaces—came into existence. I strove to close the gap that separated the background of most of my students from this "alien" subject matter. But, most importantly, I wanted them to learn this history as the intermingled stories of a great variety of people full of weaknesses and strengths, who stumbled and rose many times in their collective and individual lives. I wanted students to see the peoples of the Middle East as historical actors like the rest of humanity, and not caricatures like the ones displayed far too often in Western popular media. Yet, despite my best attempts I found at the end of each semester that the students still clung to some of the stereotypes, and they still regarded the peoples who have lived in this region as the equivalent of historical stick figures.

Frustrated with this outcome, I began to experiment with the use of documents composed—orally or in a written format—by individuals or groups from the Middle East. It soon became evident that these experiments were producing positive results. Rather than speak of "Middle Easterners," students were compelled to speak, for example, of 'Adel Zua'ayter (a representative to the Syrian Congress of 1920 from the Palestinian town of Nablus) and his views about giving Syrian women the right to vote. In grappling with the debates surrounding these issues, the students came to understand the multiplicity of opinions that existed with regard to this issue. Furthermore, through a reading of the debate that rages for two hours, my students were exposed to the complex relationship between impending European colonial rule and the local social, political, cultural, and religious factors. Regardless of whether they agreed with one or the other positions proclaimed in this particular debate, the students came to appreciate that all the participants were human beings who were subject to larger forces of history, at the same time that they were trying to shape the course of history.

From this beginning, it occurred to me that it might be worthwhile to expand the scope of the primary sources to cover a longer time frame, as well as more geographical areas and subject matter. The result is this book.

While the pedagogical rationale for the book may be apparent by now, there remains the task of explaining the logic of its organization and the criteria for the selection of documents. There is no doubt that a book such as this one can be organized in a myriad of ways. However, in outlining its structure I was concerned with accomplishing two goals. First, I wanted this collection of documents to fit easily within the structure of most modern Middle Eastern history courses being taught in the United States today. Reflecting the outline of Middle Eastern history textbooks, most courses follow a roughly chronological order that begins with a treatment of the nineteenth century and the encounter with European imperialism. From there the narrative progresses to cover the construction of nations, the emergence of post-independence states, the Palestinian-Israeli conflict, the Iranian revolution and the rise of Islamic political movements, and ending with the Gulf War and its aftereffects. Similarly, this book is divided into four parts that roughly follow the same chronological order.

After a brief introductory chapter providing guidance on how to read a primary source, particularly in this subject area, Part I presents various documents from the nineteenth century that lay the groundwork for political reforms and responses to colonialism, as well as economic, social, and cultural changes. Part II presents documents on the making of nations in the aftermath of World War I, and the construction of nationalist ideas as well as the propagation of nationalist ideas at the popular level. Part III focuses on the emergence of the bureaucratic state in the Middle East and North Africa, and its impact upon political and social life in the region. The Palestinian-Israeli conflict contains within it many of these preceding themes, and so has been woven throughout the remaining chapters where it fits within the chronological framework.

Finally, the book concludes with a long section that examines the Middle East today. I have not included documents on the Gulf War because these abound and are easily accessible, and because from the perspective of the Middle East and North Africa the war was a symptom and catalyst of larger changes within the society, economy, and polity of these two areas. But this section does include articles on the aftermath of the terrorist attacks of September 11, 2001, and it concludes with assessments of globalization and its impact on Arab culture, and the effect of cultural pluralism in the Middle East and North Africa.

My concern in organizing the text was not simply to duplicate the timeline of a course in Middle Eastern history, however. I also wanted to introduce thematic approaches within the chronological organization. For example, in the first section of the book I have included—in addition to the traditional political and economic texts—documents that address the cultural changes that were taking place in the Middle East and North Africa toward the end of the nineteenth century. These documents seek to show students the process through which the Middle East and North Africa were changing (or not changing) along social and cultural lines, the causes of these changes, and their architects. I have tried to include such social and cultural documents throughout the collection in an attempt to present the student with more than the predominant political narrative. Thus, the discussion of homosexuality in Egypt brings marginal groups into the mainstream of history and compels us as readers to understand democratic change in a new context of sexual freedoms or lack thereof. In my estimation, this mixture of political and economic documents on the one hand and social and cultural texts on the other will provide a more complete and complementary collection.

This leads me to a second issue. No collection of primary sources will cover every conceivable subject in full. However, I would like to explain briefly another rationale for the selections that have been included. As mentioned previously, I tried to obtain a balance in the *type* of documents that were included. This balance was reached after subjecting the table of contents to several external revisions in which its strengths and weaknesses were noted by anonymous colleagues from various disciplines and with various geographical interests. As a result, I have attempted to include texts from Iran, North Africa, Turkey, and the Middle East. With this attempt at breadth, I tried to find and include documents that fit within the overall theme of the chapter and the chronology of the section. For example, within the topic of Islamic responses to nationalism, I included a selection by Hassan al-Banna from Egypt and another by Shaykh Ben Badis and the Association of Ulama of Algeria.

While by no means exhaustive in coverage, these two selections still provide students with a comparative basis. This is especially the case when these two documents are read in concert with the document entitled *The Proposed Enfranchisement of Muslims in Algeria.* In addition, some documents will allow students to read how one subject was treated in the early part of the nineteenth century, and how this same subject is seen at the end of the twentieth century. This comparative perspective adds another historical dimension to the collection by allowing students to observe changes over time. Moreover, I have sought to include documents that reach across various sectors of society—presenting in the process the point of view of some elites as well as the opinions of people from the lower classes.

I hope that through the use of these documents students will gain a greater appreciation for the humanity of Middle Eastern and North African history and will see them as less foreign than they might have otherwise.

In compiling and editing a book this diverse in coverage I quickly came to know the limitations of my knowledge and the need for a great deal of assistance from colleagues within the field of Middle Eastern Studies. These colleagues were most generous and responsive to my far too frequent requests for help, and this book is so much the richer because of their selfless contributions. They include Abbas Amanat, Julia Clancy-Smith, James Gelvin, Joshua Landis, Afsaneh Najmabadi, Donald Quataert, John Ruedy, Sarah Shields, and Elizabeth Thompson. The reviewers of the manuscript were most helpful in providing me with constructive criticism about the content, breadth, and organization of the manuscript. I thank them all for improving this book: Jere Bacharach, University of Washington; Carol L. Bargeron, Southwest Texas State University; Corinne Blake, Rowan University; John Calvert, Creighton University; Julia Clancy-Smith, University of Arizona; Hafez Farmayan, University of Texas; Cengiz Kirli, Purdue University; Stephen L. McFarland, Auburn University; Sarah Shields, University of North Carolina; and John VanderLippe, SUNY–New Paltz. I would also like to acknowledge the support I received from the History Department at North Carolina State University as well as the College of Humanities and Social Sciences while working on this project. I would be most remiss not to mention the amazing technical support personnel at CHASS who worked tirelessly for three days and two nights to bring back three-years worth of work by recovering the manuscript from the jaws of computer failure. The staff of the D.H. Hill library were equally generous in responding to my incessant demands for more and more arcane titles and articles.

My editors at Houghton Mifflin were a treasure trove of kindness, professionalism, competency, and empathy. They are Jean Woy, who first saw merit in my idea for this reader and who struggled with me through several iterations of its composition; Fran Gay, who had the responsibility of making the idea come to reality by gently prodding me to meet long overdue deadlines; and Lindsay Frost, who was the model of efficiency in turning the hundreds of disparate pages into this manuscript. I would also like to thank my copyeditor, Pat Herbst, who was most diligent in turning awkward phrases into flowing prose, and in catching contradictions and errors.

Finally, I would like to acknowledge the incredible support I received throughout this project from my wife, Jodi, and children, Lauren and Micah. Their love, humor, and joyful spirits shone through during the darkest moments when I thought all was lost and that I would need to recommence the project from the start.

A. K.

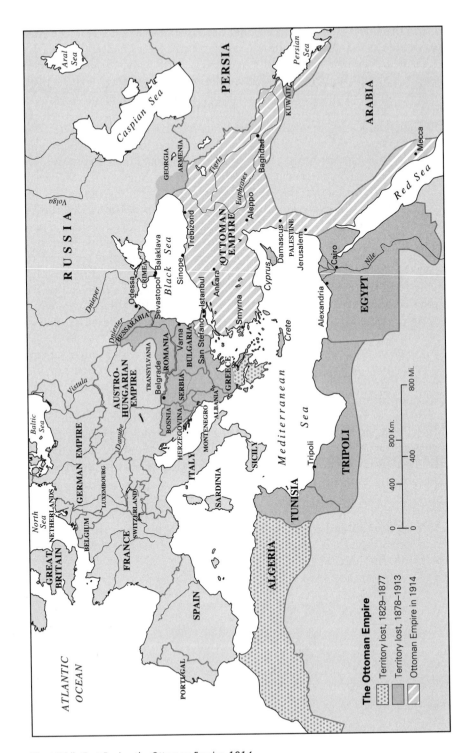

The Middle East During the Ottoman Empire, 1914

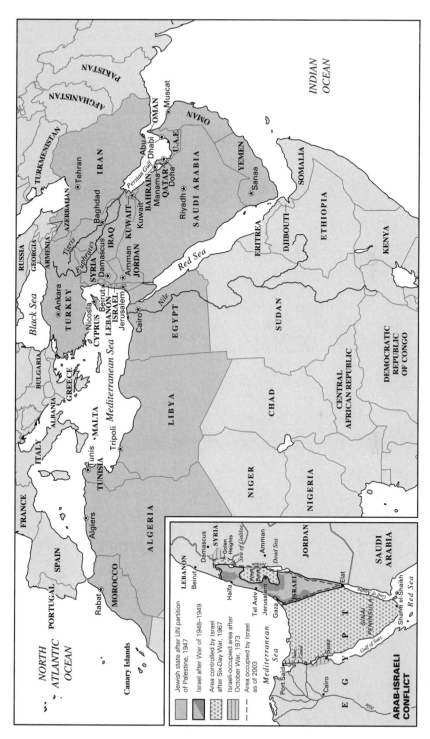

The Middle East Today

SOURCES IN THE HISTORY OF THE
Modern Middle East

INTRODUCTION:

How to Read a Primary Source

Primary sources offer fleeting glimpses into the past; they record the concerns, thoughts, and remarks of people from bygone eras. The relevance of these words or images to our own historical understanding—grounded as it is in our own time—is not always straightforward. In the following pages we consider how to approach such documents.

Every primary source presents a particular perspective. The author or authors of the source were trying to present their own point of view about a certain subject. Even when we think that a document has an objective tone, we must remind ourselves that the author was not objective, because he or she was working under the influence of strong, unavoidable cultural assumptions. Observing that all primary sources are tinged with bias, however, does not in any way call into question their value as ways to reconstruct the past. Actually, our awareness of their bias forces us to use them advisedly and carefully, rather than dismissing them or accepting them without comment. The biases of an author reveal quite a bit about some of the customs and ideas of the time period in which he or she was working. Thus, we not only can use the *explicit* content of a document to draw out a picture of a particular event, but we also can add our own *inferential* understanding of the mind-set of the author and, possibly, of persons around the author.

Another limitation to be aware of is that a primary source provides only a snapshot, at best, of a small part of a much larger historical tableau. Historians must guard against overestimating the implications of any single document by isolating it from its general context. In fact, the relevance of any document becomes apparent only when we clearly understand the context in which it was written.

With these caveats in mind, let us now examine a specific document.

United States Consulate,
Beirut, January 28th, 1885

Honorable Alvey A. Adee,
3rd Assistant Secretary of State
Washington D.C.

 The year of 1884 will be remembered by the American communities in this Consular district with pain and distrust toward the Turkish Authorities. During the year, a number of complaints were made by Americans and American protégés (employés [sic]) in this Consular district against the arbitrary and illegal actions of the Turkish Authorities. Each complaint was carefully examined by me, and in all cases, proved well founded, before the matter was brought before the Turkish Authorities. In no instance, however, has a Turkish subject been punished, or the slightest satisfaction been given. From more than three years experience in Turkey, I am convinced that it is not the policy of the Turkish government to bring to justice a Turkish subject for any misdemeanor or unlawful act committed against an American citizen, residing in this part of the country. Letters addressed to the Governor General on important business wherein American interests were concerned have been left unanswered for months. I have complained on occasions to Constantinople of the discourtesy of the officials in not answering my letters, but little if any improvement has been made in this respect. When answers have been received relative to complaints against the illegal actions of the Authorities towards Americans, almost invariably the principal points have been ignored, and no Turkish subject has been punished, as stated above. On the other hand, the Authorities have been most energetic in making difficulties where American interests have been involved. Within the last few months schools and places of worship, which have been in existence for fifteen and twenty years, have been closed notwithstanding the petitions of the Turkish Protestant congregation and the protests of the Missionaries. One of the most flagrant acts recently has been the seizing and sealing (by the Governor's seal on the doors) of buildings which are the property of Dr. W. W. Coddy, American citizen, where schools have been taught; (no complaint has even been made against any one connected with these schools.) I have requested the Governor General to allow the schools to be reopened until such time as the Authorities may choose to grant a permission for continuing the same, and that the people be allowed to worship [as] heretofore. I have demanded that the seal be removed from the door of the building and the property be delivered up to the owner, Dr. Eddy or his agent; but as yet the Governor General of Syria Hamdi Pasha, has paid no attention to my letter on the subject, nor do I think that he will take any notice of the matter further than to say that the schools must have permits from the Authorities before they will be allowed to be opened; (these permits they are not likely to grant.) The matter has been referred by me to Constantinople for such action as our Minister may deem proper to take in the premises relative to the seizure of the property referred to. In conversation with the Political Director of Syria (a kind of Grand Advisor to the Governor General) about the unfriendly action of the Authorities towards American interests in Syria, I mentioned that as for the American Missionaries they give their lives and spend large sums of their countrymen's money in educating and civilizing the people without the least return in any sense; that we receive neither commercial nor any other benefit [from] the expenditure on the work done. His answer was: "If I close all your schools and colleges what can you do?" Such expressions from one in his position shows [*sic*] plainly that there is a deep feeling of unfriendliness towards American commercial and other interests. As you are aware the war in the Soudan [Sudan] is becoming a serious affair. No one seems to have any correct idea of what will be the end, but the feeling is that sooner or later England will fund and guarantee the interest on the Egyptian debt, and when the war [between Britain and Egypt] is over, quietly settle down there for good. After this, it is the general impression in the Levant that Europe will begin to divide up Turkey. Outside of the French Colony it is not thought that France is likely to get any territory in Turkey. Italy and Greece will accept whatever the Powers may choose to give them. All agree that the division will be a difficult matter, but repeat what has been said for years that Turkey can not go on much longer as she is bankrupt and great dissatisfaction is manifested in the Army as well as by the people all over the country. It is believed by many Turks that the unwise and illegal actions of this Government to all Foreigners will hasten the downfall of the Ottoman Empire. The foregoing is the feeling existing amongst the most enlightened clan of the Levant, and I submit the same for whatever it may be worth. The enclosed article, with translation will give you a pretty correct idea of the feeling of the Mussulmans [*sic*] in Turkey toward Christians in general and English in particular. The "Thamarat il-Finoon" is the official organ of the Moslem population in this part of the country, and the article was not published without the approval of the Governor General of Syria.

I am your most dedicated servant
John T. Robison

PS: The foregoing with enclosures are private but there is no objections [*sic*] to your making any use of them that you deem proper.

After reading any document, we should be able to answer four basic questions:

1. Who wrote the document?
2. Who was the document intended for?
3. When was the document written?
4. Why was the document written?

In this case, the first three questions are rather easy to answer. The author of the document is John T. Robison, the U.S. consul general—an official diplomatic representative of the government of the United States—in Beirut. Robison is writing to Alvey A. Adee, the third assistant secretary of state, in Washington, D.C. We can surmise that Adee is the State Department's officer in charge of the region that includes Beirut and possibly the Ottoman Empire as a whole. We also can surmise that Adee's rank, *third* assistant secretary, places him low within the hierarchy of the department. (The State Department assigned a *first* assistant secretary of state to oversee U.S. relations with England. Adee's rank indicates the relative importance of the Beirut post to the American foreign policy establishment. The Beirut district—if not the whole Ottoman Empire—ranked rather low in importance.) The document was penned on January 28, 1885.

After reaching those easy conclusions, we face the more difficult task of understanding the purpose and historical significance of the letter. Why did Robison bother to send a dispatch informing his superior in Washington about the closing of American schools and missions? On the one hand, a cynic might propose that Robison had nothing better to do, so he inflated a minor event into a diplomatic incident. On the other hand, the letter could have been motivated by the need to illustrate to the State Department the low regard of the Ottoman Empire for the United States. In fact, Robison clearly indicates the Ottoman position when he quotes the governor of Syria as saying: "If I close all your schools and colleges what can you do?" This comment seals and highlights the list of grievances Robison described earlier in the passage: namely, that American missions and schools in the district of Beirut were closed for no obvious reason—at least none disclosed to American personnel—and that all of his appeals for a resolution of this "injustice" were ignored. Robison gives the impression that the "Turkish" (Ottoman) officials were arbitrary and selective in their suppression of American missionary activities and did not interfere with French or British interests.

Of course, readers should not accept Robison's argument at face value. We do not need to believe that the Ottoman governor in Beirut had no rational reasons for his actions. In fact, Robison himself provides clues to the governor's reasons farther down in his letter (more on this later). What we can accept as a historical certainty is that Robison believed that the Americans in Beirut were subjected to unfair and arbitrary Ottoman actions.

Why did Robison bother establishing the fact that the Ottomans held American power in such low regard? He was probably incensed at the Ottoman dismissal of himself as a representative of the U.S. government—and at what he regarded as flagrant impoliteness. However, we should not be satisfied with this answer. We need to place the letter within a broader context. To understand Robison's distress about the closing of mission schools, we need to ask what purpose served by those institutions did he consider so important that he decided to write his report. Mission schools—the ones he mentions are American Presbyterian missions—were intended by their founders and financial backers to convert individuals to a particular type of Christianity. In most cases, missionaries found that education provided the easiest means to achieve that end. Rather than simply proselytizing in a predominantly Muslim land, the missionaries used education to attract local boys and girls to American culture and ideas in the hope that they would be converted to Christianity. The role of the schools in spreading American ideas is what made these schools so important to Robison; he viewed them as a tool to help establish the American presence and promote American interests in the Ottoman Empire. Young men and women who graduated from the mission schools would have acquired knowledge of American English, American history and geography, and American political ideas and culture. Later, this knowledge would predispose at least some of them to cultivate commercial and political relations with the United States. Furthermore, as educated individuals living in a place and time when illiteracy was widespread, they were likely to attain positions of importance in Ottoman society. Together, those two factors might promote American influence and interests in that region. Robison knew that mission schools were outposts of American influence that helped—deliberately or otherwise—develop and increase the reach of American industry and commerce. By closing the schools, the Ottoman governor of Syria was in essence limiting the ability of the United States to expand economically and politically into the Ottoman Empire.

Establishing this context helps us to understand the second part of Robison's letter. Right after quoting the governor's dismissive statement, Robison shifts to a discussion of the pending dissolution of the Ottoman Empire. At first glance this change of subject seems a non sequitur. What does the closing of mission schools have to do with the rumored European plans to subdivide the Ottoman Empire? Given the broad context just established, we see that Robison's comments make a great deal of sense. Robison, the representative of American interests in Beirut, was concerned about American influence in that region and would have viewed the pending breakup of the empire as posing a threat to that influence. If the europeans did succeed in their plans, American influence in the empire would decline. Notice that Robison does not say that, in the event of a breakup, any Ottoman provinces would be given to the United States, but he does say that Italy and Greece—both much smaller and less powerful than the United States—would be handed some slices of the empire. In other words, the letter as a whole was intended to present the U.S. State Department with an assessment of American influence in a potentially important area. In Robison's estimation, neither the Ottoman government nor the European powers (Britain, France, and Russia—in that order) were giving

American interests a great deal of attention, nor did they hold American influence and power in great esteem.

Furthermore, we can surmise that some Ottoman government officials considered mission schools detrimental to Ottoman interests. This opinion could have derived simply from xenophobia, as Robison suggests. Or it could be that some Ottoman officials saw all foreign mission schools as outposts undermining Ottoman power and authority but decided to close only the American schools because they lacked the power to enforce the decision on the French or British. These observations are speculations that should be verified. Nonetheless, Robison's allusion to the negative "feeling of the Mussulmans [*sic*] in Turkey [read: Ottoman Empire] toward Christians in general and English in particular" confirms our tentative analysis.

Thus, in addition to providing some information about one particular historical event, this document provides a glimpse into much larger issues. Analyzing its wording and placing it in a broader context provide some information about relations between the United States, and to a lesser extent the European powers, and the Ottoman government. We sense feelings common among some officials and part of the Muslim population in the Ottoman Empire toward foreign missionaries and their schools and toward the European powers. Also, this document makes us privy to some of the thoughts of one individual—John T. Robison. Most of this information becomes evident not from a literal understanding of Robison's words but from the posing and answering of a series of *why* questions that turn this isolated document into a glimpse of a wider and more relevant past. As you read the documents assembled in the remainder of this book, your task will be to use this strategy.

PART I

The Middle East and North Africa in the Nineteenth Century

The story of the nineteenth century in the Middle East and North Africa has generally been told as the history of an encounter between a dominant Europe and a slumbering Middle East. The date usually given for the beginning of this encounter is 1798—the year Napoleon invaded Egypt and the first time since the Crusades (1098–1242) that a European army occupied land in the Middle East. In this narrative, an imperialist Europe bent on worldwide expansion came to dominate the Middle East and North Africa over the course of the nineteenth century, either through physical occupation (the French in Algeria in 1832, the British in Egypt in 1887) or through control over the economic routes and markets in the two regions. This political and economic control led to cultural and social crises in practically every part of the Ottoman Empire, Iran, Egypt, and North Africa. First individuals and then social groups began to ask questions about the reasons for the ascendancy of Europe and the forced submission of the Middle East and North Africa. Different groups arrived at different answers.

Those who were educated in Europe or in European schools came to believe that the answer lay in the modernity of European political, social, economic, and cultural systems. A minority within this new *franji* (European) educated elite believed that the only way to defend themselves against European domination was to emulate the Europeans in schooling, social customs, political institutions, and economic approaches. A much larger number within this new elite believed that a combination of indigenous traditions and European ideas would best serve the purpose of "uplifting" their societies and nations. In fact, some religious reformers, like Jamal al-Din Al-Afghani and Muhammad 'Abduh, concluded that this process of selective modernization needed to be applied not only to the secular aspects of life but also to Islam—

7

the religion of the majority of the people residing in the Middle East and North Africa.

Opposing these views were a wide variety of individuals and groups who believed that any imitation of Europe was undesirable. For religious and secular reasons they argued that what worked for Europe would not work for the Middle East and North Africa. They vociferously argued that following in the footsteps of Europe would lead their societies down the road of permanent European domination. Muslims who believed that their society was ordained by Allah (*God,* in Arabic) warned that abandoning "authentic" tradition was anathema to God.

Although this traditional narrative is fairly accurate in depicting the history of the nineteenth century in the Middle East and North Africa, it tends to skew our image of the period in several important ways. The first and most obvious of these is the notion that the regions were made up of ossified societies and peoples that had not changed—or changed hardly at all—since medieval times. The familiar version of the story assumes that because Europe and the Ottoman Empire followed separate historical paths, and because Europe attained a technological edge in the nineteenth century, Europe was ahead (far ahead in some estimates) of the Middle East and North Africa in terms of morals and civilization. This assumption is very much the same as the assumption that European writers—and some Middle Eastern authors—espoused with little evidence to justify British and French attempts to dominate the region.

Second, the usual account assumes an omnipotent Europe able to impose its will on the peoples of the Middle East and North Africa in a uniformly transformative fashion. Any variations and subtleties in the history of the encounter between Europe and these two regions are lost amid such gross assumptions. More critically, this version of the story fails to acknowledge that the encounter was as transformative to England and France as it was to any of the regions where those European powers succeeded in attaining some semblance of influence. Finally, the familiar narrative fails to allow for the fact that even individuals who embraced European ways did so on their own terms, manipulating and changing those ways to fit the particular problems facing them in places such as Tehran, Cairo, and Algiers.

None of these critiques of the traditional narrative rejects the fact that European contact with the peoples of the Middle East and North Africa was a catalyst for historically important changes. Rather, they signal the need for a more balanced perspective on these changes, to place them in their proper context and thus evaluate them as one element of the history of these areas, not as the only element. The primary sources included in this part of the book are meant to provide exactly this type of nuanced image of Middle Eastern and North African history. They are meant to illustrate that peoples in this region sought and, to varying degrees, maintained control over their individual and collective lives in the face of larger forces—which they did not always understand.

This section is divided into three chapters. "Central Political Reforms and Local Responses" deals with political reforms and reactions to these reforms on the part of the Ottoman populace during the nineteenth century. It includes edicts of the Tanzimat period (Ottoman reforms), a satirical assessment of similar Iranian reforms, and a text from a major Muslim reformer who was concerned with modernizing Islam—Jamal al-Din Al-Afghani.

In the chapter titled "Economic Changes," the same theme of reform is carried over into the realm of economic changes that took place in the nineteenth century. It includes several economic treaties between various Middle Eastern political entities and European powers, as well as documents about local oppositions to some of these economic changes. Finally, "Social and Cultural Reformulations" focuses on the rise of a modern middle class through the construction of new concepts of woman, marriage, and family. The framers of these new ideas considered them essential for the creation of a modern nation and a healthy society that would be the equal of European societies in every respect, and yet remain Egyptian, Iranian, Algerian, Lebanese, and so on.

CHAPTER 1

Central Political Reforms and Local Responses

The military defeats suffered by the Ottoman Empire in the eighteenth century and the invasion of Egypt by Napoleon in 1798 ushered in a new era in the Middle East and North Africa. It appeared to local observers that European forces suddenly were more powerful and certainly were more expansionist. By no means did this perception lead local inhabitants to assume the overall superiority of European culture, politics, or civilization. The defeats, however, did result in a certain amount of soul-searching by government officials and intellectuals. Many responses were proposed and sometimes adopted, though not always successfully. One of the lessons drawn out of the defeats by some Ottoman officials was the need to modernize the empire and its bureaucracy.

The Tanzimat was a period of reform that began in the 1830s and lasted through the dissolution of the Ottoman Empire after World War I (*tanzimat* is a Turkish word meaning "reorganization" or "restructuring"). In response to the decreasing military, political, and economic power of the empire, reformers (first the Young Ottomans, and later the Young Turks) embarked on a series of programs to modernize the imperial government and the way officials related to subject people across the various lands under imperial rule.

The notion of "modernity" was not easily or completely definable, but to government officials—especially those trained in Europe or European schools—modernity meant an increase in central government control and a shift from treating the population as "subjects" to treating them as "citizens."

Without assuming radical and rapid changes, we can still observe that such changes were attempted by studying the first three documents in this chapter. The first document, the *Hatt-I-Serif* decree, proposed a reform project to secularize the Ottoman courts and bring a greater degree of central control over the administration of the empire. The second was an attempt to transform the sociopolitical organization of the Ottoman Empire from the *millet* (sectarian communities) system to one of Ottoman citizens subject to the secular laws of the empire. The third document is an imperial decree presented to an Ottoman official in the province of Mosul (in modern-day northern Iraq) with regard to the nomadic tribes that predominated in the region. The opinion of the Bedouins expressed here provides valuable clues as to how some Ottoman officials understood the goals of the Tanzimat.

The fourth document, from the writings of the satirist Mirza Malkum Khan, provides glimpses of internal criticism of the Iranian government's and Islamic intellectuals' responses to European incursions. Malkum satirizes both groups and lampoons their efforts as half-hearted attempts to hold on to bygone days and waning powers. Although the great majority of the Iranian population probably disagreed—or at best partially agreed—with him, his satire is still important because it provides a critical perspective on the encounter between the Middle East and Europe.

Responding to Tanzimat reforms as well as to the growth of European cultural influence in the Middle East and North Africa, several Muslim intellectuals and religious reformers sought to influence the outcomes of these changes in ways that fit their own worldview. Two key Islamic voices responding to European imperialism are those of Jamal al-Din Al-Afghani (document 5) and his disciple Muhammad 'Abduh. Both men confronted an environment in which Islam and local cultures faced external pressure and criticism—direct and indirect. While some Muslim thinkers preferred to reject all attempts at reconciliation with European ways of life, these two sought some accommodation between the technological superiority of the West and their notion of Islamic society, traditions, and mores. Regardless of the degree of their success or failure, both thinkers were influential in shaping this cross-civilization dialogue and remain icons in the Muslim world.

The last document in this chapter indicates how after some seventy years of reform one minority—the Jewish community in Baghdad—evaluated the modernization of the Ottoman Empire.

1.   The Hatt-I-Serif Decree Initiates the Tanzimat, or Reform, Period in the Ottoman Empire, November 3, 1839

In the Tanzimat period of Ottoman history, attempts were made to modernize the empire and enable it to withstand European imperialist pressures. The aim of the Hatt-I-Serif decree—clothed as it was in the religious legitimacy of the Shari'a—was to allow the Ottomans to establish a stronger central government by means of reforms in the tax collection and military service systems. The purpose of these reforms was to weaken provincial governors' holds on their territories and simultaneously provide the central Ottoman government with more resources with which to face the European military and political might. The reforms were never fully implemented, but more important than any immediate changes was the fact that this decree initiated the period of Tanzimat, which lasted through the end of World War I, and whose impact went beyond military and political matters to touch social and cultural aspects of life in the Ottoman Empire.

All the world knows that since the first days of the Ottoman State, the lofty principles of the Kuran and the rules of the Şeriat were always perfectly observed. Our mighty Sultanate reached the highest degree of strength and power, and all its subjects [the highest degree] of ease and prosperity. But in the last one hundred and fifty years, because of a succession of difficulties and diverse causes, the sacred Şeriat was not obeyed nor were the beneficent regulations followed; consequently, the former strength and prosperity have changed into weakness and poverty. It is evident that countries not governed by the laws of the Şeriat cannot survive.

From the very first day of our accession to the throne, our thoughts have been devoted exclusively to the development of the empire and the promotion of the prosperity of the people. Therefore, if the geographical position of the Ottoman provinces, the fertility of the soil, and the aptitude and intelligence of the inhabitants are considered, it is manifest that, by striving to find appropriate means, the desired results will, with the aid of God, be realized within five or ten years. Thus, full of confidence in the help of the Most High and certain of the support of our Prophet, we deem it necessary and important from now on to introduce new legislation to achieve effective administration of the Ottoman Government and Provinces. Thus the principles of the requisite legislation are three:

1. The guarantees promising to our subjects perfect security for life, honor, and property.
2. A regular system of assessing taxes.
3. An equally regular system for the conscription of requisite troops and the duration of their service.

Indeed there is nothing more precious in this world than life and honor. What man, however much his character may be against violence, can prevent himself from having recourse to it, and thereby injure the government and the country, if his life and honor are endangered? If, on the contrary, he enjoys perfect security, it is clear that he will not depart from the ways of loyalty and all his actions will contribute to the welfare of the government and of the people.

If there is an absence of security for property, everyone remains indifferent to his state and his community; no one interests himself in the prosperity of the country, absorbed as he is in his own troubles and worries. If, on the contrary,

Translated by Halil Inalcik, from the Osmanli text in *Takvim-i Vekayi* as reproduced in *Tanzimat* (Istanbul, 1940) after p. 48; checked, against the text in Latin Turkish characters in A. Şerif Gözübüyük and Suna Kili, eds., *Türk Analyasa Metirleri* (Ankara, 1957), pp. 3–5, a text that appeared in *Düstür*, 1st ser. 1: 4–7. This document may also be found in J. C. Hurewitz, *The Middle East and North Africa in World Politics* (New Haven, Conn.: Yale University Press, 1975), pp. 269–271.

the individual feels complete security about his possessions, then he will become preoccupied with his own affairs, which he will seek to expand, and his devotion and love for his state and his community will steadily grow and will undoubtedly spur him into becoming a useful member of society.

Tax assessment is also one of the most important matters to regulate. A state, for the defense of its territory, manifestly needs to maintain an army and provide other services, the costs of which can be defrayed only by taxes levied on its subjects. Although, thank God, our Empire has already been relieved of the affliction of monopolies, the harmful practice of tax-farming [*iltizam*], which never yielded any fruitful results, still prevails. This amounts to handing over the financial and political affairs of a country to the whims of an ordinary man and perhaps to the grasp of force and oppression, for if the tax-farmer is not of good character he will be interested only in his own profit and will behave oppressively. It is therefore necessary that from now on every subject of the Empire should be taxed according to his fortune and his means, and that he should be saved from [any] further exaction. It is also necessary that special laws should fix and limit the expenses of our land and sea forces.

Military matters, as already pointed out, are among the most important affairs of state, and it is the inescapable duty of all the people to provide soldiers for the defense of the fatherland [*vatan*]. It is therefore necessary to frame regulations on the contingents that each locality should furnish according to the requirements of the time, and to reduce the term of military service to four or five years. Such legislation will put an end to the old practice, still in force, of recruiting soldiers without consideration of the size of the population in any locality, more conscripts being taken from some places and fewer from others. This practice has been throwing agriculture and trade into harmful disarray. Moreover, those who are recruited to lifetime military service suffer despair and contribute to the depopulation of the country.

In brief, unless such regulations are promulgated, power, prosperity, security, and peace may not be expected, and the basic principles [of the projected reforms] must be those enumerated above.

Thus, from now on, every defendant shall be entitled to a public hearing, according to the rules of the Şeriat, after inquiry and examination; and without the pronouncement of a regular sentence no one may secretly or publicly put another to death by poison or by any other means. No one shall be allowed to attack the honor of any other person whatsoever. Every one shall possess his property of every kind and may dispose of it freely, without let or hindrance from any person whatsoever; and the innocent heirs of a criminal shall not be deprived of their hereditary rights as a result of the confiscation of the property of such a criminal. The Muslim and non-Muslim subjects of our lofty Sultanate shall, without exception, enjoy our imperial concessions. Therefore we grant perfect security to all the populations of our Empire in their lives, their honor, and their properties, according to the sacred law.

As for the other points, decisions must be taken by majority vote. To this end, the members of the Council of Judicial Ordinances [Meclis-i Ahkam-i Adliyye], enlarged by new members as may be found necessary, to whom will be joined on certain days that we shall determine our Ministers and the high officials of the Empire, will assemble for the purpose of framing laws to regulate the security of life and property and the assessment of taxes. Every one participating in the Council will express his ideas and give his advice freely.

2. Sultan Abdul Majid's Islahat Fermani Decree Reaffirms the Privileges and Immunities of Non-Muslim Communities in the Ottoman Empire, February 18, 1856

On February 18, 1856, Sultan Abdul Majid issued a decree that aimed to make equal all of the citizens of the Ottoman Empire regardless of their religion. Although in part this reform was an attempt to please the British, it was also a serious attempt to transform the population of the empire from "subjects" to "citizens." By so doing, the reforming elites of the empire hoped to deter the rise of nationalist movements based on religion, such as the one that had separated Greece from the empire in 1829. Moreover, the decree was intended to limit the ability of the European powers (most notably France and Russia) to claim the right to protect their coreligionists in the empire from religious discrimination. Although this decree did not stop such interventions—in 1861, for example, French troops landed in Lebanon to protect the Catholics of the area—it marks a historical moment of transformation in the nature of the empire.

Let it be done as herein set forth.

To you, my Grand Vizier Mehemed Emin Aali Pasha, decorated with my imperial order of the medjidiye of the first class, and with the order of personal merit; may God grant to you greatness and increase your power.

It has always been my most earnest desire to insure the happiness of all classes of the subjects whom Divine Providence has placed under my imperial sceptre, and since my accession to the throne I have not ceased to direct all my efforts to the attainment of that end.

Thanks to the Almighty, these unceasing efforts have already been productive of numerous useful results. From day to day the happiness of the nation and the wealth of my dominions go on augmenting.

It being now my desire to renew and enlarge still more the new institutions ordained with a view of establishing a state of things conformable with the dignity of my empire and the position which it occupies among civilized nations, and the rights of my empire having, by the fidelity and praiseworthy efforts of all my subjects, and by the kind and friendly assistance of the great powers, my

United States, 46th Congress, special session (March 1881), Senate, Executive Documents, vol. 3, no. 3, *The Capitulations*, by E. A. Van Dyck, pt. 1, pp. 108–111. This document may also be found in J. C. Hurewitz, *The Middle East and North Africa in World Politics* (New Haven, Conn.: Yale University Press, 1975), pp. 315–318.

noble allies, received from abroad a confirmation which will be the commencement of a new era, it is my desire to augment its well being and prosperity, to effect the happiness of all my subjects, who in my sight are all equal, and equally dear to me, and who are united to each other by the cordial ties of patriotism, and to insure the means of daily increasing the prosperity of my empire.

I have therefore resolved upon, and I order the execution of the following measures:

The guarantees promised on our part by the Hatti-Humayoun of Gulhané, and in conformity with the Tanzimat, to all the subjects of my empire, without distinction of classes or of religion, for the security of their persons and property, and the preservation of their honor, are to-day confirmed and consolidated, and efficacious measures shall be taken in order that they may have their full entire effect.

All the privileges and spiritual immunities granted by my ancestors *ab antiquo,* and at subsequent dates, to all Christian communities or other non-Mussulman persuasions established in my empire, under my protection, shall be confirmed and maintained.

Every Christian or other non-Mussulman community shall be bound within a fixed period, and with the concurrence of a commission composed *ad hoc* of members of its own body, to proceed, with my high approbation and under the inspection of my Sublime Porte, to examine into its actual immunities and privileges, and to discuss and submit to my Sublime Porte the reforms required by the progress of civilization and of the age. The powers conceded to the Christian patriarchs and bishops by the Sultan Mahomet II and to his successors shall be made to harmonize with the new position which my generous and beneficent intentions insure to these communities.

The principle of nominating the patriarchs for life, after the revision of the rule of election now in force, shall be exactly carried out, conformably to the tenor of their firmans [Ottoman imperial decrees] of investiture.

The patriarchs, metropolitans, archbishops, bishops, and [rabbis] shall take an oath, on their entrance into office, according to a form agreed upon in common by my Sublime Porte and the spiritual heads of the different religious communities. The ecclesiastical dues, of whatever sort or nature they be, shall be abolished and replaced by fixed revenues of the patriarchs and heads of communities, and by the allocations of allowances and salaries equitably proportioned to the importance, the rank, and the dignity of the different members of the clergy.

The property, real or personal, of the different Christian ecclesiastics shall remain intact: the temporal administration of the Christian or other non-Mussulman communities shall, however, be placed under the safeguard of an assembly to be chosen from among the members, both ecclesiastics and laymen, of the said communities.

In the towns, small boroughs, and villages where the whole population is of the same religion, no obstacle shall be offered to the repair, according to their original plan, of buildings set apart for religious worship, for schools, for hospitals, and for cemeteries.

The plans of these different buildings, in case of their new erection, must, after having been approved by the patriarchs or heads of communities, be submitted to my Sublime Porte, which will approve of them by my imperial order, or make known its observations upon them within a certain time. Each sect, in localities where there are no other religious denominations, shall be free from every species of restraint as regards the public exercise of its religion.

In the towns, small boroughs, and villages where different sects are mingled together each community inhabiting a distinct quarter shall, by conforming to the above-mentioned ordinances, have equal power to repair and improve its churches, its hospitals, its schools, and its cemeteries. When there is question of their erection of new buildings, the necessary authority must be asked for, through the medium of the patriarchs and heads of communities, from my Sublime Porte, which will pronounce a sovereign decision according that authority, except in the case of administrative obstacles.

The intervention of the administrative authority in all measures of this nature will be entirely gratuitous. My Sublime Porte will take energetic measures to insure to each sect, whatever be the number of its adherents, entire freedom in the exercise of its religion. Every distinction or designation pending to make any class whatever of the subjects of my empire inferior to another class, on account of their religion, language, or race, shall be forever effaced from administrative protocol. The laws shall be put in force against the use of any injurious or offensive term, either among private individuals or on the part of the authorities.

As all forms of religion are and shall be freely professed in my dominions, no subject of my empire shall be hindered in the exercise of the religion that he professes, nor shall he be in any way annoyed on this account. No one shall be compelled to change their religion.

The nomination and choice of all functionaries and other employees of my empire being wholly dependent upon my sovereign will, all the subjects of my empire, without distinction of nationality, shall be admissible to public employments, and qualified to fill them according to their capacity and merit, and conformably with rules to be generally applied.

All the subjects of my empire, without distinction, shall be received into the civil and military schools of the government, if they otherwise satisfy the conditions as to age and examination which are specified in the organic regulations of the said schools. Moreover, every community is authorized to establish public schools of science, art, and industry. Only the method of instructions and the choice of professors in schools of this class shall be under the control of a mixed council of public instruction, the members of which shall be named by my sovereign command.

All commercial, correctional, and criminal suits between Mussulmans and Christians, or other non-Mussulman subjects, or between Christian or other non-Mussulmans of different sects, shall be referred to mixed tribunals.

The proceedings of these tribunals shall be public; the parties shall be confronted and shall produce their witnesses, whose testimony shall be received without distinction, upon an oath taken according to the religious law of each sect.

Suits relating to civil affairs shall continue to be publicly tried, according to the laws and regulations, before the mi[x]ed provincial councils, in the presence of the governor and judge of the place.

Special civil proceedings, such as those relating to successions or others of that kind, between subjects of the same Christian or other non-Mussulman faith, may, at the request of the parties, be sent before the councils of the patriarchs or of the communities.

Penal, correctional, and commercial laws, and rules of procedure for the mi[x]ed tribunals, shall be drawn up as soon as possible and formed into a code. Translations of them shall be published in all the languages current in the empire.

Proceedings shall be taken, with as little delay as possible, for the reform of the penitentiary system as applied to houses of detention, punishment, or correction, and other establishments of like nature, so as to reconcile the rights of humanity with those of justice. Corporal punishment shall not be administered, even in the prisons, except in conformity with the disciplinary regulations established by my Sublime Porte, and everything that resembles torture shall be entirely abolished.

Infractions of the law in this particular shall be severely repressed, and shall besides entail, as of right, the punishment, in conformity with the civil code, of the authorities who may order and of the agents who may commit them.

The organization of the police in the capital, in the provincial towns and in the rural districts, shall be revised in such a manner as to give to all the peaceable subjects of my empire the strongest guarantees for the safety both of their persons and property.

The equality of taxes entailing equality of burdens, as equality of duties entails that of rights, Christian subjects, and those of other non-Mussulman sects, as it has been already decided, shall, as well as Mussulmans, be subject to the obligations of the law of recruitment.

The principle of obtaining substitutes, or of purchasing exemption, shall be admitted. A complete law shall be published, with as little delay as possible, respecting the admission into and service in the army of Christian and other non-Mussulman subjects.

Proceedings shall be taken for a reform in the constitution of the provincial and communal councils in order to insure fairness in the choice of the deputies of the Mussulman, Christian, and other communities and freedom of voting in the councils. My Sublime Porte will take into consideration the adoption of the most effectual means for ascertaining exactly and for controlling the result of the deliberations and of the decisions arrived at.

As the laws regulating the purchase, sale, and disposal of real property are common to all the subjects of my empire, it shall be lawful for foreigners to possess landed property in my dominions, conforming themselves to the laws and police regulations, and bearing the same charges as the native inhabitants, and after arrangements have been come to with foreign powers.

The taxes are to be levied under the same denomination from all the subjects of my empire, without distinction of class or of religion. The most prompt and energetic means for remedying the abuses in collecting the taxes, and especially the tithes, shall be considered.

The system of direct collections shall gradually, and as soon as possible, be substituted for the plan of farming, in all the branches of the revenues of the state. As long as the present system remains in force all agents of the government and all members of the medjlis shall be forbidden under the severest penalties, to become lessees of any farming contracts which are announced for public competition, or to have any beneficial interest in carrying them out. The local taxes shall, as far as possible, be so imposed as not to affect the sources of production or to hinder the progress of internal commerce.

Works of public utility shall receive a suitable endowment, part of which shall be raised from private and special taxes levied in the provinces, which shall have the benefit of the advantages arising from the establishment of ways of communication by land and sea.

A special law having been already passed, which declares that the budget of the revenue and the expenditure of the state shall be drawn up and made known every year, the said law shall be most scrupulously observed. Proceedings shall be taken for revising the emoluments attached to each office.

The heads of each community and a delegate, designated by my Sublime Porte, shall be summoned to take part in the deliberations of the supreme council of justice on all occasions which might interest the generality of the subjects of my empire. They shall be summoned specially for this purpose by my grand vizier. The delegates shall hold office for one year; they shall be sworn on entering upon their duties. All the members of the council, at the ordinary and extraordinary meetings, shall freely give their opinions and their votes, and no one shall ever annoy them on this account.

The laws against corruption, extortion, or malversation shall apply, according to the legal forms, to all the subjects of my empire, whatever may be their class and the nature of their duties.

Steps shall be taken for the formation of banks and other similar institutions, so as to effect a reform in the monetary and financial system, as well as to create funds to be employed in augmenting the sources of the material wealth of my empire. Steps shall also be taken for the formation of roads and canals to increase the facilities of communication and increase the sources of the wealth of the country.

Everything that can impede commerce or agriculture shall be abolished. To accomplish these objects means shall be sought to profit by the science, the art, and the funds of Europe, and thus gradually to execute them.

Such being my wishes and my commands, you, who are my grand vizier, will, according to custom, cause this imperial firman to be published in my capital and in all parts of my empire; and you will watch attentively and take all the necessary measures that all the orders which it contains be henceforth carried out with the most rigorous punctuality.

3.   An Ottoman Government Decree Defines the Official Notion of the "Modern" Citizen, June 19, 1870

Derived in part from knowledge about the way the French, British, and Austrian governments functioned, and in part from local needs and established customs, these Tanzimat reforms attempted to extend the reach of the Ottoman government internally while allowing it to face external threats. This document seeks to draw an irrevocable distinction between "primitive" nomadic tribes—Bedouins—and "urbane" people who live in cities and villages. It makes strong value judgments about each category and provides a clear-cut recommendation for dealing with the Bedouins. Pay particular attention to the language used to describe each group, and question the characterizations. Think about likely reasons behind the creation of the two categories. Do not assume that the author is describing reality in an objective manner. What ideological motivation do you think lies behind this depiction of the Bedouin way of life?

To the model of proverbs and peers, His Excellency Firhan Pasha Zayd ʿAlwa. It is known that if one compares the tribes and people who live in the lifestyle of Bedouins [nomadic tribes] with those urbane people who live in the cities and villages, one will note the complexity in the customs of city-folk. In contrast, it will be noted that in comparison to the original creation of man and his internal self, the way of life of Bedouins is simple. In fact, the primitive and original state of man is most likely the same as that of the Bedouin. However, God has graced human beings with a characteristic that is absent from any other [species]. According to this characteristic, man cannot remain in his original state of creation but should prepare all that is needed for his food, drink, and clothing, and after this he must gather knowledge and develop commerce and other human necessities. He seeks to obtain other necessities as well, and every time he reaches a stage of acquisition, then he sees the need to advance and progress beyond what he had in the past. [. . .] Thus, it is apparent that even if the first state of man is to be a Bedouin, urbanity is a characteristic that cannot be separated from him. For the human being has become civilized [. . .] and the virtues of humanity cannot be attained except through the path of urbanization and civilization. Those who surpass their brethren and control all elements of this world, completely or partially, are those who live in the cities and who are civilized.

After proving that this is the case, we would like to explain and specify the reasons those people demand to remain in this state [of being Bedouins]. They remain in this state of deprivation of the virtues of humanity and the characteristics of civilization for several reasons. The first is that these people are ignorant of the state of the world and the nations. Because of their ignorance we have

Ottoman government decree issued to the Amir of Shamr, His Excellency Firhan Pasha, June 19, 1870. Ottoman archives of Directorate General of State Archives at the Prime Ministry (Tapu Tahrir: Mosul, 1869–1872). Translated by Akram Khater.

found our fathers desiring to stay unchanged in the state to which they were born. Secondly, the basis of the wealth of the tribes and clans is animals—in particular camels—and since it is difficult to manage and raise animals and camels in the cities—where they cannot find pasture—the people remain in their original state of being. [. . .] The third reason is that the mentioned peoples are like wild animals who enjoy what they have gotten used to in terms of stealing and raiding the property of others of their own people and killing them. This has become a reason for their wildness and their insistence on staying in the state of Bedouinism. It should be obvious that the first reason—which is ignorance and illiteracy—is an ugly and unacceptable characteristic in all the creatures of this world. And the second reason is the subordination [to tradition] characteristic of animals, and it is contrary to the image according to which man was created, for God has created the human being to be the most honorable of all creatures, and He made all breathing creatures subservient to him. He who is a Bedouin has become accustomed to the opposite of this natural order, so that although he used to be over other creatures, he has become subservient.

The truth is that this fallen state is an insult to humanity, and accordingly if we investigate the immense harm these tribes cause to each other, we will find that it has no equivalence in magnitude. For the human being has been commanded to protect those of his kind and treat them well, and is not commanded to do the opposite. In fact, all the religions command this [good treatment of others], and in particular the Mohammedan Shari'a. After proving that this is contrary to what has been commanded and is prohibited in all religions and in the Mohammedan Shari'a, then anyone with intelligence will see that harming people and robbing them of their money and their cattle is contrary to humanity and Islam. He who dares to commit that which we have mentioned must be punished. In addition, we see that this implies that since living as a Bedouin [. . .] leads to these harmful results, then no one should stay in that state of being, especially since we have arrived at a time and epoch [. . .] where to stay in this fallen and immoral state of existence appears as an ugly habit in the eyes of the world. For these explained reasons, these people cannot stay even for a short period in this state, and these tribes and clans should be settled and gain good human characteristics. It is imperative upon the Sublime Government to facilitate the emergence of these moral characteristics. This is particularly the case since those tribes and clans that have been settled during the past two years have faced difficulties and material needs, and they have remained in their original state because they are deprived of access to agriculture and commerce. Thus, and in order to feed their children, they have dared to attack the fields belonging to the inhabitants of the cities and towns. And in that case the government will have to reimburse the farmers for their losses and to dispatch imperial troops to punish the perpetrators, all of which costs money. Thus, and before matters reach this state, we would advise to give the lands that extend from Tikrit [village in Iraq] to the borders of Mosul [main city in northern Iraq] and that are located east of the Tigris River to the Shamr clan. Furthermore, we recommend that these lands be designated as a Mutassarifiya [provincial government within the Ottoman Empire] and be named as Sandjak [province] of Shamr, and that they [the clan of Shamr] be settled in these lands until they dig the necessary canals to the Tigris and reclaim the lands and plant them like other people. Once it is apparent that they are settled, then this place should be designated as a Mutassarifiya, like the Mutassarifiya of al-Muntafak, and this Mutassarifiya should be placed under your authority, O, Pasha! [. . .] Because those [people] are used to being Bedouins, and because it will be difficult to sever those ties all at once, then we should grant some of them with animals a permit to pasture their animals on some of the lands, provided that they return to their places of residence. In order to encourage development of these lands, we should exempt those who reclaim the lands and dig the ditches and canals from all but the Miri tax. [. . .] Once this Sandjak is formed according to what has preceded, and a Mutassarifiya is subsequently established, then troops should be sent to keep the peace, and the Mutassarif should be assigned a deputy and a tax collector and all that he requires in terms of government officials. [. . .]

This official Ottoman decree has been issued by the ministry of the Vilayet of Baghdad, and let it be known to all.

4.   Mirza Malkum Khan Satirizes Iran's Central Government and Religious Elites, 1880s

Like some of his contemporaries in Istanbul and Cairo, Mirza Malkum (1834–1898) was a political satirist who skewered existing political regimes and popular beliefs for their irrationality and corruption. Like writers such as Yaqub Sannu (in Egypt), Malkum was well traveled and well educated. Although he was born in Iran, he spent only ten years there. His father was a scion of the Armenian community in Iran, a community that during the nineteenth century was commercially powerful due to its connections to European mercantile interests. Malkum claimed descent from Jean-Jacques Rousseau through a distant grandmother. Malkum's father was originally Christian; he converted to Islam for personal and practical reasons. Throughout his life, Malkum proclaimed himself a Muslim. However, one scholar (Hamid Algar) argues that this profession was insincere at best and that Malkum used his proclamation of faith as a way to hide and justify his later criticisms and attacks on the Islamic faith.

Malkum's writings and lectures—some of which were delivered while he was living in England—seem to indicate his interest in an Islamic renaissance. Educated in France at the Armenian school from the age of ten, Malkum went on to study natural sciences and engineering, but his main focus of interest came to be political science. His studies, at least in his own opinion, made him an authority on the foundation of European civilization and on the reforms necessary for "civilizing" Iran. Usually writing from outside Iran, he was an effective critic of practices within the

Hamid Algar, *Mirza Malkum Khan* (Berkeley: University of California Press, 1973), pp. 300–308. Copyright © 1973 The Regents of The University of California. Reprinted by permission.

*country and among the Iranian people, but living as an expatriate was also a dis-
advantage because it prevented him from fully grasping the intricacies of Iranian
society and culture and to a certain extent colored his judgments with Western conceptions of his native land.*

*This selection from Malkum's writings provides a sampling of the political at-
tacks that Malkum launched in his newspaper, Qānūn, and the exaggerations in
which he was prone to indulge. The letters he quotes are fictitious and provide him
with stereotypical foils for his critiques of the religious and political establishments.*

*According to Hamid Algar, the following example of the journal Qānūn was
probably published in 1891. It represents Malkum's style of fabricating support for
his position and exaggerating the problems in Iran to the point of crisis. It is interesting to note, as does Hamid Algar in his book on Malkum, that Malkum's critiques
of Shah Nasr ad-Din are always indirect.*

We can convey to all supporters of the Law[1] the happy tidings that nowadays
all manner of thoughts are astir in Iran. Utterances are being made and courageous deeds performed that a few years ago none would have thought possible.

According to reliable information, a group of army officers and commanders has unanimously submitted the following declaration to the guardians of
the state:

> O guardians of the state!
> To what chaotic and miserable condition you have reduced Iran!
> Why do you thus harass our wretched people? What law, what faith
> can justify all this jailing, torturing, killing, and plundering? How
> much longer are we soldiers to cause misery to our people at your be-
> hest? What shame and humiliation we suffer at your hands as reward
> for our obedience and endurance: see in what scandalous way you have
> made of our military ranks and salaries a source of disgrace to the na-
> tion! You must think us entirely devoid of shame and honor to appoint
> your lowliest domestic servants not only over us, the commanders of
> the army, but over the minister of war, the offspring of the shah him-
> self.[2] There are men among us whose ancestors, for fourteen genera-
> tions, have sacrificed themselves in the service of the state, and now,
> without the slightest qualm, you force them, for the sake of a few filthy
> *shāhīs*[3] salary, to go and kiss the shoes of some dirty youth in your

---

[1]Malkum's use of the words *qānūn* and *ādamīyat* in his journal is deliberately ambiguous:
they might convey either their general senses of "law" and "humanity" respectively, or,
more narrowly, designate his newspaper and the secret society that undertook its distribution, the League of Humanity. In order to retain some sense of ambiguity in English, I have
translated the words in question and spelled them with capital letters. [All footnotes in this
selection are Algar's.]

[2]The minister of war was Kāmrān Mīrzā Nā'ib us-Salṭana, third son of Nāṣir ud-Dīn Shāh
and governor of Tehran.

[3]*Shāhī:* a unit of currency equivalent, in the Qajar period, to one twentieth of a *qirān*.

*ābdārkhāna*⁴ seventy times a day! Until today, we have been completely blind and unaware of our rights and duties. We imagined that the salaries we begged out of you with a thousand humiliations [literally, cuckoldries], you had somehow inherited from your fathers and that you bestowed them on us as an act of grace. But now we realize that our salaries are taken from the taxes which we, the people of Iran, pay for the protection of our rights and which you scandalously misuse to make prisoners of our nation. That time is past when we thought you to be our lords and masters and, deceived by your promises, subjected the property, life, and faith of the nation to your idiotic vagaries! The roaring flood of your oppressive deeds, the laments of the people, and the voice of Law have finally awakened us. Now we well understand that the Compassionate Lord did not create us for slavery to such as you! Now we are fully aware that, in accordance with the Law of God, we soldiers must be protectors of the people's rights, instead of ravening beasts unleashed by you to torture and trample underfoot our brothers in religion and fellow countrymen, at your whim and pleasure! Now we clearly realize that all this wretchedness of Iran is due to our apathy, neglect, and lack of union! We warn you that we have grasped the meaning and power of union, and we have become Men.⁵ We are no longer alone, that you might continue to incite us against each other and make us the executioners of our people. Henceforth, instead of being your lowly slaves and the torturers of the nation, we shall be the proud servants of the people of Iran and protectors of the rights of all true Men. We shall still sacrifice our lives, but it will be for the sake of our human rights, not for the shameful rule of injustice which you regard as your eternal fief! Awake, o guardians of evil, for we soldiers have become Men!

One of the ministers of Iran, who has wasted his life in service to the state and the desire for its progress and advancement and who now in utter disgust eagerly awaits his death, has written a brief description of the present state of Iran. He says in conclusion:

"Do not imagine that the men who rule the state themselves gain any benefit from the ruinous situation created by their stupidity. It is true that they appear to enjoy many privileges, but in reality they, and all who follow in their

---

⁴*Ābdārkhāna:* the room or outhouse in which a servant prepares coffee, tea, sherbet, or a water pipe for his master and his guests. Amīn us-Sulṭan's father was, of course, Nāṣir ud-Dīn Shāh's *ābdār,* the servant entrusted with these tasks, and Malkum's repeated references to the *ābdārkhāna* are intended as a reminder to all of Amīn us-Sulṭans lowly origin. It is implied that with his appointment to the premiership, the ministry has in effect been transformed into an *ābdārkhāna.*
⁵On the implications of the phrase "to become a man" (*ādam shudan*), see [Algar, 1973], p. 229.

wake, are the most wretched of us all. Which of our ministers can sleep tranquilly at night? What king other than our shah is imprisoned by servants and a prey to [material] needs? Everyone knows that this monarch, whose doorman is meant to be Darius and whose bodyguard reputedly consists of Khusrau and Alexander,[6] trembles in fear by night and day, is surrounded by executioners and has more difficulty supporting his family than his humblest servant! Were ever the children of some black slave in America as poor and distraught as the progeny of Fath 'Ali Shah?[7] Is there anyone in the land who has suffered more oppression than the children of 'Abbas Mirza?[8] Is there any humiliation and degradation[9] that has not constantly been visited on the brothers of the present shah?[10] As for his sons, ask them themselves: what hellish hovels they must go to in order to pay with their liver's blood for a crust of bread graciously bestowed on them by the servants of the *abdarkhana*! And what should I say concerning the sufferings endured by that noble being who has had the misfortune to see himself designated heir to the throne in this day and age? You must surely be aware that there is not a peasant in the whole of Iran who is at such a loss to secure his daily bread as this high-born prince! Where can one openly declare that in this same province of Azerbayjan where the appointees of the *abdarkhana* waste the salaries of twenty brigades on frivolous amusement, the future king of Iran does not even have a decent room in which to sit? It is because of things such as this that I say all one can do is to spit and then go and leave them all behind."

No, your Excellency. One must remain to become a Man, and by the propagation of Humanity to deliver one's progeny and nation from this ocean of catastrophe.

Another minister writes:
"It was well said that one should fear a government that has no shame. See the lengths to which their unprincipled shamelessness has gone! The guardians

---

[6]An allusion to the fulsome epithets bestowed on Nasir ud-Din Shah in panegyric poetry, in official documents and court chronicles.

[7]Fath 'Ali Shah had a particularly numerous progeny. For a full account of his reproductive achievements, see Ahmad Mirza 'Adud ud-Daula, *Tarikh-i 'Adudi*, ed. Husayn Kuhi Kirmani (Tehran, 1327 solar/1948), *passim*.

[8]That is, 'Abbas Mirza, the eldest son of Fath 'Ali Shah who predeceased his father in 1833.

[9]Malkum uses the expression *pisi varid kardan*, a colloquialism meaning "to trouble, to vex, to expose to disgrace" (see Muhammad 'Ali Jamalzada, *Farhang-i Lughat-i 'Ammiyana* [Tehran, 1341 solar/1962], p. 46). *Pisi* literally signifies leprosy, and Malkum's use of the expression is intended to emphasize the helpless and undignified state in which the shah's brothers find themselves. Much of the effectiveness of *Qanun* resided in the unprecedented literary use of vulgarisms such as this.

[10]Among the brothers of Nasir ud-Din Shah, 'Abbas Mirza Mulkara had a particularly disturbed career. He spent thirty years in exile in Baghdad under British protection, and, although later able to effect a reconciliation with his brother and return to Iran, he was constantly regarded with distrust and suspicion. See his autobiography, *Sharh-i Hal*, ed. 'Abd ul-Husayn Nava'i (Tehran, 1325 solar/1946).

of the realm now sit and forge blatant lies about well-tried servants of the state, lies which, as any child can see, prove only their stupidity and will end in their disgrace. Ask any of the celebrated European travelers whether he has ever encountered among some savage tribe a whore who would thus knowingly encompass her own disgrace by inventing transparent lies? A set of men who have made themselves the fountainhead of all the vices in the world, who continually surround themselves with mountainous heaps of scandal and disgrace—how dare they cause personal accusations to be printed in a newspaper![11] If the men of Law should wish to publish and reveal the deeds of these authors of Iran's misfortune, which one of them would ever dare, crouching in the corner of his stable, to show his head and face the stench of scandal and disgrace? But for such revelations there is no need: the pens of Humanity will pay no attention to the vices of these foremost scoundrels of the age. It is better to entrust their punish merit to the just verdict of the people of Iran."

A high-minded prince writes as follows:

"O men of Law! We members of the royal house are sincerely gratified at your efforts and intentions. The true meaning of service to the state and gratitude for favor received is precisely that which your eloquent pen sets forth. A thousand congratulations on your sense of honor and learning! The Qajar dynasty will be in your debt for all eternity! Even the blind can see that under present circumstances our monarchy is doomed. But none of us has dared to express the truth of the matter clearly, and it is you who has carried off the ball of manly courage. Continue to write, and write in harsh, straightforward terms, for our sleep of apathy is too deep to be dispelled by normal speech. Our monarch, as everyone is aware, is tired and imprisoned in his ābdārkhāna. It is as if he has abdicated and handed Iran over to these vicious rogues. If there is anything that can bring us to our senses, it is the whiplash of eloquent discourse. If today the monarch does not appreciate your manner of speaking the truth, be sure that the rush of events will soon prove, and his own imperial intuition confess, that the men of Law are the true well-wishers of the monarchy. So write on, noble servants of the state, write on! For our only hope lies in the popular enthusiasm that the spirit of Humanity has brought forth in the land of Iran."

O exalted prince!

We are performing our duty of service to the state; what are you doing? You can perform a thousand deeds for the salvation of the ship of state; why do you sit thus idly? You should have realized by now that although the foundation of the monarchy used to be the idiocy of the people, its preservation will henceforth be possible only through following the dictates of justice and the principles of Humanity. Who is better equipped than you to propagate those principles? Instead of waiting for the efforts of others to reform affairs, show some zeal yourself, and be the vanguard and protector of Humanity. You have

---

[11]Doubtless an angry allusion to the article published, by royal command, in the journal *Irān*. See [Algar, 1973], p. 180.

no excuse for delay in assuming this sacred task: all men of conscience are prepared [to help you], and the methods of propagation are inscribed in the breast of every self-respecting man. In accordance with these methods, and, using your intelligence and skill, gather together the Men you see around you, and attract them to your circle. Then appoint the more accomplished among them to be Trustees of Humanity[12] and encourage them in turn to found as many new circles as possible. Do not hesitate, for if you now grasp the grandeur of your destiny, you can without difficulty, by the spark of your words and the model of your example, kindle the light of Humanity in this realm, attain your highest goal and be a source of pride to Men until the end of time.

A respected merchant whose spirit soars high on account of Humanity writes from Tabriz:

"You can have little idea how the ministers of Tehran fear *Qānūn* and Humanity. They open everyone's letters, and anyone who has so much as glanced at *Qānūn* is arrested and asked why he has become a Man. The wise ones of Tehran seem to think they are extirpating the very names of *Qānūn* and Humanity from Iran, and they still imagine that *Qānūn* is a newspaper the contents of which become useless and outdated if it fails to arrive by post. They have not yet realized that if *Qānūn* comes by post or muleteer, today or next year, its contents will always be fresh. The more strictly it is prohibited, the more effective will be its ideas. Now the best present which can be brought from abroad is a page of *Qānūn*. Thanks to the measures of those wise men, the saddlebags of travelers and the pockets of pilgrims are stuffed to overflowing with copies of *Qānūn*. The day before yesterday, one of my partners found a thousand copies of *Qānūn* at the bottom of a crate of sugar that had just been brought from the customs. A trader in Salmās[13] found two hundred copies in a roll of broadcloth. What need, then, for new laws [to prevent the entry of *Qānūn*]? The copies which are already circulating among men of insight are enough to resurrect a graveyard. You can scarcely imagine how well some of our accomplished and learned men explain and expound on the principles of Humanity. Their commentary on each line of *Qānūn* is enough to fill a book. One of the great *mujtahids* openly says that the reading of *Qānūn* is the alchemy of union. The devil of disunity cannot penetrate the house where a page of *Qānūn* is to be found.[14]

"In short, men's thoughts are in a remarkable state of turmoil, and how, indeed, might it be otherwise? Did the people of Iran ever take an oath to lie abjectly beneath the kicks of a pitiless bunch of ruffians? The spirit of Iran everywhere bears witness that soon this edifice of tyranny shall collapse, and the banner of divine justice shall be hoisted throughout the realm."

---

[12]On the *Auṣiyā-yi Ādamīyat*, see [Algar, 1973], p. 233.

[13]A city in Azerbayjan, situated between Tabriz and Lake Riḍā'īya.

[14]This sentence is deliberately phrased to sound like a religious pronouncement, as if it were actually taken from the *fatvā* of a *mujtahid*.

Answers

H.A.   It has been sent. Always inform us of arrival.

M.‘A.   The injustice committed against your own person you may naturally forgive. But as for the injustice inflicted by the wild beasts[15] of the state on your brothers in Humanity—to avenge it is incumbent on every Man.

A.T.   Send more to the *‘atabāt*.

A.O.   The words of the vultures[16] are not worthy of attention.

Sh.M.   Consider these two brigades already prepared to sacrifice themselves for Humanity.

S.D.   God is greatest!

Declaration of the Guardians of the Victorious Ābdārkhāna

O people of Iran, what senseless words are these you now see fit to utter? Law, union, the protection of rights—what does all this mean? What law could be better than the sword of our executioners? What rights could be clearer than ours to enjoy your slavery? If you really wish, like other peoples, to reform and order your affairs anew and if—may God forbid—the people of Iran are to gain some honor and respect, then what is to become of our proprietary rights over you and your consecrated duties of servitude to us? Have not the vultures of our treasury explained to you a thousand times that whatever you have—life, property, religion, honor—all belongs to us? These shameless people who have started to speak of law are such unlettered idiots that we have been unable to find a particle of meaning in all the words they write, despite our learning and intelligence. It is for this very reason that in our tender concern for your welfare we anxiously seek to prevent your eyes from alighting on their writings. We do not doubt that with your sincere and slavish devotion to our angelic selves you will never look for unity, for unity is disbelief according to the norms by which we rule. If you wish to be sensible, you should exert yourselves to the utmost to be as far apart from and as hostile to each other as possible. It is in particular necessary for some of you to be Babis so that we can rip open their stomachs as a warning to others and confiscate their property with a plausible excuse. It is also highly desirable for you to be divided into a number of parties such as Shaykhī,[17] Mutasharri‘,[18] Shi‘i, Sunni, and Dahrī,[19] which insult, curse, and torment each other. For then you become quite oblivious of

---

[15]*Jānvarān:* the counterpart in Malkum's terminology, of *ādamān* ("men"), designating Malkum's enemies, Amīn us-Sulṭān and those who carried out his instructions.

[16]*Lāshakhūrān:* another term denoting Malkum's adversaries.

[17]See p. 282, n. 5 [in Algar, 1973].

[18]Mutasharri‘: one who binds himself to strict observance of the religious law (*sharī‘a*), in contradistinction to the Sufi who might exhibit antinomian tendencies.

[19]Dahrī: approximately, "materialist," "believer in eternal time." The word was originally applied to crypto-Manicheans, but its sense was later expanded to include any kind of heresy or disbelief.

your human rights, and without any trouble we can mount you like asses and load you with the burdens of disgrace to our heart's desire. Do not imagine that we will fail to appreciate your self-sacrificing services. Be sure that if ever you are as talented as Qā'im Maqām and serve the state as faithfully as he did, or if you are as skillful and devoted in restoring the fortunes of the monarchy as Mīrzā Taqī Khān,[20] without delay we shall ungrudgingly extend to you the same manful treatment we did to them. And if, God forbid, one of you should still persist in idle talk despite these oaths of ours, then know for certain that he shall immediately be marked as an ingrate, a traitor, and an infidel.

Of course, in your hearts you will in all justice agree that all the duties we assign you in your slavery correspond precisely to that Islam which we have produced especially for our own protection. Who observes the principles of our Islam better than we ourselves? See how firmly we have silenced your *mujtahids* and caused them humbly to submit to the raging beasts who are our servants! See how powerfully and thoroughly we have extirpated every trace of just practice and equitable behavior throughout the well-guarded land [of Iran]![21] Is there anyone who has ever sold the rights of the state and the means of livelihood of the people so cheaply to foreigners as we have done? The scandal and disgrace of bribes, the drunken arrogance of power, the invention of all kinds of foul sport, the squandering of the Muslims' treasury,[22] was ever there an age in which these evils were more flourishing? How is it possible that despite all these manifest bounties you are not night and day engaged in praying for the perpetuation of our wise and skillful rule? If, in accordance with the customs of this lofty institution, the beasts of state should plunder at their will your rights and all your possessions and reduce you to a state of abject beggary worse than that of any savage tribe, why should you grieve and sorrow? Do you not see how strictly we have forbidden the newspaper *Akhtar*[23] to say a word on matters such as these? And if we are able to expel you from your homeland whenever we choose, without interrogation, and to cut off your ear and nose and head without a trial, then what cause is there for surprise? Do you not know that our Bounteous Lord has created your entire being solely for our pleasure? So, o people of Iran, instead of following the path of error and seeking out the laws of God, try to appreciate our acts of compassion to our subjects, and ponder on your inherently slavish state. Be proud that we have made

---

[20]Here, as in his letter to *The Times* of March 16, 1891 (see [Algar, 1973,] p. 180). Malkum is again attempting to identify himself implicitly with two ministers who had given their lives for the sake of reform.

[21]*Mamālik-i Maḥrūsa:* the conventional designation for Iran in official documents and chronicles, here intended satirically.

[22]In order to arouse religious feeling, Malkum uses the expression *bayt ul-māl*, the term by which the treasury of the Islamic state was designated in the lifetime of the Prophet, instead of the usual *khazāna*.

[23]On the vicissitudes of *Akhtar*, see [Algar, 1973], pp. 186–187.

of the land over which Jamshīd[24] used to reign a blot on the history of the age and thus proven and recorded the extent of your dignity and honor. In gratitude for this bounty, fall upon the earth and kiss those *gīva's*[25] of the blessed *ābdārkhāna* which have trampled under their filthy heels such a nation as Iran and aroused the wonder of all mankind!

In reply to this proclamation of the present rulers of Tehran, the Spirit of Humanity cries out in tones that penetrate to every corner of the earth:

"O Iran of lofty fortune! It is not your allotted portion in this world to suffer the disgrace of slavery now imposed upon you! For centuries you were the throne on which the glory of Humanity reposed; why should you today lie buried in the graveyard of abjection? Where are those lions of heavenly lineage who bequeathed as a trust to your virtue and honor, glory and felicity in this world and the hereafter? Arise, o champion of wounded heart, for the days of darkness are at an end, and the sun of knowledge has illumined the world from East to West."

5. Jamal al-Din Al-Afghani Answers Ernest Renan's Criticism of Islam, May 18, 1883

Many scholars consider Jamal al-Din Al-Afghani to be one of the most prominent Islamic thinkers and political activists of the nineteenth century. In his lifetime many areas with large Muslim communities came under the direct or indirect control of the European imperial powers. This political, economic, and cultural subjugation prompted him to write various tracts that sought to explain the decline of the Islamic world historically, to defend Islam against its detractors (European and local), and to present a blueprint of sorts for a modernism that would fit within the boundaries of Islamic values.

Al-Afghani was born in 1838 in a town 180 miles from Kabul, Afghanistan, to a distinguished family. He was trained as a religious scholar and became fluent in various languages, including Arabic and Farsi. When he was eighteen, he began a series of travels that took him from India to Iran, the Ottoman Empire, Egypt, and France, where he lived long enough to become exposed to the philosophies and political ideas of the time. He died in 1897 in the Ottoman Empire under suspicious circumstances.

Al-Afghani believed that Islam was not incompatible with science and rationality, as some thinkers (including Ernest Renan, the French philosopher to whom he responds in this document) argued. Rather, Al-Afghani maintained, rigid interpretations of religion and the weight of local traditions made the Islamic world appear "backward," and, according to Al-Afghani and his disciple Muhammad 'Abduh, believers ought not abandon Islam but seek to interpret its scriptures from the

---

[24]A legendary king of pre-Islamic Iran, generally equated with Solomon.

[25]*Gīva*: A kind of canvas shoe, with a sole made of pieces of rag pressed together, commonly worn by peasants in Iran.

perspective of modern society. This ijtihad *(loosely translated as "rational interpretation") would free Islamic societies from outworn traditions and become an engine for social, economic, educational, and political change. At the same time, Islam would provide the necessary moral guidelines to restrain science from transgressing ethical boundaries.*

In this selection, Al-Afghani responds to Ernest Renan's attacks on Islam. Try to identify Al-Afghani's main ideas and to evaluate his arguments. What do you think of his vision of Islam? What are the limitations of that vision? To what extent do you think it would have been possible to apply Al-Afghani's ideas?

Sir,

I have read in your estimable journal of last March 29 a talk on Islam and Science, given in the Sorbonne before a distinguished audience by the great thinker of our time, the illustrious M. Renan, whose renown has filled the West and penetrated into the farthest countries of the East. Since this speech suggested to me some observations, I took the liberty of formulating them in this letter, which I have the honor of addressing to you with a request that you accommodate it in your columns.

M. Renan wanted to clarify a point of the history of the Arabs which had remained unclear until now and to throw a live light on their past, a light that may be somewhat troubling for those who venerate these people, though one cannot say that he has usurped the place and rank that they formerly occupied in the world. M. Renan has not at all tried, we believe, to destroy the glory of the Arabs which is indestructible; he has applied himself to discovering historical truth and making it known to those who do not know it, as well as to those who study the influence of religions in the history of nations, and in particular in that of civilization. I hasten to recognize that M. Renan has acquitted himself marvelously of this very difficult task, in citing certain facts that have passed unnoticed until this time. I find in his talk remarkable observations, new perceptions, and an indescribable charm. However, I have under my eyes only a more or less faithful translation of this talk. If I had had the opportunity to read it in the French text, I could have penetrated better the ideas of this great thinker. He receives my humble salutation as an homage that is due him and as the sincere expression of my admiration. I would say to him, finally, in these circumstances, what al-Mutanabbi, a poet who loved philosophy wrote several centuries ago to a high personage whose actions he celebrated: "Receive," he said to him, "the praises that I can give you; do not force me to bestow on you the praises that you merit."

M. Renan's talk covered two principal points. The eminent philosopher applied himself to proving that the Muslim religion was by its very essence opposed to the development of science, and that the Arab people, by their nature, do not like either metaphysical sciences or philosophy. This precious plant,

Nikki R. Keddie, *An Islamic Response to Imperialism: Political and Religious Writings of Sayyid Jamāl ad-Dīn "al-Afghānī"* (Berkeley: University of California Press, 1968), pp. 181–187. Reprinted by permission of the author.

M. Renan seems to say, dried up in their hands as if burnt up by the breath of the desert wind. But after reading this talk one cannot refrain from asking one-self if these obstacles come uniquely from the Muslim religion itself or from the manner in which it was propagated in the world; from the character, man-ners, and aptitudes of the peoples who adopted this religion, or of those on whose nations it was imposed by force. It is no doubt the lack of time that kept M. Renan from elucidating these points; but the harm is no less for that, and if it is difficult to determine its causes in a precise manner and by irrefutable proofs, it is even more difficult to indicate the remedy.

As to the first point, I will say that no nation at its origin is capable of let-ting itself be guided by pure reason. Haunted by terrors that it cannot escape, it is incapable of distinguishing good from evil, of distinguishing that which could make it happy from that which might be the unfailing source of its un-happiness and misfortune. It does not know, in a word, either how to trace back causes or to discern effects.

This lacuna means that it cannot be led either by force or persuasion to prac-tice the actions that would perhaps be the most profitable for it, or to avoid what is harmful. It was therefore necessary that humanity look outside itself for a place of refuge, a peaceful corner where its tormented conscience could find repose. It was then that there arose some educator or other who, not having, as I said above, the necessary power to force humanity to follow the inspirations of rea-son, hurled it into the unknown and opened to it vast horizons where the imag-ination was pleased and where it found, if not the complete satisfaction of its desires, at least an unlimited field for its hopes. And, since humanity, at its origin, did not know the causes of the events that passed under its eyes and the secrets of things, it was perforce led to follow the advice of its teachers and the orders they gave. This obedience was imposed in the name of the supreme Being to whom the educators attributed all events, without permitting men to discuss its utility or its disadvantages. This is no doubt for man one of the heaviest and most humiliating yokes, as I recognize; but one cannot deny that it is by this religious education, whether it be Muslim, Christian, or pagan, that all nations have emerged from barbarism and marched toward a more advanced civilization.

If it is true that the Muslim religion is an obstacle to the development of sci-ences, can one affirm that this obstacle will not disappear someday? How does the Muslim religion differ on this point from other religions? All religions are intolerant, each one in its way. The Christian religion, I mean the society that follows its inspirations and its teachings and is formed in its image, has emerged from the first period to which I have just alluded; thenceforth free and indepen-dent, it seems to advance rapidly on the road of progress and science, whereas Muslim society has not yet freed itself from the tutelage of religion. Realizing, however, that the Christian religion preceded the Muslim religion in the world by many centuries, I cannot keep from hoping that Muhammadan society will succeed someday in breaking its bonds and marching resolutely in the path of civilization after the manner of Western society, for which the Christian faith, despite its rigors and intolerance, was not at all an invincible obstacle. No, I can-not admit that this hope be denied to Islam. I plead here with M. Renan not the cause of the Muslim religion, but that of several hundreds of millions of men, who would thus be condemned to live in barbarism and ignorance.

In truth, the Muslim religion has tried to stifle science and stop its progress. It has thus succeeded in halting the philosophical or intellectual movement and in turning minds from the search for scientific truth. A similar attempt, if I am not mistaken, was made by the Christian religion, and the venerated leaders of the Catholic church have not yet disarmed so far as I know. They continue to fight energetically against what they call the spirit of vertigo and error. I know all the difficulties that the Muslims will have to surmount to achieve the same degree of civilization, access to the truth with the help of philosophic and scientific methods being forbidden them. A true believer must, in fact, turn from the path of studies that have for their object scientific truth, studies on which all truth must depend, according to an opinion accepted at least by some people in Europe. Yoked, like an ox to the plow, to the dogma whose slave he is, he must walk eternally in the furrow that has been traced for him in advance by the interpreters of the law. Convinced, besides, that his religion contains in itself all morality and all sciences, he attaches himself resolutely to it and makes no effort to go beyond. Why should he exhaust himself in vain attempts? What would be the benefit of seeking truth when he believes he possesses it all? Will he be happier on the day when he has lost his faith, the day when he has stopped believing that all perfections are in the religion he practices and not in another? Wherefore he despises science. I know all this, but I know equally that this Muslim and Arab child whose portrait M. Renan traces in such vigorous terms and who, at a later age, becomes "a fanatic, full of foolish pride in possessing what he believes to be absolute truth," belongs to a race that has marked its passage in the world, not only by fire and blood, but by brilliant and fruitful achievements that prove its taste for science, for all the sciences, including philosophy (with which, I must recognize, it was unable to live happily for long).

I am led here to speak of the second point that M. Renan treated in his lecture with an incontestable authority. No one denies that the Arab people, while it was still in the state of barbarism, rushed into the road of intellectual and scientific progress with a rapidity only equaled by the speed of its conquests, since in the space of a century, it acquired and assimilated almost all the Greek and Persian sciences that had developed slowly during several centuries on their native soil, just as it extended its domination from the Arabian peninsula up to the mountains of the Himalaya and the summit of the Pyrenees.

One might say that in all this period the sciences made astonishing progress among the Arabs and in all the countries under their domination. Rome and Byzantium were then the seats of theological and philosophical sciences as well as the shining center and burning hearth of all human knowledge. Having followed for several centuries the path of civilization, the Greeks and Romans walked with assurance over the vast field of science and philosophy. There came, however, a time when their researches were abandoned and their studies interrupted.

The monuments they had built to science collapsed and their most precious books were relegated to oblivion. The Arabs, ignorant and barbaric as they were in origin, took up what had been abandoned by the civilized nations, rekindled the extinguished sciences, developed them and gave them a brilliance they had never had. Is not this the index and proof of their natural love for sciences? It is true that the Arabs took from the Greeks their philosophy as they stripped the Persians of what made their fame in antiquity; but these sciences, which they usurped by right of conquest, they developed, extended, clarified, perfected, completed, and coordinated with a perfect taste and a rare precision and exactitude. Besides, the French, the Germans, and the English were not so far from Rome and Byzantium as were the Arabs, whose capital was Baghdad. It was therefore easier for the former to exploit the scientific treasures that were buried in these two great cities. They made no effort in this direction until Arab civilization lit up with its reflections the summits of the Pyrenees and poured its light and riches on the Occident. The Europeans welcomed Aristotle, who had emigrated and become Arab; but they did not think of him at all when he was Greek and their neighbor. Is there not in this another proof, no less evident, of the intellectual superiority of the Arabs and of their natural attachment to philosophy? It is true that after the fall of the Arab kingdom in the Orient as in the Occident, the countries that had become the great centers of science, like Iraq and Andalusia, fell again into ignorance and became the center of religious fanaticism; but one cannot conclude from this sad spectacle that the scientific and philosophic progress of the Middle Ages was not due to the Arab people who ruled at that time.

M. Renan does do them this justice. He recognizes that the Arabs conserved and maintained for centuries the hearth of science. What nobler mission for a people! But while recognizing that from about A.D. 775 to near the middle of the thirteenth century, that is to say during about five hundred years, there were in Muslim countries very distinguished scholars and thinkers, and that during this period the Muslim world was superior in intellectual culture to the Christian world, M. Renan has said that the philosophers of the first centuries of Islam as well as the statesmen who became famous in this period were mostly from Harran, from Andalusia, and from Iran. There were also among them Transoxianan and Syrian priests. I do not wish to deny the great qualities of the Persian scholars nor the role that they played in the Arab world; but permit me to say that the Harranians were Arabs and that the Arabs in occupying Spain and Andalusia did not lose their nationality; they remained Arabs. Several centuries before Islam the Arabic language was that of the Harranians. The fact that they preserved their former religion, Sabaeanism, does not mean they should be considered foreign to the Arab nationality. The Syrian priests were also for the most part Ghassanian Arabs converted to Christianity.

As for Ibn-Bajja, Ibn-Rushd (Averroes), and Ibn-Tufail, one cannot say that they are not just as Arab as al-Kindi because they were not born in Arabia, especially if one is willing to consider that human races are only distinguished by their languages and that if this distinction should disappear, nations would not take long to forget their diverse origins. The Arabs who put their arms in the service of the Muslim religion, and who were simultaneously warriors and apostles, did not impose their language on the defeated, and wherever they established themselves, they preserved it for them with a jealous care. No doubt Islam, in penetrating the conquered countries with the violence that is known,

transplanted there its language, its manners, and its doctrine, and these countries could not thenceforth avoid its influence. Iran is an example; but it is possible that in going back to the centuries preceding the appearance of Islam, one
would find that the Arabic language was not then entirely unknown to Persian
scholars. The expansion of Islam gave it, it is true, a new scope, and the Persian
scholars converted to the Muhammadan faith thought it an honor to write their
books in the language of the Koran. The Arabs cannot, no doubt, claim for
themselves the glory that renders these writers illustrious, but we believe that
they do not need this claim; they have among themselves enough celebrated
scholars and writers. What would happen if, going back to the first period of
Arab domination, we followed step by step the first group from which was
formed this conquering people who spread their power over the world, and if,
eliminating everything that is outside this group and its descendants, we did
not take into account either the influence it exercised on minds or the impulse
it gave to the sciences? Would we not be led, thus, no longer to recognize in
conquering peoples other virtues or merits than those that flow from the material fact of conquest? All conquered peoples would then regain their moral autonomy and would attribute to themselves all glory, no part of which could be
legitimately claimed by the power that fructified and developed these germs,
Thus, Italy would come to say to France that neither Mazarin nor Bonaparte
belonged to her; Germany or England would in turn claim the scholars who,
having come to France, made its professorships illustrious and enhanced the
brilliance of its scientific renown. The French, on their side, would claim for
themselves the glory of the offspring of those illustrious families who, after
[the revocation of] the edict of Nantes, emigrated to all Europe. And if all Europeans belong to the same stock, one can with justice claim that the Harranians and the Syrians, who are Semites, belong equally to the great Arab family.

It is permissible, however, to ask oneself why Arab civilization, after having thrown such a live light on the world, suddenly became extinguished; why
this torch has not been relit since; and why the Arab world still remains buried
in profound darkness.

Here the responsibility of the Muslim religion appears complete. It is clear
that wherever it became established, this religion tried to stifle the sciences and
it was marvelously served in its designs by despotism.

Al-Siuti tells that the Caliph al-Hadi put to death in Baghdad 5000 philosophers in order to destroy sciences in the Muslim countries down to their roots.
Admitting that this historian exaggerated the number of victims, it remains
nonetheless established that this persecution took place, and it is a bloody stain
for the history of a religion as it is for the history of a people. I could find in the
past of the Christian religion analogous facts. Religions, by whatever names
they are called, all resemble each other. No agreement and no reconciliation are
possible between these religions and philosophy. Religion imposes on man its
faith and its belief, whereas philosophy frees him of it totally or in part. How
could one therefore hope that they would agree with each other? When the
Christian religion, under the most modest and seductive forms, entered Athens
and Alexandria, which were, as everyone knows, the two principal centers of

science and philosophy, after becoming solidly established in these two cities its first concern was to put aside real science and philosophy, trying to stifle both under the bushes of theological discussions, to explain the inexplicable mysteries of the Trinity, the Incarnation, and Transubstantiation. It will always be thus. Whenever religion will have the upper hand, it will eliminate philosophy; and the contrary happens when it is philosophy that reigns as sovereign mistress. So long as humanity exists, the struggle will not cease between dogma and free investigation, between religion and philosophy; a desperate struggle in which, I fear, the triumph will not be for free thought, because the masses dislike reason, and its teachings are only understood by some intelligences of the elite, and because, also, science, however beautiful it is, does not completely satisfy humanity, which thirsts for the ideal and which likes to exist in dark and distant regions that the philosophers and scholars can neither perceive nor explore.

6.   Baghdadi Jews React to the Modernization of the Ottoman Empire, May 28, 1908

In 1908 the Committee of Union and Progress (commonly known as the Young Turks) came to power in Istanbul and remained in control of the Ottoman Empire until its dissolution in 1918. Since its formation in exile in Paris in 1889, the CUP had presented itself as a liberal organization seeking to decentralize political power and championing political rights and a greater degree of equality among the ethnically and religiously varied citizenry of the empire. Although the CUP became increasingly oppressive—thus alienating many early supporters—at least at first it offered the promise of freedoms unparalleled in the history of the Ottoman Empire. This document is a report by a teacher from the Alliance Israélite Universelle, a French Jewish organization that aimed to modernize non-European Jews by establishing French-language schools amidst those communities. He describes the reaction of Jews in Baghdad, Iraq, to the arrival of the CUP to power. Highly contemptuous of the local Iraqi Muslims, his words give—perhaps—an exaggerated image of the glee of the local Jews, as well as the writer's take on Muslims' feelings about the CUP and the reasons behind them.

Baghdad, 28 May 1909

[. . .]

The Christians and the Jews both gave a very enthusiastic welcome to the new regime.[1] The Jews especially had anxiously followed every turn taken in the combat being waged between autocracy and freedom; they knew instinctively that their fate depended on the outcome of this battle. For them the triumph of liberty was not simply the fulfillment of a spiritual and intellectual

_____

[1] A reference to the Young Turks, who came to power in 1908. [All footnotes in this document are Rodrigue's.]

aspiration; it was a question of life itself. This triumph represented a safeguard against an arbitrary government and protection against the fanaticism of the population, which, from that moment, lost all official sanctioning of its harassment of the Jews.

Although the non-Muslims joyously greeted the news of the constitution, the majority of the Muslims were cold and hostile. The reason for their discontent must be attributed to various causes:

The Muslims already sensed that the new regime would strike heavy blows against their fanaticism. The dream of a good Muslim would be to see Islam triumph throughout the world, and toward this dream he must eliminate the infidel, whatever the means. With the freedom granted by the constitution, the good Muslim finds himself obliged to hold his hatred in check, and he can no longer indulge in methodical persecutions. The Muslims cannot conceive that the infidels should benefit from the same rights as they. Jews, their equals, brothers of the Muslims: what an upheaval in their way of thinking! To their eyes it is quite audacious to consider treating Muslims on an equal footing with the infidels; the latter are for them *kefirs,* impure beings, execrated by God, and must disappear from the face of the earth.

By protecting the Jews from the ill-will and injustice of the Muslims, the constitution has exasperated them. They find their hands are tied and they are forced to maintain a certain respect, at least an apparent respect, for the infidels. [. . .]

During the long months which followed the promulgation of the constitution, and especially during the recent unrest in Constantinople after the coup d'état of Abdul Hamid, the non-Muslims were not always certain of what tomorrow would bring. They feared renewed aggressions and their fear contributed quite a bit to the spreading of alarming rumors. Among themselves they were saying the Muslims would certainly be moved by what was happening in Constantinople and that, reactionaries by nature, they would lend a hand to the reactionaries in the capital in striking a decisive blow to the liberal institutions. [. . .]

Since the definitive victory of the Committee for Union and Progress, there has been more light on the horizon and more sense of security in the city. As the reactionaries are no longer in a position to take advantage of an equivocal situation, they are forced to resign themselves. They did not receive the news of Abdul Hamid's ousting with great enthusiasm, but they could not manifest their discontent very openly. They no longer have the support of the government, which had no other choice but to take a liberal attitude.

Will the new regime have a profound effect on the conscience of the population? Is it an answer to the hopes of the people? Will they know how to put their new rights to good use? The Christians and the Jews, although they have

Archives of the Alliance Israélite Universelle, Irak I.C.4. This document may also be found in Aron Rodrigue, *Images of Sephardi and Eastern Jewries in Transition: The Teachers of the Alliance Israélite Universelle, 1860–1939* (Seattle: University of Washington Press, 1999), pp. 263–265.

not been well prepared for liberty, have fervently aspired to it. They have suffered tyranny too long not to embrace liberty fully. Their spirits are finally released: their lives and their possessions protected. It is only a question of time and education before they are able to profit from the changes which have taken place in the country.

[. . .]

In no other country are the laws more in advance of habits and customs than in Mesopotamia. The social condition of the Muslims is very backward, and as the Muslims are the majority, the backlash is felt among the Jews and the Christians. One example of this is the extreme scorn and disdain which the Muslim feels toward women; to him they are inferior beings who must be left to wallow in ignorance and in tedium. Women are made to take care of the home and to be slaves to the masters . . .

[. . .]

And so we see that the Muslims are the stumbling block to all progress; they are a dead weight which also drags down the rest of the population. Since they are enemies of all innovation, they look with a critical eye upon any effort on the part of the others to create a better life. Thus, they would like to stop the others from wearing European dress. This is considered a sign of civilization to them. They also want to put a stop to the habit of caring for one's personal appearance. They are capable of stoning a Turkish subject should he wear a hat. The others must model themselves after the Muslims, and even remain at a lower level than they.

To bring down this bastion of fanaticism and ignorance and to bring thousands of individuals back to life and to action, the new government must put all of its efforts in the instruction and education of the masses. The only way to purify the contaminated air which stifles the city is to allow new air to come in. Thus, they should organize a system of instruction which answers modern needs and is based on modern ideas. The government will no doubt meet with stubborn resistance on the part of the *ulemas* [Muslim clergy], who run the Islamic schools and who see to it that the Koran is not open to close examination. But the government is stronger than they are, and it must firmly impose its will.

[. . .]

The victory won by the Committee for Union and Progress will be a simple illusion if the Committee does not manage to institute an educational system throughout the empire. Liberty will be simply a word devoid of meaning, and even a source of danger, if the population is not prepared to deal with it wisely. This preparation will come only when the population becomes aware of its own rights and potentials.

[. . .]

A. Franco

CHAPTER 2

Economic Changes

The Industrial Revolution, which took off first in England in the early eighteenth century and later in continental Europe, had dramatic effects on the Middle East and North Africa. Based as it was on the rapid production and consumption of textiles, this revolution required two main ingredients to succeed: markets and raw materials. Factory owners in Birmingham and Lyons—among other places—needed ever expanding markets if they were to continue accumulating wealth and capital. At first, England and the rest of Europe provided adequate outlets for the yards of manufactured textiles, but by the nineteenth century this was no longer the case. Thus, many manufacturers cast glances at markets farther afield, including those located within the Ottoman Empire and Iran.

The fact that the Ottoman Empire and Iran entered the nineteenth century with a military considerably weaker than that of the European states made it easy for the latter to gain access to Ottoman markets. The first document, a treaty between Russia and Iran, exemplifies the direct relationship between European military power and their economic gains in the Middle East. Partly in exchange for expelling Muhammad 'Ali (governor of Egypt) from Ottoman lands he had occupied in the early 1830s, the British government extracted serious economic concessions from the Ottomans through the Treaty of Balta Liman (1838). The agreement (document 2) provided for the abolition of all monopolies within the Ottoman Empire—monopoly was a tool that Muhammad 'Ali used to develop the Egyptian economy—and granted all foreign goods entering the empire the very low tariff rate of 3 percent. Other Europeans states soon followed Britain's lead and wrested from the empire equally favorable trade agreements, all of which opened the empire more than ever to European goods.

The economic inequality resulting from such agreements was compounded by the financial strain of modernizing the imperial army and bureaucracy. The Tanzimat reforms were driven in part by the political and military losses that the empire suffered at the hands of various European powers. Some of the funding for modernization came from tax increases in the provinces, but provincial governors struggled—many times successfully—to retain local control over their resources. Thus, the imperial government found it necessary to borrow more and more money from European banks and governments, which were eager to provide short-term, high-interest loans. The onerous foreign debt and state mismanagement of the borrowed funds and of state budgets brought Egypt and the Ottoman Empire to the brink of bankruptcy. Fearing default on the various loans threatened by Khedive Isma'il in Egypt, England and France intervened militarily in Egypt and politically in the Ottoman Empire to force the establishment of a public debt administration in each. Dominated by European powers, these administrations took direct control of the state budgets, in Egypt (document 3) and the Ottoman Empire.

Iran, too, did not escape European advances. In the nineteenth century it became the scene of a political tug of war between Russia and England. In 1857 the British prevailed on Shah Nasir al-Din to grant them commercial concessions similar to those granted by Egypt and the Ottoman Empire. While Russia sought to gain greater political control over Iran—at least the northern parts of it—England sought to promote economic development that would strengthen the central government of Iran while at the same time providing the British with an economic advantage over the Russians. The shah of Iran attempted to manipulate this rivalry to his advantage by providing concessions to the British and the Russians alternately. For example, in 1872 Baron Julius de Reuter obtained exclusive rights to develop all railways, canals, and dams in Iran in addition to extensive privileges in mining and agriculture. In this way, Shah Nasir al-Din exchanged the long-term development of Iran for modest initial fees and royalties.

Documents 4 through 7 provide examples of economic agreements between the Ottoman and the Iranian governments, on the one hand, and various European interests, on the other. From central governments in the Middle East and North Africa, European governments and companies extracted potentially lucrative agreements. Among the outcomes of such agreements were European control of the Suez Canal (document 4) and the establishing of the Imperial Bank of Persia by Britain (document 5). However, the Europeans' ability to capitalize on such opportunities was not guaranteed. The Ottoman and Iranian central governments had little effective control over outlying regions of their territories. Moreover, although government officials in Istanbul and Tehran may have agreed to certain concessions, their provincial counterparts in Mosul or Tabriz were not always willing to cooperate. Whether seeking to protect their local power and sources of wealth or to defend the principle of sovereignty, local authorities often hindered the implementation of these agreements. Also, local populations both passively and actively resisted what they considered to be the unfair terms of the concessions, some of which posed threats to their economic well-being. Ordinary people resented the intrusion of foreigners and their local agents.

Documents 6 and 7, about the French tobacco monopoly and tobacco smuggling, provide clues to the relationship among European interests and Ottoman and Iranian imperial and local interests. The complexity of this relationship should keep us from accepting the notion that technological superiority guaranteed Europeans unfettered access to the economies of the Middle East and North Africa. Rather, it appears that negotiation, frustration, and failure were as much part of this history as Europeans' success in achieving their imperialist and capitalist goals. Also, it is important to note that the Europeans were able to win concessions not simply because of their industrial superiority. In subtle and blunt ways, France, England, and Russia parlayed their military might into political influence that led to economic benefits for European merchants and industrialists.

1. The Treaty of Peace and Commerce (Treaty of Turkmanchai) Between Iran and Russia, February 10–22, 1828

Throughout the nineteenth century, the Russian Empire sought to expand its influence south into the Middle East, toward warm-water ports, and to counter British and French interests encroaching into that area. More so than either Britain or France, the Russian Empire used military campaigns to conquer territory and to encourage the Ottomans and the Persians to sign treaties advantageous to Russian interests. From 1826–1828 the Russians conducted successful campaigns against the army of the shah of Iran and forced the shah to sign a peace treaty in the village of Turkmanchai, in the province of Azerbaijan, that permitted them to annex the provinces of Erivan and Nakhichevan. Moreover, the treaty allowed the Russians exclusive naval rights over the Caspian Sea. Annexed to these political elements of the treaty were commercial concessions giving the Russians greater access to local Iranian markets. This is an example of the deliberate and direct use of European military power to extract political and economic gains at the expense of indigenous governments.

1. The Treaty of Peace

ART. I.   There will be, dating from this day, peace, friendship and perfect understanding between His Majesty the Emperor of all the Russias on one hand, and His Majesty the Shah of Persia on the other, their Heirs and Successors, their States and their respective Subjects, in perpetuity.

ART. II.   Considering that the hostilities taken place between the High Contracting Parties, and happily terminated today, have brought to an end the obligations which the Treaty of Gulistan imposed upon them, His Majesty the

British and Foreign State Papers, 33-884. This document can also be found in J. C. Hurewitz, *The Middle East and North Africa in World Politics* (New Haven, Conn.: Yale University Press, 1975), pp. 232–237.

Emperor of all the Russias and His Majesty the Shah in Shan [King of Kings] of Persia have judged it appropriate to replace the said Treaty of Gulistan by the present Clauses and Stipulations, which are designed to regulate and to consolidate more and more the future relations of peace and friendship between Russia and Persia.

ART. III.   His Majesty the Shah of Persia, both in his name as in that of his Heirs and Successors, cedes in entire ownership to the Russian Empire the Khanate of Erivan on both sides of the Araxe, and the Khanate of Nakhitchevan. In consequence of this cession, His Majesty the Shah undertakes to turn over to the Russian Authorities, within six months at the latest, from the date of signature of the present Treaty, all the archives and all public documents concerning the administration of the two Khanates above-mentioned.

ART. IV.   The two High Contracting Parties agree to establish, as the frontier between the two States, the following line of demarcation: In parting from the point of the frontier of the Ottoman States, the nearest in a straight line from the summit of the little Ararat, this line will continue to the summit of this mountain from whence it will descend to the source of the river known as the Lower Karassou which flows from the southern side of the Little Ararat and it will follow its course until its discharge in the Araxe, opposite Cherour. Arrived at this point, this line will follow the bed of the Araxe to the Fortress of Abbas-Abad; around the exterior works of this place which are situated on the right bank of the Araxe, there will be traced a radius of a half agatch, or three versts and a half from Russia, which will extend in all directions; all the land which will be enclosed in this radius will belong exclusively to Russia and will be demarked with the greatest exactitude in the space of two months, dating from this day, From the locality where the eastern extremity of this radius will have rejoined the Araxe, the frontier line will continue to follow the bed of this river to the ford of Jediboulouk, from whence the Persian Territory will extend the length of the bed of the Araxe for a distance of three agatch or twenty-one versts from Russia; arrived at this point, the frontier line will traverse in a direct manner the plain of Moughan to the bed of the river known as Bolgarou, to the place situated at three agatch or twenty-one versts below the conjunction of the two small rivers known as Odinabazar and Sarakamyche. From there, this line will reascend from the left bank of the Bolgarou to the junction of the said rivers Odinabazar and Sarakamyche and will extend the length of the right bank of the river of Odinabazar to its source and from there to the summit of the heights of Djikoir so that all the waters which flow towards the Caspian Sea will belong to Russia, and all those [whose] watershed is of the Persian side will belong to Persia. The limit of the two States being marked here by the crest of the mountains, it is agreed that the declination from the side of the Caspian Sea will belong to Russia and that their opposite slope will belong to Persia. From the crest of the heights of Djikoir, the frontier will follow the summit of Kamarkouia, the mountains which separate the Talyche from the district of Archa. The crests of the mountains, separating on all sides the watershed, will determine here the frontier line in the same manner as stated above concerning the distance included between the source of the Odinabazar and the summits of Djikoir. The frontier line will follow thereafter, from the summit of Kamarkouia, the crests of the mountains which separate the district of Zouvante from that of Archa to the limit of that of Welkidji, always conforming to the principle enunciated in connection with the watershed. The district of Zouvante, with the exception of the part situated on the opposite side of the summit of the said mountains, will fall in this way in division to Russia. Beginning with the limit of the district of Welkidji, the frontier line between the two States will follow the summits of Klopouty and of the principal chain of mountains which traverse the district of Welkidji to the northern source of the river called Astara, always observing the principle relative to the watershed. From there the frontier will follow the bed of this river to its discharge in the Caspian Sea, and will complete the line of demarcation which will separate in future the respective possessions of Russia and Persia.

ART. V.   His Majesty the Shah of Persia in testimony of his sincere friendship for His Majesty the Emperor of all the Russias, solemnly recognizes by the present Article, both in his name as in that of his Heirs and Successors to the throne of Persia, as belonging forever to the Russian Empire, all the countries and all the islands situated between the line of demarcation designated by the preceding Article on the one side, and the crest of the mountains of the Caucasus, and the Caspian Sea on the other, as well as the peoples, nomads and others who inhabit these countries.

ART. VI.   With a view to recompensing the considerable sacrifices that the war, which occurred between the two States, has occasioned to the Russian Empire, as well as the losses and damages which have resulted therefrom for Russian subjects, His Majesty the Shah of Persia undertakes to make them good by means of a pecuniary indemnity. It is agreed between the two High Contracting Parties that the total of this indemnity is fixed at ten kupours of silver tomans or 20,000,000 silver roubles and that the method, the terms and the guarantees of payment of this sum will be regulated by a special arrangement which shall have the same force and value as if it were inserted word for word in the present Treaty.

ART. VII.   His Majesty the Shah of Persia having judged it fitting to appoint as his Successor and Heir Presumptive his August Son Prince Abbas Mirza, His Majesty the Emperor of all the Russias, with a view to giving to His Majesty the Shah public evidence of his friendly dispositions and of his desire to contribute to the consolidation of this order of succession, undertakes to recognize as from today, in the August Person of His Royal Highness Prince Abbas Mirza, the Successor and Heir Presumptive of the Crown of Persia and to consider Him as the Legitimate Sovereign of this Kingdom from his ascension to the throne.

ART. VIII.   Russian merchant vessels will enjoy, as in the past, the right to navigate freely on the Caspian Sea and along its coasts and to land there. They will find in Persia aid and assistance in case of shipwreck. The same right is accorded to Persian merchant vessels to navigate on the old footing in the Caspian Sea and to enter Russian Rivers where, in case of shipwreck, the Persians will receive reciprocally aid and assistance.[1]

As for war vessels, those which bear the Russian military flag being *ab antiquo* the only ones which have had the right to navigate on the Caspian Sea, this same exclusive privilege is, for this reason, equally reserved and assured today, so that, with the exception of Russia, no other Power shall be able to have war vessels on the Caspian Sea.

ART. IX.   His Majesty the Emperor of all the Russias and His Majesty the Shah of Persia, having at heart to strengthen by all means the ties so happily reestablished between them, are agreed that the Ambassadors, Ministers, and Chargés d'Affaires, who may be reciprocally delegated near the respective High Courts, whether to discharge a temporary Mission or to reside there permanently, will be received with the honors and distinction befitting their rank and conformable with the dignity of the High Contracting Parties, as with the sincere friendship which unites them and conformable with the customs of the country. An understanding to this effect will be reached by means of a special Protocol regarding the ceremonial to be observed by both sides.

ART. X.   His Majesty the Emperor of all the Russias and His Majesty the Shah of Persia, considering the reestablishment and the extension of commercial relations between the two States as one of the first benefactions which the return of peace should produce, have agreed to regulate in a perfect accord all provisions relative to the protection of commerce, and to the safety of the respective subjects, and to embody them in a separate Act annexed hereto, drawn up between the respective Plenipotentiaries and which is and will be considered as forming an integral part of the present Treaty of Peace.

His Majesty the Shah of Persia reserves to Russia, as in the past, the right of appointing consuls or commercial agents wherever the good of commerce will demand it, and he undertakes to endow these consuls and agents, none of which shall have a suite of more than ten persons, with the protection, the honors and the privileges belonging to their public character. His Majesty the Emperor of all the Russias promises on His side to observe a perfect reciprocity in respect of the consuls and commercial agents of His Majesty the Shah of Persia. In case of well-founded complaint on the part of the Persian Government against one of the Russian consuls or agents, the Minister or Chargé d'Affaires of Russia, residing at the Court of His Majesty the Shah, and under the immediate

---

[1]On 24 November 1869, a decision of the Council of the Empire of Russia was published, prohibiting the establishment of companies for the navigation of the Caspian Sea, except by Russian subjects, and the purchase by foreigners of shares in such companies (Sir Edward Hertslet, *Treaties, etc., concluded between Great Britain and Persia.* London: Butterworths, 1891). [All footnotes in this document are Hurewitz's.]

orders of whom they will be placed, will suspend him from his functions and will confer provisionally the office upon whom he will deem fitting.

ART. XI.   All the affairs and suits of the respective subjects, suspended by the intervention of the War, will be resumed and terminated in accordance with justice after the exclusion of Peace. The debts that the respective subjects may have the one in favor of the other, as well as to the treasury, will be promptly and entirely liquidated.

ART. XII.   The High Contracting Parties agree by common accord in the interest of their respective subjects to fix a term of three years in order that those among them who (own) immobile property on both sides of the Araxe may have the right to sell or exchange it freely. His Imperial Majesty of all the Russias excepts, however, from the benefit of this provision, so far as it concerns Him, the former Sardar of Erivan, Houssein Khan, his brother Hassen Khan and Kerim Khan, the former Governor of Nakhitchevan.

ART. XIII.   All prisoners of war made in one way or another, whether in the course of the last War, or before, as well as the subjects of the two Governments reciprocally fallen into captivity, at no matter what time, will be freed within a period of four months and, after having been provided with food and other necessary objects, they will be directed to Abbas Abad in order to be turned over there into the hands of Commissioners, respectively charged with receiving them and to decide upon their eventual return to their homes The High Contracting Parties will undertake the same in respect of all prisoners of War and all Russian and Persian subjects reciprocally fallen into captivity, who may not have been freed within the period above-mentioned, whether by reason of the isolated distance where they are to be found, or for any other cause or circumstance. The two Governments reserve expressly the unlimited right to reclaim them at no matter what time, and they obligate themselves to restore them mutually in the measure that they may present themselves for that purpose, or in the measure that they may reclaim them.

ART. XIV.   The High Contracting Parties will not demand the extradition of fugitives and deserters who shall have passed under their respective jurisdiction before or during the war. At the same time, in order to prevent the mutually prejudicial consequences which might be able to result from the correspondence which some of these deserters may seek to hold with their former compatriots, or vassals, the Persian Government undertakes not to tolerate in its Possessions, situated between the Araxe and the line formed by the River known as Tohara, by Lake Urumiah, by the River called Djakatou and by the River known as Kizil-Ozane, to its descent into the Caspian Sea, the presence of individuals who will be designated now by name or who may be nominated to it in the future. His Majesty the Emperor of All the Russias promises equally on His side not to permit Persian deserters to establish themselves or to remain fixed in the Khanats of Karbag or of Nakhitchevan or in the part of the Khanat of Erivan situated on the right bank of the Araxe. It is, however, understood, that this clause is and will only be obligatory in respect of individuals possessing a public character of a certain dignity, such as the Khans, the Begs and the spiritual leaders or mullahs, whose personal example, intrigues and clandestine correspondence may be able to exercise a pernicious influence on their former compatriots, those formerly under their administration or their vassals. In so far as concerns the mass of the population in the two countries, it is agreed between the High Contracting Parties that the respective subjects who shall have passed or who may pass in the future from one State into the other, will be free to establish themselves or to sojourn wherever the Government under whose domination they will be placed will find it proper.

ART. XV.   With the beneficent and salutary aim of restoring tranquility in his States and of removing from his subjects all that may aggravate the evils which have brought on them the war to which the present Treaty has put an end so happily, His Majesty the Shah accords a full and complete amnesty to all the inhabitants and functionaries of the province known as Azerbaijhan. No one of them, without exception of category, may be either pursued, nor molested for his opinions, for his acts or for the conduct which he may have pursued, either during the war or during the temporary occupation of the said province by Russian troops. There will be, moreover, accorded them a period of one year dating from this day in order to transport themselves freely with their families from Persian States into Russian States, to export and to sell their movable property, without the Governments or the local authorities being able to place the least obstacle in the way thereof, nor to deduct previously any tax or any recompense on the goods and objects sold or exported by them. As for their immovable property there will be accorded a term of five years to sell or to dispose thereof as may be desired. There are excepted from this amnesty those who may have rendered themselves culpable within the period of time above-mentioned of one year of some crime, or misdemeanor liable to penalties punished by the Courts.

ART. XVI.   Immediately after the signature of the present Treaty of Peace, the respective plenipotentiaries will hasten to send the necessary notices and injunctions in all localities for the immediate cessation of hostilities.

2. The Commercial Treaty

ART. I.   The two High Contracting Parties desiring to make their respective subjects enjoy all the advantages which result from a reciprocal liberty of commerce, have agreed upon the following:

Russian subjects provided with passports in proper order shall be able to engage in commerce throughout the whole extent of the Persian Kingdom, and to proceed equally in the neighboring States of the said Kingdom.

In reciprocity thereof Persian subjects shall be able to import their merchandise into Russia, either by the Caspian Sea or by the land frontier which separates Russia from Persia, to exchange it or to make purchases for exportation, and they will enjoy all the rights and prerogatives accorded in the States of His Imperial Majesty to the subjects of the most favored friendly Powers.

In case of the decease of a Russian subject in Persia, his movable and immovable property, as belonging to the subject of a friendly Power, will be turned over intact to his relatives or associates, who will have the right to dispose of the said property as they may judge fitting. In the absence of relatives or associates the disposition of the said property will be confided to the Mission or to the Consuls of Russia without any difficulty on the part of the Russian authorities.

ART. II. Contracts, bills of exchange, bonds and other written instruments between the respective subjects for their commercial affairs will be registered with the Russian Consul and with the Hakim (Civil Magistrate) and there, where there is no Consul, with the Hakim alone, so that in case of dispute between the two parties one can make the researches necessary in order to decide the difference in conformity with justice.

If one of the two parties without being provided with the documents drawn up and legalized as stated above, which will be valid before every court of justice, should desire to institute a suit against the other in producing only proofs of testimonials, such pretensions will not be admitted at all unless the defendant himself may recognize the legality thereof.

Every undertaking entered into between the respective subjects in the forms above prescribed will be religiously observed and the refusal to give satisfaction therein which may occasion losses to one of the parties will give place to a proportional indemnity of the part of the other. In case of bankruptcy of a Russian merchant in Persia, his creditors will be recompensed with the goods and effects of the bankrupt, but the Russian Minister, the Chargé d'Affaires or the Consul shall not refuse if demanded their good offices to assure themselves whether the bankrupt has not left in Russia available properties which may serve to satisfy the same creditors.

The provisions drawn up in the present Article will be reciprocally observed in respect of Persian subjects who engage in commerce in Russia under the protection of its laws.

ART. III. With a view to assuring to the trade of the respective subjects the advantages which are the object of the previous stipulations, it is agreed that merchandise imported into Persia or exported from that Kingdom by Russian subjects and equally the products of Persia imported into Russia by Persian subjects, whether by the Caspian Sea or by the land frontier between the two States, as well as Russian merchandise which Persian subjects may export from the Empire by the same means, will be subject, as in the past, to a duty of five per cent, collected one time for all at entry or departure, and will not be subject thereafter to any other customs dues. If Russia may judge it necessary to draw up new customs regulations or new tariffs, it undertakes however not to increase even in this case the rate above-mentioned of five per cent.

ART. IV.   If Russia or Persia find themselves at war with another Power it will not be forbidden to the respective subjects to cross with their merchandise the territory of the High Contracting Parties to proceed into the confines of the said Power.

ART. V.   Seeing that after existing usages in Persia it is difficult for foreign subjects to find for rent houses, warehouses or premises suitable as deports for their merchandise, it is permitted to Russian subjects in Persia not only to rent but also to acquire in full ownership houses for habitation and shops as well as premises to store therein their merchandise.

The employees of the Persian Government shall not be able to enter by force in the said houses, shops or premises, at least without having recourse in case of necessity to the authorization of the Russian Minister, Chargé d'Affaires or Consul who will delegate an employee or dragoman to assist in the visit to the house or the merchandise.

ART. VI.   At the same time the Minister or the Chargé d'Affaires of His Imperial Majesty, the employees of the Russian Mission, Consuls and Dragomans, finding for sale in Persia neither the effects to serve for their clothing nor many objects of food which are necessary to them, shall be able to introduce free of tax and of dues, for their own account, all objects and effects which may be destined solely to their use.

The public servants of His Majesty the Shah residing in the States of the Russian Empire will enjoy perfect reciprocity in this regard.

Persian subjects forming part of the suite of the Minister or Chargé d'Affaires or Consuls, and necessary for their service, will enjoy, so long as they shall be attached to them, their protection on an equality with Russian subjects, but if it may happen that one amongst them renders himself culpable of some misdemeanor and that he makes himself liable thereby to punishment by the existing laws, in this case the Persian Minister or Hakim and, in his absence, the competent local authority, shall address himself immediately to the Russian Minister, Chargé d'Affaires or Consul, in the service of which the accused is to be found in order that he may be delivered to justice; and if this request is founded on proofs establishing the culpability of the accused, the Minister, Chargé d'Affaires or Consul will interpose no difficulty for the satisfaction thereof.

ART. VII.   All suits and litigations between Russian subjects will be subject exclusively to the examination and decision of the Russian Mission or Consuls in conformity with the laws and customs of the Russian Empire; as well as the differences and suits occurring between Russian subjects and those of another Power where the parties shall consent thereto.

When differences or suits shall arise between Russian subjects and Persian subjects, the said suits or differences will be brought before the Hakim or Governor and will be examined and judged only in the presence of the Dragoman of the Mission or the Consulate.

Once juridically terminated, such suits may not be instituted a second time. If, however, the circumstances were of a nature to demand a second examination, it may not take place without notification to the Russian Minister, Chargé d'Affaires or Consul and in this case the affair will only be considered and judged at the Defter, that is to say, in the Supreme Chancellery of the Shah at Tabriz or at Teheran, likewise in the presence of a Dragoman of the Russian Mission or Consulate.

ART. VIII.   In case of murder or other crime committed between Russian subjects the examination and the decision of the case will be the exclusive concern of the Russian Minister, Charge d'Affaires or Consul by virtue of the jurisdiction over their nationals conferred upon them.

If a Russian subject is found implicated with individuals of another nation in a criminal suit he cannot be pursued nor harried in any manner without proofs of his participation in the crime, and in this case even as in that where a Russian subject may be accused of direct culpability, the courts of the country may only proceed to take cognizance and give judgment concerning the crime in the presence of a delegate of the Russian Mission or Consulate, and if they are not to be found at the place where the crime has been committed, the local authorities will transport the delinquent there where there is a constituted Russian Consul or Agent.

Testimonies for the prosecution and for the defense of the accused will be faithfully collected by the Hakim and by the Judge of the locality, and invested with their signature; transmitted in this form there where the crime has to be judged, these testimonies will become authentic documents or parts of the suit unless the accused proves clearly their falsity.

When the accused shall have been duly convicted and sentence shall have been pronounced, the delinquent will be turned over to the Minister, Chargé d'Affaires or Consul of His Imperial Majesty who will return him to Russia to receive there the punishment prescribed by the laws.

ART. IX.   The High Contracting Parties will take care that the stipulations of the present Act may be strictly observed and fulfilled, and the Governors of their Provinces, Commandants and other respective authorities will not permit themselves in any case to violate them, under penalty of a grave responsibility and even of dismissal in case of complaint duly proven.

2.   The Treaty of Balta Liman Gives the British Economic Advantages Within the Ottoman Empire, August 16, 1838

Despite the economic prowess of English industrialists, their access to the vast markets of the Ottoman Empire was limited by the system of tariffs and monopolies in existence throughout most of the Middle East and North Africa. Although from the perspective of the English, these practices were prohibitive of "free trade," in fact they also protected local economies and workers from being overwhelmed by European goods. All of this changed in 1838 with the signing of the Treaty of Balta Liman. At the time the Ottoman Empire was feeling militarily threatened by the expansionist ambitions of Muhammad 'Ali, the governor of Egypt. By 1833, in large part because of his modernized army, Muhammad 'Ali had extended his control to all of Syria and appeared to be threatening Anatolia, the heartland of the Ottoman Empire. Britain considered Muhammad 'Ali a threat because of his attempts to foster a local industrial revolution at the expense of European imports. The Ottomans signed the Treaty of Balta Liman in exchange for British military support in ousting Muhammad 'Ali from Syria and severely curtailing his regional power. In exchange Britain, and subsequently France and the Netherlands, gained almost unfettered access to the markets of the empire—an outcome that had momentous repercussions on the economy of the Middle East and North Africa for years to come.

ART. I.   All rights, privileges, and immunities which have been conferred on the subjects or ships of Great Britain by the existing Capitulations and Treaties, are confirmed now and for ever, except in as far as they may be specifically altered by the present Convention: and it is moreover expressly stipulated, that all rights, privileges, or immunities which the Sublime Porte now grants, or may hereafter grant, to the ships and subjects of any other foreign Power, or which may suffer the ships and subjects of any other foreign Power to enjoy, shall be equally granted to, and exercised and enjoyed by, the subjects and ships of Great Britain.

ART. II.   The subjects of Her Britannic Majesty, or their agents, shall be permitted to purchase at all places in the Ottoman Dominions (whether for the purposes of internal trade or exportation) all articles, without any exception whatsoever, the produce, growth, or manufacture of the said Dominions; and the Sublime Porte formally engages to abolish all monopolies of agricultural produce, or of any other articles whatsoever, as well as all *Permits* from the local Governors, either for the purchase of any article, or for its removal from one place to another when purchased; and any attempt to compel the subjects of Her Britannic Majesty to receive such *Permits* from the local Governors, shall be considered as an infraction of Treaties, and the Sublime Porte shall immediately punish with severity any Vizirs and other officers who shall have been guilty of such misconduct, and render full justice to British subjects for all injuries or losses which they may duly prove themselves to have suffered.

ART. III.   If any article of Turkish produce, growth, or manufacture, be purchased by the British merchant or his agent, for the purpose of selling the same for internal consumption in Turkey, the British merchant or his agent shall pay, at the purchase and sale of such articles, and in any manner of trade therein, the

Great Britain, *Parliamentary Papers, 1839*, vol. 50: pp. 291–295. This document may also be found in J. C. Hurewitz, *The Middle East and North Africa in World Politics* (New Haven, Conn.: Yale University Press, 1975), pp. 265–266.

same duties that are paid, in similar circumstances, by the most favoured class of Turkish subjects engaged in the internal trade of Turkey, whether Mussulmans or Rayahs.

ART. IV.   If any article of Turkish produce, growth, or manufacture, be purchased for exportation, the same shall be conveyed by the British merchant or his agent, free of any kind of charge or duty whatsoever, to a convenient place of shipment, on its entry into which it shall be liable to one fixed duty of nine per cent, *ad valorem*, in lieu of all other interior duties.

Subsequently, on exportation, the duty of three per cent., as established and existing at present, shall be paid. But all articles bought in the shipping ports for exportation, and which have already paid the interior duty at entering into the same, will only pay the three per cent. export duty.

ART. V.   The regulations under which Firmans are issued to British merchant vessels for passing the Dardanelles and the Bosphorus, shall be so framed as to occasion to such vessels the least possible delay.

ART. VI.   It is agreed by the Turkish Government, that the regulations established in the present Convention, shall be general throughout the Turkish Empire, whether in Turkey in Europe or Turkey in Asia, in Egypt, or other African possessions belonging to the Sublime Porte, and shall be applicable to all the subjects, whatever their description, of the Ottoman Dominions: and the Turkish Government also agrees not to object to other foreign Powers settling their trade upon the basis of this present Convention.

ART. VII.   It having been the custom of Great Britain and the Sublime Porte, with a view to prevent all difficulties and delay in estimating the value of articles imported into the Turkish Dominions, or exported therefrom, by British subjects, to appoint, at intervals of fourteen years, a Commission of men well acquainted with the traffic of both countries, who have fixed by a tariff the sum of money in the coin of the Grand Signior, which should be paid as duty on each article; and the term of fourteen years, during which the last adjustment of the said tariff was to remain in force, having expired, the High Contracting Parties have agreed to name conjointly fresh Commissioners to fix and determine the amount in money which is to be paid by British subjects, as the duty of three per cent upon the value of all commodities imported and exported by them; and the said Commissioners shall establish an equitable arrangement for estimating the interior duties which, by the present Treaty, are established on Turkish goods to be exported, and shall also determine on the places of shipment where it may be most convenient that such duties should be levied.

The new tariff thus established, to be in force for seven years after it has been fixed, at the end of which time it shall be in the power of either of the parties to demand a revision of that tariff; but if no such demand be made on either side, within the six months after the end of the first seven years, then the tariff shall remain in force for seven years more, reckoned from the end of the preceding seven years; and so it shall be at the end of each successive period of seven years.

3. An Egyptian Khedival Decree Establishes a European-Controlled Public Debt Administration, May 2, 1876

By the second half of the nineteenth century, France, Britain, and Russia had established their political and economic influence within the Ottoman Empire, Iran, Egypt, Algeria, and Tunisia. The growth of foreign influence reduced the power of governments vis-à-vis European consuls and the governments and commercial interests they represented. Some local governments—most notably in the Ottoman Empire and Egypt—attempted to reverse their fortunes by consolidating the power of their rule and at the same time seeking ways to modernize their bureaucracies, armies, and economies. These expensive projects, however, could not be solely supported by tax revenue collected from a primarily peasant population. Thus, some of these governments acquired loans from European banks. The loans were meant to fund the laying down of railroad track, the digging of irrigation canals, "modern" education, and the outfitting of new armies. Generally, the loans were of the high-interest, short-term type, because of the risk of default that the lending banks faced or claimed to face. With the influx of large amounts of money came the potential for, and the reality of, corruption and financial mismanagement, particularly in governments where independent oversight was nonexistent.

In Egypt, the thoughtful and thoughtless projects of Khedive Isma'il dragged the country into serious indebtedness. His initial attempt to service the outstanding and ballooning loans through selling the Egyptian shares in the Suez Canal Company and through new generous tax laws for the wealthy landowners of Egypt only postponed the seemingly inevitable bankruptcy of the government. Facing the prospect of Egyptian default on the loans, Italian and French advisers pressured Isma'il to issue the following edict establishing a European-controlled public debt administration that would manage Egypt's finances and the servicing of its debt at a rate of 7 percent. The British, however, balked at this arrangement and later forced the issuance of a decree (dated November 18, 1876) that placed all of Egypt's finances under French and British control.

We, the Khedive of Egypt, desiring to take definitive and opportune measures for obtaining the unification of the different debts of the State and those of the Daira Sanieh, and also desiring the reduction of the excessive charges resulting from these debts, and wishing to bear solemn testimony to our firm intention to secure every guarantee to all persons interested, have resolved to

Great Britain, *Parliamentary Papers, 1876*, vol. 83, pp. 71–72. This document may also be found in J. C. Hurewitz, *The Middle East and North Africa in World Politics* (New Haven, Conn.: Yale University Press, 1975), pp. 185–187.

establish a special Treasury charged with the regular service of the public debt, and to appoint to its management foreign Commissioners, who at our request will be indicated by the respective Governments as fit officials to fill the post to which they will be appointed by us in the quality of Egyptian officials, and under the following conditions. Having consulted our Privy Council, we have decreed, and do hereby decree, as follows:—

ART. 1. A Treasury of the Public Debt is established, charged with receiving the funds necessary for the interest and the redemption of the debt, and with applying them to this object exclusively.

ART. 2. The officials, the local Treasuries, or the special Administrations, after collecting, receiving, or accumulating the revenues specially devoted to the payment of the debt, are or shall be in future charged to pay them into the Central Treasury or to keep them at the disposal of the Intendants of Public Expenditure ("Ordonnateurs des Dépenses de l'Etat"). The Intendants of Public Expenditure are, by virtue of the present Decree, bound to pay these revenues on account of the State Treasury into the special Treasury of the Public Debt, which will be considered in this respect as a special Treasury. These officials, treasuries and administrations can only procure a valid discharge by means of the vouchers which will be delivered to them by the said Treasury of the Public Debt. Any other order or voucher will not be valid. These same officials, treasuries or administrations will every month send to the Minister of Finance a statement of the receipts or collections made by themselves directly or paid in by the receivers of the revenues specially devoted to the debt and the payments made into the special Treasury of the Public Debt. The Minister of Finance will communicate these statements to the Administration of the Treasury of the Public Debt.

The Treasury of the Public Debt shall receive from the Daira Sanieh the entire sum necessary for the interest and redemption of the amount of its unified debt, and it shall likewise receive the funds for the yearly payment due to the English Government, and representing the interest on the Suez Canal shares.

ART. 3. If the payments of the revenue devoted to the debt be insufficient to meet the half-yearly charges, the special Public Debt Department will demand from the Treasury, through the intermediary of the Minister of Finance, the sum required to complete the half-yearly payments; the Treasury will have to deliver this sum a fortnight before the payments are due. If the funds in hand constitute a surplus over the amount necessary for the payment of the interest and the sinking fund, the special Treasury of the Public Debt will pay this surplus at the end of each year to the general Treasury of the Exchequer. The Treasury of the Pubic Debt will submit its accounts, which will be examined and reported upon according to law.

ART. 4. The suits which the Treasury and its Directors, on its behalf, acting in the name and in the interests of the creditors, mostly of foreign nationality, may consider they have to bring against the financial administration represented by the Minister of Finance in so far as regards the guardianship of the guarantees of the debt which we have confided to the said Treasury, will be brought in the terms of their jurisdiction before the new tribunals which, in conformity with the agreement entered into with the Powers, have been instituted in Egypt.

ART. 5. The Commissioners selected as stated above will have the direction of the special Treasury of the Public Debt. They will be appointed by us for five years, and will sit in Cairo. Their functions may be continued after the five years have expired, and in case of the death or resignation of one of them the vacancy will be filled by us in the manner of the original appointment. They may intrust one of themselves with the functions of President, and the latter will notify his nomination to the Minister of Finance.

ART. 6. The cost of exchange, insurance, and conveyance of specie abroad, as well as the commission for the payment of the coupons, will be borne by the Government. The Directors of the Treasury will come to a previous arrangement with the Ministers of Finance with regard to all these operations, but the Minister will decide whether the despatch of these sums is to be effected in specie or by letters of exchange.

ART. 7. The Treasury will not be allowed to employ any funds, disposable or not, in operations of credit, commerce, industry, &c.

ART. 8. The Government will not be able, without an agreement with the majority of the Commissioners directing the Treasury of the Public Debt, to effect in any of the taxes specially devoted to the Debt any changes which might result in a diminution of the revenue from these taxes, At the same time, the Government may farm out one or several of these taxes, provided that the contract entered into insure a revenue at least equal to that already existing, and may also conclude Treaties of commerce introducing modifications in the Customs duties.

ART. 9. The Government undertakes not to issue any Treasury Bonds or any other new bonds, and not to contract any other loan of any nature whatsoever. This same engagement is entered into in the name of the Daira Sanieh. Nevertheless, in case the Government, from urgent national reasons, should find itself placed under the necessity of having recourse to credit, it may do so within the limits of strict necessity, and without doing anything to affect the employment of the revenues set apart for the Treasury of the Public Debt, or to cause their diversion from their destination. These totally exceptional loans can only be contracted after an agreement on the subject with the Commissioners directing the Treasury.

ART. 10. In order that the arrangements stated in the preceding article shall not place obstacles in the way of the Administration, the Government may open a running account with a bank to facilitate its payments by means of anticipations to be regulated in accordance with the year's receipts. The debit or credit balance will be settled at the end of each year. This current account must never be overdrawn during the year by more than 50,000,000 fr.

4. Convention on Free Navigation of the Suez Canal Between the European Powers and the Ottoman Empire, October 29, 1888

The Suez Canal was a crucial part of European-dominated international trade. The British, in particular, were constantly and acutely concerned with maintaining links to the economically critical South Asian parts of their empire. In the wake of the 'Urabi revolt, which threatened to topple Khedive Tawfiq in Egypt, the British and the French became alarmed at the prospect of restricted access to the Suez Canal. Thus, in 1882 the British landed an expeditionary force, which defeated the 'Urabi forces opposing the khedive and restored calm to Egyptian politics. The intervention was meant to be a brief military operation, but the British remained in power in Egypt until 1956. The Convention on Free Navigation has to be read against this backdrop. The "Powers" mentioned in this document are Austria, Germany, Italy, the Netherlands, the Ottoman Empire, Russia, and Spain, in addition to Britain and France, all of whom signed the convention in 1888. However, the convention did not become fully operational until 1904, when French reservations about the power it gave the British, who were occupying Egypt, were allayed.

ART. I.   The Suez Maritime Canal shall always be free and open, in time of war as in time of peace, to every vessel of commerce or of war, without distinction of flag.

Consequently, the High Contracting Parties agree not in any way to interfere with the free use of the Canal, in time of war as in time of peace.

The Canal shall never be subjected to the exercise of the right of blockade.

ART. II.   The High Contracting Parties, recognizing that the Fresh-Water Canal is indispensable to the Maritime Canal, take note of the engagements of His Highness the Khedive towards the Universal Suez Canal Company as regards the Fresh-Water Canal; which engagements are stipulated in a Convention bearing date the 18th March, 1863, containing an *exposé* and four Articles.

They undertake not to interfere in any way with the security of that Canal and its branches, the working of which shall not be exposed to any attempt at obstruction.

ART. III.   The High Contracting Parties likewise undertake to respect the plant, establishments, buildings, and works of the Maritime Canal and of the Fresh-Water Canal.

Great Britain, *Parliamentary Papers, 1889*, Commercial no. 2, C. 5623. This document may also be found in J. C. Hurewitz, *The Middle East and North Africa in World Politics* (New Haven, Conn.: Yale University Press, 1975), pp. 455–456.

ART. IV.   The Maritime Canal remaining open in time of war as a free passage, even to the ships of war of belligerents, according to the terms of Article I of the present Treaty, the High Contracting Parties agree that no right of war, no act of hostility, nor any act having for its object to obstruct the free navigation of the Canal, shall be committed in the Canal and its ports of access, as well as within a radius of 3 marine miles from those ports, even though the Ottoman Empire should be one of the belligerent Powers.

Vessels of war of belligerents shall not revictual or take in stores in the Canal and its ports of access, except in so far as may be strictly necessary. The transit of the aforesaid vessels through the Canal shall be effected with the least possible delay, in accordance with the Regulations in force, and without any other intermission than that resulting from the necessities of the service.

Their stay at Port Saïd and in the roadstead of Suez shall not exceed twenty-four hours, except in case of distress. In such case they shall be bound to leave as soon as possible. An interval of twenty-four hours shall always elapse between the sailing of a belligerent ship from one of the ports of access and the departure of a ship belonging to the hostile Power.

ART. V.   In time of war belligerent Powers shall not disembark nor embark within the Canal and its ports of access either troops, munitions, or materials of war. But in case of an accidental hindrance in the Canal, men may be embarked or disembarked at the ports of access by detachments not exceeding 1,000 men, with a corresponding amount of war material.

ART. VI.   Prizes shall be subjected, in all respects, to the same rules as the vessels of war of belligerents.

ART. VII.   The Powers shall not keep any vessel of war in the waters of the Canal (including Lake Timsah and the Bitter Lakes).

Nevertheless, they may station vessels of war in the ports of access of Port Saïd and Suez, the number of which shall not exceed two for each Power.

This right shall not be exercised by belligerents.

ART. VIII.   The Agents in Egypt of the Signatory Powers of the present Treaty shall be charged to watch over its execution. In case of any event threatening the security or the free passage of the Canal, they shall meet on the summons of three of their number under the presidency of their Doyen, in order to proceed to the necessary verifications. They shall inform the Khedivial Government of the danger which they may have perceived, in order that that Government may take proper steps to insure the protection and the free use of the Canal. Under any circumstances, they shall meet once a year to take note of the due execution of the Treaty.

The last-mentioned meetings shall take place under the presidency of a Special Commissioner nominated for that purpose by the Imperial Ottoman Government. A Commissioner of the Khedive may also take part in the meeting, and may preside over it in case of the absence of the Ottoman Commissioner.

They shall especially demand the suppression of any work or the dispersion of any assemblage on either bank of the Canal, the object or effect of which might be to interfere with the liberty and the entire security of the navigation.

ART. IX.   The Egyptian Government shall, within the limits of its powers resulting from the Firmans, and under the conditions provided for in the present Treaty, take the necessary measures for insuring the execution of the said Treaty.

In case the Egyptian Government should not have sufficient means at its disposal, it shall call upon the Imperial Ottoman Government, which shall take the necessary measures to respond to such appeal; shall give notice thereof to the Signatory Powers of the Declaration of London of the 17th March, 1885; and shall, if necessary, concert with them on the subject.

The provisions of Articles IV, V, VII, and VIII shall not interfere with the measures which shall be taken in virtue of the present Article.

ART. X.   Similarly, the provisions of Articles IV, V, VII, and VIII shall not interfere with the measures which His Majesty the Sultan and His Highness the Khedive, in the name of His Imperial Majesty, and within the limits of the Firmans granted, might find it necessary to take for securing by their own forces the defence of Egypt and the maintenance of public order.

In case His Imperial Majesty the Sultan, or His Highness the Khedive, should find it necessary to avail themselves of the exceptions for which this Article provides, the Signatory Powers of the Declaration of London shall be notified thereof by the Imperial Ottoman Government.

It is likewise understood that the provisions of the four Articles aforesaid shall in no case occasion any obstacle to the measures which the Imperial Ottoman Government may think it necessary to take in order to insure by its own forces the defence of its other possessions situated on the eastern coast of the Red Sea.

ART. XI.   The measures which shall be taken in the cases provided for by Articles IX and X of the present Treaty shall not interfere with the free use of the Canal. In the same cases, the erection of permanent fortifications contrary to the provisions of Article VIII is prohibited.

ART. XII.   The High Contracting Parties, by application of the principle of equality as regards the free use of the Canal, a principle which forms one of the bases of the present Treaty, agree that none of them shall endeavour to obtain with respect to the Canal territorial or commercial advantages or privileges in any international arrangements which may be concluded. Moreover, the rights of Turkey as the territorial Power are reserved.

ART. XIII.   With the exception of the obligations expressly provided by the clauses of the present Treaty, the sovereign rights of His Imperial Majesty the Sultan, and the rights and immunities of His Highness the Khedive, resulting from the Firmans, are in no way affected.

ART. XIV.   The High Contracting Parties agree that the engagements resulting from the present Treaty shall not be limited by the duration of the Acts of Concession of the Universal Suez Canal Company.

ART. XV.   The stipulations of the present Treaty shall not interfere with the sanitary measures in force in Egypt.

ART. XVI.   The High Contracting Parties undertake to bring the present Treaty to the knowledge of the States which have not signed it, inviting them to accede to it.

5.   The Concession for the Imperial Bank in Iran, January 30, 1889

In order to establish modern economies able to compete in the European-dominated international market, many of the central governments in the Middle East and North Africa sought to create modern central banks, to issue bank notes and make loans to the state and private institutions. Many of these banks established their own industrial, mining, and commercial interests funded through the financial dealings of the bank. The concession for the Imperial Bank in Iran, signed on January 30, 1889, was one such attempt to establish a modern banking institution. The idea originated with Baron Julius de Reuter, who in 1872 had received from the Iranian government a general concession guaranteed by a £40,000 sterling note. As the Russian and British rivalry over Iran intensified, the English government mediated various disagreements between Reuter and the Iranian government. Out of these negotiations emerged the 1889 concession.

The difficulties pending for a long time between the Government of His Imperial Majesty the Shah of Persia and Baron Julius de Reuter having been definitely overcome and the concession granted to the said Baron Julius de Reuter on 25 July 1872 annulled, the following has been mutually agreed upon:

ART. 1.   By the present concession the Government of His Imperial Majesty the Shah of Persia grants to Baron Julius de Reuter and his associates or representatives the right to found a state bank in the Persian Empire under the name of Imperial Bank of Persia. This right is granted for a period of sixty years from the date of signature of the present concession by His Imperial Majesty the Shah. The seat of the association and the residence of the Bank shall be established at Tehran, and the Bank may establish branches in other cities in Persia or abroad. In order to develop Persia's commerce and augment its wealth, the Imperial Bank, aside from the purposes that an institution of credit serves, may undertake on its own behalf or on behalf of a third [party], any kind of

---

Translated from the French text in Iran, Archives of the Ministry of Foreign Affairs, Tehran. This document may also be found in J. C. Hurewitz, *The Middle East and North Africa in World Politics* (New Haven, Conn.: Yale University Press, 1975), pp. 457–461.

financial, industrial, or commercial endeavor it believes favorable to this end, on condition that none of these enterprises shall be contrary to the treaties, laws, customs, or religion of the country and that the Persian Government shall be informed in advance. The Imperial Bank shall not have the right to accept a mortgage, or to buy immovable [property such as] lands, villages, etc., in the territory of the Empire, with the exception of land needed for the construction of a suitable establishment in Tehran and branches in the provinces. It is equally forbidden for the Bank to discount or to make advances on Government drafts that shall not have been drawn on the Bank.

ART. 2.   The capital of the Imperial Bank shall be 100 million francs, or £4 million sterling. Consequently, a certain number of securities may be created that the Bank shall issue in series. The Bank shall be considered established when the first series of 25 million francs, or £1 million sterling, has been subscribed. The subscription shall be opened in various capitals, such as Tehran, Berlin, London, Paris, Saint Petersburg, and Vienna, if the governments of the several Powers permit it. The securities shall be [payable] to the bearer and the Bank may also issue registered securities. The Bank, when it is judged advantageous, may augment its capital and the number of its securities on agreement with the Government.

ART. 3.   The Imperial Bank shall have the exclusive right as State Bank to issue notes payable to the bearer on demand. It shall never issue notes amounting to more than 20 million francs, or £800 thousand sterling, without informing the Persian Government. In order to further the development of public credit and place a limit on the circulation of silver money, while augmenting that of gold, the Imperial Bank accepts in principle the establishment of a single standard based on the *toman*, but within ten years after the Bank's establishment the Government of His Imperial Majesty and the Directors of the Bank shall agree on the most proper ways and means to attain this end. However, taking into consideration the demands of the actual monetary situation, the issuance of Imperial Bank notes shall be based primarily on the silver *kran*.

These notes shall be accepted by all agents and employees of the Imperial Government and shall be [considered] legal tender in all transactions in Persia. However, should the Bank not be able to redeem one of these notes, the circulation of Bank notes shall be forbidden throughout the Empire and the Bank shall be forced to redeem all its notes. To guarantee this reimbursement, the Bank expressly promises to maintain for two years from the time it begins its operations a cash balance equal to half [the value] of its notes in circulation, and after this period of two years, equal to at least one-third. The difference between the cash balance in specie and the amount of the notes issued shall be guaranteed by the titles to movable and immovable valuables belonging to the bank and deposited in its coffers in Persia.

The Imperial Bank shall be obligated to pay its notes on sight at the place of their issuance. Nevertheless, its branches' notes may be reimbursed in Tehran. The bank notes shall be in the Persian language. Paper money [of denominations] less than two tomans may not be issued without the authorization of the Government. The bank notes shall carry a sign or stamp indicating their inspection by the Persian Government and shall be signed by a Director or Administrator and by the principal cashier of the establishment where they were issued.

The Government of His Imperial Majesty the Shah pledges not to issue any sort of paper money for the duration of this concession nor to authorize the creation of any other bank or establishment having similar privileges.

ART. 4.   The Imperial Government does not guarantee the capital of the Bank. It may, if it wishes, subscribe to it or promote the subscription of Persian subjects to the amount of one-fifth of the capital called for, or [it may choose not to] participate in any way.

The division of the capital into securities, the number and value of bank notes conforming to the provisions of Article 3 of the present instrument, the organization and administration of the Bank, the nomination of managers and employees of the Bank in Persia or abroad, and the financial management of the Bank with the profits that it may make or the losses it may suffer shall be entirely in the hands of the concessionaire and his associates or representatives, at their risk and peril.

The Government of His Imperial Majesty the Shah shall exercise its high surveillance on the Bank by appointing an Imperial High Commissioner. This High Commissioner shall have the right to acquaint himself with the management of the Bank and to see that the affairs of the Bank are conducted in conformity with this instrument of concession. He shall officially attend General Meetings as well as gatherings of the Council of Administration at Tehran whenever invited. He shall control the issuance of bank notes with strict observance of the provisions of Article 3 of the present concession. He shall supervise relations between the Bank and the Imperial Treasury. He may not interfere with the administration and management of the Bank's affairs and his duties shall not impose any responsibility on the Imperial Government.

ART. 5.   The purpose of [establishing] this Bank as a national institution being the public welfare and the welfare of the State, the Government of His Imperial Majesty grants it the military protection indispensable to the security of its principal seat and branches.

The Government as protector of the enterprise shall facilitate, wherever possible, the acquisition of necessary lands and sites upon which the Bank shall establish its principal seat and branches, intervening equitably between [the Bank] and the landowners. The Bank, its premises and branches, shall be entirely exempt from any kind of tax or duty. The same shall be true for its securities, notes, receipts, and checks and for all documents emanating from it on its affairs and transactions. But if the Imperial Government should introduce a stamp tax the Bank shall not accept any bill of exchange or other instrument circulating in Persia without a State stamp.

ART. 6.   The Imperial Bank shall facilitate the payments of the Imperial Treasury in Persia or abroad. For each service the Government demands of [the

Bank] the Government and the Bank's Directors shall mutually determine the commission to be paid to the Bank. After its establishment and the payment of its capital, the Imperial Bank undertakes to lend the Government of His Imperial Majesty the Shah for a period of ten years the sum of 1 million francs, or £40 thousand sterling, at an [interest] rate of 6 percent. The interest and amortization, shall, according to His Imperial Majesty's wishes, be deducted from the 6 percent of the Bank's net profits assured to the Government by Article 7 of the present instrument. Moreover, the Bank, after its establishment, shall also place itself at the disposal of the Imperial Government for all loans or advances that [the Imperial Government] may need, against such collatoral as may be agreed upon in each case by the Imperial Government and the Bank. Otherwise, these advances or loans shall be considered an equivalent guarantee for the sum of the notes issued. The Government shall repay these loans or advances within a period specified by the respective conventions. The total interest shall be discharged regularly at the end of each Persian fiscal year, to wit, on 20 March. The first of these advances above the aforementioned sum of 1 million francs shall be 5 million francs, or £200,000 sterling, at the current rate of exchange, i.e., at the rate of 8 percent.

ART. 7.   At the end of each Persian fiscal year, on 20 March, the Imperial Bank must turn over to the Government of His Imperial Majesty the Shah, or transfer to his credit, 6 percent of the annual net profits. Should this share of the profits, fixed at 6 percent, not reach an annual sum of 100 thousand francs, or £4 thousand sterling, the Bank must furnish the balance, charging it [alone] or the total sum to its trade expenses without the right of any deduction whatsoever in the said share of profits resulting from the balance sheet of the following year.

ART. 8.   The guarantee of £40 thousand sterling that was deposited in 1872 in the Bank of England by Baron Julius de Reuter shall serve the Persian Government as a guarantee for the establishment of the Imperial Bank. The day after its establishment, the Persian Government shall return to the said Baron the aforementioned sum of £40 thousand sterling. If the Imperial Bank is not founded within a period of nine months from His Imperial Majesty's signature of the present instrument, the said guarantee shall fall to the Persian Government, and the present concession shall be considered null and void [*non avenues*] unless a war erupts in Europe between the Great Powers or Persia finds itself engaged [in war] or in any other situation [caused by] an act of God.

ART. 9.   At the moment of the establishment of the Imperial Bank, its principal Administrators shall publish the statutes by which the Bank is to be regulated. These statutes must conform strictly to the stipulations of the present concession. After the establishment of the Bank the said statutes may be modified only by the decision of a General Assembly of stockholders, who in any modifications must always respect the stipulations of the present instrument.

ART. 10.   The Imperial Bank shall be under the high protection of His Imperial Majesty the Shah and of his Government for the exercise and maintenance of the rights granted to it by the present concession, and [the Bank] pledges to respect the general laws of the country in their entirety. Should a dispute arise between the Persian Government and the Bank or between the Bank and individuals, the two parties shall each choose one or two arbitrators and the decision of these arbitrators shall be final. Should the votes be split, the said arbitrators shall name a referee to judge in the last instance.

ART. 11. The Imperial Bank being ready immediately to undertake the sacrifices necessary to employ the resources of the country for the exploitation of its natural wealth, the Persian Government grants to the said Bank, for the entire duration of the present concession, the exclusive and definitive privilege to exploit throughout the Empire mines of iron, copper, lead, mercury, coal, petroleum, manganese, borax, [and] asbestos [that] belong to the State and [have] not previously [been] ceded to other [parties]. As an annex to the concession the Persian Government shall give Baron de Reuter an official list of the mines already granted, on the day the present [instrument] is signed. [Since] mines of gold, silver, and precious stones, etc., belong exclusively to the State, [any] Bank engineers who [should] discover them shall be obliged immediately to inform the Government of His Imperial Majesty the Shah. Except for indispensable engineers and foremen, all the minor laborers that the Bank may engage shall be chosen from among the subjects of His Imperial Majesty the Shah. The Persian Government shall, by all the means in its power, aid the Bank to procure labor at the price prevailing in the country. All mines that the Bank may not have begun to exploit ten years from its establishment shall be considered abandoned and the State may dispose of them without the concessionary Bank being able to [oppose its actions].

ART. 12. The land necessary for the exploitation of these mines and the establishment of a means of communication with the nearest and most rapid lines of transport shall be given to the Imperial Bank from State lands. The Imperial Government shall aid the Bank by all the means in its power to deal with individual landowners in the most favorable conditions, should there be any along the said road of communications. The materials necessary for the exploitation shall enter Persia without any duty whatsoever. The lands and buildings of the said exploitations shall be free of all duties and taxes.

ART. 13. The Persian Government shall levy an annual premium of 16 percent on the net profits of all mines exploited by the Imperial Bank. At the expiration of the term of the present concession the lands exploited by the mines, with their buildings, offices, and material, shall be returned to the Persian Government according to the general rules followed by the Powers who have stipulated the most favorable conditions in this matter.

ART. 14. In return for the rights guaranteed to him by the present contract, Baron Julius de Reuter formally and completely renounces without reserve all other rights and privileges that had been granted him by the previous concession of 25 July 1872 [which is] annulled by the present [instrument]. . . .

6.   The Concession for the Tobacco Monopoly in Iran, March 8, 1890

A British company headed by Major G. F. Talbot sought and obtained a concession from the government of Shah Nasir al-Din to produce, locally sell, and export all tobacco in Iran. This concession included tunbaku, *the tobacco, used widely by Iranians in their water pipes. Unhappiness with the monopolistic terms of the concession and the fact that it constrained one of the pleasures of Iranian daily life coalesced with rising frustration in Iran against European domination and intervention. The financially disadvantageous terms of the agreement fueled local anger against the "sale of the country" to foreigners. Many historians consider the revolt against the concession to be the beginning of the nationalist Iranian movement that culminated fifteen years later in the constitutional revolution.*

The monopoly of buying, selling, and manufacturing all the tootoon and tobacco in the interior or exterior of the Kingdom of Persia is granted to Major Talbot by us for fifty years from the date of the signing of this Concession, in accordance with the following stipulations:—

1. The concessionnaires will have to pay 15,000*l.* per annum to the exalted Imperial Treasury whether they benefit or lose by this business, and this money shall be paid every year, five months after the beginning of the year.

2. In order merely to ascertain the quantities of tootoon and tobacco produced in the protected provinces (of Persia) the concessionnaires will keep a register of the cultivators who wish to work under the conditions of this Concession, and the Persian Government will issue strict orders to the local Governors to compel the cultivators of tobacco and tootoon to furnish such a registration.

Permission for sale, &c., of tootoon, tobacco, cigars, cigarettes, snuff, &c., is the absolute right of the concessionnaires, and no one but the proprietors of this Concession shall have the right to issue the abovementioned permits.

The Guilds of the sellers of tobacco and tootoon who are engaged in this trade will remain permanent in their local trade and transactions, on condition of possessing permits which will be given to them by the concessionnaires.

3. After deducting all the expenses appertaining to this business and paying a dividend of 5 percent. on their own capital to the proprietors of this Concession, one quarter of the remaining profit will yearly be paid to the exalted Imperial Treasury, and the Persian Government will have the right to inspect their (the concessionnaires') yearly books.

4. All the materials necessary for this work which the proprietors of this Concession import into the protected provinces (Persia) will be free of all customs duties, taxes, &c.

Great Britain, *Parliamentary Papers, 1892,* Vol. 79, pp. 211–213. This document may also be found in J. C. Hurewitz, *The Middle East and North Africa in World Politics* (New Haven, Conn.: Yale University Press, 1975), pp. 462–463.

5. Removal and transfer of tootoon and tobacco in the protected provinces (of Persia) without the permission of the proprietors of this Concession is prohibited, except as such quantities [as] travellers may have with them for their own daily use.

6. The proprietors of this Concession must purchase all the tootoon and tobacco that are produced in the protected provinces and pay cash for it. They must purchase all the tobacco, &c., fit for use that is now in hand, and the price that is to be given to the owner or the producer will be settled in a friendly manner between the producer or the owner and the proprietors of this Concession, but in case of disagreement between the parties the case will be referred to an Arbitrator accepted by both sides, and the decision of the Arbitrator will be final and will be carried out.

7. The Persian Government engages not to increase the revenues, taxes, and customs that are now levied on tootoon, tobacco, cigars, cigarettes, and snuff for fifty years from the date of the signing of the Concession, and the proprietors also undertake that all the customs that the Persian Government now obtain from tobacco shall be continued as they are.

8. Any person or persons who shall attempt to evade (the rules) of these Articles will be severely punished by the Government, and any person or persons found to be secretly in possession of tobacco, tootoon, &c., for sale or trade, will also be fined [and] severely punished by the Government. The Government will give its utmost help and support in all the business of the proprietors of this Concession, and the proprietors of this Concession undertake in no way to go beyond their own rights consistent with these Articles.

9. The proprietors of this Concession are permitted, should they wish, to transfer all their rights, Concessions, undertakings, &c., to any person or persons, but, prior to this, they must inform the Persian Government.

10. The producer or owner of tootoon and tobacco, whenever his crop of tobacco and tootoon is gathered, shall at once inform the nearest agent of the proprietors of this Concession of the quantity, in order that the proprietors of this Concession may be able to carry out the engagement in above-mentioned Article 6, and to purchase it quickly.

11. The proprietors of this Concession have no right to purchase lands, except to the necessary extent, for store-houses and abodes, and what may be necessary to carry out this Concession.

12. The cultivators, in accordance with certain conditions which will be made in conjunction with the Government, are entitled to be given an advance to a limit for their crop.

13. If, from the date of the signing of this Concession until one year, a Company to carry it out is not formed, and the work does not begin, this Concession will be null and void, except that war or such like may prevent the formation of a Company.

14. In case of misunderstanding arising between the Persian Government and the proprietors of this Concession, that misunderstanding shall be referred to an Arbitrator accepted by both sides, and in case of the impossibility of consent to the appointment of an Arbitrator, the matter will be referred to the

arbitration of one of the Representatives, resident at Tehran, of the Government of the United States, Germany, or Austria, to appoint an Arbitrator, whose decision shall be final.

15. This Concession is exchanged in duplicate with the signature of His Imperial Majesty, registered in the Foreign Ministry, between Major Talbot and the Persian Government, and the Persian text of it is to be recognized.

7. Tobacco Smuggling and the French Régie Monopoly in the Ottoman Empire, 1895

In 1881, under pressure from England and France, the Ottoman Empire relinquished control over its internal finances to a European-dominated public debt administration, and by the end of the century, several European companies were attempting to profit from Ottoman political weakness by negotiating monopolies or quasi-monopolies over various parts of the Empire's economy. These negotiations were hardly between equals, for the Empire was in serious financial trouble because of the cost of modernization, trade that favored European countries, Ottoman mismanagement of funds, European usurious loan practices, and so on. The French Régie Cointeresse des Tabacs de l'Émpire Ottoman acquired a monopoly over the purchase and sale of tobacco produced in the Empire. Much to the chagrin of the company, however, the monopoly was undermined by local government authorities and popular resentment. This document is a 1895 company report detailing some of the difficulties. Though highly subjective in tone (condemning Ottoman inaction and the brazenness of local smugglers), this report mentions real sources of opposition to the French monopoly.

We have already noted the inaction of the authorities with regard to our requests, especially in Nazareth, where the hostility of the local governor has paralyzed our operations:

In the same town we have been refused all assistance despite our incessant demands. Our Koldjis [inspectors] cannot—without risking imprisonment—carry out any seizure operation [of contraband] as long as the smugglers are constantly released by the authorities.

Our searches are constantly hindered, which keeps us from carrying out these operations. The greatest protection is afforded to cultivators with the effect of increasing the value of their tobacco. The [Ottoman] authorities refuse to name, according to the terms of Article 26 of the Réglement [the agreement between the Ottoman government and the private-public French tobacco company], a representative for the sale of tobacco at the commercial price.

Bestand des Politischen Archivs des Auswartigen/Aktengruppe: Turkei 110. Translated by Akram Khater.

Our warehouse in Derende was pillaged, and in the warehouses of Hafil, Beharenzen, Karkala, and Direiki considerable quantities of tobacco were completely destroyed.

One case of tobacco was pillaged between Deliktach and Sivas, and our office in Gurun was besieged in an attempt to pillage it. We have lost in Tokat 15,000 kilograms of tobacco.

The smugglers are very powerful in Nazareth.

In Tokat we have encountered everywhere armed resistance. The Koldjis and the police wanted to carry out a search operation in the village of Moubad, where 170 bales of contraband tobacco were discovered. However, the villagers repulsed them after attacking and injuring many of the agents who were part of that expedition.

A note sent by the general administration [of the French tobacco company] to the [Ottoman] Ministry of Interior has remained unanswered.

In Amassia, the governor has expressly acknowledged that search operations are impossible.[. . .]

This sentiment of hostility reveals itself in all contacts between the [Ottoman] authorities and our employees, and all measures are taken to make more difficult the exercise of our monopoly [over tobacco].

In Trebizonde a convoy of more than 160 loads was attacked in Platana by bands of 100 or 200 smugglers armed with rifles, and they confronted with impunity our Koldjis and fired upon them.

An imperial order decreeing the mobilization of imperial troops against these bands has not been executed, and the local authorities want an order for each particular case [of smuggling activity].[. . .]

The Régie [French tobacco company with monopoly over tobacco commerce in the Ottoman Empire] does not have sufficient means to interdict such expeditions. Moreover, when on more than one occasion we attempted to carry out such operations, the local authorities intervened and punished the Koldjis, even though the latter were serving the interests of the [Ottoman] state.

If our Koldjis have the misfortune of injuring a smuggler, then they are considered criminals and punished with hard labor.

At Cheiran a real battle took place between the smugglers and our inspectors, with one Koldji killed. The smugglers were able to continue their work of importing great quantities of tobacco, because Saadedin Pasha [the local Ottoman governor] disarmed our Koldjis and kept them from pursuing the smugglers.

CHAPTER 3

Social and Cultural Reformulations

The social and cultural manifestations of the economic and political interactions between Europe and the Middle East and North Africa during the nineteenth century had a profound impact on the latter two regions. This is not to imply that the cultures of those regions were previously isolated before their encounter with Europe. Nor is it to imply that those cultures were static replications of past traditions and customs. Rather, during the nineteenth century the extent and rate of interaction between the indigenous cultures of the Middle East and North Africa, on the one hand, and Europe, on the other, increased dramatically. Furthermore, the superior military, political, and economic power that Britain and France—the two main imperial powers—wielded made this interaction one of unequal proportions. In many important ways it was an interaction that was more conflictual than consensual.

This cultural encounter was brought about through the arrival of unprecedented numbers of European merchants, warships, diplomats, and missionaries in the Middle East and North Africa. It also was an outcome of the dispatch of students from Istanbul and Cairo to Paris and London, where they were to study French and English, among other subjects. Among many of the educated indigenous elites, these interactions, as well as the decisive military defeats of Ottoman and Egyptian troops, raised serious and critical questions about their societies and the reasons for their weakness in the face of superior European technologies. The answers to these questions were hardly uniform. A few intellectuals argued that only complete emulation of European ideas would ensure the future of the region. Others took the exact opposite position, contending that any turning away from existing norms would mean further surrender to European designs. Between these poles was a wide range of opinion. What is striking about this debate—it raged throughout the nineteenth century but was particularly intense in the last two decades—was its concentration on gender roles. Regardless of the ideological position taken, commentators infused the definition of the roles of men and women with heightened importance for society and nation.

This debate sheds some light on the transformation of societies in the Middle East and North Africa. Having lived in Paris in the 1820s, the Egyptian author of the first document draws a vivid, implicit contrast between Parisian and Egyptian ways of life. The next six documents cover various topics in the ongoing discussion about social and cultural change: women's role in management of the home (document 2), advocacy of expanded rights for the "new woman" (document 3), the need to bring "enlighted" and "modern" notions about work, education, and family life to remote Jewish communities (document 4), advocacy of education for girls (documents 5 and 6), and the need to end the actual and metaphorical veiling of Muslim women (document 7). It is important to remember that advocates of change were not the only people expressing their views. Indeed there was a great deal of opposition to many of the proposed changes. The simple fact that article after article arguing for change continued to be written indicates that changes were not coming about very quickly.

1.   Rifa'a Tahtawi Reflects on Paris, Its People, Their Ideas, and Lives in the 1820s

Shaykh Rifa'a Raf'i al-Tahtawi (1801–1873) was born into a wealthy landowning family in Tahta, Upper Egypt. After Muhammad 'Ali assumed power in Egypt in 1805, Tahtawi's family (like other elite families) was driven out of their home and into poverty. However, Rifa'a proved to be an outstanding student, and his intellectual ability gained him admission to Al-Azhar University, an old and distinguished Islamic university. After graduating in 1823, he spent two years teaching at Al-Azhar and reading European books at the house of his mentor Shaykh Hassan Muhammad al-Attar. Subsequently he was assigned to be the Imam (religious leader) of an educational mission that Muhammad 'Ali was sending to France— then the center of science and the arts. Determined to be more than an Imam, Tahtawi immersed himself in the study of French and in the translation of Western books into Arabic. He wrote about his experiences in France and his contact with Parisian society and intellectual circles in his book, Takhlis al-Ibriz fi Tafseel Bariz (A Paris Profile), first published in 1839. This excerpt from that book reveals a bit about the cultural interaction between one Muslim from Egypt and elements of French culture.

Shaykh Rifa'a Raf'i al-Tahtawi, *Takhlis al-Ibriz fi Tafseel Bariz* (A Paris Profile) (Cairo: Mustafá al-Bābī al-Halabī, 1958), pp. 30–34. Translated by Akram Khater.

Chapter Two: Speaking of the People of Paris

You should know that Parisians are Christians with intelligent minds and impressive understanding and depth of thought with regard to difficult issues. They are not like Coptic Christians [members of an Egyptian Christian sect], who are naturally inclined to ignorance and lack of wisdom. Neither are they prisoners of tradition. Rather, they always wish to know and understand the origins of things, to the point that even ordinary people know how to read and write and enter into deep discussions, according to their capacity. The common people in this country are not like those in most uncivilized countries. Knowledge about all the sciences, arts, and handicrafts is recorded in books. Even the lowliest of crafts requires of its practitioner the ability to read and write in order to master his trade. Every artist has to create in his art something never created before, and—in addition to seeking profit—artists are motivated in their innovative endeavors by the desire for good reputation and distinction.[. . .]

The inclination of French women is to seek after new things and to love change in all things, but especially in the manner of dress. They can never settle [on a single style of clothing], and styles are always changing among them. This does not mean that they completely change their clothes; instead they mix and match various elements. For example, they do not exchange a hat for a turban, but they sometimes wear a hat for a while, and then after a time they change to a hat of another style or color.

They [men and women] are characterized by their lightness of spirit and demeanor. Thus you may find a French notable running along the road like a child. They are also prone to shifts in mood—from happiness to sadness and back, and from seriousness to jocularity and back—to the point that an individual may do many contradictory things in a single moment. But this occurs only in trivial matters; on serious issues such as their political views, their opinions do not change. Everyone remains faithful to their beliefs and opinions, which they hold throughout their lives. Because they love France, they travel a great deal, even spending many years traveling between the East and the West, and they may even risk their lives to benefit their country.[. . .]

They also like foreigners and seek their company, particularly if the foreigner is wearing expensive clothes. This leads them to ask about the country [of foreigners] and the traditions of their people.[. . .] And it is common for souls to seek after that which they do not possess.

They offer solace with their words and deeds but not with their money. However, they do not refrain from lending—not giving—money to their friends, unless they are certain that they will not get their money back. They are more miserly than generous toward others, and we mention this in our chapter about their traditions, in the section about hospitality.[. . .] They generally fulfill all their obligations, and they never ignore their duties, for they are always working whether they are rich or poor. [. . .] They love a good reputation and shun self-aggrandizement and hatred, for they are—as they describe themselves—more pure in heart than sheep. When angry, they are fiercer than tigers, and if one of them becomes angry, then he may prefer death to life; hardly any time passes without someone killing himself because of poverty or love. One of their most outstanding characteristics is trustworthiness and absence of treachery. [. . .] They are spendthrifts, wasting their money on sinful pleasures and entertainment and gambling. Their men are slaves to their women and obey their orders. [. . .] Some say that women in the East are like the furniture of the house and French women are like spoiled children. [. . .]

French men do not think ill of their wives even though they may have many great faults, but if one of them (even a notable) found evidence that his wife had committed adultery, he would leave her. [. . .]

Among their good characteristics is their disinclination toward homosexuality and the love of young men, for this is something that is at odds with their nature and moral sense. In their speech and poetry they do not mention homosexual love. It is not proper in the French language to say that a man fell in love with a boy, for such a relationship is considered taboo. If a Frenchman translated one of our books, he would alter the text to say that "I fell in love with a girl," as opposed to a boy as in the original. The French consider homosexuality as a fallen state of being, and they are right, for each of the sexes is attracted to a trait that is found in the opposite sex, just as magnets attract iron and electricity attracts things. If two people of the same sex are attracted to each other, the natural state of being is upset, and for the French this behavior is so offensive that they rarely ever mention homosexuality in their books. [. . .]

Among their immoral traits is the lack of chastity among the women and the absence of male protection of the women's honor. [. . .] Generally, Paris is like other French and European cities in that it is full of sin, heresies, and immoral behavior, even though it may be the French Athens. [. . .] Parisians are the Athenians of this age; their minds are Roman and their ethics are Greek. [. . .] The French reject supernatural things and believe that [. . .] the purpose of religion is to help human beings do good deeds and avoid evil. They also believe that the development of a country and the advancement of its people in the literary arts and ethics make religions irrelevant and that in the advanced kingdoms peculiar laws are enacted. Among their ugly habits is their claiming that their scientists and learned men are greater and more intelligent than the prophets. They have many unseemly beliefs such as the denial by some of predestination, even though it is possible to believe in it [. . .] without abandoning the idea of free will. [. . .]

It is not acceptable among the French to employ a black slave in the kitchen and for housekeeping because they believe that blacks lack the necessary cleanliness. French women are extremely beautiful and gentle, and they excel at social interaction. They always use makeup, and they interact with men in the parks, and men and women may even get to know each other through outings in such places on Sundays or during the ballet or in ballrooms on Monday nights. [. . .]

It is said that Paris is paradise for women, fragrance for men, and hell for horses. This is because the women are endowed with either money or beauty, men are the slaves of women, and horses pull carriages day and night over the cobblestones of the streets of Paris. [...]

Chapter Five: Of the Foods of the People of Paris, and Their Manners in Eating and Drinking

[...] The slaughterhouses are located at the edge of the city and not within it, and this is for two reasons. One is to avoid the bad smells, and the second is to avoid damage by the cattle in case they escape. The French have different ways of butchering. [...] They hit the bulls on the head with iron mallets so that they become dizzy, and they repeatedly do so until the bull is dead, then slaughter it in the manner of sheep. I sent an Egyptian servant of mine as usual to the slaughterhouse to purchase some meat, but when he saw the horrible way in which the bulls were treated, he returned, thanking God for not making him a bull in the land of the French. [...] The number of their wine-houses is far too large to count, and only the lowliest of people go to these places with women prostitutes, and they are loud. [...] One day I was passing one of these places in a street in Paris when a drunkard yelled at me: "Oh Turk! Oh Turk!" And he grabbed my clothes. I was close to a confectioner's shop, so I brought him in and seated him on a chair and jokingly asked the owner, "Would you please give me candy for this man?" The shop owner responded: "This is not like your country, where it is permissible to sell and buy people." I responded that in his present state the drunkard was not a human being!

2.   *Anis al-Jalis*, an Egyptian Magazine, Defines a Vision of Women and Their Role in Society, 1899

In the last three decades of the nineteenth century, many journals and magazines dedicated partially or completely to women and their issues came into existence in the Middle East and North Africa. These magazines were published mainly in Istanbul, Tehran, Beirut, Cairo, Algiers, Tunis, and other large cities. They varied in political outlook, in content and style, and in purpose. Some focused on fashion, home economics, and the etiquette of middle-class life. Others pronounced themselves to be platforms for educating women in political, social, and cultural matters. As a group, these journals were seeking to define a particular vision of women and women's role in society. Despite their many profound disagreements, they gave a voice to women within the newly articulated modern public sphere. Most of their disparate editorials and articles maintained that women—however they and their roles were defined—were essential for the construction of a modern society and nation. The subject of these two articles from Anis al-Jalis *is women's important role in the management of the home.*

"Management of the Home," *Anis al-Jalis*, 2, nos. 3 and 4 (1899): pp. 110–112. Translated by Akram Khater.

[1]

The woman is a "sultana" [queen] in her house where she disposes freely of her judgments in whatever manner she pleases. Through its reins [which] are in her hand, she guides the home to the depths of despair or to the fertile lands of happiness. For she is either the source of its light and the herald of its peace, or the harbinger of its misery and the cause of its darkness. Every woman, even if she is of little significance or lowly status, occupies that position of authority and dominion within her home. Hence, she either makes it tranquil and herself its owner, or a hell and herself its devil. Every house, however dark and poor it may be, can borrow light from the smiles of the woman, and bliss and joy from the goodness of her morals. Thus, [the home] thrives like the bloom of the flower from the rays that her love and compassion casts over it From her attention and good care of it [the home] has the best of that which enjoys the characteristic of [being] idle. Certainly the children of the virtuous woman and her husband are crowned with happiness and they live a long life in happiness and joy. And now that the woman has become aware of her importance and realized the full magnitude of that which she was assigned then she must be a source of contentment for her relatives so that she herself will be happy. And, indeed, for her not to be deceived by the ornaments of vain glory, nor by the attention that admirers bestow upon her fleeting beauty. Rather, she must capture the heart of her husband and children and to attract them to her with the fulfillment of her desire and her hard work.

Do not suppose that the duty of a woman is limited to love and to the attraction of her hearts, for she has another more important and lofty task. It is to help in carrying the burdens of life and sharing in dealing that which has been fated for her of joy and agony. Furthermore, she cannot be judged by words but by deeds, and therefore the subjects of her government must be happy and joyful. [However, their happiness should be] on the condition that she does not assign their affairs to those who are without experience or care so as not to expose the ship of her home to danger in the tumultuous sea of life. For she is the captain of the ship guiding it with her hand, nay she is the soul of this body that cannot survive without it [the soul].

And she must be energetic with courage and patience, and she must see all with her eyesight without missing the slightest of details. If she needs guidance in a matter that is too complicated for her to manage and too difficult to solve then let her ask for help from her life's partner, that is the man who will be her greatest ally in her mission. For, even if he is the possessor of power and the one delegated to gain a livelihood on the outside, he still has within the home the grand patronage and the high perception. Let the woman, then, depend on the hear[t] of her husband and let her be guided by the light of his knowledge and intelligence to complete the important work which she does and the various duties that the natural life forces upon her.

Let the woman not ignore the truth of the task that nature has readied for her and that her upbringing has prepared her for: that is that she must be before all a mother and wife. And let her not allow the rare intelligence and wide knowledge, that she sometimes may have, to be causes for ignoring her duties. For she has duties toward others which are no less important [than those that she has toward herself]. Also, she cannot live an isolated life away from people, nor can she come short in fulfilling her duties toward them, otherwise she will expose herself to the arrows of blame and criticism.

There are many conditions and guidelines for this work and duties which cannot be completely described in one article. Rather, it requires great detail to accomplish the required goal, and for that we have decided with the permission of Allah to provide a special section for it in every section of the issues of this magazine. We will dedicate this section to speaking about the management of the home and what comes under that from other related matters. And this we do to fulfill the duties of service which we have vowed to accomplish with sincere advice, and without withholding effort or energy, and on Allah we depend.

[2]

As we promised in the previous issue, today we will include a new section to talk about the management of the house. As the readers know this is a large topic which is not limited only—as the nature of its title may indicate—to what is related to the inside of the house from cleaning it to the upkeep of its furniture. Rather, and in truth, it concerns that which is more important than that; that is everything that relates to social and familial life in all of its stages and conditions. [It includes] the coexistence of a married couple in a manner that reinforces the ties of love and harmony and that seals that contract which connects them with the seal of joy and happiness so that no misery and unhappiness would enter into their lives. [It also includes] the raising of the children and taking care of them in a way that would refine their manners and straighten their crookedness in order to improve their fate and for them to be able to make themselves and others happy in life. Among the duties of the individual toward people and himself is to clearly see his limits so that he would not transgress them. Thus he would safeguard his honor and will live respected and in security. And many other things are included under this section which makes it one of the most important subjects and the most useful because it is directly important to the individual. For this section will look at his private state and affairs and will elucidate ways for his comfort and happiness and will teach him the means to repulse misery with happiness. Thus it would be correct to call this type of work the Science of Social Chemistry for what it attempts to do in creating harmony amongst the various constituents of society. Moreover, [it would be correct to call it thus] for establishing harmony between the alienated members of the same household and for merging them into a single body that is well organized in connection and affiliation and for what that bring[s] about in terms of change from misery and bitterness in life to happiness and sweetness, and for lightening the heavy load and making the difficult easy. Thus, it would be even more appropriate to call this section the Management of Life or the World, and not the Management of the Household, for the house is in reality the world scaled down. And if it [the household] is managed well according to well organized rules then half of life—if not all of it—would be improved.

We said in the previous issue that the woman is the goddess of the house, and i[n] her hands she holds its reins leading wherever she wishes. Here we again repeat those words and add to them that the woman has the first and more exacting role in managing the house, for she alone is capable of [bringing about] the happiness of the man or his misery. And if we insist upon the need to educate the woman and to improve her status, we only do so as she can fully comprehend the full magnitude of the task assigned to her and the secret of her position vis à vis the man, and thus she would work fully aware of the responsibility that has been placed upon her shoulders. And if the man—who is enmeshed in civilization—does not spare any effort in improving the tools and equipment which he uses for his material needs and to guarantee his comfort and happiness, then should he not be concerned about that status of the woman, and she is one who cannot be dispensed with? Should he not be concerned with her well-being in order to improve his own existence? The woman, then, is the source of everything and upon her depends the luck of the man in his world. For in every home where you find a moral, rational, working and knowledgeable woman [there you will find that] happiness is its companion and the nightingale of joy sings in its space, and for every home where you find an ignorant and immoral woman you should bewail it and shed your tears for it and you should know that the companion of that home is misery and wretchedness.

It has been said in the popular sayings that the "man harvests and the woman builds." This means that the work of the man is dependent upon gain and profit at the outside and that the woman is the one who receives from him what he earns through his labor and efforts and spends it [in] its proper places as she is directed by sound mind and careful consideration that is fully aware of the conditions of the home and that is an expert in its affairs. These words are the epitome of wisdom because many ruined homes have been rebuilt thanks to the woman and the goodness of her work, and because many poor houses have become rich with the expertise of the woman and the soundness of her policy. In addition, many flourishing homes have been ruined because of what befell them from destruction by the woman, and many women have lost the most precious things that they had and that is the love of their men because of their [the women's] affliction with laziness and dereliction of their domestic duties. The truth is that there is nothing more difficult for the active and hard-working man—who spends his day laboring to gain his living—than to see next to him a lazy and ignorant woman who does nothing but spend money and waste her time, who does not wake up until after her poor husband had spent many hours in toil and work. And what is strange is that we hear many women complaining about their husbands because they are not satisfied with their lives, when if they [the women] had bothered to examine their conscience they would find that they [the women] are the cause of that complaint. So, if they [the women] wish not to hear anything of that sort, then let them begin to complete their domestic duties without neglect or carelessness. Then, they will receive in place of complaints and blame thanks, gratitude, compliments and peace.

3. Qasim Amin Argues for the Emancipation of Women in Egypt, 1900

Qasim Amin (1863–1908), a French-educated Egyptian lawyer, belonged to the upper middle classes of Egyptian society. He achieved fame/notoriety at the turn of the twentieth century for his advocacy for Egyptian women in his books The Liberation of Women *(1898) and* The New Woman *(1900). Amin, however, was more concerned with modernizing patriarchy, and making it similar to patriarchy in western Europe, than he was in achieving true equality for women. He regarded gender as a dividing line around which clustered distinctly different roles for men and women, with the latter occupied primarily if not solely with maintaining a modern house for their husbands and children. Amin never intended to imply that women—as individuals—should have access to the same education and work as men, let alone the same political rights.*

Amin argued that the "liberation" of women was an essential prerequisite for the liberation of Egyptian society from foreign domination. He based some of his arguments in The Liberation of Women *on the Qur'an. Although a few other writers—most of them women, such as Zaynab Fawwaz, Hind Nawfal, and A'isha al-Taimuriya—had written and spoken on the same subject, none had access to as widespread or public an audience as Amin, mainly because they were women. In other words, Amin was neither the first nor the last to speak of giving women more rights; rather, he became a lightning rod for the early phase of the feminist movement in Egypt and around the Middle East (his books were translated into Turkish and Farsi). He promoted the debate on women in Egypt from a side issue to a major national concern. But for broaching such a sensitive issue, he himself came under severe attack. Ironically, much of the criticism that was heaped on him was the same that he had used in an earlier book* Les Egyptiens *(1894), in which he replied to a French document that cast the status of Egyptian women in a negative light.*

In response to criticism of The Liberation of Women, *Amim wrote* The New Woman, *in which he defended his position and extended his ideas. In this book, Amin relied less on arguments based on the Qur'an and Hadith (sayings of the Prophet); he more openly used the ideas and arguments of European intellectuals. This excerpt from* The New Woman, *allows us to understand not only Amin's arguments but also the premises of the opponents of those ideas.*

In the Name of God, the Merciful, the Compassionate:

The new woman is one of the fruits of modern civilization. Her appearance in the West was a consequence of the scientific discoveries that freed the human mind from the powers of delusion, suspicion, and superstition, providing all individuals with control over their lives and charting for them a path to follow. Such changes occurred because science explored all issues, examined every idea, and rejected any proposition not proved to be in the public interest. This search resulted in abolishing the power of the clergy, eliminating the privileges of nobility, establishing a constitution for monarchies and rulers, and freeing black people from the bondage of slavery. It finally challenged most of the privileges that men had defined as theirs, which in effect had implied that women were not equal to men in any sphere.

Europeans used to have the same opinion of women that we have today: that women are inferior due to their mental deficiencies, their low status in religion, and their primary role as temptresses and agents for the Devil. They used to say that woman, "long of hair, short of mind," was created for no other reason than to serve man. European scholars, philosophers, poets, and religious leaders considered it foolish to educate women. Moreover, they scoffed at the woman who abandoned her household for intellectual pursuits. They accused such women of intruding on what they called "men's domain."

When the veil of ignorance was finally lifted from European men, they admitted that they themselves were instrumental in the inferior position of women, and that they had not allowed them to change and develop. They also realized that a woman was a human being like them, that she had the right to enjoy her freedom and to use her capabilities, and that depriving a woman of beneficial experiences was unacceptable.

These changes initiated a new phase for the Western woman. She started cultivating her mind, refining her manners, and gradually gaining her rights. She participated with men in human affairs and was a partner in their search for knowledge, a listener in church, a contributor to literary debates, a participant in scientific meetings, and a traveler to various countries. In a short time, that female who had been animal-like—decorated with ornaments, garbed in fashion, and immersed in amusement—was replaced by a new woman who was a sister to man, a companion to her husband, a tutor to her children—a refined individual.

This transformation is all we intend. We hope the Egyptian woman achieves this high status through the appropriate avenues open to her, and that she will acquire her share of intellectual and moral development, happiness, and authority in her household. We are convinced that if this goal were achieved, it would prove to be the most significant development in Egypt's history.

Holding such a belief, would it be acceptable for us to refrain from the pursuit of our goal because the general public is unaware of it, or because writers have demonstrated discontent with it, differing in opinion, being skeptical, or giving it a low priority?

Our reasons for writing are not motivated by a desire to gain the applause of the ignorant and general public. These people do not understand the clearly stated word of God when it is presented to them. In fact the only way they understand it is when its original intentions are distorted to them through the opinion of a sheikh. Such religious leaders are quite ignorant of the meaning of their religion; they are unpatriotic, and are unable to consider their country except through an ugly image of outmoded manners and ridiculous traditions. We are, however, writing to the educated individuals, especially to the young who are our future hope. They will indeed be the generation to have benefited from the exposure to a proper education, enabling them to bring the question of women to the place of concern and consideration it deserves.

It is unnecessary to discuss again the topic of the veil, since we examined it closely in *The Liberation of Women*, where we quoted passages from the Quran that clearly permit women to uncover their face and hands in addition to explaining their relationship to men. [...] It therefore seems clear that our religion does not support the opinion of those scholars who uphold the more extensive use of the veil. If indeed this issue has two sides, it is acceptable for us to give more weight to the opinion that supports human freedom and the general welfare of our society.

In a recent issue of *al-Manar*, the owner of that magazine supported our viewpoint:

> This is the legal decision regarding the debate. It is well known that the law forbade being alone with a woman who is not related. Analysis of writings covering the early period of Islam indicates that there was indeed extensive public interaction among men and women. It is sufficient for you to be aware that the women of the Prophet, God bless him and grant him salvation, who indeed were commanded to go further in the use of the veil, used to interact with men. In fact 'Aisha was even a commander in the army, directing it in the well-known Battle of the Camel. I cannot therefore imagine how an obstinate individual can insist that a woman should not interact with men other than those within the legal degree of consanguinity that precludes marriage.

This is the opinion of a man whose religious standing is well known by all. If individuals at al-Azhar concerned themselves with understanding the intent of their religion instead of their preoccupation with the analysis of verbal expression, grammar, and linguistic construction, they would have opinions no different from ours.

The inferior and backward status of Islamic countries in comparison to other countries is daily attributed in various writings to the role of the Islamic scholars. Such writings in effect describe Islamic scholars as having an inadequate understanding of their religion and not observing the precepts of Islam. However, when a different opinion is presented, potentially beneficial to society, these same writers and intellectuals turn to the religious leaders for guidance. They request a legal opinion from the same Islamic scholars, forgetting that those who resist reform are unaware of the knowledge to be gained through an understanding of contemporary disciplines that may refine their thinking, improve their moral standards, or assist them in their evaluation of various activities. These religious leaders have refused, for example, to include in their teachings knowledge from the disciplines of history or geography, unless forced. Their scope of knowledge or religious understanding means they are not in a position to provide an adequate opinion on any major concern, to say nothing of one of the most important issues in human history.

Anyone familiar with the Islamic legal system is aware that the Islamic perspective on the status of women is one to be proud of, especially when it is compared with other religious traditions. This is because Islam, some twelve centuries ago, granted women rights that have only been achieved by Western women during the past couple of centuries. In fact, Western women are still deprived of some of their rights and are presently concerned with claiming them.

Our legal system stipulates that women may manage their own resources. In addition it has urged the education and development of women and has not prohibited them from pursuing any profession or occupation. Islam has even gone so far in the equality between men and women as to permit women when necessary to be guardians over men, and to occupy the position of mufti or qadi, a position that entails the administering of justice. 'Umar ibn al-Khattab, may God be pleased with him, appointed women as supervisors in the markets of al-Medina, in spite of the availability of men, some of whom were the Companions of the Prophet. In contrast, until last year the French legal system did not grant women the right to enter the legal profession. Since our Islamic legal system, the Shari'a, protects women and grants her freedom, is it proper for us today to forget its intentions or to neglect the mechanisms that would help women to take advantage of these precious rights? Is it proper for us to waste our time in theoretical debates that only deter us from advancing toward reforming our condition?

I do not believe that such a stand is appropriate, and I hope that many of my readers will share my opinion.

[. . .]

Conclusion: The Current State of Thought on Women in Egypt

During the past few years, Egyptians have begun to be aware of their poor social condition, their faces show the pain of it, and they have recognized the urgent need for improvement. They have heard about how Westerners live, they have mixed and lived with many of them, and have learned of the extent of their progress. When they saw that Westerners enjoy a good life, broad independence, self-determination, and other prerogatives that they themselves are not permitted and without which life has no value, there awoke in them a yearning to catch up and a desire to earn some of that happiness. Leaders have appeared among us, supporting ideas that they believe will guide our country toward the path of success. One calls for work and activity, another for harmony, unity, and the elimination of all sources of disagreement, a third for patriotism and self-sacrifice, while a fourth calls for adherence to religious teachings, and so on.

But these leaders have neglected a very important point, namely that without women's involvement it will be impossible to bring about any change in society. If women gain an understanding of the meaning of these causes, and if they identify with them or are committed to them, they will be able to bring up their children in the best way possible, in the mold of human perfection.

No social condition can be changed unless education and upbringing are directed toward that change. In bringing about any kind of reform, it is not enough to identify the need for change, to order its implementation through governmental decrees, to lecture about it, to invite people to address it, or to write about it in journals and books. None of these efforts can change a country, warn it of its predicament, or transform its life: any change in a country is a result of the totality of its virtues, characteristics, moral qualities, and customs, which are not inherent in people but are acquired through upbringing, that is to say, through women.

If Egyptians wish to improve their condition, they must start at its source. They must realize that unless their household and families provide a sound environment for preparing men with the necessary qualities for success, there will be no hope of acquiring any worthwhile status among the advanced countries of the world or in the realm of human civilization. Households and families, however, cannot provide a sound environment unless their women are educated, and unless they have shared the ideas, hopes, disappointments, and activities of men.

This simple and straightforward truth, which I publicly stated last year, was considered a kind of folly by many and labeled a violation of Islam by the jurisprudents. Many school graduates thought it an excessive imitation of Western life. Some even went so far as to say that it was a felony against the homeland and religion. Their writings moreover suggested that the emancipation of Eastern women was one of the goals of Christian countries, who intended by this to bring about the destruction of Islam, and that Muslims who supported this were not Muslims. These claims and other fantasies are not understood by simple souls who listen to them or by those who are ignorant and accept them.

We do not wish to respond to such criticism except to state that if the Europeans intended to harm us, they would leave us in our present condition, because there would be no better way to achieve their goals. This is without a doubt the truth, and it will inevitably reveal itself, as truth always does, no matter what people may do to conceal or ignore it.

Anyone who contemplates our present condition will find aspects that demonstrate that our women have broken through a phase of slavery, and that only a thin veil now separates them from freedom. Thus we can see that:

1. A new perception among Egyptians has developed regarding the importance of educating their daughters.

2. Seclusion of women is gradually decreasing, and will eventually disappear.

3. Young men are reluctant to marry according to traditional patterns and are attempting to change the process so that they can become better acquainted with the person they will marry.

4. The government and some private citizens, headed by Sheikh Muhammad 'Abduh, the grand mufti of Egypt, are involved in reforming the Shari'a

courts. An examination of the important report issued by the grand mufti on the role of these courts indicates that many aspects of these reforms will affect Egyptian families. His statement on polygamy is of particular significance:

> I will raise my voice to protest against polygamy among the poor. Many a poor man has four, three, or two wives, and is unable to support them. There is constant conflict over finances and marital rights. Yet he does not divorce any of them. Conflict continues among them and among their children. As a result, neither the husband nor his wives are able to live according to God's ordinances. No one knows the harm of this to our religion and our country.

Many women whose husbands have been sentenced to hard labor for life or other long prison terms have complained this year to the Ministry of Justice over their miserable condition. They have no formal avenue through which they can terminate their marriage, and they do not have a family provider who can support them and their children. The Ministry of Justice was therefore forced to request a formal legal opinion from the grand mufti of Egypt on the legal action that could be taken by the courts on this issue. The grand mufti investigated this and similar problems and was able to provide guidance to the Ministry of Justice through eleven articles based on the Malikite school of jurisprudence. The following is a list of the articles developed for the benefit of the poor:

> I. If the husband refuses to support his wife, and if it is recognized that he has the means to do so, his estate will be used to support her. If he does not have the means to support her, and he continues not to support her, the judge will pronounce her divorced immediately. If the husband claims that he is unable to support her, and is unable to prove this, then the judge will rule that he provide support for her immediately. If the husband proves that he is unable to support his wife, the judge will give him a chance to do so within one month. If after that time the husband is unable to support his wife, the judge will pronounce her divorced from her husband.
>
> II. If the husband is sick or imprisoned and is therefore unable to support his wife, the judge will concede the time required for his recovery or release. If the husband's recovery is delayed or his prison sentence is long, and if there is fear of harm or temptation, then the judge will pronounce the wife divorced from her husband.
>
> III. If the husband is absent for a short while without leaving adequate support for his wife, the judge will declare a time limit. If the husband does not provide the necessary support, and if he is not present to provide that support after the identified time, the judge will pronounce the wife divorced from her husband. If the husband's location is unknown, or the absence is long, and if it is proven that he has no

money that he can use to support his wife, the judge will pronounce her divorced from her husband.

IV. If the absent husband has property, credit, or a deposit with someone, then the wife has the right to adequate support from that money or credit. She must prove the existence of the credit or the deposit. Her request will be granted without the necessity of a legal guardian. She will be required, however, to state under oath that she is entitled to the support from the estate of her absent husband, and to state that he has left no resources for her support, nor authorized anyone to support her.

V. The judge's decree of divorce for non-support is revocable on appeal. The husband can petition the return of his wife if his resources are established and if he is ready to support her, as long as this takes place during the legally prescribed period. If proof of his resources is not established, and he is unable to support her, then he has no right to appeal.

VI. If a husband is missing in a Muslim country, and if his wife has no news of him, she can submit an appeal to the Ministry of Justice in which she identifies the area where she believes or knows her husband to be. The Ministry of Justice is responsible at that point for locating her husband through notifications sent to governors or the police. If the police fail to find any trace of him, there will be a postponement of four years, after which she must wait the prescribed period of widowhood of four months and ten days. Then it will be lawful for her to remarry without any special ruling.

VII. If the missing man returns, or if it is established that he is alive, before the second husband consummates the marriage, and the second husband does not know that the first husband is alive, then the wife belongs to the first husband. This is the case even after the official marriage contract, or after consummation if the second husband knows that the first is alive. If it appears that the husband died during the legally prescribed period of widowhood or after it, before the second marriage contract or after it, the woman will inherit from the first husband, as long as the second husband has not consummated the marriage without knowing that the first husband is alive. If the second husband dies after consummation of the marriage without knowing that the first husband is alive, the wife does not inherit from the second husband.

VIII. A wife of a man reported missing in a battle among Muslims, and who was reported to have been present at the battle, may submit the matter to the Minister of Justice. After a search is made and he is not found, the wife may marry after the legally prescribed period of widowhood. Her first husband's property can be transferred into inheritance if nothing is known of him. If the only evidence is that he left with the army, the ruling concerning him is the same as that in the two preceding paragraphs.

IX. The wife of a man missing in a war between Muslims and non-Muslims may present the matter to the Ministry of Justice. After searching for him, a delay of one year will be imposed on her. When that year is completed, she will observe the legally prescribed period of widowhood. It is then permissible for her to remarry, and his property is changed into inheritance after the year is completed. Whenever a delay is imposed on the wife of a missing man, she is supported from his property unless she fears temptation for herself, in which case she may submit an appeal to the judge to grant a divorce as soon as the accuracy of her claim is established to his satisfaction.

X. When a disagreement between a husband and wife becomes serious and when it cannot be resolved through any of the methods stipulated by the Quran, then an appeal is presented to the district judge. It is up to him at that point to appoint two arbitrators of good reputation, one from the relatives of the husband, the second from the relatives of the wife, preferably neighbors. If the relatives prefer to be excused, the judge will appoint arbitrators who are unrelated and send them to the couple. If the arbitrators are able to reconcile the couple according to the prescribed methods, their arbitration will be acceptable. Otherwise the arbitrators should recommend divorce or submit the matter to the judge. The judge will make a decision on the basis of their recommendations. The divorce is single and irrevocable and the role of the two arbitrators is over.

XI. The wife may appeal to the judge for divorce from the husband if he harms her, and if such harm is not legally permissible, such as desertion without legal reason, beating, and cursing without legal reason. The wife must prove these things by legal methods.

The rector of al-Azhar approved this plan, and sent the mufti the following letter:

We have examined Your Excellency's speech number nineteen, delivered on the fourth of the current month, and the accompanying draft of the law that includes eleven articles based on the Maliki school. Our opinion regarding the ideas presented in this material is the same as yours. We have therefore signed it as an indication of our approval. We would also like to thank you for your concern with this important matter. Enclosed please find the signed documents.

The Poor Salim al-Bishri, the Malikite
Servant of Knowledge and the Poor at al-Azhar
6 Rabiʻ II, 1318

These two issues, polygamy and a woman's divorce rights, are among the most important problems that we drew attention to in *The Liberation of Women,* and we are very pleased that such an important scholar and wise jurisprudent as Sheikh Muhammad ʻAbduh found these issues worthy of his interest and that he supported our proposals with his resonant voice.

All these signs and others to be seen in our homes every day show that the condition of the Egyptian woman is improving and progressing. Furthermore, this movement does not spring from speculation or reflection, but is a result of dealing with Westerners and in accordance with the well-known law of natural history that stipulates that every animal adapts to its environment. The fact that our will is not central to this movement of change is reflected in the strong opposition that we encounter whenever the issue is raised, even from those who were experiencing these changes in themselves and in their homes. And this is not surprising, for it is our nature always to follow our prejudices.

We are already beyond the time when we must know what it is we want.

If our purpose in life is merely to survive for a few years, in whatever condition, noble or base, rich or poor, free or enslaved, educated or ignorant, good or bad, then I see that the freedom and education that has so far been granted to the Egyptian woman is unnecessary, and there is no reason to prevent a man from having any number of wives, or from marrying a woman every day and divorcing her the next, or from locking up his wives, daughters, sisters, mother, and grandmother if he wishes.

Women in some African and Asian countries live hidden away in their homes, seeing and seen by no one. A woman's life in some of these countries has reached such a low level that she must kill herself after her husband's death, because she must not enjoy life after he is gone. We need only look at these countries and ask them the secret of the advancement of their women in ignorance and isolation: perhaps what we find there will strengthen our pretext for tightening the seclusion and suppression of women!

But if our goal is indeed that which we read and hear about every day, namely that Egyptians wish to be a vital, advanced, and civilized nation, then we must say to them:

There is a way that will take you out of this predicament you complain of and elevate you to the highest stages of civilization, according to and beyond your wishes, and this is to free your women from the shackles of ignorance and seclusion. We are not the first to propose this idea, and we do not deserve credit for it. Other nations have used it before us and have tried it and benefited from it. Consider Western countries and you will find great differences among them. The training of the American woman, her manners, her customs, and ethical standards are different from those of the French woman, who differs again from the Russian woman. And the Italian woman has nothing in common with the Swedish or the German woman. But all these women, in spite of differences of climate, race, language, or religion, are all the same in one respect: they have their freedom and enjoy their independence.

Freedom has elevated the Western woman from her previous inferior status. When education was added, she was determined to participate alongside men in the progress of their society. This led her to take on active roles in society different to, but no less important than, those of men. The merchant who spends his day in a store selling his merchandise; the clerk who spends a few hours in a government office writing a memorandum to another department;

the engineer who builds a bridge to facilitate transportation between towns; the doctor who amputates a limb to save a life; the judge who mediates in disputes: not one of these men has the right to claim that his work is more beneficial to society than that of a woman who brings to society a man brought up to be of benefit to himself, his family, and his country.

We are not saying to you as others do: "Unite and cooperate with one another," or "Purify yourselves of the faults you know are in your character," or "Serve your family and your homeland," or any other such hot air. We know that change cannot be achieved through the advice of a leader, the orders of a sultan, the magic of a magician, or the miracles of a saint. Change, as we have noted, is brought about through the preparation of the minds of the rising generation.

This is the natural, long-term course, which is strewn with obstacles. The simplest difficulties, though, are those that end in victory and success, and the shortest routes are those that lead to the chosen destination.

4. Teachers of the Alliance Israélite Universelle Write About Child Marriages, Domestic Violence, and the Treatment of Children Among Jews in North Africa, 1902–1915

The Alliance Israélite Universelle was founded in Paris in 1860 to work "toward the emancipation and moral progress of the Jews." To advance this aim, the Alliance established schools in North Africa and the Middle East as vehicles to modernize Sephardic and Eastern Jews by transmitting Enlightenment ideas from the métropole *(Paris) to what they considered to be the peripheries of Jewish civilization. This aim, described in a special issue of the Alliance's magazine,* Cahier, *is worth quoting at length:*

> *Jews . . . lived like their Arab neighbors, far from the great currents of expansion in industry and science of the Western World, a primitive existence, made more difficult by their special legal status as Jews. . . . Always, since its beginnings more than a century ago, the Alliance sought to instill in the children not only love of culture and knowledge, but also the respect of the rights of man, and the meaning of the struggle for liberty and for the dignity of the individual. . . . The pure Jewish tradition on one hand, and the Western ideals brought over from France on the other, became the banner under which so many dedicated men and women carried out their task with such devotion.[1]*

Another aim of the organization was to support all Jews suffering from persecution because of their Judaism. The Alliance was deeply embroiled in the imperial politics of France, seeking to extend French Jewish influence to Jewish communities in any region. Moreover, it saw itself as the standard-bearer of progress and reform

---

[1]*Cahier* 16, no. 4 (1887): p. 23.

and as the savior of world Jewry from persecution. This self-image began to change only when the Zionist movement (the political movement to establish a Jewish homeland in Arab Palestine) became more powerful and effective after World War I (for documents on Zionism see the chapter "Contested Nationalisms").

The following Alliance reports from Marrakesh and Fez, in Morocco, indicate the attitudes of European Jews toward their local coreligionists (it is interesting to note that Christian missionaries and European diplomats were expressing very similar attitudes about local Christian and Muslim communities). Despite the inherently biased commentary, these documents provide valuable information about Jewish communities in North Africa. When reading these documents, keep in mind that many residents of those communities resented the Alliance's interference in their lives. Some communities succeeded in blocking the establishment of Alliance schools or prohibited their children from attending the schools. Instead of assuming that this outcome was a result of ignorance or fear, try to understand the dynamics that would have affected the relationship between the Alliance and the local Jewish communities.

A Sympathetic Account of the Condition of the Women of Marrakesh, 1902

Marrakesh, 13 August 1902

[. . .]

We have spoken on many occasions of the condition of women in the cities of the East and of Africa. Everywhere there is the same indifference to the wife on the part of the husband. Everywhere she remains in the background, happy enough if she is not being beaten or ill-treated. In Marrakesh one senses this unfortunate situation more so than anywhere else. Let us consider the case of an affluent family, in which the wife is not obliged to work to gain a living. Her existence is not for that devoid of worry. She must not—and, in any case, does not—dare raise her voice to her husband. Her opinion, good or bad, is considered worthless, and the husband, a veritable tyrant, will do whatever he pleases concerning either his wife or his children. A mother must not even think of defending her children against the authoritative hand of their father. When the father thinks it is necessary to beat his child, the mother must stand immobile in her corner, even when her maternal instincts rebel at the sight of the unjust treatment to which her son, or more often her daughter, is being subjected.

It goes without saying that even in the affluent families the wife must never be seated at the same table as her husband and male children. On Saturdays and holidays a high table, surrounded with chairs and properly arranged, is set up in the main room. The husband, the male children, and the guests take their places around it.

Archives of the Alliance Israélite Universelle, France XIV.F.25. These documents may also be found in Aron Rodrigue, *Images of Sephardi and Eastern Jewries in Transition: The Teachers of the Alliance Israelite Universelle, 1860–1939* (Seattle: University of Washington Press, 1999), pp. 85–91.

In another room, a low table with only a simple cloth for ornament is set up for the women, the girls, and the female servants. Here the female servants are treated like children of the family and eat at the same table with their mistress. Naturally, the choicest dishes are served first at the men's table. What is left, if there is anything left, is considered sufficient to feed the women.

I have had the opportunity, on several occasions, to attend family celebrations such as weddings, Bar Mitzvahs, engagements. In each of these cases, the celebration extends over a period of several days and never in any case does a woman have the right to sit at the table of honor. It is true that in my case there was an exception to the rule, and the poor ladies looked on with wide eyes when I received the honor of being served first. This was a sign of deference with which they had never been treated and they could not have been more astonished.

Even in the most respectable families polygamy is permitted and it is not surprising to see the two wives living in the same house. Each one has her own floor of the house. And what is more, they often get along quite well with each other. I currently have in class two little girls who are children of the same father but different mothers. The other day I was telling the older girl that she should be nicer to her little sister and help her with her homework once in a while. What was her response? "But she's not my sister; my mother is not her mother." I have to say that little girls only see their fathers at rare intervals here; as far as they know, their only parent is their mother! It was perfectly natural that the two girls did not see themselves as related at all.

So even though she is not obliged to work or struggle, the woman whose husband is well-off is still exposed to the ill-treatment, the indifference, and even the disdain of her husband.

How must it be for the woman who is obliged to work in order to feed her children? In this case, which is more or less the rule for the majority of women, her condition is worthy of compassion. All of the work and all of the worries of the home fall to her. The husband, for lack of any other occupation, can go out and get drunk. When he comes home, dinner must be ready and there must be food in the house. He has no thought to the manner in which his wife procures the necessary money or how hard she works for it . . . Most of them do sewing; some have struggled to save enough money to buy a sewing machine. They are paid between four and five centimes per meter of work done on the machine.

The less fortunate of them head to a square in the Arab district early in the morning and there they squat on the ground, rain or shine, and wait for the Arab women, who bring them some item to mend. In this way they try to earn some forty centimes per day.

Others embroider shoes; they are no less unfortunate. When the Sultan was in Marrakesh with his retinue, there was plenty of work and they made a good living. Since His Majesty has left our city, these poor workers have known the blackest misery and the most unhappy of lives.

The water carriers are another category of women to be pitied. They can be seen at the crack of dawn, going back and forth from the public fountain to the homes of their clients with their jars on their shoulders: this goes on until nightfall. As payment for their work they receive only a piece of bread or a bowl of soup.

On many occasions I have admired the dedication and the strength of will of the women in Marrakesh. How many times has some poor woman come to beg on behalf of her husband? The husband has borrowed money from an Arab; when the loan has come to term he does not have the money to pay. The husband is charged and brought before the *Pasha,* who of course puts the Jew in jail, and here is the miserable wife trying to move heaven and earth to have her husband freed.

No matter how she is treated or how many times she is refused, she does not become discouraged. She spends the day in the excessive heat running from place to place and from person to person, dragging her children along behind her; she has no time to earn the money to feed them. With enough begging and pleading she finally manages to gather enough money to pay off part of her husband's debt. This money serves to hold off the creditor for a month or so, when the loan will again come due and the whole process will begin again. Such scenes are repeated time and time again in the poor families, always because the husband has gotten into debt.

And do you think that the wife is rewarded for such devotion? When the husband feels so inclined he can go to the rabbi and, for one or two pesetas, divorce his wife; she is left with full responsibility for the children. Other times the husband will go off to another town and never be heard from again. Then it is up to the wife to work and struggle to make enough money to feed her children. In light of these conditions our task was perfectly clear: to make of our young girls women who are different from their mothers. We think it essential that the lessons learned in school serve to help these women. Once they have developed better judgment and a keener intelligence, they will no longer be at the mercy of their husbands' whims. Their wishes and their decisions must count for something in the running of the home. They too must be allowed to voice an opinion on questions concerning their children. Once a woman has received some instruction and has begun to develop her intellect, it will not take long for her husband to recognize that in his wife he has a companion whose advice and opinions are worthy of consideration. In this way the wife will no longer be an object of indifference or disdain to her husband but a sensible companion who can advise and assist him.

Obviously we can achieve such results only over a period of time. For now we can make sure that the girls who have spent two or three years in our school will have fewer hardships than any who have not been with us. The counsel they are given on a daily basis, as well as their lessons, will, I hope, prove to be of valuable assistance in creating their future happiness. This is our goal, and all of our efforts are aimed at the accomplishment of this task.

Because of their work, the number of matters to which they must attend, and the ever-present worries of the women of Marrakesh, they scarcely have the time to take good care of their children.

[. . .]

Education. What most surprises the parents of your girls is the cleanliness and the polite manners acquired by the children at the school.

All of our efforts in this direction have been crowned with success.

Prior to the foundation of our school the young girls one would see in the streets were dirty, unkempt, and barefoot; now they are unrecognizable, as they come to school every day perfectly presentable.

Even today, at the end of the school day, a good number of women stand in their doorways to watch the "girls from the school" pass by. There is whispering and chattering. "Look over there. So-and-so's daughter is wearing stockings and shoes; see that other one with the hat?" These little scenes are played out day after day.

At present our girls laugh about it and are amazed that, not long ago, they could have gone out of the house without stockings, sometimes even without shoes.

In my first letters to the Central Committee, I found many occasions to discuss the character of our girls: dishonest, sly, selfish. Those were the principal faults against which we had to fight. They would not hesitate an instant to accuse one of their friends, even their best friends, or to try and fool the teacher. Some progress has been made in this direction also. I am not saying that the girls are models of solidarity, cooperation, and kindness. But I have noted with satisfaction that there is no longer the same spirit of cunning and deceit among my students. Before, it was always a question of who could find the best ruse to get out of a difficult situation. There was joy on their faces when one of their classmates was being punished. Now they have stopped trying to trick their teacher, and when they have done something wrong, I am able to get at the truth of the matter, something that was impossible in the beginning.
[...]

Mrs. M. Coriat

The Population of Fez Resists the Work of the Alliance, 1903

Fez, 1 September 1903

[...]

... We are held in esteem because people know that above us is the Alliance, which for them is a charitable organization and nothing more. But to join us in running the school, to help us in overcoming the thousand problems we face here every day, to contribute with us in the work of the Alliance, to show enthusiasm for the presence of these schools, from which they are the first to benefit and which put them at an intellectual level equal to that of the other communities in the cities along the coast and in Turkey: these things they would never deign to do ...
[...]

For these good people, schools are a superfluous luxury. Only the poor, and not all of them, and some families who have traveled or who benefit from European protection send us their children. The others, the vast majority of the

Jews, stubbornly continue to send their children to vile little *Talmudei-Torah* to learn the Talmud and the Torah.

So many times I have been stunned to hear people who are considered intelligent say that the schools are totally useless in Fez, that what children need to be taught first and foremost is Hebrew and nothing else, that these children will never need to know a European language. Several of our fellow Jews still consider our schools profane and impious places.

I was given manifest proof of this attitude on the part of the Jews of Fez, and manifest proof of their fanaticism, during the *maamad* [meeting of the community council] we held to discuss whether a new school or a new *Talmud-Torah* should be founded. All the important people of Fez attended the meeting. After I had read them the letter from the Alliance and stressed the advantages which would result for the community of Fez if a new, larger school were founded to replace the thousand filthy hovels where Hebrew is so poorly taught, they responded in one voice that they would have nothing to do with such an institution. Since I know that they do not like any interference from a foreigner in their affairs, I told them that the *Talmud-Torah* would be administered entirely by them and that our only responsibility would be to direct and guide the teachers. They replied that they considered it a great sin to bring 1,000 Jewish children together. To guard against the evil eye, they told me, it is better to have smaller, unattractive, and pitiful-looking *Talmudei-Torah* of 50 to 100 children, where the evil eye would be powerless, than a large *Talmud-Torah* with 1,000 children, which would inevitably bring the worst calamities upon the Jewish community. For these good people, hygiene and good education are not important, they are afraid of the evil eye . . .

[. . .]

This obstinacy on the part of our fellow Jews in refusing to send their children to school can be traced to several sources. Fez is a city inhabited only by Muslims and Jews, all equally fanatic, all animated by hostile feelings toward foreigners, and enemies of any innovation. The sanctity of this place and the fierce fanaticism of its inhabitants have until now kept away all Europeans, the only representatives of progress. Furthermore, the difficulty of communication with the outside and the dangerous conditions of the roads have prevented our fellow Jews from traveling. They have not seen much of the world and are therefore not very appreciative of the benefits of education. To this must be added the persecutions to which the Jews have always been subjected. This is why the customs and ways of our fellow Jews in Fez have changed so little until now, and why fanaticism is still so prevalent here. And it does not look like there will soon be a change in these customs, which are so faithfully handed down from generation to generation and with which the Jews here are so comfortable and content.

[. . .]

J. Valadji

5. Articles in Iranian Magazines Emphasize the Link Between the Education of Girls and the Advancement of Iranian Society, 1907, 1909

*Like Cairo, Beirut, and Istanbul at the turn of the twentieth century, Tehran was a center for the publishing of journals, magazines, and newspapers—most of them focused on reforming society and reformulating the cultural practices of Iranians. Their names—*The True Dawn, The New Woman, The New Egyptian, *and so on—indicate their goals. Their impact varied with the extent of their distribution and readers' receptiveness to new ideas. Today, articles from these publications provide us with an idea of the debates going on at that time and help us understand how members of at least one group—the middle classes—were seeking to reshape their community, society, and nation.*

The following articles address the issue of education for girls. The writers of both contend that it is a necessity for girls to be educated if the nation is to become "civilized" and "modern." Notice that the writers use nation *and* civilization *in a new way. This raises the question of how these terms emerge and how they are understood by the emerging middle classes. Do they denote absolute ideas that apply universally or locally specific ideas that are defined with reference to local conditions and ideas?*

1. Girls' Education Is the Basis of Civilization and Moral Refinement

The best path to civilization is the education, training of girls. The first necessity of moral refinement for girls is to be educated, trained, and cultured. Every nation that wants to become civilized has to begin educating and training girls from an early age. Each nation, according to their own religious laws and practices, should provide it [education] for them with any means possible.

Indeed, these girls will become mothers themselves, and their children will socialize with one another and their habits and disposition will spread among each other. But if they have all been educated in a good manner and with moral refinement, then there can be established in that nation a higher civilization. In this manner, the nation will develop and complete its march of progress by becoming civilized.

On the other hand, if the girls (children) are trained and raised by an uneducated mother, then the bad moods, habits, and disposition will have a bad affect on the children. Along with the growth and mental maturity, an indecent manner will be formed and become a habit; and it will also spread among the children. Therefore, barbarism will develop among the people and they will never become a civilized nation. One savant says: "Every behavior that comes to view, or any word that is said, whether good or bad, will have affect on the

---

"Girls' Education Is the Basis of Civilization and Moral Refinement," *True Dawn* (February 1907).

child either directly or indirectly. And if that word or behavior was proper, it will have a positive influence, and if it was improper, indeed it could have a negative result on the child. Truly, the child's mind and soul absorbs any word and behavior, good or bad, faster than the elders."

Every character and manner, good or bad, when experienced by a child will develop inside him and will be there. When Confucius, a Chinese savant, saw the moral refinement that resulted from educating girls, he understood that it is the greatest and most desired outcome from their education. He took advantage of this idea and instituted it as a law in the Chinese nation. Thus, each girl that is educated and trained in decent manner and has not committed a sin will receive a specific amount of money from government.

One day Napoleon arrived in one of the schools in France, and told the teachers: "I have provided the best necessities for education in France. I have made any resources available for learning by any means, so why is public instruction not improving, and why are the children not learning or advancing in their knowledge?" The teachers replied: "The home school teachers in France are not educated. The reason for retrogression and the lack of children's learning is because of the uneducated and untrained mothers."

Therefore, our nation [Iran] which has taken off the tattered garment of barbarism and savagery, and has put on the sash of honor and civilization, should not neglect the importance of girls' education and culture.

2. Girls' Schooling

It is essential to build a school for boys, but schools are more important for girls because boys do not go to school before the age of eight. Rather, [boys] are raised and learn their behavior from their mothers. Thus, if the mother gains her education through schools, her children will learn good behavior and virtue from her. In contrast, if the mother has not been to school, her child is compelled to ill-natured behavior, like her.

So it is obvious that good education for a mother has a direct effect on her child. In the past, any woman who had a good education left a good name in history. In addition, a girl who was well-educated was also well-respected by her father, husband, and relatives, and at any time in history, she was well-received by the public. Nor has Islam ever banned educational advancement in the family of the Prophet, or subsequent royal families. It has never been reported that Islam has said that a girl could not obtain education or should remain ignorant. According to Islam, women are equal to men with regard to human rights. For inheritance, Islam has given the son twice [the inheritance] as that of a daughter. The reason is simple, because the man has to provide food and shelter for the woman it would have been unjustified if both had equal inheritance. It is irrational to criticize Islamic principles for not giving man and

"Girls' Schooling," *Watan*, 1, no. 1 (1909).

woman equal inheritance. If you heard that man and woman have to be equal, it is not in the matter of inheritance, but rather in education, human qualities, and equality in thoughts and opinions. The first woman believers, Khadija, and Fatima Zahra, praise be to them, because of their good qualities, chastity, and worship of God, were superior to all women throughout the world.

Ghatr Al-Tazy, the mother of Al-Muqtadir bi-Allah of the Abbasids [a medieval Islamic ruling dynasty], presided over civil trials and entertained foreign ambassadors. She earned the confidence of the Abbasids' Caliph [ruler]. Zubayda, the wife of Haroun Al-Rashid, had an abundant knowledge in literature, and one of her public works is "Zubayda's Fountain" [built] on the Road to Mecca. Moreover, she financed the renovation of the city of Alexandria.

Buran, the daughter of Hassan ibn Sahl, and the secretary of Mamoun Al-Rashid's wife, was popular for her wisdom, politeness, and generosity. She built several hospitals at her own expense in Baghdad. Her Highness, Sakina Khatoon, the daughter of Husayn, son of Ali [the cousin of the Prophet], praise upon him, was outstanding in literature and the Arabic language. In royal families, during old times and new, there were always several women who became rulers. If they were not distinguished in wisdom and knowledge, they would not have reached those ranks.

His excellency, the editor of the newspaper, *Fareedeh ol 'Alam Al-Islami Fasli-Moshamma*, has written on this matter, which I do not want to repeat. But its conclusion and observations about this matter [are] that the Iranians, in every city, according to its population, should build schools for women. By doing so they would serve humanity. And there are indications that several individuals are taking steps to fulfill this. God willing, when this promise is fulfilled I will present it.

Prosperity for Iranians.

6.   Bahithat al-Badiya Advocates Greater Educational and Economic Rights for Egyptian Women, 1909

Far too often it is assumed that Muslim women are without voice or speak only to reiterate male conservative opinions. As this document and the next demonstrate, these impressions are mistaken. Bahithat al-Badiya (1886–1918) grappled with complex issues surrounding the role of women in a rapidly changing Egyptian society. Nationalists were demanding Egypt's independence from Britain, a constitutional government, and a more modern state. Socially and culturally, things were also in flux. Egyptian intellectuals and elites debated the merits of "modernity" (which some understood as "Western") and "tradition" (understood as "Eastern")

Bahithat al-Badiya, "A Lecture in the Club of the Umma Party, 1909," in *Opening the Gate*, trans. Ali Badran and Margot Badran (Bloomington: Indiana University Press, 1990), pp. 228–238. Reprinted by permission of Miriam Cooke.

and their relationship in practical terms. To Bahithat al-Badiya, "modernity" meant greater educational and economic rights for Egyptian women, which in turn would strengthen the nation and support its march to independence. In this lecture, which she gave to a group of elite Egyptian women, she not only addressed these issues but proposed a program for change, which she spent her remaining years seeking to implement.

Ladies, I greet you as a sister who feels what you feel, suffers what you suffer and rejoices in what you rejoice. I applaud your kindness in accepting the invitation to this talk where I seek reform. I hope to succeed but if I fail remember I am one of you and that as human beings we both succeed and fail. Anyone who differs with me or wishes to make a comment is welcome to express her views at the end of my talk.

Our meeting today is not simply for getting acquainted or for displaying our finery but it is a serious meeting. I wish to seek agreement on an approach we can take and to examine our shortcomings in order to correct them. Complaints about both women and men are rife. Which side is right? Complaints and grumbling are not reform. I don't believe a sick person is cured by continual moaning. An Arab proverb says there is no smoke without fire. The English philosopher, Herbert Spencer, says that opinions that appear erroneous to us are not totally wrong but there must be an element of truth in them. There is some truth in our claims and in those of men. At the moment there is a semi-feud between us and men because of the low level of agreement between us. Men blame the discord on our poor upbringing and haphazard education while we claim it is due to men's arrogance and pride. This mutual blame which has deepened the antagonism between the sexes is something to be regretted and feared. God did not create man and woman to hate each other but to love each other and to live together so the world would be populated. If men live alone in one part of the world and women are isolated in another both will vanish in time.

Men say when we become educated we shall push them out of work and abandon the role for which God has created us. But, isn't it rather men who have pushed women out of work? Before, women used to spin and to weave cloth for clothes for themselves and their children, but men invented machines for spinning and weaving and put women out of work. In the past, women sewed clothes for themselves and their households but men invented the sewing machine. The iron for these machines is mined by men and the machines themselves are made by men. Then men took up the profession of tailoring and began to make clothes for our men and children. Before women winnowed the wheat and ground flour on grinding stones for the bread they used to make with their own hands, sifting flour and kneading dough. Then men established bakeries employing men. They gave us rest but at the same time pushed us out of work. We or our female servants, used to sweep our houses with straw brooms and then men invented machines to clean that could be operated by a young male servant. Poor women and servants used to fetch water for their homes or the homes of employers but men invented pipes and faucets to carry water into houses. Would reasonable women seeing water

Men blame any shortcomings we may have on our education, but in fact our upbringing is to blame. Learning and upbringing are two separate things—only in religion are the two connected. This is demonstrated by the fact that many men and women who are well educated are lacking in morals. Some people think that good upbringing means kissing the hands of women and standing with arms properly crossed. Good upbringing means helping people respect themselves and others. Education has not spoiled the morals of our girls, but poor upbringing, which is the duty of the home not the school, has done this. We have to redouble our efforts to reform ourselves and the young. This cannot happen in a minute as some might think. It is unfair to put the blame on the schools. The problem lies with the family. We must improve this situation.

One of our shortcomings is our reluctance to take advice from each other. When someone says something, jealousy and scorn usually come into play. We also are too quick to ridicule and criticise each other over nothing, and we are vain and arrogant.

Men criticise the way we dress in the street. They have a point because we have exceeded the bounds of custom and propriety. We claim we are veiling but we are neither properly covered nor unveiled. I do not advocate a return to the veils of our grandmothers because it can rightly be called being buried alive, not *hijab,* correct covering. The woman used to spend her whole life within the walls of her house not going out into the street except when she was carried to her grave. I do not, on the other hand, advocate unveiling, like Europeans, and mixing with men, because they are harmful to us.

Nowadays the lower half of our attire is a skirt that does not conform to our standards of modesty (*hijab*) while the upper half like age, the more it advances the more it is shortened. Our former garment was one piece. When the woman wrapped herself in it her figure was totally hidden. The wrap shrunk little by little but it was still wide enough to conceal the whole body. Then we artfully began to shrink the waist and lower the neck and finally two sleeves were added and the garment clung to the back and was worn only with a corset. We tied back our headgear so that more than half the head including the ears were visible and the flowers and ribbons ornamenting the hair could be seen. Finally, the face veil became more transparent than an infant's heart. The purpose of the *izar* is to cover the body as well as our dress and jewellery underneath, which God has commanded us not to display. Does our present *izar,* which has virtually become "a dress" showing the bosom, waist, and derrière, conform with this precept? Moreover, some women have started wearing it in colours—blue, brown and red. In my opinion we should call it a dress with a clown's cap which in fact it is. I think going out without it is more modest because at least eyes are not attracted to it.

Imams have differed on the question of *hijab.* If the getups of some women are meant to be a way to leave the home without the *izar* it would be all right if they unveiled their faces but covered their hair and their bodies. I believe the best practice for outdoors is to cover the head with a scarf and the body with a dress of the kind Europeans call *cache poussière,* a dust coat, to cover the body right down to the heels, and with sleeves long enough to reach the wrist. This is being done now in Istanbul, as I am told, when Turkish women go out to neighbourhood shops. But who will guarantee that we will not shorten it and tighten it until we transform it into another dress? In that instance, the road to reform would narrow in front of us.

If we had been raised from childhood to go unveiled and if our men were ready for it I would approve of unveiling for those who want it. But the nation is not ready for it now. Some of our prudent women do not fear to mix with men, but we have to place limits on those who are less prudent because we are quick to imitate and seldom find our authenticity in the veil. Don't you see that diamond tiaras were originally meant for queens and princesses and now they are worn by singers and dancers.

If the change that some women have made in the *izar* is in order to shed it when they go out that would be all right if these women would only uncover their faces but keep their hair and figures concealed. I think the most appropriate way to dress outside is to cover the head and wear a coat with long sleeves which touches the ground the way the European women do. I am told this is the way women in Istanbul dress when they go out shopping. But who can guarantee that we are not going to shorten it and tighten it until we transform it into something else?

The way we wear the *izar* now imitates the dress of Europeans, but we have outdone them in display (*tabarruj*). The European woman wears the simplest dress she has when she is outside and wears whatever she wishes at home or when invited to soirées. But our women are just the opposite. In front of her husband she wears a simple tunic and when she goes out she wears her best clothes, loads herself down with jewellery and pours bottles of perfume on herself . . . Not only this, but she makes a wall out of her face—a wall that she paints various colours. She walks swaying like bamboo in a way that entices passersby or at least they pretend to be enticed. I am sure that most of these showy women (*mutabarrajat*) do this without bad intentions, but how can the onlooker understand good intentions when appearances do not indicate it?

Veiling should not prevent us from breathing fresh air or going out to buy what we need if no one can buy it for us. It must not prevent us from gaining an education nor cause our health to deteriorate. When we have finished our work and feel restless and if our house does not have a spacious garden why shouldn't we go to the outskirts of the city and take the fresh air that God has created for everyone and not just put in boxes exclusively for men. But, we should be prudent and not take promenades alone and we should avoid gossip. We should not saunter moving our heads right and left. If my father or husband will not choose clothes I like and bring them to the house, why can't he take me with him to select what I need or let me buy what I want?

If I cannot find anyone but a man to teach me should I opt for ignorance or for unveiling in front of that man along with my sisters who are being educated? Nothing would force me to unveil in the presence of the teacher. I can remain veiled and still benefit from the teacher. Are we better in Islam than

Sayyida Nafisa and Sayyida Sakina—God's blessings be upon them—who used to gather with *ulama* and poets. If illness causes me to consult a doctor and there is no woman doctor should I abandon myself to sickness, which might be light but could become complicated, through neglect or should I seek help from a doctor who could cure me?

The imprisonment in the home of the Egyptian woman of the past is detrimental while the current freedom of the Europeans is excessive. I cannot find a better model [than] today's Turkish woman. She falls between the two extremes and does not violate what Islam prescribes. She is a good example of decorum and modesty.

I have heard that some of our high officials are teaching their girls European dancing and acting. I consider both despicable—a detestable crossing of boundaries and a blind imitation of Europeans. Customs should not be abandoned except when they are harmful. European customs should not be taken up by Egyptians except when they are appropriate and practical. What good is there for us in women and men holding each other's waists dancing or daughters appearing on stage before audiences acting with bare bosoms in love scenes? This is contrary to Islam and a moral threat we must fight as much as we can. We must show our disdain for the few Muslim women who do these things, who otherwise would be encouraged by our silence to contaminate others.

On the subject of customs and veiling I would like to remind you of something that causes us great unhappiness—the question of engagement and marriage. Most sensible people in Egypt believe it is necessary for fiancés to meet and speak with each other before their marriage. It is wise and the Prophet himself, peace be upon him and his followers, did not do otherwise. It is a practice in all nations, including Egypt, except among city people. Some people advocate the European practice of allowing the engaged pair to get together for a period of time so that they can come to know each other, but I am opposed to this and am convinced this is rooted in fallacy. The result of this getting together is that they would come to love each other, but when someone loves another that person does not see the faults of that person and would not be able to evaluate that person's morals. The two get married on the basis of false love and without direction and soon they start to quarrel and the harmony evaporates. In my view, the two people should see each other and speak together after their engagement and before signing the marriage contract. The woman should be accompanied by her father, or an uncle or a brother and she should wear simple clothing. Some might protest that one or two or more meetings is not enough for the two persons to get to know each other's character, but it is enough to tell if they are attracted to each other. However, anyone with good intuition can detect a person's moral character in the eyes and in movements and repose and sense if a person is false, reckless and the like. As for a person's past and other things one should investigate by talking with acquaintances, neighbours, servants, and others. If we are afraid that immoral young men would use this opportunity to see young women without intending marriage her guardian should probe the behaviour of the man to ascertain how serious he is before allowing him to see his daughter or the young woman for whom he is responsible. What is the good of education if one cannot abandon a custom that is not rooted in religion and that is harmful. We have all seen family happiness destroyed because of this old betrothal practice.

By not allowing men to see their prospective wives following their engagement we cause Egyptian men to seek European women in marriage. They marry European servants and working class women thinking they would be happy with them rather than daughters of pashas and beys hidden away in 'a box of chance'. If we do not solve this problem we shall become subject to occupation by women of the West. We shall suffer double occupation, one by men and the other by women. The second will be worse than the first because the first occurred against our will but we shall have invited the second by our own actions. It is not improbable, as well, that these wives will bring their fathers, brothers, cousins and friends to live near them and they would close the doors of work in front of our men. Most Egyptian men who have married European women suffer from the foreign habits and extravagance of their wives. The European woman thinks she is of a superior race to the Egyptian and bosses her husband around after marriage. When the European woman marries an Egyptian she becomes a spendthrift while she would be thrifty if she were married to a westerner.

If the man thinks the upper class Egyptian wife is deficient and lacking in what her western sister has why doesn't the husband gently guide his wife? Husband and wife should do their utmost to please each other. When our young men go to Europe to study modern sciences it should be to the benefit, not the detriment, of Egypt. As these men get an education and profit themselves they should also bring benefit to their compatriots. They should bring to their country that which will profit it and dispense with whatever is foreign as much as possible. If a national manufacturer of silk visits the factories of Europe and admires their efficiency he should buy machinery that would do work rapidly rather than introduce the same European-made product because if he does he will endanger his own good product.

If we pursue everything western we shall destroy our own civilisation and a nation that has lost its civilisation grows weak and vanishes. Our youth claim that they bring European women home because they find them more sophisticated than Egyptian women. By the same token, they should bring European students and workers to Egypt because they are superior to our own. The reasoning is the same. What would be the result if this happens? If an Egyptian wife travels to Europe and sees the children there with better complexions and more beautiful than children in Egypt would it be right that she would leave her children and replace them with western children or would she do her best to make them beautiful and make them resemble as much as possible that which she admired in those other children? If the lowliest western woman marrying an Egyptian is disowned by her family shall we be content with her when she also takes the place of one of our best women and the husband becomes an example for other young men? I am the first to admire the activities of the western woman and her courage and I am the first to respect those among them who deserve respect, but respect for others should not make us overlook the good of the nation. Public interest is above admiration. In many of our ways we follow the views of our men. Let them show us what they want. We are ready to follow their views on condition that their views do not do injustice to us nor trespass on our rights.

Our beliefs and actions have been a great cause of the lesser respect that men accord us. How can a sensible man respect a woman who believes in magic, superstition, and the blessing of the dead and who allows women peddlars and washerwomen, or even devils, to have authority over her? Can he respect a woman who speaks only about the clothes of her neighbour and the jewellery of her friend and the furniture of a bride? This is added to the notion imprinted in a man's mind that woman is weaker and less intelligent than he is. If we fail to do something about this it means we think our condition is satisfactory. Is our condition satisfactory? If it is not, how can we better it in the eyes of men? Good upbringing and sound education would elevate us in the eyes of men. We should get a sound education, not merely acquire the trappings of a foreign language and rudiments of music. Our education should also include home management, healthcare, and childcare. If we eliminate immodest behaviour on the street and prove to our husbands through good behaviour and fulfillment of duties that we are human beings with feelings, no less human [than] they are, and we do not allow them under any condition to hurt our feelings or fail to respect us, if we do all this, how can a just man despise us? As for the unjust man, it would have been better for us not to accept marriage to him.

We shall advance when we give up idleness. The work of most of us at home is lounging on cushions all day or going out to visit other women. How does the woman who knows how to read occupy her leisure time? Only in reading novels. Has she read books about health or books through which she can profit herself and others? Being given over to idleness or luxury has given us weak constitutions and pale complexions. We have to find work to do at home. At a first glance one can see that the working classes have better health and more energy and more intelligent children. The children of the middle and lower classes are, almost all of them, in good health and have a strong constitution, while most of the children of the élite are sick or frail and prone to illness despite the care lavished on them by their parents. On the other hand, lower class children are greatly neglected by their parents. Work causes poisons to be eliminated from the blood and strengthens the muscles and gives energy.

Now I shall turn to the path we should follow. If I had the right to legislate I would decree:

1. Teaching girls the Quran and the correct Sunna.
2. Primary and secondary school education for girls, and compulsory preparatory school education for all.
3. Instruction for girls on the theory and practice of home economics, health, first aid, and childcare.

4. Setting a quota for females in medicine and education so they can serve the women of Egypt.

5. Allowing women to study any other advanced subjects they wish without restriction.

6. Upbringing for girls from infancy stressing patience, honesty, work and other virtues.

7. Adhering to the *Sharia* concerning betrothal and marriage, and not permitting any woman and man to marry without first meeting each other in the presence of the father or male relative of the bride.

8. Adopting the veil and outdoor dress of the Turkish women of Istanbul.

9. Maintaining the best interests of the country and dispensing with foreign goods and people as much as possible.

10. Make it encumbent upon our brothers, the men of Egypt, to implement this programme.

7. Nazira Zein el-Din, an Egyptian Feminist, Comments on the Unveiling and Veiling of Women, 1928

Seeking to reclaim Islam from strictly male interpretations, Nazira Zein el-Din (born ca. 1905) offers a liberal interpretation of the religion. The daughter of a Lebanese judge, early in her life Nazira began to question traditional religious and cultural assumptions about the role of women in Islamic societies. In particular, she focused on the hijab, the veiling that some Muslim women used to cover their heads and bodies. In Turkey, secular reforms allowed women greater access to public life and permitted them to remove the veiling. In contrast, Nazira noted, in Syria unveiled women were not even permitted to leave home. In 1928 she published a treatise— excerpted here—arguing, from her research and study of Islamic texts, that Islam regards women as completely equal to men and the Qur'an does not require the veiling of women. Her book, which sparked fiery discussions in Lebanon and throughout the Arab world, can be seen as part of the dialogue about culture, religion, society, and politics in the Middle East that emerged at the end of the nineteenth century and focused in many ways on gender roles.

Two Views: One View on the Unveiled World and the Other on the Veiled World

Ladies and gentlemen, in the beginning I compared opposites, the numbers of the veiled and the unveiled. I found that the veiled are not more than a few million

Nazira Zein al-Din, *Unveiling and Veiling: Lectures and Views on the Liberation of the Woman and Social Renewal in the Arab World* (Cairo, 1928), pp. 64–69. This document may also be found in Charles Kurzman, *Liberal Islam* (New York: Oxford University Press, 1998), pp. 101–106.

Muslims living in towns. Those in the villages of the Islamic world and more than 1700 million in other nations are not veiled. They have rejected the veil that they had previously worn. I have noticed that the nations that have given up the veil are the nations that have advanced in intellectual and material life. Such advancement is not equaled in the veiled nations. The unveiled nations are the ones that have discovered through research and study the secrets of nature and have brought the physical elements under their control, as you see and know. But the veiled nations have not unearthed any secret and have not put any of the physical elements under their control but only sing the songs of a glorious past and ancient tradition. With such singing they sleep in stagnation.

I have seen many intellectuals of the nations where women are still veiled advocating unveiling, but I haven't seen anyone in the unveiled nations advocating or preferring the veil. That is, I haven't seen anyone who has tried unveiling and then has preferred the veil. Even if some Westerner in his hypocritical words makes the veil appear in a favorable light, he is only pleased with the beauty of the Oriental veil while at the same time he would reject the veiling of his mother, wife, sisters, and daughters because of the harm in the veil he favors for others.

I cannot imagine that in the advanced nations which have discovered the secrets of nature and harnessed its powers, which have not let anything pass without examining it to the fullest, where the struggle between right and wrong is continuous until right becomes victorious, nations which have produced works on social subjects we view as masterpieces of literature and sociology, have neglected to study veiling and unveiling to understand the benefits and disadvantages. I cannot think that our own ignorance brings us any greater understanding of what honor is than the unveiled nations possess in learning nor that our conduct is superior to theirs, nor that their women going outside unveiled enjoying their freedom is evidence of their lower conduct and corrupt morals.

Yes, I looked into all that and I could not but consider it evidence of their superior education and elevated conduct. When our esteemed ladies who wear the veil go to a Western country, they take off the veil and the men accompanying them do not prevent them from doing this the way they do when they are at home or after they return. This is because we have more faith in the conduct of Westerners than in our own conduct. The conduct of Westerners has been influenced by mingling with women and thus Western men have based their habits and morals on logic and reason looking to benefits and positive results while our conduct and morals are based on our customs whatever they may be.

I shall never forget a conversation between an Eastern man advocating the veil and an unveiled Western woman who enjoyed her freedom and independence. The Easterner said to the Westerner, "Our nature cannot accept your customs. Our customs are more noble than yours and our men support our women. The man according to his right walks in front of his wife but in your country the woman walks in front of the man as if she were the provider."

The Western woman said, "If you really want to protect your wife please let her go in front of you so that you can watch out for her for the way our men

do, rather than letting her walk behind you so that she would misuse her freedom and get hurt."

The Eastern man paused and said, "Truly, Westerners ground their customs in reason. Reason alone should dictate custom."

It is not fitting for us to say that we who are only a few million, most of
whom are not advanced, are more honorable than the one and a half billion
people (in the world), most of whom are more advanced than we are.

It is not honorable for us to deny our shortcomings and believe we are perfect and claim that our customs are the best customs for every time and place.
This conceit and false presumption is a barrier to the reform we seek. When the
nation feels its shortcomings, that is the first step in its advancement.

It is inconceivable that we claim to be defenders of honor while the veil is
our strongest shield. We must understand as everyone else does that honor is
rooted in the heart and chastity comes from within and not from a piece of
transparent material lowered over the face.

We have to realize, as the advanced unveiled world does, that good behavior and honor come from sound upbringing grounded in noble principles and
virtues. We are shortsighted if we think that the veil keeps evil away from
women and that those in the rest of the world exceeding one and a half billion
are all in the wrong while we are in the right.

He Who Bears Falsehood to the People
Has to Provide Evidence to Them

I have mentioned the above, ladies and gentlemen, fearful that I might be confronted by someone who does not use logic and reasoning to make his points,
but relies on untruths concerning the advanced unveiled nations. He may look
where vice is but he does not wish to rise up to see where virtue resides. He
might have seen their baser women and generalizes from them, subsuming the
noble and honorable in his generalization, and hurls accusing arrows of untruths at them even though human beings should not be like flies pouncing on
tails (of animals) and ignoring their heads.

He does not dare to lord scientific and industrial knowledge over the unveiled nations because these are tangible matters. Therefore he accuses them of
lack of morals and good conduct because these are not tangible. Thus he is
overwhelming in this even though his accusation is false.

You know gentlemen, nations are like trees whose rotten fruits fall to the
ground and vermin, humans and animals go after them. Those who are wise and
advanced look only to the good and ripe fruits, by which the tree is identified.

My antagonist seems to be ignorant of that or is playing the role of the ignorant. He wants to know the tree by the fallen fruits he sees beneath it. Moreover, he does not want to recognize that in every nation, however advanced,
there is a lower class overcome by corruption whose morals and conduct have
deteriorated because they did not have the chance to be educated and to develop so that they could reach the higher level in the nation.

Gentlemen, we should do our best to see to it that the majority in our nation are able to have an education and the means to develop. Then it would be possible for us to be proud before our nations. . . .

We should not believe everything we hear and take our evidence from falsehood, especially evidence that brings great evil to the nation by obstructing reform and maintaining continual backwardness.

We should abstain from hurling lies and falsehoods at others, which is alien to morality and decent debate and only brings down those who lie. Instead we should subscribe to truth, sound reasoning, unbiased knowledge, and correct behavior. In accordance with the will of God Almighty and the will of His Prophet, may God bless him. . . .

How Men Should Support Women

Gentlemen, you have heard the response of the Western woman to the Eastern man who was proud to support his woman and to walk in front of her. Yes, let men support women in principle. Every man supports his own wife spending money on her, but he has no authority over any other woman. A verse from the Qur'an was sent by God about this in relation to Sa'd ibn al-Rabi from al-Naqba and his wife Habiba; the words are related specifically to husband and wife. Men should know that authority is limited by the benefit deriving from it. Therefore, men should attain high moral development as God wants and society requires. This would make women strong and self-dependent, for when people have virtue, dignity, and honor they turn away from evil, not out of fear of punishment, nor because of reward, nor because of an immovable obstacle, but because evil is ugly and such a person would not allow herself to engage in lowly acts.

The Prophet, God bless him, said, "I was sent to help you attain the highest morality." Does not the highest morality come from the soul? Pieces of cloth over faces shall never be a measure of morality.

The Veil (*Niqab*) Is an Insult to Men and Women

It is not beneficial to men and women that men should just support women physically and financially, nor is it beneficial that man rule over those whom the *shari'a* [Islamic law] did not give him the right. It greatly harms the two sexes that every man continues to insult his mother, daughter, wife, and sister, suspiciously accusing them of bad morals and keeping them confined to a cage, as the venerable Qasim Amin [Egypt, 1865–1908] said, "With their wings cut off, heads bent down, and eyes closed. For him (man) is freedom and for them (women) enslavement. For him is education and for them ignorance. For him is sound reasoning and for them inferior reasoning. For him is light and open space and for them darkness and imprisonment. For him are orders and for them obedience and patience. For him is everything in the universe and for them part of the whole he has captured."

May God be merciful to Qasim and bless his pen, about which "The Poet of the Two Countries" has said, "He tears down the ugly and builds the beautiful, returning to the *sunna* [the practices of the Prophet] of the Drawer. He sheds light even when he writes with the dark water of the night."

Unfortunately, if the veil (*hijab*) implies the inability of the woman to protect herself without it, it also reveals that man, however well brought up and in spite of supporting the woman, is a traitor and a thief of honor: his evil should be feared and it is better that the woman escapes from him.

You, Man, the Supporter

If some women, because of the ignorance into which you have cast them, have not recognized the insult to them and to men by the veil, is it easy for you, the man who has kept himself free seeking perfection and good conduct, to bear this insult that comes to you and to your mother, daughter, wife, and sister?

Does the woman who escapes from you, or approaches you lowering the veil over her face, or turns her back on you, confirm your high status, as she might think and say and you might think and say, or is it a great insult? Does this constitute the woman's decorum, chastity and modesty? If so, then men should not be without these precious attributes; let them wear veils and let them meet each other and meet women lowering veils over their faces the way women do. . . .

On Man's Superiority in His Rights to Inheritance, Legal Testimony, Polygamy, and Arbitrariness in Divorce as Evidence Not to His Advantage but Against Him

I noticed in some of the articles written against women and their liberation, as well as against their removal of the veil, that the authors boast of the fact that in his Holy Qur'an, God favored men over women—mind and soul—in three different matters:

First, God made a woman entitled to inherit only half of what a man inherits.

Second, God considers her testimony (legally) worth only half of his.

Third, He, the Almighty, allowed a man to marry up to four wives and divorce them at will, without their consent.

The authors of these articles conclude from this that the woman is mentally and spiritually inferior. Hence they think that God, the Almighty, decided to favor a man over a woman in these three areas. But as far as I am concerned, I conclude otherwise. I understand the argument to be against men rather than in their favor.

Indeed, I examine Islam through the greatest words of God and the sayings of His Prophet. I then see God enthroned in greatness, freedom, equality, justice, goodness, and perfection. I become so overwhelmed and so elated that I feel my soul about to leave my body. I only wish that those who pretend to protect Islam and raise its banners would look in the same way as I do and see what I see. I wish they did not look at Islam through the narrow vision of commentaries and interpretations which interpret Islam in ways they want to see it. Islam is far beyond that. It is much greater.

God's permissibility only showed man's cruel heart, his inability to submit to truth and justice, and his immoral character, acquired from the worst pre-Islamic customs. Such a character, as is well known, is in contradiction with the nature of noble human mentality.

Man subjected to slavery those he deemed weak among women as among men, treating them according to his whims like merchandise or cattle. Had it not been for the viciousness in his mind, his misguided soul and cruel heart, God would not have granted him then such allowances that He disliked and which were meant to vanish with time.

We have thus far seen [in earlier sections of the author's book] what the woman's condition was, under the yoke of man throughout the world in general and in pre-Islamic Arabia in particular, just before the Qur'an was revealed to our Prophet, God bless him and grant him salvation.

God dislikes slavery. He dislikes polygamy and any violation of women's rights. God loathes divorce. His divine throne shakes every time the word is uttered on earth, as I will explain in detail below in a discussion of divorce [not included in this excerpt].

God revealed His holy message all filled with the spirit of freedom, justice and equality among people. He does not differentiate between them for His esteem, except on the basis of their faith in Him. How would then the Almighty condone the enslavement of His human creation in whom He instilled life, and for whom He ordered angels to bow in honor and respect? Did God, we might ask, instill life in the strong who take others into slavery but not in the weak who are enslaved by others? Of course not! God gave life to all. Yet, since the days of Adam, peace be upon him, man has disobeyed God and gone astray.

If Adam himself, who was a prophet, "disobeyed God's order and went astray," what of his male offspring who have realized their strength and became misguided by it? In their arrogant ways, they took into slavery whoever they saw as weak.

God sent His Prophet, peace and salvation be upon him, to mankind in that corrupt land of ignorance. He warned him in these holy words: "If you were rude and arrogant, people would desert you." And as goes one of the Prophet's own sayings: "Teach others, be lenient not harsh, preach but do not alienate anyone."

In his book *Al-Islam ruh al-madaniyya* [*Islam, The Spirit of Civilization*], Shaykh [Mustafa] Al-Ghalayini [Ottoman Empire-Lebanon, 1886–1945] wrote: "It was considered wise in Islam not to totally abolish some of the reprehensible traditions such as polygamy, as there were so many difficulties involved." He also went on to say: "Slavery and harsh treatment of captives are odious acts by Islamic standards. Slavery was considered inherited from the era of savageness. Politically, however, it was not ruled absolutely forbidden in those days." In fact if all those customs had been entirely abolished by God, several problems would have ensued. The least of these is that men would have broken away from God's religion and deserted His Prophet. Moreover, not many of His commandments would have been obeyed.

In pre-Islamic Arabia, women as well as male slaves were under the domination of financially powerful men who owned them and enjoyed them at will. These materialistic men used to get as infatuated with their wealth as they were with themselves. A man in those days would own as many as one hundred women and a large number of male slaves. Like property or cattle they were inherited as a part of an estate. How can we then take it for granted that they could be set free from man's ownership and made equal to him in every way, at the same time, and not in a gradual fashion? God said in the Holy Qur'an, "And if We willed it for them to either kill themselves or leave their land, only a few of them would." [Sura 4, Verse 66] Thus it was out of God's wisdom to eliminate some of these reprehensible customs, while leaving traces of them to turn men's attention to Him so they would not give up His religion and abandon His Prophet.

As for a woman's legal testimony, should the fact that it is considered worth only half of that of a man's be grounds for women's mental inferiority? If so, a non-Muslim's legal testimony for or against a Muslim is not accepted; can that also be considered evidence for non-Muslims' mental inferiority? Or was it rather a decision resulting from some unusual circumstances in those days?

In the final analysis, it was no other than God's kindness to the woman to consider her testimony worth half that of a man's. The latter interpreted it as a privilege and became satisfied with it. In reality, legal testimony is no other than a bothersome obligation. It is as if God wanted to reassure men and relieve women from such an obligation at the same time. It seems as if testimony were expressly ruled outside a woman's competence, so that only men would be called upon to testify in courts. There is no reason to believe that God decided that because of a deficiency in the woman's faith or intelligence. Women possess a great deal of goodness and spiritual righteousness, and as the Prophet's saying goes, "One good woman is better than a thousand improper men."

Through God's wisdom, the persistence of a few traces of those bad customs is a way of soothing the minds of those who practice them. His wisdom is revealed in several ways and verses. In the tradition of His Prophet, God bless him and grant him salvation, there is proof that the dangers in the persistence of such traces of vile traditions are removed. Thus their impact is reduced and they become acceptable rather than offensive.

God knew that people with insight would erase all traces of reprehensible customs, following this way the wisdom implied by those Qur'anic verses and Prophet's teachings. God was indeed aware that such wisdom was not unknown to His people. Hence he allowed the taking of slaves but was eager for their freedom, in the same way that He was yearning to abolish polygamy and end discrimination between men and women in their rights. This is one of the interpretations suggested by the famous scholar Muhammad 'Abduh [Egypt, 1849–1905].

Below however is another quotation from [Muhammad] Jamil Bayhum [Lebanon, 1887–1978], the author of *Al-Mar' a fi al-tarikh wa al-shara'i'* [*Woman in History and Religious Legal Systems*]:

> Some commentators have interpreted these opinions as implying a ban on polygamy, because allowing it must depend on fairness in treatment while such indiscriminate justice is highly improbable. But this is in no way an uncommon interpretation as long as laws are subject to considerations of culture and civilization. Just as Christians were somehow able to discover that their religion prohibits polygamy, when it actually did not object to it, it would be easy for Muslims to enact legislation forbidding polygamy, in appreciation of the general world condition, progress and the advancement of women.

Indeed that would be easier for Muslims than making laws condoning all the vile sins such as drinking alcohol, prostitution, usury and idolatry, or disapproving of some of God's ordinances like stoning, requital or other legal punishments. Such laws are constantly being enacted.

Don't you see that slavery was discontinued in Islamic countries like everywhere else and that punishment is administered to whoever engages in it? Don't you see that polygamy has become considered evil by enlightened communities around us, and that the great independent Islamic nation of Turkey has banned it and reserves for it the harshest of punishments?

Don't you see that, through government laws, Islamic countries have made a woman's legal testimony equal to a man's both in witnessing legal punishment as well as in other cases? They gave her equal right for inheriting land, and in Turkey, a woman's right is equal to that of a man for testimony in all cases and transactions, and in inheritance for any kind of property.

By enacting laws to eliminate those vile traditions, the Islamic governments were not in contradiction with God's message and the teachings of His Prophet. Those governments understood the reasoning behind those teachings. They abolished slavery and ended any discrimination between man and woman. Not only did they interpret the surface meanings of those Qur'anic verses and Prophet's teaching; but also they interpreted their essence in depth in the manner of people with insight and reason.

This is indeed an important and broad subject. To cover it with a presentation of convincing evidence would require lengthy explications that are beyond the scope of my present lecture series. God willing, I shall deal with it in a special lecture.

Nevertheless, I think that we should realize right now the reason which led to the persistence of those reprehensible customs and why they had such an impact on the absolute equality of man and woman and amongst men (as slaves and free men). Perhaps that reason is man's cruelty, his error, arbitrariness, and the evil side in his character prevailing over the good side. That is what led God's wisdom, to permit something reprehensible that He never condoned as fair and just.

Right now, we must realize that this reason for that has nothing to do with a woman's faith or her intelligence. In no way was the inequality between a helpless slave and a powerful free man a result of mental or spiritual deficiency so that inequality between man and woman in the matters mentioned should result from her mental and spiritual deficiency.

If God had truly condoned slavery, polygamy and inequality between man and woman, He would not have made the man accountable for expenditures for the woman's dowry, her support and that of her children's which are equal or greater than what she misses in inheritance. If so, indeed, God would not have established laws leading to the disappearance of slavery and the avoidance of polygamy; and His Prophet would not have preferred females over males in several matters. In fact, here are some of his sayings:

> When you give to your children, be fair in your giving and give equally. If I personally had a preference to make (in giving to my own), I would prefer giving to my daughters.

> Whoever goes to market and buys something to bring back home, especially for the females in his family, will enjoy God's care, and whoever is in God's care will be protected from all suffering.

> Purchasing a choice gift for members of your family is like giving charity. Priority should go to the females, because bringing joy to a female is like crying humbly in fear and respect of God and whoever cries in fear of God will be spared from the fires of Hell.

Therefore if females were deficient in mind and in faith, they would not be worthy of such preferential thoughts by the Prophet of God. He is much beyond preferring stupidity over intelligence, and a lack of faith over an abundance of it. He once also said, "Fear God in your treatment of the weak, slaves and women."

As for this last piece of advice given by the Prophet of God, we must stand facing Mecca, humbly and in reverence, in order to hear it. He uttered it from his death bed, at a time he was in distress, because he had not completely removed all of the differences between the slaves and the free, and between men and women. He uttered the following final words, his voice stammering, until his very last word:

> Prayer . . . Prayer . . . If any slaves are in your possession, do not burden them with what they are unable to do. God. God . . . of Women. They are in your hands. . . . You took them with God's trust.

He uttered these words and passed away. Peace be upon you, o Prophet of God, peace be upon you, o beloved of God. Peace be upon you, Lord of the first and last prophets. Peace be upon you the day you were born, the day you died, and the day you will be resurrected.

PART II

Making Nations in the Middle East, 1900–1949

A common misconception about the Middle East and North Africa is that the nations that now exist in the two regions have always been in conflict. However, conflicts there, as everywhere else, have taken place at specific points in time and for specific reasons. Recent conflicts that appear eternal—Arab-Israeli, Iraq-Iran, Iraq-Kuwait—actually derive from a twentieth-century phenomenon: nationalism.

Before World War I, the Middle East and North Africa were fluid geopolitical spaces in which peoples with various languages, cultures, and ethnicities intermingled in the cities and larger towns and many others lived in rural isolation. This description is not intended to imply the absence of territorial or communal conflicts or a static political environment. However, despite tensions that varied greatly in intensity and consequences, most people were able to live within their limited world, either coexisting with or oblivious to others. World War I and the subsequent French and British occupation of much of the Middle East helped bring fundamental changes to this geopolitical system. The basic shift was from a multicultural political community to a number of political entities *supposedly* ethnically unified (though in reality still quite varied). The expectation of ethnic unity—the most common indicator of nationalism at that time—was affirmed by the remapping of the region into "nations" with fixed borders drawn to separate, for example, the newly formed Iraq from the equally novel Syria.

For the people living in the Middle East and North Africa, this political (and cultural) remapping was disorienting and oppressive, even as it opened new possibilities. The basic premise of the mandate system was that the British and the French would remain in control until the peoples of the regions were "capable of ruling themselves." In other words, the litmus test for ending colonial domination was the ability of the newly formed entities to govern themselves as nations. Thus, for example, for the people living in Syria to free themselves from colonial rule and the arbitrary divisions imposed on them, they would need to accept the idea of the "nation of Syria" and prove to the Europeans that the new "nation" was capable of administering itself amid attempts by colonial forces to disrupt any political action or programs that could threaten their mandates.

The task of constructing a nation was perplexing to people long accustomed to being members of an empire and of small communities. None of their political experiences prepared them to conceive of a political entity that was smaller than an empire and larger than a city or village. Moreover, the continuing realities of a multiethnic and multilingual society posed immediate and obstinate obstacles to achieving the "ideal" of ethnically unified nations. In fact, the existence of different ethnic, religious, and linguistic groups in each of the new nations guaranteed from the outset a struggle over who would organize each nation and how power would be distributed. This dizzying set of puzzles was compounded by technological problems (how to reach the multitudes of people living in villages, who still formed the majority of each "national" population), economic problems (the new borders not only sundered trading links that had long sustained the local economies but also subjected the "national" economies to the whims and needs of the colonizers), political problems (what type of government and constitution to establish), and cultural problems (which sources of "tradition" to draw from to lay the foundation for the idea and "history" of the nation).

Out of these questions emerged a host of ideas about the meaning and definition of the "nation." Local groups proclaimed a culturally or religiously distinct nationalism. Thus, nationalists in Lebanon, Egypt, and Turkey insisted, respectively, that the "Lebanese," "Egyptians," and "Turks" constituted the national population, and they rejected any notion of subcultures, be they Kurdish, Armenian, Coptic, and so on. This definition of the "nation" drew strict distinctions along the borders separating each nationality. Thus, for instance in the minds and words of some Lebanese nationalists, Lebanon and Syria became essentially, incontrovertibly, and eternally separate "nations"; any similarities between them were dismissed as coincidental rather than deriving from any historical connection.

Political organizations articulating broader, geographical notions of the "nation" also emerged. The "nation" of "Greater Syria" (encompassing modern-day Iraq, Syria, Lebanon, and Israel/Palestine) was advocated by Antun Sa'adeh, founder of the Syrian Social Nationalist Party (SSNP). An appeal to a distant and unchanging past provided the underpinning for this approach. In the ideology of the SSNP, ancient Mesopotamia became directly linked to modern Syria, bypassing in the process Arab and Muslim history, not to mention the countless other peoples and cultures that had populated the region at one time or another. Imagining a still larger "nation," Pan-Arabists postulated that all "Arabs"—defined by a common language and culture—belonged together in a single nation that would re-create the glories of the past. In this formulation of the "nation," religion—specifically Islam but also Christianity and Judaism—become incidental effects of the main cause: Arabness. There also emerged a religious form of nationalism, which proposed that Islam offered the only viable and acceptable foundation for the Muslims of the Middle East. Moreover, Pan-Islamists argued that the emerging forms of secular nationalism were European imperial ploys meant to weaken the "Islamic world" (although such a unified "world" had never existed).

In addition to debating competing ideas about the characteristics of a "nation," many individuals and groups bent on imagining a singular new political entity had to deal with issues such as gender, class, and ethnicity—however obliquely. As alternative and potentially controversial political focal points, these issues had to be examined within every particular nationalist discourse. Thus, we find texts from Turkey, Iran, Egypt, Algeria, and elsewhere describing the nation as a "woman" and linking liberation of the nation to liberation of the women of the nation. The purpose of such liberation, however, was to advance the nation rather than to improve the lot of individual women. Women's status was to be improved for the sake of society and the nation, not for women's own sake. In this manner, liberation—in its gendered manifestation—was presented as a nationalist project and not as a humanistic and universal ideal. A similar process took place with regard to class and ethnicity.

Nationalist stirrings in the Middle East, then, led to rupture and discontinuity with the past. The documents in this section show the attempts by various individuals and groups to make sense of this change, to control its direction, and to build nations where there were none before. In their variety, these documents represent the myriad ideological sources of nationalism, the arguments about the form and substance of the "nation" and about the relationship between society and state, and the tension between ideas of the "nation" set forth by the intellectual and political elites and those of the popular classes. In reading these documents against each other, we can begin to appreciate the daunting complexity of the project of nation-making. As we learn about external pressures, internal dissensions, and practical difficulties, we are able to look beyond accounts that imbue these political entities with a "naturalness" that tends to flatten the political and cultural terrain and downplay conflict. In other words, the documents in the next two chapters shed light on the human drama behind the creation of Middle Eastern nations.

CHAPTER 4

Ideas of Nationalism

In the creation of nations in the Middle East and North Africa, ideas played a formative role. Some ideas reflected the political aims of the Western imperial powers. Other, indigenous ideas originated within the Middle East and North Africa and reflected the thinking and hopes of an array of intellectuals and activists. In this chapter we examine both types of ideas.

Documents 3 and 4 show the British planning and negotiating to advance their imperial interests when World War I ends. The Husayn-McMahon correspondence, an exchange of letters between the amir of Mecca and the British High Commissioner in Egypt (document 3), indicates differing visions of the future of the region. While the British were making promises—however ambiguous—to Husayn, European Zionists were seeking and obtaining support for their project of establishing a Jewish homeland in Palestine—an area that Husayn and most other Arabs understood to be included within the promised Arab kingdom. Document 4 pertains to Britain's Balfour Declaration. Document 5, from the Treaty of Sèvres (1920), details the postwar division of the Ottoman Empire and provides us with a map of European interests and goals in the region. Atatürk's speech in 1927 (document 6) provides an example of opposition toward European designs in favor of indigenous concepts of the nation.

Indigenous intellectuals and activists had their own ideas about nationhood. Most ambitious was the idea of Arabism. Proponents said that all Arabs—defined by a common linguistic, cultural, and historical heritage—belonged together in one nation. The specifics of this vision were the subject of many disagreements and much debate. The ideas of Michel 'Aflaq, however, are considered to be the founding principles of this brand of nationalism (document 11). Antun Sa'adeh (document 9) proposed a more modest physical and cultural definition of the "nation." He suggested that the "fertile crescent" (an area that includes modern-day Lebanon, Jordan, Israel, Palestine, Syria, and Iraq) was the "natural" homeland of a culture that, at least in Sa'adeh's opinion, predated Arabs and Islam. Even among those who agreed about the geographical definition of the "nation" there remained the complex task of explaining the founding principles of the nation and its constituency. Ahad Ha-Am explored these issues as they pertained to the creation of a Jewish state (document 2).

An even more delimited vision of the "nation" was proposed for Egypt, Lebanon, and Algeria. Proponents of local nationalism argued that history or natural boundaries made for "eternal" nations with "essential" qualities that distinguished them from all other surrounding areas. For example, in Egypt some intellectuals like Taha Husayn (document 10) contended that their country was uniquely Egyptian as it combined European, Pharaonic, and Arab-Muslim cultural influences. To such thinkers, this implied a distinctiveness from all their Arab neighbors that constrains nationalism in Egypt to the borders of that country. Similarly, Leo Pinsker—a Jewish intellectual from Russia—articulated the idea that Jews would never be accepted within European societies except as pariahs, so Jewish political and cultural salvation could come about only from the creation of a Jewish state that excluded all other ethnicities (document 1). This limited ethnic nationalism was born out of the persecution of Jews in Europe and out of acceptance of the basis of that persecution—the belief that ethnicities are essential and eternal and one must be dominant.

In conjunction with all these ideas, there emerged a strand of thought that engaged nationalist projects from an Islamic perspective. For people with these beliefs, like Hassan al-Banna (document 12), Islam was the primary point of political reference and identity. Thus, for them secular nationalism was a departure from accepted norms and posed a political threat. Their responses ranged from complete rejection of nationalism to an attempt to infuse various nationalist ideologies with strong Islamic content. At the same time there existed those thinkers such as 'Ali 'Abd al-Raziq (document 7) who rejected any political role for Islam and insisted on the separation between the state/nation and religion. Going one step further, Messali Hadj (document 8) proposes a Communist vision of the nation that not only sidelines religion in politics but also seeks to restructure the class hierarchy of society.

Regardless of their ideological bent, the authors of the documents in this chapter shared the common goal of bringing about a physical manifestation of their various visions of the "nation." Embedded in each definition were altruistic ideals and mundane goals deriving from self-interest. In reading these documents, try to identify each of these elements and to differentiate between them. Also, try to dissociate rhetoric from reality. In other words, read the documents as proposed ideals and not necessarily as the accepted vision of the totality of the "people."

1.   Leo Pinsker, a Jewish Intellectual, Proposes a "Jewish Homeland," 1882

Leo Pinsker (1821–1891) was a leading figure in the eastern European haskalah *(Jewish enlightenment). Along with Moshe Leib Lilienblum, Eliezer Ben Yehudah, and other Jewish intellectuals, Pinsker for many years believed that Jewish secular and liberal tradition would permit the assimilation of Jews into non-Jewish societies. He himself had studied medicine at Moscow University and had been decorated by the tsar for his medical work on behalf of the Russian army during the Crimean War. However, his outlook on the future of Jews in Russia and in other nations was radically altered by the terrible anti-Jewish pogroms that broke out in 1881.*

After the assassination of Tsar Alexander II in 1881 by revolutionaries, his successor—Alexander III—suspended the program of reforms that had been in place and attempted to isolate Russia from liberal influences. Some of the new tsar's aides argued that the revolutionary mood in Russia was the fault of Jews, who were "the primary bearers of revolutionary infection, the source of all that was vicious in modern capitalism."[1] This anti-Semitic mood and the government's desire to divert the attention of the Russian peasantry away from the real sources of their woes combined to give rise to anti-Jewish riots that were, if not state sponsored, at least unopposed by the agents of the government. The horrendous scenes of murder, rape, and pillage were made even worse by the infamous Russian laws of 1882, which restricted the livelihood of Jews as well as the places where they were permitted to reside.

Those blatantly discriminatory laws and the pogroms transformed the views of leading Jewish intellectuals. Pinsker, among others, could not sustain his belief in integration into the mainstream of European society in the face of such anti-Jewish violence and sentiment. He embraced the cause of Jewish nationalism and wrote his influential Auto-Emancipation *(1882)—a precursor to Theodore Herzl's* The Jewish State *(1896).*

"If I am not for myself, who will be for me?
And if not now, when?"
—HILLEL

That hoary problem, subsumed under the Jewish question, today, as ever in the past, provokes discussion. Like the squaring of the circle it remains unsolved, but unlike it, continues to be the ever-burning question of the day. That is

---

[1] David Vital, *The Origins of Zionism* (Oxford: Oxford University Press, 1975), p. 51.

Leon Pinsker, *Auto-Emancipation: An Appeal to His People,* By a Russian Jew, trans. Dr. D. S. Blondheim, Federation of American Zionists, 1916 (Masada, Youth Zionist Organization of America, 1939).

because the problem is not one of mere theoretical interest: it renews and revives in every-day life and presses ever more urgently for solution.

This is the kernel of the problem, as we see it: *the Jews comprise a distinctive element among the nations under which they dwell, and as such can neither assimilate nor be readily digested by any nation.*

Hence the solution lies in finding a means of so readajusting this exclusive element to the family of nations, that the basis of the Jewish question it will be permanently removed.

This does not mean, of course, that we must think of waiting for the age of universal harmony.

No previous civilization has been able to achieve it, nor can we see even in the remote distance, that day of the Messiah, when national barriers will no longer exist and all mankind will live in brotherhood and concord. Until then, the nations must narrow their aspirations to achieve a tolerable *modus vivendi.*

The world has yet long to wait for eternal peace. Meanwhile nations live side by side in a state of relative peace, secured by treaties and international law, but based chiefly on the fundamental equality between them.

But it is different with the people of Israel. There is no such equality in the nations' dealings with the Jews. The basis is absent upon which treaties and international law may be applied mutual respect. Only when this basis is established when the equality of Jews with other nations becomes a fact, can the Jewish problem be considered solved.

An equality of this kind did exist in the now long forgotten past, but unfortunately, under present conditions, the prospect that will readmit the Jewish people to the status of nationhood is so remote as to seem illusory. It lacks most of the essential attributes by which a nation is recognized. It lacks that autochthonous life which is inconceivable without a common language and customs and without cohesion in space. The Jewish people has no fatherland of its own, though many motherlands; no center of focus or gravity, no government of its own, no official representation. They home everywhere, but are nowhere at home. The nations have *never* to deal with a Jewish nation but always with mere *Jews.* The Jews are not a nation because they lack a certain distinctive national character, inherent in all other nations, which is formed by common residence in a single state. It was clearly impossible for this national character to be developed in the Diaspora; the Jews seem rather to have lost all remembrance of their former home. Thanks to their ready adaptability, they have all the more easily acquired characteristics, not inborn, of the people among whom fate has thrown them. Often to please their protectors, they recommend their traditional individuality entirely. They acquired or persuaded themselves into certain cosmopolitan tendencies which could no more appeal to others than bring satisfaction to themselves.

In seeking to fuse with other peoples they deliberately renounced to some extent their own nationality. *Yet nowhere did they succeed in obtaining from their fellow-citizens recognition as natives of equal status.*

But the greatest impediment in the path of the Jews to an independent national existence is that they do not feel its need. Not only that, but they go so far as to deny its authenticity. . . .

In the seemingly irrelevant circumstances, that the Jews are not regarded as an independent nation by other nations, rests in part the secret of their abnormal position and of their endless misery. Merely to belong to this people is to be indelibly stigmatized a mark repellent to non-Jews and painful to the Jews themselves. However, this phenomenon is rooted deeply in human nature.

Among the living nations of the earth the Jews are as a nation long since dead.

With the loss of their country, the Jewish people lost their independence, and fell into a decay which is not compatible with existence as a whole vital organism. The state was crushed before the eyes of the nations. But after the Jewish people had ceased to exist as an actual state, as a political entity, they could nevertheless not submit to total annihilation—they lived on spiritually as a nation. . . .

A fear of the Jewish ghost has passed down the generations and the centuries. First a breeder of prejudice, later in conjunction with other forces we are about to discuss, it culminated in Judeophobia.

Judeophobia, together with other symbols, superstitions and idiosyncrasies, has acquired legitimacy phobia among all the peoples of the earth with whom the Jews had intercourse. Judeophobia is a variety of demonopathy with the distinction that it is not peculiar to particular races but is common to the whole of mankind, and that this ghost is not disembodied like other ghosts but partakes of flesh and blood, must endure pain inflicted by the fearful mob that imagines itself endangered.

Judeophobia is a psychic aberration. As a psychic aberration it is hereditary, and as a disease transmitted for two thousand years it is incurable.

It is this fear of ghosts, the mother of Judeophobia that has evoked this abstract—I might say Platonic hatred—thanks to which the whole Jewish nation is wont to be held responsible for the real or supposed misdeeds of its individual members, and to be libeled in so many ways, to be buffeted about so shamefully.

Friend and foe alike have tried to explain or to justify this hatred of the Jews by bringing all sorts of charges against them. They are said to have crucified Jesus, to have drunk the blood of Christians, to have poisoned wells, to have taken usury, to have exploited the peasant, and so on. These and a thousand and one other charges against an entire people have been proved groundless. They showed their own weakness in that they had to be trumped up wholesale in order to quiet the evil conscience of the Jew-baiters, to justify the condemnation of an entire nation, to demonstrate the necessity of burning the Jew, or rather the Jewish ghost, at the stake. He who tries to prove too much proves nothing at all. Though the Jews may justly be charged with many shortcomings, those shortcomings are, at all events, not such great vices, not such capital crimes, as to justify the condemnation of the entire people. In individual cases, indeed, these accusations are contradicted by the fact that the Jews get along fairly well with their Gentile neighbors. This is the reason that the charges preferred are usually of the most general character, made up out of whole cloth, based to a certain extent on a priori reasoning, and true at best in individual cases, but not admitting of proof as regards the whole people.

In this way have Judaism and Anti-Semitism passed for centuries through history as inseparable companions. Like the Jewish people, the real wandering Jew, Anti-Semitism, too, seems as if it would never die. He must be blind indeed who will assert that the Jews are not *the chosen people,* the people chosen for universal hatred. No matter how much the nations are at variance in their relations with one another, however diverse their instincts and aims, they join hands in their hatred of the Jews; on this one matter all are agreed. The extent and the manner in which this antipathy is shown depend of course upon the cultural status of each people. The antipathy as such, however, exists in all places and at all times, whether it appears in the form of deeds of violence, as envious jealousy, or under the guise of tolerance and protection. To be robbed as a Jew or to be protected as a Jew is equally humiliating, equally destructive to the self-respect of the Jews

Having analyzed Judeophobia as an hereditary form of demonopathy, peculiar to the human race, and having represented Anti-Semitism as proceeding from an inherited aberration of the human mind, we must draw the important conclusion that we must give up contending against these hostile impulses as we must against every other inherited predisposition.

No people, generally speaking, likes foreigners. Ethnologically, this cannot be brought as a charge against any people. Now, is the Jew subject to *this* general law to the same extent as the other nationalities? Not at all! The aversion which meets the foreigner in a strange land can be repaid in equal coin in his home country. The non-Jew pursues his own interest in a foreign country openly and without giving offense. It is everywhere considered natural that he should fight for these interests, alone or in conjunction with others. The foreigner has no need to *be,* or to *seem* to *be,* a patriot. But as for the Jew, not only is he not a native in his own home country, but he is also not a foreigner; he is, in very truth, the stranger *par excellence.* He is regarded as neither friend nor foe but an alien, of whom the only thing known is that he has no home.

One *distrusts* the foreigner but does not *trust* the Jew. The foreigner has a claim to hospitality, which he can repay in the same coin. The Jew can make no such return, consequently he can make no claim to hospitality. He is not a guest, much less a welcome guest. He is more like a beggar, and what beggar is welcome! He is rather a refugee; and where is the refugee to whom a refuge may not be refused?

The Jews are aliens who can have no representatives, because they have no country. Because they have none, because their home has no boundaries within which they can be entrenched, their misery too is boundless. The *general law* does not apply to the Jews as true aliens, but there are everywhere *laws for the Jews,* and if the general law is to apply to them, a special and explicit by-law is required to confirm it. Like the Negroes, like women, and unlike all free peoples, they must be *emancipated.* If, unlike the Negroes, they belong to an advanced race, and if, unlike women, they can produce not only women of distinction, but also distinguished men, even men of greatness, then it is very much the worse for them.

Since the Jew is nowhere at home, nowhere regarded as a native, he remains an alien everywhere. That he himself and his ancestors as well are born in the country does not alter this fact in the least.

In the great majority of cases, he is treated as a stepchild, as a Cinderella; in the most favorable cases he is regarded as an adopted child whose rights may be questioned; *never* is he considered a legitimate child of the fatherland.

The German proud of his Teutonism, the Slav, the Celt, not one of them admits that the Semitic Jew is his equal by birth; and even if he be ready, as a man of culture, to admit him to all civil rights, he will never quite forget that his fellow-citizen is a Jew The *legal emancipation* of the Jews is the culminating achievement of our century. But *legal* emancipation is not *social* emancipation, and with the proclamation of the former the Jews are still far from being emancipated from their exceptional *social position.*

[. . .]

This degrading dependence of the ever alien Jew upon the non-Jew is reinforced by another factor, which makes amalgamation of the Jews with the original inhabitants of a land absolutely impossible. In the great struggle for existence, civilized peoples readily submit to laws which help to transform their struggle into a peaceful competition, a noble emulation. In this respect a distinction is usually made between the native and the foreigner, the first, of course, always receiving the preference. Now, if this distinction is drawn even against the foreigner of equal birth, how harshly is it applied to the ever alien Jew! The beggar who dares to cast longing eyes upon a country not his own is in the position of a young virgin's suitor, guarded against him by jealous relatives! And if he nevertheless prosper and succeed in plucking a flower here and there from its soil, woe to the ill-fated man! He must expect the fate of the Jews of Spain and Russia.

The Jews, moreover, do not suffer only when they meet with notable success. Wherever they are congregated in large numbers, they must, by their very preponderance, hold an advantage in competition with the non-Jewish population. Thus, in the western provinces [of Russia] we see the Jews squeezed together, leading a wretched existence in dreadful poverty, while charges of Jewish exploitation are continually pressed.

To sum up then, to the living the Jew is a corpse, to the native a foreigner, to the homesteader a vagrant, to the proprietary a beggar, to the poor an exploiter and a millionaire, to the patriot a man without a country, for all a hated rival.

[. . .]

If we already knew where to direct our steps, were we compelled to emigrate again, we could surely make a vast step forward. We must set vigorously to work to complete the great task of *self-liberation.* We must use all the resources which human intellect and human experience have devised, instead of leaving our national regeneration to blind chance. The territory to be acquired must be fertile, well-situated and sufficiently extensive to allow the settlement of several millions. The land, as national property, must be inalienable. Its selection is, of course, of the first and highest importance, and must not be left to off-hand decision or to certain preconceived sympathies of individuals, as has alas, happened lately. This land must be *uniform* and continuous in extent, for it lies in the very nature of our problem that we must possess as a counterpoise to our disposition *one single refuge,* since a *number* of refuges would again be equivalent to our old dispersion. Therefore, the selection of a permanent, national land, meeting all requirements, must be made with every precaution and confided to one single body, through a committee of experts selected from our directorate. Only such a supreme tribunal will be able, after thorough and comprehensive investigation, to give an opinion and decide upon *which of* the two continents and upon *which* territory in them our final choice should fall. Only then, and not before, should the directorate, together with an associated body of capitalists, as founders of a stock company later to be organized, acquire a tract of land sufficient for the settlement, in the course of time, of several million Jews. This tract might form a small territory in North America, or a sovereign Pashalik in Asiatic Turkey recognized by the [Ottoman] Porte and the other Powers as neutral. It would certainly be an important duty of the directorate to secure the assent of the Porte, and probably of the other European cabinets to this plan. Under the supervision of the directorate, the land purchased would have to be divided by surveyors into small parcels, which could be assigned according to the local conditions to agricultural, building, or manufacturing purposes. Every parcel laid off thus (for agricultural, house and garden, town-hall, factory, etc.) would form a lot which would be transferred to the purchaser in accordance with his wishes.

After a complete survey and the publication of detailed maps and a comprehensive description of the land, a part of the lots would be sold to Jews for an adequate payment at a price, exactly fixed in proportion to the original purchase price, perhaps a little above it. Part of the proceeds of the sale, together with the profits, would belong to the stock company, and part would flow into a fund to be administered by the directorate, for the maintenance of destitute immigrants. For the establishment of this fund the directorate could also open a national subscription. It is definitely to be expected that our brethren everywhere would hail with joy such an appeal for subscriptions and that the most liberal donations would be made for so sacred a purpose.

Each title-deed delivered to the purchaser, with his name entered and signed by the directorate and the company, must bear the exact number of the lot upon the general map so that each purchaser would know exactly the location of the piece of ground—field, or building lot—which he purchases as his individual property.

Assuredly, many a Jew, who is still bound to his old home by an unenviable occupation, would gladly grasp the opportunity to throw out an anchor to windward by such a deed and to escape those sad experiences so numerous in the immediate past

That part of the territory which would be assigned to the directorate for free distribution, against the national subscription mentioned and the expected profits, would be given to destitute but able-bodied immigrants, recommended by local committees.

Since the donations to the national subscription would not come in at once, but say in annual contributions, the colonization, also, would be carried out gradually and in a fixed order.

If the experts find in favor of Palestine or Syria, this decision would not be based on the assumption that the country could be transformed in time by labor and industry into a quite productive one. In this event the price of land would rise in proportion. But should they prefer North America, however, we must hasten. If one considers that in the last thirty-eight years the population of the United States of America has risen from seventeen millions to fifty millions, and that the increase in population for the next forty years will probably continue in the same proportion, it is evident that immediate action is necessary, if we do not desire to eliminate for all time the possibility of establishing in the New World a secure refuge for our unhappy brethren.

Every one who has the slightest judgment can see at first glance that the purchase of lands in America would, because of the swift rise of that country, not be a risky, but a lucrative enterprise.

Whether this act of national self-help on our part might turn out profitably or otherwise, however, is of little consequence as compared with the great significance which such an undertaking would have for the future of our unsettled people; for our future will remain insecure and precarious unless a radical change in our position is made. This change cannot be brought about by the civil emancipation of the Jews in this or that state, but only by the auto-emancipation of the Jewish people as a nation, the foundation of a colonial community belonging to the Jews, which is some day to become our inalienable home, our country.

There will certainly be plenty of counter-arguments. We will be charged with reckoning without our host. What land will grant us permission to settle a nation within its borders? At first glance, our building would appear from this standpoint to be a house of cards to divert children and wits. We think, however, that only thoughtless childhood could be diverted by the sight of shipwrecked voyagers who desire to build a little boat in order to leave inhospitable shores. We even go as far as to say that we expect, strangely enough, that those inhospitable people will aid us in our departure. Our "friends" will see us leave with the same pleasure with which we turn our back upon them.

Of course, the establishment of a Jewish refuge cannot come about without the support of the governments. In order to obtain the latter and to insure the perpetual existence of a refuge, the molders of our national regeneration must proceed with caution and perseverance. What we seek is at bottom neither new nor dangerous to anyone. Instead of the many *refuges* which we have always been accustomed to seek, we would fain have *one single refuge,* the existence of which, however, would have to be politically assured.

Let "Now or never" be our watchword. Woe to our descendants, woe to the memory of our Jewish contemporaries, if we let this moment pass by!

The Jews are not a living nation: they are everywhere aliens; therefore they are despised.

The civil and political emancipation of the Jews is not sufficient to raise them in the estimation of the peoples.

The proper, the only solution, is in the creation of a Jewish nationality, of a people living upon its own soil, the auto-emancipation of the Jews; their return to the ranks of the nations by the acquisition of a Jewish homeland.

We must not persuade ourselves that humanity and enlightenment alone can cure the malady of our people.

The lack of national self-respect and self-confidence of political initiative and of unity, are the enemies of our national renaissance.

That we may not be compelled to wander from one exile to another, we must have an extensive, productive land of refuge, a *center* which is our own. The present moment is the most favorable for this plan.

The international Jewish question must have a national solution. Of course, our national regeneration can only proceed slowly. *We* must take the first step. Our *descendants* must follow us at a measured and not over-precipitant speed.

The national regeneration of the Jews must be initiated by a congress of Jewish notables. No sacrifice should be too great for this enterprise which will assure our people's future, everywhere endangered.

The financial execution of the undertaking does not present insurmountable difficulties.

Help yourselves, and God will help you!

2. Ahad Ha-Am's "The Jewish State and the Jewish Problem," a Counterargument to the Idea of a Jewish State, 1897

Not all Jewish thinkers agreed with the Zionists that a Jewish state would solve the "Jewish problem" of the persecution of Jewish minorities in various European countries. Asher Zvi Ginzberg (his pen name Ahad Ha-Am is a Hebrew phrase meaning "one of the people") was one of those thinkers. Ha-Am (1856–1927) was born in the Ukraine. In 1868 he began a process of self-education that first led him through the works of Maimonides and other thinkers of the medieval Jewish enlightenment.

From there he progressed to the works of modern Jewish thinkers and finally to the wider world of Russian and German literature and philosophy. Because of a series of personal problems and disappointments, Ha-Am was very pessimistic and prone to self-doubt and was unwilling to assume a position of leadership within the emerging Zionist nationalist movement—even though he was offered the opportunity on at least two occasions. Nevertheless, he was an influential thinker whose writings and advice were sought by leaders such as Chaim Weizmann. More important, his critical essays provided a counterweight to the overly positivist ideas and programs of mainstream Zionism. In the essay reprinted here, he challenges the optimistic vision of the Zionists.

Some months have passed since the Zionist Congress, but its echoes are still reverberating in daily life and in the press. All kinds of gatherings—small and large, local and regional—are taking place. Since the delegates returned home, they have been calling public meetings and repeatedly regaling us with tales of the wonders that were enacted before their very eyes. The wretched, hungry public is listening, becoming ecstatic, and hoping for salvation. It is inconceivable to them that "they"—the Jews of the West—can fail to succeed in what they propose. Heads grow hot and hearts beat fast, and many "leaders" who had for years—until last August—lived only for Palestinian settlement, and for whom a penny donation in aid of Jewish labor in Palestine or the Jaffa School was worth the world, have now lost their bearings and ask one another: "What's the good of this sort of work? The days of the Messiah are near at hand, and we busy ourselves with trifles! The time has come for great deeds, for great men, men of the West, have enlisted in the cause and march before us."

There has been a revolution in their world, and, to emphasize it, they have given the cause itself a new name: It is no longer "Love of Zion" (Hibbat Zion), but "Zionism" (Zioniyuth). Indeed, there are even "precisionists" who, being determined to leave no loophole for error, use only the European form of the name ("Zionismus")—thus announcing to all and sundry that they are not talking about anything so antiquated as Hibbat Zion, but about a new, up-to-date movement, which comes, like its name, from the West, where people are innocent of the Hebrew language.

Nordau's address on the general condition of the Jews was a sort of introduction to the business of the Congress. It described in incisive language the sore troubles, whether material or spiritual, which beset the Jews the world over. In eastern countries their trouble is material: they must struggle without letup to satisfy the most elementary physical needs—for the crust of bread and the breath of air which are denied them because they are Jews. In the West, in lands where the Jews are legally emancipated, their material condition is not particularly bad, but their spiritual state is serious: they want to take full advantage of their legal rights, and cannot; they long to be accepted by the gentile majority and to become part of the national society, but they are kept at arm's

---

Arthur Hertzberg, ed., *The Zionist Idea: A Historical Analysis and Reader* (Garden City, N.Y.: Doubleday, 1959), pp. 262–269.

length; they hope for love and brotherhood, but they encounter looks of hatred and contempt on all sides; they know that they are in no way inferior to their neighbors in ability or virtue, but they have it continually thrown in their faces that they are of an inferior type and that they are unfit to rise to the level of the Aryans. And more to the same effect.

Well—what then?

Nordau himself did not touch on this question, which was outside the scope of his address. But the whole Congress was the answer. Beginning as it did with Nordau's address, the Congress meant this: that in order to escape from all these troubles it is necessary to establish a Jewish State.

There is no doubt that, even when the Jewish State is established, Jewish settlement will be able to advance only by small degrees, as permitted by the resources of the people themselves and by the progress of the economic development of the country. Meanwhile the natural increase of Jewish population both within the Palestinian settlement and in the Diaspora, will continue, with the inevitable result that, on the one hand, Palestine will have less and less room for the new immigrants, and, on the other hand, despite continual emigration, the number of those remaining outside Palestine will not be appreciably diminished. In his opening speech at the Congress, Dr. Herzl, wishing to demonstrate the superiority of his State idea to the previous form of Palestinian colonization, calculated that by the latter method it would take nine hundred years before all the Jews could be settled in their land. The members of the Congress applauded this as a conclusive argument. But it was a cheap victory. The Jewish State itself, do what it will, will find no way to make a more favorable calculation.

The truth is bitter, but with all its bitterness it is better than illusion. We must admit to ourselves that the "ingathering of the exiles" is unattainable by natural means. We may, by natural means, someday establish a Jewish State; it is possible that the Jews may increase and multiply within it until the "land is filled with them"—but even then the greater part of our people will remain scattered on foreign soils. "To gather our scattered ones from the four corners of the earth" (in the words of the Prayer Book) is impossible. Only religion, with its belief in a miraculous redemption, can promise such a consummation.

But if this is so, if the Jewish State, too, means not an "ingathering of the exiles" but the settlement of a small part of our people in Palestine, then how will this solve the material problem of the Jewish masses in the lands of the Diaspora?

The material problem will not be ended by the establishment of a Jewish State, and it is, indeed, beyond our power to solve it once and for all. (Even now there are various means at our disposal to alleviate this problem to a greater or lesser degree, e.g., by increasing the proportion of farmers and artisans among our people *in all lands,* etc.) Whether or not we create a Jewish State, the material situation of the Jews will always basically depend on the economic condition and the cultural level of the various nations among which we are dispersed.

Thus we are driven to the conclusion that the real and only basis of Zionism is to be found in another problem, the spiritual one.

But the spiritual problem appears in two differing forms, one in the West and one in the East, which explains the fundamental difference between western "Zionism" and eastern "Hibbat Zion." Nordau dealt only with the western form of the problem, apparently knowing nothing about the eastern; and the Congress as a whole concentrated on the first, and paid little attention to the second.

The western Jew, having left the ghetto and having sought acceptance by the gentile majority, is unhappy because his hope of an open-armed welcome has been disappointed. Perforce he returns to his own people and tries to find within the Jewish community that life for which he yearns—but in vain. The life and horizon of the Jewish community no longer satisfy him. He has already grown accustomed to a broader social and political life, and on the intellectual side the work to be done for our Jewish national culture does not attract him, because that culture has played no part in his earliest education and is a closed book to him. In this dilemma he therefore turns to the land of his ancestors and imagines how good it would be if a Jewish State were re-established there—a State and society organized exactly after the pattern of other States. Then he could live a full, complete life within his own people, and he could find at home all that he now sees outside, dangled before his eyes but out of reach. Of course, not all the Jews will be able to take wing and go to their State; but the very existence of the Jewish State will also raise the prestige of those who remain in exile, and their fellow citizens will no longer despise them and keep them at arm's length, as though they were base slaves, dependent entirely on the hospitality of others. As he further contemplates this fascinating vision, it suddenly dawns on his inner consciousness that even now, before the Jewish State is established, the mere idea of it gives him almost complete relief. It provides an opportunity for communal work and political excitement; his emotions find an outlet in a field of activity which is not subservient to non-Jews; and he feels that, thanks to this ideal, he stands once more spiritually erect and has regained his personal dignity, without overmuch trouble and purely by his own efforts. So he devotes himself to the ideal with all the ardor of which he is capable; he gives rein to his fancy and lets it soar as it will, beyond reality and the limitations of human power. For it is not the attainment of the ideal that he needs; its pursuit alone is sufficient to cure him of his spiritual disease, which is that of an inferiority complex, and the loftier and more distant the ideal, the greater its power to exalt.

This is the basis of western Zionism and the secret of its attraction. But eastern Hibbat Zion originated and developed in a different setting. It, too, began as a political movement; but, being a result of material evils, it could not be content with an "activity" consisting only of outbursts of feeling and fine phrases, which may satisfy the heart but not the stomach. Hibbat Zion began at once to express itself in concrete activities—in the establishment of colonies in Palestine. This practical work soon clipped the wings of fancy and demonstrated conclusively that Hibbat Zion could not lessen the material woe of the

Jews by one iota. One might, therefore, have thought that, when this fact became patent, the Hovevei Zion would give up their effort and cease wasting time and energy on work which brought them no nearer their goal. But, no: they remained true to their flag and went on working with the old enthusiasm, though most of them did not understand, even in their own minds, why they did so. They felt instinctively that they must go on; but, as they did not clearly appreciate the nature of this feeling, the things that they did were not always effectively directed toward the true goal, to which they were unconsciously dedicated.

For at the very time when the material tragedy in the East was at its height, the heart of the eastern Jews was sensitive to another tragedy as well—a spiritual one; and when the Hovevei Zion began to work for the solution of the material problem, the national instinct of the people felt that in this work it would find the remedy for its spiritual trouble. Hence the people rallied to this effort and did not abandon it even after it had become obvious that it was an ineffective instrument for curing the material trouble of the Jews.

The eastern form of the spiritual problem is absolutely different from the western. In the West it is the problem of the Jews; in the East, the *problem of Judaism.* The first weighs on the individual; the second, on the nation. The one is felt by Jews who have had a European education; the other, by Jews whose education has been Jewish. The one is a product of anti-Semitism, and is dependent on anti-Semitism for its existence; the other is a natural product of a real link with a millennial culture, and it will remain unsolved and unaffected even if the troubled of the Jews all over the world attain comfortable economic positions, are on the best possible terms with their neighbors, and are admitted to the fullest social and political equality.

It is not only the Jews who have come out of the ghetto; Judaism has come out, too. For the Jews the exodus from the ghetto is confined to certain countries and is due to toleration; but Judaism has come out (or is coming out) of its own accord, wherever it has come into contact with modern culture. This contact with modern culture overturns the inner defences of Judaism, so that it can no longer remain isolated and live a life apart. The spirit of our people desires further development; it wants to absorb the basic elements of general culture which are reaching it from the outside world, to digest them and to make them a part of itself, as it has done before at various periods of its history. But the conditions of its life in exile are not suitable for such a task. In our time culture expresses itself everywhere through the form of the national spirit, and the stranger who would become part of culture must sink his individuality and become absorbed in the dominant environment. In exile, Judaism cannot, therefore, develop its individuality in its own way. When it leaves the ghetto walls, it is in danger of losing its essential being or—at very least—its national unity; it is in danger of being split up into as many kinds of Judaism, each with a different character and life, as there are countries of the dispersion.

Judaism is, therefore, in a quandary: It can no longer tolerate the *Galut* form which it had to take on, in obedience to its will-to-live, when it was exiled from its own country; but, without that form, its life is in danger. So it seeks to return to its historic center, where it will be able to live a life developing in a natural way, to bring its powers into play in every department of human culture, to broaden and perfect those national possessions which it has acquired up to now, and thus to contribute to the common stock of humanity, in the future as it has in the past, a great national culture, the fruit of the unhampered activity of a people living by the light of its own spirit. For this purpose Judaism can, for the present, content itself with little. It does not need an independent State, but only the creation in its native land of conditions favorable to its development; a good-sized settlement of Jews working without hindrance in every branch of civilization, from agriculture and handicrafts to science and literature. This Jewish settlement, which will be a gradual growth, will become in course of time the center of the nation, wherein its spirit will find pure expression and develop in all its aspects to the highest degree of perfection of which it is capable. Then, from this center, the spirit of Judaism will radiate to the great circumference, to all the communities of the Diaspora, to inspire them with new life and to preserve the over-all unity of our people. When our national culture in Palestine has attained that level, we may be confident that it will produce men in the Land of Israel itself who will be able, at a favorable moment, to establish a State there—one which will be not merely a State of Jews but a really Jewish State.

This Hibbat Zion, which concerns itself with the preservation of Judaism at a time when Jewry is suffering so much, is something odd and unintelligible to the "political" Zionists of the West, just as the demand of R. Johanan ben Zakkai for "Yavneh" was strange and unintelligible to the comparable party of his time. And so political Zionism cannot satisfy those Jews who care for Judaism; its growth seems to them to be fraught with danger to the object of their own aspiration.

The secret of our people's persistence is—as I have tried to show elsewhere—that at a very early period the Prophets taught it to respect only the power of the spirit and not to worship material power. Therefore, unlike the other nations of antiquity, the Jewish people never reached the point of losing its self-respect in the face of more powerful enemies. As long as we remain faithful to this principle, our existence has a secure basis, and we shall not lose our self-respect, for we are not spiritually inferior to any nation. But a political ideal which is not grounded in our national culture is apt to seduce us from loyalty to our own inner spirit and to beget in us a tendency to find the path of glory in the attainment of material power and political dominion, thus breaking the thread that unites us with the past and undermining our historical foundation. Needless to say, if the political ideal is not attained, it will have disastrous consequences, because we shall have lost the old basis without finding a new one. But even if it is attained under present conditions, when we are a scattered people not only in the physical but also in the spiritual sense—even then, Judaism will be in great danger. Almost all our great men—those, that is, whose education and social position have prepared them to be at the head of a Jewish State—are spiritually far removed from Judaism and have no true conception of its nature and its value. Such men, however loyal to their State and devoted to its interests, will necessarily envisage those interests by the standards of the foreign culture which they themselves have imbibed; and they will endeavor, by moral persuasion or even by force, to implant that culture in the Jewish State, so that in the end the Jewish State will be a State of Germans or Frenchmen of the Jewish race. We have even now a small example of this process in Palestine.

History teaches us that in the days of the Herodian house Palestine was indeed a Jewish State, but the national culture was despised and persecuted. The ruling house did everything in its power to implant Roman culture in the country and frittered away the resources of the nation in the building of heathen temples, amphitheaters, and so forth. Such a Jewish State would spell death and utter degradation for our people. Such a State would never achieve sufficient political power to deserve respect, while it would be estranged from the living inner spiritual force of Judaism. The puny State, being "tossed about like a ball between its powerful neighbors, and maintaining its existence only by diplomatic shifts and continual truckling to the favored of fortune," would not be able to give us a feeling of national glory; the national culture, in which we might have sought and found our glory, would not have been implanted in our State and would not be the principle of its life. So we should really be then—much more than we are now—"a small and insignificant nation," enslaved in spirit to "the favored of fortune," turning an envious and covetous eye on the armed force of our "powerful neighbors"; our existence in such terms, as a sovereign State would not add a glorious chapter to our national history.

Would it not be better for "an ancient people which was once a beacon to the world" to disappear than to end by reaching such a goal as this? Mr. Lilienblum reminds me that there exist today small States, like Switzerland, which are safeguarded against interference by the other nations and are not forced to "continual truckling." But a comparison between Palestine and small countries like Switzerland overlooks the geographical position of Palestine and its religious importance for all the world. These two facts will make it quite impossible for its "powerful neighbors" (by which expression, of course, I did not mean, as Mr. Lilienblum interprets, "the Druses and the Persians") to leave it alone. Even after it has become a Jewish State, they will all still keep an eye on it, and each power will try to influence its policy in a direction favorable to itself, after the pattern of events in other weak states (like Turkey) in which the great European nations have "interests."

In sum: Hibbat Zion, no less than "Zionism," wants a Jewish State and believes in the possibility of the establishment of a Jewish State in the future. But while "Zionism" looks to the Jewish State to furnish a remedy for poverty and to provide complete tranquillity and national glory, Hibbat Zion knows that our State will not give us all these things until "universal Righteousness is enthroned and holds sway over nations and States"—it looks to a Jewish State to provide only a "secure refuge" for Judaism and a cultural bond to unite our nation. "Zionism," therefore, begins its work with political propaganda; Hibbat

Zion begins with national culture, because only *through* the national culture and *for its sake* can a Jewish State be established in such a way as to correspond with the will and the needs of the Jewish people.

3.   The Husayn-McMahon Correspondence, Negotiating the Establishment of an "Arab Kingdom" in the Middle East, 1915–1916

The ambiguity of the Husayn-McMahon correspondence has left a trail of misunderstandings and conflict with regard to the geopolitics of the modern Middle East. Husayn ibn-Ali (1855–1931) was the amir of Mecca around the time World War I broke out. His distrust of the Ottoman Committee of Union and Progress (Young Turks) and his own political ambition led him in 1915 to open negotiations with the British. Sharif Husayn (sharif is an honorary title indicating a claim to descent from the Prophet Muhammad) offered the British the possibility of his support through an "Arab" revolt against the Ottoman authorities. The term Arab *as he used it referred to the Arab tribes within the Arabian Peninsula. In return, Husayn expected British support for the establishment of an Arab kingdom under his leadership.*

Britain was very receptive to the idea, and the ensuing negotiations (July 1915–March 1916) between Sir Henry McMahon (the British High Commissioner in Egypt) and Sharif Husayn focused on the extent of the borders of the proposed Arab kingdom. A disagreement—whose resolution was postponed until after the war—arose about the Syrian coastal lands. Husayn insisted that they should be included in his kingdom. The British demurred, because they wanted to protect their own interests in those areas as well as the interests of their ally France.

1. From Sharif Husayn, 14 July 1915

Whereas the whole of the Arab nation without any exception have decided in these last years to accomplish their freedom, and grasp the reins of their administration both in theory and practice; and whereas they have found and felt that it is in the interest of the Government of Great Britain to support them and aid them in the attainment of their firm and lawful intentions (which are based upon the maintenance of the honour and dignity of their life) without any ulterior motives whatsoever unconnected with this object;

And whereas it is to their (the Arabs') interest also to prefer the assistance of the Government of Great Britain in consideration of their geographic position and economic interests, and also of the attitude of the above-mentioned Government, which is known to both nations and therefore need not be emphasized;

Great Britain, *Parliamentary Papers, 1939, Misc. No. 3*, Cmd. 5957.

For these reasons the Arab nation sees fit to limit themselves, as time is short, to asking the Government of Great Britain, if it should think fit, for the approval, through her deputy or representative, of the following fundamental propositions, leaving out all things considered secondary in comparison with these, so that it may prepare all means necessary for attaining this noble purpose, until such time as it finds occasion for making the actual negotiations:—

Firstly.—England will acknowledge the independence of the Arab countries, bounded on the north by Mersina and Adana up to the 37th degree of latitude, on which degree fall Birijik, Urfa, Mardin, Midiat, Jezirat (Ibn 'Umar), Amadia, up to the border of Persia; on the east by the borders of Persia up to the Gulf of Basra; on the south by the Indian Ocean, with the exception of the position of Aden to remain as it is; on the west by the Red Sea, the Mediterranean Sea up to Mersina. England to approve the proclamation of an Arab Khalifate of Islam.

Secondly.—The Arab Government of the Sharif will acknowledge that England shall have the preference in all economic enterprises in the Arab countries whenever conditions of enterprises are otherwise equal.

Thirdly.—For the security of this Arab independence and the certainty of such preference of economic enterprises, both high contracting parties will offer mutual assistance, to the best ability of their military and naval forces, to face any foreign Power which may attack either party. Peace not to be decided without agreement of both parties.

Fourthly.—If one of the parties enters into an aggressive conflict, the other party will assume a neutral attitude, and in case of such party wishing the other to join forces, both to meet and discuss the conditions.

Fifthly.—England will acknowledge the abolition of foreign privileges in the Arab countries, and will assist the Government of the Sharif in an International Convention for confirming such abolition.

Sixthly.—Articles 3 and 4 of this treaty will remain in vigour for fifteen years, and, if either wishes it to be renewed, one year's notice before lapse of treaty is to be given.

Consequently, and as the whole of the Arab nation have (praise be to God) agreed and united for the attainment, at all costs and finally, of this noble object, they beg the Government of Great Britain to answer them positively or negatively in a period of thirty days after receiving this intimation; and if this period should lapse before they receive an answer, they reserve to themselves complete freedom of action. Moreover, we (the Sharif's family) will consider ourselves free in work and deed from the bonds of our previous declaration which we made through Ali Effendi.

2. From Sir Henry McMahon, 24 October 1915

I have received your letter of the 29th Shawal, 1333, with much pleasure and your expressions of friendliness and sincerity have given me the greatest satisfaction.

I regret that you should have received from my last letter the impression that I regarded the question of the limits and boundaries with coldness and hesitation; such was not the case, but it appeared to me that the time had not yet come when that question could be discussed in a conclusive manner.

I have realised, however, from your last letter that you regard this question as one of vital and urgent importance. I have, therefore, lost no time in informing the Government of Great Britain of the contents of your letter, and it is with great pleasure that I communicate to you on their behalf the following statement, which I am confident you will receive with satisfaction:—

The two districts of Mersina and Alexandretta and portions of Syria lying to the west of the districts of Damascus, Homs, Hama and Aleppo cannot be said to be purely Arab, and should be excluded from the limits demanded.

With the above modification, and without prejudice of our existing treaties with Arab chiefs, we accept those limits.

As for those regions lying within those frontiers wherein Great Britain is free to act without detriment to the interest of her ally, France, I am empowered in the name of the Government of Great Britain to give the following assurances and make the following reply to your letter:—

1. Subject to the above modifications, Great Britain is prepared to recognize and support the independence of the Arabs in all the regions within the limits demanded by the Sharif of Mecca.

2. Great Britain will guarantee the Holy Places against all external aggression and will recognise their inviolability.

3. When the situation admits, Great Britain will give to the Arabs her advice and will assist them to establish what may appear to be the most suitable forms of government in those various territories.

4. On the other hand, it is understood that the Arabs have decided to seek the advice and guidance of Great Britain only, and that such European advisers and officials as may be required for the formation of a sound form of administration will be British.

5. With regard to the vilayets of Bagdad and Basra, the Arabs will recognise that the established position and interests of Great Britain necessitate special administrative arrangements in order to secure these territories from foreign aggression, to promote the welfare of the local populations and to safeguard our mutual economic interests.

I am convinced that this declaration will assure you beyond all possible doubt of the sympathy of Great Britain towards the aspirations of her friends the Arabs and will result in a firm and lasting alliance, the immediate results of which will be the expulsion of the Turks from the Arab countries and the freeing of the Arab peoples from the Turkish yoke, which for so many years has pressed heavily upon them.

I have confined myself in this letter to the more vital and important questions, and if there are any other matters dealt with in your letter which I have omitted to mention, we may discuss them at some convenient date in the future.

It was with very great relief and satisfaction that I heard of the safe arrival of the Holy Carpet and the accompanying offerings which, thanks to the clearness of your directions and the excellence of your arrangements, were landed without trouble or mishap in spite of the dangers and difficulties occasioned by the present sad war. May God soon bring a lasting peace and freedom to all peoples!

I am sending this letter by the hand of your trusted and excellent messenger, Sheikh Mohammed Ibn Arif Ibn Uraifan, and he will inform you of the various matters of interest, but of less vital importance, which I have not mentioned in this letter.

4.   The Balfour Declaration, Stating the British Government's Support for a Jewish Homeland in Palestine, and Discussions Leading to Issuing It in 1917

In November 1917 the British government issued the Balfour Declaration promising the Zionists help in establishing a Jewish homeland in overwhelmingly Arab Palestine. Many historians see this promise as one of the main causes of the subsequent Palestinian-Israeli conflict. The documents presented here detail some of the discussion that took place before the final version of the Balfour Declaration was approved by the War Cabinet—a ministerial executive committee that was a much-reduced version of the government of Prime Minister David Lloyd George.

The British Federation of Zionists (represented by Chaim Weizmann and Nahum Sokolow) lobbied the British government for support of their project. The British, however, faced the difficulty that under the secret terms of the Sykes-Picot Agreement (1916) between Britain and France, Palestine was to be governed by an international mandate and not simply by the British in the postwar era. Furthermore, the British knew from the Husayn-McMahon correspondence that many Arabs expected Palestine to be part of a postwar Arab kingdom led by Sharif Husayn himself. However, several factors tipped the balance in favor of the Zionists. First, the British wanted to ascertain that American Zionists would encourage the U.S. Congress to join the British war effort against the Germans. The War Cabinet suspected that the Germans were preparing to offer the Zionists some support. Thus, after asking the Zionists to obtain French support for a British mandate over Palestine, the War Cabinet authorized Foreign Secretary Lord Balfour to issue his declaration of support.

The following documents summarize discussions within the War Cabinet about the ramifications of supporting the Zionists. Observe that throughout these discussions no mention was made of the wishes of the Arab inhabitants of Palestine or their right to self-determination.

"The Balfour Declaration," *Times* (London), 9 November 1917, p. 1.

Foreign Office
November 2nd, 1917

Dear Lord Rothschild [a French Zionist],

I have much pleasure in conveying to you, on behalf of His Majesty's Government, the following declaration of sympathy with Jewish Zionist aspirations which has been submitted to, and approved by, the Cabinet.

"His Majesty's Government view with favour the establishment in Palestine of a national home for the Jewish people, and will use their best endeavours to facilitate the achievement of this object, it being clearly understood that nothing shall be done which may prejudice the civil and religious rights of existing non-Jewish communities in Palestine, or the rights and political status enjoyed by Jews in any other country."

I should be grateful if you would bring this declaration to the knowledge of the Zionist Federation.

Yours sincerely,
Arthur James Balfour

1. Cambon Letter to Sokolow, 4 June 1917

You were good enough to present the project to which you are devoting your efforts, which has for its object the development of Jewish colonization in Palestine. You consider that, circumstances permitting, and the independence of the Holy Places being safeguarded on the other hand, it would be a deed of justice and of reparation to assist, by the protection of the Allied Powers, in the renaissance of the Jewish nationality in that Land from which the people of *Israel* were exiled so many centuries ago.

The French Government, which entered this present war to defend a people wrongfully attacked, and which continues the struggle to assure the victory of right over might, can but feel sympathy for your cause, the triumph of which is bound up with that of the Allies.

I am happy to give you herewith such assurance.

2. Official Zionist Formula, 18 July 1917

H. M. Government, after considering the aims of the Zionist Organisation, accepts the principle of recognising Palestine as the National Home of the Jewish people and the right of the Jewish people to build up its National life in Palestine under a protection to be established at the conclusion of Peace, following upon the successful issue of the war.

H. M. Government regards as essential for the realisation of this principle the grant of internal autonomy to the Jewish nationality in Palestine, freedom of immigration for Jews, and the establishment of a Jewish National Colonising Corporation for the re-settlement and economic development of the country.

The conditions and forms of the internal autonomy and a charter for the Jewish National Colonising Corporation should, in the view of H. M.

Government, be elaborated in detail and determined with the representatives of the Zionist Organisation.

3. Minutes of War Cabinet Meeting No. 227, Minute No. 2, 3 September 1917

The War Cabinet had under consideration correspondence which had passed between the Secretary of State for Foreign Affairs and Lord Rothschild on the question of the policy to be adopted towards the Zionist movement. In addition to the draft declaration of policy included in the above correspondence, they had before them an alternative draft prepared by Lord Milner. They had also before them a Memorandum by Mr. Montagu entitled "The Anti-Semitism of the present Government."

It was suggested that a question raising such important issues as to the future of Palestine ought, in the first instance, to be discussed with our Allies, and more particularly with the United States.

On the question of submitting Lord Milner's draft for the consideration of the United States Government, Mr. Montagu urged that the use of the phrase "the home of the Jewish people" would vitally prejudice the position of every Jew elsewhere and expand the argument contained in his Memorandum. Against this it was urged that the existence of a Jewish State or autonomous community in Palestine would strengthen rather than weaken the situation of Jews in countries where they were not yet in possession of equal rights, and that in countries like England, where they possessed such rights and were identified with the nation of which they were citizens, their position would be unaffected by the existence of a national Jewish community elsewhere. The view was expressed that, while a small influential section of English Jews were opposed to the idea, large numbers were sympathetic to it, but in the interests of Jews who wished to go from countries where they were less favourably situated, rather than from any idea of wishing to go to Palestine themselves.

With reference to a suggestion that the matter might be postponed, the Acting Secretary of State for Foreign Affairs pointed out that this was a question on which the Foreign Office had been very strongly pressed for a long time past. There was a very strong and enthusiastic organisation, more particularly in the United States, who were zealous in this matter, and his belief was that it would be of most substantial assistance to the Allies to have the earnestness and enthusiasm of these people enlisted on our side. To do nothing was to risk a direct breach with them, and it was necessary to face this situation.

The War Cabinet decided that—

The views of President Wilson should be obtained before any declaration was made, and requested the Acting Secretary of State for Foreign Affairs to inform the Government of the United States that His Majesty's Government were being pressed to make a declaration in sympathy with the Zionist movement, and to ascertain their views as to the advisability of such a declaration being made.

4. Minutes of War Cabinet Meeting No. 245, Minute No. 18, 4 October 1917

With reference to War Cabinet 227, Minute 2, the Secretary of State for Foreign Affairs stated that the German Government were making great efforts to capture the sympathy of the Zionist Movement. This Movement, though opposed by a number of wealthy Jews in this country, had behind it the support of a majority of Jews, at all events in Russia and America, and possibly in other countries. He saw nothing inconsistent between the establishment of a Jewish national focus in Palestine and the complete assimilation and absorption of Jews into the nationality of other countries. Just as English emigrants to the United States became, either in the first or subsequent generations, American nationals, so, in future, should a Jewish citizenship be established in Palestine, would Jews become either Englishmen, Americans, Germans, or Palestinians. What was at the back of the Zionist Movement was the intense national consciousness held by certain members of the Jewish race. They regarded themselves as one of the great historic races of the world, whose original home was Palestine, and these Jews had a passionate longing to regain once more this ancient national home, Other Jews had become absorbed into the nations among whom they and their forefathers had dwelt for many generations. Mr. Balfour then read a very sympathetic declaration by the French Government which had been conveyed to the Zionists, and he stated that he knew that President Wilson was extremely favourable to the Movement.

Attention was drawn to the contradictory telegrams received from Colonel House and Justice Brandeis.

The Secretary was instructed to take the necessary action.

The War Cabinet further decided that the opinions received upon this draft declaration should be collated and submitted to them for decision.

5. Minutes of War Cabinet Meeting No. 259, Minute No. 12, 25 October 1917

With reference to War Cabinet 245, Minute 18, the Secretary mentioned that he was being pressed by the Foreign Office to bring forward the question of Zionism, an early settlement of which was regarded as of great importance.

Lord Curzon stated that he had a Memorandum on the subject in course of preparation.

The question was adjourned until Monday, 29th October, or some other day early next week.

6. Minutes of War Cabinet Meeting No. 261, Minute No. 12, 31 October 1917

With reference to War Cabinet 245, Minute 18, the War Cabinet had before them a note by the Secretary, and also a memorandum by Lord Curzon on the subject of the Zionist movement.

The Secretary of State for Foreign Affairs stated that he gathered that everyone was now agreed that, from a purely diplomatic and political point of view, it was desirable that some declaration favourable to the aspirations of the Jewish nationalists should now be made. The vast majority of Jews in Russia and America, as, indeed, all over the world, now appeared to be favourable to Zionism. If we could make a declaration favourable to such an ideal, we should be able to carry on extremely useful propaganda both in Russia and America. He gathered that the main arguments still put forward against Zionism were twofold:—

(*a.*) That Palestine was inadequate to form a home for either the Jewish or any other people.

(*b.*) The difficulty felt with regard to the future position of Jews in Western countries.

With regard to the first, he understood that there were considerable differences of opinion among experts regarding the possibility of the settlement of any large population in Palestine, but he was informed that, if Palestine were scientifically developed, a very much larger population could be sustained than had existed during the period of Turkish misrule. As to the meaning of the words "national home," to which the Zionists attach so much importance, he understood it to mean some form of British, American, or other protectorate, under which full facilities would be given to the Jews to work out their own salvation and to build up, by means of education, agriculture, and industry, a real centre of national culture and focus of national life. It did not necessarily involve the early establishment of an independent Jewish State, which was a matter for gradual development in accordance with the ordinary laws of political evolution.

With regard to the second point, he felt that, so far from Zionism hindering the process of assimilation in Western countries, the truer parallel was to be found in the position of an Englishman who leaves his country to establish a permanent home in the United States. In the latter case there was no difficulty in the Englishman or his children becoming full nationals of the United States, whereas, in the present position of Jewry, the assimilation was often felt to be incomplete, and any danger of a double allegiance or non-national outlook would be eliminated.

Lord Curzon stated that he admitted the force of the diplomatic arguments in favour of expressing sympathy, and agreed that the bulk of the Jews held Zionist rather than anti-Zionist opinions. He added that he did not agree with the attitude taken up by Mr. Montagu. On the other hand, he could not share the optimistic views held regarding the future of Palestine. These views were not merely the result of his own personal experiences of travel in that country, but of careful investigations from persons who had lived for many years in the country. He feared that by the suggested declaration we should be raising false expectations which could never be realised. He attached great importance to the necessity of retaining the Christian and Moslem Holy Places in Jerusalem and Bethlehem, and, if this were to be effectively done, he did not see how the

Jewish people could have a political capital in Palestine. However, he recognised that some expression of sympathy with Jewish aspirations would be a valuable adjunct to our propaganda, though he thought that we should be guarded in the language used in giving expression to such sympathy. . . .

5.   Division of the Ottoman Empire: The Treaty of Sèvres, August 10, 1920

Even before World War I ended, the British and the French (along with other Allies) had determined that the Ottoman Empire would not survive in its prewar form. In 1916, in secret negotiations (the Sykes-Picot Agreement), France and Britain agreed to divide the Arab Middle East among themselves. In 1920, diplomats at the Peace Conference of Versailles incorporated some of the ideas of Sykes-Picot into the peace settlement; the final division of the Ottoman lands was spelled out in the Treaty of Sèvres, concluded on August 10, 1920. The treaty harshly reduced the area of Ottoman control to a small portion of Anatolia (most of modern-day Turkey). The Arab lands of the Ottoman Empire were divided between the French and the British. This dismembering proved critical in shaping the nations of the modern Middle East and set the stage for later conflicts borne out of contrary expectations and aspirations among the populations of the region.

Part III: Political Clauses

Section I. Constantinople

ART. 36.   Subject to the provisions of the present Treaty, the High Contracting Parties agree that the rights and title of the Turkish Government over Constantinople shall not be affected, and that the said Government and His Majesty the Sultan shall be entitled to reside there and to maintain there the capital of the Turkish State.

Nevertheless, in the event of Turkey failing to observe faithfully the provisions of the present Treaty, or of any treaties or conventions supplementary thereto, particularly as regards the protection of the rights of racial, religious or linguistic minorities, the Allied Powers expressly reserve the right to modify the above provisions, and Turkey hereby agrees to accept any dispositions which may be taken in this connection.

Great Britain, *Treaty Series* (1920), no. 11, Cmd. 966, pp. 16–32. This document may also be found in J. C. Hurewitz, *The Middle East and North Africa in World Politics* (New Haven, Conn.: Yale University Press, 1975), pp. 220–225.

Section II. Straits

ART. 37.   The navigation of the Straits, including the Dardanelles, the Sea of Marmora and the Bosphorus, shall in future be open, both in peace and war, to every vessel of commerce or of war and to military and commercial aircraft, without distinction of flag.

These waters shall not be subject to blockade, nor shall any belligerent right be exercised nor any act of hostility be committed within them, unless in pursuance of a decision of the Council of the League of Nations.

ART. 38.   The Turkish Government recognizes that it is necessary to take further measures to ensure the freedom of navigation provided for in Article 37, and accordingly delegates, so far as it is concerned, to a Commission to be called the "Commission of the Straits," and hereinafter referred to as "the Commission," the control of the waters specified in Article 39.

The Greek Government, so far as it is concerned, delegates to the Commission the same powers and undertakes to give it in all respects the same facilities.

Such control shall be exercised in the name of the Turkish and Greek Governments respectively, and in the manner provided in this Section.

ART. 39.   The authority of the Commission will extend to all the waters between the Mediterranean mouth of the Dardanelles and the Black Sea mouth of the Bosphorus, and to the waters within three miles of each of these mouths.

This authority may be exercised on shore to such extent as may be necessary for the execution of the provisions of this Section.

ART. 40.   The Commission shall be composed of representatives appointed respectively by the United States of America (if and when that Government is willing to participate), the British Empire, France, Italy, Japan, Russia (if and when Russia becomes a member of the League of Nations), Greece, Roumania, and Bulgaria and Turkey (if and when the two latter States become members of the League of Nations). Each Power shall appoint one representative. The representatives of the United States of America, the British Empire, France, Italy, Japan and Russia shall each have two votes. The representatives of Greece, Roumania, and Bulgaria and Turkey shall each have one vote. Each Commissioner shall be removable only by the Government which appointed him. . . .

Section III. Kurdistan

ART. 62.   A Commission sitting at Constantinople and composed of three members appointed by the British, French and Italian Governments respectively shall draft within six months from the coming into force of the present Treaty a scheme of local autonomy for the predominantly Kurdish areas lying east of the Euphrates, south of the southern boundary of Armenia as it may be hereafter determined, and north of the frontier of Turkey with Syria and Mesopotamia, as defined in Article 27, II. (2) and (3). If unanimity cannot be secured on any question, it will be referred by the members of the Commission to their respective Governments. The scheme shall contain full safeguards for the protection of the Assyro-Chaldeans and other racial or religious minorities within these areas, and with this object a Commission composed of British, French, Italian, Persian and Kurdish representatives shall visit the spot to examine and decide what rectifications, if any, should be made in the Turkish frontier, where, under the provisions of the present Treaty, that frontier coincides with that of Persia.

ART. 63.   The Turkish Government hereby agrees to accept and execute the decisions of both the Commissions mentioned in Article 62 within three months from their communication to the said Government.

ART. 64.   If within one year from the coming into force of the present Treaty the Kurdish peoples within the areas defined in Article 62 shall address themselves to the Council of the League of Nations in such a manner as to show that a majority of the population of these areas desires independence from Turkey, and if the Council then considers that these peoples are capable of such independence and recommends that it should be granted to them, Turkey hereby agrees to execute such a recommendation, and to renounce all rights and title over these areas.

The detailed provisions for such renunciation will form the subject of a separate agreement between the Principal Allied Powers and Turkey.

If and when such renunciation takes place, no objection will be raised by the Principal Allied Powers to the voluntary adhesion to such an independent Kurdish State of the Kurds inhabiting that part of Kurdistan which has hitherto been included in the Mosul Vilayet.

Section IV. Smyrna

ART. 65.   The provisions of this Section will apply to the city of Smyrna and the adjacent territory defined in Article 66, until the determination of their final status in accordance with Article 83. . . .

ART. 67.   A Commission shall be constituted within fifteen days from the coming into force of the present Treaty to trace on the spot the boundaries of the territories described in Article 66. This Commission shall be composed of three members nominated by the British, French and Italian Governments respectively, one member nominated by the Greek Government, and one nominated by the Turkish Government.

ART. 68.   Subject to the provisions of this Section, the city of Smyrna and the territory defined in Article 66 will be assimilated, in the application of the present Treaty, to territory detached from Turkey.

ART. 69.   The city of Smyrna and the territory defined in Article 66 remain under Turkish sovereignty. Turkey however transfers to the Greek Government the exercise of her rights of sovereignty over the city of Smyrna and the said territory. In witness of such sovereignty the Turkish flag shall remain permanently hoisted over an outer fort in the town of Smyrna. The fort will be designated by the Principal Allied Powers.

ART. 70.   The Greek Government will be responsible for the administration of the city of Smyrna and the territory defined in Article 66, and will effect this administration by means of a body of officials which it will appoint specially for the purpose.

ART. 71.   The Greek Government shall be entitled to maintain in the city of Smyrna and the territory defined in Article 66 the military forces required for the maintenance of order and public security.

ART. 72.   A local parliament shall be set up with an electoral system calculated to ensure proportional representation of all sections of the population, including racial, linguistic and religious minorities. Within six months from the coming into force of the present Treaty the Greek Government shall submit to the Council of the League of Nations a scheme for an electoral system complying with the above requirements; this scheme shall not come into force until approved by a majority of the Council.

The Greek Government shall be entitled to postpone the elections for so long as may be required for the return of the inhabitants who have been banished or deported by the Turkish authorities, but such postponement shall not exceed a period of one year from the coming into force of the present Treaty.

ART. 73.   The relations between the Greek administration and the local parliament shall be determined by the said administration in accordance with the principles of the Greek Constitution. . . .

ART 83.   When a period of five years shall have elapsed after the coming into force of the present Treaty the local parliament referred to in Article 72 may, by a majority of votes, ask the Council of the League of Nations for the definitive incorporation in the Kingdom of Greece of the city of Smyrna and the territory defined in Article 66. The Council may require, as a preliminary, a plebiscite under conditions which it will lay down.

In the event of such incorporation as a result of the application of the foregoing paragraph, the Turkish sovereignty referred to in Article 69 shall cease. Turkey hereby renounces in that event in favour of Greece all rights and title over the city of Smyrna and the territory defined in Article 66. . . .

Section VI. Armenia

ART. 88.   Turkey, in accordance with the action already taken by the Allied Powers, hereby recognises Armenia as a free and independent State.

ART. 89.   Turkey and Armenia as well as the other High Contracting Parties agree to submit to the arbitration of the President of the United States of America the question of the frontier to be fixed between Turkey and Armenia in the Vilayets of Erzerum, Trebizond, Van and Bitlis, and to accept his decision thereupon, as well as any stipulations he may prescribe as to access for Armenia to the sea, and as to the demilitarisation of any portion of Turkish territory adjacent to the said frontier.

ART. 90.   In the event of the determination of the frontier under Article 89 involving the transfer of the whole or any part of the territory of the said Vilayets to Armenia, Turkey hereby renounces as from the date of such decision all rights and title over the territory so transferred. The provisions of the present Treaty applicable to territory detached from Turkey shall thereupon become applicable to the said territory.

The proportion and nature of the financial obligations of Turkey which Armenia will have to assume, or of the rights which will pass to her, on account of the transfer of the said territory will be determined in accordance with Articles 241 to 244, Part VIII (Financial Clauses) of the present Treaty.

Subsequent agreements will, if necessary, decide all questions which are not decided by the present Treaty and which may arise in consequence of the transfer of the said territory.

ART. 91.   In the event of any portion of the territory referred to in Article 89 being transferred to Armenia, a Boundary Commission, whose composition will be determined subsequently, will be constituted within three months from the delivery of the decision referred to in the said Article to trace on the spot the frontier between Armenia and Turkey as established by such decision.

ART. 92.   The frontiers between Armenia and Azerbaijan and Georgia respectively will be determined by direct agreement between the States concerned.

If in either case the States concerned have failed to determine the frontier by agreement at the date of the decision referred to in Article 89, the frontier line in question will be determined by the Principal Allied Powers, who will also provide for its being traced on the spot.

ART. 93.   Armenia accepts and agrees to embody in a Treaty with the Principal Allied Powers such provisions as may be deemed necessary by these Powers to protect the interests of inhabitants of that State who differ from the majority of the population in race, language, or religion.

Armenia further accepts and agrees to embody in a Treaty with the Principal Allied Powers such provisions as these Powers may deem necessary to protect freedom of transit and equitable treatment for the commerce of other nations.

Section VII. Syria, Mesopotamia, Palestine

ART. 94.   The High Contracting Parties agree that Syria and Mesopotamia shall, in accordance with the fourth paragraph of Article 22, Part I (Covenant of the League of Nations), be provisionally recognised as independent States subject to the rendering of administrative advice and assistance by a Mandatory until such time as they are able to stand alone.

A Commission shall be constituted within fifteen days from the coming into force of the present Treaty to trace on the spot the frontier line described in Article 27, II (2) and (3). This Commission will be composed of three members nominated by France, Great Britain and Italy respectively, and one member nominated by Turkey; it will be assisted by a representative of Syria for the Syrian frontier, and by a representative of Mesopotamia for the Mesopotamian frontier.

The determination of the other frontiers of the said States, and the selection of the Mandatories, will be made by the Principal Allied Powers.

ART. 95.   The High Contracting Parties agree to entrust, by application of the provisions of Article 22, the administration of Palestine, within such boundaries as may be determined by the Principal Allied Powers, to a Mandatory to be selected by the said Powers. The Mandatory will be responsible for putting into effect the declaration originally made on November 2, 1917, by the British Government, and adopted by the other Allied Powers, in favour of the establishment in Palestine of a national home for the Jewish people, it being clearly understood that nothing shall be done which may prejudice the civil and religious rights of existing non-Jewish communities in Palestine, or the rights and political status enjoyed by Jews in any other country.

The Mandatory undertakes to appoint as soon as possible a special Commission to study and regulate all questions and claims relating to the different religious communities. In the composition of this Commission the religious interests concerned will be taken into account. The Chairman of the Commission will be appointed by the Council of the League of Nations.

ART. 96.   The terms of the mandates in respect of the above territories will be formulated by the Principal Allied Powers and submitted to the Council of the League of Nations for approval.

ART. 97.   Turkey hereby undertakes, in accordance with the provisions of Article 132, to accept any decisions which may be taken in relation to the questions dealt with in this Section.

Section VIII. Hedjaz

ART. 98.   Turkey, in accordance with the action already taken by the Allied Powers, hereby recognises the Hedjaz as a free and independent State, and renounces in favour of the Hedjaz all rights and titles over the territories of the former Turkish Empire situated outside the frontiers of Turkey as laid down by the present Treaty, and comprised within the boundaries which may ultimately be fixed.

ART. 99.   In view of the sacred character attributed by Moslems of all countries to the cities and the Holy Places of Mecca and Medina, His Majesty the King of Hedjaz undertakes to assure free and easy access thereto to Moslems of every country who desire to go there on pilgrimage or for any other religious object, and to respect and ensure respect for the pious foundations which are or may be established there by Moslems of any countries in accordance with the precepts of the law of the Koran.

ART. 100.   His Majesty the King of the Hedjaz undertakes that in commercial matters the most complete equality of treatment shall be assured in the territory of the Hedjaz to the persons, ships and goods of nationals of any of the Allied Powers, or of any of the new States set up in the territories of the former Turkish Empire, as well as to the persons, ships and goods of nationals of States, Members of the League of Nations.

Section IX. Egypt, Soudan, Cyprus

1. Egypt

ART. 101.   Turkey renounces all rights and title in or over Egypt. This renunciation shall take effect as from November 5, 1914. Turkey declares that in conformity with the action taken by the Allied Powers she recognizes the Protectorate proclaimed over Egypt by Great Britain on December 18, 1914.

ART. 102.   Turkish subjects habitually resident in Egypt on December 18, 1914, will acquire Egyptian nationality *ipso facto* and will lose their Turkish nationality, except that if at that date such persons were temporarily absent from, and have not since returned to, Egypt they will not acquire Egyptian nationality without a special authorisation from the Egyptian Government.

ART. 103.   Turkish subjects who became resident in Egypt after December 18, 1914, and are habitually resident there at the date of the coming into force of the present Treaty may, subject to the conditions prescribed in Article 105 for the right of option, claim Egyptian nationality, but such claim may in individual cases be refused by the competent Egyptian authority.

ART. 104.   For all purposes connected with the present Treaty, Egypt and Egyptian nationals, their goods and vessels, shall be treated on the same footing, as from August 1, 1914, as the Allied Powers, their nationals, goods and vessels, and provisions in respect of territory under Turkish sovereignty, or of territory detached from Turkey in accordance with the present Treaty, shall not apply to Egypt.

ART. 105.   Within a period of one year after the coming into force of the present Treaty persons over eighteen years of age acquiring Egyptian nationality under the provisions of Article 102 will be entitled to opt for Turkish nationality. In case such persons, or those who under Article 103 are entitled to claim Egyptian nationality, differ in race from the majority of the population of Egypt, they will within the same period be entitled to opt for the nationality of any State in favour of which territory is detached from Turkey, if the majority of the population of that State is of the same race as the person exercising the right to opt.

Option by a husband covers a wife and option by parents covers their children under eighteen years of age.

Persons who have exercised the above right to opt must, except where authorised to continue to reside in Egypt, transfer within the ensuing twelve months their place of residence to the State for which they have opted. They will be entitled to retain their immovable property in Egypt, and may carry with them their movable property of every description. No export or import duties or charges may be imposed upon them in connection with the removal or such property.

ART. 106.   The Egyptian Government shall have complete liberty of action in regulating the status of Turkish subjects in Egypt and the conditions under which they may establish themselves in the territory.

ART. 107.   Egyptian nationals shall be entitled, when abroad, to British diplomatic and consular protection.

ART. 108.   Egyptian goods entering Turkey shall enjoy the treatment accorded to British goods.

ART. 109.   Turkey renounces in favour of Great Britain the powers conferred upon His Imperial Majesty the Sultan by the Convention signed at Constantinople on October 29, 1888, relating to the free navigation of the Suez Canal.

ART. 110.   All property and possessions in Egypt belonging to the Turkish Government pass to the Egyptian Government without payment.

ART. 111.   All movable and immovable property in Egypt belonging to Turkish nationals (who do not acquire Egyptian nationality) shall be dealt with in accordance with the provisions of Part IX (Economic Clauses) of the present Treaty.

ART. 112.   Turkey renounces all claim to the tribute formerly paid by Egypt.

Great Britain undertakes to relieve Turkey of all liability in respect of the Turkish loans secured on the Egyptian tribute.

These loans are:

The guaranteed loan of 1855;

The loan of 1894 representing the converted loans of 1854 and 1871;

The loan of 1891 representing the converted loan of 1877.

The sums which the Khedives of Egypt have from time to time undertaken to pay over to the houses by which these loans were issued will be applied as heretofore to the interest and the sinking funds of the loans of 1894 and 1891 until the final extinction of those loans. The Government of Egypt will also continue to apply the sum hitherto paid towards the interest on the guaranteed loan of 1855.

Upon the extinction of these loans of 1894, 1891 and 1855, all liability on the part of the Egyptian Government arising out of the tribute formerly paid by Egypt to Turkey will cease.

2. Soudan

ART. 113.   The High Contracting Parties declare and place on record that they have taken note of the Convention between the British Government and the Egyptian Government defining the status and regulating the administration of the Soudan, signed on January 19, 1899, as amended by the supplementary Convention relating to the town of Suakin signed on July 10, 1899.

ART. 114.   Soudanese shall be entitled when in foreign countries to British diplomatic and consular protection.

3. Cyprus

ART. 115.   The High Contracting Parties recognise the annexation of Cyprus proclaimed by the British Government on November 5, 1914.

ART. 116.   Turkey renounces all rights and title over or relating to Cyprus, including the right to the tribute formerly paid by that island to the Sultan.

ART. 117.   Turkish nationals born or habitually resident in Cyprus will acquire British nationality and lose their Turkish nationality, subject to the conditions laid down in the local law.

Section X. Morocco, Tunis

ART. 118.   Turkey recognises the French Protectorate in Morocco, and accepts all the consequences thereof. This recognition shall take effect as from March 30, 1912.

ART. 119.   Moroccan goods entering Turkey shall be subject to the same treatment as French goods.

ART. 120.   Turkey recognises the French Protectorate over Tunis and accepts all the consequences thereof. This recognition shall take effect as from May 12, 1881.

Tunisian goods entering Turkey shall be subject to the same treatment as French goods.

Section XI. Libya, Aegean Islands

ART. 121.   Turkey definitely renounces all rights and privileges which under the Treaty of Lausanne of October 18, 1912, were left to the Sultan in Libya.

ART. 122.   Turkey renounces in favour of Italy all rights and title over the following islands of the Aegean Sea; Stampalia (Astropalia), Rhodes (Rhodos), Calki (Kharki), Scarpanto, Casos (Casso), Pscopis (Tilos), Misiros (Nisyros), Calymnos (Kalymnos), Leros, Patmos, Lipsos (Lipso), Sini (Symi), and Cos (Kos), which are now occupied by Italy, and the islets dependent thereon, and also over the island of Castellorizzo. . . .

Section XIII. General Provisions

ART. 132.   Outside her frontiers as fixed by the present Treaty Turkey hereby renounces in favour of the Principal Allied Powers all rights and title which she could claim on any ground over or concerning any territories outside Europe which are not otherwise disposed of by the present Treaty.

Turkey undertakes to recognize and conform to the measures which may be taken now or in the future by the Principal Allied Powers, in agreement where necessary with third Powers, in order to carry the above stipulation into effect. . . .

ART. 139.   Turkey renounces formally all rights of suzerainty or jurisdiction of any kind over Moslems who are subject to the sovereignty or protectorate of any other State.

No power shall be exercised directly or indirectly by any Turkish authority whatever in any territory detached from Turkey or of which the existing status under the present Treaty is recognised by Turkey.

6.   Mustafa Kemal ("Atatürk") Outlines His Vision of the Recent Nationalist Past of Turkey and the Future of the Country, 1927

At the close of World War I, the Allies were intent on dismembering the Ottoman Empire, partly to punish the Ottomans for siding with the Central Powers and partly to extend British and French imperialist influence and presence into the eastern Mediterranean. According to the Treaty of Sèvres (1920), Italy and France would subdivide the southeastern region of Anatolia, an independent Armenian state centered around Erzurum would be established in the northeastern part, and Greece laid claim to extensive parts of southwestern Anatolia. The Turkish population of Anatolia was humiliated and left with an absurdly small territory to call its own. In addition, the Ottoman government was deprived of any real decision-making power; the Allies were in effect the real rulers at Istanbul, the capital.

In response to Allied occupation, various resistance groups emerged throughout Anatolia. By 1919 these disparate guerrilla groups were organized and led by army officers who were disillusioned with the armistice that the Allies forced the Ottoman sultan to sign. From the ranks of these officers emerged Mustafa Kemal (1881–1938), who slowly but surely gained absolute control of the national independence movement and later of independent Turkey.

Mustafa Kemal (known as Atatürk, which means "father of the Turks") delivered the following speech at the national convention of the People's Party of the Republic held in Ankara between October 15 and 20, 1927. He presented his version of the struggle for national independence. It is important to notice how he came to define the idea of "Turkey" and "Turk." Of equal importance is the purpose behind

---

Internet Atatürk Library, "The Speech." http://ataturk.turkiye.org/soylev/txwrdpdf/speech/pdf/spchdizi.htm (24 January 2003).

*telling such a tale. In reading the text, keep in mind that he was presenting a uni-
fying nationalistic account of the birth of Turkey. Whether "true" or not, the story
remains one of the key elements of Turkish nationalism.*

Gentlemen,

I landed at Samsun on the nineteenth day of May of year 1919. This was the
general state of affairs:

The group of Powers which included the Ottoman Government had been
defeated in the Great War. The Ottoman Army had been crushed on every
front. An armistice had been signed under severe conditions. The prolongation
of the Great War had left the people exhausted and impoverished. Those who
had driven the people and the country into the World War had fled and now
cared for nothing but their own safety. Vahdettin, the degenerate occupant of
the [Ottoman] throne and the Caliphate, was seeking for some despicable way
to save his person and his throne, the only objects of his anxiety. The Cabinet,
of which Damat Ferit Pasha was the head, was weak and lacked dignity and
courage. It was subservient to the will of the Sultan alone and agreed to every
proposal that could protect its members and their sovereign.

The Army had been deprived of their arms and ammunition, and this state
of affairs continued. The Entente Powers did not consider it necessary to respect the terms of the armistice. On various pretexts, their men-of-war and
troops remained at Istanbul. The Vilayet of Adana was occupied by the French;
Urfa, Maras, Antep by the English. In Antalya and Konya were the Italians,
whilst at Merzifon and Samsun were English troops. Foreign officers and officials and their special agents were very active everywhere. At last, on the 15th
May, that is to say, four days before the following account of events begins, the
Greek Army, with the consent of the Entente Powers, had landed at Izmir.

Christian elements were also at work all over the country, either openly or
in secret, trying to realize their own particular ambitions and thereby hasten
the breakdown of the State. Certain information and authentic documents that
fell into our hands later on prove that the Greek organization "Mavri Mira,"
established by the patriarchate in Istanbul, was forming bands, organizing
meetings and making propaganda in the Vilayets. The Greek Red Cross and
the Official Emigrants Commission supported the work of the "Mavri Mira."
The formation of Boy Scouts in the Greek schools directed by the "Mavri
Mira" were [sic] reinforced by the admission even of young men over twenty
years of age. The Armenian Patriarch, Zaven Efendi, also worked in connection with the "Mavri Mira." The preparations made by the Armenians progressed side by side with those made by the Greeks. A society called the
"Pontus" at Trabzon, Samsun, and other places along the entire Black Sea
coast, having their headquarters in Istanbul, worked openly and successfully.

Considered Means for Salvation

On account of the appalling seriousness of the situation which was apparent
everywhere, particularly in all the Vilayets, certain prominent personalities had

begun to develop countermeasures to improve the situation. This resulted in new organizations being started. Thus, for instance, there were unions or societies at Edirne and surrounding districts called "Trakya-Pasaeli." In the east, at Erzurum and Elazig, the "Union of Defense of the National Rights of the Eastern Provinces" had been formed, also with their headquarters in Istanbul. Again, in Trabzon there was a society called the "Defense of Rights" and in Istanbul a "League for the Separation of Trabzon and its District." Through the exertions of the members of this league, sub-committees had been established at Of and in the district of Lazistan.

Some of the young patriots at Izmir, who since the 13th May had noticed distinct indications of the approaching occupation of the town, had held meetings about the distressing condition of affairs during the night of the 14th, and in principle had agreed to oppose the occupation by the Greeks, which at that time was considered to be practically an accomplished fact, designed to end in annexation, and resisted it on the principle of "No Annexation." During the same night, those of the inhabitants who were able to meet at the Jewish cemetery at Izmir drew up a protest and spread it broadcast. But as the Greek troops actually landed on the following morning this attempt failed to achieve the desired result.

National Organizations and Their Political Aims

I would like to give you a short account of the object and political aims of these organizations.

I had already had a conversation in Istanbul with some of the leaders of the "Trakya-Pasaeli" Society. They considered that the breakdown of the Ottoman Empire was extremely probable. In face of the threatened danger of the dismemberment of their country, their first thought was to save Eastern Trakya and later on if possible, to form a Turco-Islamic community that would include Western Trakya. The only way by which they thought they could realize this aim was to put their trust in England or, if this was not possible, in France. With this object they tried to get in touch with certain political personalities belonging to foreign countries. It was believed that their intention was to establish a Trakya Republic.

The object of the "Defense of the National Rights of the Eastern Provinces Union," on the other hand (Art. 2 of their regulations), was to use all lawful means to ensure the free exercise and development of their religious and political rights for all elements inhabiting these provinces; to defend, if it should become necessary, the historical and national rights of the Muslim population of these provinces; to institute an impartial inquiry for the purpose of discovering the motives, the instigators and agitators implicated in the extortions and cruelties committed in the Eastern Provinces, so that the guilty ones might be punished without delay; to do their utmost to remove the misunderstandings that existed between the different elements in the country, and to restore the good relations that had formerly existed between them; and, finally, to appeal to the Government to alleviate as far as it lay in their power the misery resulting from the war.

Acting on these principles that emanated from the Central Committee in Istanbul, the Erzurum Branch decided to undertake, in defense of the rights of the Turks, to inform the civilized world by means of convincing documents that since the deportation the people had been taking no part whatever in the excesses. Further, that the property of the Armenians had been protected up to the time when the country was invaded by the Russians. On the other hand that the Muslims had been compelled to suffer from the cruelest acts of violence and that some Armenians who had been saved from deportation had, in disobedience of orders, attacked their own protectors. The Branch were doing their very best to resist any attempt to annex the Eastern Provinces.

The members of the Erzurum Branch of the "Defense of the National Rights of the Eastern Provinces" resolved, as stated in their printed report, after having studied the propaganda circulated in these provinces as well the Turkish, Kurdish and Armenian questions, from the scientific and historical point of view, to concentrate their further efforts on the following points:

1. On no account to emigrate;
2. Forthwith to form scientific, economic and religious organizations;
3. To unite in the defense of even the smallest part of the Eastern Provinces that might be attacked.

It can be seen that the headquarters of the "Defense of the National Rights of the Eastern Provinces" were far too optimistic in their expectation to succeed through civil and scientific means. They continued to exert themselves indefatigably in this direction. For the purpose of defending the rights of Muslims dwelling in the Eastern Provinces they published a French journal, which they called *Le Pays*. They acquired the right to publish a magazine called *Hadisat*. They also presented memorials to the representatives of the Entente Powers in Istanbul and tried to send a delegation to Europe.

From the foregoing statements, it appears to me to be clearly evident that the possible cession of the Eastern Provinces to Armenia was the most important reason for this Society having been formed. They anticipated that this possibility might become a reality if those who tried to prove that the Armenians were in the majority in these provinces, claiming the oldest historical rights, were to succeed in misleading the public opinion of the world by alleged scientific and historic documents and by perpetuating the calumny that the Muslim population was composed of savages whose chief occupation was to massacre the Armenians. Consequently, the Society aimed at the defense of the national and historic rights by corresponding methods and arguments.

The fear also existed that a Greek Pontic State might be founded on the shores of the Black Sea. At Trabzon several persons had formed another society with the object of protecting the rights of the Muslim population, to safeguard their existence and prevent them from falling under the yoke of the Greeks.

Their political aim and program is already sufficiently obvious from its name: "The Society for the Cession of the Territory of Trabzon," whose head office was in Istanbul. In any case, they set out with the idea of separating this district from the Central Government.

Organizations, in the Country and in Istanbul, Hostile to the National Existence

Besides these organizations, which were being formed in the manner I have described, other societies and enterprises began to make their appearance. In the provinces of Diyarbakir, Bitlis and Elazig, among others, there was a "League for the Resuscitation of the Kurds" with its head offices also in Istanbul. Their aim was to erect a Kurdish State under foreign protection.

Work was going on at Konya and the surrounding district for the formation of a league having for its object the revival of Islam—also with its offices in Istanbul. There were organizations named "Unity and Freedom" and "Peace and Salvation" throughout almost the whole country.
[. . .]

Closer Examination of the State of Affairs

Let us return to a closer examination of the facts, so that we may rapidly review them as a whole.

Morally and materially, the enemy Powers were openly attacking the Ottoman Empire and the country itself. They were determined to disintegrate and annihilate both. The Padisah-Caliph had one sole anxiety—namely, to save his own life and comfort. The members of the government had the same feeling. Without being aware of it, the nation had no longer anyone to lead it, but lived in darkness and uncertainty, waiting to see what would happen. Those who began to understand clearly the terrors and the extent of the catastrophe were seeking some means whereby to save the country, each guided by the circumstances that surrounded him and the sentiments that inspired him. The Army existed merely in name. The commanders and other officers were still suffering from the exhaustion resulting from the war. Their hearts were bleeding on account of the threatened dismemberment of their country. Standing on the brink of the dark abyss which yawned before their eyes, they racked their brains to discover a way out of the danger. . . .

Here I must add and explain a very important point. The Nation and the Army had no suspicion at all of the Padisah-Caliph's treachery. On the contrary, on account of religious and traditional ties handed down for centuries, they remained loyal to the throne and its occupant. Seeking for means of salvation under the influence of this tradition, the security of the Caliphate and the Sultanate concerned them far more than their own safety. That the country could possibly be saved without a Caliph and without a Padisah was an idea too impossible for them to comprehend. And woe to those who ventured to think otherwise! They would immediately have been looked down upon as men without faith and without patriotism and as such would have been scorned.

I must mention another point here. In seeking ways to save the situation, it was considered to be especially important to avoid irritating the Great Powers—England, France and Italy. The idea that it was impossible to fight even one of these Powers had taken root in the mind of nearly everybody. Consequently, to think of doing so and thus bring on another war after the Ottoman Empire, all-powerful Germany and Austria-Hungary together had been defeated and crushed would have been looked upon as sheer madness. . . .

Considered Means for Salvation

Now, Gentlemen, I will ask you what decision could have been arrived at under such circumstances for salvation?

As I have already explained, there were three propositions that had been put forward:

1. To demand protection from England;
2. To accept the United States of America as a mandatory Power.

The originators of these two proposals had as their aim the preservation of the Ottoman Empire in its complete integrity and preferred to place it as a whole under the protection of a single Power, rather than allow it to be divided among several States.

3. The third proposal was to deliver the country by allowing each district to act in its own way and according to its own capability. Thus, for instance, certain districts, in opposition to the theory of separation, endeavored to remain an integral part of the Empire. Others holding a different opinion already appeared to regard the dismemberment of the Empire as an accomplished fact and sought only their own safety.

My above explanations are inclusive of the leading motives of these three kinds of propositions.

My Decision

I did not think any of these three proposals could be accepted as sagacious, because the arguments and considerations on which they were based were groundless. In reality, the foundations of the Ottoman Empire were themselves shattered at that time. Its existence was threatened with extermination. All the Ottoman districts were practically dismembered. Only the fatherland, affording protection to a mere handful of Turks, still remained, and it was now suggested also to divide this. Such expressions as: the Ottoman Empire, Independence, Padisah-Caliph, Government—all of them were mere meaningless words.

Whose existence was it essential to save? And with whose help? And how?

Therefore, what could be a serious and correct resolution?

In these circumstances, one resolution alone was possible, namely, to create a New Turkish State, the sovereignty and independence of which would be unreservedly recognized.

This was the resolution we adopted before we left Istanbul and which we began to put into execution immediately after we set foot on Anadolu soil at Samsun.

Independence or Death

These were the most logical and most powerful arguments in support of this resolution:

The foundational principle is that the Turkish nation should live in honor and dignity. Such a condition can only be attained by complete independence. No matter how wealthy and prosperous a nation is, if it is deprived of its independence it no longer deserves to be regarded otherwise than as a slave in the eyes of civilized world.

To accept the protectorate of a foreign Power is to admit lack of all human qualities, weakness and incapacity. It is not at all thinkable that those who have never been in such a humiliating state will appoint a foreign master out of their own desire.

But the Turk is both dignified and proud; he is also capable and talented. Such a nation will prefer to perish rather than subject itself to the life of a slave.

Therefore, Independence or Death!

[. . .]

As for the Caliphate, it would only have been the laughing-stock in the eyes of the civilized world, enjoying the blessings of science and technology. As you see, in order to carry out our resolution, questions had to be dealt with about which the nation had hitherto known practically nothing. It was imperative that questions which were considered dangerous to discuss publicly be discussed openly. We were compelled to rebel against the Ottoman Government, against the Padishah, against the Caliph of all Muslims, and we had to bring the whole nation and the army into a state of rebellion.

Dividing the Implementation into Stages and Reaching the Aim by Degrees

It was essential that the entire nation take up arms against whoever would venture to attack the fatherland of Turks and Turkish independence. It would undoubtedly have been of little advantage if we had made clear to the public at the very beginning all the implications of a resolution of such far-reaching importance. On the contrary, it was necessary to proceed by stages, utilizing all opportunities to prepare the feeling and the spirit of the nation and to try to reach our aim by degrees. This is actually what happened. If our attitude and our actions during nine years are examined in their logical sequence, however, it becomes evident that our general behavior has never deviated from the lines laid down in our original resolution, nor from the purpose we had set out to achieve.

In order to dispel any doubts which might be entertained, one fact is urged upon us for mutual examination.

As the national struggle, carried on for the sole purpose of delivering the country from foreign invasion, developed and was crowned with success, it was natural and inevitable that it would gradually, step by step to the present day, have established all the principles and forms essential in government founded on national sovereignty. The sovereign of the dynasty who, thanks to his traditional instincts, foresaw this fatal course of historical events, declared himself from the very beginning the most embittered enemy of the national struggle. I, also from the first moment on, anticipated this historical progress. But I did not disclose all of my views although I have maintained them all the time. If I had spoken too much about future prospects our realistic endeavors would have been looked upon as dreams; and consequently from the outset it would have caused the alienation of those who—discouraged by the closeness of dangers that threatened from without—were fearful of possible changes which would be contrary to their tradition, their way of thinking and their psychology. The only practical and safe road to success lay in dealing with each problem at the right time. This was the way to ensure the development and restoration of the nation. This was how I acted.

7. 'Ali 'Abd al-Raziq, an Egyptian Religious Scholar, Argues for the Separation of State and Religion, 1928

In the 1960s the conservative Islamic thinker Sayyid Qutb argued that the only true form of government in a predominantly Islamic society is the khilafat, *or Islamic state that is distinct from a secular constitutional government. Forty years earlier, 'Ali 'Abd al-Raziq (1888–1966), a professor at Al-Azhar University in Cairo, argued the exact opposite. In a short book he contended that Islam does not prescribe a particular form of government because it is a faith and not a political ideology. This argument—which went against the general view of Islam as* deen wa-dunya *(religion and politics)—unleashed a torrent of controversy and led to the removal of 'Abd al-Raziq from his post at the university. Even Islamic modernists like Rashid Rida considered this argument to be incorrect and a threat to Islamic society.*

1

I saw then that there exist obstacles that are not easily overcome by those who are of the opinion that the Prophet, peace be upon him, in addition to the Message [which he carried], was also a political king and a founder of a political state. I saw that every time these people attempted to avoid a trap, they would

---

'Ali 'Abd al-Raziq, *al-Islam wa-usul al-hukm, bahth fi al-Khilafah wa-al-hukumah fi al-Islam* (Bayrut: Dar Maktabat al-Hayah, 1966). This document may also be found in Charles Kurzman, *Liberal Islam* (New York: Oxford University Press, 1998), pp. 29–35. Copyright © 1998 by Oxford University Press, Inc. Used by permission of Oxford University Press, Inc.

fall into the next, and each time they attempted to rid themselves of a problem, the problem would confront them again more intensely than before.

There remains before the reader just one school of thought, and I hope that the reader will find that it offers a convenient starting point. . . . This is that Muhammad, peace be upon him, was a Messenger of a religious call, full of religiosity, untainted by a tendency to kingship or a call for government, and that he did not have a government, nor did he rule, and that he, peace be upon him, did not establish a kingdom, in the political sense of the term or anything synonymous with it. For he was but a messenger like his brethren, the preceding *his equality* *w/ others* messengers. He was not a king nor the founder of a state, nor did he seek to *it's* rule. The above may not be a well-known view, and may in fact be resented by *not* *that he* many Muslims, although it has great vision and is based on strong evidence. *failed*

2

Before we proceed to prove this, we must warn readers about an error that they may fall into unless they observe [the following] accurately and carefully—namely that the Message in itself obliges the Messenger to have some kind of leadership and authority over his people, but this is nothing like the leadership of kings and the authority they have over their subjects. Therefore, one should not confuse the leadership of the Message with that of kings, since they are so different that they could be opposites. Readers have seen that the leadership of Moses and Jesus with regards to their followers was not a kingly leadership, rather it was similar to the leadership of most messengers.

3

The nature of the honest religious call obliges its carrier to have primarily a perfection of the senses, whereby he will lack nothing in his body, sentiments, or feelings, and have nothing that would repulse. And, he must have—because he is a leader—a strong presence to awe those around him, and an attraction that would make him sympathetic enough that men and women would love him. He must also have spiritual perfection, which is necessary for his communication with the other world.

The Message requires its carrier to enjoy considerable social distinction among his people: and as it has been said: "God does not raise a prophet unless he is loved by his people, and unless he commands authority over his clan."[1] The Message also requires its carrier to have the kind of strength which will prepare him to influence the minds of people so that they will in heed his call.

---

[1]As the two Shaykhs [Muslim ibn al-Hajjaj, circa 821–875, and Muhammad ibn Isma'il Bukhari, 810–870] have narrated: "Thus prophets are sent from the best families of their clans . . ." which is part of a long *hadith* [tradition of the Prophet]. See *Taysir al-wusul ila al-jami' al-usul* [*The Facilitation of Arriving at the Compendium of Fundamentals*, by 'Abd al-Rahman Ibn al-Dayba' (1461–1537)], part 3, p. 320.

For God, may He be elevated, does not take the Message lightly and does not raise a messenger of righteousness unless He wants his call to be heeded, and that its teachings be engraved on the tables of the world, eternally preserved and intermixed with the realities of this world: "We have sent no apostle but that he should be obeyed by the will of God." (Qur'an, Sura 4, Verse 64)[2] "Surely messengers have been mocked before you; but what they had mocked rebounded on the mockers themselves. Say: 'Travel in the land and see what happened to those who disbelieved.'" (Sura 6, Verse 10) "But God wished to confirm the truth by His words, and wipe the unbelievers out to the last, so that Truth may be affirmed and falsehood negated, even though the sinners be averse." (Sura 8, Verses 7–8) "Our word had already been given before to Our servants, the apostles, that they would be helped. And that certainly, Our armies will be victorious [over them]." (Sura 37, Verses 171–173) "We will certainly help Our messengers and those who believe, in this world and on the day the witnesses take the stand, the day when their excuses will not benefit the evil-doers, and the condemnation and evil abode will be theirs." (Sura 40, Verses 51–52) The status of the Message grants its carrier a wider authority than that which exists between ruler and ruled, and ever) wider than that of a father over his children.

The Messenger may tackle the politics of his people as a king would, but the Prophet has a unique duty which he shares with no one, namely to communicate with the souls embedded in bodies, and to remove visual obstacles in order to look in upon the hearts embedded in chests. He has the right, nay, he must open up the hearts of his followers in order to reach the sources of love and hate, of good and evil, the passages of thought, the places of obsessions, the origins of intentions, the repository of morality. His is open work in general politics and concealed work in managing the relationship between partners, allies, master and slave, parents and children, and those relationships that only husband and wife are privy to. He has patronage over that which is manifest and that which is latent in life, as well as the management of the affairs of body and soul, and our worldly and heavenly relationships. He directs the politics of worldly living and that of the next world. The Message gives its carrier—as it is seen and beyond the way it is being seen—the right to communicate with each soul, care for it and manage its affairs, as well as the right to unlimited free conduct for every heart.

4

Readers should note that, in addition to the above, the Message of the Prophet, peace be upon him, specialized in a myriad of things that other messengers did not deal with. For he, peace be upon him, came with a call that God chose for

---

[2][Translations of Qur'anic verses are taken, with modifications, from *Al-Qur'an: A Contemporary Translation*, translated by Ahmed Ali, revised definitive edition (Princeton, N.J.: Princeton University Press. 1988).—Editor]

him to rally the people to. And God ordained that he deliver it in its entirety, and that he preside over it in order to complete the call to religion, so that grace be established and conflict not arise, and so that all religion be to God. This Message grants its carrier the kind of extreme perfection that human nature seeks to achieve, the kind of psychological strength that is the end-limit of what God had fated for His chosen messengers, and enough of God's support that would be compatible with this great and general call. In this vein, God has said: "Great have been the blessings of God on you." (Sura 4, Verse 113) "For you are always before Our eyes." (Sura 52, Verse 48). And in the *hadith* [tradition of the Prophet]: "By God, God will never humiliate you."[3] "For—without boasting of it—of all of Adam's children, I am my Lord's favorite."[4]

For this purpose, the authority of the Prophet, peace be upon him, was, because of his Message, a general authority; his orders to Muslims were obeyed; and his government was comprehensive. For nothing that the arm of government can reach is beyond the authority of the Prophet, peace be upon him, and any imaginable kind of leadership or authority is included in the Prophet's, peace be upon him, reign over the believers.

If it is reasoned that it is possible for a messenger's authority over his people to have gradations, then I would say that Muhammad, peace be upon him, should have the right to exercise the highest possible authority of all messengers, peace be upon them, command the highest possible obedience, have the strength of the prophecy, the authority of the Message, and the influence of the honest call, which God had fated to be raised over the call to wrongdoing and to remain on earth. The authority is sent by Heaven, from God, to him whose divine revelation is delivered by Heaven's angels. This sacred power, special to those worshipers of God whom He had raised as messengers, does not hold within it the meaning of kingship, nor does it resemble the power of kings, nor can the [authority of the] sultan of all sultans approximate it. This is the true leadership of the call to God and of the delivery of His Message, not kingly leadership. It is a message and a religion; it is a prophetic government not a government of sultans.

Once again we warn the reader not to confuse the two kinds of governments, and not to conflate the two kinds of trusteeships—the trusteeship of the Messenger, on account of his being a messenger, and the trusteeship of powerful kings. The Messenger's trusteeship over his people is a spiritual trusteeship whose origin is faith from the heart, and the heart's true submission followed by the submission of the body. On the other hand, the trusteeship of the ruler is a material one. It depends on subduing bodies without any connection to the heart. While the former is a trusteeship leading to God, the latter is one for managing life's concerns and populating the earth. While the former is religion,

---

[3]Reported by 'A'isha [wife of the Prophet, circa 614–678] at the beginning of the Revelation. Recorded by the two Shaykhs.

[4]Reported by Anas [ibn Malik, a companion of the Prophet, 710–796], recorded by [Abu 'Isa Muhammad] al-Tirmidhi [collector of *hadith,* died 892].

the latter is the world. The former is divine, the latter is human. The former is a religious leadership, the latter a political one—and there is much distance between politics and religion.

5

Having said this, we would like to draw readers' attention to something else. There exist a number of words [dealing with our subject matter] that are used as synonyms, and others as antonyms. A disagreement or a difference in point of view arises as a result of such usage. In addition, this creates a confusion in judgement. Such words are "king," "sultan," "ruler," "commander" "caliph," "state," "kingdom," "government," "caliphate," and so on. If we were to ask if the Prophet, peace be upon him, was a king or not, we would be asking if he, peace be upon him, had attributes other than being a messenger. Would it be correct to state that he indeed founded, or began to found, a political unity or not? Kingship in our use of it here—and there is no embarrassment faced by the reader who may wish to call him caliph, sultan, commander, or whatever pleases him—means a ruler over a people who have political unity and who have civilization. As for "government," "state," "sultanate," or "kingdom," we mean that which political scientists mean by the English words "kingship," "state," or "government" and the like.

We do not doubt that Islam constitutes religious unity or that Muslims form a unified group: or that the Prophet called for that political unity and had in fact achieved it before his death; and that he, peace be upon him, headed this religious unity as its only prayer leader (*imam*), its strong manager, its master whose orders are never questioned. And that in the interest of this Islamic unity, he, peace be upon him, struggled with all his might, and with the victorious support of God, conquered. He, peace be upon him, received the support of God's angels until he delivered his Message and completed his trusteeship. For he, peace be upon him, had the kind of authority over his people that no king before him or after him ever had. "The Prophet is closer to the faithful than they are themselves." (Sura 33, Verse 6) "No believing men and women have any choice in a matter after God and His Messenger have decided it. Whoever disobeys God and His Messenger has clearly lost the way and gone astray." (Sura 33, Verse 36)

And he who wants to term this religious unity a state and this authority of the Prophet, peace be upon him—which was an absolute authority—a kingship or caliphate, and the Prophet himself, peace be upon him, a king, caliph, or sultan, and so on, he is free to do so. For this is a matter of semantics which should not stop us here. What is important in what we have said is the meaning, and that we have specified to the reader with precision.

The crucial thing is to find out whether the leadership of the Prophet, peace be upon him, over his people was the leadership of the Message, or a kingly leadership. And whether the different aspects of his trusteeship that we observe at times in the biography [of the Prophet], peace be upon him, were aspects of a political state, or of a religious leadership. And whether this unity over which the Prophet, peace be upon him, presided was a unity of a state and a government or a religious unity proper, not a political one. And, finally, whether he, peace be upon him, as only a messenger or a king and a messenger.

6

The Glorious Qur'an supports the view that the Prophet, peace be upon him, had nothing to do with political kingship. Qur'anic verses are in agreement that his heavenly work did not go beyond delivering the Message, which is free of all meanings of authority. "He who obeys the Messenger obeys God; and if some turn away (remember) we have not sent you as a warden over them." (Sura 4, Verse 80) "This (Book) has been called by your people a falsehood, though it is the truth. Say: 'I am not a warden over you. A time is fixed in every prophecy: you will come to know in time.'" (Sura 6, Verse[s] 66–[67]) "So follow what is revealed to you by your Lord, for homage is due to no one but God, and turn away from idolators. Had He willed it, they would not have been idolators. We have not appointed you their guardian, nor are you their pleader." (Sura 6, Verses 106–1 07) "If your Lord had willed it, all the people on the earth would have come to believe, one and all." (Sura 10, Verse 99) "Say: 'O people, the truth has come to you from your Lord, so he who follows the right path does so for himself, and he who goes astray errs against himself, and I am not a guardian over you.'" (Sura 10, Verse 108) "We have not sent you as warden over them." (Sura [17], Verse 54) "Have you considered he take his own lust as his god? Can you act as a trustee for him?" (Sura 25, Verse 43) "We have sent down this Book to you with the truth for all mankind. So, he who comes to guidance does so for himself, and he who goes astray does so for his own loss; on you does not lie their guardianship." (Sura 39, Verse 41) "If they turn away (you are not responsible); we have not appointed you a warden over them. Your duty is to deliver the message." (Sura 42, Verse 48) "We are cognisant of what they say; but it is not for you to compel them. So keep on reminding through the Qur'an whoever fears my warning." (Sura 50, Verse 45) "Remind them: you are surely a reminder. You are not a warden over them, other than him who turns his back and denies, in which case he will be punished by God with the severest punishment." (Sura 88, Verses 21–24)

As the reader can see, the Qur'an clearly prohibits the Prophet, peace be upon him, from serving as a guardian of people, or their trustee, or a subduer . . . or a dominator. Moreover, he did not have the right to force people to become believers. In addition, he who is not a guardian or a dominator is not a king; for the prerequisite to kingship is absolute domination and which constitute an authority without limits. And he who was not a trustee over his people is also not a king. For God has said: "Muhammad is not the father of any of man among you, but messenger of God, and the seal of the prophets. God has knowledge of every thing." (Sura 33, Verse 40)

[. . .]

7

If we were to go beyond God's Book to the *sunna* [practice] of the Prophet, peace be upon him, we would find the matter even clearer, and the argument more insistent:

One of the Prophet's biographers[5] narrates the story of a man who came upon the Prophet, peace be upon him, to take care of a matter. As he stood before him, an intense shiver and fear overtook him. The Prophet, peace be upon him, said: " Be calm, for I am no king nor a subduer, for I am the son of a woman of Quraysh who used to eat dried meat in Mecca." And it has been said in the *hadith* that when the Prophet was given the choice by the angel Israfil of being a king-prophet or a worshipping prophet, the Prophet, peace be upon him, looked up to [the angel] Gabriel, peace be upon him, as his consultant. Gabriel looked down to the ground, indicating humility. And as the story goes, Gabriel indicated for him to be humble. So the Prophet said: "A worshipping prophet." As is evident, this makes it very clear that the Prophet, peace be upon him, was not a king, and did not seek kingship, nor did he, peace be upon him, desire it.

Look between the two covers of the Qur'an for open or latent evidence supporting those who think that the Islamic religion has a political character, and then look for evidence, as hard as you can, among the *hadiths* of the Prophet, peace be upon him—these pure sources of religion which are within your hands, close to you. If you were to look in them for evidence or anything resembling it, you will find no proof, only guesses, and guessing does not replace Truth.

8

Islam is a religious call to God and is a school of thought, from among many such schools, which seeks to reform a certain type of people, guiding them to what will render them closer to God, may He be elevated, and opening up the path to everlasting happiness, which God had prepared for His righteous worshipers. [Islam] is a religious unity that God sought as a bond linking all people, and with which he wanted to surround all the regions of the earth. [. . .]

It is reasonable to say that the world could adopt one religion and that all human beings could be organized into one religious union. However, for the entire world to adopt one government and to be grouped in a shared political union would be foreign to human nature and have nothing to do with God's will. For this is a worldly aim, and God, may He be elevated, has rendered it a matter to be resolved by our minds, and has left people free to manage it in the

---

[5]*The Biography of the Prophet,* by Ahmad bin Zayni Dahlan, who died in the year 1304 of the *hijra* [1923 A.D.]. From the book entitled *Iktifa' al-qanu' bima huwa matbu'* [*The Contentment of the Satisfied with What Is Printed*].

manner that their minds, knowledge, interests, desires, and tendencies would guide them. God's wisdom in this aims at maintaining differences among people. "But if your Lord had pleased, He could have made all human beings into one community (*umma*). But they would still have differed from one another, except those on whom your Lord had mercy." (Sura 11, Verses 118–119) In addition, in order that competition continue among people so that [the] population [of the earth] would be achieved. "If God did not make people deter one another, this earth would indeed be depraved. But gracious is God to the people of the world." (Sura 2, Verse 251) And, so that the Book's purpose be achieved and God's will be done.

This is one of the worldly concerns on which the Prophet, peace be upon him, had denied himself the right to pass judgment or arbitration. For he, peace be upon him, stated that "you are more knowledgeable of your worldly concerns." This is a worldly concern; and the world from beginning to end, and all that it encompasses of concerns and goals, is too trivial for God to have it managed by anything beside the minds He endowed us with, and what He had placed within us of sentiments and desires, and what He had taught us of names and of what things are called; all this is too trivial for God to raise a Messenger to deal with, and it is too trivial for God's Messengers to be concerned with and occupy themselves in managing it.

[. . .]

8. The Program of L'Étoile Nord-Africaine: Full Independence for Algeria, May 28, 1933

L'Étoile Nord-Africaine (North African Star) was an organization established in France in 1924 by the French Communist Party for the purpose of attracting North African migrant factory workers. Although the specific aim of L'Étoile was to uphold the rights of "North African Muslims," this goal was couched within the rubric of universal Marxism. L'Étoile quickly became a mass party with over 100,000 members. Within about ten years of its establishment, the majority of the members were Algerian, and its goal shifted to attaining Algerian independence from France. Accordingly the party's platform and aims were tailored to fit that redefined goal, and the party abandoned the Marxist label—while holding on to some Marxist ideas of social and economic justice—in favor of a more "authentic" Islamic nationalist approach. This change occurred under the leadership of Messali Hadj, one of Algeria's foremost preindependence politicians. L'Étoile was banned several times in France and in Algeria, and party leaders alternated between exile and hiding, on the one hand, and public activism, on the other.

Translated from the French text in *L'Afrique Française* (1934), vol. 44, pp. 575–576. This document may also be found in J. C. Hurewitz, *The Middle East and North Africa in World Politics* (New Haven, Conn.: Yale University Press, 1975), pp. 441, 443–444. Reprinted by permission of the author.

This document consists of the party program announced in 1933; it is a manifesto making known the party's new political aims. To understand its ideology, pay particular attention to the language and to what is not said, as well as to what is said.

Our Program

The political program of our Etoile Nord-Africaine, maturely studied and profoundly analysed by the former provisional Executive Committee, was presented, read and approved by all the members the Association summoned in National Assembly at 4 o'clock on 28 May 1933 to 49 rue de Bretagne, Paris (3e).

The content of these articles is simple, very comprehensible, and above all wholly responsive to the aspirations of the Algerian people.

It is expressly recommended that the Algerian people read it attentively, understand it, and apply it. We should consider it as a National Pact, knitting together the whole of the Muslim Algerian population, working with devotion and sacrifice for the defense of our interests, our immediate claims, and the independence of our country.

For our salvation, for our future, for occupying a place in the world worthy of our race, let us all swear on the Quran and by Islam to work without interruption for its realization and final triumph.

This political program for Algeria is almost the same as that of Morocco and Tunisia, obviously taking into account the general position of these two countries and their political constitutions.

Political Program Adopted by the General Assembly of 28 May 1933

1. The immediate abolition of the odious *Code de l'indigénat* [stipulating the rights of natives] and all discriminatory measures;

2. Amnesty for all those imprisoned under special surveillance or exiled for an infraction of the Indigénat or a political offense;

3. Absolute freedom to travel in France and abroad;

4. Freedom of the press, association, assembly, and political and syndical rights;

5. Replacement of the Financial Delegations elected with restricted suffrage by a national Algerian parliament elected with universal suffrage;

6. Abolition of mixed communes and military territories and replacement of these institutions by municipal assemblies elected with universal suffrage;

7. Access of all Algerians to the civil service without discrimination. Equal employment [and] equal salary for all;

8. Compulsory instruction in the Arabic language. Opportunity for education at every level. Creation of new Arab schools. Simultaneous publication of all official acts in the Arabic and French languages;

9. With regard to military service, unquestioned respect for the verse of the Quranic surah that says "He who deliberately kills a Muslim is condemned to misery for eternity and deserves divine anger and damnation";

10. The application of the social and work laws. The right to unemployment aid and family allowances for Algerian families in Algeria. Immediate abolition of the Social Insurance [program];

11. Enlargement of agricultural credit to the small fallahin. More rational organization of irrigation. Development of the means of communication. Nonrefundable aid from the government for victims of periodic famines.

Second Part

1. Full independence for Algeria;
2. Full withdrawal of occupation forces;
3. Establishment of a national army.

National Revolutionary Government

1. A Constituent Assembly elected with universal suffrage;
2. Universal suffrage at every level and eligibility for all inhabitants of Algeria in every assembly;
3. The Arabic language considered as the official language;
4. The return to the Algerian state of ownership of banks, mines, railroads, ports, and public services that were taken over by the conquerors;
5. The confiscation of large estates taken over by the feudal allies of the conquerors, the colons, and the financial societies, and the return of confiscated land to the peasants. Respect for medium and small properties. The return to the Algerian state of lands and forests monopolized by the French state;
6. Compulsory free education at all levels in the Arabic language;
7. Recognition by the Algerian state of the right to form syndicates [and] coalitions, [the right] to strike, and its [obligation to] frame social laws;
8. Immediate aid to fallahin in the form or non-interest agricultural loans, for the purchase of machinery, seed, and fodder, the organization of irrigation, and the improvement of the means of communication, etc.

North African Musulmans

The paper *El-Ouma* is your paper. It defends you, instructs you, educates you, unmasks all the traitors, all the betrayers, all the enemies of our fatherland, of our cause; it will lead you on the right path without fear or failure.

By its news, it will put you in touch with the entire Islamic world. Make it live, help it, protect it, make it read, advertise it everywhere in order that it may become the flag and the rallying point for all the vibrant strength of the North African Musulmans.

9. Antun Sa'adeh Declares His Vision of "Greater Syria" or Regional Nationalism, June 1, 1935

Antun Sa'adeh (1904–1949) was born in Lebanon to a Christian family. In 1921 he left Lebanon with his siblings to join his father in Brazil. During his stay in Brazil (about nine years), he became involved with politics within the Lebanese emigrant community and published many articles in the emigrant press. He established the Free Syrians Party, which agitated against French occupation of Syria and Lebanon, and he called on the pope, the League of Nations, and the press in South America to support an independent Syria. After returning to Lebanon, he taught German at the American University in Beirut and lectured about his concept of "Greater Syria."

According to Sa'adeh, Syria—which he defined geographically as Palestine, Lebanon, Syria, and parts of Iraq—always had been a national entity with a distinct culture and civilization, separate from the Arab world. His interpretation of the history of this area—a viewpoint actively rejected by many contemporaneous intellectuals and nationalists—led him to argue that "Greater Syria" transcended Arab, Islamic, and Christian history and was the product of unique geographical features that determined its "eternal national" character.

To implement his idea of a "greater Syria," Sa'adeh established the Syrian Social Nationalist Party (SSNP) in 1934, with himself at its head as al-Za'im (leader). His ideas about nationalism were influenced by the fascist tendencies then emerging in Europe. He was executed in 1949, along with six members of the SSNP, by the Lebanese government because of an attempted coup d'état. In the speech included here, Sa'adeh announces the establishment of the SSNP, its ideology, and its goals.

Ever since the hour in which our social national ideology began to bring together thoughts and feelings, to unite the forces of youth threatened with dispersion by the political and national chaos that blanket our country, and to transform this union into a new system (*nizam*) with new methods, deriving its life from the new nationalism, namely the system of the Syrian Social Nationalist Party—ever since that hour, dawn has followed darkness and movement has come out of lethargy and the force of organization has burst out of confusion. We have become a nation after having been mere human herd, and a state resting on four fundamental pillars—freedom, duty, organization, power—which are symbolized by the four pointers on the flag of the Syrian Social Nationalist Party.

Ever since that hour we have repudiated by our actions the judgment of history and begun our true history—the history of freedom, duty, organization, and power, the history of the Syrian Social Nationalist Party, the true history of the Syrian nation.

Ever since the hour in which we united our hearts and our hands to stand or fall together for the sake of the realization of the highest ideal proclaimed in the principles of the Syrian Social Nationalist Party and in its aim—ever since

Antun Sa'adeh, "Speech of June 1, 1935 of the Leader of the Syrian Social Nationalist Party." http://www.ssnp.com (12 February 2003).

that hour we have put our hands on the plow and directed our eyes forward toward the ideal. We have become one community, one living nation seeking the beautiful free life, a nation loving life because it loves liberty and loving death when death is a path to life.

Before the Syrian Social Nationalist Party was constituted, the Syrians were not a nation in the true sense of the word. All that existed was a certain dissatisfaction with an unnatural situation which the Syrian people could not accept and in which they could not find satisfaction for their vital needs. Some people took up the leadership of this popular dissatisfaction and exploited it in order to obtain the positions they sought, and they bolstered up this leadership by the remains of family power derived from the principles of a bygone age—principles which consider the people as herds to be disposed of by certain families, dissipating the interests of the people for the sake of their personal power. And when these so-called leaders found that the family and the home were not sufficient in this age to uphold leadership, they resorted to certain words beloved by the people—the words of liberty, independence, and principles—and they played upon these words, words which are sacred when they indicate an ideal for a living nation, but which are corrupt when they fire a means for assuming leadership and a screen behind which lurk ambition and private aims.

The word "principles" should be noted in particular, for it should represent the living power and the basic needs of the nation. . . .

Thus it came to pass that in this age, which is the age of the struggle of nations for survival, and in this difficult time when the factors of corruption and division and national nullification are rampant amidst our people, the Syrian Social Nationalist Party rose, as dawn rises from the darkest hours of the night, to proclaim a new principle. This is the principle of will—the will of a people that wants sovereignty over itself and over its country (*watan*) in order to realize its lofty ideal; the will of life for a truly enduring nation. . . .

The Syrian Social Nationalist Party therefore is not a mere society or group, as may still appear to some members whom time has not yet permitted to understand the fundamental principle which the Syrian Social Nationalist Party embodies, or the need of the Syrian nation in this age. The Syrian Social Nationalist Party is indeed much more than a society which brings together a number of members, or a club which was established for a particular set of people or youth. The Party is an idea and a movement which embraces the life of a nation in its entirety. It is the renovation of a nation which some imagine to have collapsed forever because the various factors which have conspired against its national spirit have been so great that an ordinary nation could have hardly borne their impact and still preserve its existence or the hope of surviving. It is the rise of an extraordinary nation—a nation unique in its capacities, surpassing in its powers, rich in its characteristics—a nation which does not accept the grave as its place in the sun. . . .

From now on, our will guides the rudder. Every member of the Syrian Social Nationalist Party feels that he is being liberated from foreign hegemony and from external dominating factors because he feels that the Party is like his own independent state, which does not derive its power from a mandate or rely upon external authority. The truth, fellow comrades, is that we have bound ourselves together in this Party for the sake of a very important task, which is the establishment of our state, so that every one of us will become a subject of his independent state. This task is no doubt difficult. Will we be capable of it? The answer to this question stirs in our souls and resounds in our breasts, and may issue from our mouths. To inscribe it on the pages of history will depend upon our struggle, for history does not record hopes or intentions, but actions and facts. And I do not doubt, with these faces displaying the manifestations of power and resolution before me, that our actions and our facts confirm the judgment of our will, which does not know incapacity.

Within the Party, we have liberated ourselves from foreign authority and from external factors, but we still have to deliver our nation and liberate our whole country. In this important work we shall meet many difficulties, internal and external, which we must overcome, beginning with the first, namely, the internal, because we cannot overcome the external difficulties completely except after having conquered the internal ones. The first internal difficulty which confronts us is the lack in our community of deep national traditions to be reared on and to hold to. Our personal selves are always in conflict with our general self in all that has to do with our national causes and the way we meet them. Add to this the conflicting traditions derived from our sectarian organizations, and the effect of these traditions in resisting the national unity of the people.

I must declare here that the Syrian Social Nationalist Party has found a means of overcoming these difficulties by its system (*nizam*) which breaks down both the traditions that oppose the unity of the nation and individual psychologies which opposes the psychological individuality of the nation. Our final success depends, in fact, upon our understanding of this truth and upon the application of the four pillars of the Party which bind us indissolubly, namely freedom, duty, organization, and power. . . .

Likewise, I have on this occasion to declare that the system (*nizam*) of the Syrian Social Nationalist Party is not a Hitlerite or a Fascist system, but that it is purely a Syrian system which does not stand on unprofitable imitation, but on basic originality which is one of the characteristics of our people. It is the system which is indispensable for the molding of our national life, and for the preservation of this remarkable renaissance (*nahda*) which will change the face of history in the Near East and liberate it from the influence of the reactionary forces which cannot be trusted and which may constitute a serious danger, threatening every renovating movement with corruption under the auspices of the traditional parliamentary system that is powerless to reform itself.

Embodied in the principles of the Syrian Social Nationalist Party is the way of liberating our thoughts from decadent beliefs and fancies which have prevented us from seeking what we ought to seek. Such is the fancy, cultivated by a group of spiritually weak and mentally sterile people, that we are a weak nation incapable of doing anything and with no hope of achieving a purpose or a desire and that the best that we can do is to recognize our incapacity and let our national self disappear from among the nations and be content with any state which we attain. The members of the Syrian Social Nationalist Party have liberated themselves from such false fancies and have taken upon themselves to liberate the rest of the nation from them. This is a responsibility incumbent upon every member of the Syrian Social Nationalist Party, a responsibility which is greater than all other responsibilities, a responsibility in comparison with which every other responsibility is small indeed. As the sense of this responsibility develops and grows, there grows with it the living force of every member of our group.

The rising Syria [which] is built on the new national forces represented by the Syrian National Party will be different from the old Syria laid down by tradition, given over to the fancies of those who have lost their national spirit and their self-confidence. The Syria of the Syrian Social Nationalist Party is the Syria of national unity organized in such a way as to make the abilities stored up in it a general force capable of achieving what it wants. We have full faith that the spirit created by our principles will achieve a final victory and overcome all the internal difficulties. If this needs time, it is because time is a necessary condition for every important achievement.

As for the external difficulties, these become small once we overcome the internal ones and once the will of our nation is crystallized in our system (*nizam*) which guarantees its unity and prevents the divisive forces prevalent outside the Party from infiltrating into our solid unity for which we are ready to sacrifice everything. At this juncture, I do not wish to deal with our external problem as a whole. This I shall do on another occasion which I hope will be soon. Now, I shall merely mention a general principle which applies to the whole of our history, namely, that the destiny of Syria has been decided by external bargaining without the actual participation of the Syrian nation itself. It is on this principle that the big powers rely on in their rivalry to spread their influence upon us. I wish to declare now that the establishment of the Syrian Social Nationalist Party and its continuous growth will take it upon themselves from now on to dispel such fancies from the heads of ambitious politicians.

We feel now the existence of a strong Italian propaganda in this country in particular, and in the Near East in general. We feel a similar propaganda from Germany and similar ones from other countries. The Leadership of the Syrian Social Nationalist Party warns all its members against failing prey to foreign propaganda. We recognize that there are considerations which call for the establishment of friendly relations between Syria and foreign nations, in particular the European states, but we do not believe in the principle of propaganda. Syrian thought must remain free and independent. When it comes to foreign relations, we are always ready to clasp the hands that are extended to us with a frank, good intention and in a situation of common understanding and agreement.

The foreign states which desire to establish solid, free relations with us should recognize in the first place our right to live and should be ready to respect this right. Otherwise, the new Syria will not remain silent in the face of political maneuvers intended to lead our nation to make the political mistakes which were committed in the past and which have done her so much harm.

The task of preserving our national revival is among the most important tasks of the Syrian Social Nationalist Party and we shall not fail to undertake it in the best possible way. Foreign propaganda may spread in the chaos of parties, but when it reaches the Syrian Social Nationalist Party i[t] finds a solid barrier through which it cannot pass because the Syrian Social Nationalists form a Party which is not built on anarchy and because they follow only the policy decided upon by their party. They are not a disordered group but an organized force.

I repeat once more this organized force will change the face of history in the Near East. Our forefathers witnessed the conquerors of the past and trod on their remains. But we, we shall put an end to conquests.

Amidst the confusion of irresponsible talk and shouting spread all over this nation, the Syrian Social Nationalists undertake their work with calmness and confidence; and the spirit of the Syrian Social Nationalist Party is growing in the body of the nation and it is organizing its groups. The day shall come, and that day is near, when the world will see a new sight and an event: the sight of men clad in black sashes on gray suit[s], with sharpened spears shining above their heads; men walking behind the banners of the Red Tempest carried by giants of the army. The forests of spears will advance in well-organized ranks and the Syrian nation shall have a will which cannot be checked. For this is destiny.

10.   Taha Husayn Writes of Egypt as a Mixture of Pharaonic, Arab, and Western Cultures, 1938

In seeking to create nations, Arab intellectuals engaged in a process of imagining historical unity within their respective geographical areas. This exercise entailed the construction of a national identity that was as much cultural as it was political. For some this culture was "purely" Arab; for some it was grounded in a particular religion. A few others looked toward European cultures in their search for a coherent cultural model. A number of intellectuals did not see culture as "pure" in any real sense but believed that it consisted of cross-currents of various subcultures and ideas. Among this last group was the Egyptian write Taha Husayn (1889–1973).

Born into modest circumstances and blinded by illness at the age of two, in 1902 Taha Husayn enrolled in Al-Azhar University, the leading orthodox center for Islamic learning. Feeling stifled by the conservative intellectual atmosphere that predominated there, in 1908 he transferred to the newly established and secular Cairo University. After finishing his doctoral work, he traveled to France and studied

Taha Husayn, *The Future of Culture in Egypt*, trans. Sidney Glazer, American Council of Learned Societies, Near Eastern Translation Program, no. 9 (New York: Octagon Books, Farrar, Straus and Giroux, 1975), pp. 1–4, 7, 15, 21–22. Reprinted by permission of Hippocrene Books, Inc.

at the Sorbonne. From these experiences he forged a very independent and analytical mind. His intellectual work embroiled him in several controversies about religion and its role in society and politics. One of his most impressive works is Mustaqbal al-thaqafah fi Misr *(The Future of Culture in Egypt), from which the following selection is excerpted.*

1

The subject to be treated in this discourse is the future of culture in Egypt, now that our country has regained her freedom through the revival of the constitution and her honor through the realization of independence. We are living in an age characterized by the fact that freedom and independence do not constitute ends in themselves, but are merely means of attaining exalted, enduring, and generally practical goals.
[. . .]
Like every patriotic educated Egyptian who is zealous for his country's good reputation, I want our new life to harmonize with our ancient glory and our new energy to justify both the opinion we entertained of ourselves while we were seeking independence and the opinion held by civilized nations when they recognized our independence and cordially welcomed us to Geneva.
[. . .]

2

I do not like illusions. I am persuaded that it is only God who can create something from nothing. I therefore believe that the new Egypt will not come into being except from the ancient, eternal Egypt. I believe further that the new Egypt will have to be built on the great old one, and that the future of culture in Egypt will be an extension, a superior version, of the humble, exhausted, and feeble present. For this reason we should think of the future of culture in Egypt in the light of its remote past and near present. We do not wish, nor are we able, to break the link between ourselves and our forefathers. To the degree that we establish our future life upon our past and present we shall avoid most of the dangers caused by excesses and miscalculations deriving from illusions and dreams.

At the outset we must answer this fundamental question: Is Egypt of the East or of the West? Naturally, I mean East or West in the cultural, not the geographical sense. It seems to me that there are two distinctly different and bitterly antagonistic cultures on the earth. Both have existed since time immemorial, the one in Europe, the other in the Far East.

We may paraphrase the question as follows: Is the Egyptian mind Eastern or Western in its imagination, perception, comprehension, and judgment? More succinctly put—which is easier for the Egyptian mind: to understand a Chinese or Japanese, or to understand an Englishman or a Frenchman? This is the question that we must answer before we begin to think of the foundations on which we shall have to base our culture and education. It seems to me that the simplest way to do this is by tracing the complicated development of the Egyptian mind from earliest times to the present.

The first thing to note is that, so far as is known, we had no regular, sustained contacts with the Far East that could have affected our thinking and political or economic institutions. The available archaeological remains and documents reveal little more than that Egyptians at the end of the Pharaonic period evinced some desire to explore the Red Sea coasts, which they left only with great caution, chiefly for the sake of goods from India and South Arabia. Their attempts were tentative, unorganized, and ephemeral.

The contacts between ancient Egypt and the lands of the East scarcely went beyond Palestine, Syria, and Mesopotamia, that is, the East that falls in the Mediterranean basin, but there is no doubt that they were strong and continuous and that they exerted an influence on the intellectual, political, and economic life of all the countries involved. Our mythology relates that Egyptian gods crossed the Egyptian frontiers in order to civilize the people in these regions. Historians tell us that the kings of Egypt at times extended their sway over them. Ancient Egypt was a major power politically and economically not only in comparison with her neighbors, but with the countries that cradled the European civilization with which we are examining our kingship.

It would be a waste of time and effort to set forth in detail the ties binding Egypt to the ancient Greco-Aegean civilization. School children know that Greek colonies were established in Egypt by the Pharaohs before the first millennium B.C. They also know that an Eastern nation, Persia, successfully invaded our country at the end of the sixth century B.C. But we resisted fiercely until the Alexandrian era, having recourse at one time to Greek volunteers, and at another time allying ourselves with the Greek cities.

The meaning of all this is very clear: the Egyptian mind had no serious contact with the Far Eastern mind; nor did it live harmoniously with the Persian mind. The Egyptian mind has had regular, peaceful, and mutually beneficial relations only with the Near East and Greece. In short, it has been influenced from earliest times by the Mediterranean Sea and the various peoples living around it.

[. . .]

5

Islam arose and spread over the world. Egypt was receptive and hastened at top speed to adopt it as her religion and to make the Arabic of Islam her language. Did that obliterate her original mentality? Did that make her an Eastern nation in the present meaning of the term? Not at all! Europe did not become Eastern nor did the nature of the European mind change because Christianity, which originated in the East, flooded Europe and absorbed the other religions. If modern European philosophers and thinkers deem Christianity to be an element of the European mind, they must explain what distinguishes Christianity from Islam; for both were born in the geographical East, both issued from one noble source and were inspired by the one God in whom Easterners and Westerners alike believe.

[. . .]

9

In order to become equal partners in civilization with the Europeans, we must literally and forthrightly do everything that they do; we must share with them the present civilization, with all its pleasant and unpleasant sides, and not content ourselves with words or mere gestures. Whoever advises any other course of action is either a deceiver or is himself deceived. Strangely enough we imitate the West in our everyday lives, yet hypocritically deny the fact in our words. If we really detest European life, what is to hinder us from rejecting it completely? And if we genuinely respect the Europeans, as we certainly seem to do by our wholesale adoption of their practices, why do we not reconcile our words with our actions? Hypocrisy ill becomes those who are proud and anxious to overcome their defects.

[. . .]

12

Other objectors to Western civilization use two lines of argument, one dangerous, the other ridiculous. Sometimes they assert that it is ultra-materialistic and a source of misery both to Europe and to the rest of the world. At other times they insist that Europe is tired of her own civilization, as evidenced by the number of writers, scholars, and philosophers who are turning away from it and seeking nourishment in the spirituality of the East. Why then, they ask, should we abandon the good that the Europeans themselves desire for the evil that they are rejecting?

Certainly, there is a good deal of materialism in European civilization, but it is absurd to deny that it possesses spiritual content. The brilliant successes of modern science and the inventions that have changed the face of the earth spring from imaginative and creative minds. European history is replete with men like Descartes and Pasteur, who cheerfully devoted their time and effort to ideas alone. Besides scientists and scholars, there are such men as airplane test-pilots who expose themselves to horrible injury and even death in order to extend man's mastery over nature

Yes, we know of writers, poets, and philosophers who are tired of European civilization; yet they will sacrifice their lives for it. Some of them look toward the East, or appear to do so, but you can be sure that they would flatly refuse to live like Easterners. Dissatisfaction with modern life is a characteristic of men who are alive and progressing. Submissive contentment is a characteristic of lazy, decadent people. When Europeans tell us that their civilization is materialistic and hateful, they are either truthful—in which case we know that they seek its improvement—or lying, their purpose being to induce us to shun this civilization so that they may retain all its benefits for themselves, while we remain stationary, clinging to our spiritual civilization which makes us their slaves.

Moreover, what is this spiritual East? It is assuredly not our Near East which, as previously noted, is the cradle of the mind that I have been lauding. This area was also the source of divine religions adopted both by Europeans and Easterners—Christians, Jews, and Muslims alike. Can these religions be spirit in the East and matter in the West?

No, the spiritual East by which some Europeans are fascinated is clearly not the Near East but the Far East. It is the East of India, China, and Japan with religions and philosophies that scarcely resemble our own. In all seriousness, do we want to embrace the religion, philosophy, and motive-forces of the Chinese just when they are rapidly Westernizing themselves? Years ago, for example, China applied to the League of Nations for experts to organize its educational system on the European pattern. The country, as is well known, is being pulled in two directions, one toward the democratic Western League, the other toward Russia and communism.

This talk of a spiritual East is sheer nonsense. Egyptians who deride European civilization and praise the spirituality of the East are joking, and they realize it. They would be the last to choose to live like the Chinese or Hindus. Nevertheless, their arguments are dangerous and demoralizing, particularly to the youth, who are thereby led away from the European civilization which they know toward the Eastern civilization they do not know. Stories about the East and West are told only by those with a superficial understanding of both. The younger generation must be protected from such false knowledge, and the best, if not only, method is to provide them with a sound education.
[. . .]

11. Syrian Michel 'Aflaq Addresses the Relationship Between Arabism and Islam, 1943

Michel 'Aflaq (b. 1912) was a Christian and a member of the emerging urban middle class in Damascus, Syria. He received a "modern" education in secular schools and colleges in Syria and continued his university education in Europe. His experience with French colonialism, the corruption and inefficacy of many of the traditional political elites, and his exposure to socialism in Paris, where he attended university during the early 1930s, prompted him to articulate a new political vision for Syria and for the Arab world as a whole.

Michel 'Aflaq, *Choice of Texts from the Ba'th Party's Founder's Thought* (Florence: Cooperativa Lavoratori, 1977), pp. 71–83. Translated by Akram Khater.

'Aflaq and fellow student Salah al-Bitar argued for nationalist independence from colonialism, for a united and singular Arab nation, and for justice and equality among all social classes. After they returned to Syria, both men began to attract a following among students at the high school where they taught. After Syria's independence in 1946, 'Aflaq formed a political party, known as Ba'ath (Renaissance), based on the aforementioned principles and dedicated to the resurgence of Arab civilization. In the speech quoted here, he addresses the complex relationship between Arabism and Islam, seeking to harmonize seemingly opposing ideas. Despite his Christian background—and in opposition to many other Christians who were if not antagonistic then at least suspicious of a state dominated by Islam—'Aflaq believed that Arabism and Islam could not be separated, but at the same time he maintained that Arabism as an ideology preceded and was superordinate to Islam and thus should be the basis for the modern Arab nation.

[. . .] Today, we are facing the contradiction between our glorious past and the shameful present. The Arab personality used to be a complete whole, with no difference between its soul and mind, between its words and actions, between its private and public morals, and Arab life was complete. [. . .] But today we know only the schizophrenic psyche, and we know only a partial and impoverished life; if the mind enters it then the spirit leaves it, and if emotion exists in it then reason departs from it. [. . .] It [current Arab life] is always deprived of some fundamental power, and it is time for us to remove this contradiction so that we can regain the unity of the Arab character. [. . .]

Our relationship to our heroic ancestors is nothing more than a formality, and the connection between our modern history and our glorious past is not organic but parasitic. Today we must revive within us the traits and perform the tasks that [. . .] make our relationship a legitimate reality. We must remove whatever we can of the stumbling blocks of inertia and decadence until the original glorious blood flows in us once again. [. . .]

Islam Is a Permanent Experience and Readiness

Sirs: The Islamic movement embodied in the life of the Prophet is not simply a historical event for Arabs that can be explained in time and place and through reasons and results. Rather, and because of its depth, power, and reach, it is directly linked with the absolute life of Arabs. In other words, it is a truthful image and an eternal symbol of the nature of the Arab spirit and its rich potential and original direction. [. . .] Islam is the vital jolt that moves the internal forces of the Arab nation [. . .] removing out of its path the dams of tradition and the shackles of norms. Thus, it reestablishes the connection of that nation with the deeper meanings of the universe [. . .] and it begins to express its excitement and wonder with new words and glorious works, and it cannot remain bounded within and so it overflows with thought and action onto other nations. [. . .]

This experience [early Islamic history] is not a historical event that is to be mentioned simply out of pride and to tell a story; it is a constant readiness within the Arab nation—if Islam is correctly understood—to rise every time matter controls the soul and appearances overcome substance. It divides within in order to achieve higher unity and proper harmony, and it is an experience meant to strengthen its morals every time they softened. [. . .] Within this experience is repeated the heroic epic story of Islam with all of its chapters of preaching, persecution, emigration, war, victory, and failure, until the final victory of Truth and Faith [this is the sequence of events of the life of Prophet Muhammad].

The life of the Prophet—which embodies the Arab spirit in its absolute truth—cannot be known in the mind but through living and experiencing it. Therefore, this knowledge cannot be a beginning but a result. The Arabs, ever since they lost their vitality—that is, hundreds of years ago—have been reading the story of the life [of the Prophet] [. . .] without understanding it, because to comprehend its meaning requires an extreme level of passion and of depth and honesty of feeling that they do not yet have. [. . .]

The spirits of our heroes have left and deserted us a long time, because heroism is no longer an Arab trait. One fears that this blind aggrandizement of the Prophet is an expression of inability and impotence more than it is an appreciation of greatness. Our era is so far from heroism that we have come to regard it [heroism] with fear and wonder, as if it is from a world different from ours. In reality, the true appreciation of heroism can emanate only from sharing and [. . .] experiencing it. No one who has not achieved at least a meager level of heroism in life can truly appreciate the Hero.

Until now we have looked upon the life of the Prophet from the outside, as a wonderful picture made for us to appreciate and to sanctify. We must begin to look at it from the inside, to live it. Every Arab at the present time can live the life of the Arab Prophet, even if with the ratio of a pebble to a mountain, or a drop of water to the sea. It is natural that any man—no matter how great—will not be able to accomplish what Muhammad did. But it is also natural that any man—no matter how limited his ability—can be a miniature version of Muhammad, as long as he belongs to the nation that gathered its forces to produce Muhammad or, more to the point, as long as this man is a member of the nation that Muhammad gathered all of his forces to produce. [. . .]

Islam Is the Renewal and Completion of Arabism

An Arab man received a heavenly message, so he began to call people to it. The only people around him were Arabs, and few heeded his call. But many fought against it, so he emigrated with the Believers. The polytheists fought him until Truth vanquished and all believed in him. The epic of Islam cannot be separated from its natural stage, which is the land of the Arabs, and from its heroes, and they are all Arabs. The idolaters of the Quraish [a powerful tribe in Mecca that opposed the Prophet] were as necessary for Islam as the Believers, and those who fought the Prophet contributed to the victory of Islam as much as those who aided and supported him. God is capable of revealing the Qur'an to his

Prophet in one day, but that required more than twenty years. He is capable of making his religion victorious and to lead all of humanity to it in one day, but that did not happen in less than twenty years. He is capable of revealing Islam centuries before it appeared and to any nation of his creation, but he revealed it at a particular time and he chose for that the Arab nation and its Arab Prophet-Hero. The glaring truth, then, is that the choice of the Arabs to deliver the message of Islam was because of their fundamental character and virtues. The choice of the epoch in which Islam was revealed was because the Arabs had matured enough to accept this message and to carry it to the world. Postponing the victory of Islam for those many years was meant to allow Arabs to arrive at the truth by themselves and through their personal experiences within the world, and after trials and pains, despair and hope, failure and victory. In other words, faith had to emanate from within the depths of their souls so that it would be the True Faith mixed with experience and connected to the essence of life. Islam, then, was an Arab movement and its meaning was the renewal and completion of Arabism. The language of Islam was Arabic, the Islamic perspective was that of the Arab mind, the virtues that Islam advocated were apparent or inherent Arab virtues, and the vices that it struggled against were Arab vices on their way to extinction. The Muslim at that time [seventh century A.D.] was none other than the Arab, but the new, complete, and advanced Arab. [. . .]

The Humanity of Islam

Does this mean that Islam was founded only for Arabs? If we say that, then we depart from the truth and go against reality. For every great nation that has deep connections with the eternal truths strives toward universal eternal values. Islam [. . .] is in its reality Arab and in its ideal humanistic.

Arabs are unique among all other nations in the following characteristic: their national awakening was intimately connected to a religious message, or put another way, this message revealed the national awakening. Arabs did not expand for the sake of expansion, and they did not conquer lands simply for economic reasons or racial motivation or from a desire to control and enslave. Rather, they did so to fulfill a religious duty full of truth, guidance, compassion, justice, and charity. They spilled their own blood for its cause. [. . .] Since the connection between Arabism and Islam is intimate, and since we see in Arabism a body whose spirit is Islam, then there is no fear that the Arabs will be extremists in their nationalism. It will not become the fanaticism of colonialism and imperialism. [. . .]

It is only natural that Arabs will not be able to perform this duty unless they are a rising strong nation, because Islam can be embodied only in the Arab nation and its virtues, morals, and talents. The first duty that the humanity of Islam demands is that Arabs should be strong and sovereign.
[. . .]

Arabs and the West

A century and a half ago the West and Arabs encountered each once again through Bonaparte's campaign in Egypt. That genius symbolized this contact by hanging placards on which were written Qur'anic verses next to the Rights of Man. Since that time Arabs (or their foreign leaders) have pushed their modern renaissance in that dubious direction. They stretch themselves, the texts of their history, and the Qur'an beyond the breaking point in order to demonstrate that the principles of their civilization and ideology are not different from the principles of Western civilization, and that they preceded Westerners in announcing and applying these principles. This can only mean one thing: They stand as the defendant vis-à-vis the West, admitting the validity of Western values and their superiority. The fact is that the Western invasion of the Arab mind—coming as it did at a time when that mind had dried up to such an extent that it was an empty mold—allowed that civilization to fill this mold with its ideas and meanings. [. . .] We do not disagree with Europeans about the principle of liberty, but we disagree with their understanding of the meaning of liberty.

Europe, today as in the past, is afraid of Islam. But it knows now that the power of Islam (which in the past expressed the power of the Arabs) is reborn in a new guise, which is Arab nationalism. Therefore it has directed all of its weapons against this new power, while we see it [Europe] befriending and supporting the traditional form of Islam. Illiterate Islam, which is limited to superficial worship and banal and meaningless symbols, is becoming Europeanized, today in thought and tomorrow in thought and name as well. The day will come when the nationalists will find themselves to be the only defenders of Islam. [. . .]

The Honor of Arabism

Among the European concepts that have invaded the modern Arab mind are two ideas about nationalism and humanism that entail great error and danger. The idea of absolute nationalism in the West is logical in its attempt to separate nationalism from religion because religion entered Europe from the outside— it is foreign to its nature and history. [. . .] Islam is not a foreign ideology for the Arabs, nor is it a moral abstraction; it reveals more than anything else their existential feelings and their outlook on life, and it is the strongest expression of the unity of their personality, in which language merges with feeling and thought, and reflection with work. [. . .] Our nationalism is a living complex organism, and any separation of its parts can threaten it with death. [. . .] Arab Christians will know, when their nationalism is fully awakened and they reclaim their authentic heritage, that for them Islam is a national culture in which they must immerse themselves until they understand and love it. [. . .] If reality is still far from this wish, then the new generation of Arab Christians must undertake the task of accomplishing this with courage [. . .] sacrificing their pride and private interests, since nothing is equal to Arabism and the honor of belonging to it.

Abstract Humanism

The second danger is that of the European idea of abstract humanism, which considers all of humanity to be similar without any roots in the land and not subject to time, whereby the reforms and changes that derive out of the needs of one people can be applied to another.

[. . .] Some believe today that simply applying some reforms to the conditions of the Arabs is sufficient to rejuvenate the nation. We find in this a sign of decadence because it is a reversal of perspective when the [. . .] result takes the place of the reason. The fact is that reforms must derive from specific roots, as flowers emerge from a tree. This root is spiritual before anything else: it is the belief of the nation in its message. [. . .]

The New Arab Generation

Sirs: Today we celebrate the memory of the Hero of Arabism and Islam. Islam is nothing more than the outcome of agonies, the pains of Arabism, and these agonies have come back to the land of the Arabs with a vengeance that the Arabs of pre-Islamic times did not know. May it bring forth in us today a cleansing and reforming revolution such as the one whose banner was carried by Islam. [. . .]

We, the new Arab generation, are carrying a message, not policy, belief, and ideology, not theories and discourses. We are not afraid of the local nationalist factions that are supported by foreign weapons, driven by racial hatred against Arabs, because God, nature, and history are with us. They do not understand us because they are strangers to us, strangers to truth and heroism; they are fake, artificial, and contemptible. The only people who understand us are those who have experienced and understood Muhammad's life from within, as an ethical experiment and historical event. [. . .]

12. Hasan al-Banna Proclaims Egyptian Nationalism and the Religious Basis for an Islamic State, 1949

Hasan al-Banna (1906–1949) grew up in an Egypt that was in many ways a British colony. He came of age at a time when it appeared that the European "West" was directly or indirectly dominating Muslim societies. This hegemony was accompanied by attacks on Islam from colonial quarters, as well as from indigenous and secular groups and individuals. In 1928, amid the political chaos and cultural confusion in Egypt— and in the larger Islamic world—al-Banna established the Muslim Brotherhood.

This political party was dedicated to restoring Egyptian independence from the British and—perhaps more important—to the social and political regeneration of Egypt through the establishment of a "truly" Islamic polity and society.

By this al-Banna meant the reconstruction and reestablishment of the type of polity that existed briefly after the death of the Prophet Muhammad, when religious leadership and political leadership were ostensibly one and the same. Furthermore, and in addition to having a believing Muslim lead the umma, al-Banna believed that such a polity could come into existence only when Islamic laws—and only Islamic laws—govern society. The Brotherhood, however, did not look to the past for the specifics of its program. Rather, it was a thoroughly "modern" phenomenon that sought to reinterpret the Shari'a within the technological, economic, political, and social contexts of the twentieth century. Like his Pakistani counterpart Mawdudi, al-Banna argued that the fact that the loudspeaker, was invented in the West should not deter a Muslim from using it—after making it an "Islamic loudspeaker." Al-Banna remained the Supreme Guide of the Muslim Brotherhood until his assassination by the Egyptian government in 1949. In this document he spells out some of his ideas for creating an Islamic nation in Egypt.

A Bold Step but a Successful One

Excellency,

. . . [I]t would be inexcusable for us to turn aside from the path of truth—the path of Islam—and to follow the path of fleshly desires and vanities—the path of Europe. Along the path of Europe are to be found outer show and cheap tinsel, pleasures and luxuries, laxity and license, and comforts that captivate the soul, for all of these things are loved by the soul, as the Almighty says: "Made beautiful for mankind is the love of fleshly desires for women, and children, and heaped-up mounds of gold and silver, and branded horses, and cattle, and tilled land. That is the comfort of this world" [Q.3:14].

But the path of Islam is glory, impregnability, truth, strength, blessedness, rectitude, stability, virtue, and nobility. Follow it along with the *umma,* may God grant you success! "Say: 'Shall I inform you of something better than that? For those who are godfearing in the presence of their Lord, there are Gardens beneath which rivers flow, they being in them forever, and purified spouses, and the approbation of God. God is aware of His worshippers'" [Q.3:15].

Luxuries only annihilate nations, and her comforts and coveted possessions have only convulsed Europe: "And when We wish to destroy a city, We command its men of wealth, and they commit transgression in it, and the sentence against it is justified, and We destroy it utterly" [Q.3:16].

God (Blessed and Almighty is He!) sent His Apostle as a mercy to the worlds until the Day of Resurrection, and sent His Book with him as a light and a guidance until the Day of Resurrection. The leadership of the Apostle

Five Tracts of Hasan al-Banna (1906–1949): A Selection from the Majmu 'at Rasa'il al-Imam al-Shahid Hasan al-Banna, trans. Charles Wendell, *Near Eastern Studies,* vol. 20 (Berkeley: University of California Press, 1978), pp. 75–77. Reprinted by permission.

(May God bless and save him!) survives in his Sunna, and the authority of the Qurʾān is secure through his proof. Humanity is marching inevitably toward them both, with the might of the mighty and the humility of the humble, from near and from afar, so that God's Word should be realized: "that He may make it triumphant over every religion" [Q.9:33].

Be the first to come forward in the name of God's Apostle (May God bless and save him!) bearing the vial of Qurʾānic healing, to save the tormented, sick world! It is a bold step, but one crowned with success, God willing (Blessed and Almighty is He!), for God is victorious in His affairs: "Then the believers will rejoice in God's succor. He succors whom He will, for He is the Mighty, the Merciful" [Q.30:4–5].

Some Steps Toward Practical Reform

Excellency,

Having given a clear presentation of the spiritual mood that should prevail within the nation in its modern renaissance, we would like to point out, by way of conclusion, some of the practical manifestations and results which this mood should dictate. We are going to mention here only the broadest topics, since we are well aware that each one of these questions demands extensive and intensive study, taxing the energies and capacities of specialists. We know too that we have not yet plumbed all the puzzling problems and demands of the nation, nor all the manifestations of the renaissance. We do not believe that the fulfillment of these demands is a mere trifle which can be accomplished overnight, and we know that before many of them there are manifold obstacles which will require vast patience, great wisdom, and keen determination. We know all this and can take it in our stride. And besides this, we know that where there is genuine resolve, the way will be made plain, and that if a strong-willed nation chooses the path of goodness, it shall, by God Almighty's will, attain what it desires. Stride forward, and God will be with you! Following are the principal goals of reform grounded on the spirit of genuine Islam:

First: Political, judicial, and administrative:

(1) An end to party rivalry, and a channeling of the political forces of the nation into a common front and a single phalanx.

(2) A reform of the law, so that it will conform to Islamic legislation in every branch.

(3) A strengthening of the armed forces, and an increase in the number of youth groups; the inspiration of the latter with zeal on the bases of Islamic *jihād.*

(4) A strengthening of the bonds between all Islamic countries, especially the Arab countries, to pave the way for practical and serious consideration of the matter of the departed Caliphate.

(5) The diffusion of the Islamic spirit throughout all departments of the government, so that all its employees will feel responsible for adhering to Islamic teachings.

(6) The surveillance of the personal conduct of all its employees, and an end to the dichotomy between the private and professional spheres.

(7) Setting the hours of work in summer and winter ahead, so that it will be easy to fulfill religious duties, and so that keeping late hours will come to an end.

(8) An end to bribery and favoritism, with consideration to be given only to capability and legitimate reasons [for advancement].

(9) Weighing all acts of the government in the scales of Islamic wisdom and doctrine; the organization of all celebrations, receptions, official conferences, prisons and hospitals so as not to be incompatible with Islamic teaching; the arranging of work-schedules so that they will not conflict with hours of prayer.

(10) The employment of graduates of Al-Azhar in military and administrative positions, and their training.

Second: Social and educational:

(1) Conditioning the people to respect public morality, and the issuance of directives fortified by the aegis of the law on this subject; the imposition of severe penalties for moral offenses.

(2) Treatment of the problem of women in a way which combines the progressive and the protective, in accordance with Islamic teaching, so that this problem—one of the most important social problems—will not be abandoned to the biased pens and deviant notions of those who err in the directions of deficiency or excess.

(3) An end to prostitution, both clandestine and overt: the recognition of fornication, whatever the circumstances, as a detestable crime whose perpetrator must be flogged.

(4) An end to gambling in all its forms—games, lotteries, racing, and gambling-clubs.

(5) A campaign against drinking, as there is one against drugs: its prohibition, and the salvation of the nation from its effects.

(6) A campaign against ostentation in dress and loose behavior; the instruction of women in what is proper, with particular strictness as regards female instructors, pupils, physicians, and students, and all those in similar categories.

(7) A review of the curricula offered to girls and the necessity of making them distinct from the boys' curricula in many of the stages of education.

(8) Segregation of male and female students; private meetings between men and women, unless within the permitted degrees [of relationship], to be counted as a crime for which both will be censured.

(9) The encouragement of marriage and procreation, by all possible means; promulgation of legislation to protect and give moral support to the family, and to solve the problems of marriage.

(10) The closure of morally undesirable ballrooms and dance-halls, and the prohibition of dancing and other such pastimes.

(11) The surveillance of theatres and cinemas, and a rigorous selection of plays and films.

(12) The expurgation of songs, and a rigorous selection and censorship of them.

(13) The careful selection of lectures, songs, and subjects to be broadcast to the nation; the use of radio broadcasting for the education of the nation in a virtuous and moral way.

(14) The confiscation of provocative stories and books that implant the seeds of skepticism in an insidious manner, and newspapers which strive to disseminate immorality and capitalize indecently on lustful desires.

(15) The supervision of summer vacation areas so as to do away with the wholesale confusion and license that nullify the basic aims of vacationing.

(16) The regulation of business hours for cafés; surveillance of the activities of their regular clients; instructing these as to what is in their best interest; withdrawal of permission from cafés to keep such long hours.

(17) The utilization of these cafes for teaching illiterates reading and writing; toward this end, the assistance of the rising generation of elementary schoolteachers and students.

(18) A campaign against harmful customs, whether economic, moral, or anything else; turning the masses away from these and orienting them in the direction of ways beneficial to them, or educating them in a way consonant with their best interests. These involve such customs as those to do with weddings, funerals, births, the *zār*, civil and religious holidays, etc. Let the government set a good example in this respect.

(19) Due consideration for the claims of the moral censorship, and punishment of all who are proved to have infringed any Islamic doctrine or attacked it, such as breaking the fast of Ramadān, willful neglect of prayers, insulting the faith, or any such act.

(20) The annexation of the elementary village schools to the mosques, and a thoroughgoing reform of both, as regards employees, cleanliness, and overall custodial care, so that the young may be trained in prayer and the older students in learning.

(21) The designation of religious instruction as a basic subject in all schools, in each according to its type, as well as in the universities.

(22) Active instigation to memorize the Qur'ān in all the free elementary schools; making this memorization mandatory for obtaining diplomas in the areas of religion and [Arabic] language; the stipulation that a portion of it be memorized in every school.

(23) The promulgation of a firm educational policy which will advance and raise the level of education, and will supply it, in all its varieties, with common goals and purposes; which will bring the different cultures represented in the nation closer together, and will make the first stage of its process one dedicated to inculcating a virtuous, patriotic spirit and an unwavering moral code.

(24) The cultivation of the Arabic language at every stage of instruction; the use of Arabic alone, as opposed to any foreign language, in the primary stages.

(25) The cultivation of Islamic history, and of the national history and national culture, and the history of Islamic civilization.

(26) Consideration of ways to arrive gradually at a uniform mode of dress for the nation.

(27) An end to the foreign spirit in our homes with regard to language, manners, dress, governesses, nurses, etc.; all these to be Egyptianized, especially in upper-class homes.

(28) To give journalism a proper orientation, and to encourage authors and writers to undertake Islamic, Eastern subjects,

(29) Attention to be given to matters of public health by disseminating health information through all media; increasing the number of hospitals, physicians, and mobile clinics; facilitating the means of obtaining medical treatment.

(30) Attention to be given to village problems as regards their organization, their cleanliness, the purification of their water supply, and the means to provide them with culture, recreation, and training.

Third: the economic:

(1) The organization of *zakāt* in terms of income and expenditure, according to the teachings of the magnanimous Sacred Law; invoking its assistance in carrying out necessary benevolent projects, such as homes for the aged, the poor, and orphans, and strengthening the armed forces.

(2) The prohibition of usury, and the organization of banks with this end in view. Let the government provide a good example in this domain by relinquishing all interest due on its own particular undertakings, for instance in the loan-granting banks, industrial loans, etc.

(3) The encouragement of economic projects and an increase in their number; giving work to unemployed citizens in them; the transfer of such of these as are in the hands of foreigners to the purely national sector.

(4) The protection of the masses from the oppression of monopolistic companies; keeping these within strict limits, and obtaining every possible benefit for the masses.

(5) An improvement in the lot of junior civil servants by raising their salaries, by granting them steady increases and compensations, and by lowering the salaries of senior civil servants.

(6) A reduction in the number of government posts, retaining only the indispensable ones; an equitable and scrupulous distribution of the work among civil servants.

(7) The encouragement of agricultural and industrial counseling; attention to be paid to raising the production level of the peasant and industrial worker.

(8) A concern for the technical and social problems of the worker; raising his standard of living in numerous respects.

(9) The exploitation of natural resources, such as uncultivated land, neglected mines, etc.

(10) Priority over luxury items to be given to necessary projects in terms of organization and execution.

This is the message of the Muslim Brotherhood. We submit it, and place ourselves, our talents, and all we possess in the hands of any committee or government desirous of taking a step forward, hand in hand with an Islamic nation, toward progress and advancement. We will answer the call, and we are prepared to sacrifice ourselves. We hope that by so doing we will have fulfilled our trust and said our piece, for religion means sincerity toward God, His Apostle, His Book, the Imāms of the Muslims, and their community at large. God is our sufficiency; He is enough; and peace to His chosen worshippers!

CHAPTER 5

Contested Nationalisms

Every nation emerges from the interplay of ideas, but the implementation of those ideas depends on the goodwill and willingness to compromise of a sizable number of people. Dealing with the political, economic, and social implications of the new nationalist labels—"Turkish," "Syrian," "Iranian," "Algerian," and so on—was hardly a straightforward process. Nationalism brought with it the *ideal* of increased and in some cases equal political participation by the citizenry. Thus, the shift from being a subject in an empire or monarchy to a citizen of a republic—however imperfect—was momentous and required a great deal of intellectual adjustment and political imagination from the elites and general public alike. Moreover, this shift had to be accomplished amid ideological conflicts, in which political and religious leaders sought to attract individuals and groups to their various causes and conceptions of the "nation." Unfortunately, we have very little historical documentation that chronicles these changes and their impact. The documents in this chapter provide a few examples of the public discourse that accompanied the emergence of nations in the Middle East and North Africa.

We read (document 11) about the violent confrontation between two groups in Alexandretta—a region contested between Syria and Turkey, two post–World War I nations. One group advocated annexing the region to Turkey; the other proclaimed its allegiance to Arab Syria. What is ironic about this incident is that both groups of individuals were ethnically Kurds, not Arabs or Turks. This profusion of identities belies simplistic notions of either Turkish nationalism or Arab nationalism even as the various protagonists adhered to one or the other of those causes. An article from a Syrian newspaper published in the capital city of Damascus (document 5) also sheds light on the discrepancy between ideals and reality by charging that some "Syrians" were not ardent enough in their nationalism. While the writer argues that this lack of patriotism borders on treason, for us it is evidence of a difference of opinion among "Syrians." The article exposes the possibility of resistance to the construction of a specific definition of "Syrian" identity—very much in the same manner that the notion of being "American" has undergone many historical changes.

Perhaps no place embodies the conflict over the definition of the "nation" more than Palestine. There, the aspirations of two different peoples—Jews and Arabs—came clashing together in a most painful manner that still generates repercussions. Each community presented its claim to the land as the only valid claim. Zionist Jews submitted to the postwar Peace Conference at Versailles a memorandum detailing Jewish rights to the land on the basis of a historical title (document 2). The Resolution of the General Syrian Congress in July 1919 attested to and championed the Arab claim for the benefit of the European powers meeting in Versailles (document 3). The Arabs based their claim to Palestine on the fact that they have been inhabiting the land for centuries. Departing from either of these narrowly focused definitions of Palestine was a third view that envisioned the land as capable of housing Arabs and Jews under the rubric of a bi-national state. Document 12 provides examples of this latter idea as well as of the Arab aspirations for Palestine. In this contest over nations, as in many others, the desire of the local populations was not always the only consideration. External influences were at times paramount in shaping nations, as is illustrated by U.S. support for Israel (document 13). Similar tensions were at work between Turkey and Syria over the ownership of Alexandretta (document 11).

Conflict over national identity was not always limited to exchanges of words or a few blows. In attempting to create the mythology of a singular ethnicity within the "nation," nationalists sought to ignore the existence of multi-ethnic communities. For some nationalists, any proclamation of a separate identity other than the proposed national one was considered a threat to the essense and existence of the "nation." At times this led to terrible events such as the killing of Armenians in Turkey between 1915 and 1917, described by Henry Morgenthau, the American ambassador to Turkey (document 1). The accusation that genocide occurred in Turkey is hotly contested by most Turks, who reject that notion as pure propaganda—as did Atatürk (see document 6 in the chapter "Ideas of Nationalism"). Regardless of this denial, historical evidence does prove that some form of ethnic cleansing took place.

Summarizing some of the conflicting visions of the "nation" is a report compiled by the King-Crane Commission, dispatched by President Woodrow Wilson to poll inhabitants of the Middle East about their views of their political future (document 4). This American commission gathered myriad opinions indicating the range of people's ideas about nationalism shortly after World War I.

A document from Tunisia provides an even more detailed map of the complexity and contradictions inherent in nationalist movements and projects (document 10). The Jewish community in Tunisia—which had lived within the larger Arab milieu and spoke Arabic for many centuries—came in contact with the Zionist project around the turn of the twentieth century. Zionism—Jewish political nationalism—presented this community of Jews with the opportunity to support the idea of a Jewish nation based on ethnicity/religion. At the same time, the Alliance Israélite Universelle—a French Jewish philanthropic

organization—was actively seeking to attract these Jews toward political identi-
fication with France. Last but not least, the historical relationship of this Jewish community to Tunisia itself created a third political identity in competition
with the other two. Some members of the Jewish community in Tunisia attempted to strike a compromise among these ideas; others simply adhered to
one ideology.

Similarly, in Algeria and the "Greater Syria," the definition of the citizen
within the nation was a subject of great controversy. In Algeria (documents 7,
8, and 9), there was a tug of war between French colonial authorities that sought
to naturalize Algerians as French citizens and Algerian intellectuals who rejected French naturalization on the premise that it would deny Algerian independence. At the constitutional conference in "Greater Syria" the debate was
centered on the relationship between gender and citizenship (document 6).
What quickly emerges as a central issue is the conflict of affording women
equal political rights within a socially conservative "nation."

The documents in this chapter clearly show the difficulty of defining nationalism at the popular level. They help us assess simplistic nationalist narra-
tives that seek to erase all competing ideologies in favor of one dominant idea
of the "nation." Furthermore, they highlight some of the tools necessary to articulate political consciousness and the vision of a newly proposed collective
political entity. In other words, some of these documents clearly show the
modernity of nationalism, which, paradoxically, its proponents claimed was an
"eternal" presence in history.

1.   Henry Morgenthau Recounts Aspects of Nationalist-Driven Ethnic Cleansing of Armenians in Turkey, 1915

*The massacre of large numbers of Armenians (up to one million according to some
estimates) is a very dark period in the history of the Ottoman Empire. It also is a
hotly contested subject between the Armenian community and the Turkish government, producing lawsuits and a great deal of rhetoric.*

*The Turkish government and its supporters argue that the number of Armeni-
ans said to have been killed is inflated, and they deny that there was any systematic attempt to eradicate that ethnic community. They also contend that those
Armenians actually killed were not innocent civilians but traitorous combatants recruited by Armenian political organizations collaborating with Russia for the purpose of establishing an Armenian homeland in parts of the Ottoman Empire.
Armenians and their supporters completely and vociferously disagree with this char-
acterization. They contend the Committee of Union and Progress (the Young Turks)
began a campaign of ethnic cleansing against Armenians in 1915. A major part of*

Henry Morgenthau, *The Murder of a Nation* (New York: Armenian General Benevolent Union of
America, 1915), pp. 30–43, 50–54, 64–67.

this campaign was the expulsion of Armenians from their homes in Anatolia and into the Syrian desert. Along the way they were attacked, robbed, and killed, and countless numbers of people starved on what was in effect a death march.

Aside from the differing accounts of what transpired, these events offer a clear example of the fault lines present in nationalist projects centered on a pure and singular ethnic definition of the "nation." Reprinted here is an excerpt from a book authored by Henry Morgenthau, the U.S. ambassador to Turkey between 1913 and 1916. Morgenthau describes some of the atrocities and explains the nationalist logic behind the Armenian genocide.

The destruction of the Armenian race in 1915 involved certain difficulties that had not impeded the operations of the Turks in the massacres of 1895 and other years. In these earlier periods the Armenian men had possessed little power or means of resistance. In those days Armenians had not been permitted to have military training, to serve in the Turkish army, or to possess arms. As I have already said, these discriminations were withdrawn when the revolutionists obtained the upper hand in 1908. Not only were the Christians now permitted to bear arms, but the authorities, in the full flush of their enthusiasm for freedom and equality, encouraged them to do so. In the early part of 1915, therefore, every Turkish city contained thousands of Armenians who had been trained as soldiers and who were supplied with rifles, pistols, and other weapons of defense. The operations at Van once more disclosed that these men could use their weapons to good advantage. It was thus apparent that an Armenian massacre this time would generally assume more the character of warfare than those wholesale butcheries of defenseless men and women which the Turks had always found so congenial. If this plan of murdering a race were to succeed, two preliminary steps would therefore have to be taken: it would be necessary to render all Armenian soldiers powerless and to deprive of their arms the Armenians in every city and town. Before Armenia could be slaughtered, Armenia must be made defenseless.

In the early part of 1915, the Armenian soldiers in the Turkish army were reduced to a new status. Up to that time most of them had been combatants, but now they were all stripped of their arms and transformed into workmen. Instead of serving their country as artillerymen and cavalrymen, these former soldiers now discovered that they had been transformed into road labourers and pack animals. Army supplies of all kinds were loaded on their backs, and, stumbling under the burdens and driven by the whips and bayonets of the Turks, they were forced to drag their weary bodies into the mountains of the Caucasus. Sometimes they would have to plough their way, burdened in this fashion, almost waist high through snow. They had to spend practically all their time in the open, sleeping on the bare ground—whenever the ceaseless prodding of their taskmasters gave them an occasional opportunity to sleep. They were given only scraps of food; if they fell sick they were left where they had dropped, their Turkish oppressors perhaps stopping long enough to rob them of all their possessions—even of their clothes. If any stragglers succeeded in reaching their destinations, they were not infrequently massacred. In many instances Armenian soldiers were disposed of in even more summary fashion, for it now became almost the general practice to shoot them in cold blood. In almost all cases the procedure was the same. Here and there squads of 50 or 100 men would be taken, bound together in groups of four, and then marched out to a secluded spot a short distance from the village. Suddenly the sound of rifle shots would fill the air, and the Turkish soldiers who had acted as the escort would sullenly return to camp. Those sent to bury the bodies would find them almost invariably stark naked, for, as usual, the Turks had stolen all their clothes. In cases that came to my attention, the murderers had added a refinement to their victims' sufferings by compelling them to dig their graves before being shot.

[. . .] The Young Turks displayed greater ingenuity than their predecessor, Abdul Hamid. The injunction of the deposed Sultan was merely "to kill, kill," whereas the Turkish democracy hit upon an entirely new plan. Instead of massacring outright the Armenian race, they now decided to deport it. In the south and southeastern section of the Ottoman Empire lie the Syrian desert and the Mesopotamian valley. Though part of this area was once the scene of a flourishing civilization, for the last five centuries it has suffered the blight that becomes the lot of any country that is subjected to Turkish rule; and it is now a dreary, desolate waste, without cities and towns or life of any kind, populated only by a few wild and fanatical Bedouin tribes. Only the most industrious labour, expended through many years, could transform this desert into the abiding place of any considerable population. The Central Government now announced its intention of gathering the two million or more Armenians living in the several sections of the empire and transporting them to this desolate and inhospitable region. Had they undertaken such a deportation in good faith it would have represented the height of cruelty and injustice. As a matter of fact, the Turks never had the slightest idea of reëstablishing the Armenians in this new country. They knew that the great majority would never reach their destination and that those who did would either die of thirst and starvation, or be murdered by the wild Mohammedan desert tribes. The real purpose of the deportation was robbery and destruction; it really represented a new method of massacre. When the Turkish authorities gave the orders for these deportations, they were merely giving the death warrant to a whole race; they understood this well, and, in their conversations with me, they made no particular attempt to conceal the fact.

All through the spring and summer of 1915 the deportations took place. Of the larger cities, Constantinople, Smyrna, and Aleppo were spared; practically all other places where a single Armenian family lived now became the scenes of these unspeakable tragedies. Scarcely a single Armenian, whatever his education or wealth, or whatever the social class to which he belonged, was exempted from the order. In some villages placards were posted ordering the whole Armenian population to present itself in a public place at an appointed time—usually a day or two ahead, and in other places the town crier would go through the streets delivering the order vocally. In still others not the slightest warning was given. The gendarmes would appear before an Armenian house and order all the inmates to follow them. They would take women engaged in their domestic tasks without giving them the chance to change their clothes. The police fell upon them just as the eruption of Vesuvius fell upon Pompeii; women were taken from the washtubs, children were snatched out of bed, the bread was left half baked in the oven, the family meal was abandoned partly eaten, the children were taken from the schoolroom, leaving their books open at the daily task, and the men were forced to abandon their ploughs in the fields and their cattle on the mountain side. Even women who had just given birth to children would be forced to leave their beds and join the panic-stricken throng, their sleeping babies in their arms. Such things as they hurriedly snatched up—a shawl, a blanket, perhaps a few scraps of food—were all that they could take of their household belongings. To their frantic questions "Where are we going?" the gendarmes would vouchsafe only one reply: "To the interior."

In some cases the refugees were given a few hours, in exceptional instances a few days, to dispose of their property and household effects. But the proceeding, of course, amounted simply to robbery. They could sell only to Turks, and since both buyers and sellers knew that they had only a day or two to market the accumulations of a lifetime, the prices obtained represented a small fraction of their value. Sewing machines would bring one or two dollars—a cow would go for a dollar, a houseful of furniture would be sold for a pittance. In many cases Armenians were prohibited from selling or Turks from buying even at these ridiculous prices; under pretense that the Government intended to sell their effects to pay the creditors whom they would inevitably leave behind, their household furniture would be placed in stores or heaped up in public places, where it was usually pillaged by Turkish men and women. The government officials would also inform the Armenians that, since their deportation was only temporary, the intention being to bring them back after the war was over, they would not be permitted to sell their houses. Scarcely had the former possessors left the village, when Mohammedan *mohadjirs*—immigrants from other parts of Turkey—would be moved into the Armenian quarters. Similarly all their valuables—money, rings, watches, and jewellery—would be taken to the police stations for "safe keeping," pending their return, and then parcelled out among the Turks. Yet these robberies gave the refugees little anguish, for far more terrible and agonizing scenes were taking place under their eyes. The systematic extermination of the men continued; such males as the persecutions which I have already described had left were now violently dealt with. Before the caravans were started, it became the regular practice to separate the young men from the families, tie them together in groups of four, lead them to the outskirts, and shoot them. Public hangings without trial—the only offense being that the victims were Armenians—were taking place constantly. The gendarmes showed a particular desire to annihilate the educated and the influential. From American consuls and missionaries I was constantly receiving reports of such executions, and many of the events which they described will never fade from my memory. At Angora all Armenian men from fifteen to seventy were arrested, bound together in groups of four, and sent on the road in the direction of Caesarea. When they had travelled five or six hours and had reached a secluded valley, a mob of Turkish peasants fell upon them with clubs, hammers, axes, scythes, spades, and saws. Such instruments not only caused more agonizing deaths than guns and pistols, but, as the Turks themselves boasted, they were more economical, since they did not involve the waste of powder and shell. In this way they exterminated the whole male population of Angora, including all its men of wealth and breeding, and their bodies, horribly mutilated, were left in the valley, where they were devoured by wild beasts. After completing this destruction, the peasants and gendarmes gathered in the local tavern, comparing notes and boasting of the number of "giaours" that each had slain. In Trebizond the men were placed in boats and sent out on the Black Sea; gendarmes would follow them in boats, shoot them down, and throw their bodies into the water.

When the signal was given for the caravans to move, therefore, they almost invariably consisted of women, children, and old men. Any one who could possibly have protected them from the fate that awaited them had been destroyed. Not infrequently the prefect of the city, as the mass started on its way, would wish them a derisive "pleasant journey." Before the caravan moved the women were sometimes offered the alternative of becoming Mohammedans. Even though they accepted the new faith, which few of them did, their earthly troubles did not end. The converts were compelled to surrender their children to a so-called "Moslem Orphanage," with the agreement that they should be trained as devout followers of the Prophet. They themselves must then show the sincerity of their conversion by abandoning their Christian husbands and marrying Moslems. If no good Mohammedan offered himself as a husband, then the new convert was deported, however strongly she might protest her devotion to Islam.

At first the Government showed some inclination to protect these departing throngs. The officers usually divided them into convoys, in some cases numbering several hundred, in others several thousand. The civil authorities occasionally furnished ox-carts which carried such household furniture as the exiles had succeeded in scrambling together. A guard of gendarmerie accompanied each convoy, ostensibly to guide and protect it. Women, scantily clad, carrying babies in their arms or on their backs, marched side by side with old men hobbling along with canes. Children would run along, evidently regarding the procedure, in the early stages, as some new lark. A more prosperous member would perhaps have a horse or a donkey, occasionally a farmer had rescued a cow or a sheep, which would trudge along at his side, and the usual assortment of family pets—dogs, cats, and birds—became parts of the variegated procession. From thousands of Armenian cities and villages these despairing caravans now set forth; they filled all the roads leading southward; everywhere, as they moved on, they raised a huge dust, and abandoned débris, chairs, blankets, bedclothes, household utensils, and other impedimenta, marked the course of the processions. When the caravans first started, the individuals bore some resemblance to human beings; in a few hours, however, the dust of the road plastered their faces and clothes, the mud caked their lower members, and the slowly advancing mobs, frequently bent with fatigue and crazed by the brutality of their "protectors," resembled some new and strange animal species. Yet for the better part of six months, from April to October, 1915, practically all the highways in Asia Minor were crowded with these unearthly bands of exiles. They could be seen winding in and out of every valley and climbing up the sides of nearly every mountain—moving on and on, they scarcely knew whither, except that every road led to death. Village after village and town after town was evacuated of its Armenian population, under the distressing circumstances already detailed. In these six months, as far as can be ascertained, about 1,200,000 people started on this journey to the Syrian desert.

"Pray for us," they would say as they left their homes—the homes in which their ancestors had lived for 2,500 years. "We shall not see you in this world again, but sometime we shall meet. Pray for us!"

[. . .]

On the seventieth day a few creatures reached Aleppo. Out of the combined convoy of 18,000 souls just 150 women and children reached their destination. A few of the rest, the most attractive, were still living as captives of the Kurds and Turks; all the rest were dead.

My only reason for relating such dreadful things as this is that, without the details, the English-speaking public cannot understand precisely what this nation is which we call Turkey. I have by no means told the most terrible details, for a complete narration of the sadistic orgies of which these Armenian men and women were the victims can never be printed in an American publication. Whatever crimes the most perverted instincts of the human mind can devise, and whatever refinements of persecution and injustice the most debased imagination can conceive, became the daily misfortunes of this devoted people. I am confident that the whole history of the human race contains no such horrible episode as this. The great massacres and persecutions of the past seem almost insignificant when compared with the sufferings of the Armenian race in 1915. The slaughter of the Albigenses in the early part of the thirteenth century has always been regarded as one of the most pitiful events in history. In these outbursts of fanaticism about 60,000 people were killed. In the massacre of St. Bartholomew about 30,000 human beings lost their lives. The Sicilian Vespers, which has always figured as one of the most fiendish outbursts of this kind, caused the destruction of 8,000. Volumes have been written about the Spanish Inquisition under Torquemada, yet in the eighteen years of his administration only a little more than 8,000 heretics were done to death. Perhaps the one event in history that most resembles the Armenian deportations was the expulsion of the Jews from Spain by Ferdinand and Isabella. According to Prescott 160,000 were uprooted from their homes and scattered broadcast over Africa and Europe. Yet all these previous persecutions seem almost trivial when we compare them with the sufferings of the Armenians, in which at least 600,000 people were destroyed and perhaps as many as 1,000,000. And these earlier massacres, when we compare them with the spirit that directed the Armenian atrocities, have one feature that we can almost describe as an excuse: they were the product of religious fanaticism and most of the men and women who instigated them sincerely believed that they were devoutly serving their Maker. Undoubtedly religious fanaticism was an impelling motive with the Turkish and Kurdish rabble who slew Armenians as a service to Allah, but the men who really conceived the crime had no such motive. Practically all of them were atheists, with no more respect for Mohammedanism than for Christianity, and with them the one motive was cold-blooded, calculating state policy.

The Armenians are not the only subject people in Turkey which have suffered from this policy of making Turkey exclusively the country of the Turks. The story which I have told about the Armenians I could also tell with certain modifications about the Greeks and the Syrians. Indeed the Greeks were the first victims of this nationalizing idea. I have already described how, in the few months preceding the European War, the Ottoman Government began deporting its Greek subjects along the coast of Asia Minor. These outrages aroused little interest in Europe or the United States, yet in the space of three or four months more than 100,000 Greeks were taken from their age-long homes in the Mediterranean littoral and removed to the Greek Islands and the interior. For the larger part these were bona-fide deportations; that is, the Greek inhabitants were actually removed to new places and were not subjected to wholesale massacre. It was probably for the reason that the civilized world did not protest against these deportations that the Turks afterward decided to apply the same methods on a larger scale not only to the Greeks but to the Armenians, Syrians, Nestorians, and others of its subject peoples. In fact, Bedri Bey, the Prefect of Police at Constantinople, himself told one of my secretaries that the Turks had expelled the Greeks so successfully that they had decided to apply the same method to all the other races in the empire.

The martyrdom of the Greeks, therefore, comprised two periods: that antedating the war, and that which began in the early part of 1915. The first affected chiefly the Greeks on the seacoast of Asia Minor. The second affected those living in Thrace and in the territories surrounding the Sea of Marmora, the Dardanelles, the Bosphorus, and the coast of the Black Sea. These latter, to the extent of several hundred thousand, were sent to the interior of Asia Minor. The Turks adopted almost identically the same procedure against the Greeks as that which they had adopted against the Armenians. They began by incorporating the Greeks into the Ottoman army and then transforming them into labour battalions, using them to build roads in the Caucasus and other scenes of action. These Greek soldiers, just like the Armenians, died by thousands from cold, hunger, and other privations. The same house-to-house searches for hidden weapons took place in the Greek villages, and Greek men and women were beaten and tortured just as were their fellow Armenians. The Greeks had to submit to the same forced requisitions, which amounted in their case, as in the case of the Armenians, merely to plundering on a wholesale scale. The Turks attempted to force the Greek subjects to become Mohammedans; Greek girls, just like Armenian girls, were stolen and taken to Turkish harems and

Greek boys were kidnapped and placed in Moslem households. The Greeks, just like the Armenians, were accused of disloyalty to the Ottoman Government; the Turks accused them of furnishing supplies to the English submarines in the Marmora and also of acting as spies. The Turks also declared that the Greeks were not loyal to the Ottoman Government, and that they also looked forward to the day when the Greeks inside of Turkey would become part of Greece. These latter charges were unquestionably true; that the Greeks, after suffering for five centuries the most unspeakable outrages at the hands of the Turks, should look longingly to the day when their territory should be part of the fatherland, was to be expected. The Turks, as in the case of the Armenians, seized upon this as an excuse for a violent onslaught on the whole race. Everywhere the Greeks were gathered in groups and, under the so-called protection of Turkish gendarmes, they were transported, the larger part on foot, into the interior. Just how many were scattered in this fashion is not definitely known, the estimates varying anywhere from 200,000 up to 1,000,000. These caravans suffered great privations, but they were not submitted to general massacre as were the Armenians, and this is probably the reason why the outside world has not heard so much about them. The Turks showed them this greater consideration not from any motive of pity. The Greeks, unlike the Armenians, had a government which was vitally interested in their welfare. At this time there was a general apprehension among the Teutonic Allies that Greece would enter the war on the side of the Entente, and a wholesale massacre of Greeks in Asia Minor would unquestionably have produced such a state of mind in Greece that its pro-German king would have been unable longer to keep his country out of the war. It was only a matter of state policy, therefore, that saved these Greek subjects of Turkey from all the horrors that befell the Armenians. But their sufferings are still terrible, and constitute another chapter in the long story of crimes for which civilization will hold the Turk responsible.

[. . .]

"Suppose a few Armenians did betray you," I said. "Is that a reason for destroying a whole race? Is that an excuse for making innocent women and children suffer?"

"Those things are inevitable," he [Talaat Pasha (1874–1921), part of the CUP triumvirate who became the Prime Minister of the Ottoman Empire in 1917] replied.

This remark to me was not quite so illuminating as one which Talaat made subsequently to a reporter of the *Berliner Tageblatt*, who asked him the same question. "We have been reproached," he said, according to this interviewer, "for making no distinction between the innocent Armenians and the guilty; but that was utterly impossible, in view of the fact that those who were innocent to-day might be guilty to-morrow"!

One reason why Talaat could not discuss this matter with me freely, was because the member of the embassy staff who did the interpreting was himself an Armenian. In the early part of August, therefore, he sent a personal messenger to me, asking if I could not see him alone—he said that he himself would provide the interpreter. This was the first time that Talaat had admitted that his treatment of the Armenians was a matter with which I had any concern. The interview took place two days afterward. It so happened that since the last time I had visited Talaat I had shaved my beard. As soon as I came in the burly Minister began talking in his customary bantering fashion.

"You have become a young man again," he said; "you are so young now that I cannot go to you for advice any more."

"I have shaved my beard," I replied, "because it had become very gray—made gray by your treatment of the Armenians."

After this exchange of compliments we settled down to the business in hand. "I have asked you to come to-day," began Talaat, "so that I can explain our position on the whole Armenian subject. We base our objections to the Armenians on three distinct grounds. In the first place, they have enriched themselves at the expense of the Turks. In the second place, they are determined to domineer over us and to establish a separate state. In the third place, they have openly encouraged our enemies. They have assisted the Russians in the Caucasus and our failure there is largely explained by their actions. We have therefore come to the irrevocable decision that we shall make them powerless before this war is ended."

On every one of these points I had plenty of arguments in rebuttal. Talaat's first objection was merely an admission that the Armenians were more industrious and more able than the dull-witted and lazy Turks. Massacre as a means of destroying business competition was certainly an original conception! His general charge that the Armenians were "conspiring" against Turkey and that they openly sympathized with Turkey's enemies merely meant, when reduced to its original elements, that the Armenians were constantly appealing to the European Powers to protect them against robbery, murder, and outrage. The Armenian problem, like most race problems, was the result of centuries of ill-treatment and injustice. There could be only one solution for it, the creation of an orderly system of government, in which all citizens were to be treated upon an equality, and in which all offenses were to be punished as the acts of individuals and not as of peoples. I argued for a long time along these and similar lines.

"It is no use for you to argue," Talaat answered, "we have already disposed of three quarters of the Armenians; there are none at all left in Bitlis, Van, and Erzeroum. The hatred between the Turks and the Armenians is now so intense that we have got to finish with them. If we don't, they will plan their revenge."

"If you are not influenced by humane considerations," I replied, "think of the material loss. These people are your business men. They control many of your industries. They are very large tax-payers. What would become of you commercially without them?"

"We care nothing about the commercial loss," replied Talaat. "We have figured all that out and we know that it will not exceed five million pounds. We don't worry about that. I have asked you to come here so as to let you know that our Armenian policy is absolutely fixed and that nothing can change it. We will not have the Armenians anywhere in Anatolia. They can live in the desert but nowhere else."

I still attempted to persuade Talaat that the treatment of the Armenians was destroying Turkey in the eyes of the world, and that his country would never be able to recover from this infamy.

"You are making a terrible mistake," I said, and I repeated the statement three times.

"Yes, we may make mistakes," he replied, "but"—and he firmly closed his lips and shook his head—"we never regret."

[...]

2.   The Zionist Organization's Memorandum to the Peace Conference in Versailles Asks for Support for the Establishment of a Jewish State in Palestine, February 3, 1919

After obtaining British support for establishing a Jewish homeland in Palestine (see document 4, the Balfour Declaration, in the chapter "Ideas of Nationalism"), Zionist organizations sought to articulate and consolidate that idea into a more concrete project and brought their vision to the victorious Allies meeting in Versailles at the Peace Conference. One goal of the conference was to map the geopolitics of the postwar Middle East and Africa, so its decision about who would receive colonial control over Palestine was of momentous importance to Zionists and Arabs alike.

The Zionist project was a secular political program, but the language used in parts of this memorandum had religious connotations that the writers knew would resonate with a Western Christian audience. Of particular interest is the idea of "redemption" of a "lost" land, which implicitly dismisses centuries of Arab occupation of the region and brings to mind the logic used by nineteenth-century European imperialists to justify their occupation and colonization of the African continent. This concept of "manifest destiny" is textually linked to the idea of scientific and rational reclamation of the land, thus linking the ancient history of the Jews in Palestine (before the Diaspora of 70 C.E.) and the modernity of their European descendants.

The Zionist Organisation respectfully submits the following draft resolutions for the consideration of the Peace Conference:

1. The High Contracting Parties recognise the historic title of the Jewish people to Palestine and the right of the Jews to reconstitute in Palestine their National Home.

2. The boundaries of Palestine shall be as declared in the Schedule annexed hereto.

3. The sovereign possession of Palestine shall be vested in the League of Nations and the Government entrusted to Great Britain as mandatary of the League.

David Hunter Miller, *My Diary at the Conference of Paris* (New York, 1924), vol. 5, pp. 15–29.

4. (Provision to be inserted relating to the application in Palestine of such of the general conditions attached to mandates as are suitable to the case.)

5. The mandate shall be subject also to the following special conditions:

I. Palestine shall be placed under such political, administrative and economic conditions as will secure the establishment there of the Jewish National Home and ultimately render possible the creation of an autonomous Commonwealth, it being clearly understood that nothing shall be done which may prejudice the civil and religious rights of existing non-Jewish communities in Palestine or the rights and political status enjoyed by Jews in any other country.

II. To this end the Mandatary Power shall *inter alia*

 a. Promote Jewish immigration and close settlement on the land, the established rights of the present non-Jewish population being equitably safeguarded.

 b. Accept the co-operation in such measures of a Council representative of the Jews of Palestine and of the world that may be established for the development of the Jewish National Home in Palestine and entrust the organisation of Jewish education to such Council.

 c. On being satisfied that the constitution of such Council precludes the making of private profit, offer to the Council in priority any concession for public works or for the development of natural resources which may be found desirable to grant.

III. The Mandatary Power shall encourage the widest measure of self-government for localities practicable in the conditions of the country.

IV. There shall be for ever the fullest freedom of religious worship for all creeds in Palestine. There shall be no discrimination among the inhabitants with regard to citizenship and civil rights, on the grounds of religion or of race.

V. (Provision to be inserted relating to the control of the Holy Places).

The Boundaries of Palestine Schedule

The boundaries of Palestine shall follow the general lines set out below:

Starting on the North at a point on the Mediterranean Sea in the vicinity of Sidon and following the watersheds of the foothills of the Lebanon as far as Jisr El Karaon, thence to El Bire, following the dividing line between the two basins of the Wadi El Korn and the Wadi Et Teim thence in a southerly direction following the dividing line between the Eastern and Western slopes of the Hermon, to the vicinity West of Beit Jenn, thence Eastward following the northern watersheds of the Nahr Mughaniye close to and west of the Hedjaz Railway.

In the East a line close to and West of the Hedjaz Railway terminating in the Gulf of Akaba.

In the South a frontier to be agreed upon with the Egyptian Government. In the West the Mediterranean Sea.

The details of the delimitations, or any necessary adjustments of detail, shall be settled by a Special Commission on which there shall be Jewish representation.

Statement

The Historic Title

The claims of the Jews with regard to Palestine rest upon the following main considerations:

(1) The land is the historic home of the Jews; there they achieved their greatest development, from that centre, through their agency, there emanated spiritual and moral influences of supreme value to mankind. By violence they were driven from Palestine, and through the ages they have never ceased to cherish the longing and the hope of a return.

(2) In some parts of the world, and particularly in Eastern Europe, the conditions of life of millions of Jews are deplorable. Forming often a congested population, denied the opportunities which would make a healthy development possible, the need of fresh outlets is urgent, both for their own sake and in the interest of the population of other races, among whom they dwell. Palestine would offer one such outlet. To the Jewish masses it is the country above all others in which they would most wish to cast their lot. By the methods of economic development to which we shall refer later, Palestine can be made now as it was in ancient times, the home of a prosperous population many times as numerous as that which now inhabits it.

(3) But Palestine is not large enough to contain more than a proportion of the Jews of the world. The greater part of the fourteen millions or more scattered through all countries must remain in their present localities, and it will doubtless be one of the cares of the Peace Conference to ensure for them, wherever they have been oppressed, as for all peoples, equal rights and humane conditions. A Jewish National Home in Palestine will, however, be of high value to them also. Its influence will permeate the Jewries of the world: it will inspire these millions, hitherto often despairing, with a new hope; it will hold out before their eyes a higher standard; it will help to make them even more useful citizens in the lands in which they dwell.

(4) Such a Palestine would be of value also to the world at large, whose real wealth consists in the healthy diversities of its civilisations.

(5) Lastly the land itself needs redemption. Much of it is left desolate. Its present condition is a standing reproach. Two things are necessary for that redemption—a stable and enlightened Government, and an addition to the present population which shall be energetic, intelligent, devoted to the country, and backed by the large financial resources that are indispensable for development. Such a population the Jews alone can supply.

Inspired by these ideas, Jewish activities particularly during the last thirty years have been directed to Palestine within the measure that the Turkish administrative system allowed. Some millions of pounds sterling have been spent in the country particularly in the foundation of Jewish agricultural settlements. Those settlements have been for the most part highly successful.

With enterprise and skill the Jews have adopted modern scientific methods and have shown themselves to be capable agriculturalists. Hebrew has been revived as a living language, it is the medium of instruction in the schools and the tongue is in daily use among the rising generation. The foundations of a Jewish University have been laid at Jerusalem and considerable funds have been contributed for the creation of its building and for its endowment. Since the British occupation, the Zionist Organisation has expended in Palestine approximately £50,000 a month upon relief, education and sanitation. To promote the future development of the country great sums will be needed for drainage, irrigation, roads, railways, harbours and public works of all kinds, as well as for land settlement and house building. Assuming a political settlement under which the establishment of a Jewish National Home in Palestine is assured the Jews of the world will make every effort to provide the vast sums of money that will be needed. . . .

[Here follow a recital of the Balfour Declaration and of its endorsement by the French Foreign Minister and reference to support of Zionism and the Balfour Declaration by other allied governments.]

Great Britain as Mandatary of the League of Nations

We ask that Great Britain shall act as Mandatary of the League of Nations for Palestine. The selection of Great Britain as Mandatary is urged on the ground that this is the wish of the Jews of the world and the League of Nations in selecting a Mandatary will follow as far as possible, the popular wish of the people concerned.

The preference on the part of the Jews for a British Trusteeship is unquestionably the result of the peculiar relationship of England to the Jewish Palestinian problem. The return of the Jews to Zion has not only been a remarkable feature in English literature, but in the domain of statecraft it has played its part, beginning with the readmission of the Jews under Cromwell. It manifested itself particularly in the 19th century in the instructions given to British Consular representatives in the Orient after the Damascus Incident; in the various Jewish Palestinian projects suggested by English non-Jews prior to 1881; in the letters of endorsement and support given by members of the Royal Family and Officers of the Government to Lawrence Oliphant and finally, in the three consecutive acts which definitely associated Great Britain with Zionism in the minds of the Jews viz.—the El Arish offer in 1901; the East African offer in 1903, and lastly the British Declaration in favour of a Jewish National Home in Palestine in 1917. Moreover, the Jews who have gained political experience in many lands under a great variety of governmental systems, whole-heartedly appreciate the advanced and liberal policies adopted by Great Britain in her modern colonial administration. . . .

[Here follows a recital of the selection of Great Britain as mandatory power by the American Jewish Congress and a conference of Palestine Jews at Jaffa.]

Boundaries

The boundaries above outlined are what we consider essential for the necessary economic foundation of the country. Palestine must have its natural outlets to the seas and the control of its rivers and their headwaters. The boundaries are sketched with the general economic needs and historic traditions of the country in mind, factors which necessarily must also be considered by the Special Commission in fixing the definite boundary lines. This Commission will bear in mind that it is highly desirable, in the interests of economical administration that the geographical area of Palestine should be as large as possible so that it may eventually contain a large and thriving population which could more easily bear the burdens of modern civilised government than a small country with a necessary limitation of inhabitants.

The economic life of Palestine, like that of every other semi-arid country depends on the available water supply. It is, therefore, of vital importance not only to secure all water resources already feeding the country, but also to be able to conserve and control them at their sources.

The Hermon is Palestine's real "Father of Waters" and cannot be severed from it without striking at the very root of its economic life. The Hermon not only needs reafforestation but also other works before it can again adequately serve as the water reservoir of the country. It must therefore be wholly under the control of those who will most willingly as well as most adequately restore it to its maximum utility. Some international arrangement must be made whereby the riparian rights of the people dwelling south of the Litani River may be fully protected. Properly cared for these head waters can be made to serve in the development of the Lebanon as well as of Palestine.

The fertile plains east of the Jordan, since the earliest Biblical times, have been linked economically and politically with the land west of the Jordan. The country which is now very sparsely populated, in Roman times supported a great population. It could now serve admirably for colonisation on a large scale. A just regard for the economic needs of Palestine and Arabia demands that free access to the Hedjaz Railway throughout its length be accorded both Governments.

An intensive development of the agriculture and other opportunities of Transjordania make it imperative that Palestine shall have access to the Red Sea and an opportunity of developing good harbours on the Gulf of Akaba. Akaba, it will be recalled, was the terminus of an important trade route of Palestine from the days of Solomon onwards. The ports developed in the Gulf of Akaba should be free ports through which the commerce of the Hinterland may pass on the same principle which guides us in suggesting that free access be given to the Hedjaz Railway.

Proposals to the Mandatary Power

In connection with the Government to be set up by the Mandatary of the League of Nations until such time as the people of Palestine shall be prepared to undertake the establishment of representative and responsible Government proposals will be made in due course to the Mandatary Power to the following effect:

1. In any instrument establishing the constitution of Palestine the Declarations of the Peace Conference shall be recited as forming an integral part of that constitution.
2. The Jewish people shall be entitled to fair representation in the executive and legislative bodies and in the selection of public and civil servants. In giving such representation the Mandatary Power shall consult the Jewish Council hereinafter mentioned.

   Neither law nor custom shall preclude the appointment of a citizen of Palestine as chief of the executive.

3. That in encouraging the self government of localities the Mandatary Power shall secure the maintenance by local communities of proper standards of administration in matters of education, communal, or regional activities. In granting or enlarging local autonomy regard shall be had to the readiness and ability of the community to attain such standards. Local autonomous communities shall be empowered and encouraged to combine and cooperate for common purposes.
4. Education without distinction of race shall be assisted from public funds.
5. Hebrew shall be one of the official languages of Palestine and shall be employed in all documents, decrees and announcements and on all stamps, coins, and notes issued by the Government.
6. The Jewish Sabbath and Holy Days shall be recognised as legal days of rest.
7. All inhabitants continuing to reside in Palestine who on the   day of   , 19   , have their domicile in Palestine, except those who elect in writing within six months from such date to retain their foreign citizenship, shall become citizens of Palestine, and they and all persons in Palestine or naturalised under the laws of Palestine after the   day of   , 19   , shall be citizens thereof and entitled to the protection of the Mandatary Power on behalf of the Government of Palestine.

Land Commission

Recognising that the general progress of Palestine must begin with the reform of the conditions governing land tenure and settlement, the Mandatary Power shall appoint a Commission (upon which the Jewish Council shall have representation) with power:

a. To make survey of the land and to schedule all lands that may be made available for close settlement, intensive cultivation and public use.

b. To propose measures for determining and registering titles of ownership of land.

c. To propose measures for supervising transactions in land with a view of preventing land speculation.

d. To propose measures for the close settlement, intensive cultivation and public use of land, where necessary by compulsory purchase at a fair pre-war price and further by making available all waste lands unoccupied and inadequately cultivated lands or lands without legal owners, and state lands.

e. To propose measures for the taxation and the tenure of land and in general any progressive measures in harmony with the policy of making the land available for close settlement and intensive cultivation.

f. To propose measures whereby the Jewish Council may take over all lands available for close settlement and intensive cultivation.

g. In all such measures the established rights of the present population shall be equitably safeguarded.

The Jewish Council for Palestine

1. A Jewish Council for Palestine shall be elected by a Jewish Congress representative of the Jews of Palestine and of the entire world, which shall be convoked in Jerusalem on or before the First day of January, 1920, or as soon thereafter as possible, by the Provisional Jewish Council hereinafter mentioned.

The Jewish Congress shall determine its functions as well as the constitution and functions of the Jewish Council in conformity with the purpose and spirit of the Declarations of the Peace Conference and of the powers conferred by the mandatary power upon the Jewish Council.

2. The Jewish Council shall be recognised as a legal entity and shall have power:

a. To co-operate and consult with and to assist the Government of Palestine in any and all matters affecting the Jewish people in Palestine and in all such cases to be and to act as the representative of the Jewish people.

b. To participate in the development and administration of immigration, close land settlement, credit facilities, public works, services, and enterprises, and every other form of activity conducive to the development of the country. The organisation of Jewish education to be entrusted to such Council.

c. To acquire and hold Real Estate.

d. To acquire and exercise concessions for public works and the development of natural resources.

e. With the consent of the Jewish inhabitants concerned or their accredited representatives, to assess such inhabitants for the purpose of stimulating and maintaining education, communal, charitable and other public institutions (including the Jewish Council) and other activities primarily concerned with the welfare of the Jewish people in Palestine.

f. With the approval of the Mandatary Power and upon such terms and conditions as the Mandatary Power may prescribe, to administer the immigration laws of Palestine in so far as they affect Jewish immigration.

g. With the approval of the Mandatary Power, to issue bonds, debentures, or other obligations, the proceeds of any or all of which to be expended by the Jewish Council for the benefit of the Jewish people or for the development of Palestine.

h. The Jewish Council shall hold all of its property and income in trust for the benefit of the Jewish people.

3. A provisional Jewish Council of representatives of the Zionist Organisation, of the Jewish population in Palestine, and of such other approved Jewish organisations as are willing to cooperate in the development of a Jewish Palestine shall be formed forthwith by the Zionist Organisation. Such Provisional Jewish Council shall exercise all of the powers and perform all of the duties of the Jewish Council until such time as the Jewish Council shall be formally constituted by the Jewish Congress

4. Finally when in the opinion of the Mandatary Power, the inhabitants of Palestine shall be able to undertake the establishment of Representative and Responsible Government, such steps shall be taken as will permit the establishment of such government through the exercise of a democratic franchise, without regard to race or faith; and the inhabitants of Palestine under such government, shall continue to enjoy equal civil and political rights as citizens irrespective of race or faith. . . .

[Here follows a description of the Zionist Organization.]

3. The Resolution of the General Syrian Congress at Damascus Proclaims Arab Sovereignty over Greater Syria, July 2, 1919

In 1919, during the Peace Conference at Versailles, President Woodrow Wilson appointed an American commission headed by Henry King (president of Oberlin College in Ohio) and Chicago businessman Charles R. Crane. The purpose of the King-Crane Commission was to solicit the opinions of the local inhabitants of Syria and Palestine about their political future in light of the dissolution of the Ottoman Empire. This resolution of the General Syrian Congress formulated to provide the

King-Crane Commission with a specific and unified notion of what the "Arabs" of Greater Syria desired. The document leaves no doubt about their rejection of the Zionist project for a Jewish homeland in what the U.S. Congress—and most Arabs—regarded as Arab Palestine.

We the undersigned members of the General Syrian Congress, meeting in Damascus on Wednesday, July 2nd, 1919, made up of representatives from the three Zones, viz., the Southern, Eastern, and Western, provided with credentials and authorizations by the inhabitants of our various districts, Moslems, Christians, and Jews, have agreed upon the following statement of the desires of the people of the country who have elected us to present them to the American Section of the International Commission; the fifth article was passed by a very large majority; all the other articles were accepted unanimously.

1. We ask absolutely complete political independence for Syria within these boundaries. The Taurus System on the North; Rafah and a line running from Al Jauf to the south of the Syrian and the Hejazian line to Akaba on the south; the Euphrates and Khabur Rivers and a line extending east of Abu Kamal to the east of Al Jauf on the east; and the Mediterranean on the West.

2. We ask that the Government of this Syrian country should be a democratic civil constitutional Monarchy on broad decentralization principles, safeguarding the rights of minorities, and that the King be the Emir Feisal, who carried on a glorious struggle in the cause of our liberation and merited our full confidence and entire reliance.

3. Considering the fact that the Arabs inhabiting the Syrian area are not naturally less gifted than other more advanced races and that they are by no means less developed than the Bulgarians, Serbians, Greeks, and Roumanians at the beginning of their independence, we protest against Article 22 of the Covenant of the League of Nations placing us among the nations in their middle stage of development which stand in need of a mandatory power.

4. In the event of the rejection by the Peace Conference of this just protest for certain considerations that we may not understand, we, relying on the declarations of President Wilson that his object in waging war was to put an end to the ambition of conquest and colonization, can only regard the mandate mentioned in the Covenant of the League of Nations as equivalent to the rendering of economical and technical assistance that does not prejudice our complete independence. And desiring that our country should not fall a prey to colonization and believing that the American Nation is farthest from any thought of colonization and has no political ambition in our country, we will seek the technical and economical assistance from the United States of America, provided that such assistance does not exceed 20 years.

From the King-Crane Commission Report in *Foreign Relations of the United States: Paris Peace Conference, 1919,* vol. 12: pp. 780–781. This document may also be found in J. C. Hurewitz, *The Middle East and North Africa in World Politics* (New Haven, Conn.: Yale University Press, 1975), pp. 180–182.

5. In the event of America not finding herself in a position to accept our desire for assistance, we will seek this assistance from Great Britain, also provided that such assistance does not infringe the complete independence and unity of our country and that the duration of such assistance does not exceed that mentioned in the previous article.

6. We do not acknowledge any right claimed by the French Government in any part whatever of our Syrian country and refuse that she should assist us or have a hand in our country under any circumstances and in any place.

7. We oppose the pretentions of the Zionists to create a Jewish commonwealth in the southern part of Syria, known as Palestine, and oppose Zionist migration to any part of our country; for we do not acknowledge their title but consider them a grave peril to our people from the national, economical, and political points of view. Our Jewish compatriots shall enjoy our common rights and assume the common responsibilities.

8. We ask that there should be no separation of the southern part of Syria. known as Palestine, nor of the littoral western zone, which includes Lebanon, from the Syrian country. We desire that the unity of the country should be guaranteed against partition under whatever circumstances.

9. We ask complete independence for emancipated Mesopotamia and that there should be no economical barriers between the two countries.

10. The fundamental principles laid down by President Wilson in condemnation of secret treaties impel us to protest most emphatically against any treaty that stipulates the partition of our Syria country and against any private engagement aiming at the establishment of Zionism in the southern part of Syria; therefore we ask the complete annulment of these conventions and agreements.

The noble principles enunciated by President Wilson strengthen our confidence that our desires emanating from the depths of our hearts, shall be the decisive factor in determining our future; and that President Wilson and the free American people will be our supporters for the realization of our hopes, thereby proving their sincerity and noble sympathy with the aspiration of the weaker nations in general and our Arab people in particular.

We also have the fullest confidence that the Peace Conference will realize that we would not have risen against the Turks, with whom we had participated in all civil, political, and representative privileges, but for their violation of our national rights, and so will grant us our desires in full in order that our political rights may not be less after the war than they were before, since we have shed so much blood in the cause of our liberty and independence.

We request to be allowed to send a delegation to represent us at the Peace Conference to defend our rights and secure the realization of our aspirations.

4. The American King-Crane Commission Report Summarizes the Popular Ideas of Nationalism in the Middle East, 1919

The report of the King-Crane Commission is probably one of the most objective documents indicating the moods, uncertainties, and opinions that prevailed in the region after the war. The contradictory demands are as interesting as the agreements, because they indicate the state of flux that predominated in the Levant and Mesopotamia.

The Story of the Tour

The whole area visited by the commission during the 42 days from June 10 to July 21 is Occupied Enemy Territory under the supreme authority of General Allenby. The administration is conducted under the Turkish laws, with small local modifications, in many cases continuing in office part or all of the officials left behind by the Turks. A system of military governors and officers assigned to special duties, such as financial and medical advice, liaison work, etc., parallels the civil administration. The whole area is in four portions, known respectively as O. E. T. A. (Occupied Enemy Territory Administration) South, West, East, and North, and administered under the guidance respectively of English, French, Arab, and French officers. The order of description followed below is by these areas, and is nearly coincident with the itinerary of the commission, the only exception being that much of O. E. T. A. East was visited before O. E. T. A West. Fifteen days were spent in the South, ten in the West, fifteen in the East, and two in the North.

The Geography of the Claims

[. . .]

III. Specific Requests as Given in the Table

[. . .]

A. Territorial Limits

1. The largest percentage for any one request is that of 1,500 petitions (80.4 per cent) for United Syria, including Cilicia, the Syrian Desert, and Palestine. The boundaries of this area are usually defined as "The Taurus Mountains on the north; the Euphrates and Khabur Rivers and the line extending east of Abu

---

"King-Crane Report on the Near East," *Editor & Publisher* (New York: Editor & Publisher Co., 1922).

Kamal to the east of Al Juf on the east; Rafa and the line running from Al Juf to the south of Akaba on the south; and the Mediterranean Sea on the West." In addition to being the first plank of the Damascus program [see document 3 in this chapter] a United Syria received strong support from many Christians in all the O. E. T. As., as the number of petitions indicates.

2. In opposition to Syrian Unity, six of the nineteen pro-Zionist petitions ask for a separate Palestine, and presumably it is implied in the others.

3. In addition, two Christian groups in Palestine asked for a separate Palestine under the British, in preference to a United Syria under the French.

4. Twenty-four petitions, chiefly from Christian sources in O. E. T. A. South, asked for an autonomous Palestine within the Syrian State. For many other delegations this was doubtless implied in the general request for independence and a non-centralized government.

5. In opposition also to a United Syria are the 203 petitions (16.9 per cent) asking for an independent Greater Lebanon. One hundred and ninety-six of these came from Lebanon and 139 are copies of the French-Lebanon program.

6. The request for a United Syria is made even more emphatic by the 1,062 protests against an Independent Greater Lebanon. These include the Damascus program petitions and some from Protestant and other Christian sources in Lebanon.

7. Thirty-three Lebanese delegations representing both Moslems and Christians, fearing the economic future of a separate Lebanon, asked for autonomy within a Syrian State. Others also regarded autonomy as implied in the request for independence and a non-centralized government.

8–9. The Valley of Bekaa is usually regarded as an integral part of Greater Lebanon. Eleven petitions, however, make especial reference to its inclusion, while eight ask that the Valley remain in the Damascus area.

10–11. Similarly, while Cilicia is definitely included in the demand for a United Syria made by 1,500 petitions, two petitions asked specifically for it, while three requested that it be given to the Armenian State.

B. Independence

1. The second largest percentage of all, 1,370 (73.5 per cent), is for "Absolute Independence," the second cardinal point of the Damascus program, supported generally by all Moslem delegations. It is certain from the oral statements that accompanied the petitions that the term "Absolute Independence" was seldom used in the sense of an entire freedom from any foreign guidance, such as that of a mandatory under the League of Nations, inasmuch as the request was frequently combined with a choice of mandate, and in all but a few cases with either a choice of mandate or a request for foreign "assistance." While a few of the Young Arab clubs certainly desired freedom from all foreign control, the great majority asked for independence and defined a mandate to

mean only economic and technical assistance, because of a widespread fear that the mandatory arrangement would be used to cloak colonial annexation.

2–3. Only a slightly smaller number, 1,278 (68.5 per cent), asked for the independence of Iraq, or Mesopotamia. To these should be added 93 of the 97 petitions for the independence of all Arab countries as in only four petitions do both requests appear, and the second includes the first. The phrasing "for all Arab countries" was first used in Palestine, and dropped for the special mention of Iraq in the Damascus program. A total of 1,371 petitions, therefore, asked for the independence and economic freedom of the Iraq regions.

C. Form of Government

1–2. The establishment of a "democratic, non-centralized, constitutional" kingdom is one of the points of the Damascus program, as the number of petitions for it, 1,107 (59.3 per cent), indicate. All but five of these petitions, also, ask that Emir Feisal be made the king. These petitions were especially numerous in O. E. T. A. East, where 1,005 of 1,157 request both a kingdom and the Emir as king. This part of the program had apparently not been developed when the commission was in Palestine, as only five of 260 O. E. T. A. South petitions referred to a kingdom, and only two mentioned Emir Feisal.

3. A request for a democratic representative government, presumably of a republican character, came to the commission from 26 Christian groups in O. E. T. A. West, and eight groups in O. E. T. A. East, a total of 34 (1.8 per cent). This request was usually made in opposition to the Moslem idea of a Syrian kingdom under Feisal.

4. The request for proper safe-guarding of the rights of minorities included in the Damascus program was also made by many of the Christian groups in Lebanon. The total is 1,023 (54.9 per cent). This request received a more united support from both Moslems and Christians than any other, except anti-Zionism.

5–6. Five requests for the retention of Arabic as the official language (rather than Hebrew) and ten requests for the abolition of foreign capitulations (officially annulled by the Turks, but without sanction of the Powers) came from scattered points in O. E. T. A. South.

7. Nineteen (1.02 per cent) petitions were received for the autonomy of all the provinces of Syria. This is in addition to the separate requests for autonomy of Lebanon and Palestine. Once more it should be said that many regarded a large measure of local autonomy as implicit in the general idea of a democratic, non-centralized government, but these nineteen groups made special reference to it.

D. Choice of Mandate

With regard to choice of mandate, five classes of requests had to be distinguished, as shown in the tables [not included]. In addition to definite requests for a given nation as the mandatory power, a few groups gave their preference, "if a mandatory is obligatory," i.e., rather under protest, while the great majority asked for "assistance" rather than a mandatory, because of a misunderstanding, and the fear referred to above that a "mandate" is a convenient cloak for colonial aggression. Petitions of these three classes have therefore been grouped in the summary as "Total first choice." In addition preferences for second choice of mandate and "assistance" have been tabulated.

1. The total of the petitions asking for Great Britain as first choice is 66 (3.5 per cent). Forty-eight came from Palestine; 13 are from Greek Orthodox delegations, and four from the Druses. The second choice total is 1,073 (57.5 per cent), due to the 1,032 requests for British "assistance" if America declined, in accordance with the Damascus program.
2. The French total for first choice is 274 (14.68 per cent), all but 59 of them from the Lebanon district. The second choice total is three.
3. The 1,064 requests for American "assistance" according to the Damascus program, with 57 selections of America as mandatory power, and eight more if a mandate is obligatory, make up the first choice total of 1,129 (60.5 per cent). The second choice total is 11.
4. Twenty-three petitions received at Jenin, Haifa, and Nazareth just before the Damascus program was adopted, left the choice of mandate to the Syrian Congress. This means, therefore, an additional 23 for American first choice and British second choice total.

E. Zionism

1–2–3. The petitions favoring the Zionist program have been analyzed above in the discussion of programs. In opposition to these are the 1,350 (72.3 per cent) petitions protesting against Zionist claims and purposes. This is the third largest number for any one point and represents a more widespread general opinion among both Moslems and Christians than any other. The anti-Zionist note was especially strong in Palestine, where 222 (85.3 per cent) of the 260 petitions declared against the Zionist program. This is the largest percentage in the district for any one point.
[. . .]

I. The Area Under British Occupation (O. E. T. A. SOUTH)

1. NARRATIVE.   Owing to changes of plan at a late date, the commission arrived in Jaffa at a time when the British authorities were not expecting it, and the program followed there was arranged mainly without their help. The endeavor was made to ascertain the opinions and desires of every important group, sect, and organization, of a few well-informed representative individuals, and of significant minorities of sub-divisions, especially in cases where

there seemed to be disposition, for any reason, to suppress these. Because of the numerous sub-divisions of the Christians and particularly of the Roman Catholics, it was inevitable that from the beginning the commission would give a disproportionate number of interviews and amount of time to them. The commissioners had prepared a statement of their purposes, to be found elsewhere in this report, which was read to important groups, and given to the press in lieu of interviews. Care was taken to make it clear, in response to frequent questioning, that the policy of the United States in regard to accepting a mandate anywhere was unformed and unpredictable, and that the commission had no power of decision. Automobiles were secured from the American Committee for Relief in the Near East, in order to be as little as possible dependent upon others than Americans. Word was given out that the commission would not accept general social invitations or consent to demonstrations. [. . .]

Zionism

[. . .]

E. We recommend, in the fifth place, serious modification of the extreme Zionist program for Palestine of unlimited immigration of Jews, looking finally to making Palestine distinctly a Jewish State.

(1) The Commissioners began their study of Zionism with minds predisposed in its favor, but the actual facts in Palestine, coupled with the force of the general principles proclaimed by the Allies and accepted by the Syrians, have driven them to the recommendation here made.

(2) The commission was abundantly supplied with literature on the Zionist program by the Zionist Commission to Palestine [see document 4 in this chapter]; heard in conferences much concerning the Zionist colonies and their claims; and personally saw something of what had been accomplished. They found much to approve in the aspirations and plans of the Zionists, and had warm appreciation for the devotion of many of the colonists and for their success, by modern methods, in overcoming natural obstacles.

(3) The commission recognized also that definite encouragement had been given to the Zionists by the Allies in Mr. Balfour's often quoted statement [and] in its approval by other representatives of the Allies. If, however, the strict terms of the Balfour Statement [see document 4 in the chapter "Ideas of Nationalism"] are adhered to—favoring "the establishment in Palestine of a national home for the Jewish people," "it being clearly understood that nothing shall be done which may prejudice the civil and religious rights existing in non-Jewish communities in Palestine"—it can hardly be doubted that the extreme Zionist Program must be greatly modified.

For "a national home for the Jewish people" is not equivalent to making Palestine into a Jewish State; nor can the erection of such a Jewish State be accomplished without the gravest trespass upon the "civil and religious rights of existing non-Jewish communities in Palestine." The fact came out repeatedly in the Commission's conference with Jewish representatives, that the Zionists looked forward to a practically complete dispossession of the present non-Jewish inhabitants of Palestine, by various forms of purchase.

In his address of July 4, 1918, President Wilson laid down the following principle as one of the four great "ends for which the associated peoples of the world were fighting": "The settlement of every question, whether of territory, of sovereignty, of economic arrangement, or of political relationship upon the basis of the free acceptance of that settlement by the people immediately concerned and not upon the basis of the material interest or advantage of any other nation or people which may desire a different settlement for the sake of its own exterior influence or mastery." If that principle is to rule, and so the wishes of Palestine's population are to be decisive as to what is to be done with Palestine, then it is to be remembered that the non-Jewish population of Palestine—nearly nine-tenths of the whole—are emphatically against the entire Zionist program. The tables show that there was no one thing upon which the population of Palestine were more agreed than upon this. To subject a people so minded to unlimited Jewish immigration, and to steady financial and social pressure to surrender the land, would be a gross violation of the principle just quoted, and of the people's rights, though it kept within the forms of law.

It is to be noted also that the feeling against the Zionist program is not confined to Palestine, but shared very generally by the people throughout Syria as our conferences clearly showed. More than 72 per cent—1,350 in all—of all the petitions in the whole of Syria were directed against the Zionist program. Only two requests—those for a united Syria and for independence—had a larger support. This general feeling was only voiced by the "General Syrian Congress," in the seventh, eighth, and tenth resolutions of the statement. (Already quoted in the report.)

The Peace Conference should not shut its eyes to the fact that the anti-Zionist feeling in Palestine and Syria is intense and not lightly to be flouted. No British officer, consulted by the commissioners, believed that the Zionist program could be carried out except by force of arms. The officers generally thought that a force of not less than 50,000 soldiers would be required even to initiate the program. That of itself is evidence of a strong sense of the injustice of the Zionist program, on the part of the non-Jewish populations of Palestine and Syria. Decisions, requiring armies to carry out, are sometimes necessary, but they are surely not gratuitously to be taken in the interests of a serious injustice. For the initial claim, often submitted by Zionist representatives, that they have a "right" to Palestine, based on an occupation of 2,000 years ago, can hardly be seriously considered.

There is a further consideration that cannot justly be ignored, if the world is to look forward to Palestine becoming a definitely Jewish state, however gradually that may take place. That consideration grows out of the fact that Palestine is "the Holy Land" for Jews, Christians, and Moslems alike. Millions of Christians and Moslems all over the world are quite as much concerned as the Jews with conditions in Palestine, especially with those conditions which touch upon religious feeling and rights. The relations in these matters in Palestine are most delicate and difficult. With the best possible intentions, it may be doubted whether the Jews could possibly seem to either Christians or Moslems proper guardians of the holy places, or custodians of the Holy Land as a whole.

The reason is this: The places which are most sacred to Christians—those having to do with Jesus—and which are also sacred to Moslems, are not only not sacred to Jews, but abhorrent to them. It is simply impossible, under those circumstances, for Moslems and Christians to feel satisfied to have these places in Jewish hands, or under the custody of Jews. There are still other places about which Moslems must have the same feeling. In fact, from this point of view, the Moslems, just because the sacred places of all three religions are sacred to them, have made very naturally much more satisfactory custodians of the holy places than the Jews could be. It must be believed that the precise meaning, in this respect, of the complete Jewish occupation of Palestine has not been fully sensed by those who urge the extreme Zionist program. For it would intensify, with a certainty like fate, the anti-Jewish feeling both in Palestine and in all other portions of the world which look to Palestine as "the Holy Land."

In view of all these considerations, and with a deep sense of sympathy for the Jewish cause, the commissioners feel bound to recommend that only a greatly reduced Zionist program be attempted by the Peace Conference, and even that, only very gradually initiated. This would have to mean that Jewish immigration should be definitely limited, and that the project for making Palestine distinctly a Jewish commonwealth should be given up.

There would then be no reason why Palestine could not be included in a united Syrian State, just as other portions of the country, the holy places being cared for by an International and Inter-religious Commission, somewhat as at present under the oversight and approval of the Mandatary and of the League of Nations. The Jews, of course, would have representation upon this commission.

The recommendations now made lead naturally to the necessity of recommending what power shall undertake the single Mandate for all Syria. [...]

5. A Writer for *al-Asima*, the Syrian Government Newspaper, Seeks to Establish the Popular Idea of the "Nation," October 23, 1919

At a time when Syria was plunged into political chaos in the wake of World War I, many writers attempted to create a sense of certainty about the future of the nation. Some Syrian elites had thrown their political support behind the concept of an Arab kingdom to be led by Amir Faisal, the son of Sharif Husayn (see document 3 in

Muhib al-Din al-Khatib, "Public Opinion," *al-Asima*, 23 October 1919, vol. 1, no. 69. Translated by Akram Khater.

the chapter "Ideas of Nationalism"). Other elites saw in the arrival of French man-date forces the possibility of maintaining their power. And still others were indecisive about which path to take and whom to support. The Syrian public held equally mixed feelings.

Writing in the midst of this confusion, Muhib al-Din al-Khatib, the author of this article, tries to strike a note of certainty. Notice the language he uses to describe the "nation," the juxtaposition of individual and communal interests, and the way in which he tries to resolve the tension between "old" and "new." Throughout, he is seeking to establish a popular idea of the "nation." What audience was he ad-dressing, and why did he find it necessary to strongly juxtapose the individual and the "nation"?

Public Opinion

It would be a grave mistake to measure the general public by the actions of some individuals, and to assume those to represent the average citizen. Those who deeply explore these matters will note that the general population has a communal spirit that overcomes individual interests and erases their narrowly-focused designs and desires. The nation has an independent collective person-ality that is stronger than partial personalities, and the latter will and should dissolve into the first in the case of contradiction of interests.

The public spirit and that of the nation are derived from history and are led by the hands of the past. As long as history is filled with glorious events, and as long as the past contains beneficial models for the present and future then you can be certain that the masses will move forward. One need not doubt those who presently appeal to the true glory and who demand the right renaissance, and who preach eternal future happiness. Whoever opposes this—because of illegitimate designs and purpose or self-interest—will be swept away by the public spirit just like garbage is swept away by raging torrents of water.

In many of my previous articles I have criticized the shortcomings of some individuals in their duty toward this nation, and complained about their lack of initiative in many matters that they should have exerted more effort in accom-plishing. This would have been particularly the case had they risked few exist-ing privileges for greater and desired benefits, and had they sacrificed unworthy and temporary comforts in order to arrive at eternal happiness and peace. How-ever, regardless of how much I may have complained and criticized, I do not mean to imply that the shortcomings of those individuals will keep the nation from achieving ambitions, or will keep it from progressing to the social level worthy of a nation with an honorable past and glorious history. It will achieve its ambitions in any case, and it will occupy its deserved place whether we wished it or not. This is ordained by the spirit of the nation and the needs of its people that derive from its past and history. However, the agreement of its in-dividuals to perform their duties, and the cooperation of all of its people in these tasks will hasten the process of arriving at the results and will make the nation more respectable in the eyes of outsiders.

I have said that the spirit of the people and their personality are indepen-dent from those of the individuals. This is easily apparent to anyone who contemplates these issues, because the individual derives his decision from his selfish interests, and he expends his effort toward that end. But the people derive their decisions from their past, extracting from it a general purpose, then the masses exert themselves in achieving this ancient goal. There are individuals with enough foresight to see an intersection between their personal interests and the general good, and thus [they] would work toward that goal in conjunction with the masses. But there are others who are short-sighted and cannot see the point of intersection, and thus they work for a purpose other than the general good. Those are the ones of whom I have complained, even though I believe they are too weak to counter the tide of public opinion.

I heard someone yesterday faulting the Syrian public opinion because it is ever changing. I see these changes as evidence of the sensitivity of public opinion to the various stages that public policy has gone through. Whoever knows the Syrian people intimately, and who listens to them intently, will know with certainty that the public opinion in these lands is composed of two main elements: the first is its historical traditions to which the Syrian public adheres to faithfully, and these traditions are firmly established regardless of the shape it may take, and it will never dissipate or disappear. The illiterate old woman, the religious scholar and the enlightened youth are all equal in respecting the historical traditions and to safeguard the public good. No one can even contemplate that the people will lose faith in this central tenet of our society, or that these traditions will be influenced by the changes in our environment and world. The second element is subjective and of limited duration and is formed of the total of internal and external influences, and will evolve according to various stages and according to the changes in these influences. Many people are mystified by its evolution because they do not know that the people will filter all external influences through the sieve of its traditions. . . .

Thus, the Syrian public opinion combines the two characteristics of change and continuity. It adopts continuity from its belief in past traditions and loyalty to its eternal goal. At the same time it leans toward change because of its flexibility with regard to the demands of our time, trying throughout to balance the new requirements with the old traditions. . . . This is the secret behind the optimism of the Syrian people. . . . The Syrian people contains [*sic*] all the characteristics of change and forward movement because these characteristics are decreed by God in His creation, and that which God decrees cannot be changed.

6.   Women and the Vote in Syria: A Parliamentary Debate About the Relationship Between Gender and Citizenship in the Proposed State, April 25, 1920

This document is a transcription of the proceedings of a Syrian parliamentary session during which delegates to the Greater Syria Conference were attempting to compile a constitution. Their purpose for doing so was to thwart European (French and British) efforts to claim political control over the region. In the course of the discussions, delegates posed questions about the meaning of the Syrian "nation" and its implications. Notice that a multitude of opinions were being presented from various parts of "Greater Syria"— Palestine, Lebanon, and Syria.

On the 25th of April, 1920, Article 79—which specifies the characteristics of the voter—of the Basic Constitution was to be discussed. Lebanon's delegate (District of al-Kharoub-Sheheem), Mr. Ibrahim Al-Khatib, stood up and suggested giving the right to vote to women who had come of age and who had finished their secondary education. Subsequently, a clamor and uproar went through the hall which was interrupted by an impromptu and eloquent speech by the legal scholar Shaykh Sa'id Murad al-Ghazi (delegate of Gaza). [He spoke] about the right of the woman to vote, and the fact that the Islamic Shari'a has specified that the woman should govern, work, be knowledgeable and eloquent. [He concluded] by asking, then how could she not be a voter? At this point, the Secretary of the Conference invited Mr. Izzat Druza (Nablus) to debate Ibrahim al-Khatib's suggestion.

Shaykh 'Abd al-Qadir al-Kilani (Hama) spoke to the young men of the Conference saying, "The Europeans have walked the path of modernization for 300 years, and their traditions do not prohibit the woman from participating in any activity, yet show me one country of the countries of Europe which has given women that right [voting right]?"

VOICE: (*from the floor of the Conference*) England, Sweden.

So he responded to them, "If you want the uplifting of women then open schools for them. Giving the woman the right to vote means her right to be a delegate, so do you want amongst you female delegates?"

SA'ADALLAH AL-JABIRI: Why not? She already goes to the market and buys . . .

AL-KILANI: The presence of the woman as voter or delegate with this ignorance and immorality is harmful, but when the good morals are developed then we can look into the matter [of voting rights for women].

SA'ADALLAH AL-JABIRI: I note the words of the gentleman, that he sees no reason in the end that should keep her from voting.

AL-KILANI: Yes, yes then we will look Into the matter positively, the *hijab* is indeed an innovation, but when some demanded that it be removed the ignorant rabble began to follow the [unveiled] women mocking them. We are afraid that this decision [about voting?] will cause social and political unrest. This idea [women's right to vote] is too premature, and I request that we reject it.

DA'AS AL-JURJIS (HOSN AL-AKRAD): We do not want to remain in the state of a man who has suffered from a stroke that left one half of him healthy and the other paralyzed. The nation is made up of the man and the woman.

---

al-Hawadith, 25 April 1975, pp. 47–53. Translated by Akram Khater.

Therefore, we must reflect on this suggestion [women's right to vote] with honesty and sincerity. I would like to thank Mr. Al-Kilani because I understood from him that he supports the suggestion even though he does not think it appropriate for this moment in time! It is true that 98% of our women are ignorant, which is why he [al-Kilani] made education a requirement and that is correct! Therefore, if we give only the educated woman the right to vote then he would approve of that. Turkey has given the woman the right to vote and the author Khalida Adib is about to enter the parliament. What you observed during the war (WWI) of the service of women in the army is evidence of the importance of the help of the gentler sex. And the presence of the lady in the armed services is far more important than the process of voting. And the danger that some of the present brothers see [in giving such a right to women] can be removed because a woman has the right not to give an opinion, and the lady who is careful to avoid having the pen touch her fingertips has the right to not vote.

AHMAD AL-QADAMANI (DAMASCUS): Allah has made her with half a brain.

DA'AS AL-JURJIS: It is very important to place this principle [woman's right to vote] in our Basic Law, especially given our current political situation, therefore I demand the acceptance of the suggestion and to move it to committee (*applause from the right and the middle*).

'ADEL ZU'AYTER (NABLUS): There is no doubt that each and every one of us want[s], desires, and must work to make the woman arrive at a level of advancement where she can take her right. And despite what has been said about the benefit of giving women the right to vote, I still see its approval at this moment does not coincide with the welfare of the nation. Some of the European nations have not taken this step except after it had undergone developments that lasted hundreds of years, while we are now only at the beginning of our societal life. Every nation has traditions and wise mores, and if the laws are not based upon these then it is to be feared that revolutions and unrest will break out (*applause from the middle*). Yes, it is true that the *Shari'a* [Islamic jurisprudence] may give the woman the right to vote, but it does not say that the nation is obliged to pass legislation that give the woman the right to participate in it [the electoral process]. Permission is one thing, and obligation is another. We are now in a difficult situation. We came to this place to express the opinion of the nation, and if we pass legislation that it [the nation] does not accept, and we are in our current situation, then will we have kept that trust?

VOICES: No, No . . .

'ABD AL-QADIR AL-KHATIB (DAMASCUS): I request that we table this article for discussion, until the nation can look at it, and if it supported it then it [the nation] has the final say, and if it did not support it then it has the final say as well. Educated women are far and few in between, and we cannot take the exceptions to be the basis of the law, and I beg of you not to undertake a matter that will do greater harm than good.

SUBHI AL-TAWIL (LATAKIA): The matter is purely societal and does not effect the *hijab*. And the woman if she is selected is not required to unveil herself (*applause*). Even if this election [of a woman into the Parliament] does nothing but prove a woman's right [to be elected] then it is sufficient.

AHMAD AL-QADAMANI (DAMASCUS): And from where did you get this right and from which *Shari'a*?

SUBHI AL-TAWIL (LATAKIA): An educated woman is better than a thousand ignorant men, so why would we give men the right to vote and yet deprive educated women from that same right?

AHMAD AL-QADAMANI (DAMASCUS): How many men like you are there in Latakia?

SUBHI AL-TAWIL (LATAKIA): If you have something to say then please come to the podium, and do not speak from the floor. Yes, there are very few educated girls, but it is not obligatory for them to vote. Some of the speakers have said that Europe is now trying to give women the right to vote. What is meant by that is to give them the right to sit in the seats of the Parliament But the right to vote had been given to them hundreds of years ago.

AHMAD AL-QADAMANI (DAMASCUS): We in Damascus do not want that [women voting] to be the case, so just make it so in Latakia!

SUBHI AL-TAWIL (LATAKIA): I request that an open-ballot vote be taken on the suggestion of brother Ibrahim al-Khatib.

At this point Shaykh Sa'id Murad (Gaza), the champion of women's rights, stood up, and he was received with applause. And a commotion arose that was interrupted by Riyad al-Sulh (Beirut) saying: "Before Shaykh Sa'id speaks, [let me say that] it is possible that a group of the members [of parliament] may be of different views than his, but honoring knowledge is a must therefore, gentlemen, I ask you to applaud" (*loud applause*).

SHAYKH SA'ID MURAD (GAZA): This is a very important subject that I do not deny disagreement over it. Disagreement is the *sunna* [law] of the universe. But what I would like for this matter is for you to consider to look [at it] rationally rather than with emotions. I request that we do not mix up the matter of the *hijab* with this subject at hand. What prompts me to speak about this subject is what I have read in the writings of the Westerners and their newspapers, for they have said: The East needs the West to be its guardian, because it [the East] has decreed upon itself the ignorance of its half (*uproar*). I am speaking in colloquial Arabic that everyone can understand; the Westerners say: We must be the guardians over the East, whose one half of society has been decreed to be ignorant. Therefore, I say that there is no . . . (*at this point the following members withdrew from the session: 'Abd al-Qadir al-Khatib, Muhammad al-Mujtahid, Ahmed al-Qadamani, Ibrahim al-Shaykh Hussein, Ahmad al-'Ayash, Khalil al-Talhuni*).

THE PRESIDENT: We have lost the quorum.

SA'ADALLAH AL-JABIRI: Even though the quorum is lost we particularly want to hear the words of the gentleman.

IZZAT DRUZA (SECRETARY): There is a quorum.

SHAYKH SA'ID MURAD, *continued:* We say to the Westerners from this podium words that will reach their parliaments. There are no traditions in the East that decree the ignorance of half of its people. We are also ready at every opportunity to remove this ignorance from men and women alike. Islamic jurisprudence had decided to accept the testimony of a woman, and to accept references of *hadiths* to her, and to accept her as teacher and judge in legal matters except the criminal cases. I am not speaking here of the *hijab* for it is a secondary matter. And it is as if my brothers would have me confuse the issue of voting with that of the *hijab* when the subject is clearly about a woman's right. And those who gave us the right to legislate in this parliament have given her also the right to vote. Yes, I do not deny that all laws should be in step with the spirit of the nation, and a legislation cannot be enforced unless it is distilled from the spirit of the nation. [However,] what makes this subject a problem for some of the brothers—despite my belief in their honesty, sincerity and patriotism—is that they are confusing the matter of the *hijab* with the matter of education which is the means for election. So, if you want to discuss the *hijab* then discuss it without me being a member in this session. However, the subject of women's education was discussed half a century ago and the proponents have won. And now you can see the capitals and the countries full of girls' schools. And since we are in agreement about the education of the woman, then I wanted at this point to advance the subject of election after the matter of education hoping that it will as successful as the latter. And this we progress till we arrive at the desired goal. First, we must acknowledge the right of the woman to elect a member of the parliament. And this is similar to a woman testifying, for the judge accepts the testimony of women according to their class and traditions. Similarly, we can allow women to vote in a manner that does not force her to remove the *hijab.* And all I want for Europe to understand is that—while it maybe more advanced than us in manufacture and material things—we are more civilized than it in our civil code. And if Europe wants to progress and complete its civil code, then it must turn to the East and adopt from it. And just as we do not want to deny its [Europe's] unique characteristics, it must not deny ours. I want for every citizen to be proud of his "Syrianness," in the same manner that the greatest minister in the West is proud of his patriotism. The only link of the woman's subject [with regard to the vote] is to the matter of education, and we must acknowledge that Allah has given her the same rights as he has given you. So be kind to those on earth and He who is in the heavens will be merciful to you. This is one of the pure social issues that benefits greatly from the Qur'anic text.

RAFIQ AL-TAMIMI (AL-KHALIL-HEBRON): Mr. Sa'id Murad has spoken eloquently about this subject, but despite that [I must insist] that this matter is not a religious one, but a civil one relating to social relations more than spiritual issues. In the past the woman in the West did not have a separate individuality, rather right after marriage her person was mixed with that of her husband. Thus, she had no right to buy or sell. But the West has progressed, and the civilized nations have given the woman control over of her legal rights. Europe that has been late in giving this right [voting right] must not be better than us, especially since Islam has given the woman this right 1,200 years ago. However, we can harmonize between the old and new ideologies. The right to vote is a duty that covers all the citizens. But it is deaf, for every citizen should vote, but he is not penalized if he does not cast his vote. In other words, the woman has the liberty to use or refuse this right. And we say unto the men who do not accept to give women the right to vote, that you can influence your women. However, if there exists even the smallest group of people in the country who demand the granting of such a right then we must pave the way for it. If we give women this right then this does not mean that they must go to the city hall to vote, but rather they can meet in a designated place and vote. And for this reason I agree with the suggestion of Shaykh Ibrahim al-Khatib. I congratulate this conference which has defended the woman in the previous session, and has uplifted her status, when the rabble and the insolent fools in the capital had taken a stand against the gentler sex. I congratulate this conference because it knows that a nation whose half is ignorant cannot guarantee personal liberty. If the conference, which represents the nation, cannot put a stop to the attacks of the insolent against veiled women in the streets then we can kiss freedom goodbye.

IBRAHIM AL-KHATIB: If I had known that the minds [here] were ready to accept my suggestion to this degree then I would have suggested giving the woman more than this right (*murmurs from the seats of the Free Party, to which this member belongs*) . . . Mr. President, I declare that I have withdrawn from the Free Party because of what it contains of ignoramuses.

TAWFIQ MUFARIJ (KOURA): Withdraw your comment, Withdraw your comment!!

IBRAHIM AL-KHATIB: I withdraw it. If voting was a job then we would have obliged the woman to do it, but it is right that she has a choice in using it. We have limited this right to those women who are educated, who hold secondary degrees, and we have said that they have the right to give their opinion in writing!! I insist upon my suggestion, and I request that it should be accepted . . .

MR. RASHID RIDA (PRESIDENT OF THE CONFERENCE, LEBANON): (*Long storm of applause*): This matter has been discussed from a religious and social angle. But there are more than these two perspectives, and that is the feelings and sentiments of the nation. Had we been deciding upon a lesson then it would have been necessary for every person to give their opinion. However, he who wants to pass a practical legislation in the name of the nation must pay attention to its sentiments. Many speakers have spoken about this subject [women's right to vote] from the perspective of the Shari'a, but they did not give its due. The Shari'a is a very wide topic, and while pure religious matters are based on the text, matters relating to the world are based on consideration of public interests that change according to time and place. For, if we suppose that the leaders decide that it is in the interest of the nation to give women the right to vote, then we can find a precedent for it in the Shari'a, but until now this has not occurred. . . . Then there is another matter that is worthy of consideration. For voting pre-supposes individual freedom, and here I wonder: can a woman, living under the guardianship of her husband, use the right to vote if her husband forbids her from that?

SA'ADALLAH AL-JABIRI (ALEPPO): And does he have the right to forbid her from giving testimony in the courts?

RASHID RIDA: Yes. But I am not saying that I have decided on this matter, because I have not examined it very carefully. Do you suppose that that which the woman has learned in secondary school is sufficient to allow her to gain the right to vote? The Shari'a is quite open, so that if it can be proven that giving this right will be of benefit to the nation then the Shari'a allows it. However, the nation has sent for a particular reason . . . but we must maintain our status with the nation in whose name we speak, and to know the extent of the influence of our laws on her. The ratio of educat[ed] women amongst us is less than two percent, that is less than the percentage mentioned by Mr. Al-Kilani!! I have read in many magazines that when they, in Europe, have used women in many different tasks they have discovered that she has half the strength of the man. I submit that we must fight those reactionaries who desire for the woman to remain ignorant, however no benefit can come at this time from the issue of voting. . . . You know that the general public or public opinion will not accept the establishment of that [voting rights for women]. One shout at this critical time is sufficient to cause a public uprising. Despite my respect for the opinion of the "suggester" and my belief in his patriotism and sincerity, I request that we table the issue of the woman's right to vote and not include it within the law.

MOUNAH HAROUN (LATAKIA): I reply to the gentleman, and support the opinion of Shaykh Sa'id Murad saying: I have read in the religious interpretation that Mr. Rashid Rida himself publishes the following Qur'anic verse: "And they [the women] have the same [rights] as responsibilities." This means that the rights of the woman are the same as those of the man. And in the same interpretation [we read]: "Men are the guardians of the women," and that is by one degree. Beyond that then equality is an obligation. Therefore, I say that giving the right to vote to the woman is not contrary to the Shari'a.

RASHID RIDA: It appears that I have opened for you doors to matters that have not been clarified. Mr. Mounah Haroun has taken parts of my statement so that it appears as proof for his point, when it [my statement] is proof against him. For the degree which separates men from women is the degree of guardianship. But we do not want to enter here into interpretation. Rather we say, there is not benefit in this matter, and that we do not have the time to open the door of the people for the fanatics. Ten years ago I came to Damascus [from Egypt] and gave a lecture on the issue of *Tawhid* [monotheism] and the world was turned upside down against me. Now you oblige me to say quite frankly that in taking this decision [you will cause for] speeches to be made in the mosques and in societies against the Conference, and you will open matters that are of no practical benefit to us.

TAWFIQ MUFARIJ (KOURA): If the matter was related to the Shari'a then I would not speak of it, but this matter has nothing to do with religion, and I find it strange that the debate has arrived to this stage.

'ADEI ZU'AYTER (NABLUS): You did not understand the words of Mr. Rashid. He has dealt with this issue from the perspective of public welfare and the circumstances of the country.

TAWFIQ MUFARIJ (KOURA): All religions do not oppose this matter, and if Allah has given the woman a right then how can we forbid her from using it?

DOCTOR SAYID TALI' (LEBANON): How sad the woman is . . . you are discussing her rights in the Parliament while she is being insulted on the streets!! It is nice to be talking about the rights of the woman, and we all support that but I would like to remind you of a historical incident. When Japan wanted to craft a constitution for itself it called upon specialists from all the countries, and amongst those was an expert that was applauded by the attendees [of the constitutional session]. So he went to the Prime Minister and said to him: "My legal opinions have garnered the trust of all, so I hope that you will use as basis for your constitution. So he [the Prime Minister] replied to him: "We will take that which suits our country and leave aside that which does not." If I was in Europe I would have agreed to give this right to the woman all the while supporting my opinion with proofs and evidence, but since we are in Syria then I cannot do so. Here we are enacting legislation for the whole Syrian nation, and every law that does not correspond to the spirit of the nation is useless. . . . Syria cannot bear this law [woman's right to vote] now!

RIYAD AL-SULH: When I stand at this podium I do not ask about coffeehouses and homes, and whether it is with me or against me. Principally, I submit that we should give this right to the woman, and if the cafés of Damascus do not accept this, then the other districts will accept it with pleasure. And for me the greatest thing that this Conference has done is to leave the podium free [of interference]. . . . Please know, gentlemen, that the departure of six or seven members from this hall is of no consequent to me. Rather it proves their inability to defeat the truth. Still, I see that what the brothers have propose[d] is a compromise for the two ideas . . . it is a suggestion that we temporarily table this matter for now. . . .

GEORGE HARFOUSH (BEIRUT): I would like to say to you that the misbehavior which occurred amidst the general public in Damascus because of this debate had also occurred in Europe. . . . But this Conference has proven through its work that it walks in step with the free city. . . . Tomorrow Europe will read in its newspapers that the members of the Syrian Conference have suggested giving the woman the right to vote. . . . And rest assured that with that we will have had greater impact than twenty delegations, and accordingly I support the opinion of those demanding the need to give the woman her right.

THE PRESIDENT: Do you not find that we have had enough debate?

VOICES: Enough.

THE PRESIDENT: We have the following suggestion from Uthman Sultan and Theodore Antaki and fifteen members: "We suggest not dealing with the subject of giving the woman the right to vote, and recording the suggestion in the minutes of the Conference, and leaving the legal paragraph as it currently is." Whomsoever accepts this let him raise his hand (*and here many hands were raised in support of this suggestion . . . and the session was concluded*).

7. Ferhat Abbas Appeals for the Equality of Muslim Algerians and French Algerians, February 23, 1936

Ferhat Abbas (1899–1985) was born at Taher, Algeria, and he obtained his training as a pharmacist at the University of Algiers. By 1931 he was heavily involved in politics. He was elected to the general council of Constantine in 1933, the municipal council of Setif in 1935, and the Délégations Financières [Financial Delegations] in 1936; all of these were administrative and financial assemblies to which an Algerian Muslim could be elected according to French colonial law.

Early in his political career Abbas believed that Algeria should eschew the path of Arab nationalism and instead should become a semi-independent province of France—a relationship somewhat like the current relationship between Puerto Rico and the United States. This belief stood him in contrast to other Algerian politicians—Marxist or religious—who believed that Algeria should be completely independent from France. In the letter reprinted here, which was published in one of Algeria's French colonial newspapers, Abbas appeals for equality between Algeria's indigenous peoples and the colons—*French colonists—who practically controlled the economy and government of Algeria. Abbas hoped to find some common ground between French and local Algerian culture. Other nationalists (such as the Syrian Michel 'Aflaq—see document 11 in the chapter "Ideas of Nationalism") and the great majority of colonists rejected this goal.*

After 1936, severely disappointed by the failure of the reforms instituted by the leftist French Popular Front government, Abbas gradually shifted toward an autonomist position and in 1938 founded the Union Populaire Algérienne (*Algerian Popular Union). After World War II, after serving briefly in the French army, where he experienced anti-Arab racism, he formulated a new plan for an autonomous Algeria, but the plan came to naught because France was not willing to end its control of Algeria. In 1944 Abbas founded the organization* Amis du Manifeste de Liberation (*Friends of the Liberation Manifesto) re-formed in April 1946 as the*

Ferhat Abbas, "On the Margins of Nationalism. I am France!" *Liberté*, 27 February 1936, p. 3. Translated by Akram Khater.

Union Democratique du Manifeste Algérien *(Democratic Union of the Algerian Manifesto), which called for an autonomous Algeria in federation with France and was seen as a rival and an alternative to* L'Étoile Nord-Africaine, *Messali Hadj's more radical organization (see document 8 in the chapter "Ideas of Nationalism").*

By this time the French colonial regime considered Abbas anti-French and imprisoned him on several occasions. His years in jail convinced him finally that there was no way for Algerians to attain equality within a French-controlled Algeria. Thus, in 1956, when the Algerian armed revolt against the French was in full swing, he escaped to Cairo and joined the Front de Libération Nationale *(FLN) (Front for National Liberation). However, he could not play a large role—he disagreed with the approach of the FLN leaders—and he left Cairo in 1961. Later he served in the National Assembly of independent Algeria, but his political career was circumscribed by his opposition to the ruling FLN party and several of its leaders.*

With the lightness of thought characteristic of misinformed individuals, the newspaper *Le Temps*—without doubt inspired by colonial capital or the demented notions of some politicians—has resumed the attacks against Muslim Algeria by throwing in its face all the old accusations that the colonial arsenal has been using periodically for the past fifty years: nationalism, religious fanaticism, Wahabism [Islamic fundamentalism originating in the Arabian Peninsula in the late eighteenth century].

We recall the campaign carried out against us in 1935 and the subsequent arrival of the minister of the interior here. With the intelligence of a knowledgeable man, Mr. Régnier observed the character of our action and observed the spirit of the people whom we represent. He listened carefully and observed, then returned to Paris to announce with conviction and solemnity, from the podium of the Senate tribunal: "I trust the indigenous peoples [Arabs and Berbers]."

We thought that these wonderful words would be heard by the whole world and, placing our trust in the government of the [French] Republic [which had colonized Algeria in 1836] and even in our past adversaries, we awaited reforms and real changes. We hoped for the end of the Algerian malaise. We naively confused sentiment with action, and honor with politics. By believing the beautiful promises that were made to us, we entered a game controlled by our enemies. [. . .]

These forces exerted a great effort in opposing the decision of the arbitration. [. . .] We defended ourselves in 1935. We will defend ourselves today. [. . .] The truth, once more, will overcome lies. Most of all the land: we are ready with the help of God and men, we will be victorious in recapturing the land.

It is not within my ability to defend Shaykh Ben Badis and Shaykh al-Okbi and with them all of the 'ulama' [Muslim religious and legal scholars]. The question that interests me, and that was posed by *Le Temps*, is about teaching Arabic. That language is to the Islamic religion what the church is to the Catholic religion. It [Islam] cannot survive without it. The belief of an ignorant Muslim is nothing more than a tissue of superstitions. It [the language] constitutes the cement of faith. Is it then necessary under these circumstances to affirm our attachment to the teaching of the Arabic language, the basis of our belief?

This education is closely connected to freedom of thought. The suppression or even hindering of that education is a declaration of war against the Muslim religion. It is above all a declaration of war against teaching. We must see things as they are: Wahabism and Pan-Arabism are fragile facades behind which hide the real designs of our colonial educators. The majority of people to whom they deny French education must be deprived of Arabic education. Neither French culture nor Arab culture [will benefit Algerians]. Rather, [these policies will produce] an army of [Algerian] domestic servants and non-believers who would be easy to exploit, or at least fill the prisons and camps with them.

That is not what we desire.

In a country where more than 800,000 children are deprived of schooling, all of our attention is focused on education. This concern is translated into incessant demands to the public authorities for the creation of schools. It is equally translated into the thanks that we owe to private initiatives, and in particular to the 'ulama', for the considerable number of children whom they rescued from a terrible life on the streets. [. . .]

If the 'ulama' are "racists" or "Pan-Islamist" [as the French colonial press labeled them], then we the political friends of Dr. Ben-Djelloul would be nationalists. The accusation is not new. I have discussed this question with many different individuals. My opinion is known. Nationalism is a sentiment that drives a people to live within its territorial frontiers, a sentiment that has created this network of nations. If I discovered the "Algerian Nation," then I would be a nationalist but I would not have committed a crime. Men who have died for the national ideal are honored daily and respected. My life is not more valuable than theirs, yet I will not make this sacrifice. As a nation, Algeria is a myth, and I have not discovered it. I have interrogated history; I have interrogated the dead and the living; I have visited cemeteries: no one spoke to me about it. Of course I have found the "Arab Empire," and the "Muslim Empire," which honor Islam and our race, but these empires are gone. They are the equivalent of the Roman Empire and of the medieval Holy Roman Empire. They were born for an epoch and for a humanity that no longer exist.

Can an Algerian Muslim seriously dream of building the future with the dust of the past? Don Quixotes do not belong to our century. We are not building sand castles. Therefore, once and for all, we have put aside daydreams and chimeras to link our future with that of the French project in this country [Algeria]. [. . .] The protection of this work is the primary goal of our political action. And if I am in need of a single fact to support our doctrine, I will cite one that was revealed to me in my own research. In 1918 the amount of life insurance taken out by local Algerians was barely a few hundred thousand [French] francs. Today the amount is more than 20 million francs. It seems to me that if we were anti-French nationalists, the last thing we would do is place our resources in French banks. How could I be against France when for the past twenty to thirty years I have been investing in the French economy my meager resources on which I count for my existence in my old age and to educate my children?

Enough pleasantries! Our actions and ideas are the same. No one before has seriously believed in our nationalism. What they struggled for in the name of this word is our economic and political emancipation. And we desire this double emancipation with all of our will and our social ideals.

Six million Muslims live in this land, which became French one hundred years ago. They live in slums, barefoot, without clothes or bread. From this multitude of the starving we want to create a modern society through education, by defending the peasant, and through social welfare. We want to elevate the dignity of these men and women until it is equal to that of the French.

Would any other colonial policy be more fruitful? Do not forget that without the emancipation of the indigenous population, French Algeria will not long endure. France is me, because I have the numbers [native-born Muslim Algerians outnumbered French immigrants by 6 to 1]: I am the soldier, I am the worker, I am the craftsman, and I am the consumer. To dismiss my collaboration, my well-being, and my reward for work is a terrible heresy. The interests of France are my interests from the moment that our interests become those of France.

Rational action and ideas are the obstacles [facing] feudal Algeria [a small percentage of French Algerians owned most of the land]. The provocations of the latter [French colonists] are increasing. They cause us grief because we have taken our schoolbooks seriously. Perhaps they want us to go backward, but it is too late. We are the children of the modern world, created by French spirit and effort. Our motto is "Forward!"

8. The *Projet* Blum-Violette: The Proposed Enfranchisement of Muslims in Algeria, 1936

French colonial policy was predicated on the notion of a mission civilisatrice, *a civilizing mission that would uplift supposedly inferior indigenous peoples to the heights of French culture and civilization. By the beginning of the twentieth century, assimilation was an integral part of that overall goal. The indigenous* évolués *(evolved peoples) were expected to be "like" the French in language, habits, and values. The exact means of attaining this goal were not necessarily uniform across the great variety of French colonial possessions, and it was left to the local colonial administrators to implement the goal in a manner compatible with local politics.*

In Algeria, where there was a significant and politically powerful community of

Paul-Émile Viard, *Les Droits Politiques des Indigenes d'Algerie* (Paris: Librairie du Recueil Sirey, 1937), pp. 78–82. This document may also be found in J. C. Hurewitz, *The Middle East and North Africa in World Politics* (New Haven, Conn.: Yale University Press, 1975), pp. 505, 507, 508. Reprinted by permission of the author.

French colonists, the local administration stipulated the abandonment of Islamic law—Shari'a—as a prerequisite for the political enfranchisement of Muslim Algerians, who were being subjected to French colonial rule without being able to participate in the political process of ruling the country. The following document is a bill coauthored by Maurice Violette, speaker of the French parliament, and Léon Blum, the prime minister of the Popular Front government in France. It was intended to remove the stipulation that Muslim Algerians must renounce the Shari'a before they would be enfranchised. The bill was widely denounced by the French colons of Algeria, who feared it would dilute their political, economic, and social control over that country and their influence in the French parliament. Many demonstrations were held in support of the bill by Algerian Muslims and Berbers in large towns and cities in Algeria. Ultimately, the bill never came to a vote, and the project was abandoned.

Within this document are expressions of nationalism different from the notions of the emerging nationalist movement in Algeria, which was demanding independence from French colonial rule. The bill appealed to a particular group of well-educated Algerian Muslims who were well integrated into the French economy and culture and who saw themselves as intermediaries between France and the majority of Algerians. Thus, it sheds some light on the relationship between nationalist projects and interest groups within society.

1. Explanatory Statement

The *sénatus-consulte* of 14 July 1865 and the imperial decrees of 21 April and 12 May 1866 following this *sénatus-consulte* have organized a procedure for the naturalization of native Muslims that gives them, once naturalized, the benefit of all the legislation applicable to French citizens and for the most part, according to common law, covers children yet to be born of the naturalized person.

The law of 4 February 1919 is also concerned with facilitating the naturalization of French Muslims of Algeria, introducing for this purpose in our legislature a simplified procedure, whose effectiveness the government tries to assure and with which it is determined in accordance with the lawmaker's wish to bring about all the effects the Civil Code has on naturalization.

But experience has shown that it was impossible to continue treating as subjects without essential political rights French natives of Algeria who have fully assimilated French thought but who for family or religious reasons cannot give up their personal status. Algerian natives are French. It would be unjust to refuse henceforth the exercise of political rights to those among them who are the most cultured and who have furnished important guarantees of loyalty.

It is therefore fitting to resolve the problem posed by their situation without touching their personal status. Indeed, it must not be forgotten that all rules determining personal status are set forth in the Muslims' holy book. What remains of this solemn promise made by so many governments, notably at the time of the centenary (1930), that we should not realize the urgency of this necessary task of assimilation that affects in the highest degree the moral health of Algeria.

2. The Proposed Bill

ART. 1.   The French Algerian natives of the three departments of Algeria who fulfill the conditions enumerated in the following paragraphs shall be allowed to exercise the political rights of French citizens without modification of their status or civil rights, and this shall be definitive except for the application of French legislation on the forfeiture of political rights:

1. The French Algerian natives who have left the army with an officer's rank;
2. The French Algerian native noncommissioned officers who have left the army with the rank of master-sergeant or higher after serving for fifteen years or separating with a certificate of good conduct;
3. The French Algerian natives having completed military service and obtained both the Military Medal and the *croix de guerre;*
4. The French Algerian native holders of one of the following diplomas: diploma of higher education, *baccalauréat* of secondary education, higher certificate, elementary certificate, diploma of completion of secondary studies, diploma of *médersa,* graduating diploma of a large national school or of a national school of professional, industrial, agricultural, or commercial education, as well as civil servants recruited in a competitive examination;
5. The French Algerian natives elected to the Chambers of Commerce and Agriculture or designated by the Administrative Council of the economic region and by the Chambers of Agriculture of Algeria, under the conditions stipulated in Article 2;
6. The French Algerian native financial delegates, general councillors, municipal councillors of autonomous communes, and president of *jama'al* or local councils who have held office for the duration of a mandate;
7. The French native Algerian *bashaghas, aghas,* and *qaids* who have held office for at least four years;
8. The French Algerian native commanders of the National Order of the Legion of Honor or members of this order for military reasons; [and]
9. The native workers, holders of the Labor Medal (*médaille du travail*) and the secretaries of regularly constituted workers' unions who have held office for at least ten years.

ART. 2.   The Administrative Council of the economic region of Algeria at its sessions following the entry into force of the present law shall designate by decree of the Governor General two hundred businessmen, industrialists, or artisans for each Algerian department, who shall henceforth be invested with the political rights granted by Article 1 of the present law. The three Algerian Chambers of Agriculture at their first sessions each year following the entry into force of the present law shall each designate two hundred farmers, under the same conditions and with the same aim. The Administrative Council of the economic region of Algeria, under the same conditions as above, shall designate fifty businessmen, industrialists, or artisans for each Algerian department, and the three Algerian Chambers of Commerce shall each designate fifty farmers under the same conditions and with the same aim.

ART. 3. The convictions stipulated in Articles 15 and 16 of the law of 2 February 1852, as well as any intervening repeal [of rights] of functionaries enumerated in Article 1, paragraphs 6 and 7, and removal from the ranks of the Legion of Honor and the Military Medal shall entail automatic removal from the electoral lists.

ART. 4. Every French Algerian native benefiting from the provisions of the present law may lose the benefit of the preceding provisions by the application of the provisions of Article 9, paragraph 5, of the law of 10 August 1927.

ART. 5. The provisions of the present law have no retroactive effect and apply only to French Algerian natives who at present or may in the future fulfill the conditions that it enumerates. The representation of Algeria in the Chamber of Deputies is assured in the proportion of one deputy per 20,000 registered electors or fraction of 20,000.

ART. 6. The Minister of the Interior is charged with the application of the present law.

9.   Shaykh Ben Badis Pronounces a Fatwa (Religious Edict) Against the French "Naturalization" of Algerians, August 10, 1937

The Association of the 'Ulama' of Algeria was established in 1931 by a group of Muslim 'ulama' (religious and legal scholars) under the leadership of Shaykh Ben Badis. The purpose of the organization was to rejuvenate Islam by reforming and "purifying" it of popular religious practices common in North Africa. The reformers believed that Islam could survive and indeed thrive in the modern world only if it returned to its roots —the Qur'an and Hadith—and if Islamic scholarship became infused with the modern scientific method and rationality (for similar views from the nineteenth century, see document 5 by Al-Afghani in the chapter "Central Political Reforms and Local Responses"). This belief placed the reformers on a collision course with the conservative Marabouts ("Saints") and Brotherhoods popular in the countryside.

The reformers used the mosques to attack the obscurantism, heterodoxy, superstitions, and subservience of their coreligionists. Moreover, they began to articulate through Islam a nationalist ideology that undermined French colonial power. A

Al-Basha'ir, Journal of the Association of the 'Ulama' of Algeria, 14 January 1938. Translated by Akram Khater.

book published by a member of the association—Ahmad Tawfiq al-Madani—sum-
marized their nationalist doctrine in the motto "Islam is my religion; Arabic is my
language; Algeria is my country." This slogan eventually became the official motto
of the independent Algerian state.

Because of this political activity, the French colonial administration issued an
order in 1933 denying reformist 'ulama' access to any of the official mosques. In re-
sponse, a wave of agitation and unrest ensued during the next few years. French
authorities closed Al-Hadith, *a madrassa (religious school) opened in Tlemcen by*
Shaykh Ibrahimi, a reformist 'ulama.' In response, the journal of the association—
Al-Basha'ir—published this fatwa (religious edict) by Shaykh Ben Badis against the
French "naturalization" of Algerians.

In the name of God, the Most Merciful and Compassionate,

So that our Muslim brothers will know:

1. The action of acquiring a non-Muslim nationality implies the abandonment of Islamic law. Even the renunciation of a single precept of the Qur'an
leads, according to the doctrine accepted by all of the 'ulama' of Islam, to apostasy. A naturalized person is thus an apostate.

According to French civil laws, the children of a naturalized French person
are fully French. Therefore, neither they nor their descendants will know the
privileges granted to the followers of Islam, because of actions taken by their
parents, actions that we find reprehensible. The naturalized person cannot purify himself of this mistake, of this sin, except by sincerely repenting and by
penitence accompanied by a complete return to Islamic law.

But after becoming subject to French civil laws through naturalization,
how can someone return to an environment that he voluntarily abandoned? In
our opinion, there is one way for this to happen: the person must leave the
country where he is subject to French laws and move to a country where he
would be subject to Islamic legislation. If he does not want to leave but affirms
the sincerity of his contrition, we cannot believe him. It is our duty to refuse
him the benefits of our rituals.

2. A person who is condemned by a Muslim *qadi* [judge] conforming to
the precepts of Islam, and who seeks to overturn the judgment by appealing to
a foreign jurisdiction [. . .] is also an apostate. If he desires to merit the graces
of God again, he must desist from his appeals and submit completely to the
sentence of the Muslim judge.

3. Whoever provides testimony according to clauses contrary to the teachings of Islam is also an apostate.

4. He who marries a non-Muslim woman risks the lives of his offspring. He
deprives them of all the advantages and privileges reserved by Islam for its followers. If the marriage is concluded with complete knowledge of the consequences that may follow, then the spouse should be considered an apostate. If the
marriage is consummated under duress [. . .] then the sin is less but is still con-
demnable because the naturalized placed his children in a dangerous situation.

May God forgive us our sins, and may we always walk along the straight
path.

10.   Nationalism and the Jewish Community in Tunisia, March 5, 1938

The Alliance Israélite Universelle *and the Zionist movement had a rather complex relationship. Although both were intent on improving the lot of Jews throughout the world, they followed quite different—and at times contradictory—paths. The Al-liance approached its task from a European perspective, seeking to "modernize" the Jews of the Middle East and North Africa by inculcating them with an "enlight-ened" French education.* Alliance *members believed that this education and the re-sulting closer relations with France would allow the Jews of these two regions to attain greater rights within their respective nations or countries. The Zionists, in contrast, believed that the only solution for the "Jewish problem" was the creation of a* separate *nation for Jews (in the "Ideas of Nationalism" chapter, see document 1, Leo Pinsker's 1882 appeal). The Alliance report reprinted here provides an ex-ample of the clash of these two views in the Jewish community of Tunisia.*

Tunis, 5 March 1938

Antisemitism and Zionism in Tunisia: How They Affect the School

. . . Yes, antisemitism exists in the Regency. The relations between Jews and Arabs are certainly satisfactory, but there are certain indications which do not escape the notice of those who are aware and which suggest that there are cur-rents of discontent on the part of the Arabs toward the Jews. This discontent is especially caused by the jealousy of the Arabs when they see too many Jews succeeding in commerce and in the liberal professions (most of the business-men, lawyers, and doctors in Tunis are Jewish) and little by little taking over the life of the nation. The Destourian movement[1] serves only to increase and spread this discontent. They resent not only the French but also the Jews. Ob-viously, antisemitism does not figure directly in the program of the *Destour,* but it is implied. A violent spirit of chauvinistic nationalism and a call for "Na-tional Awakening" animate the Tunisian youth of today and dictate to them quite unfavorable sentiments toward the Jews.
[. . .]
At the same time, it is no less certain that Zionism, too, exists and is rapidly developing. The Jewish daily newspapers, *La Nouvelle Aurore, Tel-Aviv,* and *La Semaine Juive,* regularly devote long articles to this topic. They comment at length on the activities of the Zionist movement, its efforts, its successes, the obstacles it faces in Palestine; they keep the public informed of the situation of

---

[1]The Tunisian nationalist movement.

Archives of the Alliance Israélite Universelle, Tunisie I.G.3. This document may also be found in Aron Rodrigue, *Images of Sephardi and Eastern Jewries in Transition: The Teachers of the Alliance Israélite Universelle, 1860–1939* (Seattle: University of Washington Press, 1993), pp. 252–256. Copyright © 1993. Reprinted by permission of University of Washington Press.

the Jews in the various countries and show how that situation is daily growing worse. What is most distressing is that this movement is not simply a Zionist movement but rather a party with clearly Revisionist tendencies: often it is only a question of Mr. Jabotinsky and his projects. And this movement has grown even among the Boy Scouts. It is saddening to observe that these troops of Jewish Scouts are becoming involved in politics. This is damaging not only to the Scouts themselves but to the entire population.

Thus the two movements growing stronger and stronger in Tunisia are Zionism and antisemitism. Are these two movements opposed? Should we believe that the former encourages the latter or that it is a remedy to it? Is it because of Zionism that antisemitism is developing? Is Zionism the solution to antisemitism? Are the Jews here justified in lending themselves to such a degree to political preoccupations of this nature?

Without trying to give a direct answer to such delicate questions, I will limit myself to applying these questions to what can be seen in the school. [...]

In general terms, all of our students, like most young people today—this is the *"mal du siècle"*—are taken with politics, and this is regrettable. Under the pretext of keeping informed, they scour the newspapers and become passionately involved in public and international issues. In this way, they waste a good portion of their time, often to the detriment of their studies and sound thinking. Indeed, through this kind of reading they acquire a mass of misguided opinions, which they take for Gospel and of which it is very difficult to rid them.

This is also true for my pupils, who are older adolescents preparing for the *brevet élémantaire.* Among them are several Muslims affiliated with the Destourian party ... When I am giving my course on civics (in the second year of preparation for the diploma), there are always a few of them who point out certain so-called inequities or injustices which make them indignant. I cannot help but notice that the same idea is always behind these remarks: "make room for the Tunisians who are living in the streets and dying of hunger while scores of Frenchmen and Jews occupy all the respected positions."

Although I never allow myself to become involved in politics in the classroom and I do not tolerate the slightest allusion to this subject, I make it my duty to reply to these remarks, to analyze them, and to refute them. I believe that if these young people have been led astray in their circle of family and friends, it is up to us to show them the truth. Most often I succeed in convincing them and in disposing them toward higher sentiments and more just ideas.

The Jews live side by side with the Muslims, and on excellent terms. The Jews too, in their way, take an interest in politics. Obviously in their circle of family and friends, the sole topic of conversation is Zionism. How could they keep from talking about it, from discussing it at length, from considering all the possibilities and all the theories, and from enumerating all the solutions? Their minds are so steeped in these ideas that they cannot help but expose their personal sentiments, sometimes even in their compositions. Allow me to tell you about one case:

I had assigned the following topic (again it is a question of the students in the second year of preparation for the diploma), which is, as it happens, a regular topic in the program: "What emotions, what dreams does the word *partir!* [to leave] suggest to you?" A few spoke about Palestine and discussed the ideal of every Jew, to leave one day for the Holy Land. Thus far there could be nothing more legitimate and natural. But they did not stop there. "Why should I work for this ungrateful land?" I am quoting word for word from one composition, "Why pour out my efforts here while my country awaits me? I do not want to live in exile and sacrifice myself for foreigners . . ."

Such ideas denote a special mentality. If the students speak about this even in their school compositions, that means that they certainly talk about this among themselves and with their Muslim friends. What might happen when these Muslims, strongly influenced by Destourian ideas (therefore nationalistic and antisemitic ideas), revolt and challenge their Jewish friends so full of misunderstood Zionist ideas? This is what will happen: the relations between them, which have been excellent up until now, will become more and more strained and will contribute to profound dissension between the two sections of the Tunisian population. On the one side, the Arabs will spread the word that the Jews are foreigners, who have only to leave, that this is not their home, and that they are living as parasites. On the other side, the Jews, continuing along these lines, will neglect even their most basic civic duties.

Such is, then, the precise state of mind of our students today, and such are the serious consequences in which it may result.

[. . .]

How can we struggle effectively against such a situation? Should we systematically speak out against both the Destourian movement and Zionism? Is it wise to tell our students, even in an indirect and discreet manner: "You are both wrong; give up these ideas." In so doing, would we not risk shocking them and deeply wounding the sentiments they hold most dear?

It would appear that the solution lies elsewhere; this solution is twofold: 1. It is our duty to strengthen the civic and moral education of our students. They should understand that the first duty of the Jew is to the country in which he lives. Because they have the privileges accorded all citizens, it is right that they also accept the duties of citizens and carry them out fully. Even more than this: the Jews must always regulate their behavior and their lives in such a manner that they not become targets for those malicious minds who are always looking for faults and who never fail to generalize them. I would like to quote here a few of the noble words spoken by the Chief Rabbi of Geneva, Mr. Poliakoff, who visited our school when he was in Tunis and left an elevated moral teaching in the minds of our older students: "My dear children! Never forget that the Jews are closely bound together. The slightest fault, the slightest questionable affair on the part of one, is quickly generalized and attributed to all . . . We have a heavy burden to bear: for centuries the name Jew has been a synonym for coward, thief, usurer; this name represented all moral baseness. It is through our actions and our conduct that we can show the world the injustice that has been done to us and that we suffer still today. You must lead lives that are dignified, irreproachable, and exemplary from a moral, civic, and religious point of view. Then those who seek only to denigrate and belittle us, to deny us our very existence, will be able to find no fault in you . . ."

And so the first duty of any Jew is to be a "good citizen," worthy of the country in which he lives and worthy of his glorious heritage.

2. But it is not enough to give the students a solid civic and moral base. They must also be turned away from politics, which is the source of contention, disorder, and so many fruitless, if not tragic, discussions. The mind of the adolescent, just beginning to awaken, has need of nourishment. He seeks it out, and because most often he is surrounded by discussions of politics, he turns to politics himself. But could not this active mind and this hunger for learning, which are typical of the adolescent, be put to other, more profitable use?

Since he has this passion for all that is new to him and for all that is capable of awakening, strengthening, and developing his most pure and noble sentiments, why not warn him against the wrong road and show him the right path, the path rich in positive results?

And what path could this be?

This path has just been discovered by the students at the *Lycée Carnot* in Tunis: they founded a paper, which they write, edit, and publish entirely on their own. All questions of politics are excluded; the paper treats topics in literature, the arts, the sciences, sports, and anything that has to do with daily life. The first issue has already come out, and to judge by the favorable opinion of the public and the encouragement offered by the authorities concerned, this paper promises to prosper for a long time to come.

Does not an initiative such as this deserve to be imitated? Could we not do something along those lines, obviously on a more modest scale, with some of our students? We could encourage the students in their French (a subject in which they are generally quite weak), lead them toward sound and instructive reading, introduce them to literary masterpieces rather than insipid serial novels, develop in them artistic taste and sensibility (some of them are gifted in this area; they have shown me their sonnets and their sketches, and they are quite good), talk with them about sports, which so fascinate them, and speak to them of friendship and brotherhood between Arab and Jewish classmates. And as we do all this, we would be stimulating a spirit of healthy competition, which could bring only good results. Is not this the most effective way to turn them away from politics completely and to channel their growing energy in a manner that is both instructive and enjoyable? . . .

These are the solutions resulting from my reflections on antisemitism and Zionism and their effects on the school.

[. . .]

M. Cohen

11.   The Contest for Alexandretta Between Syria and Turkey, May 1938

For much of its premodern history, Alexandretta, with its capital city Antioch, was considered as part of Bilad al-Sham, *the area known today as Syria. In 1920 the sanjak (province) of Alexandretta was awarded to Syria by the League of Nations in the guise of a French mandate. In 1936 Alexandretta became the subject of a complaint to the League of Nations by Turkey, which claimed that the privileges of the Turkish minority in the sanjak were being infringed. (In 1921 there were only 87,000 Turks amid a population of 220,000 that was primarily Arab). In 1937 the sanjak was given autonomous status by an agreement, arranged by the League, between France (the mandatory power in Syria) and Turkey. Riots broke out between the various "national" and "ethnic" groups (primarily Arabs and Turks but also Kurds and Armenians). The result, in 1938, was the establishment of joint French and Turkish military control. In 1939, France transferred the sanjak to Turkey, and it became Hatay province. The transfer was the outcome of a highly contested and suspect referendum. Turkish peasants had been trucked into Antioch to vote, and Arabs had boycotted the election because they said it was fraudulent. After the votes were counted, close to fourteen thousand Armenians, who had fled Turkey because of the anti-Armenian genocide of 1914, left Hatay province and moved to Lebanon. Most historians agree that France's motivation for ceding the province to Turkey, despite Hatay's Arab majority, was to persuade Turkey to side with the Allies against Germany in the event of war.*

The letter and deposition included here refer to the 1938 rioting and indicate the complexity of the subject of national identity.

[1]

Request No. 912
Received: 16 May 1938
Responded: 17 May 1938

Kirik-Han May, 15, 1938

To the President of the Commission
League of Nations, Antioch
Sir,

We undersigned, in the name of Arab in habitants of the villages of Keferkale and Ak Kouyou, in the district of Mourad Pasha, most humbly request your energetic protection against an armed Turkish band which has been raiding these two villages during the nights of the 13th and 14th Inst. The band is composed of the following Turkish proprietors of the district: Reshid Agha of Yeni Keuy, Abdullah Agha of Ak Pounar, Ahmed Agha of Jingil Aghlou and

League of Nations Archives, Geneva, Switzerland. Translated by Akram Khater.

Mohamed Riza of Keferkale. These people having with them about another six of their men and being armed to teeth are menacing us to be murdered in case we vote for Arabs which is our nationality. Since five days the villages of Keferkale and Ak Kouyou have been called to report to your Bureau at Mourad Pasha for inscription. Turks have reported, but we Arabs are being prevented to proceed there by this armed band.

In the name of justice we request your high protection against these aggressors and your energetic intervention to give safety to proceed to Mourad Pasha to vote there to our Arab nationality.

We remain Sirs, Your most obedient servants.

Hussein Bin Mohamed of Keferkale
Matar Edelli of Ak Kouyou
Ahmed el Gedro of Ak Kouyou

[2]

Alexandretta Police
Rayhaniyye Station

Deposition of Plaintiff Sido bin Dawuud
a Taxi driver stationed at Rayhaniyye

Half an hour after I began working in front of the Karim's Coffeehouse, when I saw Haydar Hassan Misto, and his brothers Uthman and Abdu and a fourth person whose name I do not know, going to the Arabs' club in Rayhaniyye. They were followed by more than 20 of their friends. They all shouted, "We are looking for the boss (Agha)." When they did not see him, the four individuals I mentioned first said, "here is one of the children of the one we are looking for," and they pulled out their revolvers that they were carrying and pointed them at me. Mr. Halafi Shaykh Mustafa Ramadan, Abu Omar Kassir and many other individuals whose names I cannot recall intervened on my behalf.

My witnesses are: Abdo from the neighborhood, . . . The aggressors and I are all from a Kurdish tribe. They asked why I was wearing a hat, and why I do not join the Arabs' club. I responded by saying that I am simply a taxi driver. Amongst those of them who carried weapons was a certain Khalil who I recognized . . . and he has three gold-crowned teeth.

5/10/1938

12.   The Arab Case for Palestine and the Case for a Binational State, March 1946

Zionists believed overwhelmingly that the only way to ensure a secure future for Jews was to establish a Jewish homeland in Palestine. Arabs in Palestine were thoroughly opposed to that idea. They considered Palestine to be their ancestral home. They constituted a clear majority there and fervently believed that the establishment of a Jewish state would deprive them of their sovereign rights and dispossess them of their land and livelihood. Moreover, they considered Palestine to be part of the larger Arab culture and civilization and believed that the creation of a Jewish state would undermine that relationship. Any proposal to divide the land between Jews and Arabs was seen by the Arabs as a gross injustice, taking what was rightfully Arab and giving it to foreigners who only recently immigrated into Palestine.

A small minority among Zionists within and outside Palestine worried that the establishment of a Jewish homeland in Palestine would indeed be unjust. From the perspective of this small group, the moral authority of Zionism and Judaism would—at least in the long run—be undermined if an unacceptable state were forcibly imposed on the Arabs. Concern for the future relations between Arabs and Jews led a few Jews and Arabs to propose a binational state in which the two communities could coexist.

The Arab case and the case for a binational state are made in the following documents.

The Arab Case for Palestine: Evidence Submitted by the Arab Office, Jerusalem, to the Anglo-American Committee of Inquiry, March 1946

The Problem of Palestine

1. The whole Arab People is unalterably opposed to the attempt to impose Jewish immigration and settlement upon it, and ultimately to establish a Jewish State in Palestine. Its opposition is based primarily upon right. The Arabs of Palestine are descendants of the indigenous inhabitants of the country, who have been in occupation of it since the beginning of history; they cannot agree that it is right to subject an indigenous population against its will to alien immigrants, whose claim is based upon a historical connection which ceased effectively many centuries ago. Moreover they form the majority of the population; as such they cannot submit to a policy of immigration which if pursued for long will turn them from a majority into a minority in an alien state; and they claim the democratic right of a majority to make its own decisions in matters of urgent national concern. . . .

2. In addition to the question of right, the Arabs oppose the claims of political Zionism because of the effects which Zionist settlement has already had

---

Evidence Submitted by the Arab Office, Jerusalem, to the Anglo-American Committee of Inquiry, March 1946.

upon their situation and is likely to have to an even greater extent in the future. Negatively, it has diverted the whole course of their national development. Geographically Palestine is part of Syria; its indigenous inhabitants belong to the Syrian branch of the Arab family of nations; all their culture and tradition link them to the other Arab peoples; and until 1917 Palestine formed part or the Ottoman Empire which included also several of the other Arab countries. The presence and claims of the Zionists, and the support given them by certain Western Powers have resulted in Palestine being cut off from the other Arab countries and subjected to a regime, administrative, legal, fiscal and educational, different from that of the sister-countries. Quite apart from the inconvenience to individuals and the dislocation of trade which this separation has caused, it has prevented Palestine participating fully in the general development of the Arab world.

First, while the other Arab countries have attained or are near to the attainment of self-government and full membership of the U.N.O., Palestine is still under Mandate and has taken no step towards self-government; not only are there no representative institutions, but no Palestinian can rise to the higher ranks of the administration. This is unacceptable on grounds of principle, and also because of its evil consequence. It is a hardship to individual Palestinians whose opportunities of responsibility are thus curtailed; and it is demoralizing to the population to live under a government which has no basis in their consent and to which they can feel no attachment or loyalty.

Secondly, while the other Arab countries are working through the Arab League to strengthen their ties and coordinate their policies, Palestine (although her Arab inhabitants are formally represented in the League's Council) cannot participate fully in this movement so long as she has no indigenous government; thus the chasm between the administrative system and the institutions of Palestine and those of the neighbouring countries is growing, and her traditional Arab character is being weakened.

Thirdly, while the other Arab countries have succeeded in or are on the way to achieving a satisfactory definition of their relations with the Western Powers and with the world-community, expressed in their treaties with Great Britain and other Powers and their membership of the United Nations Organization, Palestine has not yet been able to establish any definite status for herself in the world, and her international destiny is still obscure.

3. All these evils are due entirely to the presence of the Zionists and the support given to them by certain of the Powers; there is no doubt that had it not been for that, Arab Palestine would by now be a self-governing member of the U.N.O. and the Arab League. Moreover, in addition to the obstacles which Zionism has thus placed in the way of Palestine's development, the presence of the Zionists gives rise to various positive evils which will increase if Zionist immigration continues.

The entry of incessant waves of immigrants prevents normal economic and social development and causes constant dislocation of the country's life; in so far as it reacts upon prices and values and makes the whole economy dependent upon the constant inflow of capital from abroad it may even in certain circumstances lead to economic disaster. It is bound moreover to arouse continuous political unrest and prevent the establishment of that political stability on which the prosperity and health of the country depend. This unrest is likely to increase in frequency and violence as the Jews come nearer to being the majority and the Arabs a minority.

Even if economic and social equilibrium is re-established, it will be to the detriment of the Arabs. The superior capital resources at the disposal of the Jews, their greater experience of modern economic technique and the existence of a deliberate policy of expansion and domination have already gone far toward giving them the economic mastery of Palestine. The biggest concessionary companies are in their hands; they possess a large proportion of the total cultivable land, and an even larger one of the land in the highest category of fertility; and the land they possess is mostly inalienable to non-Jews. The continuance of land-purchase and immigration, taken together with the refusal of Jews to employ Arabs on their lands or in their enterprises and the great increase in the Arab population, will create a situation in which the Arab population is pushed to the margin of cultivation and a landless proletariat, rural and urban, comes into existence. This evil can be palliated but not cured by attempts at increasing the absorptive capacity or the industrial production of Palestine; the possibility of such improvements is limited, they would take a long time to carry out, and would scarcely do more than keep pace with the rapid growth of the Arab population; moreover in present circumstances they would be used primarily for the benefit of the Jews and thus might increase the disparity between the two communities.

Nor is the evil economic only. Zionism is essentially a political movement, aiming at the creation of a state: immigration, land-purchase and economic expansion are only aspects of a general political strategy. If Zionism succeeds in its aim, the Arabs will become a minority in their own country; a minority which can hope for no more than a minor share in the government, for the state is to be a Jewish state, and which will find itself not only deprived of that international status which the other Arab countries possess but cut off from living contact with the Arab world of which it is an integral part.

It should not be forgotten too that Palestine contains places holy to Moslems and Christians, and neither Arab Moslems nor Arab Christians would willingly see such places subjected to the ultimate control of a Jewish Government.

4. These dangers would be serious enough at any time, but are particularly so in this age, when the first task of the awakening Arab nation is to come to terms with the West; to define its relationship with the Western Powers, and with the westernized world community on a basis of equality and mutual respect, and to adapt what is best in Western civilization the needs of its own genius. Zionist policy is one of the greatest obstacles to the achievement of this task: both because Zionism represents to the Arabs one side of the Western spirit and because of the support given to it by some of the Western Powers. In fact Zionism has become in Arab eyes a test of Western intentions towards them. So long as the attempt of the Zionists to impose a Jewish state upon the

inhabitants of Palestine is supported by some or all of the Western Governments, so long will it be difficult if not impossible for the Arabs to establish a satisfactory relationship with the Western world and its civilization, and they will tend to turn away from the West in political hostility and spiritual isolation; this will be disastrous both for the Arabs themselves and for those Western nations which have dealings with them.

5. There are no benefits obtained or to be expected from Zionism commensurate with its evils and its dangers. The alleged social and economic benefits are much less than is claimed. The increase in the Arab population is not primarily due to Zionist immigration, and in any case would not necessarily be a sign of prosperity. The rise in money wages and earnings is largely illusory, being offset by the rise in the cost of living. In so far as real wages and the standard of living have risen, this is primarily an expression of a general trend common to all Middle Eastern countries. The inflow of capital has gone largely to raising money prices and real estate values. The whole economy is dangerously dependent upon the citrus industry. The benefits derived from the establishment of industries and the exploitation of the country's few natural resources have been largely neutralized by the failure of Jewish enterprises to employ Arabs.

The Zionist contention that their social organizations provide health and social services for the Arab population is exaggerated; only a minute proportion of the Arabs, for example, are looked after by Jewish health organizations. Even if true it would prove nothing except that the Government was neglecting its responsibilities in regard to the welfare of the population. Arab voluntary social organizations have grown up independently of Jewish bodies and without help from them. Even in so far as social and economic benefits have come to the Arabs from Zionist settlement, it remains true on the one hand that they are more than counterbalanced by the dangers of that settlement, and on the other that they are only incidental and are in no way necessary for the progress of the Arab people. The main stimulus to Arab economic and social progress does not come from the example or assistance of the Zionists but from the natural tendency of the whole Middle Eastern areas, from the work of the Government and above all from the newly awakened will to progress of the Arabs themselves. The Arabs may have started later than the Jews on the road of modern social and economic organization, but they are now fully awake and are progressing fast. This is shown in the economic sphere for example by the continued development of the Arab citrus industry and financial organizations, in the social sphere by the growth of the labour movement and the new Land Development Scheme.

If any proof were needed of this, it could be found in the progress made during the last three decades by the neighbouring countries. None of the Arab countries is stagnant today: even without the example and capital of the Zionists, they are building up industries, improving methods and extending the scope of agriculture, establishing systems of public education and increasing the amenities of life. In some countries and spheres the progress has been greater than among the Arabs of Palestine, and in all of them it is healthier and more normal.

The Zionists claim further that they are acting as mediators of Western civilization to the Middle East. Even if their claim were true, the services they were rendering would be incidental only: the Arab world has been in direct touch with the West for a hundred years, and has its own reawakened cultural movement, and thus it has no need of a mediator. Moreover the claim is untrue: so long as Jewish cultural life in Palestine expresses itself through the medium of the Hebrew language, its influence on the surrounding world is bound to be negligible; in fact, Arab culture today is almost wholly uninfluenced by the Jews, and practically no Arabs take part in the work of Jewish cultural or educational institutions. In a deeper sense the presence of the Zionists is even an obstacle to the understanding of Western civilization, in so far as it more than any other factor is tending to induce in the Arabs an unsympathetic attitude towards the West and all its works.

6. Opposition to the policy of the Zionists is shared by all sections of the Palestinian Arab people. It is not confined to the townspeople but is universal among the rural population, who stand to suffer most from the gradual alienation of the most fertile land to the Jewish National Fund. It is felt not only by the landowners and middle class but by the working population, both for national reasons and for reasons of their own. It is not an invention of the educated class; if that class have seen the danger more clearly and sooner than others, and if they have assumed the leadership of the opposition, that is no more than their duty and function.

Moreover not only the Arab Moslem majority are opposed to Zionism but also and equally the Arab Christian minority who reject Zionism both because they share to the full in the national sentiments of other Arabs and because as Christians they cannot accept that their Holy Places should be subject to Jewish control, and cannot understand how any Christian nation could accept it.

7. The sentiments of the Palestinian Arabs are fully shared by the other Arab countries, both by their Government and their peoples. Their support has shown itself in many ways: in Pan-Arab Conferences, in the moral and material support given by the whole Arab world to the revolt of 1936–39, in the diplomatic activities of Arab Governments, and most recently in the formation of the Arab League, which has taken the defense of Palestine as one of its main objectives. The members of the Arab League are now taking active measures to prevent the alienation of Arab lands to the Zionists and Jewish domination of the economic life of the Middle East. . . .

8. In the Arab view, any solution of the problem created by Zionist aspirations must satisfy certain conditions:

i. It must recognize the right of the indigenous inhabitants of Palestine to continue in occupation of the country and to preserve its traditional character.

ii. It must recognize that questions like immigration which affect the whole nature and destiny of the country, should be decided in accordance with democratic principles by the will of the population.

  iii. It must accept the principle that the only way by which the will of the population can be expressed is through the establishment of responsible representative government. (The Arabs find something inconsistent in the attitude of Zionists who demand the establishment of a free democratic commonwealth in Palestine and then hasten to add that this should not take place until the Jews are in a majority.)

  iv. This representative Government should be based upon the principle of absolute equality of all citizens irrespective of race and religion.

  v. The form of Government should be such as to make possible the development of a spirit of loyalty and cohesion among all elements of the community, which will override all sectional attachments. In other words it should be a Government which the whole community could regard as their own, which should be rooted in their consent and have a moral claim upon their obedience.

  vi. The settlement should recognize the fact that by geography and history Palestine is inescapably part of the Arab world; that the only alternative to its being part of the Arab world and accepting the implications of its position is complete isolation, which would be disastrous from every point of view; and that whether they like it or not the Jews in Palestine are dependent upon the goodwill of the Arabs.

  vii. The settlement should be such as to make possible a satisfactory definition within the framework of U.N.O. of the relations between Palestine and the Western Powers who possess interests in the country.

  viii. The settlement should take into account that Zionism is essentially a political movement aiming at the creation of a Jewish state and should therefore avoid making any concession which might encourage Zionists in the hope that this aim can be achieved in any circumstances.

9. In accordance with these principles, the Arabs urge the establishment in Palestine of a democratic government representative of all sections of the population on a level of absolute equality; the termination of the Mandate once the Government has been established; and the entry of Palestine into the United Nations Organization as a full member of the working community.

Pending the establishment of a representative Government, all further Jewish immigration should be stopped, in pursuance of the principle that a decision on so important a matter should only be taken with the consent of the inhabitants of the country and that until representative institutions are established there is no way of determining consent. Strict measures should also continue to be taken to check illegal immigration. Once a Palestinian state has come into existence, if any section of the population favours a policy of further immigration it will be able to press its case in accordance with normal democratic procedure; but in this as in other matters the minority must abide by the decision of the majority.

Similarly, all further transfer of land from Arabs to Jews should be prohibited prior to the creation of self-governing institutions. The Land Transfer

Regulations should be made more stringent and extended to the whole area of the country, and severer measures be taken to prevent infringement of them. Here again once self-government exists matters concerning land will be decided in the normal democratic manner.

10. The Arabs are irrevocably opposed to political Zionism, but in no way hostile to the Jews as such nor to their Jewish fellow-citizens of Palestine. Those Jews who have already entered Palestine, and who have obtained or shall obtain Palestinian citizenship by due legal process will be full citizens of the Palestinian state, enjoying full civil and political rights and a fair share in government and administration. There is no question of their being thrust into the position of a "minority" in the bad sense of a closed community, which dwells apart from the main stream of the State's life and which exists by sufferance of the majority. They will be given the opportunity of belonging to and helping to mould the full community of the Palestinian slate, joined to the Arabs by links of interest and goodwill, not the goodwill of the strong to the powerless, but of one citizen to another.

It is to be hoped that in course of time the exclusiveness of the Jews will be neutralized by the development of loyalty to the state and the emergence of new groupings which cut across communal divisions. This however will take time; and during the transitional period the Arabs recognize the need for giving special consideration to the peculiar position and the needs of the Jews. No attempt would be made to interfere with their communal organization, their personal status or their religious observances. Their schools and cultural institutions would be left to operate unchecked except for that general control which all governments exercise over education. In the districts in which they are most closely settled they would possess municipal autonomy and Hebrew would be an official language of administration, justice and education.

11. The Palestinian State would be an Arab state not (as should be clear from the preceding paragraph) in any narrow racial sense, nor in the sense that non-Arabs should be placed in a position of inferiority, but because the form and policy of its government would be based on a recognition of two facts: first that the majority of the citizens are Arabs, and secondly that Palestine is part of the Arab world and has no future except through close co-operation with the other Arab states. Thus among the main objects of the Government would be to preserve and enrich the country's Arab heritage, and to draw closer the relations between Palestine and the other Arab countries. The Cairo Pact of March, 1945, provided for the representation of Palestine on the Council of the Arab League even before its independence should be a reality; once it was really self-governing, it would participate fully in all the work of the League, in the cultural and economic no less than the political sphere. This would be of benefit to the Jewish no less than the Arab citizens of Palestine, since it would ensure those good relations with the Arab world without which their economic development would be impossible.

12. The state would apply as soon as possible for admission into U.N.O., and would of course be prepared to bear its full share of the burdens of establishing a world security-system. It would willingly place at the disposal of the

Security Council whatever bases or other facilities were required, provided those bases were really used for the purpose for which they were intended and not in older to interfere in the internal affairs of the country, and provided also Palestine and the other Arab states were adequately represented on the controlling body.

The state would recognize also the world's interest in the maintenance of a satisfactory regime for the Moslem, Christian and Jewish Holy Places. In the Arab view however the need for such a regime does not involve foreign interference in or control of Palestine: no opportunity should be given to Great Powers to use the Holy Places as instruments of policy. The Holy Places can be most satisfactorily and appropriately guarded by a Government representative of the inhabitants, who include adherents of all three faiths and have every interest in preserving the holy character of their country.

Nor in the Arab view would any sort of foreign interference or control be justified by the need to protect the Christian minorities. The Christians are Arabs, who belong fully to the national community and share fully in its struggle. They would have all the rights and duties of citizens of a Palestinian state, and would continue to have their own communal organizations and institutions. They themselves would ask for no more, having learnt from the example of other Middle Eastern countries the dangers of an illusory foreign "protection" of minorities.

13. In economic and social matters the Government of Palestine would follow a progressive policy with the aim of raising the standard of living and increasing the welfare of all sections of the population, and using the country's natural resources in the way most beneficial to all. Its first task naturally would be to improve the condition of the Arab peasants and thus to bridge the economic and social gulf which at present divides the two communities. Industry would be encouraged, but only in so far as its economic basis was sound and as part of a general policy of economic development for the whole Arab world; commercial and financial ties with the other Arab countries would so far as possible be strengthened, and tariffs decreased or abolished.

14. The Arabs believe that no other proposals would satisfy the conditions of a just and lasting settlement. In their view there are insuperable objections of principle or of practice to all other suggested solutions of the problem.

1. The idea of partition and the establishment of a Jewish state in a part of Palestine is inadmissible for the same reasons of principle as the idea of establishing a Jewish state in the whole country. If it is unjust to the Arabs to impose a Jewish state on the whole of Palestine, it is equally unjust to impose it in any part of the country. Moreover, as the Woodhead Commission showed, there are grave practical difficulties in the way of partition; commerce would be strangled, communications dislocated and the public finances upset. It would also be impossible to devise frontiers which did not leave a large Arab minority in the Jewish state. This minority would not willingly accept its subjection to the Zionists, and it would not allow itself to be transferred to the Arab state. Moreover, partition would not satisfy the Zionists. It cannot be too often

repeated that Zionism is a political movement aiming at the domination at least of the whole of Palestine; to give it a foothold in part of Palestine would be to encourage it to press for more and to provide it with a base for its activities. Because of this, because of the pressure of population and in order to escape from its isolation it would inevitably be thrown into enmity with the surrounding Arab states and this enmity would disturb the stability of the whole Middle East.

2. Another proposal is for the establishment of a bi-national state, based upon political parity, in Palestine and its incorporation into a Syrian or Arab Federation. The Arabs would reject this as denying the majority its normal position and rights. There are also serious practical objections to the idea of a bi-national state, which cannot exist unless there is a strong sense of unity and common interest overriding the differences between the two parties. Moreover, the point made in regard to the previous suggestion may be repeated here: this scheme would in no way satisfy the Zionists, it would simply encourage them to hope for more and improve their chances of obtaining it. . . .

The Case for a Bi-national State*

The Arab Contention

The Arabs say that "the existence of the Jewish National Home, whatever its size, bars the way to the attainment by the Arabs of Palestine of the same national status as that attained, or soon to be attained, by all the other Arabs of Asia" (Royal Commission, p. 307). That is so. And they ask if they are not as fit for self-government as the Arabs of other countries. They are.

Arab Concessions

But the whole history of Palestine shows that it just has not been made for uni-national sovereign independence. This is an inescapable fact which no one can disregard. Although the Arabs cannot have a uni-national independent Arab Palestine, they can enjoy independence in a bi-national Palestine together with their Jewish fellow-citizens. This will afford them a maximum of national freedom. What the bi-national State will take away from them is sovereign independence in Palestine. There are other Arab States with sovereign independence. But we contend that the sovereign independence of tiny Palestine, whether it be Jewish sovereignty or Arab sovereignty, is a questionable good in this post-war period, when even great States must relinquish something of their sovereignty and seek union, if the world is not to perish. We contend that for this Holy Land the idea of a bi-national Palestine is at least as inspiring as that of an Arab sovereign Palestine or a Jewish Sovereign Palestine.

---

*Reprinted from M. Buber and J. L. Magnes, *Arab-Jewish Unity* (London: Victor Gollancz Ltd., 1947).

Jewish Concessions

On the other hand, the bi-national Palestine would deprive the Jews of their one chance of a Jewish State. But this bi-national Palestine would be the one State in the world where they would be a constituent nation, i.e. an equal nationality within the body politic, and not a minority as everywhere else. The absence of a Jewish State would make more difficult direct access by the Jewish people to U.N.O. To compensate for this, some form should be devised for giving the Jewish people a recognised place within the structure of the United Nations Organisation.

Nevertheless, the concessions the Jews would have to make on these matters are, we think, more far-reaching than the concessions the Arabs of Palestine would have to make. But the hard facts of the situation are that this is not a Jewish land and it is not an Arab land—it is the Holy Land, a bi-national country—and it is in the light of such hard facts that the problem must be approached.

The Advantages of a Bi-National Palestine

Before proceeding to outline our suggestions as to the political structure of the bi-national Palestine, we should like finally to point out some of the advantages of bi-nationalism based on parity in a country which has two nationalities.

FAILURE OF MINORITY GUARANTEES

1. The breakdown of the minority guarantees provided for in the Versailles Peace treaties is proof that in a bi-national country the only safeguard for a minority is equality with the majority. There is no prospect of peace in a country where there is a dominant people and a subordinate people. The single nation-State is a proper form for a country where there is but one legally recognised nationality, as, for example, the United States. But in countries with more than one recognised nationality—and they are numerous in Europe and in Asia—bitterness is engendered among the minority because the civil service, the military, the economic key positions, foreign affairs, are in the hands of the ruling class of the majority nation. Parity in a multi-national country is the only just relationship between the peoples.

SWITZERLAND

2. The multi-national state is an effective method of affording full protection for the national languages, cultures and institutions of each nationality. That there can be full cultural autonomy combined with full allegiance to the multi-national political state is proven in Switzerland's history for more than 100 years. The Swiss are divided by language, religion and culture; nor do the linguistic and religious groupings coincide in the various cantons. Yet all of these divergencies have not been obstacles to political unity. This is a newer form of democracy which is as important for multi-national states as the more familiar form of democracy is for uni-national states. The Swiss example is most relevant to Palestine, although there are, of course, many points of difference.

OTHER MULTI-NATIONAL COUNTRIES

The Soviet Union is a newer example of a multi-national State. The new Yu-goslav State is an attempt at multi-national federalism. Professor Seton Watson outlines a bi-national solution of the age-long problem of Transylvania. Rou-manian domination, Hungarian domination, partition had all been tried with-out success.

BI-NATIONALISM A HIGH IDEAL

3. In many senses the multi-national state represents a higher, more modern and more hopeful ideal than the uni-national sovereign independent State. The old way of having a major people and a minor people in a State of various na-tionalities is reactionary. The progressive conception is parity among the peoples of the multi-national State. The way of peace in the world to-day and to-morrow is through federation, union. Dividing up the world into tiny national-istic sovereign units has not been the success the advocates of self-determination had hoped for at the end of the First World War. (Cobban, *National Self-Determination.*) The peoples who have been placed by fate or by history in the same country have warred with one another for domination throughout the centuries. The majority have tried to make the State homogeneous through keeping down the minority nationalities. The federal multi-national State, based on the parity of the nationalities, is a most hopeful way of enabling them to retain their national identity, and yet of coalescing in a larger political frame-work. It results in separate nationalities, yet a single citizenship. This is a noble goal to which the youth of multi-national countries can be taught to give their enthusiasm and their energies. It is a modern challenge to the intelligence and the moral qualities of the peoples constituting multi-national lands.

13.   President Harry Truman's Statement Supporting Jewish Immigration into Palestine, October 4, 1946

In August 1945 U.S. President Truman wrote Clement Atlee, the British prime minis-ter, asking him to lift the British government's restrictions on Jewish immigration into Palestine, and to issue admission permits for 100,000 Jews. Truman wrote this letter—which was leaked to the press—partly because of his and most Americans' sympa-thy for the plight of the Jews of Europe in the wake of the Holocaust. Also, his move was calculated to help New York City Democrats attract the Jewish vote in the up-coming mayoral election. Ernest Bevin, the British foreign secretary, was disturbed by what he regarded as unilateral American statements not helpful to the situation in the Middle East. Yet, given Britain's need for American financial aid for post–World War II reconstruction, Bevin was reluctant to criticize American foreign policy publicly.

Michael Cohen, *Palestine and the Great Powers, 1945–1948* (Princeton, N.J.: Princeton University Press, 1982), pp. 58–59.

Thus, in an attempt to contain American policy, he proposed the formation of the Anglo-American Committee of Inquiry to explore "the possibility of relieving the position [of Jews] in Europe by immigration to other countries outside of Europe." The final version of the group's mandate, however, amended under American pressure, said that the committee's aim was "to make estimates of those who wish or will be impelled by their conditions to migrate to Palestine or other countries outside of Europe."[1] Despite that change, Bevin made it clear—in private and public—that the British government did not regard Palestine as the solution to the Jewish refugee problem and that he envisaged a Palestinian and not a Jewish state in Palestine. This position convinced David Ben-Gurion and other Zionist leaders that military operations against the British were necessary. Violent attacks by the Zionist paramilitary organizations Irgun and Lehi soon began to take their toll on the British, who responded increasingly in kind. At the same time, the Arab population of Palestine, which still amounted to double the number of Jews, rejected any proposal that would deny the Arab character of the country. Some Zionist leaders were willing to accept partition plans, but the Arab leadership considered such proposals unjust.

As the conflict intensified, the Anglo-American Committee of Inquiry tried to strike a compromise. On the one hand, members called for the admission of 100,000 Jewish immigrants into Palestine and the removal of land sale restrictions that had been in place since the 1939 White Paper (a British policy statement issued on May 17, 1939, that questioned the creation of a Jewish homeland in Palestine in the face of Arab opposition). On the other hand, members stated that any attempt to establish an independent state or states in Palestine would lead to civil strife. Instead, the committee envisioned a binational state in which Arabs and Jews would share power equally. On the day the committee made its recommendation (April 30, 1946), Truman announced U.S. support for the part of the report that recommended allowing 100,000 Jews to emigrate to Palestine, as well as allowing the Zionists to purchase land there more freely. In some ways, Truman timed his unilateral and abridged announcement to lead up to the 1946 U.S. congressional elections.

I have learned with deep regret that the meetings of the Palestine Conference in London have been adjourned and are not to be resumed until December 16, 1946. In the light of this situation it is appropriate to examine the record of the administration's efforts in this field, efforts which have been supported in and [out] of Congress by members of both political parties, and to state my views on the situation as it now exists.

It will be recalled that, when Mr. Earl Harrison reported on September 29, 1945, concerning the condition of displaced persons in Europe, I immediately urged that steps be taken to relieve the situation of these persons to the extent at least of admitting 100,000 Jews into Palestine. In response to this suggestion the British Government invited the Government of the United States to cooperate in setting up a joint Anglo-American Committee of Inquiry, an invitation which this Government was happy to accept in the hope that its participation would help to alleviate the situation of the displaced Jews in Europe and would assist

---

[1]Michael Cohen, *Palestine and the Great Powers, 1945–1948* (Princeton, N.J.: Princeton University Press, 1982), pp. 58–59.

in finding a solution for the difficult and complex problem of Palestine itself. The urgency with which this Government regarded the matter is reflected in the fact that a 120-day limit was set for the completion of the Committee's task.

The unanimous report of the Anglo-American Committee of Inquiry was made on April 20, 1946, and I was gratified to note that among the recommendations contained in the Report was an endorsement of my previous suggestion that 100,000 Jews be admitted into Palestine. The administration immediately concerned itself with devising ways and means for transporting the 100,000 and caring for them upon their arrival. With this in mind, experts were sent to London in June 1946 to work out provisionally the actual travel arrangements. The British Government cooperated with this group but made it clear that in its view the Report must be considered as a whole and that the issue of the 100,000 could not be considered separately.

On June 11, I announced the establishment of a Cabinet Committee on Palestine and Related Problems, composed of the Secretaries of State, War, and Treasury, to assist, me in considering the recommendations of the Anglo-American Committee of Inquiry. The alternates of this Cabinet Committee, headed by Ambassador Henry F. Grady, departed for London on July 10, 1946, to discuss with British Government representatives how the Report might best be implemented. The alternates submitted on July 24, 1946 a report, commonly referred to as the "Morrison plan," advocating a scheme of provincial autonomy which might lead ultimately to a bi-national state or to partition. However, opposition to this plan developed among members of the major political parties in the United States—both in the Congress and throughout the country. In accordance with the principle which I have consistently tried to follow, of having a maximum degree of unity within the country and between the parties on major elements of American foreign policy, I could not give my support to this plan.

I have, nevertheless, maintained my deep interest in the matter and have repeatedly made known and have urged that steps be taken at the earliest possible moment to admit 100,000 Jewish refugees to Palestine.

In the meantime, this Government was informed of the efforts of the British Government to bring to London representatives of the Arabs and Jews, with a view to finding a solution to this distressing problem. I expressed the hope that as a result of these conversations a fair solution of the Palestine problem could be found. While all the parties invited had not found themselves able to attend, I had hoped that there was still a possibility that representatives of the Jewish Agency might take part. If so, the prospect for an agreed and constructive settlement would have been enhanced.

The British Government presented to the Conference the so-called "Morrison plan" for provincial autonomy and stated that the Conference was open to other proposals. Meanwhile, the Jewish Agency proposed a solution of the Palestine problem by means of the creation of a viable Jewish state in control of its own immigration and economic policies in an adequate area of Palestine instead of in the whole of Palestine. It proposed furthermore the immediate issuance of certificates for 100,000 Jewish immigrants. This proposal received

wide-spread attention in the United States, both in the press and in public fo-
rums. From the discussion which has ensued it is my belief that a solution
along these lines would command the support of public opinion in the United
States. I cannot believe that the gap between the proposals which have been put
forward is too great to be bridged by men of reason and good-will. To such a
solution our Government could give its support.

In the light of the situation which has now developed I wish to state my
views as succinctly as possible:

1. In view of the fact that winter will come on before the Conference can be resumed I believe and urge that substantial immigration into Palestine cannot
   await a solution to the Palestine problem and that it should begin at once.
   Preparations for this movement have already been made by this Government and it is ready to lend its immediate assistance.

2. I state again, as I have on previous occasions, that the immigration laws of
   other countries, including the United States, should be liberalized with a
   view to the admission of displaced persons. I am prepared to make such a
   recommendation to the Congress and to continue as energetically as possible collaboration with other countries on the whole problem of displaced
   persons.

3. Furthermore, should a workable solution for Palestine be devised, I would
   be willing to recommend to the Congress a plan for economic assistance for
   the development of that country.

In the light of the terrible ordeal which the Jewish people of Europe endured during the recent war and the crisis now existing, I cannot believe that a
program of immediate action along the lines suggested above could not be
worked out with the cooperation of all people concerned. The administration
will continue to do everything it can to this end.

PART III

The Rise of Postindependence States, 1950–2000

European colonialism, which tore at the fabric of society, nationalist projects that sought forcibly to create new "authentic" nations, and the economically debilitating effects of World War II left most countries in the Middle East and North Africa in a state of chaos. The old political landowning elites, leftovers from the Ottoman era, and the new middle-class elites, formed in the second half of the nineteenth century, proved incapable of providing the majority of the people with a unifying goal or with solutions to very real economic and social problems. For example, in the 1930s and 1940s King Farouk and his coterie in Egypt appeared completely incapable—and at times unwilling—to eject the British from Egypt. Furthermore, their conspicuous consumption stood in stark contrast to the poverty that predominated among peasants and the urban poor. Nor were most middle-class political parties much more effective. The Wafd Party—which presented itself as the party of the "people"—emerged from World War II with very little credibility. After twenty years at the helm of Egyptian political life, the Wafd appeared no closer to achieving complete and true independence for Egypt. Furthermore, the entanglement of its leadership in a series of political corruption scandals, and the unwillingness of these leaders to enact any laws that would ameliorate the lives of the peasants, bankrupted the political fortunes of the party.

The confusion was compounded by the dearth of national institutions that could bring some semblance of unity and order to most of the new nations in the Middle East and North Africa. In large part, this situation stemmed from the goals of the mandate powers. France, for instance, refrained from investing in a civil service infrastructure capable of independently administering Syria and Lebanon. French colonial fiscal policies were crafted primarily to benefit the economy of France, not to encourage the economies of Lebanon and Syria to grow independently. Such policies—meant to prolong the presence of the colonial powers—kept most countries from establishing visible national institutions that would cut across the various dividing lines in society (class, gender, ethnicity, religion, etc.). The one institutional exception was security organizations—the military or the police.

Security organizations were national institutions in which individuals from all walks of life could participate on equal terms. An 'Alawi Muslim from the environs of Latakia, a Sunni Muslim from Damascus, a Greek Orthodox Christian from Aleppo, and a Druze from the Golan could join the same Syrian army, wear the same uniform, march side by side in parades, and salute the same flag. Membership in the army did not eliminate divisiveness or overcome communal loyalties. But the army became one of the most visible symbols of Syria's status as a "nation." From outside Syria and from within, the army presented an image of unity and order that contrasted sharply with the political chaos that reigned in civil society during the 1930s and later. The army appeared "clean" in the face of rampant political corruption; it seemed strong while the civilian politicians seemed ineffective; it was national when the political leadership was sectarian; and it was composed of ordinary people, not the ruling elites.

Those contrasts were heightened by the loss of Palestine to the Zionists in 1948. Although the soldiers and officers of the various Arab regiments that fought in that war performed fairly well, the war was perceived to have been lost because of the ineptitude of Arab general commands, the lack of real support from Arab capitals, and the outdated weapons with which Arab regimes had armed their troops. This humiliation convinced many officers in various Arab armies that the time had come to overthrow the old political regimes and provide a new direction for the "nation."

During the 1950s and early 1960s this conclusion inspired action in various parts of the Middle East. In Egypt in 1952, for example, Gamal Abdel Nasser and the Free Officers overthrew King Farouk and established a "revolutionary" government whose self-avowed goal was to rescue the nation from colonialism and restore its national dignity. Over the following years, this goal also motivated military leaders who rose to power in Iraq, Libya, Syria, Algeria, and Yemen. The widespread desire to bring an end to years of humiliating and oppressive colonialism is understandable. The appeal of such a goal is especially apparent when we take into consideration the European "Orientalist" traditions, which throughout the nineteenth century and later characterized the Middle East and North Africa as backward. Also for people in Egypt and elsewhere, a strong, unified, and coherent government offered a welcome reprieve from the pervading chaos. Thus, despite some strong opposition to the idea of military rule, Nasser in Egypt, Hafez al-Assad in Syria, and other leaders elsewhere were seen as potential saviors of the beleaguered "nation"—an impression that these leaders strongly encouraged.

In the case of Nasser, this impression became more powerful after he successfully nationalized the Suez Canal in 1956 and refused to back down in the face of British, French, and Israeli military aggression. (The importance of this moment in Arab history can be gauged by the incredible success of the movie *Nasser '56,* produced in 1993 in the wake of the Gulf War, which retold the story of Nasser and his victory in very positive terms.) This success legitimized for a while the emergence of single-party rule centered on the cult of the *za'im* (leader). In the new state, the leader and the nation began to become indistinguishable. The belief was widespread that only the za'im could possibly know what was good for the people, and anyone who opposed him or his ideas was considered a traitor to the "nation."

One of the leader's goals was indeed to improve the lives of the people of the nation (if for no other reason than to keep them from revolting). Nevertheless, a state defined in this manner had little legitimacy. This paternalistic approach was sustainable only as long as the benefits of authoritarianism seemed to outweigh its detriments. While opportunities for a better life were available to large numbers of people, the state could justify and people would tolerate political authoritarianism and the rejection of any opposition—legitimate or otherwise. However, this situation could not be sustained for long. Economically, states all across the Middle East and North Africa soon proved incapable of properly managing the economy. From conservative regimes such as Iran and Saudi Arabia to "revolutionary" states such as Egypt and Algeria, ruling elites faltered in their handling of the economy. Corruption, graft, overly ambitious projects, lack of economic diversity, overpopulation, and a residue of economic dependence on the West combined to create serious economic crises at various times for various states. Politically, many of these states also faltered—albeit at different times and for different reasons. For instance, in 1967 Egypt, Syria, and Jordan suffered a humiliating defeat at the hands of the Israeli army. This defeat of conservative (Jordan) and "revolutionary" (Egypt and Syria) regimes alike destroyed the credibility of leaders who had based their claims to legitimacy on the premise that they were advancing their countries. Within forty-eight hours, superior Israeli military technology emptied years of military parades and bombastic speeches of any meaning. The facades that had provided flimsy excuses for the suppression of various freedoms and for sordid human rights records came crashing down, leaving the ruling elites exposed to criticism from all angles.

The chapters in this section attempt to document in a variety of ways the emergence and initial success of these states, as well as the challenges they faced. Included here are documents that highlight attempts to create dominant state ideologies leaving little room for any opposing ideas. Also presented are critiques of these types of states—of their failures to fulfill their promises and to improve the lives of their peoples.

CHAPTER 6

Restricting Authority

The struggle to create modern nations between the two world wars was a politically exhausting and debilitating struggle between competing ideologies and groups that sometimes presented radically different visions of the "nation" to the population at large. In Egypt, this period of experimentation with democratic processes is known as the "Liberal Experiment." Between 1926 and 1939, Egypt experienced widespread freedom of the press, a plethora of political parties ranging from communists on the left to Muslim Brothers on the right, and a series of public elections. Unfortunately, for most Egyptians this experiment was ultimately a failure. Consecutively elected parliaments failed to provide relief for the economic woes of either the peasants—still the majority of the population—or the workers. Most remained impoverished and subject to exploitation by landowners, bankers, and industrialists. Politically, the electoral process was severely undermined and tarnished, because King Farouk dissolved the Egyptian parliament whenever he deemed its goals to be at odds with his desires, and the occupying British forces constantly interfered in the selection of the Egyptian cabinet. Also, the corrupt practices of the once-popular Wafd Party convinced most Egyptians that the democratic process was a farce.

If this experiment in Egypt—where a "modern" bureaucratic state had been in existence since the beginning of the nineteenth century—failed to fulfill people's aspirations for a politically independent and economically healthy nation, the situation was even worse elsewhere in the Middle East and North Africa. In countries such as Syria and Iraq, the population was far more ethnically, religiously, and linguistically diverse than in Egypt, and modern governing institutions were much less numerous than in Egypt. In places such as Syria and Algeria, the colonial powers (France in these cases) prevented most of the indigenous population from participating in the administration of the country. These factors, in addition to economic hardship resulting from years of colonial rule and economic mismanagement, increased the complexity of nation building and intensified the political chaos.

World War II worsened this situation, leaving most countries in the Middle East and North Africa greatly impoverished. Without a Marshall Plan but with ongoing and intensified European extraction of local resources, the peoples of these countries were pushed farther down the economic ladder. Most of the indigenous ruling elites—whose hallmark was conspicuous consumption—were increasingly viewed as illegitimate rulers. For many in the Middle East, the crisis of political legitimacy came to a head with the loss of Palestine to the Zionists in 1948. When the creation of Israel was announced in May of that year, the armies of Transjordan, Syria, and Egypt (with some volunteers from Iraq and Saudi Arabia) announced that they would soon retake the land for the Arabs. Unfortunately for them, the first Arab-Israeli war led to an even greater loss, as Israel claimed 73 percent of Palestine, as opposed to the 50 percent allocated by the United Nations' 1948 partition plan. This devastating loss highlighted the gap between the bombastic rhetoric of the Arab ruling elites and their actual ability to create modern nations capable of safeguarding the interests of their peoples.

In the wake of this defeat, political opposition to the ruling elites intensified and discontent grew on the streets of Cairo, Amman, Damascus, and Baghdad. Most of these nascent nations appeared to teeter on the brink of disintegration. Against this chaotic background, the military in these countries seemed islands of strength, stability, and unity. From the armed forces emerged a new group of political activists. Generally, they were officers—such as Gamal Abdel Nasser of Egypt—who had risen into the middle ranks of the military from a humble socioeconomic background. Their allegiance was to the "nation" and not primarily to a political party. They were still untarnished by the political and financial corruption sullying the ruling elites, and they had the military wherewithal to at least overthrow the existing government. And this is what transpired throughout the 1950s in Egypt, Syria, and Iraq, and later in the 1960s in Libya, Algeria, and Yemen.

Elsewhere in countries such as Iran, Jordan, and Morocco, the state was controlled by a monarchy that based its rule in large part on its army and on support from Western powers. Saudi Arabia, however, offered a still different model. The power of the Saudi monarchy derived from the alliance between the tribe of Bin Saud, originally from the eastern region of modern-day Saudi Arabia, and the Wahabis, members of an ultraconservative religious reformist movement that emerged in the eighteenth century in the same region of the country. Their symbiotic relationship was based on the religious legitimacy that the Wahabis gave to the Saudi monarchy and the willingness of the Saudis to allow the Wahabis to instill their retrograde vision of Islam within the kingdom.

Thus, by the 1960s, the great majority of the countries in the Middle East and North Africa were authoritarian states. Even Israel, which proclaimed itself a democratic state, limited the privilege of full political participation by definition and in practice to its Jewish citizens—some would argue to Jews of European descent—thus politically marginalizing its Arab citizens.

Included in this chapter are documents that examine the rise of authoritarianism in various countries. Excerpts of the confidential diary of Asadollah Alam, Iran's court minister between 1969 and 1977, provide invaluable glimpses into the ambitions and follies of the shah of Iran, Muhammad Reza Pahlavi (document 1). In document 2, Saddam Hussein, the authoritarian president of Iraq, proclaims his notion of history as a tool for "educating" the masses and particularly children about the revolution. This document illustrates the power of rhetoric in authoritarian discourse; such power is in many ways far more effective than military weapons and oppression. The constitution of Saudi Arabia (document 3) explains the claim of the ruling House of Saud to a religious source of legitimacy and highlights the nature of Saudi rule. Document 4 is an interview with a human rights activist in Turkey who discusses the army's role in shaping the political process in that country.

In most of these documents we find that behind the rise of the authoritarian state in the Middle East is the personification of the nation. Many rulers came to see themselves as the embodiment of the "nation" and their wishes and desires as the wishes and desires of the "people." The greater their illegitimacy, the more oblivious they became to what their people really hoped for, and the more they came to believe in their own fiction or in some fiction constructed by their sycophantic entourages.

1. Asadollah Alam's Diary Details Some Elements of the Shah of Iran's Rule in 1976 and 1977

Asadollah Alam descended from the non-Qajar aristocracy that ruled the eastern provinces of Iran before the rise of the Pahlavi dynasty to the monarchy. After the fall of Muhammad Mosaddeq—the nationalist prime minister of Iran—in August 1953 as a result of an American-concocted coup d'état, Shah Muhammad Reza Pahlavi (1919–1980) was reinstated to power, and he was finally able to implement his vision of unlimited personal power within Iran. Alam shared and even encouraged the shah's view of government. Alam's first task—which he carried out successfully—was to promote the social reforms known as the White Revolution, to be implemented under the sole leadership of the shah. This move was an attempt to remove any constitutional blocks to the absolutism that the shah so desired and that Alam supported wholeheartedly. Alam was responsible for violently putting down several revolts against the regime of the shah, first by tribal leaders in the Fars region and then by religious clergy led by Ayatollah Ruhollah Khomeini (document 3 in the chapter "Crisis of the State" is a 1975 denunciation of the shah by Khomeini). These successes, however, only set the stage for the weakening and down-

Asadollah Alam, *The Shah and I: The Confidential Diary of Iran's Royal Court, 1966–1977*, ed. Alinaghi Alikhani, trans. Alinaghi Alikhani and Nicolas Vincent (London: I. B. Tauris & Co., 1991), pp. 508–510, 515–516, 523–527, 540, 542–543, 545–546, 547, 549, 550. Reprinted by permission of I. B. Tauris & Co Ltd, London.

*fall of the shah. The quite successful social reforms opened a host of educational op-
portunities to a greater number of Iranians than ever before, and a generation of
educated young people grew up expecting and then demanding more political
rights and a greater say in the governing of the country. These demands ran in the
face of the autocratic tendencies of the shah, which were encouraged by Alam. By
the end of his regime—in the late 1970s, about which Alam writes here—the shah
had become politically isolated and insulated from the mounting opposition to his
rule, and the violence of his police machine—the Savak—barely kept in him power.*

Friday, 10 September [1976]

. . . Met the Israeli representative this evening. Discussed joint action to persuade the US Senate to accept arms sales to Iran. He suggested that HIM [His
Imperial Majesty] raise the issue with Shimon Perez, the Israeli Defence minister, who is due to be received tomorrow. He also told me that Senator Hubert
Humphrey is considering making a tour of the Middle East; Iran, Israel and
Saudi Arabia in particular . . . It would be a good idea if our Washington ambassador could extend an invitation along these lines, since it would help our
position in regard to arms. He stressed that we must act quickly if we're to
forestall Saudi Arabia and so be the first to attract the senator's attention . . .

Tuesday, 14 September

Audience. Discussed the race for the US presidency, where Carter seems still to
be leading. We then turned to the underlying reasons for the hostility shown us
by the American media. I remarked that the Americans are fools and that their
opposition to our arms purchases shows them bowing to Soviet propaganda. If
they had any sense they would be crying out for us to buy more not less
weapons, since it would increase our dependence on the USA to an even
greater extent. "Quite so," HIM replied. "Soviet propaganda is remarkably effective and the Americans are even more remarkably stupid. Combine these
two factors and you arrive at the present débâcle; every single congressman and
pundit acting directly contrary to their own best interests." . . .

Princess Ashraf has again asked the government to pay the expenses of her
trip to England, greatly to HIM's annoyance. He instructed me to notify every
member of the Imperial family that such impertinent requests to the government will be severely dealt with in future.

This afternoon I received a prominent American journalist named Helen
Copley; a supporter of ours. We spent an hour discussing the Information
Plan. She suggested we set up a special news agency in the USA, the better to
influence public opinion . . .

Saturday, 18 September

Audience . . . HIM asked me to write to Ardeshir Zahedi, urging him to liaise
closely with Israel's embassy in Washington . . .

Last Wednesday on HIM's instructions, I cabled General Nassiri in Washington following his prostate operation, notifying him that the Shahanshah had most graciously agreed to pay his medical and travel expenses. Ardeshir Zahedi telephoned yesterday to say that the general had also received money from the PM and that he's now bewildered whether he has HIM to thank for this second payment. "The PM said nothing about it to me," HIM remarked with a smile.

It seems our PM takes a keen interest in the well-being of the men from Savak! . . .

Sunday, 19 September

Audience. HIM declared he felt better today than he's felt for many years . . .

Shahriar Shafiq,[1] HIM's nephew by his sister Princess Ashraf, presently an officer in the navy, was at last night's dinner. He and HMQ [Her Majesty the Queen] spent the entire time moaning on about Tehran's chaotic traffic congestion, the incompetence of municipal bureaucracy in Bandar Abbas, and so forth. I told HIM I strongly disapprove of such talk; fair enough if they raised these problems during the day, but they're not appropriate topics for the dinner table and do nothing but damage to HIM's health. Even Hitler spent his evenings listening to music, even at the height of the war. HIM gave a wry smile as if to say such things are beyond his power to change . . .

Reported that Danny Chamoun, the son of the former Lebanese President, has asked for an audience in order to pass on a message from his father. "I'd be ill-advised to receive him in present circumstances," HIM remarked. "His father has grown old and more than a little mad." I pointed out that the old man put up a brave resistance to the left-wingers . . . "Quite so," HIM replied, "but the determination with which he acted merely proves the degree of his madness." . . .

Met the Israeli representative after lunch. He predicts the US-presidential elections will be a very close-run affair . . .

[. . .]

Sunday, 17 October

. . . Discussing our image abroad, HIM referred to an interview he gave recently to Mike Wallace of NBC.[2] "The bloody man's questions were incredibly hostile. He more or less forced me into declaring that the USA is controlled by the Jews and that it's this same influence which has persuaded Carter to oppose

---

[1]The son of Ahmad Shafiq, an Egyptian, who was the second husband of Princess Ashraf. A graduate of the British Royal Naval College, Dartmouth, Shahriar was regarded as a competent and straight-forward military officer, unaffected by and uninterested in Court life. He was assassinated in Paris in December 1979 amid speculation that the revolutionary regime in Tehran regarded him as a threat. [All footnotes in this document are Alikhani's.]

[2]See Mike Wallace, *Close Encounters* (New York, 1985), pp. 334–335.

our purchasing arms." ... "Tell the Israelis," HIM said, "that the bastard was so malicious I had no choice but to speak my mind. He more or less dragged it out of me." I reminded him that everyone, the Court press department, our Jewish advisers and myself, had pleaded with him not to receive this man Wallace. Yet he insisted on going ahead and just look where it's led us. "There's no use wringing our hands," he replied. "What's done is done. But tell Ardeshir Zahedi that he's not to arrange interviews with such vultures ever again." Here too, I pointed out that it's a standing order of our new campaign that no one is to arrange foreign press interviews for HIM. It was for precisely this reason we asked for the Foreign Minister to be admitted to our steering committee. HIM finally approved this last suggestion ...

Monday, 18 October

Audience ... Some time ago HIM's sister, Princess Fatemeh, asked for a 707 army plane to fly her, Mrs Diba and seventy other ladies on pilgrimage to Mashad. Knowing what HIM's reaction would be I avoided reporting the matter whilst we were in Birjand. However last night the Princess telephoned to press her claim and I was forced to raise it at today's audience. HIM was furious. "Do they suppose the military have nothing better to do," he said, "than to act as courier to a bunch of redundant old bags in search of God's mercy?" He was so angry that we both kept a tense silence for quite some time. I bitterly regretted having raised the matter.

I asked whether his skin rash was any better. He now believes it was due to the calcium tablets he was taking and has noted a marked improvement since he gave them up. His doctors are due to give him a blood test next week, but he rejected my suggestion that they bring along a dermatologist, saying that the rash is due to some sort of internal reaction not to any problem with his skin.

Reported that Princess Shahnaz has asked for a three-fold increase in salary. "Has she gone mad?," HIM replied. "I said raise her salary, not treble it! I'd never be able to justify it to the others. They'd all be clamouring to follow suit." ... He added that he intends making a tour of inspection of the Tehran barracks next Thursday afternoon. I pointed out that since next Wednesday is a religious holiday, everything will be shut down until the Saturday after.[3] In any case military offices are always closed on Thursday afternoons. He did nothing more than smile by way of reply; in other words warning me to mind my own business ...

There have been municipal elections across the country. Despite being allowed greater licence than normal, people in Tehran seemed utterly indifferent to the whole thing. Of the city's 5 million inhabitants, only about 70,000 bothered to vote. Since the Rastakhiz Party made no attempt to drum up attendance at the polling stations, it only goes to show that nobody's particularly interested in these elections. A worrying sign ...

---

[3]Thursday and Friday constitute the weekend in Iran.

Monday, 22 November

... Met Yankelovich together with the deputy head of the information and press department of Israel's Foreign Ministry. Between them they have drawn up a lengthy report on Iran's image in the western media. Most interesting and yet alarming to discover how little we really knew of the situation. I am pleased that it is I who should have the responsibility of passing the real facts on to HIM.

Thursday, 25 November

Audience. Amongst other things, reported that Princess Shahnaz was expecting to lunch with the Egyptian Vice-President during her trip to Cairo, but at the last moment Sadat himself telephoned to invite both her and the Vice-President to be his guests ...

Remarked that when I bid farewell to HMQ yesterday on her departure for Egypt, I found her surrounded by the usual bunch of ill-mannered dimwits. It's only to be expected they should turn up in Kish, Nowshahr, Birjand, even in Amman, but really Cairo is another matter altogether. Their Majesties enjoy a special relationship with Egypt which these people can only jeopardize ... "But what's to be done?" HIM replied. "HMQ is genuinely attached to them. Even her mother has warned her, several times, yet she was told to mind her own business so harshly she daren't raise the subject ever again." ...

"Incidentally," he said, "I don't suppose you've heard about President Tito's latest statement? He's announced that Yugoslavia needs a strong military defence and can no longer rely on the promises of outsiders." I remarked this seemed very much in line with what HIM has been saying about Iran. "Precisely," he said. "We have to alert the Iranian public to this issue. My political testament consists of little else; above all it emphasizes that the army is the very cornerstone of this country's future. The testament needs to be made public." I replied that it would be better to wait until the Crown Prince's twentieth birthday.

"The other day," HIM continued, "I was asked by the US ambassador why Amouzegar had been appointed Secretary-General of the Party. I explained that Amouzegar is an excellent administrator; he's not a freemason, and I can trust him. No one is perfect, of course. Amouzegar also happens to be extremely mean. He's envious of other people's success and over keen to be generous towards his brothers and his family. But then, as I say, nobody is perfect." ...
[...]

Friday, 26 November

... Talked for an hour this afternoon with Joseph Kraft, an American journalist who has been a good friend to Iran. He told me the Carter administration is bound to turn against us, as our policies are mutually incompatible. During his election campaign Carter declared it undesirable that there should be any further military build-up in the Middle East; he blamed Iran for the rise in oil prices, and attacked our record on human rights . . . I asked Kraft what we might do to overcome this problem. In his opinion, HIM should visit Carter at the White House as soon as possible. In addition we should dismiss our ambassador in Washington; he's too obviously a supporter of the former regime and has turned our embassy into something not far short of the Playboy Club.

I expressed surprise that Carter should be so taken in by the propaganda of our enemies. Our political prisoners are communists, and in this country communist activity is illegal. To say that we deny political liberty is merely to parrot the slogans of our enemies . . . As for our re-armament, I presume Carter has sufficient intelligence not to rush to hasty judgments. We're spending so much money on US military supplies that no US government, let alone the arms manufacturers, could afford to deny us . . . I added that even if Carter is foolish enough to opt for confrontation, we are not lacking in the means to retaliate. The USA has no monopoly over arms manufacture, and we can always turn to France or Germany, or exchange our gas for Soviet hardware . . .

I didn't bother pointing out the extent to which HIM has the support of his nation. The internal situation is sound. The workers and the farmers are content and the middle classes grow richer day by day. Set against this, what does it matter if a few so-called intellectuals express opinions at odds with our own. In any case what do these blasted dissidents hope to gain? Education and the health service are already free. People are allowed a large degree of control over their own affairs. "Mr Joseph Kraft," I said, "you are a friend of Iran. But if you have been sent here to bully us, I must tell you bluntly that we give not a damn for other peoples' opinions. You can rest assured HIM has no intention of visiting the USA either in the immediate future or for some time to come."

Kraft remarked that, though he'd already met the PM and most of the cabinet, no one had spoken to him as harshly as me. I replied I had done no more than express an honest opinion to someone I assumed to be a friend. It was up to him to interpret my words in whatever way he chose. "Sure," he said, "but the opinions you express are really those of the Shah." I replied that having been granted an audience himself he was already in a position to judge how closely my views accord with those of my Shahanshah. I told him, however, that I had been given no prior briefing and that in any case HIM accounts the entire subject as of very little significance. Kraft was amazed at this, remarking that what I had said about HIM visiting the USA was more or less word for word what the Shah himself had told him.

Saturday, 27 November

Audience . . . Reported my conversation with Kraft. HIM was pleased with the way I'd handled it. "How can they ignore the prestige of my country?," he said. "How can they think of throwing up business worth $4 billion a year; likely to top $50 billion over the coming decade? I only wish the PM and the cabinet had spoken as you did." He went on to say that we are in the midst of negotiations with the Soviet Minister of Foreign Trade for the supply of Russian long-range artillery. "And we can turn to Western Europe for tanks and aircraft. Then we shall set how these American gentlemen react."

Met the Israeli representative after lunch. He told me that Yankelovich is seriously concerned that his report has offended HIM.

Again met Kraft. He claims that the US embassy here is misleading our government in claiming that Carter has no alternative but to fall into line with previous American policy towards Iran. Apparently the senators who were here recently disbelieved the US ambassador's stories about close relations between Iran and Israel. They asked Kraft to check up on the matter. "And," he said, "I had to tell them that everything was just as the ambassador told them. Even so it gives you a good idea how much faith our senators put in the word of their own officials." . . .

Sunday, 28 November

Audience . . . Described the findings by our press department on Yankelovich's report of American public opinion.[4] HIM almost exploded with rage, saying, "How can the bastard have dared be so impertinent? His report was based on wholly negative assumptions. It was not his business to question whether the country enjoys political liberty, nor whether torture is employed against political prisoners. He should not concern himself with whether we are contributing to peace in the Middle East." I replied that the question of peace was entirely valid, and that Yankelovich's other points were all the subject of intense interest in the USA and therefore of relevance to a report on US opinion. He and his associates must be allowed to diagnose the problem if they're to prescribe a remedy "We shall see," said HIM, "but in my opinion he and his colleagues are being manipulated by the oil companies. They're out to frighten us." I replied that as far as I can tell there is no evidence to support such an allegation. "Very well," HIM said more angrily than ever, "if you're too blind to see what's been going on, then it's pointless my trying to explain it to you." Again I did my best to point out that it was we ourselves who asked Yankelovich and his firm to study our image in the West, to show us where we were going wrong and to suggest improvements . . . But HIM remained silent and I thought it best to change the subject. Even then his sullen mood persisted and he did no more than snap out brief comments on the matters I had to report . . .

---

[4] "A Study of the Attitudes of the American Public and Leadership Towards Iran," based on interviews with leading figures in American business, politics, the media, etc. The Court's press department worked closely with the American public relations consultants, agreeing with their methods and findings.

Wednesday, 1 December

Audience . . . Reported that Amnesty International's survey of Iran is extremely hostile. "Quite so," HIM remarked. "But Parviz Radji, our ambassador in London, has answered their criticisms very well." I pointed out that Amnesty's report has received considerable publicity world-wide, but that Radji's remarks merited no more than a brief reference from the BBC. "Fair enough," he replied, "you must cable Radji immediately. Tell him if his statement isn't published, then he must bring it out himself via advertising space in the newspapers." I also had to report that West German radio has broadcast criticisms of Savak. This put HIM in a worse mood still . . .

Tuesday, 14 December

Audience . . . Cautiously and with a great deal of apprehension I submitted Yankelovich's latest report, setting out proposals for the internal structure of our Information Plan. HIM read it through carefully and without any sign of annoyance. He then instructed me to ensure it's implemented. I was not unduly surprised by this. HIM is a complex individual. He knows very well that Yankelovich can be of service in improving our foreign propaganda, particularly given his influence with Carter and the American Jewish community . . .
[. . .]

Tuesday, 10 May 1977

Audience . . . Kermit Roosevelt, a CIA agent involved in the downfall of Dr. Mosaddeq in August 1953, plans to publish an account of the coup. I reported that I've now examined the book and found it most undesirable. It portrays HIM as a waverer, forced into various crucial decisions, for example the appointment of General Zahedi as Prime Minister, by pressure from Roosevelt. The man is . . . hoping to present himself as a hero. HIM said he had no idea the book contained so much nonsense. He agreed I must try to prevent publication . . .

Thursday, 12 May

Audience . . . The telephone rang in the midst of our conversation. Clearly it was to report an enormous fire at an oil field somewhere. I was alarmed and, contrary to my usual discretion, asked HIM for details. "Oh, it's nothing disastrous," he said. "It's in Saudi Arabia. Why else do you suppose I sat here so relaxed?" I told him he's enjoying an extraordinary spell of luck. First, the cold winter in the USA, then the storms in the Gulf, and now this fire; the Americans are having little success in sabotaging our oil policy . . . "Quite so," he agreed. "What's more, Carter is beginning to see sense. He's no longer preaching the same old nonsense he did during the election."

[. . .]

Saturday, 21 May

Audience . . . Much to HIM's disgust the new US ambassador, William Sullivan, has issued a statement to Congress, referring to the existence of religious opposition groups here in Iran . . . "Doesn't he realize these people are Islamic Marxists, mere Soviet puppets," HIM said. I replied that, whilst various of them may well be manipulated by the Soviets, or for that matter by Washington, there are others who act solely out of ignorant fanaticism . . . HIM remarked that he had no objection to girls wearing scarves at school or university; "But veils are out of the question . . . Tell my private secretariat to inform the government accordingly." . . .

Monday, 23 May

Audience . . . Reported a meeting I held yesterday with the British ambassador Sir Anthony Parsons. He is favourably impressed with the new British Foreign Secretary, David Owen, a man in his early thirties. The ambassador has explained to him that it's pointless to accuse Iran of violating human rights. We've granted substantial social improvements to our people over the past few years; a move unprecedented elsewhere in the world. The foreign media judge us from too narrow an angle . . .

Referring to Carter's speech of last night, HIM said, "He's announced he's willing to supply weapons to NATO, Israel, the Philippines, South Korea, Australia and New Zealand without any conditions attached; he didn't so much as mention Iran. Does he suppose that, strategically speaking, Iran is less significant than a country like New Zealand? Perhaps the Americans and the Soviets have devised some scheme to divide the world between themselves." I replied that this was quite out of the question. The Americans will never abandon us. As for Carter's pronouncements, they're intended merely to impress American public opinion. Like it or not, these idiot Americans are convinced we're violating human rights . . .

Sunday, 29 May

Audience . . . Discussing the USA, I remarked I'd been impressed by the latest letter HIM received from Carter. It indicates he's slowly starting to see sense. "He had no choice," HIM said . . .

[Writing on 24 May 1977 President Carter, in the warmest terms, thanked the Shah for accepting an invitation to visit Washington the following November.]

HIM remarked that, when he was in the southern suburbs a couple of days ago, he saw thousands of women wearing the veil . . . "These bloody mullahs don't dare admit that Islam and Marxism are at opposite ends of the spectrum," he said. "Why did Ayatollah Khonsari beat about the bush for such a long time and then, in the end, decide against speaking out?" I replied that they all go in fear of their lives. "Have they nothing better to think of than saving their own skins?" HIM asked. "Of course not," I said . . .
[. . .]

Wednesday, 8 June

Audience . . . Reported that Carter has given an interview to an American magazine, stating he is delighted by the excellent relationship between the USA and Saudi Arabia. "Quite so," HIM remarked. "People are always pleased to have a lackey." I suggested Carter really is doing his best to get on with us. "I have no cause for complaint," HIM said.

He then told me he had good news. "I've decided to give up attending my sisters' dinner parties, and to cease inviting that bunch of creeps to the palace. They had begun to get on my nerves. Every time we played bridge or *belote,* and someone laid down a card, some other bloody fool would interrupt to ask a personal favour . . . I told HMQ my decision last night. She was not at all pleased." . . . I congratulated him, pointing out that I've been begging him to do this for the past ten years.

Sunday, 11 June

A reception this morning in the gardens of the Niavaran Palace, attended by 500 members of the Association of Scholars and Intellectuals. In theory they're supposed to examine policy problems and submit their findings to the government . . . The Association was established at a time when HIM was anxious to provide some sort of balance, other than the Mardom party, to the power of Iran Novin. Its members seem oblivious to the fact they've been made redundant by the introduction of single party politics . . .

Audience . . . Referring to this morning's reception HIM said, "I have to cater to the vanity of these people. Not that I don't appreciate their hard work. Their organization should be kept going for the rest of this year." I said I had no objection to this, although the poor devils clearly don't realize how superfluous they have become. "What do you mean?," HIM snapped back. I explained my reasoning. He was disconcerted to find that I'd guessed his motives from the very start . . .

Sunday, 12 June

Audience . . . The Imperial Air Force is at daggers drawn with Iranair over which one of them is responsible for servicing HIM's private jet. I have looked into the matter, and the air force have sent in a report justifying their claim. "Then they probably deserve to be in charge," HIM said. "Form a committee and get things sorted out. Maybe the plane ought to be a joint responsibility." [. . .]

Friday, 17 June

. . . Ayatollah Khonsari telephoned to complain that the city of Qom is without water or electricity. I contacted HIM who told me to inform the PM who duly promised to send someone to investigate. I told him that this simply isn't good enough; hunger and thirst are serious matters, not to be glossed over in his usual way . . . He grew a little abashed at this and promised to take action. [. . .]

Sunday, 26 June

Audience . . . Asked about the report by the International Red Cross; their President was granted an audience yesterday. "It's still confidential and for our eyes only," HIM said. "But even so it claims that out of 3,000 political prisoners, 900 bear signs of torture. Precisely the same figure was given by the Commission I myself appointed. The report goes on to say that signs of torture have vanished altogether over the past few months." . . . I told him that in my view this is serious news indeed, and only goes to show that the dissidents had real cause for protest. We can only hope no word of it gets out. "It's for our eyes only," HIM repeated. "No one can leak it, save we ourselves." I pointed out that, nowadays, nothing can be considered secret, and that it's a pity we did nothing to improve prison conditions on our own initiative. He made no attempt to reply . . .
[. . .]

Tuesday, 28 June

Audience. Reported meeting the US ambassador yesterday. He suggested we inform the American public about recent improvements in the way political prisoners are handled. "Why can't they do it themselves?," HIM asked. "Their media should pass on news of what we've been doing." I replied they have no reason to help us. Indeed, their media claims the improvements are due solely to pressure from Carter.

We then turned to Yankelovich and the Information Plan which HIM rejected . . . "MG craved a role as part-time ambassador in Washington and part-time Foreign Minister," HIM said. "He wanted Yankelovich made our secret political representative in the USA." I've long known HIM harboured such ideas, hence my decision in Paris a few months ago to drop the entire affair. Who knows, even I might have fallen under his suspicions . . .

As we were talking news came through of an attempt to assassinate Saddam Hussein of Iraq. Apparently he escaped with only a slight scratch to the eye . . . I remarked that his death would have been a grave disappointment to us. "Quite so," HIM replied. "But for him, there'd have been no compromise over the Shatt al-Arab." . . .

Wednesday, 29 June

. . . Escorted HMQ to the airport, ostensibly on her way to attend the summer seminar at Aspen, Colorado, though her real reason for going is to establish personal contact with Rosalind Carter, the President's wife . . .

2.   Iraq's Saddam Hussein Proclaims History as a Tool for Educating the Masses About the Revolution and Comments on the Role of Women in the Revolution, 1975, 1978

One of the most striking aspects of authoritarian government is not the use of physical violence to achieve its goals and to minimize opposition but rather the attempt to shape citizens' views about a broad range of subjects. This hegemonic approach to the hearts and minds of the populace, coupled with the technical ability to interfere on such an intimate and daily basis, distinguishes the post–World War II governments in the Middle East and North Africa from their prewar counterparts. The Ottomans and the Egyptian government under Muhammad 'Ali and his descendants sought to centralize power and to extend their bureaucratic influence more effectively throughout their lands. However, their ability and interest in shaping people's daily lives and thoughts was minimal at best, mainly because they regarded people simply as subjects, not citizens.

After World War II, however, ideas of citizenship and nationhood became political realities not easily ignored. Many regimes—such as the Ba'ath in Syria and Iraq, Nasser in Egypt, the shah in Iran, Israel vis-à-vis its Arab inhabitants, and the Christian ruling elite of Lebanon—attempted to shape the meaning of these ideas in a way that would bolster their power to rule. Mass media offered the most effective means of spreading their interpretations of "citizen" and "political participation" while excluding opposing ideas. Although these regimes were never completely successful in squelching opposition and contrarian ideas, they enjoyed a large measure of success.

In the following selections, ideas of the "citizen" and the "nation" are set forth in speeches by Saddam Hussein (b. 1937), perhaps the most notorious of the authoritarian rulers in the Middle East and North Africa. Hussein's childhood and upbringing and exposure to colonial rule seem to have convinced him that maintaining absolute control upheld by violence was the best strategy for governing a fractious nation like Iraq. He applied this logic ruthlessly as an operative in the Ba'ath Party, as vice president of that party, and as president of Iraq. Upon attaining power in 1979, Hussein immediately purged the party of any opponents through execution and exile. On one chilling occasion, he convened the Ba'ath leadership in a hall and called the names of individuals whom he considered to be "traitors" to the cause. Those individuals were immediately taken outside and they "disappeared" before the eyes of the remaining delegates. Scenes of men pleading for their lives and Hussein dabbing away crocodile tears were recorded on film and shown to all party members. Hussein's attempt to strike fear in the hearts of his opponents resembled Stalinist methods of controlling access to information and shaping ideas to fit state propaganda. The speeches included here indicate the worldview that Hussein projected to Iraq in the years before he became president.

1. On Writing History

"We must not speak about the writing of history in isolation from current times and circumstances" *Saddam Hussein's Pronouncement in discussing the Report of the National Educational Committee for the Correction of School Curriculum, 1975*

It is only that several things should be taken into consideration in modern curriculums: age, the educational and scientific capabilities of the students and pupils; thus one does not say the same things—in terms of content and approach—to high school students as one would to elementary school students.

When we speak to young children, who have limited scientific understanding, we must speak about some political or historical issues that we wish for them to internalize, in the absolute without any qualifications. For example, when we speak of Arab unity we must not occupy the little student with details and to engage him in a discussion of whether we are indeed a single nation or not. It is enough to speak of the Arab as one nation assuming that to be an absolute reality, with a brief summary about the role that colonialism played in dividing the [Arab] countries and nation in order to weaken it and maintain control over it. We should also portray the path to unity through struggle in a simplified form as well. Thus, when we speak about the Ba'ath Arab Socialist Party [the party that brought Hussein to power and that he leads] as a leading party, we should speak about it to the children as if it is an absolute reality. As to the details of why and how it became a leading party then we can show that through a discussion about the accomplishments of the party, the role of the party in saving the Iraqi people, and through a discussion of the Revolution without fatiguing the students at this stage with complicated theoretical, philosophical or political analyses. This is especially the case with the generation that did not live through the period preceding the Revolution of 17–30 June, 1968 [which brought the Ba'ath to power] . . . Discussing the Revolution, and the Arab Ba'ath Socialist Party without speaking of the dark era that preceded the revolution—in social, political, economic, cultural and military terms—will not provide [a] historical and objective context for understanding the Revolution. The June revolution is great because of the accomplishments it attained from 18–30 June 1968 until now; but its greatness appears greater when we understand what preceded the revolution. It is important to speak of the dark period which preceded the revolution in detail so that coming generations will

Saddam Hussein, *On Writing History* (Beirut: Dar al-Tal'ia, 1979). Translated by Akram Khater. Reprinted by permission of the American Committee on Jerusalem.

understand the greatness of their revolution. We must avoid speaking in detail about matters that are constantly and rapidly changing because they will appear small in later stages. . . .

Here I find it necessary to speak, educate and concentrate on the fact that Iraq is part of the Arab nation more than speaking about the Iraqi people being part of the Arab nation. In this manner we can achieve our goal without upsetting opposing nationalist tendencies amongst the other part of our people.

In our national education we must speak about self-rule [for the minorities]. And when we address the subject of self-rule we must not get lost in too many details so as not to make the administrative structure of self a "Chinese Wall" that separates the Arab from the Kurd in Iraq. For instance, when we speak about Iraqi folklore we do not see it necessary to speak about Kurdish folklore, and another that is Arab and a third that is Turkish . . . etc. Rather, it should be presented simply as Iraqi folklore. So we would say for example: this is a dance from the South of Iraq from al-Nassiriya [an Iraqi town], and this is a dance from al-Sulaymaniya [another city]. . . . Exaggerated actions to show that we care about local nationalisms [within Iraq] will cause immense harm in our short- and long-term plans. . . . To take for example our starting point, by way of imagining equality between the Arab and others, as saying that the Arab wears the *'iqaal* (one type of headdress) and the Kurd wears *laffat* [another type of headdress] around the head . . . is a big mistake because this image will have negative psychological effects and will lead to dangerous ideological and political results. Perhaps there is someone who is purposely plotting to maintain a Chinese wall that separates our people psychologically and mentally. . . .

When we speak about our people's nationalist sacrifices we must not limit our discourse to talking about political and military actions. Rather we need to point to the big sacrifices that the citizens have done, and continue to perform, in the field of production and other activities in order to build up the nation. He who endangers himself to save a machine is worthy of mentioning with pride in order to strengthen the tendency to consider work a basic tenet in the honor and progress of the nation . . . and to strengthen the tendency among the sons of our people to safeguard the socialist property.

2. The Revolution and the Woman

. . . When we want to speak about the liberation of the woman and her historical role in building society, and about the equality in rights between her and the man, how should we approach this subject?

There are certain known givens with regard to the starting position in this subject. When we discuss the practical aspects of this subject, it is assumed that we are in agreement about the basic premises which make equality between the man and the woman, for the purpose of building the society with a combined effort, a given since it is one of our basic principles. . . .

Saddam Hussein, *The Revolution and the Woman* (Beirut: Dar al-Tal'ia, 1979). Reprinted by permission of the American Committee on Jerusalem.

But should we continually immerse ourselves in the details of daily work, by talking about the ability of the woman . . . in order to prove that the woman, like the man can grasp every opportunity and can do anything? Is this correct? I think this approach is wrong. . . . Rather than approach this matter within such a context, we should approach from a different perspective, not to escape the basic premise but to use objective premises to support our argument. . . . In this manner we concentrate on equality in rights, balance of rights; we concentrate on rejecting the idea that places the woman in a secondary position [to the man]; we reject the feudal and tribal mentality and perspective; we reject the idea which makes the woman subservient to the man. . . . This approach is better than saying that a woman can equally do anything that a man can, because then you will find someone who says: therefore, we must apply military service on women, because that is one of the conditions of equality, and it is one way to prove that men and women are equal in capabilities. . . .

Thus, at the same time that women cannot permanently serve in the Armed Forces in a widespread manner, and particularly in the active units, men cannot take over the role of raising and nurturing children as the women do. In the same manner that the man is distinguished from the woman by serving in the army, the woman [is] distinguished from him in nurturing children, and both are central roles in our society.

My advice to all the women of Iraq is to concentrate on the proper manner of dealing with this subject, and which . . . makes the man support the woman in this direction rather than oppose her. . . . Our discourse on the woman and her role in society should be balanced, and that our perspective on this subject should be balanced as well. There has been talk here, in this place, and in other places whereby some of you have asked to lift the guardianship off women since they have become mature enough to take care of themselves. And others have asked for this guardianship to continue using the excuse that we should take into consideration the particular circumstances of the woman. . . . One time we speak of her as a weak creature . . . and at other times we speak of her as the leader of society. One time we speak of the lack of the special circumstances, as we call them, for the woman to perform her duties in the countryside and the factory, and in building roads and bridges, and at another time we reject the mentality which distinguishes in a hierarchical fashion between man and woman with regard to job and educational opportunities. Our discourse about the woman and her role in our society should be balanced!

Why, for example, did we in 1976 approve the training of women in the popular army when it was not approved in 1970? We have not ceased, and have not ignored our initial and revolutionary position about changing society, but we postponed the application of these ideas until we could prepare the groundwork to accomplish our goals without great losses. . . .

We must not offer colonialism a technical opportunity, since it no longer has a strategic opportunity to oppose the Revolution. Therefore, it and its agents have been seeking technical opportunities through the mistakes that we commit, either in hurrying matters too much or in postponing too long. . . .

It is vital that you concentrate on self-criticism [of women]. For when we concentrate on the shortfall of women with regard to their duties, and this is initiated by the General Union of Iraqi Women [an arm of the Ba'ath Party] as was done in this report, then we are not belittling the historic role of women in building society.

3. The Constitution of Saudi Arabia Bases the Legitimacy of the Ruling House of Saud on Religion, 1992

Many of the more conservative regimes in the Middle East and North Africa, such as Saudi Arabia and Morocco, are monarchies. In the twenty-first century, this political system appears to outsiders as well as to citizens of these countries as an anomaly—a fact not lost on the ruling families. In an era of democratic reforms sweeping the globe, their political legitimacy is questioned in muted and loud tones. In the case of Saudi Arabia, the ruling family—the Sauds—deflects some of the criticism through the "carrot" of a welfare state that provides services to Saudi citizens. The "stick" part of this formula is strict control over information, political expression, and access to power. Both the "carrot" and the "stick" are made possible by oil wealth, which allows the state to provide free education and health care and to guarantee employment, while it uses a secret police force to maintain control over dissidents.

In many ways such an arrangement is made possible by the help of an outside power. Many people in the Middle East and North Africa consider Saudi Arabia and other monarchies as little more than puppets of the United States. Whether because of direct involvement in the oil industry, or because of military support, the United States is seen as the mainstay of the Saudi regime. The authoritarian control exercised by the Saudis is justified in this excerpt from the Saudi constitution—a constitution that is the regime's most "liberal" compromise.

(Adopted on: March 1992)
(Adopted by Royal decree of King Fahd) (ICL Document Status: Oct 1993)

Chapter 1 General Principles

Article 1

The Kingdom of Saudi Arabia is a sovereign Arab Islamic state with Islam as its religion; God's Book and the Sunnah of His Prophet, God's prayers and peace be upon him, are its constitution, Arabic is its language and Riyadh is its capital.
[...]

Constitution of Saudi Arabia, http://www.the-saudi.net/saudi-arabia/saudi-constitution.htm (27 January 2003).

Chapter 2 [Monarchy]

Article 5

- (a) The system of government in the Kingdom of Saudi Arabia is that of a monarchy.
- (b) Rule passes to the sons of the founding King, Abd al-Aziz Bin Abd al-Rahman al-Faysal Al Sa'ud, and to their children's children. The most upright among them is to receive allegiance in accordance with the principles of the Holy Koran and the Tradition of the Venerable Prophet.
- (c) The King chooses the Heir Apparent and relieves him of his duties by Royal order.
- (d) The Heir Apparent is to devote his time to his duties as an Heir Apparent and to whatever missions the King entrusts him with.
- (e) The Heir Apparent takes over the powers of the King on the latter's death until the act of allegiance has been carried out.

Article 6

Citizens are to pay allegiance to the King in accordance with the holy Koran and the tradition of the Prophet, in submission and obedience, in times of ease and difficulty, fortune and adversity.

Article 7

Government in Saudi Arabia derives power from the Holy Koran and the Prophet's tradition.

Article 8 [Government Principles]

Government in the Kingdom of Saudi Arabia is based on the premise of justice, consultation, and equality in accordance with the Islamic Shari'ah.

Chapter 3 Features of the Saudi Family

Article 9

The family is the kernel of Saudi society, and its members shall be brought up on the basis of the Islamic faith, and loyalty and obedience to God, His Messenger, and to guardians, respect for and implementation of the law, and love of and pride in the homeland and its glorious history as the Islamic faith stipulates.

[. . .]

Article 13

Education will aim at instilling the Islamic faith in the younger generation, providing its members with knowledge and skills and preparing them to become useful members in the building of their society, members who love their homeland and are proud of its history.

Chapter 4 Economic Principles

Article 14

All God's bestowed wealth, be it under the ground, on the surface or in national territorial waters, in the land or maritime domains under the state's control, are the property of the state as defined by law. The law defines means of exploiting, protecting, and developing such wealth in the interests of the state, Its security and economy.
[...]

Article 17

Property, capital, and labor are essential elements in the Kingdom's economic and social being. They are personal rights which perform a social function in accordance with Islamic Shari'ah.

Article 18

The state protects freedom of private property and its sanctity. No one is to be stripped of his property except when it serves the public interest, in which case fair compensation is due.

Article 19

Public confiscation of money is prohibited and the penalty of private confiscation is to be imposed only by a legal order.
[...]

Article 39 [Expression]

Information, publication, and all other media shall employ courteous language and the state's regulations, and they shall contribute to the education of the nation and the bolstering of its unity. All acts that foster sedition or division or harm the state's security and its public relations or detract from man's dignity and rights shall be prohibited. The statutes shall define all that.
[...]

Article 43 [Royal Courts]

The King's Court and that of the Crown Prince shall be open to all citizens and to anyone who has a complaint or a plea against an injustice. Every individual shall have a right to address the public authorities in all matters affecting him.

Chapter 6 The Authorities of the State

Article 44

The authorities of the state consist of the following: the judicial authority, the executive authority, the regulatory authority. These authorities cooperate with each other in the performance of their duties, in accordance with this and other laws. The King shall be the point of reference for all these authorities.

Article 45

The sources of the deliverance of fatwa in the Kingdom of Saudi Arabia are God's Book and the Sunnah of His Messenger. The law will define the composition of the senior ulema body, the administration of scientific research, deliverance of fatwa and its (the body of senior ulemas) functions.

Article 46

The judiciary is an independent authority. There is no control over judges in the dispensation of their judgements [*sic*] except in the case of the Islamic Shari'ah.
[. . .]

Article 57

(a) The King appoints and relieves deputies of the prime minister and ministers and members of the Council of Ministers by Royal decree.
(b) The deputies of the prime minister and ministers of the Council of Ministers are responsible, by expressing solidarity before the King, for implementing the Islamic Shari'ah and the state's general policy.
(c) The King has the right to dissolve and reorganize the Council of Ministers.

Article 58

The King appoints those who enjoy the rank of ministers, deputy ministers and those of higher rank, and relieves them of their posts by Royal decree in accordance with the explanations included in the law. Ministers and heads of independent departments are responsible before the prime minister for the ministries and departments which they supervise.

Article 59

The law defines the rules of the civil service, including salaries, awards, compensations, favors and pensions.

Article 60

The King is the commander-in-chief of all the armed forces. He appoints officers and puts an end to their duties in accordance with the law.

Article 61

The King declares a state of emergency, general mobilization and war, and the law defines the rules for this.
[…]

Article 68 [Consultative Council]

A Consultative Council is to be created. Its statute will specify how it is formed, how it exercises its powers and how its members are selected.

Article 69

The King has the right to convene the Consultative Council and the Council of Ministers for a joint meeting and to invite whoever he wishes to attend that meeting to discuss whatever matters he wishes.

4.   Human Rights Activist Yilmaz Ensaroglu Discusses the Role of the Army in Turkey, 1997

Modern Turkey was established as a constitutional republic by an authoritarian army led by Mustafa Kemal (Atatürk) (see document 6 in the chapter "Ideas of Nationalism"). The legacy of Kemalism can be summarized as popular secular nationalism overseen and "protected" by statist economic and military policies. Kemalism sought to create a "modern" society whose characteristics are strictly "defended" by the military. This paradox has led to several periods of army intervention in civilian

*politics, and even periods of army rule. In the 1960s and 1970s, Turkey was em-
broiled in what many consider its worst constitutional and civil rights crisis. The document included here implicates the army in the use of death squads in the earlier
period and in the more recent army "coups." It is an interview with Yilmaz Ensaroglu, president of Mazlum Der, a Turkish human rights organization. Yilmaz
Ensaroglu also acted as deputy president of the same organization between 1992
and 1996. Originally from the eastern province of Agri, Ensaroglu is an imam hatip
graduate who was active in labor union movements before becoming a human
rights activist. He served a prison term for charges of having violated former constitutional Article 163 banning fundamentalist activities.*

Rights Were Curbed More with Each New Constitution in Turkey

President of Mazlum Der, the Organization for Human Rights and Solidarity
with the Oppressed, Yilmaz Ensaroglu, stated that human rights violations in
Turkey have a legal basis and that more limitations were brought on freedoms
and rights with each new constitution.

The following interview is the third of its kind on human rights and covers
the views of the conservative-religious section's approach to human rights violations, which isn't actually much different from those speaking for "secular"
human rights associations. Ensaroglu said the word *Mazlum* (the suffering,
the oppressed) was often confused with *Muslim* and wanted to stress that it
wasn't so.

Malzum Der however was established in 1991, at the time of the foundation of the Human Rights Association (IHD), to defend the rights of the believers and the religious sectors of society. These sectors felt the other human
rights associations were pro-leftist and didn't care much for the defense of the
rights of others. Today Mazlum Der has close cooperation with the IHD. Ensaroglu said: "Mazlum Der was established not as a human rights association to
compete with the others but on the contrary as one which will cooperate by
filling up the gaps left by the others."

- Let's start with the general question as to how you assess developments regarding human rights in Turkey, whether there has been any improvement?

I personally don't think that there have been improvements because in our
country the individual's rights and liberties can be limited, for the sake of the
state, according to constitutional provisions. This is our system. Whereas, constitutions in other countries, are social agreements guaranteeing the rights and
liberties of the individual. In our case, human rights and liberties are curbed
with the Constitution. It is a great pity that there is a legal basis for a large section of human rights violations. And we see that certain verdicts are given with
very subjective assessments of our judges, and most recently, decisions go even
beyond subjective assessments, and decisions against the existing laws are being given—laws are altogether suspended.

- Since when has this been happening?

I would say in the past one-and-a-half or two years. And in the past six months there has been a renewed escalation especially against the freedom of thought and expression.

- Why? Is it because of a certain fear that there may be threats against the state?

Well the fear has always been there and our problem is actually this fear—the state's fear, not of the individuals. From the beginning there is a structure which takes the state as the ultimate and sacred being. This structure has also chosen an official race, language and official religion. Such a system was formed and it was called democracy. But when you look at it, this democracy isn't really functioning either in Parliament, nor in political parties. . . .

- Also in the Welfare Party [Refah]?

Of course, I am not making any discrimination. I am talking of all the parties represented in Parliament. But we don't know the exact structure of some other parties which aren't represented in Parliament, so I am talking about those that we know. A so-called oligarchic structure exists in all the parties in Parliament. Deputies aren't elected there because they have the support of the people but because their party nominated them. They are appointed there by their chairmen and these deputies in Parliament therefore cannot voice the problems of the people. They simply obey the chairman.

- Is democracy interrupted at that point?

Yes, and what happens then? I think, for years, the country has been run with the policies defined by a couple of bureaucrats through a couple of feudal leaders.

- Who are these feudal leaders?

They are the party chairmen. I mean the bureaucrats decide on the policies and define these policies, and the party leaders put these policies into application.
    When a Refah deputy was attacked by police forces nobody reacted because he was from Refah, then after some time another deputy was attacked in the May 1 demonstrations, and because this deputy was from the Republican People's Party, everyone said he was a leftist anyway, so nobody defended him. Then a day came when a whole group of deputies were kicked out of Parliament. . . . This is actually the credibility, the honour of Parliament that we should seriously be concerned about.

- Then there isn't any meaning in asking whether this government is any better than the other or vice versa?

Exactly, there is no meaning in asking whether there has been any improvements in human rights with this government or the previous one. I suggested to the EU term president when speaking with us, that it was useless for them to go and speak with government officials. I said they should go and speak with the National Security Council instead. I am terribly ashamed when I say this but there is such a problem in my country . . . the most typical example is the practice of the Emergency Rule. All parties when in opposition say the Emergency Rule should end, then the same party which has said this in opposition comes to power and in power it defends its continuance.

- Well this government at least ended the practice in many provinces. . . . However shouldn't we then have no political parties?

Maybe it is much better, because we will then know that is the problem in the Turkish system. But this isn't the case and we have a Parliament, we call our system democratic, we have deputies but all the policies are framed at the National Security Council—by the military bureaucracy. I mean even a party which remained determined to oppose those policies for years when in opposition—you know that the Refah had always voted against the extension of the Emergency Rule Region in the Southeast—when in power started saying that the Emergency Rule was needed.

- This is a universal trend. We are trying to find the answer to the question as to how we can overcome this. As to how shall we achieve a free society not a chaotic one.

That is true. I think we can achieve a free society when such a consciousness is spread all over the society. In Turkey, people aren't fully aware of their rights and the state is seen as sacred. Even if individuals are against this state, still at the back of their mind they feel it is not correct to be against it. The state should be brought down to act as a tool which serves the happiness and comfort of the citizens.

Also, the state shouldn't just respect but should be based on human rights; its reason of existence should be human rights. When we look at our constitutional history we see that with each new constitution, rights have been more and more curbed. And the 1982 Constitution defines human rights as being "within the limits brought by this Constitution."

- Do you have an explanation for that?

I think the main factor behind this notion is that in Turkey the majority of the elite and the bureaucracy do not know the people. The elite and the people are strangers to each other and this isn't something new but a trend that has been continuing since the Ottoman period. And at this point there are serious differences in the values of the elite and the people. The state has always wanted to shape people instead of serving them. And within such an understanding, in our case "limitation" becomes the rule and "freedom" an exception.

- Isn't it up to the political parties to change this situation? And you as an association defending the human rights of the believers of society, why haven't you pressed the Welfare Party to do certain things to change the situation while they were in office? For example Refah violated the right of women to be elected to Parliament; didn't you do anything against this?

To tell the truth we haven't conducted any specific work on Refah. But whenever we have certain statements or bulletins, we send it to all parties in Parliament, and naturally to Refah. I personally do not know to what degree the women in Refah wanted to become candidates in the elections. I haven't looked into that.

But I want to say that our association somehow has always had good relations with opposition parties but when they have come to power, disagreements have started. It has been the same case with Refah. We had many disagreements when that party came to power. Double standards hold true for all.

- Generally speaking, can you make your voice heard?

As I said double standards are everywhere, and it doesn't make any difference whether it is the leftists, rightists or religious groups. . . . All have this double standard unfortunately. Therefore whenever we brought up human rights violations when Refah was in power, pro-Refah newspapers wouldn't even print that news.

We voiced a very strong reaction against the Metin Goktepe incident and said that we felt ashamed because of the attitude of the press towards a colleague. But none of the newspapers, including the one Goktepe was working for, gave any place to our association's reaction. Only the daily *Cumhuriyet* covered our reaction, and how, we don't still know. Our biggest problem is that the public doesn't know us very well.

- What are other ways of making yourself known?

Of course the best way is through the media. But we try with extra effort to attend conferences and debates and make use of various platforms. However, I see with regret that the outside world—of course this may be due to other reasons—follows our activities more. Whenever we issue a report and—if by chance the *Turkish Daily News* also publishes it—the next day at least five embassies call us and ask for the full text of that report.

We all know that the outside world is closely following human rights in Turkey. And now for the first time our own officials are contacting us, calling us and trying to learn our views. This is a very important development, an important progress. And we want this approach to continue.

- Can we say that Europe's close interest to human rights in Turkey is also alerting our officials on the subject, that this is a positive development?

Yes of course, and also human rights shouldn't be made an issue of national pride. I say this to foreigners and I tell them that it is our right to also show the same sensitivity vis-à-vis human rights violations in their countries.

I tell them that if I am talking very openly about human rights violations in my country then you should also be as open with me about, for example, the situation of Turks in German prisons.

[. . .]

CHAPTER 7

Crisis of the State

Authoritarian regimes in the Middle East and North Africa have tried to consolidate their power through repression, populist economic and social policies, and propaganda. But the voices of opposition—religious and secular—as well as shifting political circumstances around the world have kept these regimes from completely attaining their goals.

Perhaps one of the most effective voices of opposition throughout the Middle East and North Africa has been that of Islamic political movements. In part their effectiveness is due to the fact that most states in those areas have succeeded in suppressing leftist secular opposition. The relative ease of this repression is due to the secular nature of those opposition movements, which leaves members open to the false but damaging charge of being atheists or unbelievers. Such labels limit the basis of popular support for leftist ideas and programs among populations that tend to be overwhelmingly religious—even if only at the cultural level. Furthermore, the socialist and intellectual language of leftist organizations makes their ideas and programs inaccessible and—perhaps more important—irrelevant to the majority of the peoples of the region.

By contrast, none of these states ever has been fully able to silence the religious right. Most of them instituted governmental restrictions on places of worship, required licenses for clerics, and jailed, tortured, and killed religious dissidents. Nevertheless, the ubiquity of religious institutions and the lack of any acceptable formal religious hierarchy provided those on the religious right with a good deal of maneuvering space and staying power. Furthermore, the states—even the most self-avowedly secular ones—sought "moderate" religious support at various critical moments in order to shore up their disintegrating legitimacy. Thus, as the Syrian philosopher Sadiq al-ʿAzm notes in document 2, the government of Nasser appealed to religion as a way to distract attention away from the humiliating defeat Egypt suffered in 1967—a defeat for which he initially accepted responsibility (document 1). Nasser's successor—

Anwar el-Sadat—employed the religious opposition as a bulwark against the leftist elements in the country that opposed him.

It is this cynical employment of religion that accounts for the preponderance of religious criticism of the state and its abuse of power. Among the best known of these opposition figures is Ayatollah Ruhollah Khomeini, who was a teacher of Islamic theology in Qom, the religious capital of Iran. There was a consistent stream of criticism of the rule of the shah in Iran, but Khomeini denounced the regime as un-Islamic (document 3). This charge resonated far more strongly among religious students, peasants, and the urban poor than attacks on the shah by a leftist party like the Tudeh. The language that Khomeini used contained references to Islamic history and traditions with which even the uneducated were familiar and comfortable. Thus, it appeared that Khomeini and other religious opposition figures were providing an indigenous call for justice and were presenting an Islamic alternative to a shah supported by the "West." The report from the American embassy in Iran (document 5) highlights further how this message resonated with the majority of Iranians, and the platform of the Islamic Salvation Front (document 7) incorporates the same type of religious language into the definition of Algeria and by extension into the definition of the legitimate ruler of that nation. Also included in this chapter is the introduction to an Islamist book about an attack by the Syrian regime against its own people in Hama (document 6). Although this is a highly biased and charged essay, it is a very important source for understanding how Islamists viewed the ruling regimes in the Middle East. The language found in this document is used almost universally by Islamic opposition movements.

Of course, not all opposition was or is religion based. In the documents about the Lebanese civil war (document 4), we find two disparate views about the definition of the "nation" and the distribution of state power. The definitions serve as road maps to the distribution of political, economic, and cultural power. In Lebanon, criticism of the state was based on the belief that in its pre-1975 incarnation it provided power for Christians at the expense of Muslims. The near demographic parity of these two communities as well as the radicalization of politics in the region (a consequence of the Arab-Israeli conflict) brought about calls for change in state institutions and in both domestic and foreign policy. However, as with any demand for change, the reluctance of the dominant group to abandon its hold on authority was as strong as the desire of the opposing side to change the balance of power.

Challenges to the distribution of power within the state also have emerged in the past thirty years in Israel. From its beginning in 1948, Israel has been defined as a "Jewish state." However, from its inception, Israel also has been home to a growing minority of Arab citizens. From the perspective of this Arab community, the Jewish-state definition of Israel is insulting: it ignores the presence of the Arabs and relegates them to the position of second-class citizens. By the end of the 1970s the Arab community not only had grown numerically—in relation to the larger Jewish community—but also had become more educated and articulate in its rejection of its alienated status. The growing demand for meaningful recognition as equals is apparent in shifts in voting, as Arabs withdraw support for Jewish-Israeli parties and vote instead for Arab-Israeli parties. Not only in electoral politics but in every avenue of social, cultural, and economic affairs have Arabs found their voice. Thus, more and more Arab-Israeli writers write in Hebrew about their experiences, in direct or oblique criticism of what they perceive as racism against them. The last document in this chapter is one example of this cultural manifestation of opposition to the definition of Israel as a Jewish state.

1. Egyptian President Gamal Abdel Nasser Resigns from Office Following the 1967 Arab-Israeli War, June 9, 1967

In 1967, in six days, Israeli armed forces were able to defeat Egyptian, Syrian, and Jordanian forces in a decisive manner and to conquer more Arab land—including Egypt's Sinai Peninsula. This outcome was profoundly shocking to the psyches of ordinary people and leaders alike—at least before excuses began to be fabricated to explain away the humiliation of so swift a loss. The shock was all the worse because the preceding decade had seemed full of promise—for "modernization" of society and the state, for an Arab renaissance with Nasser at the helm, and even for the possibility that at least part of Palestine would be recaptured. The war of 1967 crushed these dreams and exposed the emptiness of promises made (read Halim Barakat's novel Days of Dust *[1974] for a painfully eloquent description of the mood that prevailed on the "Arab street" during this war). Nasser's resignation speech was an acknowledgment—albeit fleeting—of his personal failure and by extension the failure of the state that he led. Many historians argue that this speech marks the start of the dissolution of the postindependence army-ruled states.*

Brothers, at times of triumph and tribulation, in the sweet hours and bitter hours, we have become accustomed to sit together to discuss things, to speak frankly of facts, believing that only in this way can we always find the right path however difficult circumstances may be.

We cannot hide from ourselves the fact that we have met with a grave setback in the last few days, but I am confident that we all can and, in a short time, will overcome our difficult situation, although this calls for much patience and wisdom as well as moral courage and ability to work on our part. Before that, brothers, we need to cast a glance back over past events so that we shall be able to follow developments and the line of our march leading to the present conditions.

"Nasser's Resignation Broadcast," BBC Radio Monitoring Service, Cyprus. From Voice of the Arabs Radio, Cairo, 9 June 1967.

All of us know how the crisis started in the Middle East. At the beginning of last May there was an enemy plan for the invasion of Syria and the statements by his politicians and all his military leaders openly said so. There was plenty of evidence concerning the plan. Sources of our Syrian brothers were categorical on this and our own reliable information confirmed it. Add to this the fact that our friends in the Soviet Union warned the parliamentary delegation, which was on a visit to Moscow, at the beginning of last month, that there was a premeditated plan against Syria. We considered it our duty not to accept this silently. This was the duty of Arab brotherhood, it was also the duty of national security. Whoever starts with Syria will finish with Egypt.

Our armed forces moved to our frontiers with a competence which the enemy acknowledged even before our friends. Several steps followed. There was the withdrawal of the United Nations Emergency Force and the return of our forces to the Sharm al Shaykh post, the controlling point in the Straits of Tiran, which had been used by the Israeli enemy as one of the after-effects of the tripartite aggression against us in 1956. The enemy's flag passing in front of our forces was intolerable, apart from other reasons connected with the dearest aspirations of the Arab nation.

Accurate calculations were made of the enemy's strength and showed us that our armed forces, at the level of equipment and training which they had reached, were capable of repelling the enemy and deterring him. We realised that the possibility of an armed clash existed and accepted the risk.

Before us were several factors—national, Arab and international. A message from the US President Lyndon Johnson was handed to our Ambassador in Washington 26th May asking us to show self-restraint and not to be the first to fire, or else we should have to face grave consequences. On the very same night, the Soviet Ambassador asked to have an urgent meeting with me at 05.30 [as broadcast] after midnight. He informed me of an urgent request from the Soviet Government not to be the first to open fire.

In the morning of last Monday, 5th June, the enemy struck. If we say now it was a stronger blow than we had expected, we must say at the same time, and with complete certainty that it was bigger than the potential at his disposal. It became very clear from the first moment that there were other powers behind the enemy—they came to settle their accounts with the Arab national movement. Indeed, there were surprises worthy of note:

1. The enemy, whom we were expecting from the east and north, came from the west—a fact which clearly showed that facilities exceeding his own capacity and his calculated strength had been made available to him.

2. The enemy covered at one go all military and civilian airfields in the UAR. This means that he was relying on some force other than his own normal strength to protect his skies against any retaliatory action from our side. The enemy was also leaving other Arab fronts to be tackled with outside assistance which he had been able to obtain.

3. There is clear evidence of imperialist collusion with the enemy—an imperialist collusion, trying to benefit from the lesson of the open collusion of

1956, by resorting this time to abject and wicked concealment. Nevertheless, what is now established is that American and British aircraft carriers were off the shores of the enemy helping his war effort. Also, British aircraft raided, in broad daylight, positions on the Syrian and Egyptian fronts, in addition to operations by a number of American aircraft reconnoitering some of our positions. The inevitable result of this was that our land forces, fighting most violent and brave battles in the open desert, found themselves at the difficult time without adequate air cover in face of the decisive superiority of the enemy air forces. Indeed it can be said without emotion or exaggeration, that the enemy was operating with an air force three times stronger than his normal force.

The same conditions were faced by the forces of the Jordanian Army, fighting a brave battle under the leadership of King Husayn who—let me say for the sake of truth and honesty—adopted an excellent stand; and I admit that my heart was bleeding while I was following the battles of his heroic Arab Army in Jerusalem and other parts of the West Bank on the night when the enemy and his plotting forces massed no less than 400 aircraft over the Jordanian front.

There were other honourable and marvellous efforts. The Algerian people, under their great leader Hawwari Bumedien, gave without reservation and without stinting for the battle. The people of Iraq and their faithful leader Abd ar-Rahman Arif gave without reservation or stinting for the battle. The Syrian Army fought heroically, consolidated by the forces of the great Syrian people and under the leadership of their national Government. The peoples and governments of Sudan, Kuwait, Yemen, Lebanon, Tunisia and Morocco adopted honourable stands. All the peoples of the Arab nation, without exception, adopted a stand of manhood and dignity all along the Arab homeland; a stand of resolution and determination that Arab right shall not be lost, shall not be humiliated, and that the war in its defence is advancing, regardless of sacrifice and setbacks, on the road of the sure and inevitable victory. There were also great nations outside the Arab homeland who gave us invaluable moral support.

But the plot, and we must say this with the courage of men, was bigger and fiercer. The enemy's main concentration was on the Egyptian front which he attacked with all his main force of armoured vehicles and infantry, supported by air supremacy the dimensions of which I have outlined for you. The nature of the desert did not permit a full defence especially, in face of the enemy's air supremacy. I realised that the armed battle might not go in our favour. I, with others, tried to use all sources of Arab strength. Arab oil came in to play its part. The Suez Canal came in to play its part. A great role is still reserved for general Arab action. I am fully confident that it will measure up to its task. Our Armed Forces in Sinai were obliged to evacuate the first line of defence. They fought fearful tank and air battles on the second line of defence.

We then responded to the cease-fire resolution, in view of assurances contained in the latest Soviet draft resolution, to the Security Council, as well as French statements to the effect that no one must reap any territorial expansion from the recent aggression, and in view of world public opinion, especially in Asia and Africa, which appreciates our position and feels the ugliness of the forces of international domination which pounced on us.

We now have several urgent tasks before us. The first is to remove the traces of this aggression against us and to stand by the Arab nation resolutely and firmly; despite the setback, the Arab nation, with all its potential and resources, is in a position to insist on the removal of the traces of the aggression.

The second task is to learn the lesson of the setback. In this connection there are three vital facts: (1) The elimination of imperialism in the Arab world will leave Israel with its own intrinsic power; yet, whatever the circumstances, however long it may take, the Arab intrinsic power is greater and more effective. (2) Redirecting Arab interests in the service of Arab rights is an essential safeguard: the American Sixth Fleet moved with Arab oil, and there are Arab bases, placed forcibly and against the will of the peoples, in that service of aggression. (3) The situation now demands a united word from the entire Arab nation; this, in the present circumstances, is irreplaceable guarantee.

Now we arrive at an important point in this heartsearching by asking ourselves: does this mean that we do not bear responsibility for the consequences of the setback? I tell you truthfully and despite any factors on which I might have based my attitude during the crisis, that I am ready to bear the whole responsibility. I have taken a decision in which I want you all to help me. I have decided to give up completely and finally every official post and every political role and return to the ranks of the masses and do my duty with them like every other citizen.

The forces of imperialism imagine that Jamal Abd al-Nasser is their enemy. I want it to be clear to them that their enemy is the entire Arab nation, not just Jamal Abd al-Nasser. The forces hostile to the Arab national movement try to portray this movement as an empire of Abd al-Nasser. This is not true, because the aspiration for Arab unity began before Abd al-Nasser and will remain after Abd al-Nasser. I always used to tell you that the nation remains, and that the individual—whatever his role and however great his contribution to the causes of his homeland—is only a tool of the popular will, and not its creator.

In accordance with Article 110 of the Provisional Constitution promulgated in March 1964 I have entrusted my colleague, friend and brother Zakariya Muhiedin with taking over the [post] of President and carrying out the constitutional provisions on this point. After this decision, I place all I have at his disposal in dealing with the grave situation through which our people are passing.

In doing this I am not liquidating the revolution—indeed the revolution is not the monopoly of any one generation of revolutionaries. I take pride in the brothers of this generation of revolutionaries. It has brought to pass the evacuation of British imperialism, has won the independence of Egypt and defined its Arab personality, and has combated the policy of spheres of influence in the Arab world; it has led the social revolution and created a deep transformation in the Egyptian reality by establishing the people's control over the sources of their wealth and the result of Arab action; it recovered the Suez Canal and laid down the foundation of industrial upsurge in Egypt; it built the High Dam to bring fertile greenness to the barren desert; it laid down a power network over the whole of the north of the Nile Valley; it made oil resources gush out after a long wait. More important still, it gave the leadership of political action to the alliance of the people's working forces, the constant source of renewed leaderships carrying the banners of Egyptian and Arab struggle through its successive stages, building socialism, succeeding and triumphing.

I have unlimited faith in this alliance as the leader of national action: the peasants, the workers, the soldiers, the intellectuals and national capital. Its unity and cohesion and creative response within the framework of this unity are capable of creating—through work, serious work, difficult work, as I have said more than once—colossal miracles for this country in order to be a strength for itself, for its Arab nation, for the movement of national revolution and for world peace based on justice.

The sacrifices made by our people and their burning spirit during the crisis and the glorious pages of heroism written by the officers and soldiers of our armed forces with their blood will remain an unquenchable torch in our history and a great inspiration for the future and its great hopes. The people were splendid as usual, noble as their nature, believing, sincere and loyal. The members of our armed forces were an honourable example of Arab man in every age and every place. They defended the grains of sand in the desert to the last drop of their blood. In the air, they were, despite enemy supremacy, legends of dedication and sacrifice, of courage and willingness to perform the duty in the best way.

This is an hour for action; not an hour for sorrow. It is a situation calling for ideals and not for selfishness or personal feelings. All my heart is with you, and I want all your hearts to be with me. May God be with us all, a hope in our hearts, a light and guidance. Peace and the blessing of God be with you.

2. Sadiq al-'Azm, an Arab Intellectual, Critiques the Arab State and Clergy for Their Use of Religion, 1968

In 1967 Sadiq al-'Azm was a professor of philosophy at American University in Beirut when the Arab armies of Egypt, Syria, and Jordan suffered a humiliating defeat at the hands of the Israelis. Like many Arabs, al-'Azm was shocked by the swift and disastrous course of the war (which lasted a mere six days), especially after years of propaganda about progress and modernization in Egypt, the self-declared standard-bearer of the "progressive" Arab states. Like other Arabs, al-'Azm sought explanations for this abysmal turn of events.

Some Arabs presented a religious justification for the failure—namely, that Muslims had strayed from the path of God and God punished them by abandoning them at their time of great need. However, as a secular intellectual, Sadiq al-'Azm rejected this explanation and posited that the problem lay in exactly that type of thinking. He—and others such as the Syrian poet Adonis—argued that religion in the Middle East hinders rationality and produces fatalism and a culture that is shackled to the past. Moreover, the disillusioned al-'Azm argued, although some Arab states had constructed facades of modernism based on equality, progress, and democracy, they remained hamstrung by backward-looking religious thought. He

*criticized these states for manipulating religious ideas to gain legitimacy and re-
main in power while maintaining their authoritarian rule. Al-'Azm wrote the following criticism of the state, religion, and their relationship in 1968 for the Arab journal
Arab Studies.*

Those who know the editorials of Muhammad Hasanayn Haykal about the
state of the Arab world after the defeat of June 1967 may remember that the famous [Egyptian] editorialist has said on more than one occasion that undoing
the effects of [Israeli] aggression without resorting to war and military power
will require nothing short of a miracle. Then he added that our age is not an age
of miracles. . . . However, circumstances seem to belie Haykal with regard to
his comments about miracles since on June 5, 1968 *Al-Ahram* [Egypt's leading
and semi-official daily newspaper] carried the press release of Pope Kyrallis the
Sixth [the Coptic Christian pope] in which he declared and affirmed the truth
of the apparition of the Virgin Mary at al-Zaytoun Church. Furthermore, *Al-
Ahram* carried a photo on its front page that it declared to be a photographic
recording of the Virgin or her shadow that had appeared. . . .

Soon after, the whole Egyptian press became immersed in a sudden religious hallucination and it adopted "this great national issue" and began to publicize it and to exert itself in "finding scientific evidence" for the existence of
miracles. The Egyptian press searched for scientists and university professors
who would testify that the appearance of the Virgin is a scientific fact that cannot be doubted. . . . Furthermore, the press made quite clear that the apparition
of the Virgin has long term political, social, and touristic implications for the
Arab masses in Egypt and with regard to reclaiming the land occupied after
June 5 [1967]. . . .

Naturally, this religious hysteria has been reflected in Lebanon, and *Al-
Anwar* [a Lebanese daily] has begun publicizing the phenomenon. So it was
that it [the newspaper] appeared with news of a serious scientific study that
proves "that the apparition of the Virgin in Cairo is a factual truth." . . .

The dangerous aspect of this sudden religious phenomenon within Arab
media is not the traditional belief in miracles that is prevalent amongst the
people, and the belief in the appearance of the Virgin and in her ability to do so
at will. The stories and tales of supernatural and healing miracles are as old as
humanity, and it is not limited to one religion. . . . However, the dangerous aspect in the subject of the apparition of the Virgin is that this popular movement . . . did not follow a spontaneous course whereby the believers would go
on pilgrimage to the said church and some would be healed, others would die,
and still others would believe and that would be the end of the story; as all such
stories should end. The course of events was exactly the opposite of that in
Egypt where the government's agencies—its press, media and ministries—

Sadiq Jalal al-'Azm, "The Miracle of the Appearance of the Virgin Mary and Removing the Evidence of
[Israeli] Aggression," *Critique of Religious Thought* (Beirut: Dar al-Tal'ia for Publication, 1968), pp. 151–
179. Translated by Akram Khater. Reprinted by permission of the American Committee on Jerusalem.

adopted the story of the apparition of the Virgin and publicized it and concluded from it what it wished in terms of political and touristic implications. Thus it transformed it into a religious hysteria that has swept the great majority of citizens. . . . It would have been easy [to dismiss this event] if the media that publicized this religious fever was that of a reactionary Arab country seeking to cover its material and intellectual deficits . . . under the cloak of religiosity and by linking defeat and victory to supernatural powers beyond human control. But what is really tragic is that this task was carried out by a press overseen and directed by the Arab Socialist Union [of Egypt]. . . . All that we heard in the aftermath of the [Arab] defeat [of June 1967] about modern science and technology and the scientific method in thinking, planning and preparing ourselves, and about rationality in our words, declarations and behaviors, has gone up in smoke in a single moment as a result of the effect of this religious hysteria. . . . Let it be known that the preoccupation of the Arab masses with supernatural events and miracles and their stories in the second half of the twentieth century, and particularly in these difficult times, will never help us in successfully resolving our pressing worldly problems, and will not help us attain our vital national rights regardless of whether the Virgin was angry or not about the loss of Jerusalem [to the Israelis].

In this essay I would like to present some basic comments and reflections about what have been called the miracle of the appearance of the Virgin. I will base my research on the press releases and commentaries that [have] been published about it either officially or semi-officially for the purpose of uncovering several important facts included in those releases and for the purpose of supporting what I said at the beginning of this article. . . . In other words, I want to make evident the fabrications . . . that are part of what has been said and published about the apparition of the Virgin in Cairo in the hope of presenting a humble effort toward inviting the Arab mind to return once again to measured, rational and objective thought . . . and to move away from the waves of religious hysteria and . . . demagoguery that [have] wasted enough of Arab time and efforts. . . .

We can find the political implications of this large religious phenomenon in various sections written about the apparition of the Virgin and its relationship to the removal of the effects of the [Israeli] aggression and liberating occupied Arab lands. *Al-Ahram* printed the following headline on its second page: "The apparition of the Virgin indicates that God will help us be victorious and that Heaven has not abandoned us." In other words, after all that has happened it is still asked of Arabs to beseech Heaven for victory and to beg the Almighty for it instead of asking Arabs to depend on themselves. . . . It was declared during the packed press conference that followed the appearance of the Virgin at this time and specifically in Egypt that:

> "We have said that the saints and martyrs appear to the believers at the greatest time of need to support and encourage them. It [is] for that reason that the Virgin has come to strengthen the will of the blessed and believing Egyptian people . . . to call upon them to cling to its

beliefs in this particular time when atheist calls are ringing. . . ." (*Al-Ahram*, p. 3)

It is clear from this . . . that the Virgin did not appear to call upon the Arab people of Egypt to uphold its revolution and to deepen its commitment to its socialism . . . to respond to the Israeli challenge. Rather she came to ask this people to hold on to worn-out and inherited traditions and supernatural ideology that dominate the mind; that is to face the future by returning to the past instead of surging forward. . . .

Does the Virgin have to descend from Heaven for the Arabs to realize that the liberation of Palestine is a matter of the greatest importance? . . . Do the Arabs today need comfort and soothing talk or criticism, rejection and concern that would fuel them in facing occupation and the serious challenges surrounding them? . . .

In the face of such talk it should be clear to every Arab that the crisis generated by the defeat is not an immediate crisis at all. It is [a] vital and existentialist crisis that threatens the Arab being in its entirety, and that Arabs should prepare themselves to face this crisis not as a passing moment but as a continuous problem that will become worse. . . . Any other interpretation of this crisis which seeks to make light of its dangers and intensity is nothing more than trickery and gratuitous flattery. Contrary to what Father Gregorius said, neither miracles nor the appearance of the Virgin . . . will truly uplift the morale of the Arab people and will regain its confidence in its current leadership. . . .

(4) Frankly, it seems to me that the intellectual, cultural and scientific standards of the clerical system within the Egyptian Coptic church are very low. . . . This has become clear to me after looking into announcements by clerics . . . about the miracle of the apparition of the Virgin. Following are some examples about what I mean:

(a) During a meetings at the Ma'alaqa Church . . . Father Samuel gave a speech in which he emphasized "a historical and scientific truth" which is that during the time of the Fatimids [11–12th centuries] al-Muqattam mountain was in a location [other] than its current one. However, the Caliph [Fatimid ruler] asked one of the patriarchs of the Coptic church to move the mountain from its old location to where it is now. . . ."

We would propose to the respected Patriarchs, on this occasion, to carry al-Muqattam mountain as soon as possible and to place it directly over Israeli military central command during the meeting of their general staff, and this would be of great benefit for the Arab cause. . . .

(d) One of the Bishops participating in the press conference said the following about the scientific explanation for the appearance of the Virgin:

"Scientifically, it has been proven that every person has his own 'ethereasness' that cannot be erased and that can be embodied at any moment in the shape of ethereal atoms that takes the full appearance of the individual. . . . For example, science has been able to photograph tens of men or women that died hundreds of years ago. If all of this requires sophisticated electronic equipment . . . then I think that

saints and martyrs do not need any of this. . . . belief will suffice."
(*Al-Ahram*, p. 3)

One does not need to be an accomplished scientist or an expert in electronics and
"ethereals" to realize that this [is] nothing more than nonsense. It is more pathetic and dangerous than myths because it claims to speak in the name of science
and in a language that appears reasoned. . . . It is shameful for the Arab mind in
the second half of the twentieth century to repeat such nonsense. . . . Is this the
cultural guidance that the Arab masses need after the Defeat [of June 1967]?

3.   Ayatollah Ruhollah Khomeini Denounces the Rule of the Shah of Iran, 1975

*Ayatollah Ruhollah Khomeini (1900–1989) was one of the architects and leaders of
the revolution that overthrew Shah Muhammad Reza Pahlavi of Iran in 1979. After
settling in the city of Qom (the main center for Shi'ite Islamic learning in Iran) in
1923, Khomeini began to lecture and write on Islamic ethics and law. In the early
1960s he quickly gained prominence among seminary students and then attracted
a larger audience in Iran when he began to criticize the shah and his government. In
speeches and essays Khomeini contended that the shah's government was illegitimate because it did not follow the precepts of Islam, and because it allowed Western
influences to dilute what he regarded as Iran's authentically Islamic heritage. His
opposition to the shah and his growing popularity soon attracted the attention of
the shah's secret police—the Savak. His persistent and strident denunciations
of the shah's corruption, oppression of the masses, and compromising of Iran's sovereignty led to his arrest in 1963 by the Savak and his exile to Turkey in 1964. A year
later, he was allowed to reside in the city of Najaf in southern Iraq.*

*From exile, Khomeini continued to exhort his followers to oppose the shah and
to critique the Iranian state. In 1975, the shah planned a celebration of the twenty-
five hundredth anniversary of the Persian Empire. He intended the festival to legitimate his weak regime by linking it to a long heritage of kings who predated
Islam. Khomeini condemned the upcoming celebration. The staging of this event
and Khomeini's critique were critical steps toward revolution. In reading this document, try to understand Khomeini's points within the context of the shah's government, which many Iranians considered illegitimate, and to decipher the alternative
view of government that Khomeini was presenting. (For an insider's view of the
shah in 1976 and 1977 see document 1 in the chapter "Restricting Authority.")*

Now, according to numerous letters and reports I have received, one of the unfortunate aspects of the present situation in Iran is that a large number of

Ayatollah Ruhollah Khomeini, "The Incompatibility of Monarchy with Islam," in Hamid Algar, *Islam
and Revolution* (Berkeley, Calif.: Mizan Press, 1981), pp. 201–208. Reprinted by permission.

people have died of hunger. While these tragic circumstances and conditions prevail, millions of tumans are to be spent celebrating in honor of the monarchy. According to reports, 80 million tumans are to be spent on decorating and lighting up Tehran alone. Experts have been invited from Israel to take care of the arrangements—from Israel, that stubborn enemy of Islam and the Qur'an, which a few years ago attempted to corrupt the text of the Qur'an, and now imputes to the Qur'an unworthy statements, which our students abroad vigorously refute and deny (may God strengthen them). Israel, which is at war with the Muslims and plans to occupy all the lands of Islam up to Iraq and (God forbid) to destroy the noble shrines of Islam! Israel, which set fire to the Masjid al-Aqsa, a crime that the Iranian regime tried to cover up with all sorts of propagandistic proposals to rebuild the mosque! Israel, which has turned more than a million Muslims into refugees and occupied the lands of the Muslims! That state is now to arrange the celebrations for the Iranian monarchy, and that state is supplied with Iranian oil by tankers. Ought the people of Iran to celebrate the rule of a traitor to Islam and the interests of the Muslims who gives oil to Israel? Who was responsible for the events of Khurdad 15; who killed, according to one of the *'ulama,* four hundred people in Qum alone; who had fifteen thousand people massacred throughout Iran; who sent his agents to Fayziya Madrasa to insult the Qur'an and Imam Ja'far (upon whom be peace)? They set fire to the students' turbans, threw some of them off the roof of the building, and behaved scandalously, filling the prisons with our patriots. Many of these best sons of our people were tortured to death in prison by his agents. Are we now to honor the rule of such a monarch with a celebration?

What benefit have our people ever derived from such rulers that we should now celebrate and light up our cities? Are we to commemorate Agha Muhammad Qajar, that bloodthirsty savage? Or the monarch who massacred people in the mosque of Gauhar Shad in such numbers that the walls were stained with blood and the gates of the mosque had to be closed so that none might see the spectacle?

[. . .]

Only recently, because of a slogan uttered in the university that ran counter to his lowly inclinations, he sent his bandits to the university and had them beat the students atrociously. According to reports that reached here, some female students needed surgery as a result of the blows and wounds they received. Their only crime was opposing the twenty-five hundredth anniversary celebrations and saying, "We have no need of this festival. Put an end to the hunger of our people; do not celebrate over the corpses of our people."

[. . .]

Are we not to protest that the oil belonging to Iran and Islam is sold to a state at war with the Muslims? Why is Israel able to gain influence in the affairs of a Muslim country? Of course, the answer will be, "We are given orders, and we have no choice but to obey. These are our orders, and we have to carry them out." The Shah himself in one of his speeches, which was later reproduced in a book, stated, "The allies, after occupying Iran, thought it fitting that I should be in control of affairs, and they agreed to my accession to the throne." May God curse them for thinking it fitting and casting us into disaster! Naturally, someone who is a puppet has to serve his masters; he cannot do otherwise. And they follow their desires and appetites ("They eat as the beasts eat"); they care not where their nourishment comes from nor how it is obtained. As long as their needs and requirements are met, the world may drown in blood and fire, and entire peoples may be destroyed.

Are we not to speak out about these chronic ailments that afflict us? Not to say a single word about all these disasters? Is it incompatible with our position as religious scholars to speak out? Were not the Prophet and the Commander of the Faithful, 'Ali (peace be upon both of them) religious scholars, and did they not preach long sermons? In the Shaqshaqiya sermon about a certain person who made illicit use of the money belonging to the community, far harsher and more uncompromising expressions occur than those we have used. How is it that now, when it is the turn of the present generation of religious scholars to speak out, we invent excuses and say that it is "incompatible" with our status to speak out?

[. . .]

If the 'ulama of Qum, Mashhad, Tabriz, Isfahan, Shiraz, and the other cities in Iran were to protest collectively today against this scandalous festival, to condemn these extravagances that are destroying the people and the nation, be assured that results would be forthcoming. There are more than 150,000 students and scholars of the religious sciences in Iran. If all these scholars, authorities, proofs of Islam, and ayatullahs were to break the seal of silence and make a collective protest to remove the endorsements of their silence from the list of crimes committed by the regime, would they not achieve their aims? Would the authorities arrest them all, imprison and banish them, destroy them? If they were able to, they would destroy me before anyone else, but their interests do not permit them to do so.

Would that they did destroy me, so that I might no longer be tormented by the tragic state of our country. The tyrannical regime imagines that I am very happy and satisfied with my life, and so they think they can threaten me. But what life is this that I lead? Death as soon as possible would be better than this life; then I might join the presence of the Most Noble One in the hereafter and be delivered from this life of misfortune. What life is it that I lead, constantly hearing the cries and moans of our oppressed and tyrannized people? The crimes committed by this tyrannical regime and the acts of treachery against Islam and the Muslims have robbed me of all peace. News constantly arrives to the effect that the prisons are full of patriots, that innocent people are dying from the effects of pitiless torture, that bandits and ruffians are attacking the university to kill and wound the students, and that girls are being tortured by having boiling water poured on their heads. It is just like the time of Ibn Ziyad and Hajjaj, when if it was thought that someone might be a follower of the Shi'a, he was seized and destroyed. So, too, they attack and arrest and torture now on the strength of mere suspicion. Nobody's life is safe. If someone offers religious advice or utters a word from the pulpit, he is immediately carried off to prison. If someone distributes a few copies of a critical pamphlet, they arrest him and take him off to some unknown destination.

[...]

Come to your senses; awaken Najaf! Let the voice of the oppressed people of Iran be heard throughout the world. Protest to the government of Iran by letter and telegraph. It costs nothing to write a letter; for God's sake, write to the Iranian government. Tell them to abandon this abominable festival, these scandalous extravagances. If these latest excesses are not prevented, still worse misfortunes will descend upon us and we will be confronted with even more distasteful events. Every day new events are created, new disasters for the wretched people of Iran. They even have a special expert for dreaming up these events, these idiotic spectacles. If matters continue on their present course, we will be faced with events in the near future that none of us can even imagine.

[...]

It is the duty of the Muslim people of Iran to refrain from participation in this illegitimate festival, to engage in passive struggle against it, to remain indoors during the days of the festival, and to express by any means possible their disgust and aversion for anyone who contributes to the organization or celebration of the festival. Let the festival organizers know that they are despised by the Islamic community and by all alert peoples throughout the world, that they are hated by all lovers of freedom, and that Islam and the Muslims are repelled by the very notion of monarchy.

It is also your duty to make your opposition to this festival known by any means at your disposal and to pray for your fellow Muslims—those wretched, starved, and hungry people in Iran—for those who suffer imprisonment, torture, and banishment; for those innocent girls who have severe wounds inflicted on them. Pray for them and for all victims of the Iranian regime, and ask God Almighty to grant them His aid.

And peace be upon you.

4. Documents About One of the Major Political Arguments Underlying the Lebanese Civil War, 1975

In April 1975 civil war broke out in Lebanon. It lasted until 1989, although some observers contend it continues today albeit in a nonmilitary manner. On the surface, the war appeared to be an internal conflict, but it was far more than that.

The war was a manifestation of regional conflicts. These antagonisms—some of them between Arabs, others between Arabs and Israelis—played out in Lebanon because the absence of a strong central government there facilitated external interference and the flow of weapons, both of which fed a bloodbath lasting nearly two decades.

The war in Lebanon threatened the whole region because it was caused by a deeply flawed political system. One group in Lebanon—Maronite Christians—dominated the political, economic, and social sectors of the whole country. This type of imbalance was not unique to Lebanon; it was the norm throughout a region where democracy was a fleeting dream for most. Thus, the outbreak of civil war in Lebanon caused serious alarm in other countries in the region that suffered from similar imbalances. Many countries began to warn of possible "Lebanonization" of their own internal politics.

On a fundamental level, the war in Lebanon represented a crisis in the national identity of a country born—like most other Middle Eastern and North African countries—in the wake of independence from European colonial rule. In Lebanon, the implications of the national mythologies constructed in the first half of the twentieth century were coming home to roost. Lebanon's identity as a "nation" was precariously maintained for some twenty years by means of the "National Charter," which established the power-sharing formula that permitted Christians to maintain a slim margin of control over the government. However, in the early 1970s, the changing demographics of the country (Muslims began to outnumber Christians), the intensification of the Palestinian-Israeli conflict (over 300,000 Palestinians living in refugee camps in Lebanon were demanding the right to fight Israel across Lebanese borders), and economic crises, which polarized the country's population more than ever between haves and have-nots, coalesced to severely test the formula. Ultimately, the pressure became so great that civil war broke out.

The following documents present Muslim and Christian visions of Lebanon. Muslim views are presented by the prime minister, Rashid al-Sulh, and by Muhsin Salim. Pierre Gemayel, the head of the main right-wing Christian party, and one of his advisers, N.T., respond. Besides shedding light on a critical issue in Lebanon, this exchange of opinions conveys tensions unsettling all nations of the region—tensions resulting from differing visions of the "nation" and from unequal access to state power and benefits.

Statement of the Prime Minister of Lebanon, Mr. Rashid al-Sulh, in the Resignation Session in the Parliament, May 15, 1975

[. . .]
Dear Members of the Parliament,
[. . .]

I wish today to present you with a statement to clarify my position with regard to the current events, because of its critical importance. . . .

At noon on the 13th of April a horrendous crime was committed in Ayn al-Rumaneh [a suburb of Beirut] against a bus carrying Lebanese and Palestinian citizens. . . .

It is clear that the Phalangist party [right-wing Christian party led by Pierre Gemayel] is fully responsible for the massacre, and for the subsequent complications, and for the material and moral damages that befell the country as a result. And this was clear from the first moment of the ugly crime, and

Harb al-sanatayn, 1975–1976/al-Nahār (Bayrūt: Dār al-Nahār, 1976). Translated by Akram Khater.

because the party refused to condemn the crime, and refused to turn over those responsible for it for three days, then its subsequent and clear declaration of responsibility through handing over two of those who committed the massacre and its promise to hand over others.

The real dimension of the Phalangist responsibility for the event becomes clear when we tie it to its precedents, and to the attempts that followed it to expand the resulting conflict and to turn it into a widespread confrontation between the Lebanese and the Palestinians, and even among the Lebanese themselves.

For a long time the Phalangist party has been politically and materially and practically preparing in all of its measures for such actions.

The memoranda that were issued with or without occasion, have dealt with the issue of the Palestinian presence on Lebanese soil, and openly call for opposing it and agitate against this presence with a consistent and constant call to go outside the official government policy regulating the Lebanese-Palestinian and Lebanese-Arab relations. . . .

All this intense political preparation which sought to inflame sectarian hatred, was accompanied by feverish military preparations with the establishment of an armed militia which obtained its weapons from known quarters, as affirmed by the Chief Muslim Mufti of the Lebanese Republic. . . . This was premised on the notion that the Palestinian fighters had weapons, when everyone knows that it is directed against the Israeli enemy, while the other weaponry has no other purpose but to prepare to strike against the Palestinian resistance movement, and to create internal conflicts that will drive the country toward chaos in order to protect sectarian and isolationist privileges that most of the Lebanese have come to reject.

[. . .]

Dear Members of the Parliament,

I must in conclusion frankly and clearly present to your esteemed parliament what I deem to be important conclusions that my tenure as prime minister has only confirmed. These are conclusions that derive from the convictions of the great majority of the Lebanese. The sectarian privileges which form the basis of the Lebanese political system have become, in light of the developments in Lebanon and its relationship to its Arab milieu, a stumbling block which prohibits any progress and threatens to . . . undermine that which the builders of independence had constructed [a united nation].

It is this reality which prohibits the real sharing of power and the proper distribution of authority within the various parts of government . . . and it prohibits the establishment of a proper democratic parliamentary representation, and keeps us from strengthening the army and enabling it to perform its natural role as the defender of the nation. . . . this is what prohibits the establishment of real equality between the citizens in a manner that will eradicate abject poverty and will improve those neglected areas [mostly in the predominantly Muslim areas].

. . . We are confronted with only two options for escaping this deteriorating situation: establish a new formula within the context of the current political system and in light of the present demographic and social status of the Lebanese religious sects. Or, establish a new democratic formula within the context of the requirement for a national renaissance at the social, political and economic levels; a formula that will lead eventually toward the secularism of the state institutions and to social justice and total development at the same time. . . .

I and the nationalist groups choose without any hesitation the second option which derives from the logic of history, and the reality of our nation and the spirit of the times and the outlook of the new generation.

Thus, it is imperative to deal with the country's situation in a radical manner that will come into effect in stages according to the following principles:

First, implement real democratic reform that guarantees correct distribution of power among the various elements of government, and that affords the possibility of establishing political representation that reflects the true popular will through democratic reforms of the election legislation.

Second, commit to the common Arab requirements for facing the Zionist enemy . . . by supporting the Palestinian people and its struggle with all possible means, regardless of the sacrifices. . . .

Third, reform the law organizing the army and subject it to political authority and maintain sectarian balance in its ranks and provide it with all the necessary human and material requirements so that it will be able to perform its basic national duty, and avoid dragging it into internal matters. . . .

Message of Pierre Gemayel, Leader of the Christian Right-Wing Phalangist Party, to the Muslims of Lebanon, June 24, 1976

My Muslim Brothers,

This voice, the voice of a human being who persists in proclaiming—amidst the wave of despair, and despite the state of disintegration that has overwhelmed the people and all institutions—the civilized character that has defined the facade and core of Lebanon.

It is a voice from the heart and soul, indeed it is an act of faith that I had decided to undertake without being appointed by anyone to do so, and without any formalities. It appears to me that the proclamation of this faith, in all sincerity, is better than all the arbitrations and resolutions meant to resolve the conflict that outnumber the days of this crisis, and that has until now succeeded only in widening and deepening the feeling of despair.

In any case, Lebanon is now in need of something like a miracle in order to survive the evils of division and to be re-born again . . . and is there anything other than faith that can bring about miracles?!

. . . [The faith I speak of is] faith in Lebanon of course, and faith on the part of his children in the first place. If they lack this burning faith then it is certainly dead. If it burns in their bosoms then it is alive and will not die. The miracle of which I speak is not of divine provenance, but it derives from the labor of man. In any case, the borders of countries have not been recorded in the Bible or the Qur'an, and neither the Qur'an nor the Bible has stated that Lebanon is for the Christians or Muslims, or for both parties. And God, all glory to him, has not taken sides with these people or those.

According to these basic facts, the Muslims and Christians of Lebanon do not have the right to disagree because of God. Rather it is their duty to unite in him, because He is the God of all of humanity, and because He is—before people began to interject Him in their earthly conflicts—the absolute good, beauty and love. In addition, Christians and Muslims do not have the right to bring religion into their conflicts about Lebanon. Neither Islam nor Christianity can dictate consecrating this land for themselves. It goes without saying that monopolizing Lebanon by this or that group is not one God's commands. . . . Rather the spirit of monopoly is one of the earthly sins. . . .

The role of the Lebanese, Christians and Muslims, in this circumstance is one of the most important roles. The message has not been given to anyone else. . . . And if each people are assigned a role or task in this world through which to perform a service to all of humanity, then the Lebanese have no better role than this one through which they can serve themselves, their religions, man, liberty and all the other human values. Islam does not need another Islamic country, nor does Christianity need another Christian addition. . . .

[He goes on to discuss the Palestinian armed presence in Lebanon and argues that it is the cause of the civil war raging in the country.]
[. . .]

While the Christians have demanded that the Palestinians' ability to interfere in Lebanon's internal politics should be stopped, you [the Muslims] have insisted upon allowing to proceed along the same path. . . . There is no alternative at this [juncture] from the return to real sovereignty [for Lebanon] and there is no alternative to demarcating these boundaries [between Palestinian refugee camps and the rest of Lebanon]. So, is this possible if your cooperation is not more forceful than your acquiescence with chaos [PLO fighters carrying out military operations against Israel from Lebanese soil]? And is this possible if you do not declare in some form this solidarity [with the demands of the Christians] and if you do not affirm it?

It is for this purpose that I address you today, appealing to your conscience, pleading with you to save this nation that is threatened with division and dissolution. I hope that you will be today as you were in the forties when you decided to build with your Christian brothers a nation that is not like all the other countries, and nation that is not like all the other nations. I cannot imagine your ambition today to be for anything less than an ideal nation that Islam, Christianity, Arabism and all of humanity so desperately need. The matter rests with your decision. Indeed the salvation of this nation has never depended upon this decision as it does today. So declare [your allegiance to an independent Lebanon] as you declare your faith in God daily, and you will receive from the Christians all the gratitude, love, and loyalty.

Response of Muhsin Salim to the Call of Pierre Gemayel

To the Honorable Lebanese Shaykh [honorific title]:

Your latest appeal, which was broadcast through "The Voice of Lebanon" [radio station] on the 24 of June, 1976, calls for rejuvenating the unique Lebanese formula [sectarian division of political power with Christians maintaining a slight margin over Muslims] upon [a] new basis and for the return of the brotherly cooperation between the Muslims and Christians in the nation, and to work to remove from Christians their fear about the subject of Arabism which they have been advocating lately. It appears that this appeal, which emanates from the bottom of your heart and from the purity of your Lebanese feeling, has received positive reactions among the Muslims who care ever so much about the unity of the land and people of Lebanon, and about proclaiming its true Arab cultural identity, and that Lebanon should remain the land of liberty and humanity as you demanded in your appeal.

What I would like to say to you on this occasion, in response and as a comment on your aforementioned appeal, is the natural response for every Lebanese Muslim who lives in the land of Lebanon and who loves his country and wishes to safeguard its free and independent existence. Your appeal, O honorable Shaykh, penetrated to the depth of our essence [the Lebanese Muslims], it has occupied our thoughts and reflections, and has received a good response. This is so not only because it was issued by you but also because it expresses the essence of our thoughts, worries and fears about the unknown future and destiny of this nation if we—as Muslims and Christians—do not agree upon a common factor to save our nation from destruction and extinction.

But how we do we put the appeal into effect? This is the question that we posed to ourselves when we heard the appeal, since you did not tell us—the Muslims in Lebanon—what we should do and from whence we must begin to revive the Lebanese formula around which the Lebanese were united in the past.

You did not tell us what practical steps the Muslims in Lebanon must take so that Lebanon will return to its sovereignty and authenticity, in a manner that would be acceptable to their Christian brothers.

The Lebanese Muslims, whom you addressed in your last appeal and in the wake of the disaster that befell them and all their Lebanese brothers recently, wish you had specified in a later statement how you see the process for reviving the Lebanese formula. What are the foundations upon which it should be based, and what methods must be adopted to practically and clearly designate the Arab identity of Lebanon in a manner that would be acceptable to all the Lebanese equally, Muslims and Christians? I believe that the subject of Lebanon's identity and specifying its Arabness in a responsible and practical manner is one of the most important subjects that occupy the Lebanese at the present time. It may be that this subject lies at the center of all the other numerous problems and issues that concern the Lebanese.

If the Arab identity of Lebanon can be specified in a clear and frank manner . . . which is acceptable to all the Lebanese groups and particularly the

Muslim ones, then we can find a solution to all the other issues since it will become secondary in relation to this fundamental problem.

The Lebanese have been satisfied to use the expression coined by the past Riyad al-Sulh, the prime minister of the first independent government in Lebanon, in his first governmental statement, which states that "Lebanon has an Arab facet." This extremely brief expression has been considered to be the basis and formula through which the Lebanese deal with Arabism.

Since the establishment of the Arab League in 1945, and the entrance of this country as a permanent member, and throughout the 30 years that Lebanon have participated in the work and decisions of the Arab League, we have not heard once that Lebanon stood in opposition to any of the League's decisions. This confirms Lebanon's attachment to its Arabness, and to [its] commitment to really and effectively share with all Arabs in their national stances. As for Palestine, which is the biggest Arab cause, Lebanon was and remains the one carrying its banner in all venues to the point that Lebanon was the voice of all the Arabs in defending it at the podium of the United Nations. . . . How can Lebanon turn away from its Arabness when its language and heritage are Arabic, when it is completely [linked] to the Arab world, when it exists in an Arab milieu and its destiny is an Arab destiny, and its economy an Arab economy, and its outlooks are Arab, and everything about it definitely states that it is an inseparable part of the Arab world.

However, and in addition to all of this, Lebanon has a particular characteristic that sets it apart from any other Arab country . . . and unique features that Lebanon cannot and must not ignore because they are intimately linked to its unique personality and glorious and great history. . . .

Isn't it strange that no one objects when Arab Egypt takes pride in its ancient and Pharaonic history, and objects when Lebanon takes pride in its ancient history and heritage, and accuses it of denying its Arabness. . . .

So, O Venerable Lebanese Shaykh,

We are with you in your appeal, and are ready to revive the unique Lebanese formula which unites the Lebanese in a unified Lebanon upon new foundations that are just and equal and that are nurtured by love and mutual trust.

But before we discuss any other subject we must begin from the beginning, and the beginning here is the agreement to specify the identity of Lebanon and its Arabness in a scientific and national fashion, without any confusion. . . . This can only be achieved by establishing a committee of Lebanese scholars, intellectuals and politicians from all sects to agree upon drawing a document that provides a scientific and political definition for the identity of Lebanon.

Response by N.T. to Muhsin Salim's Letter to Pierre Gemayel

1. We applaud your desire—presented in your letter to Shaykh Pierre Gemayel—to find the "practical steps that the Lebanese Muslims must take in order for Lebanon to return to its unity in a manner acceptable to their Christian brothers." However, we wish this was the desire of all Muslims, leaders

and followers, knowing all the while that if it were thus then they [the Muslims] would have exhausted every means to achieve it.

2. You say in your letter: "Before anything else we need to specify clearly and frankly the identity of Lebanon and its Arabness . . . for the Arabness of Lebanon is the thorniest of issues and the basis of disagreement among the Lebanese." We have two comments on your statement:

FIRST OBSERVATION. Presenting the problem in this manner assumes that Lebanon is an orphan with no identity, and that it needs an identity other than [t]his. My dear sir, this assumption needs correction. At least half of the Lebanese—and perhaps you are among them—believe that Lebanon is an independent political entity that exists on its own and that does not require description or definition because it is in their eyes a complete nation and their aspirations and dreams stop at its borders. They are only loyal to it, they do not contemplate any cause or problem in the far or near world but from the perspective of its interests, and every time the interests of Lebanon conflict with any others they will unhesitantly champion the cause of Lebanon. . . . They believe in Lebanon the way they believe in God who is only known as "He is He."

Those see that the identity of Lebanon cannot be the subject of debate, argument or disagreement. The question about the identity of Lebanon cannot be posed any more than a question can be posed about the identity of France or Germany or the Soviet Union or others. . . .

The fact is that there is in Lebanon a second group of citizens who consider Lebanon to be a part of a larger whole, and that it is a temporary stage that must be transcended at the earliest opportunity. This group also believes that any conflict between the interests of Lebanon and those of the "larger whole" or even those of another part of this whole, must be resolved by sacrificing the interests of Lebanon.

Here is the real problem: the issue of loyalty to Lebanon; is it an absolute loyalty that Lebanon deserves or a conditional and temporary one which ranks lower than loyalty to Syrian or Arab nationalism?

SECOND OBSERVATION.   You demand, on one hand, commissioning a committee of scholars, intellectuals and politicians "to agree upon drawing a document that provides a scientific and political definition for the identity of Lebanon." Then, on the other hand, you link this identity with Arabism when you ask about "the method that should be adopted to define the Arab identity of Lebanon in a clear and scientific manner. . . ."

It seems to me that you have already pre-determined the decision which you ask the committee to make. Thus, you cannot imagine but an Arab identity for Lebanon. Will you then permit us to ask you: why do you ignore all the multitudes of those Lebanese who reject any other name for their Lebanon, not out of arrogance or animosity to anyone but for fear that the appellation will lead into the unknown. They are afraid that [such adjectives] will empty Lebanon of its contents and fill it with another unknown entity, a content that can be described as explosive in the tragic manner we have witnessed for the past sixteen months. . . .

"The unique character" and "unique characteristics which are linked to Lebanon's unique personality, history and civilization," are due—as you know, my dear sir—to the multi-ethnic nature of this country. Its varied cultural groups did not meet accidentally, but were gathered across a long history by one unifying factor which is their desire for liberty and their revolt against the oppressive rule of the majority and their intent to hold on to their unique identities. . . .

This pluralism, that is concomitant with the creation of Lebanon, has a progressive and civilizational value that supersedes Arabism, and all other one-faceted values. Thus, it would be unjust and wrong not to benefit from its wealth by finding political and cultural frameworks to guard and protect it and to highlight its great civilizational wealth.

To take as a point of departure the imposition of an Arab identity, and it is the cultural identity of but one group, on all of Lebanon is a rejection of this pluralism and an attempt by the few to control the whole and to absorb it. It is an act of oppression and hegemony that is rejected and fought by all sects who see in it a threat to its liberty, and therefore to its existence.

In addition, we do not understand this insistence on forcing Arabism on Lebanon. What is the use of it, when you know that the concept of Arabism is unclear, and it is difficult to make the concept of all? . . .

If Arabism is a common language, then there is no disagreement that Lebanon was given the language of the Arabs. . . .

If Arabism is a matter of geographical belonging from which are derived common regional interests, such as the European nature of France, Italy, Germany . . . then geography and the natural relations between countries and people are realistic matters that are not objects of disagreements. . . .

If Arabism is free commitment to common causes, then your letter clearly indicates that Lebanon has rendered special service to the causes of the Arabs, at times beyond its capacity . . . and despite all of this commitment the Arabists of Lebanon are still not satisfied. . . .

Will Arabism be something other than all of this, other than language, geography and free commitment to common causes? Are there any concepts left other than race and religion that can be attached to it? The first is not reasonable, and the second is not acceptable to non-Muslims. So, are you going to force the unity of race and religion?

You say: "I believe that the subject of Lebanon's identity, and specifying its Arabness . . . is one of the most important subjects that occupy the Lebanese at the present time. . . ."

No my dear sir! It is not the identity of Lebanon—or the gender of angels—that today tops the concerns of the Lebanese! Lebanon is burning; it is being torn apart, and raped. The most important matter is that Lebanon should continue to exist as a nation for a free people.

The role of the Muslims, quite simply, is to prove at least once that their loyalty to Lebanon is above and beyond their loyalty to any other cause, nationalism or ideology. . . .

5.   American Consular Documents Reveal U.S. Diplomats' Assessment of the Revolution in Iran, 1978

Who knew what was happening in the months leading up to and following the 1979 revolution in Iran? Secret American documents published after the takeover of the United States embassy in Tehran in November 1979 contain a wealth of first-hand day-to-day accounts and analyses. These documents, which normally would have been declassified decades from now, were obtained by the New York Public Library and are available for all to see. The document reprinted here gives an indication of what was going through the minds of American diplomats and analysts. It is an analysis of Iranians' feelings toward the shah of Iran written by a political officer at the U.S. consulate in Shiraz on September 23, 1978. It is striking to read the political officer's astute remarks about the political situation, yet his conclusions appear in retrospect to be far off the mark. This document and the excerpts from the diary of the shah's court minister (document 1 in the chapter "Restricting Authority") let us glimpse the complexity of the U.S.-Iranian relationship and its consequences for the people and government of Iran.

Department of State
AIRGRAM
Classification: Confidential
Message reference No.: A-23
To: Department of State
Info: AMCONSULS Isfahan and Tabriz (via internal pouch)
From: AMCONSUL Shiraz   Date: 9/23/78
Drafted by: Political officer Victor L. Tomseth
Subject: Political attitudes in southern Iran

SUMMARY AND INTRODUCTION.   Recent conversations with a variety of people in southern Iran have revealed considerable unanimity as regards [to] dislike for the regime headed by the Shah but little unity on other issues including the place of Islam.

The discontent is undoubtedly profound, but aside from students of the radical left who advocate overthrow of the Shah and establishment of a republic, few people can agree on a constructive alternative to the government as it has been practiced for the last 15 years.

From http://www.iranian.com/Jan 96/History/USA1.html (10 January 2003).

Calls for early elections free from manipulation are heard fairly frequently. However, thoughtful Iranians, even those whose dislike for the present regime is intense, concede that in the absence of constraints on who can run and under what conditions, elections are likely to produce a Majles whose members will be incapable of uniting on any issue other than their grievances with the past government.

Under such circumstances, it seems inevitable that despite lack of enthusiasm for his leadership, the Shah will continue as Iran's ultimate political arbitrator. END SUMMARY AND INTRODUCTION.

It has been extremely difficult to find anyone in southern Iran with a good word for the Shah in recent days. Iran's population profile gives some indication why.

Almost half of all Iranians have been born since 1963, the last time the country faced an economic or political crisis of significance. Almost two thirds have been born since 1953, the last time an alternative to the Shah's rule was a serious possibility.

Few people among this group are impressed with comparisons of then and now, comparisons that have profound meaning for someone who has seen Iran transformed from a poverty-stricken country whose sovereignty was ignored by the great powers to one of the world's wealthier and more influential nations and who played a key role in that transformation. The post-1953 generation has been promised the millennium and its comparisons are made by that standard.

Even those old enough to remember the old days of 1953 and earlier have their grievances with the regime. These range from the secularization of the state to the arrogance of high government officials to the collapse of the real estate market to corruption to continuing (and often growing) inequities in Iranian society.

The Shah and his advisors have not been unaware of sources of discontent such as those enumerated above, and have usually reacted to them.

However, sometimes actions taken to alleviate pressures building in one area (e.g., controls on real estate speculation designed to curtail the number of overnight millionaires and close the gap between rich and poor) have created new pockets of unhappiness (i.e., among land owners, not all of whom by any means count their holdings in numbers of villages, who hoped to sell their properties for enough money to send their children off to college or for a retirement nest egg).

Other times, the determination to modernize Iran has led to decisions (e.g., giving women the vote) which were known would be opposed (i.e., by religious conservatives).

Change always poses a threat to vested interests, but it does not follow that the changes the Shah has wrought in Iran were foreordained to produce a degree of opposition to his rule which is now so manifest among the Iranian populace.

Rather it would appear that the manner in which these changes were effected has often been a more fundamental factor in the reaction to them than the changes themselves. Iranians seem overwhelmingly to resent having been excluded from virtually all political decisions of the last 15 years.

As one middle-aged Iranian, who says he remembers what it was like during Mossadeq's time, put it, "It bothered me less that the government decided to impose [an] exit tax on Iranians leaving the country than it did to have (former Minister of Information Darioush) Homayoun announce the decision without going to the trouble of consulting the Majles whose members in accordance with the constitutions are supposed to represent the interests in government."

Another, a businessman, referring to government interference in the hours shops can be open, said: "We Persians for the most part retain a 'hand-to-mouth mentality,' the heritage of the time when Iran was still a poor country. Small shopkeepers are thus inclined to maintain hours convenient to housewives whose habits are conditioned by the memory of a former day when they might not have known at noon when buying bread for lunch where the money would come from to buy the ingredients for dinner.

"In practice, we may not work more than the forty-hour week common in the West, but we do not like to be told by Harvard-educated bureaucrats who think they know better than we what is best for us [and] how and when to work it."

Aside from their commonly shared unhappiness with their government, however, Iranians in southern Iran are deeply divided on most other issues. Rural people, for example, while they may be deeply religious, are generally uninterested in the agitation for the return of Ayatollah Khomeini which has taken place in many urban areas.

They are inclined to view the issue as irrelevant to their major concerns—the weather, the availability of water, the price of wheat, etc. Recent arrivals from the countryside in cities where religious agitation has taken place, on the other hand and notwithstanding the attitudes of their rural relatives, have often figured prominently in such activities.

The explanation for this seeming contradiction appears to lie in the trauma they experience in trying to adjust to urban life. Frequently, their religion is the only institution familiar to them in their new surroundings, and they are thus highly susceptible to the religious emotionalism that surrounds a cause such as Khomeini's.

The business community, too, is divided on the religious issue. The more fervent among its members have willingly closed their shops in protest against the government and in mourning for fallen martyrs, often at great financial loss.

Others have usually closed as well, but often more in fear of retaliation for not closing than in sympathy for the causes espoused by the ulema. They may take their religion seriously and dislike the regime every bit as much as the fanatics, but they are also concerned about their businesses and they resent the disruptions frequent closures bring.

Contempt for the Islamic fundamentalists is perhaps even more profound than opposition to the regime among many members of the modernist element of society in southern Iran.

An Ahvaz banker characterized those who had participated in religious demonstrations (and numerous bank trashings) in that city as "illiterate Arabs who had taken leave of their senses under the influence of religious leaders hardly less ignorant than themselves."

A senior military officer in Shiraz described the clergy in general as the worst of Iranian society, lazy louts who entered religious schools for no more noble reason than to avoid conscription.

An American-trained engineer at Shiraz's Iran Electronics Industries in comparing Reza Shah (whom he admires) to Ataturk concluded that the latter was a greater leader because he had gotten rid of all of Turkey's ulema whereas Reza Shah had made the mistake of leaving some alive. His mastery of historical fact might have been shaky, but he left no doubt where he stood on the religious issue.

Lack of unanimity on the place of Islam is paralleled on secular political issues as well. Aside from those who have demanded the Shah's ouster and the establishment of a republic (a view which still seems to be confined to relatively small minorities on the extreme left and right in southern Iran), few Iranians seem to have considered alternatives to the kind of leadership he has provided.

Critiques are usually limited to where he has failed with little consideration given to how past deficiencies might be rectified. There does seem to be a consensus that the present Majles and all those who have served in governments during the past 15 years are discredited. Accordingly, early elections free from government manipulation are frequently advocated.

Thoughtful Iranians, however, recognize that there is as yet little of the discipline required for orderly elections present in their country. Most of the parties and political groupings which have emerged in recent weeks are held together by no more reliable glue than the personalities of their leaders.

Under the circumstances, these Iranians concede that elections without limitations on who can run and the size of parties which can field candidates are likely to produce a Majles whose membership would be an assemblage of mini-parites incapable of uniting on any issue other than the inadequacy of past governments, hardly a viable alternative to the Shah.

In sum, Iran is confronted with a difficult dilemma. Many Iranians, if southern Iran can be taken as representative of the rest of the country, are dissatisfied with the character of the leadership they want in its place.

Further, short of violent revolution and the imposition of a regime which in all likelihood would be every bit as autocratic as the Shah's, the Iranian people do not appear at this time to possess the self-discipline to find a way out of their predicament.

Thus, it seems that by default, the Shah will continue as the ultimate arbitrator of Iran's political future.

6.   The Massacre of the Muslim Brothers of Syria in Hama, 1982

In February 1982, for twenty-seven consecutive days, elements of the Syrian army surrounded the city of Hama and unleashed their full power on the inhabitants. Tens of thousands were killed; many more were injured. This harsh attack on civilians and militias alike came as an immediate response to an attack by the Muslim Brotherhood on a military college in which approximately fifty-four cadets had been killed. From a wider perspective, the massacre was one of numerous attempts by the regime of Hafez al-Assad to quell mounting opposition to its authoritarian rule.

The Muslim Brotherhood was a Sunni political group whose members were dedicated to establishing an "Islamic state" according to their definition of that concept. Their animosity to the regime in Syria derived from the fact that it was dominated by 'Alawi Muslims—a Shi'ite Islamic sect that most Sunnis considered heretical. (For information about the ideology of the Muslim Brotherhood by Hasan al-Banna, see document 12 in the chapter "Ideas of Nationalism.")

The following document is the introduction to one of the very few books written about the Hama massacre. The writer clearly opposes the Assad regime and sympathizes with the Muslim Brotherhood, so his representation of the regime must be seen as not necessarily objective. The book describes in as much detail as possible the attack on Hama, but its purpose is to present propaganda against the Assad regime. This does not mean that the details are necessarily inaccurate but that the presentation cannot be taken as absolutely true. The writer presents his position in stark terms, allowing readers to understand the Muslim Brotherhood's point of view.

[. . .] People have read and heard many things about tragic events in modern times, but they have not encountered a tragedy of such significance or depth. . . . They have not heard or known of a tragedy like the tragedy at Hama.

We must not forget that Hama faced the Crusaders and other invaders; that is why the Ayyubid kings adopted Hama as their first capital. Although the hordes of Crusaders approached the other principal cities of Syria, these hordes could not approach Hama.

During the French mandate, Hama remained a thorn in the side of the French and continued—for a quarter of a century—to fight and struggle against them. France punished Hama by depriving it of the means of development and left it a backward rural city. It was prevented from establishing institutions and from entering the industrial age; yet despite all of this, the people of Hama increased in strength.

Thus, it is not surprising that the current regime [of Hafez al-Assad] found Hama to be a stumbling block on the path of the conspiracy that the Syrian regime planned to carry out in order to neutralize Syria's central role in the Middle East. As [Miles] Copeland stated [in *The Game of Nations: The Amorality of Power Politics* (1969)], and as others like him have said, Syria

---

Hama: The Tragedy of This Era That Has Surpassed the Massacres of Sabra and Santilla (Cairo: Dar al-'Itsam Publishing House). Translated by Akram Khater.

represents a source of trouble for the American Empire. . . . It is for this reason that Copeland and other intellectuals and ideologues in the Western intelligence services have tried to neutralize this role, trying all means in the process: military coups, depending upon agents who were sometimes leaders and at other times on secret agents; but they did not succeed. Then finally they established this regime [Assad] to put an end to Syria's traditional role.

Because Hama was an obstacle to this terrible plot, reports leaked from the institutions of the Syrian regime that said that Hafez al-Assad and his band were planning evil things for this city appear logical. They wanted to erase it from the face of the map, to reconstitute its demographic makeup and thus rid themselves of opposition from this city, and to make Hama an example for other Syrian regions—or so they thought!

In this book the reader will read about the executive decree issued by the High Security Council—two months before the tragedy—giving Rifa'at, the brother of Hafez al-Assad and his partner, a free hand in enforcing martial law and providing him with 12,000 members of the Defense Companies to attack the northern cities and "purify" them of opposition. Hama was to be the first area of operations. Members of the High Security Council said to Rifa'at: You may kill up to 5,000 without requesting anyone's approval. They identified 100 families that he could wipe out, and they permitted him to commit mayhem— which is nothing new for him, but this time it was to be done under the guise of governmental decree.

Two years before the tragedy of February, the reader will note, the authorities allowed their agents and men to commit crimes in this city . . . to the point of attacking and killing children.

The intelligent reader will certainly be aware of the meaning of the changes that Hafez al-Assad has made in the Syrian penal code, which used to require no more than one month in prison for someone carrying a rifle without a permit. Hafez al-Assad increased the penalty from one month to five years; then in a new decree he increased the penalty to twenty years or even execution—all this in attempt to deprive people of the means to resist.

The reader will also be aware of the media blackout that Hafez al-Assad imposed on the events in Hama in order to isolate the city from the rest of the provincial governments and public opinion. The full scope of this conspiracy will be apparent when the reader learns the size of the repressive security force that camped within the city at that time (Military Intelligence, National Security Intelligence, Politburo) in addition to the encampment of the 47th Armored Division in the suburbs of the city and the introduction of the 21st Mechanized Division on the third day of the events in order to continuously and rapidly support and augment the regime's forces and militias. [. . .]

Two months before the events, the people of Hama were saying: We die every day, or a part of the city dies[. . . .] How long will this continue?

Each house was searched more than ten times. Soldiers of Hulegu [a thirteenth-century Mongol invader] would barely have left a house before others reentered. But what most offended the city were attacks on the honor and dignity of the people. Women were not safe from the soldiers' shameful and dishonorable behavior. Children often were killed in front of their parents. If an informer told the soldiers, "I saw a man enter this building, and he did not leave," they would force their way into the apartments within the building, and if they searched and did not find any fighters, they would destroy the building on top of those living in it. Many innocent families were killed in this manner, and all the while Hafez al-Assad was claiming that all was quiet in Syria and that he had eradicated a gang of Muslim Brothers. [. . .]

The reader will realize that the people of Hama faced a plot to exterminate them and believed that they had reached the end of the road. So residents of the city of all sects and groups, young and old, children and women alike, rose against the regime to defend their land, their lives, and their honor. Christians stood shoulder to shoulder with Muslims. The Christians of Syria distinguished themselves in a way that will have a great impact on the future of Syria and the region. [. . .]

The Syrian army suffers from the same problems as the civilians. It has been diverted from its primary mission, safeguarding the nation and its borders, to become a tool of oppression. Moreover, assassinations within its ranks have not ceased, because internal opposition [to al-Assad's regime] has not stopped and will not stop.

Hafez al-Assad wanted to give supporters of his sectarian regime control over various parts of the army. [. . .] In January 1982—shortly before the events in Hama—he executed fifty officers, and the regime covered up the executions by inventing a story about an attempted coup. In reality, the operation was simply a mop-up of officers whose loyalty was in doubt.

The suffering of the Syrian army is compounded because members of the military suffer from the same sectarian discrimination that afflicts the civilian population: discrimination on the basis of religion, persecution of anyone with an independent voice, demeaning behavior with no reason or cause, and repression that reaches a criminal level. At the same time, the army is used to kill its own members or to kill the people of neighboring countries, such as the Lebanese and Palestinians.

The Syrian army will remain, from the point of view of the Syrian people, a positive nationalist element that will participate in turning the tide [against al-Assad] in the final determining hours. Despite all the executions and all the wounds, it will remain a national army that will erase its dishonor [. . .] and will join with the people in solidarity. [. . .]

As for the Syrian cities—specifically at the time of the massacre in Hama— they stood in solidarity with each other through the unity of the people, but they were in no position to rise in support of Hama because the people were not armed and because of the intense media blackout. Nevertheless, the city of Aleppo attempted to go on strike as an expression of protest [against the attacks on Hama], but the regime threatened it with bombardment and destruction. Nuhad al-Qadi, the mayor of Aleppo, announced to the merchants: "Whosoever goes on strike will be hung in front of his store." Damascus also attempted to go on strike, but Hafez al-Assad summoned all members of the chambers of commerce to his palace and threatened whoever dared to strike with the same fate. It is important to note that the [French] foreign occupiers did not dare to say such things.

Perhaps the explosion of a car in the Ministry of Information building and at the center for the distribution of the regime's newspaper *al-Ba'ath* on February 18, 1982, in the capital Damascus is the best evidence of the solidarity of other Syrian cities with Hama. Michael Frenchman, former editor of *The [London] Times* newspaper, recounted that he was in the office of Zuhayr Kana'an, the deputy minister of information, when the explosion took place. Frenchman said that he was talking with the deputy about "how calm Damascus was that day" when the loud explosion occurred!

But that was not all. Other things happened that were comic and disgusting at the same time. After Hama was destroyed, the regime—using its usual, well-known police-state methods—organized the population of the villages of Jabal al-Alawi in a supportive demonstration, and a representative of Hafez al-Assad asserted: "Those are the people of Hama celebrating its destruction! They are dancing on the bodies of their children!"

Did this creature, who stood before a city that was destroyed on top of its people, know anything about decency [. . .]?

People speak of Nero, who burned his capital, Rome, two thousand years ago in order to enjoy the sight of fire, and we do not know whether this is a true or fictional story. However, a thousand years from now, people will say that Syria—during a bizarre period—was ruled by a deviant sect that lacked ethical values, standards, and beliefs and had no loyalty for the people or the nation, and that its traitorous leader declared, without a hint of hesitation, that the people of Hama were demonstrating in support of him after he destroyed their city around them.

In fact, the tragedy of Hama is one indicator of the corruption of the whole regime. Today in Syria it is impossible for an honest citizen—someone who fears and knows God—to achieve any position of note within the power structure. Rather, a person can obtain a position of power in Syria only through immorality, corruption, or apostasy, or by placing oneself above the values and heritage of the nation. There are some high-ranking party members in Syria, who know this truth and who secretly cooperate and dialogue with the opposition. They are pathetic, for not one of them dares to pray, and some of them even refrain from fasting during Ramadan in order to stay in power and to show that they are worthy of their responsibilities within the regime of Hafez al-Assad.

O Arabs and Muslims, people and governments.

O rulers of this world and O people of this earth.

O Man in every place [. . .] remember your responsibility toward the Syrian people.

O rulers of the Arab world, do not forget to take into consideration the future of your relationship to the Syrian people.

It is a dangerous thing for you to adopt silence and this acquiescent position.

The people of Syria know with certainty that the regime in Syria is tempo-rary and does not represent the wishes of any individual in the nation. The regime itself acknowledges this point. Otherwise, what is the meaning of its at-tempt to safeguard its rule by destroying a whole city?

7. The Platform of the Islamic Salvation Front in Algiers Bases Its Ideology on Respect for Islamic Values, June 18, 1995

The Islamic Salvation Front (FIS) was founded in Algiers on February 18, 1989, and was legalized by the Interior Ministry on September 16, 1989. It centers its ideol-ogy on strict respect for Islamic values. This means legislators in parliament have to defer to the imperatives of the Shari'a in all fields. Before the first round of the De-cember 1991 parliamentary elections, some FIS leaders spoke of banning secular and socialist parties if the FIS won a majority of the seats. Far from being homoge-neous, however, the FIS is marked by philosophical dissension between the Djazaara clan (the "Djazarists," supporters of dialogue and gradual Islamization, close to the Egyptian Muslim Brothers) and the Salaafiya clan (the "Salafists, "sup-porters of the radical Islamization of Algerian society and more internationalist).

The FIS is Algeria's leading political party. It rapidly attracted young unem-ployed and marginalized Algerians, an important segment of the population. In the June 12, 1990, local elections, it won 54.3 percent of the vote, demonstrating its strength in a large number of regions. The FIS subsequently won 47.3 percent of the vote (there was an abstention rate of 41 percent) during the first round of the parlia-mentary elections of December 26, 1991. The FIS party benefited from a single-member voting system in two rounds, based on an arbitrary division of constituencies to favor large voting blocs (the government designed this system to weaken the po-sition of the democratic parties).

Two months after the army's show of strength interrupted the electoral process on January 11, 1992, the FIS was outlawed. The local governments it controlled were dissolved, the mosques it controlled were depoliticized, and FIS activists were jailed. Party members reorganized in exile (in Europe and the United States) and illegally in Algeria.

The Army of Islamic Salvation (AIS), the FIS's armed branch, became active in July 1992, attacking the army and public targets. The AIS is also responsible for murdering intellectuals. Links between the FIS and the most violent armed Islamic groups remain tenuous. Some Islamist leaders condemn in increasingly strong terms the bloody acts committed by the GIA (French acronym for Armed Islamic Group) against the civilian population. In this document, the FIS outlines its vision for ending the bloody crisis that was tearing apart Algeria. It presents a framework for allowing the FIS leadership to reenter the political mainstream and to distance itself from the GIA and its terrorist acts.

The Islamic Salvation Front Platform. http://www.medea.be/en/index058.html (February 2002). Trans-lated by Akram Khater. Reprinted by permission of Medea Institute.

In the Name of Allah, the Most Merciful and Compassionate, Algeria, June 18, 1995.

The Necessary Principles and Procedures to Exit the Crisis

The Algerian people is adherent to its noble religion, and its Arab and Amazaghit [Amazight] heritage, and continues to follow the civilizational and cultural path of its nation with all their Islamic, Arab, North African and national dimensions, and is loyal to his glorious history and his immortal revolutions for independence, and to the sacrifices of past generations, The unity of the nation has been built, and has lasted across generations, upon these unchanging givens and solid foundations.

Algerians have reclaimed their sovereignty and independence from French colonialism after great sacrifices through which they sought to "establish the sovereign social democratic republic of Algeria within the boundaries of Islamic principles," as was specified in the communiqué of November 1, 1954. Thus, they became worthy of reclaiming their legitimate right to be led by choice not through force, through agreement not oppression, and through the good not the evil.

Then, political pluralism and public rights became a public right after the events of October 5, 1988. When the current crisis led to neglect of the people's wishes, and to depriving Algerians of the sources of their liberty, and the increase in the bloody confrontation between Algerians, then there is no hope for exiting this crisis except through a return to legitimacy, in the shadow of unity, security liberty, and justice in all their political, economic, social and cultural dimensions.

Since the previous attempts have not succeeded in arriving at the pursued legitimate and just political solution, then it has become necessary to establish as follows the necessary principles and procedures for exiting the crisis:

1. Principles

a. Islam is the religion of the Algerian nation and state, and is the source of its ideology, [morality] and legislations. It must remain above all other considerations because of its position among the foundations of the nation.

b. It is necessary to maintain the Algerian identity in its Islamic, Arab and Amazight dimensions, and to reject any conflict between these three fundamental principles upon which the unity and legitimacy of the nation is built.

c. It is necessary to work according to the Constitution of 23 February, 1988, until it is changed or amended through popular will expressed by legitimate methods.

d. Respect political pluralism within the context of national values.

e. Respect human rights, and guarantee individual and communal freedoms in the political, social and religious spheres, as well as the freedom of expression; all within the context of the nation's values and its founding principles.

f. The right of the people to choose its leaders, representatives, and its goals through free elections.

g. Guarantee the respect of political succession through the method of free selection by the Algerian people, through plural elections.

h. Refrain from using violence as a means to stay in power or to gain access to it, and the right of the people to defend his selection through legal means.

i. Isolate the institutions of the National Popular Army from political issues and struggles, to hold them to their constitutional duties.

2. Procedures

a. Remove the Prohibition of the Islamic Salvation Front.

b. Remove the state of emergency and all extra-legal measures, and allow the police to resume its normal security operations, and to free the work in the arenas of politics, media, social and missionary from any fetters.

c. Stop the confrontations between the two sides, after expanding the process of consultation to include all whose participation will be necessary in reaching decisions, and to postpone dealing with all unresolved issues relating to the conflict until legitimate rule has been established.

d. Compensate all victims of the crisis.

e. Release all prisoners, and stop legal and extra-legal executions, and cease all pursuits of individuals and groups, with returning civil and political rights to all.

f. Appoint a neutral government that would be given the task to organize elections and [manage] civil matter[s], and to establish a committee to oversee the implementation of the agreement, and that would regulate all the procedures of return to legitimate rule [. . .]

g. Work to re-establish normal life, and lift all emergency rules, particularly in the field of the media, and to encourage all political and social forces to [safeguard civil liberties.]

h. Announce the agreement in total transparency according to the manner agreed upon by the two parties.

3. Initial Procedures (The Authorities will commit to implement these immediately after implementing the initial agreement.)

a. Release the older prisoners and the active leadership, and remove all restraints in order to allow them to seriously pursue a solution.

b. Close all prisons in the desert, and release all women prisoners.

c. Improve the situation of the prisoners.

d. Cease from escalating the official media campaign.

e. The way the media handles these procedures will be regulated by the two parties.

4. Basic Observation

This document is the result of discussions of the *shuyukh* of the Islamic Salvation Front, who are part of the permanent leadership of that organization. It is the end result of an arduous series of contacts and discussions with representatives of the interim government. It represents preliminary suggestions, and includes necessary principles and procedures for ending the crisis. After discussions with the government, the latter must allow the *shuyukh* to expand the consultation about the preliminary agreement—that is the result of these discussions—to anyone whose participation they [the *shuyukh*] deem necessary for making the decision or implementing it, so that the agreement will be finalized.

The *Shuyukh* [Imprisoned]: Madani Abbasi, Ali Ben Hadjm Abd al-Qadir Hashani; [Free]: Abd al-Qadir Khamkham, Ali Jaddi, Kamal Qammazi, Umar Abd al-Qadir.

8.   Report on Arab Israelis: Breaking the Stranglehold of Alienation, October 27, 2000

In June 1948 Israel was founded as a "Jewish state." However, this narrowly focused designation was immediately undermined by the presence of a steadily growing Arab minority. As the percentage of Arabs within the Israeli population has grown, Arabs' visibility in society and politics has increased. After remaining politically quiet and rather invisible through the 1970s, the Arab community has begun to assert its political weight by voting for Jewish Knesset (Israeli parliament) members sympathetic to the causes of Arabs in Israel or for Arab-Israeli candidates.

Culturally, the moment when many Israeli Jews came to acknowledge the presence of Arabs in their midst was the publication of Anton Shammas's novel Arabesques *in 1986. Shammas, an Arab Israeli, wrote in Hebrew.* Arabesques *is a fictionalized memoir and account of his childhood and life in the so-called Jewish state, whose definition erases his memories of his Palestinian roots and denies his right to exist as a full citizen. The maelstrom that erupted around the publication of the book and the accolades it received brought to Israeli national consciousness questions about the nature of the state and its definition. Since that time, the discussion has increased in intensity with the numerical growth of the Arab community and the increase in Arabs' social, economic, and cultural influence.*

At the beginning of the confrontation between Palestinians in the Occupied Territories and the Israeli army that started in September 2000, many Arab Israelis took to the streets to protest Israeli policies in the Territories and, at the same time, to protest their own status as second-class citizens. These demonstrations and the heavy-handedness of Israeli police efforts to put them down ignited once more the discussions about the definition of the "state" of Israel and its relationship to the Arab citizens. The following document, which appeared in Ha'aretz, *a center-leftist Israeli newspaper, is an example of these discussions about an ongoing crisis.*

From the heights of the Katzir settlement, standing on the ridge that overlooks Wadi Ara from the southwest, the picture is clear. From here, looking down onto the Arab villages in the valley, "it isn't difficult to understand why the Arabs feel strangled, and why they are bursting with rage," says Shuli (Shalom) Dichter, co-director of Sikkuy, an association involved in the struggle for equal rights for the Arab citizens of Israel. Dichter, a resident of Wadi Ara, explains that government strategy regarding the Arab communities in the region is one of enclosure, i.e., of restricting the potential for Arab growth by means of a belt of Jewish settlements on the south side of the valley, and a wide stretch of land, the disputed al-Roha lands that the Israel Defense Forces commandeered more than two years ago for public purposes, to the north. "That's the whole story," Dichter says, "both from a physical and from a consciousness-symbolic point of view."

For Dichter, the story dates back to his childhood. He grew up on Kibbutz Ma'anit, at the entrance to Wadi Ara, with the slogan that Ma'anit "plowed the first furrow of Jewish settlements" on the western slopes of the hills of Samaria. Founded in 1942 by the Hashomer Hatzair movement, the kibbutz, according to Dichter, was intended to drive a wedge between the settlements of Wadi Ara and those of the Triangle region and to upset the closely-knit, rural Arab web that existed there.

In 1948, the Arab settlements of Wadi Ara absorbed numerous refugees from the Jezreel Valley and expanded significantly. The population of these set-tlements continued to increase as a result of natural growth. Since the estab-lishment of the state, the Arab population has increased sixfold; the land it occupies, on the other hand, has shrunk by some 40 percent. There has not been a single new Arab settlement established in Israel since 1948.

Wadi Ara is still licking its wounds from the outburst of violence in the area at the beginning of the month [October 2000]. Vandalized by the demonstrators, the traffic lights at some of the crossroads along Road 65 are still not functioning. Electricity and telephone services in the villages are not yet fully operational be-cause the Israel Electric Corporation and Bezeq technicians are afraid to enter them. Jewish suppliers are not sending goods to the stores. Some of the towns are still flying black flags in memory of residents killed in the riots.

Dichter's car passes by the peace-and-coexistence sukka (a hut tradition-ally constructed for the Jewish festival of Tabernacles). The sukka was set up by the Menashe local council, most residents of which are Jewish, at the south-ern entrance to the valley. "Together, we will halt the destruction," boasts a large banner above the sukka. Dichter laughs: "We'll love you, but don't run riot any more," he spits out mockingly. The old format of coexistence has been destroyed, he says, and it's a good thing. Dichter proposes building on the ruins with an alternative relationship between Jews and Arabs in Israel.

In June of this year, the association headed by Dichter—together with his Arab co-director, Dr. Assad Ganem, a political science lecturer at The University of Haifa—published its annual report on equality and the integration of Arab citizens within the state. The report systematically reviews one government ministry after another, revealing the Jewish majority's discrimination against the Arab minority, which makes up 18.6 percent of the population of the country. The so-called coexistence between Jews and Arabs in Israel has been based on the very discrimination that cries out from the pages of the report.

This basis—the "fragile texture of the relationship" between Jews and Arabs and between Arab citizens and the establishment—is "an exhausted structure that cannot be relied on," writes Dichter in the preface to the report. Preserving this fragile texture, he writes, is tantamount to maintaining a status quo of inequality, which "certainly does not ensure stability in the relations between the citizens."

Dichter was not surprised by the outburst of rage among Arab citizens of the country. The "delicate tissue" of the relations between the two nationalities in Israel has been stretched, like a membrane, across a reality of inequality, injustice and oppression, he says. Now, "the coexistence has turned out to be a bluff that has blown up in our faces"; it has existed in the framework of a controlling relationship—an uneven relationship between a ruling majority and a ruled minority.

These same sentiments were expressed among Arab Israelis years ago, filtering through into the public consciousness. Jews who are involved in contacts and dialogue with Arabs are also beginning to internalize this awareness now. One of them is Ronen Dori, a resident of Katzir and principal of the Mevo'ot Iron comprehensive high school that serves the Jewish settlements in the area.

Some three years ago, Dori's school joined a project known as YAMI (the Hebrew acronym for "children teaching children"), which was designed to promote understanding between Arab and Jewish children. The Arab children were to teach Arabic to the Jewish children, while the Jewish children were to teach Hebrew to their Arab compatriots.

The equation soon proved to be flawed: The Arab children already knew Hebrew; the Jewish children found it difficult to communicate with their Arab counterparts, believing them to be conservative and too patriotic; the Arab children couldn't free themselves of nationalist and political rhetoric.

The Jewish children, Dori says, felt they were making a huge sacrifice just by agreeing to visit Umm al Fahm. After the customary cordialities, their Arab hosts told them exactly how they felt about the Jewish public. Among other things, one of the Arab students said that if they could, the Palestinian citizens of Israel would wipe out the Jews. The Jewish students, most of whom live on the kibbutzim of the Hashomer Hatzair movement, were shocked. "Concerned parents called after the meetings and said: 'What's going on here? You have turned our children into fascists,'" Dori recalls.

"Rather than bringing people closer together," Dori says, "the project erected walls of alienation." He and his colleagues decided, therefore, that before trying to bring the two populations closer together, it would be best to first focus on laying the groundwork for such a process by dedicating two school hours a week to discussions on civics, tolerance, differences and identity. The other teachers and school principals involved in the YAMI project adopted a similar approach.

"I realized that the perception of coexistence that formed the basis of the project was wrong; coexistence hadn't proved itself. It hadn't got us anywhere because we hadn't touched on the nerve center of the Arab society," Dori says. He adds that the next stage in the relationship between the two nations "must be full participation of the Arab Israelis, with affirmative action and complete equality. Our quality of life as Jews in this country will be influenced by the living conditions of our friends no less than by our own living conditions—not just from an economic point of view, but from all aspects. Participation will bring responsibility, and responsibility is the basis for good citizenship."

A village of some 36,000 residents, which was declared a city but looks like a refugee camp bursting at the seams, Umm al Fahm is sorely lacking in land and adequate infrastructure. The municipality has an overall deficit of some NIS 25 million, with a current deficit of around NIS 3.5 million. The municipal tax collection rate is a mere 11 percent.

Based on the figures accompanying a four-year development program for the Arab sector, approved this week by the government, this is the typical profile of an Arab local council, providing public services accordingly. The buildings in Umm at Fahm are so "tightly packed" that some of the alleyways between them aren't wide enough for four-wheel vehicular transport.

Umm at Fahm's distress is particularly stark in relation to the conditions at the nearby cooperative settlement, Mei Ami. The Jewish settlement is spacious and green. Each of the 50 families lives in a handsome, single-storey house. In the afternoons, the moshav is empty and quiet.

Mei Ami and Umm al Fahm are separated by the access road to the Jewish settlement, along which the residents of Mei Ami are making every effort to preserve a distance from the houses of the Arabs—something like a demilitarized zone. One of the houses of Umm al Fahm that is located near the road is that of Khaled Mahamid. For the past three years, the owner's son, attorney Ra'id Mahamid, has been fighting against a petition that was submitted to the High Court of Justice by members of the Jewish settlement. The petitioners want the court to order the authorities to carry out a demolition order that was issued against a portion of Mahamid's house; the reason for the demolition order: renovation work that the Mahamid family did inside the house itself. Mahamid consulted with the local planning and building committee, which told him that renovations inside a house do not require a permit. The regional committee thought otherwise.

Mahamid's house was built in the late 1950s. The road to Mei Ami was paved in the early 1970s. After the road was paved, a number of residents of

Umm al Fahm, Mahamid's neighbors, renovated and enlarged their houses, while others built new ones; the residents of Mei Ami complained. The legal authorities approved demolition orders, but did not implement them.

In 1995, the management committee of Mei Ami petitioned the High Court of Justice, demanding that the houses be demolished. A separate petition was filed with regard to the Mahamid family home, which was renovated in 1997. The petition was upheld and the court granted the authorities a number of extensions for the implementation of the order; the last of which comes to an end in December. The Mahamid family is living in fear: Any day now, a demolition team could come and tear down their house.

The Mahamid family home is just one of the 20,000 houses in the Arab sector over which a demolition order hangs. The authorities issue such orders, but in most cases, they are not carried out. There's no need to; a "marked" house, with the demolition axe at its neck, conveys a message to others to refrain from any building in the vicinity.

The most popular medical clinic in Umm al Fahm is the al-Nur clinic of the Islamic Movement. It is located on the ground floor of a large mosque in the "city" and is equipped with one of the three mammography instruments that exist in Arab settlements (the other two are in Nazareth). There are 62 such machines in Jewish towns and cities in Israel, despite the fact that the incidence of breast cancer among Arab women is higher than that among Jewish women. The clinic is so proud of its mammography unit that it still boasts the celebratory banners that were posted to mark the opening of the unit more than 18 months ago.

The willingness of Arab women to undergo checkups has increased significantly over the past two years, but for most of them, access to mammography is problematic. Three machines are simply not sufficient for a population of almost two million people.

At the entrance to Umm al Fahm—across from the petrol station that was torched and is yet to be renovated, and opposite the junction at which youths confronted police for more than a week—lies the al-Babur restaurant. Prior to the recent violent incidents, most of its patrons were Jewish Israelis. Today, for the most part, the restaurant is empty. Brothers Nassat and Hussam Abbas, dejected in the face of the losses they have suffered since Rosh Hashanah, wonder whether relations between Jews and Arabs in Israel have reached a point of no return. Nassat is convinced that the past situation will soon be restored and that Jews will return to dine in their restaurant. Hussam is not so sure. "This time, it was different," he says. "This time, people were killed—many people."

Shuli Dichter believes there is a chance, but that it does not lie in returning to the status quo of the past. On the contrary, he says, "despite all the pain, now is the time for goodwill," now is the time in which coexistence can be based on a profound recognition of the fact that living together also includes an element of conflict between two communities with different national identities. In fact, he says, the state now has the power to channel the national conflict between the two communities toward a democratic, parliamentary, civic struggle, with full participation for all.

It's possible, Dichter says, "if only the state would recognize the collective rights of the Arabs, just as it recognizes those of the Jews." And this includes everything—from signposts and the names of junctions and streets, to the equal distribution of resources.

PART IV

The Middle East Today

The 1991 Gulf War ushered in a new phase in the history of the Middle East. The war was the culmination of a series of crises that thoroughly discredited and delegitimized most of the authoritarian states in the Middle East. After 1967 the military or military-supported states in the Middle East came under mounting criticism for their mismanagement of national economies, their brutal political oppression, their suppression of freedom, and their political and military ineptitude. Alternative ideas previously considered by only a few groups or intellectuals gained popularity during the last three decades of the twentieth century. These ideas can be loosely grouped into three categories: political Islam, secular minority-group ideas, and economic reform.

Political Islam first appeared in the living rooms of America in 1979, in news reports of blindfolded Americans being held hostage by a group of bearded and jubilant students in Tehran. Since that time, Islam has acquired the reputation of being a religion of fanaticism, irrationality, and hatred of the "West." In popular media the word *jihad*—mistranslated as "holy war"—has been used repeatedly to connote those tendencies and to position "Islam" as the new threat—after the collapse of the Soviet Union—to Western civilization. [In reality, *jihad* means "struggle" and can manifest itself in three different ways. The most important of these manifestations is the act of cleansing oneself from sin. The least important of these is "jihad of the sword" or war, which is to be conducted only in the defense of Muslims and strictly prohibits killing noncombatants.]

Widespread acceptance of these notions is unfortunate, because they are not correct. This is not to deny that some Muslims carry out acts of violence and justify them in the name of their religion. Such groups of extremists have always existed across the spectrum of secular and religious ideologies, but the existence of such groups among Muslims, for example, should not be interpreted to mean that all Muslims are prone to violence. A moment of reflection reveals that such a generalization is as absurd as the idea that all Christians, Jews, or Buddhists are of one nature and one nature only. The notion that Islamic groups are anti-Western, medieval, or traditional is equally unfortunate. Indeed, many members of Islamic political movements are fully immersed in the modern world. Rather than seeking to retreat from it to a premodern existence, their intent is to shape modernity according to their understanding of religion and its precepts.

Apart from these considerations is the complicated task of understanding why Islamic political movements have acquired prominence and attracted a greater following since the 1970s. Instead of dismissing such movements, we must try to understand—even if we happen to disagree with and disapprove of their goals and tactics—who they are, what they seek, and how they came about.

One of the first clues to the rise of vibrant Islamic political movements is to be found in the crisis of the state—the theme of the chapter "Crisis of the State." The emergence of military dictatorships, and of regimes dependent on military support, such as Iran or Turkey, in many countries of the Middle East and North Africa considerably limited the opportunity for political expression and opposition. For example, during the 1960s and 1970s, the shah's government established single-party rule in Iran, and the rubberstamp Iranian parliament made a mockery of constitutional government. Moreover, the shah's secret police—the notorious Savak—established an extensive spy network whose sole purpose was to monitor, arrest, torture, and sometimes kill opponents of the regime. This trend, common throughout the Middle East and North Africa, left only a few public spaces where people could voice their discontent. Among the most prominent were mosques or religious institutions, which could be controlled or co-opted to some extent but, unlike secular political parties and their offices, not closed or suppressed.

In addition, at various times, many countries in these regions underwent severe economic crises. Part of the blame can be placed at the feet of ruling elites who mismanaged state funds through incompetence and corruption. However, other structural problems also contributed to these downturns. Rapid population growth, especially among the young in the second half of the twentieth century, meant that a diminishing percentage of the population had to produce enough to feed and satisfy the needs of an increasingly larger segment of society. More to the point, as young men and women finished their education, they expected jobs that would allow them to live independent lives (their own apartments, marriage, children, and so on). Unfortunately, even the strongest economies could not have accommodated this surge in the labor force, and the economies of Egypt, Algeria, and Syria were hardly strong. For example, Algeria's main source of hard currency was (and still is) the export of petroleum. As oil prices took a downturn in the 1980s, state revenues also plummeted. This meant that services, which the state had been providing (such as subsidies of food, transport, and fuel), had to be cut severely, and it was the Algerian lower classes who bore the brunt of the cuts. Simultaneously, the one safety valve—emigration to France—that in the 1960s and 1970s had allowed hundreds of thousands of young Algerians to escape poverty was being shut. Economic hard times in France and an intolerant mood of racism against Arabs meant that few Algerians were allowed to immigrate into France during the latter part of the 1980s. Together the decrease in oil prices and the closing off of French borders to Algerians left hundreds of thousands of young Algerian men and women jobless and penniless. The unemployment rate in Algeria in 1989 was 36 percent, and it was double that among the eighteen-to-twenty-five age group. This situation left many frustrated and angry, and as they searched for reasons for their dilemma, they focused on their government as the culprit.

The globalization of Western—particularly American—culture also had some detrimental effects on many societies in the Middle East and North Africa (for documents pertaining to this issue, see the chapter "The Future of the Middle East and North Africa"). The spread of American pop music, fashion, food chains, and movies and television brought a set of values at times jarring to many local sensibilities. For example, the 1970s television show *Dallas* was one of the most popular shows in Egypt. On Thursday evenings the streets of Cairo were nearly empty as people followed the unfolding soap opera of immense wealth, unbridled greed, barely concealed sex, and betrayal. Although all these themes were, of course, familiar to the elites of Egypt, they remained private matters, not public displays as on *Dallas.* The show contradicted the premises of public morals in Egyptian society and created tension between local values inculcated through upbringing and foreign values projected from television sets. Some Egyptians found this tension threatening because it represented a loss of "authenticity" and morality. Without necessarily agreeing with such dire and one-sided assessments, we can still understand the reasons for and costs of such tension on society. What complicated this cultural clash— whether perceived or real—was the imbalance in power behind the cultural representations. *Dallas,* Coca-Cola, and McDonald's arrived in these societies with far more polished images (even if the content left much to be desired) than the images of any local products; foreign companies sometimes dwarfed their local counterparts. Only those few Egyptians who had disposable income could afford to drink Coke, eat at McDonald's, and wear Nike shoes. Thus, Western products became expensive icons of cultural superiority and symbols of class divisions and gave rise to further tension.

Islamic political movements became popular after 1967 because—for many of the lower classes—they held the promise of resolving these tensions. Various Islamic political movements applied the vague notion that "Islam is the Solution" to political, economic, and cultural problems. Modern Islamic thinkers such as Sayyid Qutb, Ayatollah Khomeini, and Abbas Madani gave a political voice to people who had been deprived of one. Their ideology promised a more equitable distribution of income without resorting to communism, and it provided the framework for an "authentic" and strong culture. Beyond these vague promises, there existed (and still exists) a very wide spectrum of

Islamically based programs. In fact, the very meaning of Islam as a way of life continues to be debated throughout the Islamic world. Thus, we cannot speak of a singular Islamic political movement or aim.

The forces that help explain the rise of Islamic political movements also produced secular movements that were suspicious of the Islamists and rejected the imposition of religious solutions and ideas on society. Since the 1970s, feminists, environmentalists, homosexuals, and ethnic minorities have sought to deal with the same issue as the Islamists, but from a secular perspective. The fact that they have not been as successful, organized, or well financed as the Islamists does not detract from their critical role in shaping the regions today. Their voices, ideas, and arguments indicate the diversity of opinion in the Middle East and North Africa. The existence of these various viewpoints is evidence of the expansion of the call for democracy. There have always been such voices, but now they are more vocal and determined. They are achieving gains not thought possible only twenty years ago. For example, in Iran (which is seen by the United States as a theocratic and medieval state) democracy is flourishing in astonishing ways—from an overwhelming 96 percent turnout for elections to an astounding number of magazines and newspapers that insistently (despite frequent closures) demand reforms and greater freedoms. Even in Syria, where the Assad state has long been able to dominate public discourse, new public intellectual "salons" were held in 2000 to demand a loosening of government control over freedom of speech and political opposition.

Running somewhat in tandem with these new movements is the attempt to construct new types of economies throughout the two regions. This movement—labeled *khaskhasa,* or privatization—is made up of private and public initiatives (with a great deal of encouragement from the United States, the European Union, and the World Bank) that seek to turn state-owned institutions and factories into privately and semi-privately held interests. The privatization movement extends from public utilities to banks and factories. Several factors are propelling it. Most notable is the fact that in the rush toward globalization of trade and commerce, with few exceptions (Tunisia and Israel) the states of the Middle East and North Africa lag far behind the economies of the so-called Asian Tigers, the United States, and Europe. This economic trend has political ramifications that threaten the hold of the ruling elites, so the concern for creating a more open economy has been growing steadily among them. Less cynically, most governments do express some level of concern for the welfare of the population and consider the lack of economic opportunities to be detrimental to the nation as a whole.

Yet the trend toward privatization has also raised some serious concerns. Critics argue that it is nothing more than a process that is opening their countries further to American and European economic dominance. They concede that privatization may help a small segment of society, but they contend that its overall cost for the less fortunate majority is too high. Globalization too seems to be nothing more than a continuation and intensification of "Western" domination, which is generating a sense of alienation among young men and women.

Thus, the shift toward a more privatized economy appears to have contradictory and controversial impacts on the societies of the Middle East.

The documents in this part of the book highlight the historical forces and ideas explored in this introduction. These documents cover the spectrum from a sampling of the writing of one of the most influential and revolutionary Islamic political thinkers of the twentieth-century—Sayyid Qutb—to a feminist interpretation of the rights of women in Islam; from the comments of homosexuals in Egypt to the complaints of Arab soccer players in Israel; and from the declaration of the Iranian Communist party to a discussion of the impact of globalization on the Middle East.

CHAPTER 8

Islamic Political Movements Since 1964

Until 1979 most Americans were ignorant of Islam in its multiple manifestations. The Iranian revolution of that year and later events brought this ignorance to an abrupt end. Unfortunately, this new encounter resulted from violence. Islam acquired a reputation for violence in the American media because of a series of attacks by "Muslims" on American interests culminating in the atrocities of September 11, 2001. Subsequently, many pundits, academics, and foreign policy experts told American audiences that the only interaction with "Islam" was through violence. Hollywood released one film after another depicting dark-skinned, supposedly Arabic-speaking terrorists attacking the United States. Mutual distrust created a chasm that was widened by ignorance. "Why do they hate us?" asked people on both sides of the divide.

This chapter presents some documents intended to achieve three goals. The first is to explain the rise of Islamic political movements (the "Islamists") in the Middle East and North Africa as a phenomenon of the late twentieth century. The second is to present liberal views of Islam that are at odds with the more extreme interpretations of that religion. The third is to present the most extreme Islamist vision—that of Usama Bin Laden and the World Islamic Front (document 6). All of these documents together show the breadth of interpretation within modern Islamic movements.

A variety of Islamic political movements emerged in the late 1960s and became viable and credible political movements after the 1980s. Scholars do not agree on a single reason that led to the rise of Islamist movements, but most agree that common historical political, economic, and cultural factors are behind the emergence of most of them. In the postindependence period, most state regimes ruling over a majority of Muslims tended to be authoritarian. This was most definitely the case in the Middle East, as we saw in the preceding part of this book. The political repression practiced to varying degrees by these regimes minimized legitimate political opposition and almost completely crushed secular liberal and leftist opposition. In some cases, such as in Egypt, the state achieved this outcome through an alliance with "moderate" Islamists, who provided the state with legitimacy and support in its repressive campaigns. In other places, such as Iran, repression extended to religious as well as secular opposition. This repression, carried out by pro-Western and pro-Soviet regimes alike, discredited not only the regimes themselves in the eyes of the majority of the population, but also the regimes' supporters: the United States and the Soviet Union. Thus, there emerged a movement seeking an "authentic" form of political expression that would not fall into either camp. Islam—or, more accurately, politicized Islam—provided this new ideology.

The concept of political Islam is not new. Throughout Islamic history there have been self-consciously Islamic movements whose purpose was to renew and reform Islam in a manner that would recapture the presumed utopia of Medina at the time of the Prophet. While most of these movements did not intend to re-create the time of the Prophet, they did seek to rediscover the "purity" of original Islam as they assumed it was when Muhammad was the leader of the umma, the community of believers. This idealized past gave impetus over the course of Islamic history to a variety of movements that can be labeled reformist. In the eighteenth century one such movement—the Wahabis—swept through the Arabian Peninsula seeking to eradicate popular forms of Islam and unify Muslims under its strict interpretation of the religion. Other such movements coursed through West Africa, Libya, and Sudan during the nineteenth century. The Muslim Brotherhood was yet another such movement in Egypt during the first half of the twentieth century.

This genealogy of political movements contains the common thread of attempts to renew the religion (a tendency found in every religion). Yet despite the universalist claims of these movements, each was solidly grounded in its own local historical circumstances. Moreover, the articulation of a new Islamist ideology—presented most clearly and radically by Sayyid Qutb (document 1)—did not mean that every Muslim joined one of these organizations. Membership began to swell only as the economic well-being of the region took a sharp downturn in the 1980s because of the fall of oil prices and a general worldwide recession. These economic hard times meant that many university-educated men were hard-pressed to find employment and start families. Frustration over their economic misery—accentuated by the conspicuous consumption of the ruling elites—drove some *but not all* of these young men to seek meaning for their lives in different venues. The most extreme tended to join extremist Islamic movements that promised justice and equality in the wake of an anticipated Islamic revolution. The Iranian revolution of 1979 stood as proof that such a revolution was possible even against the most powerful of Westernized and Western-supported regimes.

The rise of globalization with its overwhelmingly Westernized culture threatened to rob people in the Middle East and North Africa of their identity and to replace it with a consumption-driven one. This threat was real to people on the receiving end of American products ranging from lurid TV shows such as *Dallas* and *Baywatch* to Nike shoes and Levi's jeans. This cultural onslaught was another factor that propelled some to seek refuge and certainty in their Islamic faith.

Yet all of these factors did not produce a common notion of what "Islam" is and how it pertains to daily life. Conservative Muslim thinkers argued that Islam contains a blueprint for a state and society that is culturally authentic, politically just, and economically equitable. This vision, however, was difficult to implement to the satisfaction of all, and many ideas emerged about the meaning of an "Islamic state." Conservatives insisted that the process leading to the attaining of an Islamic state had to be legal and peaceful. A small minority disagreed. They argued that there could be no negotiations with non-Muslims or with heretical Muslims (the extremists themselves decided what constituted "heresy"). Nor could there be any accommodation of multiple points of view about the nature of the state in a predominantly Islamic country. Instead, they contended, a fundamentalist re-creation of the early Islamic society and state offered the only possible solution to the woes mentioned previously. Also there emerged at this time a group of Muslims who sought to interpret Islam as a liberal religion quite compatible with modern politics, society, and economy. They still saw in it a means to create a distinct and strong identity in the face of external threats. And they insisted that this identity would allow Muslims to engage the world in a dignified dialogue rather than turn inward into an isolated and xenophobic space.

The documents presented in this chapter cover this vast expanse of interpretation and help us to understand that Islam, like Christianity or the elusive "West," is far from monolithic. Sayyid Qutb (document 1) and his successor Usama Bin Laden (document 6) articulate a new and militant vision of jihad that exhorts Muslims to understand and use their religion as an activist political ideology facing a hostile world composed of heretics and unbelievers. Confronting this particular interpretation are the more humanistic and liberal views of the Iranian thinkers Ali Shari'ati (document 2) and Mehdi Bazargan (document 3), who see Islam as a religion that promotes social justice and allows for liberal thought. Fatima Mernissi (document 4) goes one step further and argues that Islam has been misinterpreted from a conservative male perspective, thus rendering its application oppressive to women. She argues that a proper understanding of the teachings of the Qur'an and of the Prophet would in fact provide Muslim women with greater freedoms and rights than they currently enjoy in most Muslim societies. According to Farag Foda (document 5), an Egyptian journalist who was assassinated for his secular views, Islam should remain an issue of personal faith with little if any role in public life. His caustic editorials about Islamic conservatives and extremists sought to highlight the absurdities of modern religious politics and thought in Egypt. Finally, Ehsan Ahrari and Muna Shuqair (document 7) reflect from differing perspectives on the events of September 11, 2001. While acknowledging that the perpetrators of these terrorist attacks were religious extremists who are the products of

secular events, the two authors differ in their explanation for the reasons behind the emergence of such groups. Ehsan Ahrari argues that these aberrant individuals and groups are signs—and products—of the internal flaws of
un-democratic Arab societies that have been saddled by authoritarian, corrupt,
and incompetent regimes. Muna Shuqair, on the other hand, argues that U.S.
policies in the Middle East and North Africa are at least in part responsible for
engendering the anger and hostility that led to the events of September 11.

1. Egyptian Writer Sayyid Qutb Articulates a New, Influential Vision of Jihad, 1964

*Sayyid Qutb (1906–1966) is arguably the most influential writer on political Islam
to have emerged in the last fifty years. Qutb seems to have provided many modern
Islamic political groups with their ideological justification for opposing—sometimes
violently—the state and for rejecting its authority as "un-Islamic." In the early part
of his life (before the 1950s) Qutb was a moralist who wrote essays exhorting Muslims to adhere to the ethical values of Islam in their daily existence. However, after
spending two years in the United States (1948–1950), and after being introduced
to the writings of another Islamic political writer, Sayyid Mawdudi, he became convinced that only the establishment of an Islamic state would allow for the existence
of a just and moral society. In other words, he came to the conclusion that individual morality could not survive or even be perfectly attained as long as the society
and the state remained in a state of immorality. Thus, upon his return to Egypt, he
joined the Muslim Brotherhood (see document 12, about Hasan al-Banna, in the
chapter "Ideas of Nationalism") and became chief editor of the Brotherhood newspaper. In 1954—when the Brotherhood was outlawed on the pretext that it was
trying to overthrow the Egyptian government—Qutb was sentenced to fifteen years
in jail, of which he served ten. During this period his ideas about the Islamic state
and society fully matured, and when he was released in 1964 (because of the in-
tercession of many Muslim figures), he wrote his most famous work,* Milestones.
*Because of this book he was arrested a second time and sentenced to death for in-
citing Muslims to revolt against the secular government of Gamal Abdel Nasser.*

When writers with defeatist and apologetic mentalities write about "Jihaad in
Islam," and try to remove this 'blot' from Islam, they mix up two things: first,
that this religion forbids the imposition of its belief by force, as is clear from
the verse: "There is no compulsion in religion" (2:256), while on the other hand
it tries to annihilate all those political and material powers which stand between people and Islam, which force one people to bow before another people
and prevent them from accepting the sovereignty of God. These two principles

Sayyid Qutb, *Milestones* (Lahore: International Islamic Federation of Student Organizations, 1977), pp.
102–114, 131–140.

have no relation with each other nor is there room to mix them. In spite of this, these defeatist-type people try to mix the two aspects and want to confine Ji-haad to what today is called "defensive war." The Islamic Jihaad has no rela-tionship to modern warfare, either in its causes or in the way in which it is conducted. The causes of Islamic Jihaad should be sought in the very nature of Islam and its role in the world, in its high principles, which have been given to it by God and for the implementation of which God appointed the Prophet—peace be on him—as His Messenger and declared him to be the last of all prophets and messengers.

This religion is really a universal declaration of the freedom of man from servitude to other men and from servitude to his own desires, which is also a form of human servitude; it is a declaration that the sovereignty belongs to God alone and that He is the Lord of all the worlds. It means a challenge to all kinds and forms of systems which are based on the concept of the sovereignty of man; in other words, where man has usurped the Divine attribute. Any sys-tem in which the final decisions are referred to human beings, and in which the sources of all authority are human, deifies human beings by designating others than God as lords over men. This declaration means that the usurped authority of Allah be returned to Him and the usurpers be thrown out—those who by themselves devise laws for others to follow, thus elevating themselves to the status of lords and reducing others to the status of slaves. In short, to proclaim the authority and sovereignty of God means to eliminate all human kingship and to announce the rule of the Sustainer of the universe over the entire earth. In the words of the Qur'an,

"He alone is God in the heavens and in the earth." (43:84)

"The command belongs to God alone. He commands you not to wor-ship anyone except Him. This is the right way of life." (12:40)

"Say: O People of the Book, come to what is common between us: that we will not worship anyone except God, and will not associate any-thing with Him, and will not take lords from among ourselves besides God; and if they turn away, then tell them to bear witness that we are those who have submitted to God." (2:64)

The way to establish God's rule on earth is not that some consecrated people—the priests—be given the authority to rule, as was the case with the rule of the Church, nor that some spokesmen of God become rulers, as is the case in a "theocracy." To establish God's rule means that His laws be enforced and that the final decision in all affairs be according to these laws.

The establishing of the dominion of God on earth, the abolishing of the dominion of man, the taking away of sovereignty from the usurper to revert it to God, and the bringing about of the enforcement of the Divine Shari'ah and the abolition of man-made laws cannot be achieved only through preaching. Those who have usurped the authority of God and are oppressing God's crea-tures are not going to give up their power merely through preaching; if it had been so, the task of establishing God's religion in the world would have been very easy for the Prophets of Allah! This is contrary to the evidence from the history of the Prophets and the story of the struggle of the true religion, spread over generations.

This universal declaration of the freedom of man on the earth from every authority except that of God, and the declaration that sovereignty is God's alone and that He is the Lord of the universe, is not merely a theoretical, philosophical and passive proclamation. It is a positive, practical and dynamic message with a view to bringing about the implementation of the Shari'ah of God and actually freeing people from their servitude to other men to bring them into the service of God, the One without associates. This cannot be attained unless both "preaching" and "the movement" are used. This is so because appropriate means are needed to meet any and every practical situation.

Because this religion proclaims the freedom of man on the earth from all authority except that of God, it is confronted in every period of human history—yesterday, today or tomorrow—with obstacles of beliefs and concepts, physical power, and the obstacles of political, social, economic, racial and class structures. In addition, corrupted beliefs and superstitions become mixed with this religion, working side by side with it and taking root in peoples' hearts.

If through "preaching" beliefs and ideas are confronted, through "the movement" material obstacles are tackled. Foremost among these is that political power which rests on a complex yet interrelated ideological, racial, class, social and economic support. Thus these two—preaching and the movement—united, confront "the human situation" with all the necessary methods. For the achievement of the freedom of man on earth—of all mankind throughout the earth—it is necessary that these two methods should work side by side. This is a very important point and cannot be over-emphasized.

This religion is not merely a declaration of the freedom of the Arabs, nor is its message confined to the Arabs. It addresses itself to the whole of mankind, and its sphere of work is the whole earth. Allah is the Sustainer not merely of the Arabs, nor is His providence limited to those who believe in the faith of Islam. Allah is the Sustainer of the whole world. This religion wants to bring back the whole world to its Sustainer and free it from servitude to anyone other than God. In the sight of Islam, the real servitude is following laws devised by someone, and this is that servitude which in Islam is reserved for God alone. Anyone who serves someone other than God in this sense is outside God's religion, although he may claim to profess this religion. The Prophet—peace be on him—clearly stated that, according to the Shari'ah, "to obey" is "to worship." Taking this meaning of worship, when the Jews and Christians "disobeyed" God, they became like those who "associate others with God."

Tirmidhi has reported on the authority of 'Adi bin Hatim that when the Prophet's message reached him, he ran away to Syria (he had accepted Christianity before the Prophet's time), but his sister and some of the people of his tribe became prisoners of war. The Prophet—peace be on him—treated his sister kindly and gave her some gifts. She went back to her brother and invited him to Islam, and advised him to visit the Prophet—peace be on him. 'Adi agreed to this. The people were very anxious to see him come to Medina. When he came into the presence of the Prophet, he was wearing a silver cross. The Prophet—peace be on him—was reciting the verse, "They (the People of the Book) have taken their rabbis and priests as lords other than God." 'Adi reports: "I said, 'They do not worship their priests.'" God's Messenger replied, "Whatever their priests and rabbis call permissible, they accept as permissible, whatever they declare as forbidden, they consider as forbidden, and thus they worship them."

This explanation of the above verse by the Prophet—peace be on him—makes it clear that obedience to laws and judgments is a sort of worship, and anyone who does this is considered out of this religion. It is taking some men as lords over others, while this religion has come to annihilate such practices, and it declares that all the people of the earth should become free of servitude to anyone other than God.

If the actual life of human beings is found to be different from this declaration of freedom, then it becomes incumbent upon Islam to enter the field with preaching as well as the movement, and to strike hard at all those political powers which force people to bow before them and which rule over them, unmindful of the commandments of God, and which prevent people from listening to the preaching and accepting the belief if they wish to do so. After annihilating the tyrannical force, whether it be in a political or a racial form, or in the form of class distinctions within the same race, Islam establishes a new social, economic and political system, in which the concept of the freedom of man is applied in practice.

It is not the intention of Islam to force its beliefs on people, but Islam is not merely "belief." As we have pointed out, Islam is a declaration of the freedom of man from servitude to other men. Thus it strives from the beginning to abolish all those systems and governments which are based on the rule of man over men and the servitude of one human being to another. When Islam releases people from this political pressure and presents to them its spiritual message, appealing to their reason, it gives them complete freedom to accept or not to accept its beliefs. However, this freedom does not mean that they can make their desires their gods, or that they can choose to remain in the servitude of other human beings, making some men lords over others. Whatever system is to be established in the world ought to be on the authority of God, deriving its laws from Him alone. Then every individual is free, under the protection of this universal system, to adopt any belief he wishes to adopt. This is the only way in which "the religion" can be purified for God alone. The word "religion" includes more than belief; "religion" actually means a way of life, and in Islam this is based on belief. But in an Islamic system there is room for all kinds of people to follow their own beliefs, while obeying the laws of the country which are themselves based on the Divine authority.

Anyone who understands this particular character of this religion will also understand the place of Jihaad bis saif (striving through sword), which is to clear the way for striving through preaching in the application of the Islamic movement. He will understand that Islam is not a "defensive movement" in the narrow sense which today is technically called a "defensive war." This narrow meaning is ascribed to it by those who are under the pressure of circumstances and are defeated by the wily attacks of the orientalists, who distort the concept of Islamic Jihaad. It was a movement to wipe out tyranny and to introduce true freedom to mankind, using resources according to the actual human situation, and it had definite stages, for each of which it utilised new methods.

It we insist on calling Islamic Jihaad a defensive movement, then we must change the meaning of the word "defense" and mean by it "the defense of man" against all those elements which limit his freedom. These elements take the form of beliefs and concepts, as well of political systems, based on economic, racial or class distinctions. When Islam first came into existence, the world was full of such systems, and the present-day Jahiliyyah also has various kinds of such systems.

When we take this broad meaning of the word "defense," we understand the true character of Islam, and that it is a universal proclamation of the freedom of man from servitude to other men, the establishment of the sovereignty of God and His Lordship throughout the world, the end of man's arrogance and selfishness, and the implementation of the rule of the Divine Shari'ah in human affairs.

As to persons who attempt to defend the concept of Islamic Jihaad by interpreting it in the narrow sense of the current concept of defensive war, and who do research to prove that the battles fought in Islamic Jihaad were all for the defense of the homeland of Islam—some of them considering the homeland of Islam to be just the Arabian peninsula—against the aggression of neighboring powers, they lack understanding of the nature of Islam and its primary aim. Such an attempt is nothing but a product of a mind defeated by the present difficult conditions and by the attacks of the treacherous orientalists on the Islamic Jihaad.

Can anyone say that if Abu Bakr, 'Umar or 'Othman had been satisfied that the Roman and Persian powers were not going to attack the Arabian peninsula, they would not have striven to spread the message of Islam throughout the world? How could the message of Islam have spread when it faced such material obstacles as the political system of the state, the socioeconomic system based on races and classes, and behind all these, the military power of the government?

It would be naive to assume that a call is raised to free the whole of humankind throughout the earth, and it is confined to preaching and exposition. Indeed, it strives through preaching and exposition when there is freedom of communication and when people are free from all these influences, as "There is no compulsion in religion"; but when the above-mentioned obstacles and practical difficulties are put in its way, it has no recourse but to remove them by force so that when it is addressed to peoples' hearts and minds, they are free to accept or reject it with an open mind.

Since the objective of the message of Islam is a decisive declaration of man's freedom, not merely on the philosophical plane but also in the actual

conditions of life, it must employ Jihaad. It is immaterial whether the homeland of Islam—in the true Islamic sense, Dar ul-Islam—is in a condition of
peace of whether it is threatened by its neighbours. When Islam strives for
peace, its objective is not that superficial peace which requires that only that
part of the earth where the followers of Islam are residing, remain secure. The
peace which Islam desires is that the religion (i.e., the law of the society) be purified for God, that the obedience of all people be for God alone, and that some
people should not be lords over others. After the period of the Prophet—peace
be on him—only the final stages of the movement of Jihaad are to be followed;
the initial or middle stages are not applicable. They have ended, and as Ibn
Qayyim states: "Thus, after the revelation of the chapter 'Bra't,' the unbelievers were of three kinds: adversaries in war, people with treaties, and Dhimmies.
The people with treaties eventually became Muslims, so there were only two
kinds left: people at war and Dhimmies. The people at war were always afraid
of him. Now the people of the whole world were of three kinds: one, the Muslims who believed in him: two, those with whom he had peace (and from the
previous sentence we understand that they were Dhimmies): and three, the opponents who kept fighting with him."

These are the logical positions consonant with the character and purposes
of this religion, and not what is understood by the people who are defeated by
present conditions and by the attacks of the treacherous orientalists.
[. . .]

As we have described earlier, there are many practical obstacles in establishing God's rule on earth, such as the power of the state, the social system and
traditions and, in general, the whole human environment. Islam uses force only
to remove these obstacles so that there may not remain any wall between Islam
and individual human beings, and so that it may address their hearts and minds
after releasing them from these material obstacles, and then leave them free to
choose to accept or reject it.

We ought not to be deceived or embarrassed by the attacks of the orientalists on the origin of Jihaad, nor lose self-confidence under the pressure of present conditions and the weight of the great powers of the world to such an
extent that we try to find reasons for Islamic Jihaad outside the nature of this
religion, and try to show that it was a defensive measure under temporary conditions. The need for Jihaad remains, and will continue to remain, whether
these conditions exist or not!

In pondering over historical events, we should not neglect the aspects inherent in the nature of this religion, its declaration of universal freedom, and
its practical method. We ought not to confuse these with temporary needs
of defense.

No doubt this religion must defend itself against aggressors. Its very existence in the form of a general declaration of the universal Lordship of God and
of the freedom of man from servitude to any being other than God, and its organising a movement under a new leadership other than the existing jahili leadership, and its creating a distinct and permanent society based on the Divine

authority and submission to One God, is sufficient cause for the surrounding jahili society, which is based on human authority in some form or another, to rise against it for its own preservation and for the suppression of Islam. Clearly, under these conditions, the newly-organised Islamic community will have to prepare itself for defense. These conditions inevitably occur and come into existence simultaneously with the advent of Islam in any society. There is no question of Islam's liking or disliking such a situation, as the struggle is imposed upon Islam; this is a natural struggle between two systems which cannot co-exist for long. This is a fact which cannot be denied, and hence Islam has no choice but to defend itself against aggression.

But there is another fact which is much more important than this fact. It is in the very nature of Islam to take initiative for freeing the human beings throughout the earth from servitude to anyone other than God; and so it cannot be restricted within any geographic or racial limits, leaving all mankind on the whole earth in evil, in chaos and in servitude to lords other than God.

It may happen that the enemies of Islam may consider it expedient not to take any action against Islam, if Islam leaves them alone in their geographical boundaries to continue the lordship of some men over others and does not extend its message and its declaration of universal freedom within their domain. But Islam cannot agree to this unless they submit to its authority by paying Jizyah, which will be a guarantee that they have opened their doors for the preaching of Islam and will not put any obstacle in its way through the power of the state.

This is the character of this religion and this is its function, as it is a declaration of the Lordship of God and the freedom of man from servitude to anyone other than God, for all people.

There is a great difference between this concept of Islam and the other, which considers it confined to geographical and racial limits, and does not take any action except out of fear of aggression. In the latter case, all its inherent dynamism is lost.

To understand the dynamism of Islam with clarity and depth, it is necessary to remember that Islam is a way of life for man prescribed by God. It is not a man-made system, nor an ideology of a group of people, nor a way of life peculiar to a given race. We cannot talk about external reasons for Jihaad unless we overlook this great truth and unless we forget that the fundamental question here is the sovereignty of God and the obedience of His creatures, it is impossible for a person to remember this great truth and still search for other reasons for Islamic Jihaad.

The true estimate of the difference between the concept that war was forced upon Islam by Jahiliyyah because its very nature demanded that jahili societies would attack it, and the concept that Islam takes the initiative and enters into this struggle, cannot be made in the early stages of its movement.

In the early stages of the Islamic movement it is difficult to discriminate between these two concepts, because in either case Islam will have to do battle. However, in the final stages, when the initial battles are won, the two concepts make a great difference—a great difference in understanding the purposes and the significance of the Islamic message. And herein lies the danger.

There is also a great difference in the idea that Islam is a Divinely-ordained way of life and in the idea that it is a geographically-bounded system. According to the first idea, Islam came into this world to establish God's rule on God's earth, to invite all people toward the worship of God, and to make a concrete reality of its message in the form of a Muslim community in which individuals are free from servitude to men and have gathered together under servitude to God and follow only the Shari'ah of God. This Islam has a right to remove all those obstacles which are in its path so that it may address human reason and intuition with no interference and opposition from political systems. According to the second idea, Islam is merely a national system which has a right to take up arms only when its homeland is attacked.

In the case of either concept, Islam has to strive and to struggle; but its purposes and its results are entirely different, both conceptually and practically.

Indeed, Islam has the right to take the initiative. Islam is not a heritage of any particular race or country; this is God's religion and it is for the whole world. It has the right to destroy all obstacles in the form of institutions and traditions which limit man's freedom of choice. It does not attack individuals nor does it force them to accept its beliefs; it attacks institutions and traditions to release human beings from their poisonous influences, which distort human nature and which curtail human freedom.

It is the right of Islam to release mankind from servitude to human beings so that they may serve God alone, to give practical meaning to its declaration that God is the true Lord of all and that all men are free under Him. According to the Islamic concept and in actuality, God's rule on earth can be established only through the Islamic system, as it is the only system ordained by God for all human beings, whether they be rulers or ruled, black or white, poor or rich, ignorant or learned. Its law is uniform for all, and all human beings are equally responsible within it. In all other systems, human beings obey other human beings and follow man-made laws. Legislation is a Divine attribute; any person who concedes this right to such a claimant, whether he considers him Divine or not, has accepted him as Divine.

Islam is not merely a belief, so that it is enough merely to preach it. Islam, which is a way of life, takes practical steps to organise a movement for freeing man. Other societies do not give it any opportunity to organise its followers according to its own method, and hence it is the duty of Islam to annihilate all such systems, as they are obstacles in the way of universal freedom. Only in this manner can the way of life be wholly dedicated to God, so that neither any human authority nor the question of servitude remains, as is the case in all other systems which are based on man's servitude to man.

Those of our contemporary Muslim scholars who have been defeated by the pressure of current conditions and the attacks of treacherous orientalists, do not subscribe to this characteristic of Islam. The orientalists have painted a picture of Islam as a violent movement which imposed its belief upon people by the sword. These vicious orientalists know very well that this is not true, but by this method they try to distort the true motives of Islamic Jihaad. But our Muslim scholars—these defeated people—search for reasons of defense with which to negate this accusation. They are ignorant of the nature of Islam and of its function, and that it has a right to take the initiative for human freedom.

These research scholars, with their defeated mentality, have adopted the Western concept of "religion," which is merely a name for "belief" in the heart, having no relation to the practical affairs of life, and therefore they conceive of religious war as a war to impose belief on peoples' hearts.

But this is not the case with Islam, as Islam is the way of life ordained by God for all mankind, and this way establishes the Lordship of God alone—that is, the sovereignty of God—and orders practical life in all its daily details. Jihaad in Islam is simply a name for striving to make this system of life dominant in the world. As far as belief is concerned, it clearly depends upon personal opinion, under the protection of a general system in which all obstacles to freedom of personal belief have been removed. Clearly this is an entirely different matter and throws a completely new light on the Islamic Jihaad.

Thus, wherever an Islamic community exists which is a concrete example of the Divinely-ordained system of life, it has a God-given right to step forward and take control of the political authority, so that it may establish the Divine system on earth, while it leaves the matter of belief to individual conscience. When God restrained Muslims from Jihaad for a certain period, it was a question of strategy rather than of principle; this was a matter pertaining to the requirements of the movement and not to belief. Only in the light of this explanation can we understand those verses of the Holy Qur'an which are concerned with the various stages of this movement. In reading these verses, we should always keep in mind that one of their meanings is related to the particular stages of the development of Islam, while there is another general meaning which is related to the unchangeable and eternal message of Islam. We should not confuse these two aspects.

2. Iranian Intellectual Ali Shari'ati Examines Man from the Viewpoint of Islam, 1968

Like many secular and religious Iranian thinkers, Ali Shari'ati (1933–1977) grew up in the middle of the twentieth century aware of the economic, political, and social problems that embroiled Iran. He experienced the abject poverty of the lower classes during his years at the Teacher's Training College. He was well aware of the

Ali Shari'ati, "Man and Islam," *On the Sociology of Islam,* trans. Hamid Algar (Berkeley, Calif.: Mizan Press, 1968), pp. 70–81, a translation of *Insan va Islam,* a lecture given at the Petroleum College of Abadan. The introductory paragraph has been omitted. Reprinted by permission.

political dissatisfaction with the shah of Iran and the criticism of the shah's author-itarian rule (see Khomeini's denunciation of the shah—document 3 in the chapter "Crisis of the State"). However, one of the elements that distinguished Shari'ati was the eclectic nature of his education. After receiving his degree from the Teacher's College, he received a scholarship to complete his graduate studies at the Sorbonne, from which he received a doctorate in sociology in 1965. Upon his return to Iran he was immediately arrested on the charges that he had participated in anti-shah po-litical activities in Paris. After being released, he taught sociology at Mashhad Uni-versity and attracted a large following. After he was expelled from the university, he continued to lecture at Hussein-e-Ershad Religious Institute. While there, he became extremely popular: literally thousands of students attended his lectures, and his first book sold over sixty thousand copies in its first edition despite government attempts to limit its availability.

This popularity was due to the fact that Shari'ati was an intellectual who sought to understand the problems of Muslim societies and to find solutions deriv-ing as much from that context as from his understanding of Western ideas. He be-lieved and argued that Islam and Islamic history contain within them the means to modernize Islamic societies. Indeed, he did not regard "Western" humanitarian val-ues to be at odds with Islamic religious ideas and practices—as some other secular intellectuals postulated. Rather, he contended that the two could and should inter-mingle as long as this interaction takes place in a manner that does not dilute or dismiss Islamic values. The popularity of these ideas and his implied and open criti-cism of the shah's regime led to his expulsion from Iran in 1977 to London, where he was assassinated by the Savak, the shah's secret police.

The question of man is the most important of all questions. The civilization of today is based upon humanism, the nobility of man and the worship of man. It is believed that the religions of the past crushed the personality of man and compelled him to sacrifice himself to the gods. They forced him to regard his own will as totally powerless when confronted by the will of God. They com-pelled him always to be seeking something from God by way of prayer, sup-plication and entreaty. The philosophy of humanism is, then, a philosophy that, since the Renaissance, has opposed religious philosophies—philosophies founded on belief in the unseen and supranatural realm—and its aim has al-legedly been to restore nobility to man. The roots of humanism lie in Athens, but as a universal philosophy, it has become the basis of the modern civilization of the West. In reality, it arose as a reaction to scholastic philosophy and me-dieval Christianity.

My purpose tonight is to examine—within the limits of my capability and the present occasion—the question of man from the viewpoint of our religion, Islam, and to seek an answer to the question: what kind of a phenomenon does Islam see in man? Does it see in man a powerless creature whose ultimate aim and ideal is to stand helpless before God? Does Islam deny man all notion of nobility? Or, on the contrary, does belief in Islam itself impart a form of no-bility to man, and make an acknowledgement of his virtues? This is the topic I wish to discuss.

In order to understand the place of "humanism" in different religions, and the concept of man that each of them holds, it is best to study the philosophy of the creation of man that each has set forth. However, I do not have the opportunity now to examine all the religions of East and West from this point of view. I will speak only of the philosophy of creation that exists in Islam and those pre-Islamic religions of which Islam is the continuation—the religions of Moses, Jesus and Abraham.

How is the creation of man explained in Islam or the Abrahamic scriptures, of which Islam is the culmination and perfection? Can we deduce the status and nature of man from the manner in which the creation of man is described in the Qur'an, the Word of God, or in the words of the Prophet of Islam? From examining the story of Adam—the symbol of man—in the Qur'an, we can understand what kind of a creature man is in the view of God and therefore in the view of our religion. By way of introduction, let me point out that the language of religion, and particularly the language of the semitic religions, in whose prophets we believe, is a symbolical language. By this we mean a language that expresses meaning through images and symbols—the most excellent and exalted of all the languages that men have ever evolved. Its value is more profound and eternal than that of expository language, i.e., the clear and explicit language that expresses meaning directly. A simple and straightforward language, one deprived of all symbol and image, may be easier for purposes of instruction, but it has no permanence. For, as the celebrated Egyptian philosopher Abd ar-Rahman Badawi has pointed out, a religion or philosophy that expounds all of its ideas and teachings in simple, one-dimensional and straightforward language will not be able to survive. Those addressed by religion or philosophy represent different types and classes—both the common folk and the educated. The audience of a religion is, moreover, not a single generation or age, but different and successive generations which follow upon each other throughout history. They inevitably differ with each other with respect to way of thought, level of thought, and angle of vision. The language that a religion chooses in order to convey its concepts must, then, be a versatile and multifaceted language, each aspect and facet of which addresses itself to a particular generation and class of men. If the language be monofaceted, it will be comprehensible only to a single class, and totally without value for all other classes; accessible to one generation, but beyond the reach of the next. It will be impossible to extract any new meaning from it. It is for this reason that all literary works written in symbolic language are immortal. For example, the poems of Hafiz are immortal, and whenever we read them we deduce a new meaning from them, in proportion to the depth of our thought and taste and outlook. But the history of Bayhaqi is something different, as is, too, the *Gulistan* of Sa'di. When we read the *Gulistan,* its meaning is quite apparent to us, and we enjoy its verbal beauty and structure. But many of the ideas it contains are outmoded, precisely because it is clear what Sa'di had to say, and what he had to say is false! But the style of Hafiz is multi-faceted and symbolical; depending on his taste and manner of thought, everyone can interpret its symbols in a certain sense, thus deducing new meanings from the text.

It is for this reason that religions must employ a symbolic language; they are addressed to different human types and different generations of men. There are numerous concepts in religion that were not clearly understood at the time of their appearance. If religion had *not*, on the one hand, expressed its ideas in common, familiar language, it would have been incomprehensible to the people of that age; but if it *had* expressed its ideas in common language, religion would have had no meaning in later times. It was therefore necessary that religion should speak in images and symbols that would become comprehensible with the development of human thought and science. Symbolism represents the highest of styles in European literature—symbolism, which is the art of speaking in symbols and images and concealing profound ideas in images that apparently mean something else but have an inner significance that man can discover in accordance with his own degree of profundity.

It was necessary, then, that the story of the creation of Adam, of man, be told in symbolic fashion, so that today, after fourteen centuries of progress in the human and natural sciences, it should still be readable and comprehensible.

How was man created, in the view of Islam?

First God addresses the angels, saying, "I wish to create a viceregent for Myself upon earth." See how great is the value of man according to Islam! Even the post-Renaissance humanism of Europe has never been able to conceive of such exalted sanctity for man. God, Who in the view of Islam and all believers, is the greatest and most exalted of all entities, the creator of Adam and the master of the cosmos, addresses the angels and presents man to them as His viceregent. The whole mission of man according to Islam becomes evident from this divine address. The same mission that God has in the cosmos, man must perform on earth as God's viceregent. The first excellence that man possesses is, then, being God's representative on earth.

The angels cry out saying, "You wish to create one who will engage in bloodshed, crime, hatred and vengeance." (Since before Adam, there had been other men who, like the man of today, busied themselves in bloodshed, crime, corruption and sin, and the angels wished to remind God that if He were to create man again and grant him a second opportunity on earth, man would again engage in bloodshed and sin.) But God replies, "I know something that you do not know," and then sets about the task of creating man.

It is at this point that the symbolic aspect of the narrative begins. See what profound truths concerning man are hidden beneath these symbols! God desires to create a viceregent for Himself out of earth, the face of the globe. One might expect that the most sacred and valuable of materials would have been selected, but God chose, on the contrary, the lowest of substances. The Qur'an mentions on three occasions the substance from which man was fashioned. First it uses the expression "like potter's clay" (55:14); that is, dry, sedimentary clay. Then the Qur'an says, "I created man from putrid clay" (15:26), foul and evil-smelling earth; and finally it uses the term *tin*, also meaning clay (6:2,

23:12). So God set to work, and willed to create a viceregent for Himself; this precious viceregent He created out of dry clay, and then He inhaled some of his own spirit into the clay, and man was created.

In human language, the lowest symbol of wretchedness and baseness is mud. No creature exists in nature lowlier than mud. Again in human language, the most exalted and sacred of beings is God, and the most exalted, sacred and noble part of every being is its spirit. Man, the representative of God, was created from mud, from sedimentary clay, from the lowliest substance in the world, and then God inhaled into him not His blood or His body— so to speak—but His spirit, the most exalted entity for which human languages possess a name. God is the most exalted of beings, and His spirit is the most exalted entity conceivable, the most exalted concept that could ever arise in the human mind.

Thus man is a compound of mud and divine spirit, a bi-dimensional being, a creature with a dual nature, as opposed to all other beings which are one-dimensional. One dimension inclines to mud and lowliness, to stagnation and immobility. When a river overflows, it leaves behind a certain muddy sediment that lacks all motion and life, and the nature of man, in one of its dimensions, aspires to precisely this state of sedimentary tranquility. But the other dimension, that of the divine spirit, as it is called in the Qur'an, aspires to ascend and to mount up to the highest summit conceivable—to God and the spirit of God.

Man is composed, then, of two contradictory elements, mud and the spirit of God; and his splendor and importance derive precisely from the fact that he is a two-dimensional creature. The distance between his two dimensions is the distance between clay and the spirit of God. Every man is endowed with these two dimensions, and it is his will that enables him to decide either to descend toward the pole of sedimentary mud that exists in his being, or to ascend toward the pole of exaltation, of God and the spirit of God. This constant striving and struggle takes place in man's inner being, until finally he chooses one of the poles as the determinant for his destiny.

After thus creating man, God taught him the names. (As will be apparent to you, I am paraphrasing the verses of the Qur'an as I proceed.) What does this teaching of the names mean? It is not yet certain. Everyone has expressed a certain opinion, and every commentator has suggested his own interpretation. Everyone has interpreted it according to his own outlook and way of thought. But whatever be the correct explanation, there can be no doubt that the verse centers on the notion of teaching and instruction. When the creation of man was completed, God taught His viceregent the names so that man became a possessor of the names. Then the angels cried out in protest, "We were created of smokeless fire and man was created of clay; why do you prefer him to us?" And God replies, "I know something you do not know; fall down at the feet of this two-dimensional creature of mine." All the angels of God, great and small, are commanded to fall down in prostration before this creature.

This is true humanism. See how great is the dignity and stature of man; so great, indeed, that all the angels, despite their inherent superiority to man and the fact that they are created of light while he is created of mud and clay, are commanded to fall down before him. God tests them because of their protest, and asks the angels concerning the names; they do not know the names, but Adam does know them. The angels are defeated in this test, and the excellence of Adam—which lies in his knowledge of the names—becomes apparent. This prostration of the angels before Adam serves to clarify the Islamic concept of man. Man knows certain things that the angels do not know, and this knowledge endows man with superiority to the angels despite the superiority of the angels to man with respect to race and origin. In other words, the nobility and dignity of man derive from knowledge and not from lineage.

Another point to be considered is the creation of woman from the rib of man, at least according to the translations usually made from the Arabic.[1] But the translation "rib" is incorrect, and the word so translated has the real meaning, in both Arabic and Hebrew, of "nature, disposition or constitution." Eve—that is, woman—was created, then, out of the same nature or disposition as man. Since the word has been mistranslated as "rib," the legend arose that woman was created from the left rib of Adam, and therefore all women are lacking one rib!

A great man like Nietzsche said that man and woman were created as totally separate creatures, and only came to resemble each other because of their constant association through history. The ancestries of man and woman he held to be totally different. Almost all scholars and philosophers have conceded that man and woman are of the same stock, yet they have always tried to belittle the nature of woman and present the nature of man as superior. But the Qur'an says, "We have created Eve from the same nature or disposition as Adam; man and woman proceed from the same substance."

Another remarkable matter concerning the creation of man is that God summons all of His creation, all the phenomena of nature such as inanimate objects, plants, animals, and tells them, "I have a trust that I wish to offer to all of you—earth, heavens, mountains, oceans and beasts." They all refuse to accept it, and instead, man accepts it. It is thus clear that man has another virtue and excellence, deriving from his courageous acceptance of the Trust that God offered to all beings and they rejected. Man is not only the viceregent of God in this world and on this earth, but also—as the Qur'an makes clear—the keeper of His Trust. Now what is the meaning of the Trust? Everyone says something different. Maulana Jalal ad-Din Rumi says that the Trust means man's will, his free will, and this is also my opinion.

It is by means of his will that man attains superiority over all other creatures in the world. He is the only being able to act counter to his own instinctual nature, something no animal or plant can do. For example, you will never

---

[1]The creation of Eve is not directly mentioned in the Qur'an, so the author is presumably referring to accounts such as that given in Kisa'i's *Qisas al-Anbiya*, Cairo, 1312, pp. 18 ff. (TR.) [All footnotes in this document are Algar's.]

encounter an animal voluntarily engaging in a two-day fast, or a plant committing suicide out of grief. Plants and animals can neither render great services nor commit treachery. It is not possible for them to act in a way different from that in which they have been created. It is only man who can rebel against the way in which he was created, who can defy even his spiritual or bodily needs, and act against the dictates of goodness and virtue. He can act either in accordance with his intelligence or in opposition to it. He is free to be good or to be evil, to resemble mud or to resemble God. Will is, then, the greatest property of man, and the affinity between God and man is apparent from this fact.

For it is God Who inhales into man some of His own spirit and makes of him the bearer of His Trust, and man is not merely the viceregent of God upon earth but also His relative—if the expression be permitted. The spirits of God and man both possess an excellence deriving from the possession of will. God, the only entity and being possessing an absolute will and capable of doing whatever it wishes, even in contradiction to the laws of the universe, inhales some of His spirit in man. Man can act like God, but only to a certain degree; he can act against the laws of his physiological constitution only to the extent permitted by his similarity to God. This is the aspect held in common by men and God, the cause of their affinity—free will, the freedom for man to be good or evil, to obey or rebel.

The following conclusions can be drawn with regard to the philosophy of the creation of man in Islam:

All men are not simply equal; they are brothers. The difference between equality and brotherhood is quite clear. Equality is a legal concept, while brotherhood proclaims the uniform nature and disposition of all men; all men originate from a single source, whatever their color.

Secondly, man and woman are equal. Contrary to all the philosophies of the ancient world, man and woman were created out of the same substance and material at the same time and by the same Creator. They share the same lineage, and are brothers and sisters to each other, descended from the same mother and father.

Thirdly, the superiority of man to the angels and the whole of creation derives from knowledge, since man learned the names and the angels fell in prostration before him; despite the superiority of their descent to that of man, they were compelled to humble themselves before him.

More important than all this, man's being stretches out over the distance between mud and God, and since he possesses will, he can choose either of the two opposing poles these represent. Again since he possesses will, a certain responsibility comes into being. From the point of view of Islam, man is the only being responsible not only for his own destiny but also for the fulfillment of a divinely entrusted mission in this world; he is the bearer of God's Trust in the world and in nature. It is he who has learned the names—and, in my opinion, the proper meaning of "names" is the truths of science, since the name of a thing is its symbol, its defined, conceptual form. The teaching of the names by God means, therefore, the bestowal of the ability to perceive and comprehend the scientific truths inherent in the world. Through this primordial instruction by God, man gained access to all the truths existing in the world, and this constitutes a second great responsibility for man. Man must fashion his destiny with his own hands. Human society is responsible for its own fate, and the human individual is responsible for his own fate: "Yours is what you acquire and theirs is what they acquire" (Qur'an, 2:134). The fate of past civilizations is no more and no less than what they brought down on themselves, and your fate will consist exactly of what you are now fashioning with your own hands. Man thus has a great responsibility toward God, since he possesses free will.

Here we must add this observation, that history has witnessed a great tragedy; namely, man has not been recognized as a two-dimensional being. In contrast with other religions that posit God and the Devil to exist within nature in mutual combat, Islam teaches that only one force exists in nature—the force of God. But within man, Satan wages war against God, and man is their battlefield. The dualism of Islam, unlike religions of the past, posits the existence of two "deities," two hypostases, in the inner being and disposition of man, not in nature. Nature knows only of a single hypostasis; it belongs to the realm, and is subject to the will, of a single power, the power of God. In Islam, Satan is not a contestant with God; he is a contestant against man, or rather against the divine half of man. And since man is a two-dimensional creature composed of God and of clay, he has need of both elements. The religion and ideology that he needs to believe in and to found his life upon must fulfill both kinds of need and pay both of them due attention. The tragedy is that history tells a different tale. History tells us that all societies and civilizations were oriented exclusively either to the hereafter and renunciation of this world, or to this world of dust. The civilization of China began by being oriented to this world, by giving primacy to pleasure and beauty and striving to enjoy the gifts of nature to the full, as the life of the Chinese aristocracy testifies. Then came Lao Tse, bringing a religion exclusively oriented to the hereafter, and emphasizing the spiritual and other-worldly dimension of man. Indeed, he led the Chinese so far in that direction, that a people who had lived purely for the sake of pleasure became monks, gnostics and mystics. He was succeeded by Confucius, who reoriented society toward this world and summoned the Chinese to the pleasures of worldly life, causing them to revert to their former preoccupations.

India, the land of rajas and legends, was oriented to the other world by the teachings of the Vedas and the Buddha, devoting itself to abstemiousness, monasticism and mysticism. It is for this reason that India is now famous for men sleeping on beds of nails, or subsisting for forty days on a single date or almond, for remaining behind the progress of civilization.

In Europe, ancient Rome devoted itself to murder and bloodshed, to establishing political mastery of the world, to accumulating all the wealth of Europe and Asia; it immersed itself in enjoyment and pleasure, in gladiator fights and the like. Then came Jesus, who directed society to concentrate on the hereafter, so that Rome changed its orientation from pleasure and worldliness to asceticism and contemplation of the hereafter, the ultimate result of this being the Middle Ages. The medieval world was one of war and bloodshed and military ascendance on the one hand; and one of monasteries, nunneries and retreats, on the other. Europe was delivered from this orientation only by the Renaissance, which caused the pendulum to swing in the other direction. Today we see that European civilization is so worldly in its orientation, and so exclusively defines the purpose of man's life as pleasure and enjoyment, that, as Professor Chandel has put it, the life of contemporary man consists only of making the tools of life. This is the idiocy of the contemporary philosophy of man, the result of a purpose-free technology. The whole meaning of civilization has been robbed of any ideal, and the world has gone so far in the direction of worldliness that it almost seems as if another Jesus were needed.

As is apparent from the philosophy of man in Islam, he is a two-dimensional being and needs, therefore, a religion which will also be two-dimensional and exert its force in the two different and opposing directions that exist in man's spirit and human society. Only then will man be able to maintain his equilibrium. The religion needed is Islam.

Why Islam?

In order to understand any religion, one must study its God, its Book, its Prophet, and the best individuals whom it has nurtured and raised.

First, the God of Islam is a two-dimensional God. He has the aspect of Yahwa, the god of the Jews, who interests himself in human society, in the affairs of this world, who is stern, severe in punishment, and tyrannical, and also the aspect of the god of Jesus, who is compassionate, merciful and forgiving. All of these divine attributes can be found in the Qur'an.

As for the book of Islam, the Qur'an, it is a book that like the Torah contains social, political and military provisions, even instructions for the conflict of warfare, the taking and setting free of prisoners; that is interested in life, in building, in prosperity, in struggling against enemies and negative elements; but it is also a book that concerns itself with the refinement of the soul, the piety of the spirit, and the ethical improvement of the individual.

The Prophet of Islam also possesses two contrasting aspects, aspects which would be contradictory in other men, but in him have been joined in a single spirit. For he was a man constantly engaged in political struggle against his enemies and the disruptive forces in society, concerned with building a new society and a new civilization in this world; and also a guide leading men to a particular goal; that is, also a man of prayer, piety and devotion.

And then three men trained by him—Ali, Abu Dharr and Salman—were supreme examples of two-dimensional men. They were both men of politics and battle, struggling for a better life and constantly present in circles of discussion and learning, and also men of piety and purity, not less than the great monks and mystics of the East. Abu Dharr was a man of politics and piety; the reflections of Abu Dharr concerning the nature of God can serve as a key to the understanding of the Qur'an. Look at all the Companions of the Prophet; they were all men of the sword, concerned with improving their society, men of justice, and at the same time, great men of thought and feeling.

The conclusion I wish to draw is this: in Islam man is not humbled before God, for he is the partner of God, His friend, the bearer of His trust upon earth. He enjoys affinity with God, has been instructed by Him, and seen all of God's angels fall prostrate before him. Two-dimensional man, bearing the burden of such responsibility, needs a religion that transcends exclusive orientation to this world or the next, and permits him to maintain a state of equilibrium. It is only such a religion that enables man to fulfill his great responsibility.

3.   Iranian Liberal Mehdi Bazargan Advocates Freedom as a Vital Necessity for Government and Religion, 1974

Mehdi Bazargan (1907–1995) was one of the leading liberal Islamic thinkers in Iran. Throughout his life, he attempted to achieve democracy within Iranian politics, as well as within the conservative Shi'a clerical establishment. While Shah Muhammad Reza Pahlavi was in power through the 1960s and 1970s, Bazargan maintained his opposition to that regime through organizations like the Iranian Human Rights Association, which he cofounded in 1977. After the 1979 revolution, Khomeini appointed Bazargan to the position of prime minister, only to work constantly against his policies. This led Bazargan to leave the government in frustration and to spend the twilight of his political life in opposition to the radical Islamic government and the attempts by the conservative clerics to maintain a stranglehold on power in Iran.

Freedom as a Vital Necessity for Government and Religion

Let me reiterate: freedom means freedom to oppose, criticize, and object—even if the criticism is untrue and unjust. Where there is freedom there are opponents and currents that disturb routine stability and normalcy. Otherwise, freedom would be meaningless and useless.

This notion of freedom is hard for many zealous—if sincere—people to digest, as they consider such a freedom unwise and deleterious to the survival of the nascent Islamic Republic [of Iran]. They may even consider it a blunder on their part to have allowed this notion of freedom to prevail in the constitution of the Islamic Republic of Iran.

Mehdi Bazargan, *Din va Azad: Bazyayi-ye arzesh'ha* (Religion and Liberty) (Tehran: Netzahe Azadi-ye Iran, 1983), pp. 59–88. This document, translated by Mohammad Sadri, can also be found in Charles Kurzman, *Liberal Islam* (New York: Oxford University Press, 1996), pp. 81–84. Reprinted by permission.

However, omniscient, compassionate God has not only sanctioned freedom in many affairs, he has made it the very foundation of survival and revival in the world. Let me elaborate on this point.

Opposition, the Cause of Movement and Life

In general, an object in a given force field will, of necessity, behave in a calculable and predictable way. For any object, whether a stone, a plant, or a human society, force means movement. For example, a piece of metal that is released within earth's gravitational field will fall in a straight line. Its position and velocity are calculable at every moment. Similarly, the behavior of a human being who is motivated only by the demands of his or her appetite is predictable. However, if in the place of one force, two or more forces are introduced—for example if a powerful magnet is placed in the path of the falling piece of metal—its trajectory and velocity will change. It will, to use a poetic expression, be freed from the slavery of a single cause of motion. The scenario is most intriguing when the affected object has the power to choose its level of susceptibility to the external influences. That is, when it has "free will." In this case, the person whose choice is not readily predicable and calculable for others—or even for oneself—could be said to possess "free will."

Therefore, freedom requires, as the case of Satan's temptations teach us, the existence of an oppositional force, along with a power of choice on behalf of the individual or the society. Opposition promulgates movement and change, which may, in turn, lead to decline or progress, depending on the choice of the agent involved.

Motion and change in the case of inanimate objects, even constructed objects such as machines, lead to erosion and deterioration (in the jargon of thermodynamic theory, the increase of entropy). In other words, inanimate objects aim at final rest and quiet. However, objects endowed with life, particularly human beings, thrive on movement and opposition. They acquire new capabilities and aptitudes and accumulate experience and virtue because of opposition and change. Movement, a result of need, agitation, and love, is a blessing and a source of survival and evolution, while rigidity is a cause of stasis, decline, and death. Animals and human beings, once they feel need, danger, or attraction, tend to move, willy-nilly, either toward the object of their desire or away from the source of danger. Therefore, without opposition, as a source of motivation or agitation there would be no progress.[1] The oppositional motivator can lead to reform and revival.[2]

---

[1] See my '*Eshq va parastesh, ya termodinamik-e ensan* [*Love and Worship, or the Thermodynamics of Humanity*].

[2] It is obvious that opposition in this context is an external force, different from materialist-dialectical opposition, involving an internal antithesis that is said to be inevitable, global, and social.

Our Islamic Revolution, our nationalist struggles, revivalist Islamic associations and movements, the earlier Constitutional Revolution of Iran—the awakening and activism of the Eastern countries in general after several hundred years of slumber and humiliation—were all the result of the encounter with Western civilization. The wondrous European Renaissance too was a result of conflicts, dissatisfactions, and objections to medieval Christian hegemony.

Similarly, the missions of the prophets were in the past the source of conflicts that revolutionized towns and tribes that were wallowing in the darkness of idolatry and the cesspool of corruption and inequity.

Conflict, one of whose quintessential representations for human beings is Satan, is the cause of a plethora of blessed events, from the natural cycle of life here on earth to the higher cycle of resurrection in the hereafter. The Qur'an frequently compares the colossal events of Judgment Day with seasonal rain and the revival of life on earth. Rain itself is the result of atmospheric disturbances and opposing forces of cold and warm weather systems. The science of meteorology has established, through hourly reports from weather stations, that rain-bearing continental weather fronts are comprised of successive fronts of dense clouds. These clouds are the result of expanding, rising, and condensing warm tropical weather and its collision with the cold and heavy weather systems that flow from the northern regions. The heavy winds occupy the lower areas and push the warm humid weather up.[3]

The Opponents of Freedom

The opponents of freedom resort to the adage: "A head that does not ache does not need to be wrapped." Their argument goes like this: We know we are on the true path. We believe in Islam and possess good will and proper judgment. What need is there for further inquiry and learning? We can simply devote ourselves, body and soul, to the realization of the true doctrine. The entire nation and its leadership support this endeavor, Why should we let the enemies of God and the republic, the supporters of America, or those who do not follow our line—in short, people of suspicious intent or judgment—to muddy the waters, confuse minds, disturb society, and weaken the government? Such freedom and criticism will provide fodder for foreign radio propaganda which will, in turn, cause our youth to hesitate or deviate from the straight path. It is thus better to remove all the impediments from the path of the revolution and to conduct our affairs quickly and effectively—that is, without the nagging distractions of free expression and opposition.

These gentlemen, even if they are sincere, are deluded and naive about their own monopoly of the truth and about the notion of freedom. Freedom is

---

[3]See [my] book *Bad va baran dar Qur'an* [*Wind and Rain in the Qur'an*] where many verses (more than 115 passages) are quoted that bear witness to this argument. [A series of citations follows.—Editor]

not a luxury; it is a necessity. When freedom is banished, tyranny will take its place.

In the first place, those whose belief system is based on reason and truth are not afraid of opponents' criticism and propaganda. In the words of Sa'di [Persian poet, 1184–1292], "He who has clear accounts, has no fear of accountants."

Secondly, freedom of expression, opposition, and criticism awakens the negligent and holds back treason, monopoly, and tyranny. If the objections are unjustified, let the accused respond and thus dispel the clouds of suspicion and slander. This will strengthen the national resolve. The Qur'an considers such examinations as the means of separating the good from the bad.[4] Conversely, suppression of freedom is an indication of a fundamental weakness or flaw in the government's intentions or actions. Consider the following Qur'anic debate: a believer in the pharaoh's family reasons with his affluent and powerful kin to listen to the message of Moses: "If he is a liar, his lie will be his own loss; but in case he speaks the truth, some of what he predicts will befall you." (Sura 40, Verse 28) In response, the pharaoh reiterates the argument of all dictators, tyrants, and zealots: "I show you only what I see (is right); and guide you but to the right path." [Sura 40, Verse 29] How can people exercise their religious obligation to call others to virtue and to warn them against vice in an Islamic society, without the freedom of conscience and expression, and in the absence of political and legal security? These are duties that Muslims are recommended to fulfill lest evil-doers dominate them and their prayers remain unanswered.

Thus the survival of a just system and its progress on the path of virtue and excellence is guaranteed by the freedom of expression and legal opposition. The protection of religion against abuse, ignorance, superstition, and deviance, too, requires that the mace of excommunication and compulsion be removed from society and the media. It is necessary to avoid painting a varnish of religiosity and godliness on human affairs, save that which necessarily and authentically belongs to religion. It is also necessary that some room is left for reflection and maneuver in all debates.

We have established, under the rubric of "Religion and Nation," that God addresses people themselves immediately and directly, without intermediaries. Everyone is directly responsible, and people's reason, knowledge, thought, perception, reflection, and will are the ultimate arbiter. We have the Qur'anic injunction, "If you do not know, then ask the keepers of (knowledge and) remembrance," (Sura 21, Verse 7) which indicates that it is proper to inquire, and to augment one's knowledge. In the meantime, the Qur'an has envisioned, without censure, the existence and expression of disagreements and differences of opinion among the faithful. It recommends the disagreements with the

---

[4]Sura 3, Verse [141]: "This is so that God may try the faithful and destroy the unbelievers." Sura 3, Verse [154]: "God had to try them to bring out what they concealed in their breasts, and to bring out the secrets of their hearts, for God knows your innermost thoughts."

rulers to be referred to the Prophet and to God; which in our days, would mean the body of religious knowledge.[5]

Disagreement becomes unacceptable and disruptive only when it takes place at the executive level and when the responsible managers, instead of harmony and disciplined cooperation, engage in discord and in-fighting, each playing their own tune and doing their own thing. The principle of division of powers and their mutual non-interference and orderly checks and balances pervades Iran's old and new constitutions, and those of other parliamentary democratic systems. People and their representatives have a right to discuss, investigate, supervise, and decide public affairs within certain limits and without interfering in the progress, rigor, and effective management of the executive affairs as determined by the legislature. And now let me address the questions that were posed earlier:

The First Question

Has Islam abandoned people to do whatever they please? Is there no responsibility and restraint in this world?

Being free and autonomous is one thing, and being responsible for one's beliefs and actions quite another. God has given us freedom of opinion and action within certain parameters, but He has given us plenty of warning through His messengers and holy books, that rebellion, disbelief, and injustice will have dire results that will follow from our actions both in this life and in the hereafter. The consequences may be heeded and avoided beforehand, or they may be understood only after they have materialized, as stated in Sura 30, Verse [41]: "Corruption has spread over land and sea from what men have done (and do) themselves that (God may let) them taste a little bit of what they have done: They may come back [to the right path]."

God bestows both freedom and guidance concerning the consequences of actions. His mercy is infinite and His vengeance great. Thus freedom exists; so do responsibility and restraint. The choice is ours.

The Second Question

Should the Islamic government and the religious scholars in the leadership not check crime and treason? Should chaos and license rule?

---

[5]The text of Sura 4, Verse [59], is as follows: "O you who believe, obey God, and obey the Prophet and those in authority among you; and if (mutual opposition occurs and) you are at variance over something, refer this (matter and disagreement) to God and the Messenger [...]" It is noteworthy that on five or six other occasions the faithful are told to obey God and the Prophet; only in this occasion is the phrase "those in authority" added, and that is qualified by the phrase "among you" (which could mean elected rulers). It is further stipulated that in case there appears a disagreement between the people and the rulers it should be referred to the other two authorities [God and the Prophet].

First, the issue of individual liberty in violation of others' rights has been addressed in the first question. Absolute freedom of choice, as we understand it in the Qur'an, prevails in the relationship of God and man—not in that of society and the individual, where mutual rights and responsibilities are at stake. God may forgive transgression against His laws but, as we know, God cannot forgive people for transgressing against the rights of people. We do not enjoy the same level of freedom in our dealings with other people as we do in our personal relationship with God.

Second, religious scholars, as religious scholars, have no rights or responsibilities save those delegated to them within the democratic system of the Islamic government.

Third, self-defense and the prevention of injustice and corruption in an Islamic society are not only warranted but required. The principle of "neither inflicting nor suffering harm" is paramount in Islam, both on the individual and the societal level. Since everyone is entitled to enjoy a measure of freedom and honor, the freedom of all is necessarily limited. Furthermore, being a beneficiary of social privileges creates mutual responsibilities that the Islamic government, derived from people's will, is duty-bound to supervise.

The details of this issue and the form of intervention of the state and participation of the people, which should be exercised with utmost justice and mercy, are a separate discussion that should be analyzed under the rubric of Islamic government.

4. Moroccan Feminist Fatima Mernissi Argues That Islam Has Been Misinterpreted on the Subject of the Position of Women, 1988

Fatima Mernissi, born in Morocco in 1940, is widely recognized—by supporters and detractors—as a leading Muslim feminist. Trained as a psychologist, she became famous because of her radio show, on which she dealt openly and critically with the position of women in Moroccan society. Later, she proceeded to critically analyze the sources of women's oppression in Arab and Islamic societies. While painting at times with a far too broad scholarly brush, she nonetheless presented one of the first systematic critiques of Islamic practices from within the religion. Other feminists, such as the Egyptian Nawal al-Saadawi, had come to the conclusion that religion is at the root of Arab patriarchy. Mernissi, in contrast, contended from the beginning that misunderstanding or misapplication of the true meaning and intent of Islam and its Prophet had led to the rise of patriarchy. Thus, she argued, there is no inherent conflict between Islam and modernity, but rather between modernity and conservative interpreters of the religion.

Fatima Mernissi, The Veil and the Male Elite: *A Feminist Interpretation of Women's Rights in Islam,* ed. Mary Jo Lakeland (Reading, Mass.: Perseus Books, 1991). This document may also be found in Charles Kurzman, *Liberal Islam* (New York: Oxford University Press, 1996), pp. 112–114, 119–121, 126. Reprinted by permission of Perseus Books Publishers, a member of Perseus Books, L.L.C.

"Can a woman be a leader of Muslims?" I asked my grocer, who, like most grocers in Morocco, is a true "barometer" of public opinion.

"I take refuge in God!" he exclaimed, shocked, despite the friendly relations between us. Aghast at the idea, he almost dropped the half-dozen eggs I had come to buy.

"May God protect us from the catastrophes of the times!" mumbled a customer who was buying olives, as he made as if to spit. My grocer is a fanatic about cleanliness, and not even denouncing a heresy justifies dirtying the floor in his view.

A second customer, a schoolteacher whom I vaguely knew from the newsstand, stood slowly caressing his wet mint leaves, and then hit me with a *hadith* [tradition of the Prophet] that he knew would be fatal: "Those who entrust their affairs to a woman will never know prosperity!" Silence fell on the scene. There was nothing I could say. In a Muslim theocracy, a *hadith* is no small matter. The *hadith* collections are works that record in minute detail what the Prophet said and did. They constitute, along with the Qur'an (the book revealed by God), both the source of law and the standard for distinguishing the true from the false, the permitted from the forbidden—they have shaped Muslim ethics and values.

I discreetly left the grocery store without another word. What could I have said to counterbalance the force of that political aphorism, which is as implacable as it is popular?

Silenced, defeated, and furious, I suddenly felt the urgent need to inform myself about this *hadith* and to search out the texts where it is mentioned, to understand better its extraordinary power over the ordinary citizens of a modern state.

A glance at the latest Moroccan election statistics supports the "prediction" uttered in the grocery store. Although the constitution gives women the right to vote and be elected, political reality grants them only the former. In the legislative elections of 1977, the eight women who stood for election found no favor with the six and a half million voters, of whom three million were women. At the opening of Parliament, there was not one woman present, and the men were settled among their male peers as usual, just as in the cafes. Six years later, in the municipal elections of 1983, 307 women were bold enough to stand as candidates, and almost three and a half million women voters went to the polls. Only 36 women won election, as against 65,502 men![1]

To interpret the relationship between the massive participation of women voters and the small number of women elected as a sign of stagnation and backwardness would be in accordance with the usual stereotypes applied to the Arab world. However, it would be more insightful to see it as a reflection of changing times and the intensity of the conflicts between the aspirations of women, who take the constitution of their country seriously, and the

---

[1]Morocco, Ministère de l'Artisanat et des Affaires Sociales, *Les Femmes marocaines dans le développement économique et social, décennie 1975–1985* [*Moroccan Women in Social and Economic Development, the Decade 1975–1985*].

resistance of men, who imagine, despite the laws in force, that power is necessarily male. This makes me want to shed light on those obscure zones of
resistance, those entrenched attitudes, in order to understand the symbolic—
even explosive—significance of that act which elsewhere in the world is an
ordinary event: a woman's vote. For this reason, my misadventure in a
neighborhood grocery store had more than symbolic importance for me. Revealing the misogynistic attitude of my neighbors, it indicated to me the path I
should follow to better understand it—a study of the religious texts that
everybody knows but no one really probes, with the exception of the authorities on the subject: the *mullas* [religious scholars] and *imams* [prayer leaders].

Going through the religious literature is no small task. First of all, one is
overwhelmed by the number of volumes, and one immediately understands
why the average Muslim can never know as much as an *imam*. [Muhammad ibn
Isma'il] Al-Bukhari's [810–870] prestigious collection of traditions, *Al-Sahih
(The Authentic)*, is in four volumes with an abstruse commentary by one
[Muhammad ibn 'Abd al-Hadi] al-Sindi [died 1726], who is extremely sparing
with his comments.[2] Now, without a very good commentary a non-expert will
have difficulty reading a religious text of the ninth century. . . . This is because,
for each *hadith,* it is necessary to check the identity of the Companion of the
Prophet who uttered it, and in what circumstances and with what objective in
mind, as well as the chain of people who passed it along—and there are more
fraudulent traditions than authentic ones. For each *hadith,* al-Bukhari gives the
results of his investigation. If he speaks of X or Y, you have to check which
Companion is being referred to, what battle is being discussed, in order to
make sense of the dialogue or scene that is being transcribed. In addition, al-
Bukhari doesn't use just one informant; there are dozens of them in the dozens
of volumes. You must be careful not to go astray. The smallest mistake about
the informant can cost you months of work.

What is the best way of making this check? First of all, you should make
contact with the experts in religious science (*faqihs*) in your city. According to
moral teaching and the traditional conventions, if you contact a *faqih* for information about the sources of a *hadith* or a Qur'anic verse, he must assist you.
Knowledge is to be shared, according to the promise of the Prophet himself.
Fath al-bari by [Ibn Hajar] al-'Asqalani (he died in year 852 of the *hejira*
[1372–1449 A.D.]) was recommended to me by several people I consulted. It
consists of 17 volumes that one can consult in libraries during their opening
hours. But the vastness of the task and the rather limited reading time is enough
to discourage most researchers.

The schoolteacher in the grocery store was right: the *hadith* "those who
entrust their affairs to a woman will never know prosperity" was there in al-
'Asqalani's 13th volume, where he quotes al-Bukhari's *Sahih,* that is, those

---

[2]Al-Bukhari. *Al-Sahih (Collection of Authentic Hadiths)*, with commentary by al-Sindi
(Beirut, Lebanon: Dar al-Ma'rifa, 1978). The *hadith* quoted by the schoolteacher is in volume 4, p. 226.

traditions that al-Bukhari classified as authentic after a rigorous process of selection, verifications, and counter-verifications.[3] Al-Bukhari's work has been
one of the most highly respected references for 12 centuries. This *hadith* is the
sledgehammer argument used by those who want to exclude women from politics. One also finds it in the work of other authorities known for their scholarly rigor, such as Ahmad ibn Hanbal [780–855], the author of the *Musnad* and
founder of the Hanbali school, one of the four great schools of jurisprudence
of the Sunni Muslim world.[4]

This *hadith* is so important that it is practically impossible to discuss the
question of women's political rights without referring to it, debating it, and
taking a position on it. . . .

According to al-Bukhari, it is supposed to have been Abu Bakra [died circa
671] who heard the Prophet say: "Those who entrust their affairs to a woman
will never know prosperity." Since this *hadith* is included in the *Sahih*—those
thousands of authentic *hadith* accepted by the meticulous al-Bukhari—it is a
priori considered true and therefore unassailable without proof to the contrary,
since we are here in scientific terrain. So nothing bars me, as a Muslim woman,
from making a double investigation—historical and methodological—of this
hadith and its author, and especially of the conditions in which it was first put
to use. Who uttered this *hadith*, where, when, why, and to whom?
[. . .]

If one follows the principles of Malik for *fiqh* [Islamic jurisprudence]. Abu
Bakra must be rejected as a source of *hadith* by every good, well-informed Malikite Muslim.

To close this investigation, let us take a brief look at the attitude of the religious scholars of the first centuries toward that misogynistic *hadith* that is
presented to us today as sacred, unassailable truth. Even though it was collected as *sahih* (authentic) by al-Bukhari and others, that *hadith* was hotly contested and debated by many. The scholars did not agree on the weight to give
that *hadith* on women and politics. Assuredly there were some who used it as
an argument for excluding women from decision making. But there were others who found that argument unfounded and unconvincing. Al-Tabari was one

---

[3]Ibn Hajar al-'Asqalani, *Huda al-sari, muqaddimat Fath al-bari* [*The Traveller's Guide, Introduction to "The Creator's Conquest"*], commonly known as *Fath al-bari* [*The Creator's
Conquest*]. It comprises al-Bukhari's text with a commentary by al-'Asqalani. The *hadith*
that concerns us here, on the necessity of excluding women from power, is found on p. 46
of volume 13 of the edition of Al-Matba'a al-Bahiya al-Misriya (1928) and on p. 166 of volume 16 of the edition of Maktaba Mustafa al-Babi al-Halabi fi Misr (1963). (Future page
references are to the 1928 edition.)
[4]The Muslim world is divided into two parts: the Sunnis (orthodox) and the Shi'ites (literally, schismatics). Each group has its own specific texts of *fiqh* (religious knowledge), especially as regards sources of the *shari'a* (legislation and laws). The Sunnis are split between
four *madhahib* (schools). . . . The differences between them most frequently relate to details of juridical procedures.

of those religious authorities who took a position against it, not finding it a sufficient basis for depriving women of their power of decision making and for justifying their exclusion from politics.[5]

After having tried to set straight the historical record—the line of transmitters and witnesses who gave their account of a troubled historical epoch—I can only advise redoubled vigilance when, taking the sacred as an argument, someone hurls at the believer as basic truth a political axiom so terrible and with such grave historical consequences as the one we have been investigating. Nevertheless, we will see that this "misogynistic" *hadith*, although it is exemplary, is not a unique case.

Throughout my childhood I had a very ambivalent relationship with the Qur'an. It was taught to us in a Qur'anic school in a particularly ferocious manner. But to my childish mind only the highly fanciful Islam of my illiterate grandmother, Lalla Yasmina, opened the door for me to a poetic religion.... This dual attitude that I had toward the sacred text was going to remain with me. Depending on how it is used, the sacred text can be a threshold for escape or an insurmountable barrier. It can be that rare music that leads to dreaming or simply a dispiriting routine. It all depends on the person who invokes it. However, for me, the older I grew, the fainter the music became. In secondary school the history of religion course was studded with traditions. Many of them from appropriate pages of al-Bukhari, which the teacher recited to us, made me feel extremely ill at ease: "The Prophet said that the dog, the ass, and woman interrupt prayer if they pass in front of the believer, interposing themselves between him and the *qibla* [the direction of Mecca]."[6]...

By lumping [woman] in with two familiar animals, the author of the *hadith* inevitably makes her a being who belongs to the animal kingdom. It is enough for a woman to appear in the field of vision for contact with the *qibla*—that is, the divine—to be disturbed. Like the dog and the ass, she destroys the symbolic relation with the divine by her presence. One has to interrupt one's prayer and begin again.

Arab civilization being a civilization of the written word, the only point of view we have on this question is that of Abu Hurayra [died 678]. According to [Shams al-Din] Ibn Marzuq [1311–1379], when someone invoked in front of 'A'isha the *hadith* that said that the three causes of interruption of prayer were dogs, asses, and women, she answered them: "You compare us now to asses and dogs. In the name of God, I have seen the Prophet saying his prayers while I was there, lying on the bed between him and the *qibla*. And in order not to disturb him, I didn't move."[7] The believers used to come to 'A'isha for verification of what they had heard, confident of her judgment, not only because of her closeness to the Prophet, but because of her own abilities:

---

[5]'Asqalani, *Fath al-bari*, volume 13, p. 47.
[6]Bukhari, *Sahih*, volume 1, p. 99.
[7]Bukhari, *Sahih*, volume 1, p. 199.

I have seen groups of the most eminent companions of the Prophet ask her questions concerning the *fara'id* [the daily duties of the Muslim, the rituals, etc.], and Ibn 'Ata' said: "'A'isha was, among all the people, the one who had the most knowledge of *fiqh,* the one who was the most educated and, compared to those who surrounded her, the one whose judgment was the best."[8]

Despite her words of caution, the influence of Abu Hurayra has nevertheless infiltrated the most prestigious religious texts, among them the *Sahih* of al-Bukhari, who apparently did not always feel obliged to insert the corrections provided by 'A'isha. The subject of many of these *hadith* is the "polluting" essence of femaleness.

To understand the importance for Islam of that aspect of femaleness, evoking disturbance and sullying, we would do well to look at the personality of Abu Hurayra, who, as it were, gave it legal force. Without wanting to play the role of psychoanalytical detective, I can say that the fate of Abu Hurayra and his ambivalence toward women are wrapped up in the story of his name. Abu Hurayra, meaning literally "Father of the Little Female Cat," had previously been called "Servant of the Sun" ('Abd al-Shams).[9] The Prophet decided to change that name, which had a very strong sense of idolatry about it. "Servant of the Sun" was originally from Yemen, that part of Arabia where not only the sun, a female star in Arabic, was worshipped, but where women also ruled in public and private life. Yemen was the land of the Queen of Sheba, Bilqis [tenth century B.C.], that queen who fascinated King Solomon [reigned 962–922 B.C.], who ruled over a happy kingdom, and who put her mark on Arab memory, since she appears in the Qur'an:

> [Hud-hud] said: "I have found (a thing) that thou apprehendest not, and I come unto thee from Sheba with sure tidings."
>
> Lo! I found a woman ruling over them, and she hath been given (abundance) of all things, and hers is a mighty throne.
>
> I found her and her people worshipping the sun instead of God. . . . (Sura 27, Verses 22–24)

Abu Hurayra came from the Yemeni tribe of the Daws.[10] At the age of 30 the man named "Servant of the Sun" was converted to Islam. The Prophet gave him the name 'Abdallah (Servant of God) and nicknamed him Abu Hurayra (Father of the Little Female Cat) because he used to walk around with a little

---

[8]Ibn Hajar al-'Asqalani, *Al-Isaba fi tamyiz al-sahaba* [*A Biographical Dictionary of the Companions of the Prophet*] (Cairo: Maktaba al-Dirasa al-Islamiya Dar al-Nahda, no date), volume 8, p. 18.

[9]'Asqalani, *Al-Isaba,* volume 7, p. 427.

[10]'Abd al-Mun'im Salih al-'Ali al-'Uzzi, *Difa' 'an Abi Hurayra* [*In Defense of Abu Hurayra*], second edition (Beirut, Lebanon: Dar al-Qalam; Baghdad: Maktaba al-Nahda, 1981), p. 13.

female cat that he adored.[11] But Abu Hurayra was not happy with this nick-
name, for he did not like the trace of femininity in it: "Abu Hurayra said:
'Don't call me Abu Hurayra. The Prophet nicknamed me Abu Hirr [Father of
the Male Cat], and the male is better than the female.'"[12] He had another reason to feel sensitive about this subject of femininity—he did not have a very
masculine job. In a Medina that was in a state of full-blown economic development, where the Medinese, especially the Jews, made an art of agriculture, and
the immigrant Meccans continued their commercial activities and managed to
combine them with military expeditions, Abu Hurayra preferred, according to
his own comments, to be in the company of the Prophet. He served him and
sometimes "helped out in the women's apartments."[13] This fact might clear up
the mystery about his hatred of women, and also of female cats, the two seeming to be strangely linked in his mind.

He had such a fixation about female cats and women that he recalled that
the Prophet had pronounced a *hadith* concerning the two creatures—and in
which the female cat comes off much better than the woman. But 'A'isha contradicted him, a Companion recounted:

> We were with 'A'isha, and Abu Hurayra was with us. 'A'isha said to
> him: "Father of the Little Cat, is it you who said that you heard the
> Prophet declare that a woman went to hell because she starved a little
> female cat and didn't give it anything to drink?"
>
> "I did hear the Prophet say that," responded Father of the Lit-
> tle Cat.
>
> "A believer is too valuable in the eyes of God," retorted 'A'isha,
> "for Him to torture that person because of a cat. . . . Father of the Lit-
> tle Cat, the next time you undertake to repeat the words of the
> Prophet, watch out what you recount."[14]

It is not surprising that Abu Hurayra attacked 'A'isha in return for that.
She might be "The Mother of the Believers" and "The Lover of the Lover of
God," but she contradicted him too often. One day he lost patience and defended himself against an attack by 'A'isha. When she said to him, "Abu Hurayra, you relate *hadith* that you never heard," he replied sharply, "O Mother,
all I did was collect *hadith*, while you were too busy with make-up and your
mirror."[15]

[...]

---

[11]'Asqalani, *Al-Isaba*, volume 7, p. 426.
[12]'Asqalani, *Al-Isaba*, volume 7, p. 434.
[13]'Asqalani, *Al-Isaba*, volume 7, p. 441.
[14]Imam [Muhammad ibn Bahadur al-] Zarkashi [circa 1344–1392]. *Al-Ijaha li-irad ma is-
tadrakathu 'A'isha 'ala alsahaba* [*Collection of 'A'isha's Corrections to the Statements of the
Companions*], second edition (Beirut, Lebanon: Al-Maktab al-Islami, 1980), p. 118.
[15]'Asqalani, *Al-Isaba*, volume 7, p. 440.

With this anecdote we come back to our point of departure, the relationship of "Father of the Little Female Cat" to femaleness and to the very mysterious and dangerous link between the sacred and women. All the monotheistic religions are shot through by the conflict between the divine and the feminine, but none more so than Islam, which has opted for the occultation of the feminine, at least symbolically, by trying to veil it, to hide it, to mask it. Islam as sexual practice unfolds with a very special theatricality since it is acted out in a scene where the *hijab* [veil] occupies a central position. This almost phobic attitude toward women is all the more surprising since we have seen that the Prophet has encouraged his adherents to renounce it as representative of the *jahiliya* and its superstitions. This leads me to ask: Is it possible that Islam's message had only a limited and superficial effect on deeply superstitious seventh-century Arabs who failed to integrate its novel approaches to the world and to women? Is it possible that the *hijab,* the attempt to veil women, that is claimed today to be basic to Muslim identity, is nothing but the expression of the persistence of the preIslamic mentality, the *jahiliya* mentality that Islam was supposed to annihilate?

5.   Egyptian Editorialist Farag Foda Critiques Islamic Movements in Egypt, 1989 and 1992

The documents in this chapter deal mainly with Islamic political movements. It is also important to note at least one example of secular criticism of such movements and their aims. Reprinted here are two essays by Farag Foda, (1947–1992), an Egyptian commentator who was assassinated by a group of extremist Islamists— al-Jihad—for his "attacks on Islam." His assassination—along with attacks on other secularists in Egypt—was meant to silence criticism of the religious right in Egypt and to limit public debate about "Islamic values" to parameters narrowly defined by the most reactionary Islamists.

1. God Forbid!

God forbid that anyone should think I would defend Egypt's Copts! Dividing Egyptians into Muslims and Copts is detestable to me. To me, Egyptians are just Egyptians and they will continue to be Egyptians until God inherits this earth and everything on it. And yet there are these aberrations in history when history deviates from its proper course here and there, but it soon comes back to its proper course because ultimately it is only what is proper that holds true.

Farag Foda, *Before the Fall,* trans. Legal Research and Resource Center for Human Rights (Cairo: Legal Research and Resource Center for Human Rights, 1992). http://www.geocities.com/lrrc.geo/Foda/fodacopt.htm (10 January 2003). Reprinted by permission.

When I speak in defense of something, I speak in defense of Egypt. I will not condone injustice for any Egyptian. I refuse to accept the proposition that one citizen has the right to testify because he is an Egyptian Muslim and another be denied that right because he is not a Muslim. (This is what Mr. Al Hamzah Di'bis stated in *Al-Nour* newspaper, citing the testimony of Mr. Ibrahim Faraj in his book about Mustafa al-Nahhas.) I also refuse to have the right to govern, to legislate, to serve in the courts or to defend the country given to one group of Egyptians and denied to another. Let me repeat: this is a country; it does not belong to one group and not another. Now that we are on the verge of the 21st century, I cannot accept the notion that someone would call upon a group of Egyptians to refrain from taking the initiative to greet another group of Egyptians. I cannot accept the notion that someone would call upon one group of Egyptians to harass the other group if they should meet. I cannot accept such an admonition on the grounds that it is based on a prophetic tradition when the authenticity of that tradition is doubtful and its lines of attribution are weaker than the threads of a spider web. I cannot accept the claim that the October War was a religious war between Muslims and Jews. The only thing I will accept is that it was a war between Egyptians and Israelis. It was in that war that the blood of Muslim Egyptians was mixed with the blood of Coptic Egyptians. The only reason both Muslims and Copts were fighting was to defend Egypt. Muslim Egyptians lost their lives, and their families laid them to rest as martyrs; and Coptic Egyptians lost their lives, and their Coptic families laid them to rest as martyrs too.

It is a most splendid thing when the two religions unite to acknowledge the ultimate sacrifice of those who were defending our dear country. But what we have here is a sickness of the heart; what we have is narrow-mindedness and stupidity that could lead the entire country to ruin. Is there anything more ruinous than for fellow countrymen to become divided because they resent each other? Is there anything more ruinous than for countrymen to become involved in civil strife, as some of them see themselves as oppressed while some see others as oppressors? And yet if one were to look at matters closely, and examine the situation with scrutiny, one would find that nothing in this situation has to do with religion or faith. Instead, one would find that this is a matter of politics. It is a rugged and difficult course built by politicians who do not care at all about the country's future as long as they can get one vote here or there. It is a rugged course built by political clergymen who do nothing but proclaim slogans and do not concern themselves with setting forth programs or particulars; the only thing they care about is toying with people's emotions in the absence of the voice of reason.

Ye who cry and moan for Islam: cry and moan no more! Islam is alive and well. The only danger to Islam comes from you when you compel the young and inexperienced to drop out of the university because its modern sciences are secular. The danger to Islam comes from your efforts to fill young people's heads with superstition, the least of which is that thunder is the fart of a great devil! You tell them that women lead us into evil and that all society is ignorant and foolish. And God only knows that you are the most ignorant and most foolish among all Muslims. Islam has been and will always be the religion of knowledge and reason. It would be better for Islam and for Muslims if people were to study biology, physics, and chemistry and spend no time studying what religion has to say [about] [. . .] someone who frees a slave who has money, or [. . .] of someone who sets an illegitimate child free. It would be better if people were to study the modern sciences rather than the case of someone who has been dyed yellow, or the matter of women wearing capes. It would be better for Islam and Muslims if young people were to study the sciences rather than interdictions against stirring up unrest in Ethiopia [or treatises about] putting out fires at night, cauterization, snuff, magical incantations, antidotes and leeches.

The fact that members of al-Jihad organization find no other way to raise funds for their organization but rob jewelry stores owned by Copts, killing the owners and seizing their property, has nothing to do with Islam. I do not want to go on at length in this vein so as not to inflame a healing wound. But this was the independent opinion issued by someone who deserves to have us scream in his face and exclaim: What Islam is this? Islam has never been a religion of terrorism. There was nothing Islamic about killing a citizen who was sitting peacefully in his store. There was nothing Islamic about killing a man and depriving his children of their father; there is nothing Islamic about destroying homes for no other reason than that those people subscribe to a religion different from your own. Homes were destroyed and an Egyptian citizen lost his life because the leader of a religious group made an erroneous independent judgment and a mistake.

Someone like me has to be saddened and distressed when he reads this strange statement by Dr. Ahmed Umar Hashim [published in *al-Liwa al-Islami* newspaper issue no. 153]: "Islam does not prohibit Muslims from doing business with non-Muslims, but it prohibits them from having close friendships with non-Muslims because close friendships can exist only between Muslims." No sir, not at all: close friendships can exist between Egyptians whether they are Muslims or Copts. It makes no difference. To say otherwise is to create disunity and division among Egyptians.

Someone like me has to be saddened and distressed when it is proclaimed that an Indian Muslim would be closer to an Egyptian Muslim than an Egyptian Copt. That is not true at all, and it will never be true. Egyptians, I mean all Egyptians, are distinguished by the love they have for their country and the loyalty they feel for their land. To say otherwise is to have an ulterior motive, a sickness in the heart, evil intentions, a grim view, and no patriotism. To say otherwise is a major offense against the country.

God only knows who is behind this vicious attack which is creating disunity among the ranks, dividing groups, frustrating our people and breaking up our solidarity.

2. Egyptian Laws, Women, and Religion

Today's speech revolves around three main issues: first, the Egyptian legislation between religious and civil laws, and second, a discussion on the *hijab*, and third, what I would call the "*fikh* of vexing."

The first issue is obviously broad and requires more than one lecture, but I shall try and be brief in presenting a case study. In today's editorial of the newspaper entitled *Al Gareeda,* an Islamic newspaper published by the Ahrar Party, there was a paragraph saying that Dr. Rifaat al-Mahgoub [then speaker of parliament] insists on ignoring Islamic Shari'a laws without showing them to the People's Assembly which would then approve them to replace local laws that permit adultery and other sins. In truth, this paragraph gives us the "case study" that we want to address today. Please note that as long as "they" lift their hands to us with a closed Book, the issue becomes complex and difficult. If we open the Book, they will find themselves in a difficult and complicated position. The problem is that in all of Egypt, no one has the courage to discuss the position of saying "No," because Islamists have succeeded in portraying those who discuss issues as apostates, and that anyone who opposes them is an atheist. People fear for no reason. I will speak today, because time is limited, about the *hodood* of adultery in Islamic Shari'a when compared to local laws. We would like to ask ourselves: is it true that local laws, meaning the ones made by people for the benefit of people, allow adultery and promiscuity? I would like to point out one fact before I proceed, and that is that if the *hodood* [sins] of adultery are applied as they exist in the *fikh* [theology] books, all vice crimes over the past 25 years will receive a "not guilty" verdict without exception. Every officer in the vice police squad should also be lashed 80 times in each of those cases, because the case is not legally valid according to Shari'a.

Second, if the proposed adultery laws are passed in the people's assembly, all rape crimes will receive a "not guilty" verdict, and those who catch the rapist will have to receive 80 lashes as well. Third, there is no shame in religion, as the saying goes, and according to religious law, there should be four witnesses who have seen the "incident" and who have seen the male organ inside the female pelvis. This would have been possible a long time ago, when there were tents that hovered with the breeze, and when people were able to see such an event happening. Today, there are houses, the doors are locked and the windows are shut. Today, four witnesses have no means of witnessing anything except through two means: one is peeping through the hole of the door, and then the second comes in and peeks, and then the third and then the fourth person, and this is, according to the *fikh* another crime. Another solution would be for him to sit with them and watch. This obviously means he is a pimp, and is yet another crime!

Excerpts from a speech given by Farag Foda on October 21, 1989, at the Arab Women Solidarity Association. Trans. Legal Research and Resource Center, http://www.geocities.com/lrrc.geo/Foda/foda.htm (10 January 2003). Reprinted by permission.

There is another point in the issue of adultery. Say a man is working in Libya, and has been there for three or two years, and his wife suddenly sends him a letter saying that she is pregnant. This is of course a classic case of adultery. But no no. Ibn Hanbal [one of the schools of thought] [said] that there is a theory of "stagnant pregnancy," where a sperm could remain in a mother's womb for three years. Medicine says this is impossible, but it is not important, because Ibn Hanbal said three years, and the woman is scot free, because her husband most probably has divine powers! This is all about the laws ignored by the People's Assembly with which Islamists claim they want to save society from the adultery that is rampant on the streets. Listen to the following cases that the proposed laws discuss (incidentally there is no stoning in Islam because the Qur'an only specified 100 lashes for adulterers, and the verse that discussed stoning preceded the verse that discussed lashing):

- What is not on the agenda of the proposed laws are kisses, hugs and harassment of women, and those are not part of the articles specifying adultery. That means that kisses in films do not fall into the boundaries of adultery. So kisses on the streets and in cinemas do not count.
- What Westerners call "Oral sex" is not in the realm of adultery either because the male organ was not in the female.
- Perverse relations between men and women also do not fall under this category, because the male organ "missed" the female's by an inch!
- A man and woman spending time in a closed place, regardless of the sounds they make, does not constitute adultery. So if they stayed three days in a furnished flat or in an hotel, it is still not adultery.
- If a man caught his wife with her lover committing adultery, this cannot be established proof, although the man is with her in bed. The story comes from a *hadith* where a man called Saad bin Adab went to the Prophet and asked him: does this mean if I find a man in bed with my wife I should go and get four witnesses? And the Prophet answered yes, so he left him in anger. This is when the verses came to the Prophet saying that in such a case a man should repeat four times as a witness that he had seen his wife, and she is brought and asked to testify also.
- Also, this brings us to the issue of marriage of pleasure, where a man and woman may marry for a certain period of time for pleasure, even for an hour, and then divorce immediately.

According to the proposed Islamic law, therefore, if people are caught committing adultery, they bring forth four witnesses to say they are married for pleasure, and there is no legal punishment for this.

It should also be remembered that when God gives an order with limitations and boundaries, he gives first certain licenses in His mercy and then if people still persist in sinning, he punishes them fiercely. Some people claim that they want us to go back to the first century after *higra* when life was pure and loyal and beautiful and good. Fine, but in that time, when the boundaries of adultery were specified, there were licenses with unlimited slaves and several wives, after which there could be a severe punishment if the man still committed adultery. You want to apply the boundaries of adultery, no, first you must open a slave market on the Pyramids street, in Al-Ataba and in Roxi, and one near Al Higaz St. Isn't that the logic behind it? One should marry one or two or three and even four women. What prevents people today from doing that is the economic crisis where one could hardly manage to marry and support even one woman, so if those people are serious about applying the Shari'a, let them first solve our problems and give us this license, and give us financial support to marry the second and the third, and unlimited finances to he who marries a fourth. There would then be four wives and unlimited slaves in Al Higaz St., so why should anyone want to commit adultery? Before talking to us about limits and boundaries, give us licenses.

By this talk I only mean one thing: as long as words are just being said without thinking, it frightens some people who will say let us just stone the offenders. But people who have real faith will think oh God, stoning people in public is a crime! They hide things in their stories and if you discuss it with them, they themselves will withdraw from it and you will discover how ignorant they were.

This is a message for those who avoid constructive discussions and those who control our media. They believe one should run away instead of confronting these issues. Although you have the answers, you will only be attempting to close a dirty wound, for it is bound to open later and the issue will never be finished. Compare this with fourth-century laws, where such laws now punish rapists with hanging! Local laws prove adultery by the mere presence in a room together or any "likelihood" of adultery. A journalist walking by the river Nile saw two people kissing and was very upset that the Shari'a is not applied in this country. We tell him all right, please apply it, and he will find that they shall not be guilty of anything.

I merely want to show here that we, the supporters of civil law, want only the benefit of our society, where human beings make their own laws and then may change them as time goes by. We reject anyone who tells us he has been inspired by God to monitor our society and its people.

Second: the issue of the *hijab*.

The truth is that I have always viewed the issue of the *hijab* as one of personal choice, where one may choose the *hijab*, the *nikab*, or at the other end of the spectrum, shorts. These are all choices that are truly private. I have always known, according to my humble knowledge, that what was mentioned in the Qur'an concerning the *hijab* was something general, and does not mention *hijab* in particular, but mentions being appropriately covered. According to my knowledge also, what discussed the particulars of the *hijab* was the *sunna*. But they start getting more and more extremist, and they tell us for instance that a woman must not even show except one eye, which is the left eye! This makes me wonder, why did God really create women's right eyes? Is it to see darkness or dreams? This is truly funny. Why didn't He create them with one eye only to avoid the earthquakes and volcanoes they create when we see both their eyes?

I have always asked myself and continue to do so to this very day: is there something wrong perhaps with my manhood? I see women all the time whose hairs are loose and who are smiling, but they do not excite in me any bad feelings. Rather, I have every respect for them. They do not make me have sexual urges or wet dreams, but make me think. I have never felt there was a devil standing there between us, but that between us there was all respectfulness and dignity and appreciation. The problem is therefore not me, and I think I am all right. It is quite the contrary: the problem is in them. It is their excessive "manhood," and we therefore advise them to take some tranquilizers or see some doctor to suppress their urges. Perhaps they should fast.

They attack women hostesses on television. Listen to this paragraph in one of their newspapers about one such hostess: "Her eyes! Oh her eyes! It explodes with pleasure. And her lips, oh her lips!"

I obviously thought when I read it, "well this man is truly sick!" The *Al Nour* newspaper made an investigative report on girls from the Girl's College. Note that this is a segregated college, and yet listen to this: a girl said that the problem is that they have to change their clothes sometimes in front of other girls, and of course among those girls are Christian girls, and the latter obviously see them, especially the ones wearing the *hijab*. This, to them, is a problem, and this is based on Ibn Katheer's interpretations where he said that Muslim women should not undress before non-Muslim women because the latter will go and describe them to their husbands! This reminds me of those who claim that in an Islamic fundamentalist state there will be paradise of freedom of belief!!

The third point I shall discuss is what I call the *fikh* of "vexation." This basically means that some people simply seek to vex us every time they see us happy. For instance, there was this song by Abdel Wahab [a famous singer] called "Don't ask why?" where he said "we do not know why we are born nor where we are going." But then this was considered heresy of course. We don't know why we were born? Why, to praise Him, why else? The singer was therefore considered an apostate and heretic and was asked to repent. Do they have anything personal against Abdel Wahab? No. They merely want to vex us because we were pleased with the song and because we enjoyed it.

Or for instance, as we all know that there is an epidemic of kidney problems, and some people need kidney transplants. But ah, they tell us that transplants are *haram* and that the patient should be left to die. Who cares? As you realize, news of the one-eyed *hijab* and news of kidney transplants might bring a heart attack to any sane person. This means going into intensive care. But one famous sheikh comes along and tells us that this will hinder God's will. Let the guy go and meet his Creator. That is to say, my father today gets a heart attack and people come from the hospital for him, but I don't allow them because our Lordship said we must leave him to meet his God. Why don't I throw him out the window then to meet his God even faster? My goodness, this is crazy.

Or for instance about AIDS patients who got it from blood transfusion. . . . Instead of being compassionate and trying to help them, a *fatwa* says we should kill them! Of course this *fatwa* was broadcast throughout the world and Muslims looked like barbarian monsters, and our scandal became a "scandal international."

Today, in the absence of real enlightened thinkers, they have succeeded in calling for the Islamic state, claiming that Islam is "state and religion." But let us see who said that: it is none other than Hassan al Banna and his followers. Today, we are governed by the law and the constitution, and they want us governed by Islam. But let us ask them, which Islam are they talking about? And which interpretation of it?

6.   Islamic Fundamentalist Usama Bin Laden Calls on Muslims to Take Up Arms Against America, 1998

Usama Bin Laden became a household name in the United States after the terrorist attack of September 11, 2001. As a young man who came from a very privileged background in Saudi Arabia—his family owned a multi-million-dollar construction company—he seemed an unlikely candidate to lead an organization—al-Qa'eda—that visited horror on the United States. However, he had been involved in a struggle to oust the Soviet Union from Afghanistan in the 1980s. He, as well as thousands of Arab Muslims who volunteered for that war, helped to defeat the Soviet army—with a great deal of help from the United States, Pakistan, and Saudi Arabia. That victory—couched in terms of a "holy war"—as well as the Iranian revolution of 1979 convinced Bin Laden and other Islamic fundamentalists that they could and should attempt a similar task in the remainder of the Islamic world. Their aim was to re-create an Islamic state that would unite the Islamic world and replace secular or quasi-Islamic governments. The fact that the majority of Muslims did not agree with their vision and certainly not with their violent tactics was not a consideration.

Intellectually isolated and xenophobic, these mujahideen *(Muslim guerrillas fighting a jihad) convinced themselves that they were fighting for Allah. Throughout the 1990s they failed to achieve their goals because many of the authoritarian governments in the Middle East and North Africa succeeded in crushing the various attempts of these activists and in exiling a majority of them. These extremists then contended that the United States was responsible for their failure because it supported un-Islamic regimes in the region. Many Arabs had grown frustrated with American foreign policy in the region during the 1990s, so it was a natural step for Bin Laden to argue that he was fighting against "America" because of its "iniquity" toward Arabs. He hoped that this transparent excuse—one that he did not care about before 1998—would ignite the frustration of the Arab world into a massive revolution in his support. The two documents presented here are an "interview" by some of his followers and an announcement of the creation of a new World Islamic Front. They reveal the worldview of Usama Bin Laden and his organization.*

"Interview with Usama Bin Laden by His Followers," *Nida'ul Islam* 15 (October–November 1996). Translated by Akram Khater.

1. Interview with Usama Bin Laden by His Followers, 1998

- What is the meaning of your call for Muslims to take up arms against America in particular, and what is the message that you wish to send to the West in general?

The call to wage war against America was made because America has spearheaded the crusade against the Islamic nation, sending tens of thousands of its troops to the land of the two Holy Mosques, over and above its meddling in its affairs and its politics and its support of the oppressive, corrupt, and tyrannical regime that is in control. These are the reasons behind the singling out of America as a target. And not exempt from responsibility are those Western regimes whose presence in the region offers support to the American troops there. We know at least one reason behind the symbolic participation of the Western forces and that is to support the Jewish and Zionist plans for expansion of what is called the Great Israel. Surely, their presence is not out of concern over their interests in the region. [. . .] Their presence has no meaning save one and that is to offer support to the Jews in Palestine who are in need of their Christian brothers to achieve full control over the Arab Peninsula, which they intend to make an important part of the so called Greater Israel. [. . .]

- Many of the Arabic as well as the Western mass media accuse you of terrorism and of supporting terrorism. What do you have to say to that?

There is an Arabic proverb that says "She accused me of having her malady, then snuck away." Besides, terrorism can be commendable and it can be reprehensible. Terrifying an innocent person and terrorizing him is objectionable and unjust, also unjustly terrorizing people is not right.

Whereas, terrorizing oppressors and criminals and thieves and robbers is necessary for the safety of people and for the protection of their property. There is no doubt in this. Every state and every civilization and culture has to resort to terrorism under certain circumstances for the purpose of abolishing tyranny and corruption. Every country in the world has its own security system and its own security forces, its own police, and its own army. They are all designed to terrorize whoever even contemplates an attack on that country or its citizens. The terrorism we practice is of the commendable kind, for it is directed at the tyrants and the aggressors and the enemies of Allah, the tyrants, the traitors who commit acts of treason against their own countries and their own faith and their own prophet and their own nation. Terrorizing those and punishing them are necessary measures to straighten things and to make them right. Tyrants and oppressors who subject the Arab nation to aggression ought to be punished. The wrongs and the crimes committed against the Muslim nation are far greater than can be covered by this interview. America heads the list of aggressors against Muslims. The recurrence of aggression against Muslims everywhere is proof enough. For over half a century, Muslims in Palestine have been slaughtered and assaulted and robbed of their honor and of their property. Their houses have been blasted, their crops destroyed. And the strange thing is that any act by them to avenge themselves or to lift the injustice befalling them causes great agitation in the United Nations, which hastens to call for an emergency meeting only to convict the victim and to censure the wronged and the tyrannized whose children have been killed and whose crops have been destroyed and whose farms have been pulverized. [...]

In today's wars, there are no morals, and it is clear that mankind has descended to the lowest degrees of decadence and oppression. They rip us of our wealth and of our resources and of our oil. Our religion is under attack. They kill and murder our brothers. They compromise our honor and our dignity and if we dare to utter a single word of protest against the injustice, we are called terrorists. This is compounded injustice. And the United Nations insistence to convict the victims and support the aggressors constitutes a serious precedent that shows the extent of injustice that has been allowed to take root in this land. [...]

- What is your relationship with the Islamic movements in various regions of the world, such as Chechnya and Kashmir and other Arab countries?

Cooperation for the sake of truth and righteousness is demanded from Muslims. A Muslim should do his utmost to cooperate with his fellow Muslims. But Allah says of cooperation that it is not absolute, for there is cooperation to do good, and there is cooperation to commit aggression and act unjustly. A Muslim is supposed to give his fellow Muslim guidance and support. He [Allah] said "Stand by your brother be he oppressor or oppressed." When asked how were they to stand by him if he were the oppressor, he answered them, saying, "by giving him guidance and counsel." It all goes to say that Muslims should cooperate with one another and should be supportive of one another, and they should promote righteousness and mercy. They should all unite in the fight against polytheism, and they should pool all their resources and their energy to fight the Americans and the Zionists and those with them. They should, however, avoid side issues and rise over the small problems, for these are less detrimental. Their fight should be directed against unbelief and unbelievers. [...]

- We heard your message to the American government and later your message to the European governments who participated in the occupation of the Gulf. Is it possible for you to address the people of these countries?

As we have already said, our call is the call of Islam that was revealed to Muhammad. It is a call to all mankind. We have been entrusted with good cause to follow in the footsteps of the Messenger and to communicate his message to all nations. It is an invitation that we extend to all the nations to embrace Islam, the religion that calls for justice, mercy, and fraternity among all nations, not differentiating between black and white or between red and yellow except with respect to their devotedness. All people who worship Allah, not each other, are equal before him. We are entrusted to spread this message and to extend that call to all the people. We nonetheless fight against their governments and all those who approve of the injustice they practice against us. We fight the governments that are bent on attacking our religion and on stealing our wealth and on hurting our feelings. And as I have mentioned before, we fight them, and those who are part of their rule are judged in the same manner. [. . .]

- In your last statement, there was a strong message to the American government in particular. What message do you have for the European governments and the West in general?

Praise be to Allah and prayers and peace upon Muhammad. With respect to the Western governments that participated in the attack on the land of the two Holy Mosques regarding it as ownerless, and in the siege against the Muslim people of Iraq, we have nothing new to add to the previous message. What prompted us to address the American government in particular is the fact that it is on the head of the Western and the crusading forces in their fight against Islam and against Muslims. The two explosions that took place in Riyadh and in Khobar recently were but a clear and powerful signal to the governments of the countries that willingly participated in the aggression against our countries and our lives and our sacrosanct symbols. It might be beneficial to mention that some of those countries have begun to move toward independence from the American government with respect to the enmity that it continues to show toward the Muslim people. We only hope that they will continue to move in that direction, away from the oppressive forces that are fighting against our countries. We, however, differentiate between the Western government and the people of the West. If the people have elected those governments in the latest elections, it is because they have fallen prey to the Western media, which portray things contrary to what they really are. And while the slogans raised by those regimes call for humanity, justice, and peace, the behavior of their governments is completely the opposite. It is not enough for their people to show pain when they see our children being killed in Israeli raids launched by American planes, nor does this serve the purpose. What they ought to do is change their governments that attack our countries. The hostility that America continues to express against the Muslim people has given rise to feelings of animosity on the part of Muslims against America and against the West in general. Those feelings of animosity have produced a change in the behavior of some crushed and subdued groups, who, instead of fighting the Americans inside the Muslim countries, went on to fight them inside the United States of America itself

The Western regimes and the government of the United States of America bear the blame for what might happen. If their people do not wish to be harmed inside their very own countries, they should seek to elect governments that are truly representative of them and that can protect their interests. [. . .]

The enmity between us and the Jews goes far back in time and is deep-rooted. There is no question that war between the two of us is inevitable. For this reason it is not in the interest of Western governments to expose the interests of their people to all kinds of retaliation for almost nothing. It is hoped that people of those countries will initiate a positive move and force their governments not to act on behalf of other states and other sects. This is what we have to say, and we pray to Allah to preserve the nation of Islam and to help them drive their enemies out of their land.

- American politicians have painted a distorted picture of Islam, of Muslims, and of Islamic fighters. We would like you to give us the true picture that clarifies your viewpoint. [...]

The leaders in America and in other countries as well have fallen victim to Jewish Zionist blackmail. They have mobilized their people against Islam and against Muslims. These are portrayed in such a manner as to drive people to rally against them. The truth is that the whole Muslim world is the victim of international terrorism, engineered by America at the United Nations. We are a nation whose sacred symbols have been looted and whose wealth and resources have been plundered. It is normal for us to react against the forces that invade our land and occupy it. [...]

- Quite a number of Muslim countries have seen the rise of militant movements whose purpose is to stand up in the face of the pressure exerted on the people by their own governments and other governments. Such is the case in Egypt and Libya and North Africa and Algiers, and such was the case in Syria and in Yemen. There are also other militant groups currently engaged in the fight against the unbelievers and the crusaders, as is the case in Kashmir and Chechnya and Bosnia and the African horn. Is there any message you wish to convey to our brothers who are fighting in various parts of the Islamic World?

[...] Tell the Muslims everywhere that the vanguards of the warriors who are fighting the enemies of Islam belong to them and the young fighters are their sons. Tell them that the nation is bent on fighting the enemies of Islam. Once again, I have to stress the necessity of focusing on the Americans and the Jews, for they represent the spearhead with which the members of our religion have been slaughtered. Any effort directed against America and the Jews yields positive and direct results, Allah willing. It is far better for anyone to kill a single American soldier than to squander his efforts on other activities.

2. Jihad Against Jews and Crusaders: World Islamic Front Statement

23 February 1998

Shaykh Usamah Bin-Muhammad Bin-Ladin

Ayman al-Zawahiri, amir of the Jihad Group in Egypt

Abu-Yasir Rifa'i Ahmad Taha, Egyptian Islamic Group

Shaykh Mir Hamzah, secretary of the Jamiat-ul-Ulema-e-Pakistan

Fazlur Rahman, amir of the Jihad Movement in Bangladesh

Praise be to God, who revealed the Book, controls the clouds, defeats factionalism, and says in His Book: "But when the forbidden months are past, then

Usama Bin Laden, "Jihad Against Jews and Crusaders," *Nida'ul Islam* 15 (October–November 1996). Translated by Akram Khater.

fight and slay the pagans wherever ye find them, seize them, beleaguer them, and lie in wait for them in every stratagem (of war)"; and peace be upon our Prophet, Muhammad Bin-'Abdallah, who said: I have been sent with the sword between my hands to ensure that no one but God is worshiped, God who put my livelihood under the shadow of my spear and who inflicts humiliation and scorn on those who disobey my orders.

The Arabian Peninsula has never—since God made it flat, created its desert, and encircled it with seas—been stormed by any forces like the crusader armies spreading in it like locusts, eating its riches, and wiping out its plantations. All this is happening at a time in which nations are attacking Muslims like people fighting over a plate of food. In the light of the grave situation and the lack of support, we and you are obliged to discuss current events, and we should all agree on how to settle the matter.

No one argues today about three facts that are known to everyone; we will list them, in order to remind everyone:

First, for over seven years the United States has been occupying the lands of Islam in the holiest of places, the Arabian Peninsula, plundering its riches, dictating to its rulers, humiliating its people, terrorizing its neighbors, and turning its bases in the peninsula into a spearhead through which to fight the neighboring Muslim peoples.

If some people have in the past argued about the fact of the occupation, all the people of the peninsula have now acknowledged it. The best proof of this is the Americans' continuing aggression against the Iraqi people using the peninsula as a staging post, even though all its rulers are against their territories being used to that end, but they are helpless.

Second, despite the great devastation inflicted on the Iraqi people by the crusader-Zionist alliance, and despite the huge number of those killed, which has exceeded 1 million. [. . .] despite all this, the Americans are once again trying to repeat the horrific massacres, as though they are not content with the protracted blockade imposed after the ferocious war or the fragmentation and devastation.

So here they come to annihilate what is left of this people and to humiliate their Muslim neighbors.

Third, if the Americans' aims behind these wars are religious and economic, the aim is also to serve the Jews' petty state and divert attention from its occupation of Jerusalem and murder of Muslims there. The best proof of this is their eagerness to destroy Iraq, the strongest neighboring Arab state, and their endeavor to fragment all the states of the region—such as Iraq, Saudi Arabia, Egypt, and Sudan—into paper statelets and through their disunion and weakness to guarantee Israel's survival and the continuation of the brutal crusade occupation of the peninsula.

All these crimes and sins committed by the Americans are a clear declaration of war on God, his messenger, and Muslims. And 'ulama' have throughout Islamic history unanimously agreed that the jihad is an individual duty if the enemy destroys the Muslim countries. This was revealed by Imam Bin-Qadamah in "Al-Mughni," Imam al-Kisa'i in "Al-Bada'i," al-Qurtubi in his interpretation, and the shaykh of al-Islam in his books, where he said: "As for the fighting to repulse [an enemy], it is aimed at defending sanctity and religion, and it is a duty as agreed [by the 'ulama']. Nothing is more sacred than belief except repulsing an enemy who is attacking religion and life."

On that basis, and in compliance with God's order, we issue the following fatwa to all Muslims:

> The ruling to kill the Americans and their allies—civilians and military—is an individual duty for every Muslim who can do it in any country in which it is possible to do it, in order to liberate the al-Aqsa Mosque and the holy mosque [Mecca] from their grip, and in order for their armies to move out of all the lands of Islam, defeated and unable to threaten any Muslim. This is in accordance with the words of Almighty God, "and fight the pagans all together as they fight you all together," and "fight them until there is no more tumult or oppression, and there prevail justice and faith in God."
>
> This is in addition to the words of Almighty God: "And why should ye not fight in the cause of God and of those who, being weak, are ill treated (and oppressed)?—women and children, whose cry is: 'Our Lord, rescue us from this town, whose people are oppressors; and raise for us from thee one who will help!'"

We—with God's help—call on every Muslim who believes in God and wishes to be rewarded to comply with God's order to kill the Americans and plunder their money wherever and whenever they find it. We also call on Muslim 'ulama', leaders, youths, and soldiers to launch the raid on Satan's U.S. troops and the devil's supporters allying with them, and to displace those who are behind them so that they may learn a lesson.

Almighty God said: "O ye who believe, give your response to God and His Apostle, when He calleth you to that which will give you life. And know that God cometh between a man and his heart, and that it is He to whom ye shall all be gathered."

Almighty God also says: "O ye who believe, what is the matter with you, that when ye are asked to go forth in the cause of God, ye cling so heavily to the earth! Do ye prefer the life of this world to the hereafter? But little is the comfort of this life, as compared with the hereafter. Unless ye go forth, He will punish you with a grievous penalty, and put others in your place; but Him ye would not harm in the least. For God hath power over all things."

Almighty God also says: "So lose no heart, nor fall into despair. For ye must gain mastery if ye are true in faith."

7.   Reflections on the Terrorist Attacks of September 11, 2001

The attacks on the World Trade Center and the Pentagon of September 11, 2001, were a cataclysmic event on many different levels. One such level is reflected in the tensions that emerged within the relationship between the Arab world and the United States. These tensions were focused on the questions—asked on both sides of this relationship—"Why do they hate us?" It was a question that was meant to explain what most—Americans and Arabs alike—agreed to be a horrendous crime and a dangerous precedent that could lead the world into more dire circumstances. The answers however were certainly not the same. Most Arabs tended to focus on the foreign policy of the United States in the Middle East and what they perceived to be its detrimental impact on the stability of the region and biases toward Israel and conservative—or in American foreign policy parlance, "moderate"—regimes. Many Arab observers, including Muna Shuqair who authored one of the two articles presented here, argued that the United States created its own worst enemy through its "arrogant" approach toward the Middle East that was centered on safeguarding its access to oil and blind support for Israel. On the other hand, many American observers, including Ehsan Ahrari who authored the first article, have argued that the terrorist attacks on the United States are clear indications of deep flaws that reside within the societies and polities of the Arab world. According to these observers, it is the authoritarian nature of these countries that creates an oppressive political environment, a deeply flawed educational system that discourages liberal thought, and economies that are grossly unjust in their distribution of wealth—and it is that un-democratic environment that produces extremists. There are certainly merits to both arguments, and it remains for you to contemplate their veracity and ability to explain the events of September 11.

1. Facing the "Real" Enemy in the Arab Middle East

The September [11, 2001,] terrorist attacks on the United States triggered a debate over "why they hate us," involving the Arab Middle East as well as the entire Muslim world. On the Arab side, the same question was asked at the popular level. However, since free debates are not allowed in authoritarian systems, the international community did not get the real flavor of that debate.

The United Nation's Human Development Program (UNDP) has done the world a great service by commissioning a report on the state of Arab societies prepared by a group of Arab intellectuals. It does not answer the "why they hate us" question for the region. However, it does underscore what is wrong with their polities, and who the real enemy is. It is not the West. It is the authoritarian rule and its perpetrators. Here are some of the highlights of that report, which can be viewed in full in PDF format at: http://www.undp.org/rbas/ahdr/:

Ehsan Ahrari, "Facing the 'Real' Enemy in the Arab Middle East," *Asia Times* (online edition), 13 July 2002. Copyright © 2002 Asia Times Online. Reprinted by permission.

- The 22-nation Arab League (280 million people) produced a combined gross domestic product of US$531.2 billion in 1999, less than the single Western nation Spain.
- The real income of the average Arab citizen was just 13.9 percent that of the average citizen of Organization for Economic Cooperation and Development (OECD) countries.
- Only 0.6 percent of the population uses the internet, and the personal computer penetration rate is only 1.2 percent.
- Arab governments' overall investment in research and development does not exceed 0.5 percent of the GNP.
- The unemployment rate across Arab countries is about 15 percent, which is "among the highest rate in the developing world."
- Manufacturing exports have remained stagnant and private capital flows have lagged those of other regions.
- Even in oil and oil-related products, which accounts for over 70 percent of export from the region, the rate of growth was only 1.5 percent per year.
- No generation of young Arabs has been as large as today's.
- Despite recent progress made on the status of women, more than half of Arab women are still illiterate. They also suffer from inequality of opportunity in employment-status, wages, and gender-based occupational segregation.

The authoritarian rulers know only too well that their very survival depends on the continued backwardness and acute economic underdevelopment of their societies. Thus, as the rest of the world becomes enlightened with the spread of the information revolution and reaps the benefits stemming from enhanced globalization and industrialization, Arab countries remain at the very bottom of those phenomena. Policies of authoritarian regimes are directly responsible for their plight.

Authoritarian rule, more often than not, is also notoriously inept, corrupt and unresponsive to popular needs. The UNDP's report makes these points in sedate bureaucratic language. Consider its following observations: "There is a substantial lag between Arab countries and other regions in terms of participatory governance." And "freedoms of expression and association are frequently curtailed. Obsolete norms of legitimacy prevail." Finally, government spending and policy changes "are evident in lack of accountability, transparency and integrity, along with ineffectiveness, inefficiency and unresponsiveness to the demands of peoples and of development." The temperate language of this report notwithstanding, it is still a scathing criticism of the state of affairs in the Arab countries, and was released at a time when the search for "what went wrong?" and "who did it to us?" is on.

Once such a biting criticism of the state of affairs of Arab polities is circulated worldwide, it is reasonable to expect that sweeping reforms will be introduced and "qualitative changes," to quote Karl Marx, will be brought about. Marx was not right about the feasibility of a classless society; however, he was definitely right about the fact that qualitative change may only be brought about as a result of a cataclysmic change and through an implosion from within, especially when the "enemy" is the regime (or, in this instance, regimes) in power. Needless to say, Marx was referring to nondemocratic societies, since democratic societies are procedurally equipped to bring about such changes through periodic elections.

However, the trouble with all societal implosions is that no one can predict the outcome. Mikhail Gorbachev's *glasnost* and *perestroika* were examples of the fact that although he only meant to reform the archaic political system, be ended up with an entirely unintended outcome—the implosion of the Soviet Union. Implosion in a country may not mean the emergence of a representative system of government. Even if some semblance of democracy emerges, still no one can be certain whether a less democratic system will become more or even less democratic, and when. Iran is a good example of this particular point. In the absence of such a certainty, an alternative would be "managed" democratic change. But which regime would be willing to bring about managed change? More to the point, who is going to persuade any government in the Arab world to bring about managed democratic change?

The continuation of the status quo in the Arab world is not acceptable, for it only postpones cataclysmic changes in most, if not all, Arab polities. It is not possible for people to suffer endlessly, especially when they see on their televisions the uplifting outcomes of globalization and industrialization in the standards of living of their European and Asian counterparts. Managed democratic change from within emerges as the only realistic option. The United States, the only declared global proselytizer for democracy, may be able to play a limited and a low-key role in this direction.

In the past, the United States has been pussyfooting around this issue in that region. President George W. Bush's insistence in his June 24 speech on the interim Palestinian state was an important development in the sense that it called for the establishment of a democratic government in the Palestinian-administered territories. However, given the highly controversial nature of that speech, there is a fear that other Arab states, wittingly or otherwise, missed that point entirely.

But if introduction of democracy in the Palestinian-administered territories becomes a successful reality, Jordan might be the next candidate. Lebanon also stands a high probability of becoming a democracy, since it does not have a strongman like Saddam Hussein of Iraq. Syria under Bishara Assad is not yet the repressive dictatorship that it was under his father, Hafiz Assad. However, given the fact that the old guard and the security apparatus created by senior Assad is still very much intact, Syria is not likely to become less authoritarian, or more democratic, any time soon. Iraq is a hopeless case of a continued tyranny. Even if Saddam is toppled, there is no certainty that Iraq will start its march toward democracy soon thereafter.

In North Africa, Morocco may be a leading candidate for managed democratic change. But the remaining states of that region are likely to remain under authoritarian repression for the foreseeable future. In fact, both Hosni Mubarak and Muammar Gaddafi are grooming their sons to be their heirs apparent. Sadly, hereditary dictatorship is also a long-standing phenomenon of the Arab Middle East.

That leaves the Gulf monarchies as the next region of challenge. However, the Persian Gulf monarchies are not uniform in their practice of authoritarian rule. Qatar, Bahrain, Oman and Kuwait are already experimenting with limited democracy, and a discreet American encouragement for enhancing the scope of that experimentation might not be a bad idea.

Saudi Arabia, the largest state of the Arabian Peninsula, remains an archetype of authoritarian rule. It is also a country where Islamic orthodoxy is extremely well entrenched. So opening up the Saudi polity will be a great challenge, and only the ruling elite of that country may be able to bring that about. The current generation of Saudi rulers, sons of King Abdel Aziz, may not be the ones to play a crucial role in that direction. A general expectation is that the grandsons of Abdel Aziz might become the harbingers of political change, However, those who support this view provide no hard evidence to prove this point.

As the stoutest obstacle to change, authoritarian rule is the real enemy, but also has great potential for becoming an equally powerful force for change. Given the magnitude of development-related changes for the Arab countries, the extant regimes had better become its initiators and managers, especially if they do not wish to be swept aside. Political change in the Arab world is coming. There is nothing uncertain about that proposition. What is questionable is whether the real enemy of change will become its promoter and manager.

2. America's Inability to Understand Sept. 11 Rests with Warped Self-Image and Perception of Values and Power

One year after September 11, 2001, America appears unable to get over the shock and the resultant feeling of general rage and need for revenge. Sections of the American people have been able to do so. But the US administration seems incapable of the rational thought needed to analyze the crisis, consider its causes and thus deal with it in a manner that prevents its repetition. The shock blinded America, wounded its pride and made it vengeful. It was deluded by its own power and will continue to be so as long as it believes that it can deal with the challenges it faces by force.

Rage and vengeance prompted America to seek to dry up the wellsprings of terrorism by war, first in Afghanistan. One year on it is preparing to attack Iraq, while signaling that Iran, Syria and Lebanon could follow. Its fury has

---

Muna Shuqair, "America's inability to understand Sept. 11 rests with warped self-image and perception of values and power," *The Daily Star,* 30 September 2002. Reprinted by permission.

even turned it against traditional friends like Saudi Arabia, on grounds that the terrorists were natural products of its education system.

The reasons for America's failure to move on from rage to reflection, and thus to a measured and wise approach to dealing with Sept. 11, have to do with its self-image and the rationale that governs its behavior as the sole superpower. America refuses, consciously and deliberately at times, unconsciously at others, to bear responsibility for its actions. It views itself in terms approaching perfection and infallibility, as though it never wronged or committed or condoned crimes against Third World peoples. It thus assumes that feelings of hatred and hostility toward it are directed at fundamental aspects of that perfection at American values of democracy, human rights, modernity, science and progress. Thus it divides the world into two: a free and democratic world at whose pinnacle it sits, and a backward and undemocratic world that necessarily opposes and hates it. In other words, the conflict is between America as it sees itself and the others as it sees them, a conflict of identities, cultures and civilizations that is totally decoupled from the historical experience of encounters between the superpower and the peoples who have suffered from its power and tyranny.

America does not understand, or does not want to understand, that it does not necessarily represent the promised model to the "Other"—including the Arab- and Islamic-"Other"—because its values of freedom and democracy have not made it into a moral force in the world. Refusal to take responsibility for one's actions conflicts with those values, as does denying others rights one reserves for oneself. So does backing repressive and oppressive regimes, turning a blind eye to crimes committed by allies, intervening in criminal ways in countries whose regimes it opposes, and assassinating leaders merely because one disagrees with their policies. Through these and other actions and biases prompted by a narrow perception of self-interest, the model America has managed to project to many peoples is a loathsome one.

The assumption that the American dream must be a universal dream disregards the fact that some peoples, groups, and individuals see only the nightmarish side of that dream and associate it with aggression, injustice and hypocrisy. Freedom cannot be a supreme value when it applies to oneself but not to others, or is decoupled from the values of equality and justice—which mandate that all peoples be viewed as being worthy of life, liberty, independence and the right to self-determination. The scientific reasoning America cherishes—and whose technological output has oppressed peoples worldwide—is also totally at odds with its division of the world into good and evil. Without attempting to define either, it appropriated good for itself and proceeded to address the world with the arrogant and reductionist logic of "with us or against us."

A sole superpower cannot be a great power without a moral message, both to earn the respect of other peoples by showing them respect, and to enable it to play a credible role as a fair arbiter in world affairs. America failed to make the transition to that role, but emerged from the Cold War still captive to its prejudice—the Arab-Israeli conflict being a case in point—to take on minor regional players that do not even begin to constitute a match for the military might it developed to confront a rival superpower.

America's new wars are not defensive. No other country could or would dare threaten it. They are to protect its interests. But treating oneself and one's interests as the same thing is wrong even from a pragmatic standpoint. A threat to some of one's interests is not a threat to oneself But that is the rationale for attacking Iraq, despite the lack of evidence that Baghdad has anything to do with Sept. 11.

The US believes Iraq's policies threaten American oil interests and Israel's security. The claim that it wants to rid the Iraqi people of a dictator who attacks them with weapons of mass destruction is merely a pretext to conceal its self-interested motives. This is tantamount to imperial days when colonial powers would start wars and redraw maps to advance their interests.

America has not managed to understand the phenomenon of Islamic terrorism. To link Islam, or even an Islamic group, to terrorism is to misconceive both. The linkage should be between a certain understanding of Islam and the behavior it inspires, which may or may not be terrorism. It is not terrorism for an Islamic group to resist an occupier, or a people to resist their occupiers or oppressors. The values of freedom and independence cannot be selectively applied or monopolized by a single people, country or religion.

Nor has America understood the relationship between terrorist activity and the religious ideological motives that may inspire it. Although nothing could justify or legitimize the horrific slaughter of innocents on Sept. 11, understanding a phenomenon does not mean condoning or judging it. It is not a matter of zealous young Muslims killing themselves to become martyrs or enter paradise. In their perception, that only happens if they strike at an aggressor who has humiliated them or their peoples and denied them their humanity. Martyrdom is only achieved against an enemy hostile to Islam and Muslims and who has attacked them and violated their sanctities.

When the phenomenon of terrorism stemming from a religious ideological world view is looked at from a cultural and political perspective, it can be understood for what it is: an expected consequence of peoples being sentenced to injustice, humiliation, despair and despondency, as perceived consequences of the direct or proxy application of the superpower's might. Such an understanding leads to the conclusion that the phenomenon needs to be tackled by a combination of political and cultural means, in addition to any security measures.

But merely using military muscle against the kind of religious-inspired terrorism that prompts groups of young men to kill themselves to wreak vengeance against America, will not eradicate the phenomenon. It will ultimately strengthen it, forcing it to retreat and conceal itself at first, before it is reconstituted in new guises and re-emerges in even more resentful and ruthless forms.

CHAPTER 9

Subaltern Groups

Although Islamic political movements have played an important role in the Middle East and North Africa, it would be a serious mistake to assume that they completely define the range of political and social movements in the regions. In fact, as a result of some of the challenges that have led to the rise of political Islam, nonreligious social movements have emerged. By their very existence or through their activism, these secular movements and groups undermine the image of state and society as monolithic. Their members, through their lifestyles and actions, try to claim and define a social space in opposition to the moral conservatism of the Islamists and the oppression of the state. In this chapter we present some of these subaltern groups.

Leftist politics has been integral to the rise of the modern Middle East and North Africa. Socialist and communist ideas have spawned political movements and have played a role in shaping the organizational structure and approaches of mainstream and right-wing politics. For example, the dedication of the Tudeh (Masses) Party of Iran to Marxist ideology has helped to shape modern Iran and its politics. Even though the party is today outlawed in Iran by the conservative government, it continues to play a subversive political role. Thus, the statement of the party's central committee—self-aggrandizing without doubt—provides a glimpse into the ideas and history of one communist organization in the Middle East and North Africa (document 8).

Stereotypes of women in the Middle East and North Africa portray them as members of a veiled community, powerless in the face of male domination. However, despite a great deal of discrimination against women in these regions, the situation for women is far more complex than the stereotypes imply. In Iran, the law requires women to wear the chador (a loose robe covering the body from head to foot and leaving only the face exposed), yet many women run for political office, vote for liberal candidates, and actively participate in every aspect of life. Women in Tunisia have far more rights than women in Algeria or Libya. In Israel, the law guarantees women many rights, but the

Jewish religious right is constantly seeking to deprive women of those very rights. What even this cursory look at the variety and complexity of women's lives reveals is that women are not passive victims of history; they challenge the status quo in small and large ways on a daily basis. Document 1, an article detailing Arab feminist action against violence targeting women, is one example of such a challenge.

Gender politics is another facet of social movements in the Middle East and North Africa. Document 2 presents an Internet discussion about education for women in Saudi Arabia and the role they ought to play after marriage. As families attempt to deal with pressing economic needs, individual desires, and collective challenges, answers to the question of whether a woman should pursue education or marriage vary considerably. The discussion about Saudi women allows us to go beyond the stereotype of these women as silent, veiled nonentities. Their voices—never silent—are ever more present with the rise of new technologies that allow them access to public spaces previously denied.

More challenging to the social structure and mores of any society is homosexuality. This is a subject that remains taboo in Egypt, although 150 years ago Rifa'a Tahtawi wrote of its ubiquity and social acceptance in Egypt (see document 1 in the chapter "Social and Cultural Reformulations"). Today the subculture of homosexuals in Egypt is seen as a challenge to heterosexuality and religious "morality" simply by its existence. A reading of document 6 allows us to appreciate the diversity of social life in places we normally view through an extremely reductionist lens.

Every country in the Middle East and North Africa has a nationalist myth of creation that projects the image of a unified people living in a unified land. Israel declared itself a "Jewish state," practically every Arab nation declared itself to be "Arab," and Turkey projects itself as singularly "Turkish." These broad ethnic designations, however, are called into question by the ethnic diversity evident in every part of the regions. If during most of the twentieth century, ethnic minorities remained silent out of fear or necessity, this is no longer the case in the twenty-first century. Minority rights have become a critical political issue in these countries, even if the ruling majority chooses to ignore the topic and its ramification for the nationalist myth.

This chapter contains three documents dealing with that issue. Document 4 is a proclamation by the Imazighen (Berbers) of Algeria decrying the designation of that country as an "Arab" nation despite the presence of a sizable non-Arab minority. This issue is especially frustrating for the Imazighen because they are descendants of the original inhabitants of the area, who predate the Arab conquest in the seventh century. Document 7 focuses our attention on Israel, where the Arab-Israeli minority actively challenges the notion that the state is simply Jewish. Their very existence stands as testimony against this exclusionary definition. In addition to voting and becoming more politically outspoken, the Arab Israelis challenge the Zionist mythology by their presence in every walk of life. Document 7 spotlights the interaction of Jewish and Arab soccer players and coaches in Israel. Document 5 describes the attempts by

Kurds in Turkey to break through the official silence about their existence as a minority group and to challenge the contention that Turkey is only for Turks.

Finally, environmental issues and politics represent a new axis of grass-roots challenges to state authority. This is demonstrated in document 3, which explores environmental activism in Egypt and Turkey.

Collectively, the documents in this chapter demonstrate that the nations of the Middle East and North Africa are not simply "Muslim" or "Jewish" or "Arab." A host of additional categories—ethnic and linguistic among others—and interests define the myriad lives there.

1. The Arab Women's Court Vows to Resist Violence Against Women, 1995 and 1998

At the beginning of the twenty-first century, Arab women, like women elsewhere, are still struggling for full equality with their male counterparts. Despite some similarities, however, the issues have changed since the early days of the Arab feminist movement, which began one hundred years ago. Today, Arab, Iranian, Turkish, and Israeli women have the right to work in the public sphere, although they still experience discrimination. Now, women in most Middle Eastern and North African nations enter the universities as a matter of course; a century ago they were fighting to gain access to secondary education. The change in women's status and power is especially apparent in the shift in feminist language over the past one hundred years. If you compare the early pronouncements in the documents in the chapter "Social and Cultural Reformulations" with the wording of this document, you will find here some new ideas and concepts that are indicators of real change.

This document derives from a website listing the accomplishments of "The Women's Court." The organization is described as follows: "the Women's Court— the Permanent Arab Court to Resist Violence Against Women—is a . . . popular court that aims at fighting all forms of violence practiced against women in Arab societies." Among its objectives are to publicize violence against women and to change laws that condone if not encourage such actions. At public hearings women lawyers from across North Africa and the Middle East convene to address particular cases with symbolic importance and to render judgments that serve as metaphors for larger issues. Much of the language of the court is symbolic; this organization does not have the legal power to enforce its decisions. Yet public pressure demands responses even from people who reject the court's claims. This document provides a glimpse of feminist activity in the Middle East and North Africa. A cursory Internet search will allow you to explore the greater scope of feminist activism there.

The Women's Court: The Permanent Arab Court to Resist Violence Against Women, "Accomplishments." http://www.arabwomencourt.org/womenscourt/accomplishments/accomplishments.htm (10 January 2003). Reprinted by permission.

Public Hearings 1995 and 1998

Prior to the establishment of the Court, and upon the initiative of the El-Taller organization, a group of Arab NGOs referred to as the Arab Women Court held a public hearing on June 29th and 30th 1995. At this hearing, 33 live testimonies of women coming from 14 different Arab countries were heard. The testimonies reported great pain and suffering and focused on the various types of social and legal crimes as well as the erroneously so-called "honor crimes."

During its first year of existence and building on the field experience of its members, the Women's Court: the Permanent Arab Court To Resist Violence Against Women realized the necessity of raising awareness on the personal status codes existing in the Arab counties in order to reveal to the public the injustice that these codes are inflicting on women. In fact, the personal status observed at both the legislative and applied levels in most Arab countries is one of the most important mechanisms for subjugating and oppressing women within the framework of gender social relations within the family. The Court decided to dedicate its second public hearing (held in Beirut, Lebanon on March 15th to 17th 1998) on these laws and to focus on four major issues: Marriage, Divorce, Custody and Alimony, and Inheritance.

Testimonies 1995

". . . I do not recall the day of my excision, said Fatima from Mauritania, "but what has remained engraved in my memory is the agony and affliction I began to feel when I grew up and became aware of the horror inflicted on my body. At the age of ten, I was taken to where a group of us, 8 to 10 years old, were awakened every day at 5 A.M. and placed before jugs containing one liter of milk each. The exercise was to have each one of us drink, under tight control, between 30 and 40 liters of milk daily. If anyone of us threw up . . . she would be forced to drink the amount she had vomited. I shall never forget the case of a friend of mine who drank herself to death. Frightened by her death, I became more obedient and soon, grew into one of the fattest girls of the group. By the following winter the second phase of the fattening process began . . . In our society, fat means beautiful and the purpose is to turn the young girl into a docile creature ready for the marriage imposed upon her.

"The third and more damaging kind of violence was forced marriage; I was given to marriage to a man much older than me, a marriage which led to divorce leaving me with children that I love."

"My name is Souad, a survivor of Sabra and Shatila massacre in Palestinian camps, in 1982, when Israel invaded Beirut.

"On Thursday, 17 September 1982 at 5 A.M., 13 soldiers backed by Israel, broke into our home. I was then sixteen. My youngest sister (hardly a year and a half old) was the first to die from a shot in her head, crying mamma . . . I was raped by three of them, one after the other . . .

"They returned again the day after and sneered at me. As they heard words of depreciation I could not withhold, they shot me, point [blank] in the breast and head.

"I did not die but fell unconscious and lost the ability to move until the third day, when I was shaken into consciousness by a voice from outside . . . My condition has not changed since the massacre. I became a cripple condemned to a wheelchair. I fear nothing and desire nothing than ultimate victory and the end of this painful drama."

Statement of Justice 1995

After listening to the live testimonies and careful review and deliberation, the panel of judges at the public hearing issued the following verdict:

> The Tribunal condemns the cultural concepts, values and regimes which deny the humanity and rights of women.

> The Tribunal believes that the unconditional joining by the Arab states to the international treaty to eliminate all kinds of discrimination against women, will strengthen the standing of the Arab women, preserve their rights, ensure equality, and help to eliminate the phenomena of violence.

> The Tribunal notices that the majority of laws implemented in the Arab states fall short in achieving equality and justice for women and fail to conform with the principles of a democratic society.

> The Tribunal believes that achieving justice requires wide rang[ing] legal and procedural reforms including among others the personal status code, the laws organizing employment, citizenship, criminal law and social security.

> The Tribunal considers killing and harming individuals under the pretext of defending honor a crime punishable by law and no special clause should be included to ease the punishment.

> The Tribunal condemns all forms of traditional practices containing discrimination or violence against women, especially excision, and considers these practices a crime.

> The Tribunal believes that Israeli occupation of the Arab land is a continuous violation of international law, human rights, and UN Security Council resolutions. The Israeli occupation is a major cause for the continuation of political violence against the peoples of the region, in particular women. Furthermore and in accordance with the Geneva accords, the Tribunal calls on releasing the illegally held prisoners in Israeli jails.

> The Tribunal calls for joint efforts to be undertaken by all those who believe in human rights in order to stop violence against women.

Statement of Rights 1995

We, the women participating in the Arab Woman Court, held in Beirut, between June 28th and 30th 1995, as testifiers and audience to these live testimonies commit ourselves and raise our voices pledging the rejection of all forms of violence practiced against women.

We reject violence because it is an abuse of women's rights, because it violates women's human dignity and because it is the worst of all forms of discrimination against them;

We pledge to cut the strings of silence which covers such violence and to put a hand of solidarity into the hands of all those who help us in our fight throughout the world, especially in the third world.

We reject all forms of violence and will fight them at the local and international levels, no matter how well it may be disguised and how justified others might claim.

We reject violence regardless of how it is categorized—political, economical, or social.

We reject violence whomever the entity carrying it out against us may be—father, brother, husband, son, governor, foreign elements, or any entity of the new world order; whether it is signed by states, religious institutions, local, regional or international bodies.

We reject all forms of violence in circumstances of war or peace.

We reject all forms of violence no matter what it is called or how it is justified.

We reject all forms of violence whether it is directed at individuals, women or organized groups, whether the act itself be legal or illegal, individual or affecting groups.

Testimonies 1998

Rania, a 23 old Jordanian woman university graduate, was forced by her parents to marry her cousin. She had no option but to flee from her parental home two weeks before the wedding day. She did so only after all methods used to express her rejection—persuasion and even resorting to [attempted] suicide—failed to bear fruit.

The result was the murder of Rania in a primitive, brutal manner just because she sought her right to free choice as guaranteed by all religious laws.

The lovely brunette was an educated young woman who spoke in a convincing manner. When she contacted the people in charge in the "People's Talk" program on Jordan's television, they gave her the pseudonym of Haneen to help her broadcast her messages to her parents. In those letters, Rania/Haneen expressed her deep love for her parents. Her maternal aunt—who appeared later to have planned to get rid of her niece—started to send messages to the TV program, claiming that Rania had been forgiven and begging her on air to come back home. In one of these messages, the father talked beseechingly to his own daughter: "come back, come back, my dear daughter."

Two weeks later, Rania was shot dead, murdered because she decided to escape, and refused to marry her cousin. The executioner of the crime—planned by the father and his kinsmen—was Rania's younger brother who is no older than fifteen years (being a minor protects him from severe sentencing).

Yet another victim of outdated tribal customs!

"I got married at the age of eighteen," said Z.B. from Syria. "My husband deprived me of the opportunity to continue my university studies, and forced me to serve his mother . . . He started to beat me to severe bleeding . . . He then drove me out of my house with no clothes and no money . . . My husband started to drink heavily and womanizing to the extent that he started to get some women into our own apartment.

"He kept insisting on the need to give birth to a son. As soon as I had given birth to our son, his attitude worsened. He prohibited me from going out of the house . . . Beating and abuse were no longer confined to our home. He began to torture me while starving my kids and myself. He began to threaten me of throwing me out of the house. One night, he severely beat me, I tried to commit suicide but was saved by my parents.

"The Court did not rule that I get an alimony, because my husband claimed to be poor . . . When my eldest daughter reached the end of her nurture age, my husband took her and started setting her against me. She now considers me repulsive and refuses to see me. Lately my husband took my other children, but two days later, he sent our young son home and said: 'I will take him back when he grows up.'

"He denies me any chance to see my daughters. I'm raising my son without any alimony and without being divorced, while expecting his father to take him away from me."

Statement of Justice 1998

After listening to numerous live testimonies, the judges at the public hearing recommended the following:

Drafting a uniform domestic civil law dealing with the personal status codes that is based on the respect of the human rights whereby all citizens would be treated in a nondiscriminatory manner.

Prompting each Arab country to join and abide by the international human rights conventions including the international convention for the elimination of all forms of discrimination against women (especially article 16 bearing on prejudices within families).

Working for the amendment of the codes enforced in the respective Arab countries to suit the provisions of the international conventions already agreed on and signed by the respective Arab nations.

Setting up institutions specialized with the purpose of looking after the victims of domestic violence, counseling, guidance and essential services tending for legal and judicial help.

Reforming judicial procedures related to domestic issues such as shortening the interval of the trials and speeding up the implementation of the judicial verdicts, reducing the court expenses, and calling on social experts aid.

Establishing a governmental fund that would disburse the divorce allowance to separated and divorced women.

Emphasizing the necessity of the independence and immunity of the jurisdiction, eliminating the exclusive and private courts. Courts must be equipped with capable personnel and staffed with women lawyers and judges. Besides, a special department for appeal must be established in quest for an amicable settlement.

Educating the public over basic human rights and relevant legal knowledge only to be included in the school civic education curriculum.

The Court also perceives that the elimination of violence and discrimination in all its forms requires the unity of the efforts of the non-governmental organizations (NGOs) with the various sections and forces concerned with the progression of society. This could take place in the frame of a broad and efficient Arab movement to exercise pressure in different directions to effect the indispensable change towards reinforcing the rights of the Arab citizen, whether man or woman, and enabling him to be his own decision maker to achieve his objectives.

Statement of Rights 1998

We, the Arab women participating in the Arab Women's Court held in Beirut from the 15th to the 17th of March 1998, have taken upon ourselves since 1995 to struggle for complete equity before the law. Our struggle is part and parcel of the international conventions, especially the international declaration of human rights and the convention of eliminating all forms of violence against women. We end our 2nd Arab public hearing with the following Statement of Rights:

We request that Arab governments fully abide by the Convention of Eliminating all forms of Discrimination Against Women (CEDAW).

We call for an equitable civil status law that would guarantee the freedom of getting married and the right to end the marriage.

We demand the prohibition of polygamy as it is a form of violence against women.

We demand that physical, psychological, and sexual violence, undeclared divorce (separation), and arbitrary divorce be categorized as crimes punishable by law.

In case of divorce, we call for an equal distribution of wealth and property and for sharing the cost of child support (when woman is employed), otherwise the father ought to bear the total cost.

We demand equal access to the children, allowing the child to choose his or her guardian.

Despite their major role in the economy, women are not equally treated when it comes to inheritance and still impeded by the prevailing norms and mentality. Therefore, we request that all obstacles, be it [*sic*] legal or traditional, be removed immediately.

2. Internet Discussion of Marriage and Education for Saudi Women, 1996

The Internet—extremely popular among Saudi Arabians in general and Saudi women in particular—offers a new venue for discussion of social issues, beyond the circle of immediate friends or family. The anonymity of the Internet permits some discussions to be far more forthright and honest than earlier discussions in the Middle East. The two sections of this document—an article and readers' comments from wide-ranging locations—exemplify this new development. Such articles are bringing to public attention new subjects or at least are providing a wider range of opinion. In either case, their impact is real.

Marriage or Education, a Dilemma for Saudi Women

If you had to choose between getting married or studying, which would you choose? As female education moves further and further every year, more and more Saudi women are faced with just this decision. The problem is particularly acute among those who are educated in highly-specialized fields. Medicine, for example, requires a minimum of six years university attendance and further degrees can take up to another five years. Most female medical students marry and have children while they are studying, but there are a few who remain single for a variety of reasons.

Many Saudi women work in their selected professions and acquire higher degrees within the framework of marriage. A laboratory technologist says, "I made it clear to my husband that I wanted to finish my education. I even put it as a clause in the marriage contract. For me, ambition is the most important element. I don't see a clear-cut choice between either marriage or education. If you really want to make them both work, you can, but it does take a lot of perseverance. Right now, I'm pushing my husband to let me go to Riyadh to get a

Dina Ibrahim, "Marriage or Education, a Dilemma for Saudi Women," *Arab News,* 29 November 1996. http://www.arab.net/arabview/articles/ibrahim2.html. Reprinted by permission.

higher degree. This means moving and changing the children's schools, but it looks like he's going to agree."

For some parents of female medical students, education is one thing but employment is another. Students tell of a colleague whose father did not object to her finishing medical school but when she finished and it was time for her to work in a hospital, he refused permission.

Fatma remains unmarried at the age of 37. She is a doctor specializing in internal medicine and has been working for the past nine years. "I was engaged once when I was 18, but I didn't want to get married so early. I wanted to finish my education and if my family had found a man who would have accepted that, I would have married him. But they didn't," she says.

Another medical student says, "The average age for marriage ranges from 20–25. After the age of 25, the quality of men looking to get married declines, so it is better to get married while a student than to wait and in the end stay unmarried or marry an older man such as a widower or even become someone's second, third or fourth wife."

Some educated women are treasured assets to younger men who are just starting out. By the time she had finished her doctoral studies, Nura was 32 and unmarried. Her mother arranged a marriage for her to a younger man whose mother was happy to marry him off to an older woman, because she had a job and could support both of them until he got on his feet.

There may be a shortage of men who are willing to support their wives until they complete their education, but they do exist. Talal Abu Jaffar considers himself a supporter of women's education. "But," as he puts it, "there are limits." He wants each of his four daughters to finish secondary school since he feels it is important for them to read and write, to learn about Islam and the Qur'an and to be knowledgeable in the sciences. This knowledge, in his opinion, is for them to pass on to their children. Once they have finished school, marriage becomes a priority. As for a college education, he says, "I will not allow my daughters to go to a college while they are still unmarried. When they marry, it is up to their husbands whether they get a college education or not."

Other men are selective about which degree their wives study for. "When we were first married, I advised my wife to stay away from medicine and sciences because they would take up too much of her time and there are no colleges or jobs for women with degrees in engineering and such. I convinced her to go to the literary side. That way, she can get a job as a teacher, but if she had gone into the sciences, she would have ended up frustrated because those are traditionally male occupations," said Abu Khalid, a legal consultant.

A woman who has a Master's Degree in English Literature and teaches at the Women's College in Dammam said, "My husband at first tried to dissuade me from getting a college degree. We were married quite young and he thought it best if I stayed at home and had children. Well, I did have three children but I certainly didn't stay at home." She managed to convince her husband to let her study and he agreed as long as it did not interfere with her domestic duties. "When I had my first son, I was in my second year as an undergraduate. It took me six years instead of four to finish my degree, but I did it and after I got it, my husband was the one who encouraged me to get a Master's Degree."

So far, the two main branches of college education with the most employment opportunities for women are either medicine or teaching. Female medical students, doctors and teachers are calling for augmentation and diversification of these opportunities. One student said, "My sister is a very talented artist, but there is no college she can attend here. If we want to send her to a fine arts program, the only alternative is to send her abroad and even if we do that, she won't find a job. Employment opportunities are very few. I chose medicine simply because I didn't want to be a teacher, not because of any real desire to be a doctor. If I could have studied computer science or business or economics, I would have been much happier because medicine is extremely stressful."

Education and employment continue to pose formidable challenges to these women. The married ones struggle to perform their duties as wives, students, mothers and career women. The unmarried ones face social and emotional friction. Nevertheless, both groups share the immense satisfaction of being able to work and study within their own unique conservative framework, thereby proving beyond any doubt that they are valuable assets in their quest to serve and complement today's Saudi society.

Feedback [from the Internet]

Selected comments we have received about this article are shown below. If you want to add your own comments, please fill in our feedback form.

ABDALLAH S. GAMAR, U.S.A.   I haven't finished the topic yet but if its all about getting married and continuing work or education I would agree if both parties agree. However I would love to get married right now or as soon as possible, if you know someone who is interested please let her e-mail me. I am working and trying to finish my college education, inshallah, in psychology. I am a male 35 light skinned.

MS. NARGIS NAQVI, MINNEAPOLIS, U.S.A.   This is an interesting subject and one that has caused a lot of confusion. My personal experience and opinion is that, Islamically, we are all supposed to obtain as much of an education as we can, men and women alike, but if it causes hurdles and problems for married women then, if their marriage is worth it, they should put that first. If husbands are unnecessarily strict then they should read some rights in Islam granted to women. In any case, women are not supposed to work unnecessarily if their husbands can provide for them (or their fathers can provide for them if they are not married), but in a place like Saudi Arabia where men and women don't mix at work, working just enhances the mind and makes one wiser to the ways of the world. They become better companions to their husbands who should be more understanding and supportive. For women with children, if education is going to cause problems like travelling to another place, etc., I feel that instead of being selfish, we can work out ways that help us be good mothers, wives and also continue with our needs in life. If education is one such need, then there are ways to acquire it without causing disturbance. Always remember the clue to a happy life: If you keep what Allah has said about our duties and responsibilities, men and women alike, then you will always make the best decision.

DR. SOMIAH ALNEMRI, VANCOUVER, CANADA   This is very complicated subject, especially to our conservative culture and society. We need to address everything with regard to Islamic teaching. In the Holy Qur'an, women are ordered to stay at home and not expose themselves like the time before Islam (*Algaheliah Alola*). On the other hand, there are other Hadiths from the Prophet Mohamed (SAW) encouraging continuous learning from early childhood to old age for mankind (male and female). That is why we need to ask our Olama—what is the extend [*sic*] of this education for women? And what is the application of that order to stay at home? Then we can get a balance between married life and education, especially for us as medical doctors.

H. S. FAISAL, RIYADH, SAUDI ARABIA   This is just a minor point with regards to the girl that studied medicine because she did not want to become a teacher. There is a computer science department for girls in King Saud University. I would like to further add that it seems to me that the problem of educating women should not exist in Saudi Arabia. First of all it is absolutely irrational to claim that educated women do not benefit their families. And second, it is the duty of every female to insist on her education and to enlighten the men in her life as to the benefits of her obtaining an education. Every woman should advocate and implement the benefits of any education from an Islamic, social and familial angle. As we are in the 20th century and heading towards the 21st century, the debate about whether or not women should be educated seems to be highly retrogressive.

ABDULLAH ALHMEED, LAWRENCE, KANSAS, U.S.A.   The question of whether a woman should sacrifice her education to get married or the other way around is a ridiculous question! As we are proceeding to the 21st century, our sisters and daughters should not be faced by this question when they want, or when the time comes, to get married. As women compose almost half of our society and have a very important role in raising our future generation, in line with men, and participating in the job market, women's education should not be a question but rather a necessity in order to improve our methods of raising our children, improving our productivity and eventually improving our society. It seems to me that educating a women [*sic*] is just as important as educating a man. I think that the doors should be open to every woman willing to complete her education without any questions. The woman's family and husband should understand that education is the corner stone for societies to progress and compete with other societies. Furthermore, working after pursuing a college degree is also as important as education Not only does work improve the economic situation of the family, but it adds another dimension of thinking for both the wife and husband. It might be true that the work of the wife causes some "organizational" problems within the family, but definitely the advantages of it would outweigh these problems. In summary, society in general and the woman's family and husband should find and establish some methods so that our girls are not faced with this tough question!

HELAL SAMARGANDY, KHOBAR, SAUDI ARABIA   Education is necessary for women as well as men. However, there are some things which MUST be taken into consideration. For example, Islamic orders and commands must be respected and followed and this is a very big subject. Also, good and bad "Al-Masalih wa Al-Mafasid" for the family, children, husband, etc. must be considered. This would bring many, many different situations. Each situation has its own sentence. However, we have to be careful about any subject related to women because our enemies (Kuffar or Munafqoon) want to damage the Islamic culture and Islam itself using any tool and one of these tools is SEX. Anything you want to do in your life requires effort and you face some resistance. Why do we raise women's problems in education or any kind of problem when this problem is a human problem. For example, many men stop their wives' education after marriage because of the feeling that it conflicts with their family's needs. Why do some women want to get everything without giving up anything. I am talking to the Muslim women: Do you want to go to Jannah? The way to that is by following Allah and his Prophet and then your husband. You can do anything as long as it does not conflict with Islamic orders.

ISHAAK EBRAHIM, JOHANNESBURG, SOUTH AFRICA   Why is this question posed? What are the sharia rulings regarding women in the workplace? Is it necessary for women to work, or can their husbands, fathers or family not support them? Does the western world dominate the way they live and think? Is Allah not the provider and sustainer? Does he not promise to provide in the holy Qur'an? It is a noted fact that career women's marriages do not last due to having affairs with colleagues. Remember, between every man and woman is the devil.

UBEDULLAH PATEL, LOS ANGELES, CALIFORNIA, U.S.A.   Bismillah Walhamdulillah Was Salaatu Was Salaam 'ala Rasulillah As-Salaam Alaikum Wa-Rahmatullahi Wa-Barakatuhu Sahabah—19th Rabi-ath-Thani 1419 (13 August 1998) I like to marry in Madina. Can you suggest me; is there any WEB site for matrimonial? Jazakallah Khair As-Salaam Alaikum Wa-Rahmatullahi Wa-Barakatuhu

3.   Grassroots Environmental Movements in Egypt and Turkey, 1997 and 2000

Although people—regardless of where they live—have always shown some level of concern about their immediate natural surroundings, not until the last quarter of the twentieth century did environmental politics emerge at the local or state level. In the Middle East and North Africa, environmental activism and concerns became publicly prominent only in the last ten years, as many "Green" parties began to influence the state environmental policies. Such pressure groups are not welcomed by states and private industries that are keen on keeping their environmental mistakes away from public scrutiny. But the immediacy and relevance of environmental issues such as air pollution and the novelty of environmental politics have allowed many nongovernmental organizations (NGOs) to use environmental issues as a way to challenge the authority of the state to make public policy. Though not always (if ever) successful, these organizations are still able to shape the public discourse; their activities force the state to acknowledge, even if only through some symbolic gesture, that it not the only arbiter of public issues. Environmental politics seems to have allowed some degree of democratization of public life in the Middle East and North Africa. The first of the two articles that follow describes the efforts of a low-income, Egyptian community to establish a "green" area in their midst, while the second article recounts the attempts of Turkish Greenpeace activists to stop industrial pollution.

1. Mobilization in a Cairo Neighborhood: Community Participation and Environmental Change

Cairo—a city upwards of 14 million inhabitants—is known to be one of the most polluted cities in the world. Although measures of pollutants in some places in Cairo exceed internationally recognized standards, popular collective action organized around environmental issues is rare. The case of Ezbet Mekawy, an industrial area in northern Cairo, and the successful struggle of the residents there to close local lead smelting factories is a reference point regarding possible forms of popular organizing in response to environmental pollution and sheds light on the limits and merits of community participation as experienced within the wider political context in Egypt.

A low-income urban industrial area, Ezbet Mekawy was originally an agricultural village in the outskirts of the Qalyubia governorate. In the 1920s, it witnessed an influx of people seeking low-income informal housing. During the 1950s and 1960s, small industrial workshops began to appear in the area. Today, remnants of the village—its maze-like, narrow unpaved alleyways, food vendors peddling from their donkey carts, garbage heaps and animals—merge with large industrial factories that have sprung up in the area. Air pollution has been but one of the negative impacts of this misguided and unplanned development process.

As early as 1968, inhabitants filed individual complaints against one of the lead smelters in the area. After the smelter was closed for two months, the owner reached an agreement with the authorities to raise the smoke stack so that emitted smoke would be carried further away from nearby houses. By the mid 1970s, the smelter extended its operation to three shifts a day, almost nonstop, using four stacks. The factory smelted up 24 tons of lead daily, 16 tons of which

Inas Tewfik, "Mobilization in a Cairo Neighborhood: Community Participation and Environmental Change," *MERIP Reports*, Winter 1997. Reprinted by permission.

were emitted into the surrounding environment in the form of black smoke laden with lead oxides and other pollutants. The problem was intensified by Ezbet Mekawy's downwind location. As one community member remembers, "If you spat, your saliva would be mixed with lead." Environmental pollution in the area caused severe health problems, including respiratory tract problems, cancer, stunted physical and mental growth, and in some cases even death.

In reaction to this situation, a group of volunteers from the neighborhood was formed in 1989 to close down the lead smelters in the area. The organizer of this community protest movement and its unofficial leader was imprisoned in 1971 for two years due to his involvement in a left, underground movement against the regime of the late President Sadat. The core organizers of the community protest identified with Nasserite beliefs. Many were members of the old socialist party or, as young men, were enlisted into Nasserite youth organizations. The political history of the community members provided a unifying frame of reference for organizing protests against the lead smelters.

Collective action was facilitated by the fact that, as one leader of the movement describes, "In times of need or crisis, we all become one. Having witnessed several deaths in their community, people were already aware of the dangers of the lead smelters. All they needed was for someone to pull these efforts together; someone to lead them forward."

Living in the same neighborhood enabled them to meet informally in the mosque after prayers, in coffee shops or on special occasions where possible actions and the latest developments could be discussed. It was decided from the start to adopt a peaceful strategy to communicate their complaints to the officials by filing official protests and enlisting the media to propagate their case to the general public and officials alike.

Throughout the struggle, various actors appeared on the scene. Both members of the People's Assembly for the area—one representing the ruling National Democratic Party and the other representing the leftist Tagammu' party—became involved in the struggle. They wrote a report on the hazardous effects the smelters posed to the community which was presented at the parliamentary discussions of the then new environmental law. Their involvement, however, was regarded by many in the protest movement as a ploy aimed at winning more votes for the coming elections.

A newly established health center (that began operating in 1992)—aimed at establishing an alternative health care system based on preventive as well as on curative services—found Ezbet Mekawy to be fertile ground for achieving these goals. Doctors at the center concentrated on providing the community members with "scientific" evidence of the negative health effects of the lead smelters through a series of soil, blood and air quality tests. In addition to this, popular perceptions and awareness of the environmental hazards of lead smelters were formed by the everyday experience of the residents. Such awareness, at its peak, was crystallized by the death of several members of the community.

The initial idea of filing a lawsuit against the governorate for granting permits for these smelters to operate in a residential area—neglecting industrial safety measures and codes for health standards which regulate the operation of these industrial outlets—was seen as tedious and without the possibility of obtaining any results in the immediate future. To justify their demands, the community members made use of an existing law that prohibits the operation of industrial outlets which prove to be affecting the public health or safety of those living in residential areas.

As knowledge of environmental issues expanded, the phrase "environmental pollution" became part of their language of protest for the first time. As a result, the problem was no longer confined to the local level—an owner who is not complying with industrial safety measures—but became regarded as an issue of public interest.

Stressing the point that these smelters were the source of environmental pollution and ill health in the area, protest letters were signed by community members and then sent to officials such as the prime minister, the president, the minister of interior, the minister of environment, the governor of Cairo, the head of the people's assembly, the minister of justice, and the minister of local administration.

After government officials failed to respond seriously to these protests, community members decided to take the battle onto the pages of newspapers and broadcast media. Stories focusing on the plight of Ezbet Mekawy quickly became an issue of interest to the broader public in Cairo especially because it fed into the public debate on a new environment law that was being prepared and discussed at that time. In addition to one television program and two radio programs, a series of articles written by and interviews with community members appeared in both government and opposition publications.

Several ideas for possible actions were debated during the course of the protests. One suggestion was to stand in front of the entrance to one of the smelters to get the attention of the police who would be forced to investigate this action. Community members refrained from doing this for fear that the police might resort to the emergency law and interpret their peaceful act as jeopardizing public safety and retaliate by jailing the participants.

Movement members decided to appeal to foreign governments with the hope that they would put pressure on their Egyptian counterpart to take more serious measures in stopping environmental pollution. When it became known that the German government had a specialized aid program directed towards environmental protection in Egypt, newspaper articles, pictures of sick children, medical reports and copies of the closure orders were prepared to be sent to Germany—an action to be taken only as a last resort. The documents were never sent.

The collective protests to close down the smelters were met with more than six closure orders from the government. None of them, however, were effectively implemented. The executive body justified its non-implementation of the orders on the grounds that 200 workers would lose their source of income and the governorate would be unable to provide an alternative location for these factories. Documents from the ministry of insurance and social affairs subsequently prove that only seven workers were legally registered in one of the factories. Moreover, the government's closure order did not oblige the governorate to provide the smelters with an area of land upon which to relocate their operations. In March 1994, work at the smelters was finally terminated when a third memo to cut off the electricity and water supplies to the smelters was issued from the governorate.

The collective action of the community had overcome several obstacles. At the local level, bureaucracy was the first impediment. While smoke poisoning from the lead smelters continued on a daily basis, protest letters took months to circulate from one government department to the other. At the same time, the owners of one of the lead smelters tried, in vain, to bribe the leader of the movement and thereby co-opt any further collective protest. Likewise, local officials were bribed to obstruct and delay the implementation of closure orders. Nevertheless, efforts to close down the smelter were successful largely because the demands did not constitute a threat to the formal power or interests of the state.

By choosing to follow legal and peaceful means in communicating their demands to officials, collective participation acted as a buffer against other possible acts of destruction and violence. While authentic collective action and participation must take place on the grassroots level, its success is largely dependent upon the responsiveness and tolerance of the state. In the case of Ezbet Mekawy, through community mobilization, residents effectively shifted the existing power structures on the micro-level of the community in order to reclaim control over their public space and mobilize around attempts to terminate the work of the lead smelting factories.

2. Environmental Protest Turns Ugly

Yarimca, Turkey, August 15, 2000 (ENS)—Fourteen people were arrested today amid a violent confrontation between Turkish police, factory security and environmental activists protesting pollution from the Petkim Chemical Complex in Izmit Bay.

Members of the environmental group Greenpeace hung a 25 meter long banner on the quayside reading "Earthquakes Strike Once, the Chemical Industry Strikes Everyday."

On August 17 last year, an earthquake hit the region. As part of its latest Mediterranean Toxic Tour, Greenpeace said it wants to highlight both the pollution caused by chemical plants in the region and the dangers of building them near seismic fault lines.

Other protesters climbed onto cranes and factory premises opening flags voicing opposition to the use of toxic substances.

According to Greenpeace, Petkim's security staff were violent towards the activists and pushed two into the water. Fourteen of the 16 Greenpeace activists dispatched from the *MV Greenpeace* are now in police custody.

"The devastation caused by the Marmara earthquake last year brought to the fore the hazards posed behind chemical plants' closed doors," said Tolga Temuge, a toxics campaigner in Turkey. "Yet, the Bay of Izmit did not die on the 17th of August of last year. It was murdered by the industry a long time ago. We are demanding zero toxic discharges and the phase-in of alternative clean technologies."

Samples taken by Greenpeace of the toxic waste pumped into the environment by Petkim repeatedly revealed substances that are included as priority contaminants for elimination from discharges into the sea under Annex I of the Barcelona Convention for the Protection of the Marine Environment and Coastal Region of the Mediterranean.

In 1975, all nations bordering the Med, except Albania, Algeria and Syria, met in Barcelona and promised to "take all appropriate measures to prevent, abate and combat pollution in the Mediterranean Sea area and to protect and improve the marine environment in the area."

This led to the Mediterranean Action Plan, launched by the United Nations, and was the beginning of what is now known as the Barcelona Convention. Today, all Mediterranean states, including the EU, are members of the Barcelona Convention.

But the convention's six protocols have yet to be ratified by all members. So far, Tunisia has ratified all protocols while Monaco, Italy and Spain have ratified all protocols except the Hazardous Waste and Offshore Protocols.

The focus of the *MV Greenpeace* Mediterranean tour is to pressure all governments in the region to ratify the Barcelona Convention.

Greenpeace's requests to the Turkish government for reliable data on the hazardous waste generated by industrial plants have proved fruitless. The group says the Turkish Ministry for Environment replied to a Greenpeace letter last month admitting that it could not provide the data.

"We urge the public to stand up and fight for their right to know," said Temuge. "We demand a Toxics Use Inventory and a Toxics Use Reduction Act to replace the poisons produced by the chemical industry which are dispersed in our food and in the tissues of our children."

The *MV Greenpeace* Mediterranean tour is the latest in a series of tours in the region that began in 1986.

4. The Imazighen (Berbers) of Algeria Decry the Pronouncement of the Country as "Arab," 1998

Before the Arabs arrived in North Africa in the seventh century, the population of the region was overwhelmingly Amazigh (Berber). Except for the coastal cities and towns, most of the land was occupied by these tribal and settled peoples. Although nearly all the Imazighen (the plural of Amazigh) *converted to Islam and many of them joined Arab armies in pushing the Muslim conquests as far as the Iberian*

Peninsula and France, they constituted a distinct ethnic group with its own culture and language (Tamazight). Berbers suffered from discrimination at the hand of Arab rulers, and in response they protested and at times revolted in opposition. In the twentieth century, this situation did not improve. As nationalist struggles for independence intensified in North Africa around the middle of the past century, the ideology of that struggle became more monocultural (see the chapter "Contested Nationalisms"). In Algeria, where the indigenous population fought against a century of French occupation and exploitation, the ruling FLN (National Liberation Front) defined Algeria as an Arab-Muslim state and nation. Hidden beneath that label is the reality of Berber (Amazigh) existence. Despite some symbolic gestures acknowledging the existence of other-than-Arab cultures in Algeria, many Berbers in Algeria (and elsewhere) consider themselves to be an oppressed minority.

For an Immediate Abrogation of the Law Pertaining to the Generalization of the Arabic Language in Algeria

Call

We, the cultural, social, women's associations . . . ; women and men gathered together this day, 21 May 1998, at the headquarters of the Tamazgha Association (Paris), having discussed the contents and consequences of the law pertaining to the generalization of the Arabic language in Algeria, and which will become effective on 5 July 1998.

In the course of the debates, the following arguments clearly emerged to justify our action against this law which must be abrogated.

This law aims at excluding Tamazight (the Berber language)—which is already marginalized by the fact that it is not recognized constitutionally—in a way that it was never excluded before. A law which prohibits individuals to express themselves in meetings, judiciary audiences, and the parliament . . . is a villainous law because it denies the human being the right to legitimately use his language.

Tamazight, which has only a small development space circumscribed in time, is being suppressed on purpose. The law pertaining to the generalization of the Arabic language is encoded in straight lines of judicial texts with an eye toward bringing about the linguistic assimilation of the Imazighen (Berbers), an objective that has been the goal of those who for decades have sought to deny the Amazigh [Berber] identity.

The Jacobinism[1] which is the ideological foundation of this law aims to efface the cultural and linguistic wealth that have been the nourishing sap for the civilization of the region [North Africa].

---

[1]Jacobins, the radical wing of the French Revolution, instituted a series of extreme social and economic reforms. They achieved historical notoriety for instituting, through local Jacobin clubs, the Reign of Terror. Jacobinism thus became synonymous with dictatorship.

Collective for the Abrogation of the Law Regarding the Arabization of Algeria. http://www.kabyle.com (May 2001). Translated by Akram Khater.

This law aims to exclude the use and employ of French at the level of public administrations, universities, hospitals, socio-economic sectors, etc. It also aims to exclude the Francophone elite, [who] are [educated] . . . in Algerian schools [and who] represent the technical and scientific cadres in all sectors.

It condemns the emigration—which is the source of financial contributions, scientific, technical and economic knowledge—to a non-return [to Algeria]; because that inhumane law aims to expel out of Algeria close to two million emigrants and their children.

That law aims then at the destruction of the socio-economic apparatus and making it "archaic" because the French language is in reality the third language in use in Algeria.

The application of the law of Arabization within the educational system has already caused irreparable damage to the level of education whose consequences are visible in Algeria in all sectors.

This law is aimed as much at both the Francophone elite and cadres as at the Amazigh. For all these reasons, we reject this unjust and irresponsible law because:

- It marginalizes an important part of Algerian men and women;
- It is an attempt to isolate Algeria from the rest of the world;
- It stops the modernization of Algeria and the attainment of democracy.

We appeal to associations, women and men, celebrities, artists, intellectuals, academics . . . who reject this law, to join the Collective created for the purpose of focusing our action around a specific point which is the abrogation of this law.

The Collective remains OPEN to all those who sympathize with this struggle.
C.A.L.A.A.
Paris, 21 May 1998.

5. A Kurdish Activist's Letter Appealing to Berna Yilmaz, the Spouse of the Turkish Prime Minister, September 27, 1998

The Kurds are an ethnic community whose ancestral homeland is divided among the modern nations of Iran, Iraq, and Turkey. Thus, the desire of Kurdish nationalists for a separate nation of their own has come into continuous and often violent conflict with the nationalist claims of those three countries. For a brief moment after World War I, with the support of President Woodrow Wilson, it appeared that the dream of

Leyla Zana, "An Open Letter to the First Lady of Turkey," 27 September 1998, American Kurdish Information Network (AKIN), trans. staff of the American Kurdish Information Network. http://kurdistan.org/Leyla/firstlady.html (27 January 2003). Reprinted by permission.

a Kurdish nation would come true, and such a state was included in the Treaty of Sèvres (see document 5 in the chapter "Ideas of Nationalism"). However, the maps drawn up after the war made no allowance for any such territory, and from the early days of the Turkish republic, the Kurds suffered persecution that resulted in—among others things—the banning of Kurdish names, language, and culture. Subsequently several Kurdish liberation movements, like the Kurdistan Workers Party (PKK), emerged for the purpose of making independent Kurdistan a reality. However, internal Kurdish conflicts, entanglement in regional politics (such as the Gulf War), and Kurdish acts of terrorism against civilians have made this dream unattainable so far. Yet there is no doubt that the plight of the Kurds and the persecution of their political leaders have captured the imagination of many foreigners.

One of those Kurdish political leaders is Leyla Zana, a Kurd elected to the Turkish parliament. In March 1994 the Turkish parliament voted to lift the parliamentary immunity of Leyla Zana and five other Kurdish MPs because they made public announcements supporting Kurdish rights and independence. The State Security Court prosecutor Nusret Demirel successfully prosecuted the accused for seeking to "separate the . . . Turkish Republic through legal ways," and they received jail sentences for their activism on behalf of the Kurds. From her jail cell, Leyla Zana wrote the following letter appealing to the wife of the Turkish prime minister.

Dear Berna Yilmaz,

Because you are the wife of Prime Minister, you probably receive hundreds if not thousands of letters from people all over the country.

Some ask for peace,

Some for work.

Other[s] share with you a problem with the hope that you will be part of its solution.

Some want to reach goals that may not be attainable.

There are still others who write you and tell you that they can not [*sic*] pay the cost of an operation for their loved ones and those who can not pay for the prescribed medication.

Some may be the relatives of deceased ones in the hospitals who may ask you to write to a hospital to let it release the body of the deceased person since they can not pay for the hospital costs. And of course, there are other letters, the ones that congratulate you for your work or recognize you for your achievements.

I thought I too would add a letter, be another one in your mail list. You don't know me or you may know me through the media or shall I say the way media has projected me.

For example, a "Bandit!," a "Terrorist!," a "Separatist!," a "Traitor!" or a convicted member of PKK. The list goes on.

I am not the least concerned to be associated with these descriptions. They, in a way, point to the alleged players on the stage whose roots go back to history. I want to refer to a bleeding geography and also to the concerted efforts of the ruling circles to deny the very existence of a people. I am referring to the struggle of those who are standing up to oppression for peace, freedom, brotherhood, democracy and labor rights. I have in mind their principled stands and how they were seen fit to assume those names. In other words, I am referring to the reality of my country, of its peoples and the state of affairs that are unfolding in it.

If it needs to be stated again, I belong to those who seek peace.

I know you through the media. Your warm disposition, friendly face, interested and humble ways that come across in numerous places. So I am writing this letter to you as a woman and also as a mother. Because I think we have at least those two things in common. But then I may be mistaken.

You may ask what prompted this letter?

A few years back, I read in an interview your views about the ongoing conflict. You were asked to comment on the war between the Turkish army and the PKK. While you did the usual, calling the question a problem of the southeast, but you also uttered the taboo words, the need for peace and a humane approach to resolve the conflict. I may not be quoting you verbatim, but I remember you saying that you did not want the mothers to cry and that you were very worried about the state of things.

These words were moving, not the usual remarks of the wife of Prime Minister. There was no disguised form of chauvinism, racism, and the talk about blood in your remarks.

Then I remember the accident/incident in which your son hurting himself in a sporting event was sent to Austria with a private plane to get proper medical care. The televised images of your sadness were real. You were distraught. You wanted to be with your son and the anxiety was showing all over your face.

It was the anxiety of a mother. Watching you, I did not want to think that you were the wife of Prime Minister, I wanted to understand you as a mother. A part of you had been hurt and you wanted to be with your son as soon as possible. And you finally got to see him.

And yet, there are mothers in Turkey, forget about being able to be with their children, do not even know where they are. They can not reach them, embrace them, smell them or touch them.

They do not even have a grave site for them, a place these mothers could shed their tears.

These mothers, for years now, every Saturday, meet in front of Galatasaray High School at noon, with pictures of their loved ones in their hands. They want to share their pain by means of peaceful sit-ins.

They do not loiter, they do not block the traffic, and they do not attack the spectators.

They want to sit there in front of that high school to voice their deadening silence about their losses.

The names of their loved ones were Mehmet, Hasan, Yavuz, Aysel and Savas at one time. But they all have one name now: disappeared ones.

The names of the mothers are Emine, Esma, Yildiz, and Pervin. Now, they have one name as well: the mothers of disappeared ones or Saturday Mothers.

Do you know what is happening to them for weeks now?

Elite police forces with their batons, shields, and guns accompanied with the sounds of siren attack these mothers, pull their hairs, haul their bodies, beat their torsos, subject them to pressurized water and force them to board the waiting busses [*sic*] for police stations. They are then kept for a few days and then released. These mothers gather in front of that high school for what they feel in their hearts. Will they ever stop coming? Dauntlessly, they come back. Their crime is to be the Saturday Mothers. Their crime is to love their sons and daughters.

You are a mother and they are mothers.

You have a son named Hasan and another named Yavuz. They had sons at one time.

You love your children. These mothers are even denied a [*sic*] opportunity to express their love for their children.

Moreover, these mothers don't want other mothers to face their predicament. In other words, they love the children of others as well. They don't want any disappearances. They love peace so that war will not consume their loved ones. And because of that, they keep coming back to the same spot for weeks and sit for hours without getting tired. In other words, their love is boundless, deep and universal.

One Saturday, I urge you, please, to go to Galatasaray High School. Go see those mothers. Take them a flower, a carnation, or a September rose, and be part of their pain. If only for a few minutes, be a Saturday Mother, be a mother of the disappeared. Don't be afraid of elite police forces. Don't be afraid of the sounds of siren that have legitimized lawlessness, injustice, and oppression. The police won't touch you. No, they will not be able to touch you. Then, believe me, you will love yourself more and your children too.

You can be one of the "first" ones to do so. You can set aside the so-called traditions of hundreds of years.

Remember that Princess Diana broke the tradition of remaining aloof, and became one of the people, and was mourned by millions when her untimely death arrived. And she lives today in the hearts of additional millions because of her principled stand against the threat of mines.

Back to our country, the cease-fire that PKK declared goes on despite the provocation, despite the silence of many in the positions of authority. You said, mothers should not cry. But mothers are still crying even as one side to this war is willing to take the road of peace.

Here is a golden opportunity for you. You can bring the crying Turkish and Kurdish mothers together. And the mothers of disappeared as well.

Or you could choose to be the mother of only Yavuz and Hasan. . . .

6. Journalist Lilian Liang Discusses Homosexuality in Egypt, 1999

One of the taboo subjects in the Middle East and North Africa is homosexuality. This unwillingness to acknowledge the existence of homosexuals—and AIDS—within society is a modern phenomenon that developed toward the end of the nineteenth century. Before that time, poetry celebrating homosexuality was common, and homosexual activities were tolerated, though not approved by everyone (see Rifa'a Tahtawi's reflections—document 1 in the chapter "Social and Cultural Reformulations"). One outcome of the "modernization" of the region was the shunning of alternative sexual lifestyles in favor of a heterosexual model based on the idea of the nuclear family. Today, the strength of the taboo is slowly diminishing. The climate of democracy that is straining to exist in the Middle East and North Africa allows a modicum of space for homosexual and other subcultures to emerge publicly. The document included here—about homosexuality in Egypt—provides a glimpse into such subcultures. Furthermore, it allows you to understand marginal democratic movements that are mostly quietly—but sometimes loudly—demanding a place in the civil societies of the regions.

Many girls at Alexandria University have fallen for the charms of 22-year-old Michael, an Egyptian art student with delicate features and green almond-shaped eyes. But he has lost count of the number of times he has refused to go out on dates—and not because he likes playing hard to get. He is just more interested in spending time with his French boyfriend. "I tell the girls straight away that it's not personal and that I am gay," he explains with a shy smile. "They are shocked in the beginning, but then we become friends."

Michael started having homosexual intercourse when he was 12 but his first steady relationship happened when he was 16. After it was over, he got depressed and had to be medicated for a year—which was when he told his family about his sexual orientation.

"Homosexuality is becoming more apparent in the Egyptian society," says Dr. Josette Abdalla, assistant professor of Psychology at the American University in Cairo (AUC). "This is in part the result of more exposure to mass media, western influences and more access to papers, satellite dishes and TV."

According to her, these factors are making Egyptians more aware of their own sexuality. The changes are happening slowly, however. Numbers and visibility are increasing, but homosexuality is still a taboo in the country. Even though everybody knows it has always existed—in literature and real life—nobody talks about it. Crossing the safe line between the familiar world of heterosexuality and venturing into the unknown of open homosexuality is still a risk most don't take.

"It is a contradictory phenomenon," explains Ted Swedenburg, assistant professor of Anthropology at University of Arkansas and a Middle East expert. "In the past, it was not very much talked about, but it was more accepted. Now, homosexuality is more visible and causing more reaction." The reaction is more of a backlash, however. Instead of becoming more liberal, society is becoming more conservative. According to Swedenburg, it could be because it is easier to deal with things when they remain out of sight.

Michael complains about the attitude towards what he thinks are the millions of homosexuals present in Egypt, including gays and lesbians. "Even if the government accepts [homosexuality] and makes it official, the people will still refuse it," he says. "They think that being gay is shameful and brings Egypt a bad reputation."

He is probably right. The reaction of society, especially the family, is still the main factor hindering homosexuals in admitting their orientation according to health care experts.

"It's a big shame to the family because it's not only about the homosexual himself," says Dr. Sanaa Nassif, HIV/AIDS program officer at Caritas Egypt. "His sister is going to be known as the sister of a homosexual and his father will be known for having a homosexual son."

Ashraf (like most quoted in this article, not his real name), a 30-year-old doctor in Cairo, preferred to spare his family from such comments. Gay for more than half of his life now, his parents still don't know about his sexual choice. Instead, they keep asking him when he will get married. "I will never tell them that I'm gay," he says. "I don't want to hurt them." Intolerance to homosexuality is not only found inside the family. Societal norms still hold a very strict position regarding sexuality and even people who have daily contact with the gay scene have a hard time accepting them. Mohammed, manager of a famous gay hangout in a Cairo five-star hotel, doesn't sympathize with his customers, despite the business they generate. "Money with a bad reputation, how good is that?" he asks. "Even prostitutes are more respectable than gays."

Hassan, a 26-year-old actor in Cairo, remembers the days when homosexuals had more freedom and less restrictions.

"Five years ago, I gave a birthday party and invited around 30 people," he recalls. "About 200 people showed up, some complete strangers. I didn't even know there were that many gays in Egypt." But despite the increasing numbers, the situation is getting worse.

In addition to prejudice, homosexuals also have to deal with police abuse—they are sometimes arrested when leaving pubs and beaten up for no apparent reason.

Ahmed, who owns a restaurant in Alexandria, has never been arrested, but prefers to play it safe. "A friend of mine was taken and forced to sign a document admitting that he was making out in the street, which was not true," he recalls. "Now every time police are out there, I call everyone to warn them."

Episodes like these usually happen only to the more affluent gays, especially because they are the ones who have money to spend in pubs and restaurants. Homosexuals from poorer segments of society meet at public places, such as Ataba Square or Ramsis Station, where the crowds make the meetings harder to spot.

"Some lower-class men become homosexuals just because they don't have enough money to afford a prostitute," says Dr. Nassif. "If they have money, they usually go for a woman."

According to her, lower-class homosexuals differ from their richer counterparts not only in the way they dress and places they go, but also in the way they behave.

"Most lower-class homosexuals don't look or behave in a feminine way," says Dr. Nassif. Unlike the high-class gay scene, they don't have feminine gestures or voices—many don't even see themselves as gays, especially if they play the more active role in sexual relations.

"If they are active, they are considered even more masculine because they are not sleeping with a woman, but with a man, who is stronger," explains Nassif.

Sometimes leading a dual life, like most homosexuals in Egypt, might cause more problems than just prejudice and rejection. In the face of these pressures, some homosexuals can't maintain the facade—and end up with serious psychological problems such as paranoia and depression. "One of my clients was so obsessed with the idea that someone would find out about him being gay that every time somebody spat near him, he thought that the person knew about it," says Dr. Nassif. "He would take it as a sign of disdain."

According to the psychiatrist, most of her clients are from poor backgrounds because they are less afraid of exposing themselves. "Because of their economic situation, many of them think they are not worthy of respect," she explains. "That sometimes makes it easier for them to seek help."

By help she means counseling, not treatment. It is common to see homosexuals denying their own identity and seeking out a "cure." One of Dr. Nassif's clients was so busy trying not to be gay he quit his job and stayed at home to avoid risky situations.

According to her, problems like these could be avoided if more information about the issue were available, especially for young people. "Because nobody talks about it, these people spend a lot of time thinking about sex and creating wrong ideas," says Dr. Nassif.

With homosexuality becoming more visible in Egypt, some believe that the solution to their dilemma lies in reversing the conservative trend in society.

"There must be more freedom," says Swedenburg. "It all comes with more freedom of expression and education." He feels homosexuals need to play a major role in the process, but steps have to be taken slowly, starting with the individual.

"I hope I'm setting the example for other people like me," says Michael. "If you accept and respect yourself, everybody will accept and respect you."

7. Arab and Israeli Soccer Players Discuss Ethnic Relations in Israel, 2000

In September 2000, Israeli-Palestinian relations rapidly deteriorated into violent conflict. The immediate cause was the visit of Ariel Sharon (at that time an Israeli ex-minister of defense considered by Palestinians to be a war criminal) to al-Haram al-Sharif—the third holiest Islamic site and a place that most Jews consider to be the site of the Temple. Sharon's visit was the spark that lit pent-up Palestinian

frustrations with the Oslo peace process. Earlier attempts at peace appeared bank-
rupt, and the gap between Arab and Jew yawned wider. In the West Bank and
Gaza, Israeli occupation forces came under attack by stone-throwing civilians and
armed Palestinian police, and Israelis sought to maintain their hold through in-
creasingly violent measures against the Palestinian population.

These tensions spilled over quickly into Israel itself, where the Arab-Israeli pop-
ulation arose in protest for two reasons: (1) to demonstrate in sympathy with Pales-
tinian Arabs in the Occupied Territories and demand an end to Israeli occupation
and (2) to express frustration at their own status as second-class citizens within the
state of Israel. Although academicians had been discussing the discriminatory na-
ture of the Israeli state and society, only a few liberal intellectuals were interested in
the topic. The majority of Israeli Jews were unaware of, or uninterested in, the plight
of the Arab Israelis.

The emotional intensity of the demonstrations caught most Israeli Jews by sur-
prise, and ultimately they were angered by what they saw as Arab-Israeli betrayal
of the state. During bitter protest demonstrations, some Arab Israelis were shot and
killed by Israeli police, and others were attacked by Jewish mobs. These events ex-
acerbated the situation, despite attempts by politicians and intellectuals to contain
the potentially explosive issue by calling for committees of inquiry into the plight of
the Arab Israelis and into the use of excessive violence by Israeli police against Arab-
Israeli demonstrators.

Arab Israelis were posing fundamental questions about the nature of the state
of Israel. Is it a Jewish state, and if it is, then where does that leave the Arab Israelis?
Furthermore, if Israel is a democracy, then how should it deal with ethnic discrimi-
nation against citizens of Arab descent, who are growing in numbers at a faster
rate than Jewish citizens of the state? This document explores the ways in which
Arab and Jewish soccer players handle these tensions and questions in order to
come up with a winning team.

Two weeks ago, having suffered three losses and four ties, Maccabi Ahi
Nazareth found itself last in the National League. The team's lackluster performance did little to improve the atmosphere in Nazareth, its mood already
dampened by the recent rioting and its harsh economic consequences. In an effort to keep from sinking to a lower league, the team's management fired coach
Samir Issa and appointed Eli Mahpoud in his place. Surprisingly, the replacement of an Arab coach with a Jewish one, even in these tense times, was accepted in Nazareth without protest. The Ahi Nazareth fans, it seems, just want
their team to stay in the National League, the second of the six divisions in Israeli soccer, under the Premier League. If nothing else, at least that. This is
Mahpoud's second stint in Nazareth. Last season, when Maccabi Ahi Nazareth
found itself in similar straits, Mahpoud came on as its coach and succeeded in
keeping it in the National League. When the season ended, he accepted the better contract offered by Maccabi Kiryat Gat. But the relationship with Kiryat
Gat proved short-lived, and Mahpoud found himself out of a job—a common

Uriya Shavit, "Playing for Keeps," *Ha'aretz*, 3 November 2000. Copyright © 2000. Reprinted by permission.

enough occurrence in the dizzying game of musical chairs that is Israeli soccer. When the offer from Nazareth came, Mahpoud agreed almost immediately.

The recent outbreak of violence, he says, had little influence on his deliberations on whether or not to accept the job. "I was worried only that the roads might be closed, and I would not be able to make it to practice. Those around me were more concerned than I was. I did not give much thought to what happened in Nazareth. I like to think positive. There are radical minorities everywhere. I don't know the city, but I do know the team and its fans, and they're wonderful people. They welcomed me warmly when I signed back on."

The first game under Mahpoud's renewed reign, played against Hapoel Jerusalem, ended in a sweet 2–1 victory. The night before, shots had been fired on the Jewish neighborhood of Gilo in Jerusalem. Only a handful of fans accompanied the Nazareth team to the game. Mahpoud says he did not know how his players would be received at Teddy Stadium. "Naturally, we were a little anxious, but in the end it was wonderful: When I sent out one of our players, the Jerusalem fans applauded. It was heartwarming."

Driving to practice from his home in Petah Tikva last week, Mahpoud was unwilling to talk politics. His radio was tuned to the all-music station Galgalatz throughout the two-hour trip to Nazareth and to local sports news on the 90-minute drive back. The fact that he coaches an Arab team is mere coincidence, as far as he is concerned. People who work in sports, he believes, should worry only about sports.

Mahpoud claims that the team's four Jewish players—Sagi Strauss, Shlomi Ben-Hamu, Arik Hangali and Emil Castiel—were similarly unaffected by the current crisis. "The rioting in Nazareth had no effect on anyone in the team, Jewish or Arab," he says. "None of the Jewish players came and said they wanted to leave. Soccer players are soccer players: they want to play."

The National League is the perennial "not quite" league. Its players earn their living playing soccer, but most of them never make it to the big money. Ahi Nazareth's Jewish players were all in the Premier League once, and they all hope to be back there someday. Some of the Arab players have also played in top "Jewish" teams. Under the great mantra of "professionalism," they can play together without stopping to worry about their identity or relationship with their communities. They all share the same dream: to go as far as they can. There are, however, some significant differences. For the Arab players, their own ethnic origin is one major obstacle on the way to making the dream come true.

Issam Issami, the team's striker, is a Druze who served in the Israeli army. He spent last season playing for Maccabi Netanya and had hoped to move to Betar Jerusalem for the current season. "I was at the Betar tryouts this summer. By the end of the first week, I felt I was not welcome there. Fans yelled curses at me during the first practice. The players didn't say anything to my face, but I knew that behind my back they were asking, 'Why did they have to bring the Arab player?' I knew what would happen if I made a mistake during the first game, that the crowd would call me a dirty Arab. Jerusalem has Jews and goys. I'm a goy to them. I spent three years in the army, and I'm a goy to them."

Is it possible that you simply weren't good enough for Betar?

"Of course that's what they'd say. But that's not what I feel. Look, it's my country. I feel that it's my country. But you won't give me the space to feel that. You act like it's not my country, not in soccer, and not in other areas."

Life as an Arab player

Mahpoud, once a star player in Hapoel Petah Tikva, was first recommended for the job by his friend Azmi Nassar, who two years ago led the Palestinian national team to third place in the Pan Arab Games. Nassar says he thought Mahpoud would work well with an Arab team. "He's an honest person, understands a lot about soccer. He has this restaurant in Petah Tikva where he works with Arab employees, and he gets along with them. I was sure he would not be patronizing or dismissive toward the Arab players."

Nassar is now coach of Bnei Sakhnin, the National League's other Arab team. Bnei Sakhnin now faces a double challenge. It is struggling not only to remain in the league, but also to maintain its status as "Israel's leading Arab team." Maccabi Ahi Nazareth is its arch-enemy. Last week the two teams played each other; Bnei Sakhnin won 2–1.

In the days preceding this much-awaited match, Mahpoud and Nassar's friendship helped take some of the sting out of the fierce rivalry. There was, however, another reason why passions did not quite rise to their expected frenzy: up until the last minute, it was not clear whether the game would even take place.

The police refused to allow the match to be held in Nazareth. When Kiryat Eliezer was suggested as an alternative site, the insurance company demanded an exorbitant security deposit. "It's hard to prepare a team for a match this way," Mahpoud said last Tuesday, during the break between morning and afternoon practice. "You have to divide up the practice load, follow a plan, and you can't do that under these conditions. The Arab teams are harmed through no fault of their own."

Do you support the Arab players' claims that they suffer from discrimination?

"People in Ahi Nazareth say that the referees are prejudiced against them. In some games I feel that it's true. I think it's mostly because we're a small team, even for the second league. But it's also true that the life of an Arab player is much harder.

"They tell me that players on rival teams curse them, calling them 'dirty Arab' and names like that. That infuriates me. I always tell them that you can't allow yourself to be affected by these provocations. This is their job, their livelihood, and they have to keep it. I also get sworn at by the fans of rival teams. When I was coaching a Jewish team, the curses were much softer. Here people yell, 'You son of a bitch, why are you coaching Arabs?'"

What about your friend Azmi Nassar?

"Azmi did not get a single offer from a Jewish team, despite his many successes. I don't know why that is. He's an excellent coach. Speaking in purely professional terms, he has what it takes to coach a Premier League team. Maybe it's because soccer is such an emotional business. If his team failed, well, you know the kind of position the administration would then be in, having hired an Arab coach."

[. . .]

Carpools and Music

Having finished their lunch, four of the Ahi Nazareth players sit around a table in a downtown restaurant and talk. Shlomi Ben Hamu lives in Herzliya, is married and has a child, and once played for Hakoah Ramat Gan and Hapoel Petah Tikva. Arik Hangali lives in Bat Yam. Last season he played for Ironi Rishon Letzion. Ashraf Suliman, the chairman's nephew, lives in Nazareth and grew up on the local team. Abed Titi, who lives in Tira, is the National League's leading goal-maker after nine rounds of playing, even though Ahi Nazareth is still a game short.

The four are friends, and not only on the soccer field. Titi, Ben Hamu and Hangali carpool to practice, meeting each day at the Netanya junction. Whoever is driving gets to choose the music, so that Ben Hamu and Hangali are constantly exposed to the latest Arab hits.

SULIMAN: We in Nazareth want good players. We don't care if they're Jewish, Arab or foreign, as long as they play well.

HANGALI: I never thought I'd end up playing for an Arab team, but from the moment I got here, I felt at home. I was treated very warmly, and I knew I was staying. You have to know how to keep sports and politics apart. We're in sports, we all have the same goal. I feel that I represent the city of Nazareth. I have no problem with that. But I also represent myself—if I don't play well, I'll disgrace myself, too. We're not repressing reality. Titi and Suliman are really our friends. If a few extremists raised some hell, is that any reason to be mad at them?

TITI: We only want peace and quiet. What does anyone, Jewish or Arab, have to gain from people being killed? Why can't we all have fun together?

SULIMAN: Iad Lawabneh, the first casualty from Nazareth, was a big fan of ours. He was killed 15 minutes before our game against Kiryat Gat began. Our management asked to have the game postponed, but it wasn't. We lost.

BEN HAMU: I had no problem playing when the riots started. I never thought of leaving the team. All in all, I know both the people here and the administration. People in my family were worried about me, said I should look into other options. But eventually, when things calmed down, those fears disappeared, too.

HANGALI: When we came to practice on the days of the rioting, we found fans waiting. They said they'd look out for us. Today, when people in Tel Aviv ask me whether I'm afraid to go to Nazareth, I laugh. What's there to be afraid of?

BEN HAMU: Joining Nazareth changed something for me. I didn't know any Arabs before, had no Arab friends. I knew nothing about their mentality. Today I get together with friends from the Arab team even after practice. We go out to eat or go bowling. Today all I want is for there to be peace.

[…]

8.   Self-Reflection by the Communist Party of Iran, 2001

Most recent articles and reports about Iran—and about the Middle East and North Africa in general—concentrate on Islamic politics, thus giving the impression that secularism and leftist politics are completely absent from the political spectrum and that all thought and action are firmly contained within the rubric of Islam. This approach to understanding these areas obscures the range of ideas that exist in practically every part of the Middle East and North Africa. Even if secular and leftist movements remain limited in their membership and overall role in public life, their voices create a counterpoint to the rightist politics of most Islamic movements and to the authoritarianism of the state.

The following document is a statement by one of the oldest leftist political parties in the Middle East—the Tudeh (Masses) Party of Iran. Founded in 1941 by a group of young Iranian Marxists, the party sought a broad variety of social and economic reforms to better the lot of workers and peasants. Partly because of its political platform, and partly because of its organizational success, Tudeh became the largest and most efficient political party in Iran. Many people in Iran believed that it would dominate the government shortly after World War II. In part, Tudeh failed to come to power because the United States and Britain were strongly opposed to the party since they believed that it would allow the Soviet Union too much influence in that oil-rich region. Reprinted here is a statement issued by the party on its sixtieth anniversary. It offers a glimpse of Tudeh's view of the history of Iran and its vision of the country's future.

Six decades of historic and heroic struggle by the party of workers, women, youth, students and intellectuals to emancipate the country from the chain of imperialism, reactions, dictatorship and to achieve democracy, freedom, independence and social justice.

Central Committee of the Tudeh Party of Iran, "Statement of the Central Committee of the Tudeh Party of Iran on the Sixtieth Anniversary of the Party," from "Nameh Mardom," Central Organ of the Tudeh Party of Iran, no. 618, 23 September 2001, reprinted in *Tudeh News,* no. 207, October 2001.

*   *   *

October 2, 2001, marks the sixtieth anniversary of Tudeh Party of Iran (TPI), the party of the working class of our country. Sixty years ago, political prisoners just released from Reza Shah's prisons, along with other freedom seeking persons in our country, founded the party. The founders of TPI were comrades of the great revolutionary and thinker, Dr. Taghi Erani. They strove to continue the path of the Social Democratic Movement and the Communist Party of Iran before them.

The appearance of TPI in the political arena of Iran was an important historical event, creating an undeniable impact on the political, cultural and social life of our country. In those days, political parties survived on the good grace of the regime and so played the role of defending internal reaction and imperialism. In contrast, TPI raised the banner for the rights of the toiling masses. From the very onset, the party faced the wrath and attacks from all those who benefited entirely from internal reaction, dictatorship and imperialism.

The Tudeh Party of Iran: Impact on the Political and Cultural Life of Our Society

The party's impact on the society can be investigated in many ways. TPI was the only political organisation in the country that [was] based on realizing the aspirations and the will of the working class. It played a unique role in organising and educating the working class. In the short period that the party enjoyed freedom of activity, it influenced the progress of our country.

When TPI stepped into the political-class struggle, Iran was a semi-feudal and semi-capitalist society, deeply influenced by a reactionary and imperialistic culture. In those days, women had no right to vote. Foreign imperialist countries imposed their policies on the government and political figures. Peasants were sold along with the land they worked on. Political and cultural backwardness, and superstition dominated Iranian society.

Within a few years of activity, our party made deep inroads into the political-cultural life of the country. The first programme of TPI, delivered to its first congress in 1944, is a historic document showing the revolutionary essence, far sightedness, intellectual clarity and progressive thinking of our party. It was the first programme of a political party in the Iranian contemporary history offering the means of achieving trade union rights, reduction of working hours to eight per day, creating a social security system, establishing land reform, right of women to elect and to be elected and gain equal rights and the right of religious and ethnic minorities.

More importantly, our party was able to organise a large social force from among the workers, women, youth and students aimed at realising these progressive aspirations. Members of our party played an outstanding role in creating organisations: the "United Central Council of the Workers and Toilers" in 1944, the first peasant unions in 1943, the "Democratic Organisation of Iranian

Women" (broadly based women's organisation dedicated to the struggle for women's rights), the "Organisation of the Tudeh Youth" in 1943 (a progressive organisation of youth and students). All these reflected clearly the effect our party had in organising a vast social struggle for fundamental change[s] in the social life of our society.

Our party has also played a major role in introducing new thoughts, particularly in introducing Marxism and Leninism to Iranians in the last six decades. The publication of hundreds of books, journals and scientific articles created a qualitative change in the familiarity of different generations in our country in differen[t] scientific fields especially in the fields of politics, economics and social sciences. Today, even after sixty years, those seeking to study the classics on Marxism in Farsi (Persian language), their main source of reference will be the publications of TPI. The reactionary and imperialist forces do not fear our party for its material strength, but because of its immense intellectual influence and its ability to influence events in the country.

The Role and Effect of the Tudeh Party of Iran in the Most Important Events of Contemporary Iranian History

A scientific study of contemporary Iranian history cannot, in all fairness ignore the key role TPI has played in the most important events of the last six decades. The degree of creativity and far sightedness displayed by our party had been enormous. Our party has utilised the experiences of democratic movements both in Iran and internationally to direct the process of events towards creating a democratic, just, free and independent Iran. Revolutionary thinking, boldness and search for new solutions to continue the process, proposing solutions and showing the way forward during extremely complex times of the democratic movement are among the unique characteristics of TPI.

The first battlefield for our party was the struggle against fascism and its destructive effect on the political life of the country. The 1940s coincided with the aggression of the united front of fascist Germany, Italy and Japan who had dreams of domination and absolute slavery around the world. In Iran, the ruling reactionaries of the time were preparing themselves to welcome the frontrunners of Nazi Germany. Poisonous and reactionary thinking of the Nazis had been disseminated amongst the Iranian people tainted with lies and anticommunist propaganda and had successfully poisoned important segments of the society.

Under these circumstances, our newly formed working class party, embarked on creating the party structures, educating its cadres in the scientific ideology of Marxism-Leninism. It also exposed the true nature of fascism and the danger threatening the sovereignty and freedom of the nations. The party also strove to unite the national forces against this danger and to organise and lead the democratic movement to push forward and consolidate the gains made in the democratic rights and freedoms. The publications of the daily "Mardom" [the people] also known as the "antifascist Mardom" and the wide ranging activities of the members of the TPI were able to transform the poisonous political climate of the country and unite the broad based population of the country against the fascism and its dangers.

Another arena of struggle for the party in those years was to unite and organise all democratic forces for the nationalisation of the oil industry and to struggle against the corrupt Pahlavi dynasty, under Moha[mm]ed Reza Shah, propped up by the imperialists. Many historical documents, some of which were recently released by imperialist countries like [the] United States and Britain's document centres, bear witness to the fact that reaction and the imperialism had viewed and targeted the party as its main enemy. Even the political opponents of TPI believed that the party had been attacked by the forces of reaction and imperialism because of its unflinching persistence in promoting the people's interests and aspirations.

Dr. Shayegan, a prominent leader of Iran's "National Front," one of Dr. Mosadegh's comrades, and also the defence lawyer of the imprisoned Tudeh Party leaders, said: "Today, I can also prove that they should not be on trial. . . . They have been contributing to this country. To understand the reality, it is necessary to understand their ideas. . . . They did not think of themselves or the interest of their families. They work for the public good. . . . They have made a wonderful class of thought, a class of educating the people. The attack against the Tudeh Party starts from this point that they were educating the people. They taught the workers and peasants the cause of their unfortunate existence, the root causes of their living conditions and what had to be done for liberation. This was the biggest crime of the Tudeh Party."

During this highly dynamic period of history, until the coup d'etat of August 18, 1953, the Tudeh Party of Iran succeeded in deepening the anti-imperialist aspect of the movement for the nationalisation of the oil industry, despite ongoing attacks by the security forces and its struggle in semi-clandestine conditions. Despite its initial opposition to Dr. Mosadegh's initial policies at the beginning of his premiership, TPI remained his sole ally. When important segments of the religious forces, under the leadership of Kashani and important members of the leadership of the "National Front," turned their back on Dr. Mosadegh and his government, the Tudeh Party stood by him to the end. It was the members of the Tudeh Party who to the last moment stood by the democratic movement and it was the Tudeh officers who sacrificed their lives and with their blood guaranteed the continuation of the democratic movement.

The coup of August 18, 1953 succeeded in bringing an absolute domination of the monarchical dictatorship entirely dependent on imperialism. TPI endured heavy losses but survived. Despite the fact that thousands of its members across the country were attacked, detained and tortured, our party, due to its deep roots among the masses, powered by the antagonistic contradictions of Iranian society, could not be brought it its knees.

Creating the underground organisation, the heroic struggles of our comrades like Comrade Tizabi, the historic trials in court of Comrade Hekmatjoo and Khavari, the struggles of comrades (like Touraj Haidari Bigvand) and later in 1970s, the founding of "Navid" underground organisation by Comrade Rahman Hatefi (Haider Mehregan) broke the fear created by the dictatorship. Thus the party was able to play its [part] in the 1979 Revolution.

The influence of "Navid" in the anti-dictatorial movement can be gauged by the fact circulation had reached hundreds of thousands on the verge of the revolution. TPI, realising the people's readiness for the final battle against the monarchy, anticipated the possibility of victory. At this point the party invited all the patriotic, nationalist and freedom fighters to unite in a united front to launch the final assault against the dictatorial regime of the Shah.

The party incessantly and without flinching for a moment, tried to unite the forces which were struggling in the same front. TPI, in its public address on July 21, 1978 offered its practical programme for a broad based front of forces which should begin overthrowing the monarchy and establish a republic that would embrace far-reaching changes in all aspects of social life.

Our party deployed all its political and organizational force behind the revolutionary struggle. Tudeh partisans fought side-by-side other progressive forces and freedom fighters in the barricades. During the first few days following the victory at the political phase of the revolution, and the total collapse of the monarchy, our party put forward the "United Front of the People" as the only way to guarantee the success, continuation and deepening of the revolution onwards to subsequent stages.

The documents of the 16th plenary session of the central committee stated: "The working class and its party, the Tudeh Party of Iran, will engage all its resources to protect the united front arising practically from all patriotic and freedom seeking sections of the society. Our party will counter all efforts of the enemy attempting to undermine this unity." Not getting a positive response to this clear invitation gave the enemies of the revolution an opportunity to attack the disjointed revolutionary forces.

Some leaders, particularly Khomeini, left the revolutionary path and along with it, the genuine and democratic aspirations of the revolution. Instead, they choose to impose on the people a backward minded, anti-democratic structure, thus stalling the revolutionary process that was underway. The influence of our party on the revolution was to such a degree that Ali Khamenei, the current supreme leader, admitted several years later (in 1993): "During a period of time and at the beginning of the revolution, everything was being manipulated by the Tudeh Party. . . . I and everyone else could feel that, just after the revolution, the Tudeh and the left, especially the Tudeh, were dominating everything and were trying to divert the path of the revolution."

But what was this diversion the supreme religious leader is referring to? Historic documents on the period just after the February 1979 revolution clearly indicates [sic] that our party was persistent in its struggle to realize the aspirations of the revolution. It transformed the political climate of the society by popularising progressive slogans: the necessity for land reform, a struggle for an affirmative employment law, opposing reactionary employment bills, mobilising the country's defences when Iraq invades Iranian territory, firmly opposing the continuation of the war after the enemy was driven back to the internationally recognised borders, standing against the bigoted attempts by the reactionaries [to] confuse their backward views with the true aims of the revolutions.

All these factors brought fear to the hearts of reaction. For these very reasons, the reactionaries mounted their assault on the gains of the revolution and our party, helping them to consolidate their despotic grip over the people. They had the complete backing of the intelligence services of the United States, Britain, Israel, Turkey and Pakistan. Thus their well-engineered and broad attack ended in the arrests and detention of thousands of our members and followers. The assault of 1983 against our party was an attack against the revolution and turning point in the fate of the revolution.

Tudeh Party of Iran in the Critical Events of Recent Years

The role and impact of the Tudeh Party of Iran on the events of the recent years in our country is another valid evidence of the creative approach of our party in relation to the events and f[i]nding solutions that have been proven right in the historical test of events.

While several political forces, influence[d] by western media, were hoping that a "pragmatic man" from within the regime will lead Iran towards "renovation" and even freedom, TPI in its Central Committee meeting in March of 1990, analysed the country's situation and the rulers maneouvers to save the regime. It concluded that: "our country has a medieval totalitarian religious regime in power. In the name of "Feghahat-e-Islam" (the absolute rule of the supreme religious leader), this regime has committed atrocious crimes and has no regard for human rights whatsoever. . . . If we accept the fact that the very concept of "Velayat-e-Faquih" . . . puts the destiny of millions of people in the hands of despots who consider themselves above any law, then we have to turn the edge of our struggle towards this fundamental obstacle.

The purpose of "freedom and peace" slogans selected in the plenary meeting of December 1981 was to broaden the spectrum of forces participating in the front to fight against the despotic rule of "Velayat-e-Faquih." Currently, both inside and outside Iran, forces and individuals opposing the principle of Velayat-e-Faquih are [many]. . . . At the same time, there are individuals and forces that presently play a certain role in the ruling regime. They have religious beliefs but there is evidence of their willingness to cooperate with other forces to dispose of Velayat-e-Faquih. [. . .] The principle of the supremacy of the rule of the spiritual leader that forms the core of the ruling regime's ideology will need to be replaced with a democratic principle, and therefore requires a fundamental change in the constitution.

Thus, the slogan "Dispose of Velayat-e-Faquih" is a tactical slogan aimed at achieving a strategic goal. The same is true of the struggle for freedom and democracy, which ultimately serves to reach that final goal. . . .

Today, eleven years after adopting this analysis, its legitimacy is evident for the vast section of political forces. It was based on such an understanding of the events in Iran, that our party, during the presidential elections of June 1997 and then June 2001, proclaimed that [it] is impossible to realise the slogans of the reform movement, achieve a civil society and freedom, while circumstances that allow the "Velayat-e-Faquih" regime to exist [prevail].

Four years after the presidential elections of June 9th 1997, and trying times, including the state-sponsored assassinations of prominent opponents of the regime, the vicious attack on the pro-reform 2nd Khordad movement (named after the date of the presidential elections of June 7th), in May, the increasing pressure on this movement to undermine its role as an organised pro-reform social force, along with the suppressing of critical press and finally the arrests of religious-national critics, have proven wrong all those theories purporting that all kinds of freedom can be had within the framework of [the] "Velayat-e-Faquih" regime.

Today, as in the past, TPI, drawing on its scientific ideology and its 60-year historic experience, believes that the future destiny of our people and achieving freedom and establishing a popular and democratic regime will be impossible unless all freedom-loving forces struggling for people's rights unite. Creating an anti-dictatorship front, relying on pro-reform social forces, i.e. the working class and other working people, the youth, students and brave women of our country, is the historical necessity of the current phase of struggle in our nation. We believe that without organising these forces, and within the framework of [the] "Velayat-e-Faquih" regime, achieving fundamental, democratic reforms and stability in our country is not possible.

Members, Supporters, and Friends of the Party!

The history of TPI is an indivisible part of the history of our people's struggle for freedom, against reaction and despotism. The history of TPI is an extension of the history of the Iranian Communist Party and the struggle that Iran's social democrats initiated a century ago. In the past sixty years, the Tudeh Party of Iran, through its class struggle and its intellectual influence and inspirational guidance, has proved to be a potent organising force and had left a remarkable legacy.

Exceptional dedication and selflessness of Tudeh partisans in the last 60 years fills the proud pages of our people's history. In spite of successive onslaughts by despotic regimes and reactionary forces in the past 60 years, the Tudeh partisans have continued to uphold the banner of struggle of the workers, resolutely. This history and struggle is not only our party's achievement, but also belongs to the history of the progressive and freedom-loving movement in our country.

However, this in no way means that the Tudeh Party of Iran has made no mistakes in its long years, while confronting enormous difficulties. The important task is to analyse and realistically rectify these mistakes in order to learn the necessary lessons from them.

The reactionary ruling regime, along with other professional anti-communists and enemies of our party continue to disseminate a massive amount of propaganda and malicious accusations against our party, as they have done in the past 60 years. But, our people can see through the dirty lies against our party. Our people are well aware of the heroic history of our party, which in more than six decades, has never rested from the struggle for their rights.

The party has endured vicious attacks by ruling regimes and imperialism, a total of tens of thousands years of imprisonment, brutal tortures, and thousands of martyrs. Not only have these failed to destroy our party, but as history testifies, the party of people's silenced heroes, the party of Ruzbeh's, Siamak's, Kayvan's and Vartan's, the party of patriotic army officers, the party of working class, and the party of martyrs of 16 Azar, the party of Tizabi's, Hekmatjoo's, Fatemeh Modaressi's, Rahman Hatefi (Mehregan)'s, and Keymanesh's, as always firmly and proudly lifts the glorious and bloodstained banner inherited from Heydar-Amughlu's and Erani's, and will not rest a moment until the victory of humanitarian ideals of the working class and working people of our country [is] achieved.

The future belongs to the oppressed people and popular movement, and Tudeh members and supporters, just as in the past six decades, will fight side-by-side [with] the people, and will persevere to establish an independent, democratic and free Iran.

> *Warmest greetings to all Tudeh martyrs and all martyrs of freedom, independence and social justice of our nation!*
>
> *Warmest salutation to all political prisoners in Iran, who are resisting in the dungeons of [the] "Velayat-e-Faquih" regime!*
>
> *Long live international solidarity of all workers and toiling people of the world!*
>
> *Forward to the establishment of an anti-dictatorship united front for freedom, independence and social justice, and to dispose of the "Velayat-e-Faquih" regime!*
>
> *Greetings on the 60th anniversary of the Tudeh Party of Iran, the party of workers and toiling people of our people!*

CHAPTER 10

The Future of the Middle East and North Africa

Previous chapters focus on the past and present of the Middle East and North Africa. In this chapter, we look to the future. The two documents presented here touch on many of the questions facing the peoples of this area.

The first document is an essay about the relationship between the Middle East and North Africa, on the one hand, and globalization, on the other. The writer summarizes feelings of distrust and ambiguity about globalization, then criticizes these misgivings as shortsighted and argues that if the region is to play a role in shaping globalization, then its peoples will have to engage with this movement actively and effectively. He contends that the future importance of the region generally, and of the Arab world in particular, depends on this engagement and its outcome.

The writer of the second document heralds the emergence of a third era in modern Arab history. He argues that democracy, demilitarization, and cultural pluralism offer the only means for the region to become an effective participant in the world and a contributor to the formation of a global civilization. While maintaining that the United States and Israel have played a detrimental role in the modern history of the Middle East and North Africa, he contends that the time has come to deal seriously and honestly with internal problems previously pushed aside because of the specter of external threats. The authoritarian nature of the states, intolerance for cultural, social, and political deviations from the mainstream, and the miserable condition of most of the local and regional economies are the most pressing issues for the future. Only by addressing these problems, practically and through the construction of a new culture, can the region advance.

1. Selection from a Roundtable Discussion of Globalization and Its Impact on Arab Culture, October 26, 2000

Globalization has raised many troubling questions in the Middle East and North Africa. Some observers wonder whether globalization means the erasing of local cultures in favor of a hegemonic Western (mostly American) culture. Others search for clues as to whether globalization will improve the lot of humanity or simply create more misery for the majority while further enriching the Northern Hemisphere. Also, globalization raises questions about national boundaries: will they be swept aside in the pursuit of global markets? To answer some of these questions, the journal of the Ministry of Culture in Bahrain convened a roundtable of Arab intellectuals, including the author of this document: George Tarabishi, an author who resides in Paris and writes extensively on the Arab world for the French and Arab press. Tarabishi's point of view on this subject is a minority opinion in intellectual circles but not in business ones. His essay highlights various aspects of the argument about globalization in the Arab world.

When Muslim theological scholars used to determine that an issue is conflictual, they meant that it is permissible to disagree about it, that *ijtihad* [the application of reason] is necessary, and that this conflict and this *ijtihad* cannot be considered heretical. It is within this specific context that I declare that globalization is a conflictual matter. [. . .]

Globalizing the World

There is no doubt that the ability to read globalization as a conflictual matter derives from its seriousness as a phenomenon, from the looseness of its meaning, and from its capacity to be loaded with conflicting meanings and values. In addition, the vastness of this phenomenon and its multiple facets allows it to take as its basis an existential duality and thus a Manichaean reading that depends on feelings and value judgments more than on knowledge. Thus, these approaches to globalization deal with it on the level of the singularities of good and evil, or love and hate, or right and left. Therefore, anyone who speaks of globalization must define first what he means. For me, globalization [. . .] means nothing more than the world becoming one. Before economy, before media, and before cultural production, the world itself is becoming globalized. We must not forget that the world, in its largest meaning, is a modern concept. Before overcoming the law of distances with modern means of transportation and communication, the world was made of worlds. The borders within these worlds were not merely geographical but also linguistic, religious, and ethnic. It was rare to imagine that each of these partial worlds was the world in its totality.

George Tarabishi, "Globalization and Its Impact on Arab Culture: Globalization as a Matter of Conflict," *al-Bahrain al-Thaqafia*, no. 26, 26 October 2000. Translated by Akram Khater.

However, this world, which is being united by globalization—and herein lies the problem—cannot be unified except on the basis of its division into two dualities of a developed world and an underdeveloped world, a world of the rich and a world of the poor, a world that produces information and knowledge and a world where there is not even the means to consume these. According to a famous United Nations description [of the world], 20 percent of the world's population owns 80 percent of its riches, and 80 percent of its people own less than 20 percent of its resources. This places four-fifths of humanity on one side and one-fifth on the other side. According to another report, 20 percent of the world's rich own 85 percent of the global production, while 20 percent of the world's poor own no more than 1.1 percent.

Contrary to a strongly held belief, the globalization of the world—on the basis of this problematic dual division—is not limited to the economic sector alone. [. . .] In addition to economic globalization—which is without doubt the most obvious and most predisposed to quantification—there is technological globalization, environmental globalization, food globalization, legal globalization, media globalization, and finally cultural globalization.

Globalizing the Arab World

If the Arab countries do not have sufficient cultural capacity to absorb globalization, then the concept of counter-globalization, as it is being propounded in the Arab cultural arena today, appears as if it is being activated under an attractive theoretical name—what we have called the mechanism of hegemony [. . .] by a sizable number of intellectuals. It is true that the person who shaped this concept—the Tunisian linguist 'Abd al-Salam al-Masdi, has himself warned against dealing in a utopian fashion with the concept. [. . .] He clearly stated: "The concept of globalization that we have constructed in our cultural discussion in the book *Globalization and Counter-Globalization* does not mean that we deny the phenomenon of globalization. Nor do we object fundamentally to its existence. Nor are we in any way calling to completely oppose it. Had we done or claimed any of these, then we would be utopian in the absolute sense of the word. What we are calling for is the introduction of a new idea where counter-globalization would be a mentality that eschews negative criticism and embraces positive criticism."

Despite this [warning], it appears that this concept [counter-globalization] [. . .] has escaped like the genie from the bottle and has acquired an ideological independence that is not related to the rational purpose that produced it. It has imposed itself with incredible speed in the Arab world as a slogan for opposition and resistance, and as an alternative or contrary globalization, which some have defined as "the true globalization as opposed to the fake globalization," others as "the humane versus the monstrous globalization," or, as Mahmud Amin al-'Alam has said, "the globalization of truth not falsehood, the globalization of liberty not enslavement and hegemony, the globalization of science, knowledge and creativity not ignorance, alienation, underdevelopment and dependency."

To draw ourselves away from the intellectually crippling gravitational pull between *globalization* and *counter-globalization,* I believe that we must be armed with both a realistic and critical awareness. This is not meant to confront and counter but to improve our chances of benefiting from its [globalization's] advantages and avoiding its negative aspects. In the large global village that the world is on the verge of becoming, the Arab world—which is more divided than ever—is in need of becoming first a regional singular village. This, I believe, is the shortest path to enter the village of globalization—or its jungle, as its opponents claim—safely.

Since one of the possible definitions of globalization is the erasure of borders, and we are dealing specifically here with cultural globalization, let us then add quickly that the borders that we think we ought to remove in the Arab world are cultural borders. We are realistic enough to realize that the political borders in the Arab world—despite our previous ideological illusions about these borders being artificial—are currently and for the foreseeable future not subject to removal. However, the Arab world is capable, despite the consecration of its divisions and its regional and national characteristics with borders, of representing a singular cultural group. If it was not for this ability, then the Arab world would not have been able to distinguish itself—and be distinguished by others—as an Arab world.

So as not to float in the ethereal world of abstraction, let us say right away that it is new communication technologies that allow for the relatively safe and effective circumvention of Arab cultural borders. The first indication of this penetration is embodied in the Arab satellite television channels, which—regardless of what has been said about their performance or funding and purpose—have succeeded, however partially, in shrinking the Arab world despite its vastness and the invincibility of its political topography.

Another example is presented to us by the capability—which has become a reality in some cases—provided by new communication technologies to publish multiple editions of the same Arabic newspaper or magazine in various Arab capitals and at the same time. If, in the near future, we can develop the spread of the Internet in the Arab world, then another aspect of internal Arab borders—and we mean regional censorship of thought and the means of exchanging it through books, journals, and newspapers—will fall or at least be circumvented. On the Internet the scissors of the censor cannot intrude.

We do not need to view the circumventing or the removal of the cultural borders as solely negative. We can envision a type of positive Arab globalization in which the Arab League—after revising its purpose toward elevating its cultural role—can play an effective role. We can envision, within this context, the establishment of an Arab network that links Arab scientific and university institutions to limit the chaos of Arab research, to lessen duplication and the waste of effort and money, and to allow for a real possibility for coordination of university research and for disseminating that research so that it benefits the Arab world and does not remain locked away collecting dust. Within this context also, we can envision a network to link Arab museums and another network to "revive" Arabic manuscripts in Arab and foreign universities and libraries and thus allow all researchers access without having to travel and waste money and time.

Proponents of the theory of Arab cultural security may object that circumvention of the borders will not be accomplished solely by Arabs but by necessity will be carried out also by "foreign" forces. [. . .] As is sometimes said in the world of strategy, the best defense is offense. Therefore, we say that the best way to confront globalization is to be present, not absent. In any case, globalization is already here, whether we like it or not. So let us learn how to participate in it. [. . .] Just as globalization has made possible the emergence of a new economic pole in the world, the Asian pole, and just as it has made possible the crystallization of a European media pole (Euro News in opposition to CNN, for example), there is nothing to keep us from anticipating the emergence of an Arab cultural pole one day. Although light-years separate us from the realization of this dream—whose accomplishment is linked to a chain of democratic, modernizing, and radical changes in the Arab world—we see no reason not to look forward to it. Why? Simply because we refuse to limit ourselves between the jaws of the Fukuyama and Huntington pincers: neither the "end of history" nor the "clash of civilizations" is preordained. We reject the thesis that history is dominated by a singular universal civilization that crushes all else, and we reject the thesis of a history that, through global conflict, reshapes the world along lines of isolated and clashing civilizational islands. We believe that the world is heading toward becoming for the first time in history a single civilization with multiple cultures. Globalization may be the tool for this dialogue between world civilization and national cultures. But this dialogue should take place on the condition—which some may say is utopian— that globalization ceases to be a tool for *hegemony* and instead becomes a tool for *participation.*

To avoid appearing as if I am simply making a play on words, allow me to say that adjusting the equation of globalization from hegemony to participation does not presume absolute equality in the shares of the partners. Globalization is closer to an incorporated company, and our position within the corporation is decided by the size of our stock portfolio. According to our demographic size, our share cannot exceed 3.4 percent; otherwise, we would become hegemonic like others. But even this level is higher than what we can arrive at in the foreseeable future. [This is so] first, because the Arab world does not enter into the company of globalization as a singular stockholder. Its portfolio is distributed among many partners, who in many instances are fighting among themselves. Moreover, the Arab world, most of which belongs to the Third World—some parts even belong to the Fourth World—is not equal to the other stockholders in the globalization company in terms of its capacity for material and intellectual production. This disparity is particularly evident vis-à-vis the large partners who—despite being numerically small—own 80 percent of humanity's material production and 95 percent of its intellectual production. We will be realistic if we dream of increasing our share, in stages, from 0.001 to 1 percent within a time frame that is no less than a quarter of a century. This 1 percent is the minimum requirement for "takeoff," as the experiences of East and Southeast Asian nations indicate. If we, some or all of us, fail to "take off" in the next quarter of a century, we must not attribute our failure in adjusting the equation of globalization to a failure of globalization itself. The formula for globalization is open and multifaceted and ever changing in its values, and if there is an unknown that is difficult to determine, it is the Arab unknown, because we are living in a period of high tension between those who support and those who oppose modernity.

[. . .] The impact of globalization on us and our participation in globalization, specifically from a cultural perspective, is a matter of *how* in addition to *how much*. If we do not take this into consideration, then we risk our role by falling into the error of separating the tool and the spirit [of globalization]. Although such a division is possible economically and technologically, and even in the media, it is not possible culturally. From a cultural point of view, globalization is not a neutral phenomenon, for it occurs within a particular culture. At a time when Arab culture, like the other cultures of the world, has no option but to engage with it [globalization], then it would appear that this engagement, in the Arab case, will be conflictual rather than cooperative. This is so because the cultural values contained within globalization appear, to a large extent, at odds with predominant Arab values.

We can describe the culture of globalization as being of this world—we do not say secular—while Arab culture is still counted within the religious segment [of cultures] and is still preoccupied with matters of the spiritual world. The culture of globalization, because it is the culture of wealthy society, has a hedonistic tendency to squeeze all pleasure from the present moment and to engage in hyper-consumption. In contrast, Arab culture [. . .] is dominated by the logic of contentment, abstention, and thrift, and spiritual saving for future dark days.

The culture of globalization—by definition a visual culture—depends on the presence of the human body and does not hesitate to uncover and denude it, particularly the female body. Arab culture, in contrast, is a culture of modesty—manifested by covering the body, particularly the female body. The two cultures also diverge greatly on the issue of sexual abstinence and permissiveness. The culture of globalism goes to extremes in allowing for sexual love, while Arab culture goes to extremes in limiting it.

These differences, among others, make the intersection of Arab culture and the culture of globalism a point of painful ruptures. But a certain measure of rupture and pain may be necessary to provide the impetus for what we will call [. . .] cultural mobility. In our estimation, cultural mobility provides the ideal escape from the dual dangers that threaten the intersection of Arab culture and the culture of globalism. These are (1) the danger of isolationism and cocooning in a suffocating parochial or fundamentalist culture and (2) the danger of being torn away from the self and being swept away by a hegemonic globalizing cultural.

Cultural mobility, which combines the restraint of authenticity and the impetus of globalizing modernity, appears more capable than any other mechanism to control the speed and direction of Arab development and to avoid the pit-falls on either side of its path. [. . .] As we all know, the discourse about roots is today considered of great value in all of the world's cultures, which feel an undeniable need to hold on to their roots for fear of being uprooted by the winds of globalization, which can also undeniably take the form of a storm. However, holding on to cultural roots does not seem to us to be sufficient or a guarantee of the minimum level—let alone the ideal level—of cultural dynamism. [. . .] National cultures, including the Arab one, in their march toward integration with the culture of globalization, need wings as much as they need roots.

Nobody can predict what will happen to the Arab world in the next twenty-five years, and how the struggle over the mother of conflicts—which is globalization in our time—will be resolved. However, the study of reality, which does not allow for miraculous transformations—[. . .] forces us to be more pessimistic about the start of this new era, without being overly pessimistic about its end.

2.   Lebanese Author Elias Khoury Argues for Democracy, Demilitarization, and Cultural Pluralism in the Middle East and North Africa, 2000

Elias Khoury has written several novels and short stories, some of which (such as his novel The Small Mountain, *1989) have been translated into English. Currently, he is the editor of the culture section in one of Lebanon's—and the Arab world's—leading daily newspapers,* Al-Nahar. *This essay is part of a collection of articles commissioned by his newspaper to celebrate the beginning of the new millennium. As an Arab-Lebanese intellectual, Khoury voices many of the feelings shared by other Arabs, elites and nonelites alike. His manifesto can be read not as the opinion of all Arabs but as the expression of a fairly powerful and common point of view.*

After the first defeat in Maysaloun [the battle where the French defeated the army of Prince Faisal and proclaimed the establishment of the French mandate over Syria] then in Palestine, and a second renaissance that became bankrupt after the defeat of the June war [1967], how do we establish an Arab culture that does not succumb to another retreat into history?

When I listen to Fairuz [a popular Lebanese singer] sing, "And we have memories in Maysaloun," I feel that Arab East there, I see it at the turn of

Elias Khoury, "Leaving Behind the Nightmare of the Arab Military Establishment: The Third Renaissance: The End of the Coup," *Al-Nahar,* 13 December 2000. Translated by Akram Khater.

the twentieth century, when the world took it from the Ottoman state to the defeat of the Arab nation project, when the minister of defense in the Faisal government died defending a kingdom [the proposed Arab kingdom] that was not born.

The memories of Maysaloun are not limited to the voice of Fairuz, but rather they merge with our consciousness of the second defeat that the Arabs were dealt in 1967, when dreams and words collapsed in six days of napalm [an incendiary explosive used by the Israelis], of loss and the crowds of new refugees. After the defeat of June, the Palestinian resistance established training camps, where a man—injured all over his body—by the name of Abu Ali Iyad led the volunteers to dream about a new beginning, before he died in the woods of Jarash and Ajloun. Between the two Maysalouns and after them, the Arabs lived a linguistic century whose main characteristic was to exchange reality with words. Perhaps the first correct word invented by modern Arab culture was *Al-Nakba* [The Disaster], which was used to describe the great defeat of 1948; and this can be attributed to our professor Constantin Zurayq [an Arab intellectual who coined the term]. Arab culture had to wait another half-century in order to give birth to another correct word that was created by the collective imagination, and it is *Intifada* [Palestinian rebellion against Israeli occupation in 1987], which was born through the rocks of children in Palestine. Perhaps these are the only two words in Arabic that are impossible to translate, not because they have no equivalent in other languages, but because translation deprives them of their uniqueness, and that is why they appeared transliterated in all the languages of the world.

The linguistic century that the Arabs have lived was a century in which language sought to trick reality. That is why the two renaissance movements at the beginning and the middle of the century were incomplete; and this lack of completion expresses in and of itself the frightening divorce between reality and language.

The first renaissance, which began in the nineteenth century and lasted through the 1930s, contained within it two symbols. The first was the rejection of Ottoman oppression and the call for the establishment of constitutional governments. The second symbol was the call for the independence and unity [of Arabs].

Between the two symbols, the first renaissance period failed the test of naming the historical moment in which it was born. It did not see in the defeat of the East by an ascending European power a point of departure for the establishment of the new and different. Rather it saw itself as an extension of the past. After the grand linguistic renaissance—which was started by al-Shidyaq, the two Yazijis, and the Burstanis [nineteenth-century intellectuals from Lebanon]—and after the literary modernization period founded by [Arab] emigrant authors, Arab culture found itself prisoner to the past in both its linguistic and religious dimensions. Ideas and thought thus remained bounded by borders drawn by Al-Afghani and Muhammad 'Abduh [see document 5 in the chapter "Central Political Reforms and Local Responses"]. Moreover, politics remained in the realm of dreaming about the rebirth of a golden era that had been trampled by the hooves of the Mongols [in the thirteenth century] long ago, before it was completely destroyed by the Mamluks.

This intellectual, linguistic, and political prevarication produced an incomplete first renaissance. Soon after the end of World War I this renaissance found itself incapable of building independence and unity. Faisal's experiment in independence was defeated in Syria, so it moved to Iraq to become its own contradiction. The Egyptian experiment, which was embodied in the 1919 revolution, fell because it could not achieve the dream of national independence [from the British], leaving to a young army officer by the name of Gamal Abdel Nasser the task of leading Egypt into independence, before he himself fell in the wake of the second defeat by Israel.

The first renaissance was born incomplete because it embodied a new consciousness that could not find social forces to support it. Despite its ability to reconcile various ideas and interests, this renaissance was far ahead of the social groups that carried it. Thus, consciousness was defeated by reality, and no new historical forces emerged to lead the Arab East toward unity and independence. [. . .]

Perhaps this impotence was represented in the suppression of two books: *Islam and the Principles of Government* by Ali 'Abd al-Raziq, and Taha Hussein's *Jahili* [pre-Islamic] *Poetry*. With these two there emerged confusion about the relationship between renaissance, on the one hand, and society and political elites, on the other. Moreover, it made clear how the wasted revolutions that colored the beginning of the Arab century with the blood of defeat led the Arabs toward their Grand Defeat of 1948.

The first renaissance was created by a mixture of intellectuals from different ideologies: nationalists, Islamists, enlightened secularists, liberals, and socialists. However, the second renaissance was principally built by armies, and it depended on nationalist ideology after adding to it a socialist flavor.

The idea of rebirth that was preached by the pioneers of the first renaissance was embodied in young officers from rural backgrounds, who—in turn—produced the markers of the Nasserite experiment: rural reform, nationalization of the Suez Canal, Syrian-Egyptian unity. [. . .]

However, the distinction of the second renaissance was its relationship to culture and intellectuals. In the beginning it was established by marginalizing the liberals; then it placed the communists in prisons, and finally it destroyed the Islamic trend. Thus, it destroyed the political and cultural elites in order to establish a direct relationship between the Leader and the masses—a relationship whose only conduits were government secret police and intelligence services.

The Officers could only avail themselves of the culture currently available to them, so they mixed [Sati] al-Husi and [Michel] 'Aflaq [see document 11 in the chapter "Ideas of Nationalism"] with an Arabized Marxism, and they depended on a Mamluk tradition [of authoritarian rule and patron-client politics] that Muhammad 'Ali could not destroy despite his famous feast at the Citadel [when he assassinated most of the Mamluk elites in 1805].

The effects of this mixing did not appear until the defeat of June 1967.

Before the defeat, the popularity of Nasser and his historical stature and charm were able to fill the gap between polity and society. However, when the weakness of the government of the Officers was uncovered, and their failure at war became evident, the charm turned into merciless repression. Nasser faced the demonstrations of students and their songs with impotence. Then Sadat came to establish a new era that quickly led to complete collapse. The Egyptian army needed only half a victory in the October [1973] war in order to declare its absolute rule and bring about the destruction of the political and intellectual structures that had created the first two periods of renaissance. Thus, the Islamic fundamentalist movement and thought, which swept the Arab world, emerged as a maker of the end of the stage.

This separation between culture and authority produced in Arab culture a special case called Beirut. It is a case that requires special study because it was characterized by a rich literary and intellectual milieu, and by an ability to continue the first renaissance through a cultural extension into the second renaissance that was expressed in thought, poetry, novels, theater, and art. This case existed in a margin whose weakness only became apparent during the Lebanese civil war, when it was completely destroyed by the final confrontation between the culture of the second renaissance—represented by the Lebanese left—and Arab regimes—embodied in the entrance of the Syrian forces into Lebanon in 1976. [. . .]

The second renaissance was a sharp separation between its language and its reality. It is true that it succeeded in establishing political independence (in Algeria in particular), and it is true that it dared to create a single Arab state, and it is true that it discussed the matters of development and social justice. However, it declared its impotence at three levels:

1. The first is the absence of democracy, which led—particularly after the defeat of June 1967—to destroying civil society.

2. The second is the inability to build Arab unity, and the marginalization of all kinds of common Arab efforts, until the Arab League became a Wailing Wall.

3. The third and most important level is military impotence. The second renaissance failed to build fighting armies, and this became most evident in the defeat of the military institutions in the war of 1967. The war of 1973 was arrested by the impossibility of achieving military victory [over the Israeli army], and thus it was satisfied by establishing a balance of power that was soon discarded by unilateral agreements (Camp David) and civil wars (Lebanon). The Palestinian resistance was established at the margins of defeat, with its two bloody experiments in Jordan and Lebanon. But it was as if it carried within it the elements of both resistance and collapse at the same time. The Palestinian experiment only escaped the abyss because of the Intifada, which was the first fruit of the steadfastness of Beirut [in the face of the Israeli invasion of 1982]. Despite the Oslo Agreements and the Bantustans

that were established in the West Bank and Gaza, the Intifada succeeded in declaring that the Palestinian Cause would remain the open Arab wound for a long forthcoming century.

The first renaissance was defeated in Maysaloun, but its defeat was not complete until the Palestinian Disaster, which led to the dispossession of a whole people of its land and its country.

The second renaissance was defeated in June 1967 but was only completely destroyed by the Lebanese tragedy and Iraqi horror, in which a whole people was made homeless within its own country. [. . .]

Can we now speak of a third renaissance, while we live in the darkness of decay, under the humiliation of siege and the death of dreams?

Can the Arabs emerge from their second defeat, when their country is either occupied or practically occupied and they are being led to a peace with Israel that is neither just nor balanced?

The third renaissance will not be established simply by an optimistic will, as Antonio Gramsci suggested during his long prison stay; it will be established through the optimism of the mind. That is, it will be established through an ability to look at reality, to name it, and to admit its facts in order to change that reality.

The third renaissance is not an intellectual need like the first one, and it is not a military need like the second one. It is a life necessity. Today the Arab World is under the threat of becoming outside of history, and this is not an exaggeration. It is poised to drown in ignorance and poverty, disease and hunger.

Leaving the nightmare of the twentieth century behind rests on three basic premises:

First, democracy. We learned during the two aborted renaissance movements that change cannot occur from above, nor can it be left to kings and officers. Revolution is not an authoritarian decision carried out by intellectuals or quasi-intellectuals. Revolution is a social act that is built by the institutions of civil society, through daily work that is, in turn, premised on marrying reality with dream.

Democracy is the prerequisite for Arab thought. Arabism is not like European nationalist movements in singularity. It does not belong to the nation-state and cannot be built on race and ethnicity. It is a plural Arabism that meets in language and culture, admitting the multiple sources that have formed the civilization of the Arabic-speaking peoples. Arabism is not a dream based on a memory of a bygone past; it is many horizons that crystallize the interests of Arab societies. [. . .]

Secondly, we must abandon the old language. Language is not a substitute for reality; rather it is a means to express experience and to approach reality. The condition of the third renaissance is to name things with their proper names. The Arab world cannot enter the twenty-first century without being aware of its defeat. Yes, the renaissance begins with naming our defeat. The Arabs have been defeated by the Israeli-American project, and they must admit it if they want to resist defeat. However, if they wish to stay in the waters of stagnation, then they need only to continue calling defeat victory, humiliation pride, and kneeling standing. The old lying language was the tool that dictatorial governments used to repress their people, to humiliate them, and to lead them to poverty, hunger, and submission.

The renaissance begins by returning language to language: by starting out from the reality of the historical defeat that the Arab world suffered at the hands of the Zionist-American power, and preparing from the starting point for a long resistance whose condition is to build plural, modern, and democratic Arab societies. The battle with Israel begins after the imposed empty "Peace," and it bases itself on the notion of justice, because it is the one human value that the god of the American market cannot destroy.

Thirdly, we must bring down the Arab military establishment. The game begun by the Arab officers of the Ottoman army is over. [. . .] Armies do not fight wars but as extensions of dynamic societies. But when the armies kill and destroy society, then they are fighting a retreating war and can only fight through surrender.

The condition of the third renaissance is to abandon the mirage of revolution through coups, and of liberty through chains. The twentieth century has witnessed the greatest cultural tragedy in history, when the humanity of the socialist idea was destroyed by Marxist revolutionaries, who established the society-prison in the name of freedom.

The Arab military establishment "crowned" the defeats of the Arabs with the two disasters of Iraq [the Iran-Iraq war and the Gulf War], the massacres of Algeria [between the government and the Islamic Salvation Front—see document 7 in the chapter "Crisis of the State"], and the hunger in Sudan, among other tragedies at the end of the twentieth century.

The Arab dictatorial regimes have succeeded not only in depriving people of bread and dignity, but also in depriving them of air! Arab decay has overflowed with blood, and if Arab societies are to escape extinction, they must break the chains and declare the end of the coups.

The Arabs must begin their third democratic renaissance at the beginning of the third millennium. Arab culture has not died under the boots of soldiers, as one would suspect from the silent and depressing image of Arab cities. Culture has not succumbed to the oil, which is polluted with blood, as it would appear from the perspective of the kings [in the Gulf region] who believe that the defeats of the end of the twentieth century will return the Arabs to the defeats of its beginning. Arab culture has not ceased to produce new ideas, poetry, novels, art, cinema, and theater. These are produced in jails, in exile, and in the besieged nations.

Today, at the end of the century of defeats crowned by the surrendering "Peace" [referring to Palestinian-Israeli Oslo agreement], the Third Arab Renaissance must establish a resisting, democratic, and pluralistic peace that will build the dream of independence and freedom, thus liberating the Arabs from slavery to the idols of authority and idols of the dead language.